Christopher Wordsworth, Francis Procter, Abbey Syon

The martiloge in Englysshe after the use of the chirche of Salisbury and as it is redde in Syon with addicyons

Vol. 3

Christopher Wordsworth, Francis Procter, Abbey Syon

The martiloge in Englysshe after the use of the chirche of Salisbury and as it is redde in Syon with addicyons
Vol. 3

ISBN/EAN: 9783337257187

Printed in Europe, USA, Canada, Australia, Japan

Cover: Foto ©ninafisch / pixelio.de

More available books at **www.hansebooks.com**

HENRY BRADSHAW SOCIETY

Founded in the Year of Our Lord 1890

for the editing of Rare Liturgical Texts.

Vol. III.

ISSUED TO MEMBERS FOR THE YEAR 1891,

AND

PRINTED FOR THE SOCIETY

BY

HARRISON AND SONS, ST MARTIN'S LANE,

PRINTERS IN ORDINARY TO HER MAJESTY.

THE MARTILOGE

in Englysshe

after the Use of the Chirche of Salisbury and as it is redde in Syon With addicyons.

Printed By Wynkyn de Worde in 1526.

EDITED

WITH INTRODUCTION AND NOTES

BY

F. PROCTER, M.A.,

AND

E. S. DEWICK, M.A., F.S.A.

London.

1893.

INTRODUCTION.

IN the ancient cathedral and monastic churches of England, the Martyrology was read daily in the chapter house after prime.[1] For this reading every large church was provided with a book known as the Martyrologium, which contained not only the brief notices of saints and martyrs which were read on the day preceding their celebration and gave the name to the book, but also the records of the obits of the members of the chapter and of their benefactors, together with memoranda of various kinds.

Several of these books are still in existence. Of the Martyrologium of Christ Church, Canterbury, two copies have come down to us. The earlier, which is in the British Museum (Arundel MS., 68), is a thirteenth century MS. When this had become antiquated, an illuminated copy was made at the beginning of the sixteenth century, which is preserved in the Library of Lambeth Palace (Lambeth MS., 20). This is a large folio, still in its original leather binding, protected by plates and corner-pieces of latten. Both of these books contain an Obituarium as well as the Martyrology.

Another complete Martyrologium is that which belonged to the Brigettine monastery of Syon in Middlesex (British Museum, Add. MS., 22, 285), which will be more fully described below.

Occasionally the Martyrologium is included in the Breviarium, of which a fine example may be seen in the British Museum (Harleian MS., 2785).

These Martyrologia were adapted solely to the purposes of the particular church in which they were used. Even the Martyrology proper has its variations, according to the locality

[1] W. Maskell's *Monumenta Ritualia*, 2nd ed. 1882, vol. i. pp. clxx–clxxiv.

in which the book was to be used. They all exhibit variations and local additions which are often sufficient by themselves to indicate the church for the use of which the book was written.

Probably these variations may be sufficient to explain the reason why the Martyrologium is not found amongst the service-books printed for use in England. It may also be added that only one copy of the book was actually required in each church for the use of the reader.[1]

But though the Martyrologium was not printed for liturgical use, there is an interesting English version of it made for private use by Richard Whytford, a brother of Syon monastery, and printed by Wynkyn de Worde, as a small quarto, in 1526. Of this book about seven copies are known to be in existence, of which some are imperfect.

A reprint of this rare book is now offered to members of the Henry Bradshaw Society. Its title is:—

The Martiloge in englysshe after the vse of the chirche of salisbury/ and as it is redde in Syon/ with addicyons.

This English version was made, as the translator tells us in his preface, "for the edificacyon of certayn religyous persones vnlerned/ that dayly dyd rede the same martiloge in latyn/ not vnderstandynge what they redde." Thus the motive which led

---

[1] There is some uncertainty as to the custom of reading the Martyrology in parish churches. The Martyrologium is not among the books which parishioners were required to provide for their churches by the Constitutions of Archbishop Robert Winchelsey (Lyndewode's *Provinciale*, London, W. Bretton, 1505, fo. 137). The book is not always found in inventories of church goods, but it is found at Cherry Hinton, Trumpington, Histon, and elsewhere in Cambridgeshire, the book being sometimes a separate volume, or at other times bound up with the Processionale or Ordinale. (*Churches of Cambridgeshire*, pp. 9, 40, 60, 83, 104.)

The Rev. Christopher Wordsworth adds the following note:—

"The Martyrology did not appear in the list of seven books which an archdeacon of Sarum, in his charge, cir. 1485, required as 'sufficient boks . . . whiche ye are bownde to have.' See *Fasti Sarisb.* p. 131. Even in the account of the visitation of *prebendal* churches and their chapels by the Dean of Sarum in 1220-24 no mention is made of any martyrology either produced or required. A 'martyrologium' was one of the eight or nine books with which Bede had counselled the young priest to furnish himself before his ordination (*De remediis peccatorum* cap. i, quoted by Maskell *Mon. Rit.*, 2nd ed., 1882, Vol. I. p. xv). But I have not come across any instance of its purchase being made compulsory by authority."

to the production of this work was the same as that which gave to the same monastery *The Myroure of Oure Lady*[1] in the prologue of which the translator, addressing the "daughters of Syon," says :—"forasmoche as many of you, though ye can synge and rede, yet ye can not se what the meanynge therof ys. . . . . I haue drawen youre legende and all youre servyce in to Englyshe, that ye shoulde se by the vnderstondyng therof, how worthy and holy praysynge of oure gloryouse Lady is contente therin, and the more deuoutely and knowyngly synge yt and rede yt, and say yt to her worship."

Towards the end of the sixteenth century the Roman Martyrology was translated into Spanish with similar motives by the Jesuit Father Dionysio Vasquez,[2] who in his prologue states that it was made to meet the wants of those brethren (hermanos) of the Company of Jesus who were ignorant of Latin, with the hope that it might be useful also to others, who might be desirous to read "in a language so spread over the whole world [en una lengua tan esparzida por todo el mondo] a book so holy and profitable, which kindles our devotion by living examples, animates our weakness, warms our coolness, and consoles those distressed and tried by temptations and trials when they see the noble spirit of the glorious martyrs." It is added that no tables of the epacts and moons are given, because the book was for private use, and not for the services of the choir [porque no hauiendo de seruir esto libro en Romāce para los coros en que se dizen los horas : no lo juzgamos necessario]. The same omission will be noticed in our English *Martiloge*.

In the seventeenth century an English translation was made of the reformed Martyrologium Romanum, which the translator recommended for daily use "in every Catholick family," just as

---

[1] *The Myroure of Oure Lady*. Printed in London by Richard Fawkes, 1530. Reprinted for the E.E.T.S., 1873.

[2] *Martyrologio Romano* . . . . *Traduzido ahora nueuamente de lengua Latina en la Española : por el Padre Maestro Dionysio Vasquez de la Compañia de IESVS*, Valladolid, 1586.

its Latin orignal was used in every religious community.[1] This Martyrologe is, of course, purely Roman; there are no English saints inserted in addition to those which have a place in the Martyrologium Romanum, and there is nothing to suggest that the translator had seen the *Martiloge* of Richard Whytford.

It is now necessary to return to the *Martiloge* of Richard Whytford, and to examine its claim to be regarded as "after the vse of the churche of Salysbury/ and as it is redde in Syon."

To test the accuracy of this statement we naturally turn to the Latin Martyrologium used in Syon monastery, and now preserved in the British Museum (Add. MS., 22, 285). Some results of this comparison are given in the Notes in this volume, and it will be found that the *Martiloge* of Whytford (excluding the "addicyons") is substantially a translation of that actually in use at Syon monastery.

There are, however, some variations which seem to show that the copy used by Richard Whytford was not the same as that which has come down to us. Many of the peculiarities of spelling in the *Martiloge* are also found in the Syon Latin Martyrologium[2] (which for convenience will be referred to as A.); but on

[1] A copy before me has the title :—*The Roman Martyrologe set forth by the command of Pope Gregory XIII., and reviewved by the Avthority of Vrban VIII.* Translated out of Latin into English by G. K., of the Society of Iesvs. The second edition . . . . Printed at S. Omers by Thomas Gevbels, 1667.

[2] Examples of peculiar spellings common to the *Martiloge* and A. :—
March 19. 1. 5. *at suretyke.* apud sureticum A., for Surrentum.
Sept. 10. 1. 14. *Brydhestane.* brydhestani A., for Frithestani.
Sept. 19. 1. 5. *pluteolane.* pluteolana A., for Puteolana.
Oct. 1. 1. 12. *In the graūd port.* in portu granda A., for: in portu Ganda.

On the other hand, the following examples seem to show that the translator had before him a text which differed in some respects from A. :—
Jan. 30. 1. 3. *Innouate.* nouati A. Some MSS. of Usuard read Innouatus.
Feb. 8. 1. 3. *Coynt.* Corinthe A. Cointha is the reading of most MSS. of Usuard.
May 14. 1. 3. *two of the emperours sones.* duo philippi imperatores A. It seems probable that the translator was led into this mistake by a text with the spelling : duo filippi imperatores. By a stretch of charity towards R. Whytford, we may further suppose his text to have been : duo filii imperatoris.

the other hand there are many cases in which the *Martiloge* has a reading which is more correct than A. It will also be noticed that many of the additions to A are not found in the *Martiloge*. For example, the two feasts of St. Osmund, his deposition on Dec. 4, and his translation on July 16 are not in the *Martiloge*, though they appear to have been added to A before 1526.

Again, the two feasts of St. Thomas of Canterbury are not in the *Martiloge*,[1] though they are both in A, having been erased in the time of Henry VIII., and reinserted in the time of Queen Mary, when for a short time the "daughters of Syon" returned to their old home, and brought back their Martyrologium with them.

We may then be satisfied that the *Martiloge* is for the most part a translation of that which was daily read at Syon; but the other claim of its being " after the vse of the chirche of salisbury" remains to be considered. There is *à priori* reason for supposing that the Martyrologium used at Syon would be after the use of Salisbury, because by the Constitutions of the Brigettine Order, the brothers were ordered to sing mass and office after the use of the diocese in which any house of the order might be situated.[2] The monastery of Syon was in the diocese of London, in which the old use of St. Paul's was displaced and Sarum use ordered for adoption by Bishop Clifford in 1414,[3] the year before Henry V. granted a charter to Syon monastery, and the King himself laid the foundation stone in the presence of that bishop. Thus the Martyrologium used at Syon was doubtless regarded as being after the use of Salisbury, and the two

May 27. l. 4. *adartens*. atrebatensi A. Other MSS. read adartensi.
Nov. 19. l. 5. *Crispyne*. Cipriani A. Crispini is the reading of most MSS. of Usuard.

It may be added that *Dioclecian* is the usual spelling of the *Martiloge* (Dec. 24 and elsewhere), but that A. always uses the form Dioclicianus.

[1] The feast of St. Thomas is placed in the Addicyons on Dec. 29, but is not in the Martiloge proper.

[2] Sorores erunt sexaginta et non plures que clericos habebunt qui quotidie de tempore missam et officium quod habetur in ecclesiis cathedralibus illarum terrarum in quibus huiusmodi monasteria sunt decantabunt. Cap. X. [British Museum, Add. MS. 5208, fo. 8. b.]

[3] The original text of the mandate has been recently printed by Dr. W. Sparrow Simpson in *Proc. of the Soc. Ant. of London*, vol. xiv. p. 118.

calendars bound up with it are certainly of that use, with the slight exception that the second calendar, which contains the obits, has the Deposition of St. Erkenwald on April 30, and his Translation on November 14 (the observance of which two feasts was allowed by Bishop Clifford). There are also the three feasts of St. Bridget, viz., her Natalis on July 23, her Translation on May 28, and her Canonization on October 7, and also (in a later hand) St. Catherine of Sweden on June 25. In the Martyrology of A. the dedication of the church of Salisbury is noticed on September 30, and that of St. Paul's, London, on October 1.

But before accepting this Syon Martyrologium as after the use of Sarum, it is further desirable to compare it with other Martyrologies, which may be supposed to be of the same use. Unfortunately we have no knowledge of the original Martyrologium of the cathedral church of Salisbury, beyond a few extracts made by John Leland[1] when he saw the book in the sixteenth century, and these extracts are taken exclusively from the Obituarium There is, however, a Martyrology contained in a MS. *Breviarium ad usum Sarum* of the fifteenth century (British Museum, Harl. MS., 2785), which may be supposed to be of Sarum use. This has been partly collated in the Notes (where it is referred to as H), and it will be found that it varies considerably from the Syon version, and is, in particular, remarkable for the long notice of St. Oswald on Feb. 28.

Another Martyrology in the British Museum (Roy. MS., 2 A. xiii) has on the verso of its last leaf a list of *festa duplicia* and *festa maiora duplicia in ecclesia Sarum*, and it may be inferred that the book was intended for use in connection with Sarum rites. But in this MS. the notices of English saints differ from those in the Harleian and Syon MSS.

The Canterbury Martyrologium again, from which the extracts relating to English saints are printed in the Appendix to this volume, confines its notices of English saints in greater part to the Archbishops of Canterbury and Kentish saints, and,

---

[1] *Itinerary of John Leland,* edited by Thomas Hearne, 3rd ed., Oxford, 1769, vol. iii, p. 95.

as might have been expected, the notices of St. Thomas on the feasts of his martyrdom and his translation are unusually full. There is also a commemoration, probably peculiar to Canterbury, of the return of St. Thomas to Canterbury after his exile (Dec. 2).

Whilst these books differ amongst themselves in the notices of English saints, they all agree, in common with most mediæval Martyrologies of the Western Church, in having for their basis the Martyrology compiled in the ninth century by Usuard, a monk of Paris. From the materials consulted we cannot determine that the Martyrologe of a church following Sarum use was required to be anything more than a variant of Usuard, with additions of English saints selected according to local circumstances.

The Syon Martyrologium is of this class. It closely follows a rather corrupt text of Usuard, and has numerous variations and additions. Its most remarkable peculiarity is the long notice of St. Mary of Egypt on April 2, and the *four* feasts of St. Edward, King and Martyr, viz., on Feb. 13, Feb. 18, March 18, and June 20. Nearly all English calendars and Martyrologies record the martyrdom of St. Edward on March 18, and his translation on June 20; but the Syon book not only has these, but two additional celebrations, on Feb. 18, of the receiving (Adventus) of the Martyr's body at Shaftesbury from Wareham, and a translation on Feb. 13.

These notices are such as we should expect to find in a Martyrologium for the use of Shaftesbury, where the body of St. Edward, King and Martyr, was shrined in great honour. The Shaftesbury character of the book is confirmed by the notices of St. Elgiva, whose name appears on May 18 as Eluina in A, and in the blundered form "Elene" in the *Martiloge;* and on Dec. 21, where again we have Eluina in A, but "Ewyne" in the *Martiloge*. At the same time, as Shaftesbury is only twenty miles from Salisbury, it is just possible that these notices might have been inserted in a Salisbury Martyrology.[1]

[1] The two February feasts of S. Edward appear in the Calendar of the Red Book of Derby (*The Leofric Missal*, ed. F. E. Warren, Oxford, 1883, p. 271).

INTRODUCTION.

The Addicyons.—We have seen that the Martiloge proper is a translation of the Martyrologium which was read daily *in capitulo*. The translator has, however, supplied his readers with "addicyons" which have no liturgical authority of any kind. The names of saints given by him are in many cases not found in other Martyrologies or accredited Calendars, but are gathered, as we are told in his Preface, from the *Legenda Aurea* of Jacobus de Voragine, the *Catalogus Sanctorum* of Petrus de Natalibus, and other sources, including the *Sanctiloge*, which we might be inclined to identify with the *Sanctilogium* of John of Tinmouth, of which a copy exists in the British Museum. (Cottonian MS., Tiberius, E. 1.) But fortunately the Catalogue of the Library of the Brothers of Syon Monastery is preserved amongst the MS. treasures in the Library of Corpus Christi College, Cambridge, and we are thus enabled to see what books Richard Whytford was able to consult.

The books are all entered with the names of their donors,[1] press-marks, titles, and the first words of their second folio for the purpose of identification. The two volumes of which the Sanctilogium consisted are thus entered :—

DUCISSA CLARENCIE. 𝔐. 1.

Prima pars Sanctilogii Saluatoris de legenda et historiis sanctorum continens libros 8. cum tabula de nominibus sanctorum infra contentorum et kalendario generali secundum ordinem martilogii in principio libri.

DUCISSA CLARENCIE. 𝔐. 2.

Secunda pars Sanctilogii Saluatoris continens libros septem residuos predictorum.

---

[1] Among the names of the donors we find many times "Whytforde" who was perhaps the wealthy uncle of our Richard Whytford, also "Wynkyn," *i.e.*, Wynkyn de Worde, who presented copies of his *Ortus Vocabulorum* and *Noua legenda Anglie*, but his *Martiloge* does not appear in the Catalogue.

The name of the subsequent destroyer of the peace of Syon is also recorded amongst the donors :—

REX HENRICUS OCTAUUS.　　　　☉. 23.　　　　2° fo.. dicamus ut

Assertio septem sacramentorum aduersus Martinum Lutherum edita ab illustrissimo Rege nostro henrico. eius nominis octauo.

For the opportunity of examining this most interesting record I am indebted to the courtesy of the Rev. J. R. Harmer.

Thus we see that the *Sanctilogium Saluatoris* would have supplied suitable material for the "addicyons," and as there does not appear to have been a copy of the *Sanctilogium* of John of Tinmouth in the Syon Library, we can hardly be wrong in supposing that it was the former of these books which Richard Whytford made use of, and referred to as the *Sanctiloge.*

All the other books which are referred to in the Preface as having been used for the Addicyons are also found in this Catalogue (see Notes, p. 206).

When we begin to study the "Addicyons" it will be found that they have been put together in a somewhat careless and unsystematic manner. There is comparatively little in them which is specially English. A very large proportion of the matter has been obtained from the *Catalogus Sanctorum.* In the month of January no less than fifty-two saints out of a total of ninety-two have been taken from this book.

The saints drawn from other sources are mostly British worthies, or hermits of the desert, and in making his selection the translator seems to have been generally guided by his love of the marvellous. The wild extravagance of the legends which he relates in the "Addicyons" stands out in contrast to the comparative soberness of the Martyrology proper.[1]

As examples of want of care, we find certain saints not only mentioned in the *Martiloge* on the proper day of their celebration, but also given again in the "addicyons" either on the same day or on a day or two before or after. For example,

---

[1] The earliest Martyrologies, such as the Hieronymian, contains only the name, place, and day of the passion of the martyrs. The Martyrology of Bede has short histories added to the names, and this process was extended by Ado, archbishop of Vienne, who filled up many days left vacant by Bede. Then Usuard, a monk of Paris, towards the end of the ninth century condensed the work of Ado, and produced his Martyrology, which has been the basis of the Syon, as well as of most Western Martyrologies. For further information see Art. "Martyrology" in Smith and Cheetham's *Dictionary of Christian Antiquities,* 1880, ii. p. 1132 ; and also the learned dissertasions of Baronius in his edition of *Martyrologium Romanum,* Romæ, 1586 ; of Florentinius in his *Vetustius Occidentalis Ecclesiæ Martyrologium,* Lucæ, 1668 ; and of Sollerius in the Bollandist *Acta Sanctorum,* Junii, tom. vi.

"Grymbald" of "wynchester," in July 7, Add., is the same as "Grūbald" of "wentane" on July 8; and on this latter day St. Kilian of Wurzburg is mentioned no less than three times, viz., as Ciliane and Kyliane in the *Martiloge* proper, and again as Ciliane in the "addicyons." So, too, his companions are mentioned first as Colonare and Conace, and reappear in the "addicyons" as Colonate and Romane.

Mistakes of other kinds are not uncommon. Thus, on May 7, we find the early church of Queen Bertha described as "saynt Martyns in london"; and on November 12 we read of "Salomon and his sone Ieroboam."

We may also notice that some of the saints in the "Addicyons," such as "saynt Rowlande" and "saynt Olyuer" on June 16, and the story of Amilius and his Amicus on October 4, belong rather to the regions of romance than to hagiology; though it must be acknowledged that they are also to be found in the *Catalogus Sanctorum.*

The British Saints in the Martiloge. To facilitate comparison with other English Martyrologies it may be useful to give according to the order of the calendar a list of the British Saints in the *Martiloge*, distinguishing by italics those which occur only in the Addicyons.

    A.—Additional MS., 22, 285.
    D.—Drummond Missal.
    U denotes the names found also in Usuard's Martyrology.
    Inverted commas mark words according to the spelling of the *Martiloge.*
    Square brackets give additional particulars from other sources.

JANUARY.

5. St. Edward, K.C., at Westminster.
   Octave of St. Thomas of Canterbury.
8. *St. Wolsyn*, bishop of Sherborne.
9. Translation of St. Judocus ('Nidoke') at Winchester (wentane ')
   St. Adrian, abbot of Canterbury.
12. *St. Alred*, abbot [of Rievaulx, d. 1166].
    St Benedict Biscop, abbot of Wearmouth.
13. *St. Kentigern*, B.C.
15. *St. Dorothy* or *Sythe* [= St. Ita], in Ireland.
16. St. Fursey, C.   U.
    St. Sigybert, K.M.
    St. Henry, hermit of Coquet Island, Northumberland.
18. 'Saynt Vulstane,' B.C., 'at wyllenchester,' see Notes, Jan. 18
    St. Deicolus, abbot.
19. Translation of St. Branwallatour, B.C. [at Milton Abbas].
    St. Wulstan ('Vulstane '), B.C., at Worcester.
20. *St. Fechin* ('Fekyne'), abbot in Ireland.
29. St. Gildas ['gildas sapiens.' A.].
30. St. Batildis, Queen.

FEBRUARY.

1. St. Brigide or Bryde, V., in Ireland [' Scotlonde ']. U.
2. St. Laurence, archbishop of Canterbury ('doroberne ').
3. St. Werburg ('warburge'), V. [at Chester].
4. St. Gilbert, C. [of Sempringham].
   St. Aldate ('Eldade'), B.C. at Gloucester.
6. *SS. Mele, Melke, Munyse*, bishops, and *St. Ryoke*, abbot, all sons of St. Darerke and nephews of St. Patrick of Ireland.
   St. Fynian, abbot in Ireland.
7. St. Augulus, B.M., at London ['august ']. U.
   St. Richard, K.C., father of SS. Willibald, Winibald and Walburga.
9. *St. Theliaus*, Elios or Eliud [= St. Teilo].
10. St. Merwin ('Merpwyn')—[first abbess of Romsey].
13. Translation of St. Edward, K.M. ('confessour') [at Shaftesbury].
    St. Ermenilda [Queen of Mercia, afterwards abbess of Ely].
17. St. Finian, Pr. C., in Scotland [Fintanus].   U.
18. The Receiving ['Adventus.' A.] of St. Edward, K.M., at Shaftesbury ('sephton ').
    St. Eudelme, V. [= Ethelina, see Notes, Feb. 18].
20. *St. Wulfrick* ('Wolryke '), born near Bristol.
    St. Bolke, in Ireland.
24. St. Ethelbert ('Athelbert'), K.C.
25. *St. Walburga* ('Walpurge'), V.
28. St. Oswald, archbishop of York, at Worcester.
    St. Ayd, in Ireland.

MARCH.

1. St. David, archbishop in Wales.
2. St. Chad, B.C., at Lichfield.
   St. Cedde, B.C., brother of St. Chad.
   St. Willyam, Priest, 'in the tyme of the Emperour Henry ye thyrde.'[1]
3. St. Winwalloc ('wynewale'), abbot, C.
5. St. Cieran ('Ciaue'), in Ireland.
   St. Peran or *Keran*, in Cornwall [the same as the above].
6. *St. Kyneburga*, abbess [of Dormundcastor, now Castor, near Peterborough], *St. Kyneswide*, her sister, and *St. Tybbe*, her kinswoman.
7. *St. Esterwyne*, abbot of St. Paul's [Jarrow].
8. St. Felix, B.C., apostle of East Anglia.
   St. Fenan (Senan. D.), in Ireland.
12. St. Alphege, bishop of Winchester ('wentane').
16. *St. Fynan*, in Ireland.
    St. Abbane or *Kyryne*, 'whose syrname was Boniface,' in Scotland.
17. St. Patrick, B.C., in Ireland ('in scotlonde'). U.
    St. Withburga ('witburge'), V.
18. Passion of St. Edward, K.M.
    St. Anselm, archbishop of Canterbury.
20. St. Cuthbert, bishop of Lindisfarne. U.
24. *St. Hildelyth*, V., abbess of Barking.
    St. Sebba, K.
    St. Mackartyne (Meic Cairthinn. D.).
26. *St. Finchell* (Sinchell. D.), abbot in Ireland.
29. *St. Gundleus*, K., hermit.

[1] Cf. R. Stanton's *Menology of England and Wales*, 1887, p. 671.

APRIL.

3. St. Richard of Chichester, B.C.
4. *St. Tiernake* (Tigernach. D.), in Ireland.
7. *St. Bernake*.
11. St. Guthlac [hermit at Crowland].
13. *St. Caradoke*, Priest, hermit, at Brecknock.
15. *St. Paternus* or *Padarn*, B.C.
    St. William of Norwich, Boy-Martyr.
18. St. Lafreane (= Laisrean), abbot.
19. St. Alphege, archbishop of Canterbury, M.
21. Deposition of St. Anselm, archbishop of Canterbury.
24. St. Mellitus, B.C., archbishop of Canterbury (619-624). U
    St. Egbert, Priest.
    [*Translation of*] *St. Wilfrid*, archbishop of York.
    Invention of St. Ive.
29. Translation of St. Edmund, K.M.
    St. Wilfrid, junior, archbishop of York.
30. Deposition of St. Erkenwald, B.C., at London.

MAY.

1. *St. Walburge*, called also 'Gauburge,' V.
7. Deposition of St. John Beverley, B.C.
   St. Letard, B.C.
8. *St. Catald*, in Ireland [afterwards bishop of Tarentum].
   St. Indractus ('Indrake'), K.M., in Ireland.
10. *St. Congall*, abbot in Ireland.
    St. William, 'borne in englond.'
11. St. Fremund, K.M.
13. *St. Maeldoke*, C., in Ireland.
14. *St. Carthake*, bishop in Ireland.
15. *St. Brithwyne*, abbot of Beverley.
16. St. Brendan [or Brandon], abbot in Ireland.
    St. Carantock, called also 'Ceruach,' C., in Ireland.
18. Translation of St. 'Elene, quene and empresse' [= Elgiva,[1] queen of Edmund I].
19. St. Dunstan, archbishop of Canterbury.
20. St. Ethelbert ('Adelbert'), K.M., at Hereford.
21. St. Godric of Finchale ('fynthall').
25. St. Aldhelm, B.C., at Malmesbury ('mildunens').
26. St. Augustine, B.C., Apostle of England. U.
    Venerable Bede ('called y^e worshypfull').
28. *St. Lanfranc*, archbishop of Canterbury.

[1] Eluina. A. Cf. Martyrologium in British Museum (Roy. MS., 2 A. xiii):—In britannia apud Sheftesburiam natale sancte Ælgiue anglorum regine.
St. Ælgiva also appears on this day (May 18) in the calendars of 'The Red Book of Derby' and the Missal of Robert of Jumièges (see Warren's *Leofric Missal*, pp. 272, 280).
In the Litany of a MS. Psalter in the British Museum (Landowne, 383, fo. 147) we find Elgiua under the form Eluiua, which is not far removed from Eluina.

JUNE.

1. *St. Wistan*, K.M. at Evesham ('ewsham').
2. *St. Odo*, archbishop of Canterbury.
3. *St. Kenyne*, bishop in Ireland [Coemgin. D.].
4. St. Petrock ('Patryke'), C.
5. St. Boniface, B.M., bishop of Mainz, born in England. U.
6. St. Goodwale, B.[St. Gudwal of Cornwall, afterwards bishop of St. Malo].
7. Translation of St. Wulstan, bishop of Worcester.
   St. Colman, bishop in Ireland.
   St. Robert, abbot [of Newminster, near Morpeth].
8. *St. William*, archbishop of York.
9. St. Columba ('Columbane'), in Scotland. U.
   Translation of St. Edmund, archbishop of Canterbury.
10. St. Ithamar, [bishop of Rochester.]
    [*Translation of*] *St. Ive* ('yue').
    St. Margaret, Q. of Scotland.

b

JUNE—*continued*.

14. [Translation of] St. Brandane (or Brandon), abbot in Ireland.
15. Deposition of St. Eadburga, V. [at Pershore].
16. Translation of St. Richard, B.C., of Chichester.
17. St. Botulph, abbot.
    St. Molyng, bishop in Ireland.
20. Translation of St. Edward, K.M.
21. Translation of St. Werburg ('warburge') of Chester.
    St. 'Cassiane,' C., 'in englond.'
22. St. Alban, M.   U.
    St. Winifred ('wenefrede'), V.M.
23. St. Etheldreda ('Audre'), V.   U.
24. *St. Bartholomew* of Durham.
25. St. Kyneburga ('Keneburge'), V., at Gloucester.
    St. Amphibalus, M., with St. Alban.
    St. Milburga, V. [abbess of Wenlock].
27. St. Benignus ('Bemonus'), C., at Glastonbury.

JULY

1. *SS. Aaron* and *Julius*, MM.
2. Deposition of St. Swithun, B.C.
   St. Oudoceus ('Ondoce'), bishop of Llandaff.
5. St. Modwen, V.
   St. Anselm, C. (*Cat. Sanct.* vi. 57).
   St. Anselm, archbishop of Canterbury (*Cat. Sanct.* vi. 56).
6. St. Sexburga.
7. [Translation of St. Thomas of Canterbury, in A., but omitted in *Martiloge*.]
   St. Hedda, B.C.
   St. Ethelburga ('called Alborowe'), V.
   St. Erkengode, daughter ('sister') of St. Sexburga.
   St. Grimbald, abbot of New Minster or Hyde, at Winchester.
8. St. Grimbald, abbot at Winchester.
   St. Neot, C.
   Translation of St. Withburga ('Wydburge').
13. St. Mildred, V. [abbess of Minster].
    St. Juthware, V., 'in englond.'
15. Translation of St. Swithun, B.C.
    St. Deusdedit, archbishop of Canterbury.
16. [Translation of St. Osmund, B.C., added *secunda manu* in A., but omitted in *Martiloge*.]
17. St. Kenelm, K.M.
18. St. Eadburga.
20. *St. Arildis*, V.M. ('Aryld'), at Gloucester.
    St. Modmund, M., at Gloucester.
25. *St. Judocus*, hermit, C. [not in English calendars on this day. Cf Jan. 9 and Dec. 13].
30. *St. Tadwin*, archbishop of Canterbury.
31. St. Neot ('Neoche'), Pr., C.
    SS. Wolfade and *Rufyne*, sons of King Wolfere, MM.

AUGUST.

1. Deposition of St. Ethelwold ('Adelwold'), B.C., at Winchester.
    St. Hugh, Child-Martyr, of Lincoln.
    St. Kenede [hermit in Wales].
2. Invention of St. Alban, M.
3. *St. Wallene or Waltheof* [abbot of Melrose, d. 1159].
5. St. Oswald, K.M. U.
    St. Thomas, monk [of St. Martin's, Dover, M., 1295].
12. St. Eadwold, hermit ('Ethelwold').
18. *St. Fiacre*, C., born in Ireland [hermit near Meaux].
    St. Daygens [Dega. D.], C. in Ireland.
20. *St. Oswin*, K.M.
21. *St. Moghtewe*, abbot in Ireland.
23. *St. Eugene* [Eogain. D.], abbot in Ireland.
25. *St. Ebbe*, V. [abbess of Coldingham].
    St. Ebbe [V.M., abbess of Coldingham].
    St. Edburt, K., monk.
26. *St. Brigwin*, archbishop of Canterbury.
29. *St. Edwold*, K., hermit [near Shaftesbury].
31. St. Aidan, bishop of Lindisfarne, at Glastonbury ('glastingens').
    St. Cuthburga, V. [at Wimborne].
    St. Eanswyde, V. [at Folkestone].

SEPTEMBER.

4. Translation of St. Cuthbert.
    Translation of St. Birinus, bishop [of Dorchester].
6. *St. Maculin* [Meic Cuilinn. D.], C. in Ireland.
7. *St. Dunstan* [placed here in error, see Notes, Sept. 7].
    St. Alhmund ('Alkunde'), bishop of Hexham.
9. St. Queranus or Keranus. U.
    St. Modwen, V. [at Polesworth].
    St. Osman, V., in Ireland.
    St. Wulfhild ('wolsyld'), abbess of Barking and Horton.
10. St. Frithstan ('Brydhestane'), bishop of Winchester (909-931).
    Translation of St. Ethelwold ('Adelwold'), at Winchester.
    Translation of St. Augustine, apostle of England.
    St. Fynan or Wynyn, B.C., in Ireland.
12. *St. Albey* [Ailbus, D.], in Ireland.
16. St. Edith of Wilton ('wynchester').
    St. Ninian ('Mynyane'), B.C.
19. *St. Theodore*, archbishop of Canterbury.
25. *St. Ceolfrid* ('Golfryde'), abbot of Jarrow ('iarewe').
    St. Barry, bishop in Ireland.
26. *St. Colman Elo* ('Colmauell'), in Ireland.
28. *St. Forseus* ('Fors'), bishop in Ireland.
30. Dedication of the church of Salisbury.

OCTOBER.

1. St. Melour, son of the duke of Cornwall.
    Dedication of St. Paul's, London.
2. Deposition of St. Thomas of Hereford.

OCTOBER—*continued.*

7. St. Osyth, V.M. [at Chic, now St. Osyth, in Essex].
8. St. Iwigius ('yve'), [iui. A.]
   St. Keyna or *Reynwir*, d. of St. Breghan, 'kynge of breknoke.'
9. *St. Aymon*, archdeacon of Canterbury.
10. St. Paulinus, archbishop of York.
11. St. Canitius ('Canuke'), in Scotland.   U.
    St. Ethelburga, V. [abbess of Barking].
12. St. Wilfrid, B.C., of York.
    St. Edwin, K.M., of Northumberland.
13. Translation of St. Edward, K.C.
17. Translation of St. Etheldreda ('Awdre'), V.
    SS. Ethelred and *Ethelbright*, MM.
19. St. Frideswide, V.
    St. Ethebyne (or Ethbin), abbot in Ireland.
20. The Dedication of the church of Syon.
    St. Acca ('Akke'), B.C., of Hexham.
21. *Ordination of St. Dunstan.*
23. St. Elflede, V. [third abbess of Romsey].
25. [Translation of] St. John of Beverley, B.C.
27. *St. Abbany*, in Ireland.
29. *St. Elflede*, V. Cf. Oct. 23.
30. Ordination of St. Swithun, B.C.
31. *St. Foyllane*, B.M., of Ireland.

NOVEMBER.

2. *St. Malachi*, bishop in Ireland. Cf. Nov. 5.
   St. Herke (Erccus. D.), bishop in Ireland.
3. Translation of St. Edith, V.
   St. Winifred, V.M.
   St. Kenelm.
   St. Clitanke, M.
   St. Rumwold, C., at Buckingham.
4. St. Birnstan ('Brinstane'), bishop of Winchester.
   St. Clare, M., born at 'Orchester.'
5. St. Malachi [archbishop of Armagh, d. 1148].
6. *St. Iltute*, cousin of King Arthur.
7. St. Willibrord, bishop [of Utrecht].
8. *St. Keby*, bishop in Cornwall.
10. St. Just, archbishop of Canterbury ('Yorke').
14. Translation of St. Erkenwald, B.C.
    St. Dubricius, bishop of Llandaff.
    St. Constant, abbot in Ireland.
    St. Laurence [archbishop of Dublin (1162-1180)].
16. St. Edmund, archbishop of Canterbury, d. at Pontigny [1240].
17. St. Hugh, bishop of Lincoln.
    St. Hilda, V., abbess ('in yrelonde').
18. St. Hilda, V., abbess [of Whitby].
20. St. Edmund, K.M.
21. St. Columban, abbot.   U.
23. St. Columban, in Italy [at Bobio], a repetition of the above.
24. *St. Kenan* [Cianan. D.], in Ireland.

DECEMBER.

3. Deposition of St. Birinus, B.C.
   St. Lucius ('Lucy'), K.C.
4. [Deposition of St. Osmund, B.C., added *secunda manu* in A., but not noticed in the *Martiloge.*]
5. *St. Justinian*, hermit, M., at St. David's.
7. *St. Boecius* [Butus. D.], bishop in Ireland.
12. *St. Finian* ('Fynany'), in Ireland.
13. Deposition of St. Judocus ('Iudoke').
    St. Columba ('Columby'), abbot in Ireland.
19. *St. Samdyne* [Samthainna. D.], V. in Ireland.
21. St. 'Ewyne' (Eluina. A.), Queen. Cf. May 18.
    St. Berenwald, Pr. M., at Bampton ('betony'), Oxon.
28. *St. Alphege*, archbishop of Canterbury, M.
29. [St. Thomas of Canterbury in A., but not in *Martiloge* proper.]
    Passion of St. Thomas of Canterbury, M.
30. *St. Egwin* ('Ewgyne'), bishop of Worcester, d. 717 [at Evesham].

The greater number of the saints contained in the above lists (excluding those in the "addicyons") are found in early English Calendars. For instance, if a comparison is made with "the Red Book of Derby" (MS., C.C.C.C., No. 422), it will be seen that out of fifty-four English saints in its Calendar,[1] no less than fifty-two are also in the *Martiloge*. They are also to be found in the treatise *De Sanctis qui in Anglica patria requiescunt*, of which there are several variants in Latin and also in Anglo-Saxon.[2]

Richard Whytford. Of Richard Whytford, as the translator of the *Martiloge* and compiler of the "addicyons," it may be well to say a few words. According to Wood's *Athenæ Oxonienses* (Ed. Bliss, 1813, pp. 132-4) he was educated at Oxford, and afterwards became chaplain of Richard Foxe, Bishop of Winchester in the time of Henry VII. He is said to have been acquainted with Sir Thomas More,[3] and also with Erasmus,[4] but the only expression in the *Martiloge* which at all

[1] *The Leofric Missal* (ed. F. E. Warren), p. 272.
[2] A collation of some of these is given by F. Liebermann, *Die Heiligen Englands*, Hannover, 1889.
[3] More's *Life of Sir Thomas More*, ed. Hunter, 1828, Chap. III. p. 46.
[4] Cf. *Desiderii Erasmi Opera Omnia*, Lugd. Batavorum, folio, 1703, vol. III. p. 7, where there is a letter which appears by the Index to this work to have been addressed to Richard Whytford, but we have no certainty that this is our Richard. He is addressed as "Ricarde candidissime . . . . . . cura ut bene valeas, teque tua philosophia oblectes."

implies any sympathy with the opinions of the latter is the marginal note on April 21 (Add.), appended to the account of Ulphilas ('Gulphyle'):—"Note here how dilygent holy faders were to trāslate holy scripture ī to the moder tōgue and cōmune language."

Richard Whytford afterwards became a brother in the Brigettine monastery of Syon in Middlesex, of which an uncle of the same name, who died in 1511, had previously been a brother. The elder Richard Whytford was a wealthy clerk possessed of lands at Hope, Whitford, and elsewhere, both in Cheshire and also in Lancashire. The numerous presents of books which stand in the name of Whytford in the Catalogue of the Syon Library probably came from him.

Our Richard Whytford, the younger, was the author or translator of many books, written whilst he was a brother of Syon. A list of them is given by Bliss in his edition of Wood's *Athenæ Oxonienses*. The best known are a translation of the Rule of St. Augustine, *The Martiloge*, printed by Wynkyn de Worde in 1526, *The Pype/ or Tonne/ of the lyfe of Perfection*, printed by Robert Redman in 1532; and a translation of *Imitatio Christi*, entitled *The Folowinge of Christe*, which was printed in 1556 and again in 1585.[1]

In the *Martiloge*, as well as in other of his books, Richard Whytford signs himself in self-depreciation as "the wretche of Syon," and in *The Pype or Tonne of the Lyfe of Perfection* as "the olde wretched brother of Syon." He evidently took for his model the saint whom he describes as "a man of grete notable mekenes, so that whan a rude persone in dyspleasure called hym wretche, he lowly thanked hym" (p. 150. Cf. also p. 158).

During the troublous times of the visitation of Syon Monastery by the Commissioners of Henry VIII., Richard Whytford is several times referred to as having incurred the displeasure of these unscrupulous visitors. In one of Thomas Bedyll's letters to Secretary Cromwell, dated Aug. 28, 1534,

---

[1] This has lately been reprinted with modernized spelling and an Introduction by Dom Wilfrid Raynal, O.S.B., London, 1872.

there is a passage recounting that "on Sunday last, one Whitford, one of the most wilful of that house, preched, and wold speke no word of the Kinges Grace said title [supreme Hed of the Churche of England]; and this man hath but small lernyng, but is a greate rayler."[1]

At the suppression of Syon Monastery in 1539, Richard Whytford received a pension of eight pounds per annum,[2] and is said to have lived in retirement with William Blount, Lord Montjoy.[3] There is some uncertainty as to the exact date of his death. In the copy of *The Pype or Tonne of the lyfe of Perfection* preserved in the Library of Lambeth Palace (xxviii. 1. 6), on the verso of the first leaf, below the name of "The olde wretched brother of Syon/ Richarde Whytford," a sixteenth century hand has written, "obijt año dñi 1542°."

Richard Whytford as a translator. We have just read the opinion of Thomas Bedyll concerning Richard Whytford that he was a man of "small lernyng." Unfortunately, his work as a translator does not enable us to disprove this statement. Even after making allowance for the standard of scholarship at the beginning of the sixteenth century, we are unable to regard the learning of Richard Whytford as anything but "small." We may at once concede that he did not attempt close accuracy, but was satisfied if he could convey the general sense to his readers. Thus, he perhaps considered himself justified in rendering "cameli" by "mules" on Feb. 27, but it is not quite so easy to excuse him when he translates "in portu Romæ" by "in a gate of Rome" (Aug. 22, 23; Sept. 5), or "via Claudia" by "the village of clawde." On July 5, "que dum ad confessionem beati petri apostoli oraret" is turned into "bycause she praysed the vertue of saynt Peter," and the mistake is repeated on the following day.

Again, his knowledge of geography could not have been

---

[1] Aungier's *History and Antiquities of Syon Monastery*, 1840, p. 436.
[2] Aungier, *l.c.*, p. 90.   [3] *Ib.*, p. 535.

extensive when we find him turning the river Tiber into "the cite of tyberym" (March 24).

Our translator often gets himself into difficulties by his fondness for offering explanations of words unfamiliar to himself and to his readers. Thus he is certainly very wide of the mark when he explains the torture known as "equuleus" as "an huge instrument of metall made lyke a hors/ all full of pryckes and hote as fyre" (Feb. 6); and the "olympiades" as "a notable date amonge the iewes" (Dec. 25).

We may also notice that when he is in difficulty as to the translation of certain forms of torture, he cuts the matter short by the convenient phrase, " many variaunt and cruell turmentes " (Dec. 30, and elsewhere). On the other hand, he frequently adds expressions to the text with a view to increasing the piquancy of his narrative. Thus, on Feb. 1, "leones" becomes with him "wode and rampynge lyons." And in order to round off his sentences, descriptive phrases not found in the original are often added, such as, "that was a pyteous man and of hygh perfeccyon" (Jan. 2), "of synguler vertue and holynes" (Apr. 19), "w^t grete solempnite and moche Ioyfull honour" (March 31).

When we come to the proper names, there are many errors caused by mistakes which easily occur in reading a mediæval MS. Thus, f was read as a long s, giving us Sawster for Fawster (Feb. 6), and Sawstyne for Fawstyne (May 22), and iu was read as ni, giving "Nidoke" for "Judoke" (Jan. 9). Some mistakes of this kind had already occurred in the Latin original, and they must not all be laid upon Richard Whytford.

In treating the Latin names of persons, the translator has not been very successful in finding satisfactory equivalents in English. Thus with him "Lucy" does duty for Lucius (Dec. 3), and for Lucia (Sept. 16); so too Victor is used not only as a masculine but also for the female Victoria (Dec. 23). Occasionally we are glad to welcome the colloquial names of the sixteenth century, such as Agas for Agatha, Audry for Etheldreda, Alborowe for Ethelburga, Pernell for

Petronilla, Benet for Benedict, Effam for Euphemia, Rewle for Regulus.

But the names of places were a greater stumbling block to Richard Whytford than the names of persons. Such names as Sicilia and Cilicia, Phrygia and Frisia, Sirmium and Smyrma, are continually interchanged.

For most of the Latin names of places he was unable to give any English equivalent, but contented himself with the original word, not always changing the oblique case of the word, or the adjectival forms used in Latin for describing the see of a bishop. Thus we have such words as "trecas" for Troyes (Trecæ), "calcidy" for Chalcis, "assisiour" for Assisii, "pictauis" for Poitiers, "ephesum" for Ephesus (July 27), "arelatens" for Arles, "atrebacens" for Arras, "tolosane" for Toulouse, and "ratisponens" for Ratisbon.

Among the names of foreign places we have the vernacular English for a few of them, such as Parys, Rone (Rouen), Reme (Rheims), Orlyaunce, Naples, and a few others; and occasionally a familiar English name is made to serve for several distinct Latin ones. Thus, "Oxforde" not only represents Oxonium (Dec. 21), but also Oximæ, Exmes in Normandy, on Dec. 29, and Oxona, Burgo de Osma in Spain, on Apr. 2. So too "Venyse" does duty not only for Venetia but also for Venusia, Venosa (Oct. 24); and even "englonde" stands not only for Britannia, but also for Britannia Minor (Brittany), as in the "addicyons" on Oct. 24.

The names of places in England seem to have presented no less difficulty than the foreign ones. Even "Wentana civitas" is left as "wentane," although Syon was only separated from the diocese of Winchester by the river Thames; and Dorobernia remains as "doroberne," except on Nov. 10, where "dorobernensis" is confused with "Eboracensis," and St. Just is made "archebysshop of yorke."

The Martyrologium of Syon Monastery (British Museum, Add. MS. 22285). The history of this book is so closely connected with the fortunes of the "daughters of Syon," that a few words must be said about the monastery itself.[1]

The monastery of St. Saviour and SS. Mary the Virgin and Bridget of Syon was founded in Middlesex by King Henry V. in 1415, and was the only Brigettine house in England. Like other monasteries of this Order it was a double foundation for Sisters and Brothers, each with a separate enclosure. It was suppressed by Henry VIII. in 1539, when many of the Sisters retired to the Continent, and continued to live together according to the rule of their Order. By Queen Mary the daughters of Syon were restored to their old home in 1559, but they were dispossessed by Queen Elizabeth, when they took refuge a second time on the Continent, and resided successively at Dermond, Antwerp, and Mechlin. They removed to Rouen in 1584, but after the surrender of that city to Henry of Navarre, they again took flight and reached Lisbon in 1594, where they received a gift of houses and grounds from Isabel de Azevedo, and built a church and monastery. Here they remained until 1809, when troubles on the Continent urged them to take refuge in England, and nine sisters returned, bringing with them some books, their seals, and other relics. They at first lived in a small house at Walworth, and then at Peckham and elsewhere. Subsequently they removed to Spetisbury in Dorsetshire, and they are now settled at Chudleigh near Newton Abbot in Devonshire.

The MS. Martyrologium which had been the companion of the Sisters in all their wanderings was brought back to England in 1809, and sold to the Earl of Shrewsbury, from whose executors it was acquired for the British Museum in 1858.

Although this MS. has certainly been in the hands of the Sisters since the suppression of the monastery of Syon, in 1539, there is reason to suppose that the volume originally belonged to the Brothers. We know for certain that there were two

---

[1] A full and interesting account of Syon Monastery at Isleworth will be found in Aungier's *History and Antiquities of Syon Monastery*, London, 1840.

Martyrologia at Syon, one for the use of the Sisters, the other for the Brothers. They are referred to at fo. 17 b. of the MS. we are about to describe, in the chapter "*De exequiis pro benefactoribus librariarum,*" where it is ordered that the name of Thomas Graunte, a donor of books, is to be inscribed in each of the two Martyrologia. "Concessum est eciam quod nomen dicti Magistri Thome inseretur et inscribetur utrisque martilogiis scilicet tam sororum quam fratrum."

The reason for concluding that we have left to us the original Martyrologium of the Brothers is that the book contains the form of profession of the clerical Brothers whether *sacerdotes* or *diaconi*, and also for the lay-brothers (focarii), but there is no corresponding form for the Sisters. It will also be observed that the directions for the services for deceased members of the house and for benefactors would concern the Brothers rather than the Sisters.

We now proceed to describe the MS., which fortunately retains its fifteenth-century binding of white leather with overlapping edges. The clasp still remains. The leaves, which are of coarse vellum, measure $10\frac{5}{8}$ inches by 7 inches.

The figures in the following description of the contents refer to the modern numbering of the leaves.

> Fo. 1. Pasted into the cover there is a memorandum on paper relating to the death of St. Bridget in 1373, and the translation of her relics to the monastery of Wastein in Sweden in 1391. One bone was brought to England by Robert Bell, Confessor General of Syon, and by him enclosed in a silver gilt reliquary and presented to the monastery of Osney, near Oxford.
>
> Fo. 2. List of Abbesses of Syon beginning with the first abbess "Dña Joanna Northe," and ending with the sixteenth "Dña Birgitta Mendanha, Lusitana, 1ª."
> List of Confessors General.
>
> Fo. 3 a–4 b. Regulations for the service which was said by the Brothers for deceased Sisters and Brothers and for Henry V., founder, and other benefactors.

Fo. 5 a–10 b. Calendar of Sarum use (but only a few feasts are distinguished by being written in red).
> There are a few other entries and obits which are all in a later hand.
> x. Kal. Feb. Sancte osburge virginis. non sarum.
> vii. Kal. Jul. Canonizatio sancte katerine maius duplex.
> Non. Oct. Canonizatio beate Birgitte.
> Nov. 17. Exequie pro serenissima Maria regina Anglie. et pro D. Reginaldo Polo Cardinali. $17°$ die huius mensis. Anno dñi. $1558°$. Cum cantu.

Fo. 11, 12. Markers giving the plural forms of Soror, Focarius, Frater, Focaria, Benefactrix and other words used in reading the Obits.

Fo. 13. Rules for reading the Martyrologium, relating principally to grammar, commencing:—
> *Martilogium legatur post* de profundis *cotidie exceptis duobus diebus ante pascha et die pentecostes.*

Fo. 14. *De prima fundacione huius monasterii.*

Fo. 15. *De quibusdam exequiis singulis annis persoluendis.*

Fo. 17b. *De exequiis pro benefactoribus librariarum.*

Fo. 18 b, 19 a. The form of profession of a Brother, whether priest or deacon, promising obedience to the Confessor General, and to observe the Rule of St. Augustine, the Constitutions of St. Bridget, and also such local statutes and additions as might be made.

Fo 19 b., 20 a. The form of profession of a lay brother or focary. [Two forms are given, one more "compendious," both of them in English. They have been printed in the Introduction to *The Myroure of oure Ladye*, E.E.T.S., 1873, p. xxi.]

Fo. 21. De iacentibus in ambitibus fratrum et sororum. ab a° dñi 1485.

Fo. 21 b.–69 b. The Obituarium—consisting of a calendar, arranged with four days on each page, leaving blank spaces to be filled in from time to time with the names of Sisters, Brothers, or Benefactors.

Until about 1470 the entries are in the same hand, and have been copied from some older book. After that date, they have evidently been added from time to time. The dates range from 1422 to 1639.

The following extracts, some of which have been partly chosen to illustrate the continental wanderings of the Sisters, will show the nature of the record.

Januarii. f. 6. *Epiphania dni.*
Thomas Herberd frater laicus, 1500.
Dña Birgitta Rooke nona Abbatissa : obiit Rhotomagi in Normannia. anno dñi 1594. sepulta est ibidem in ecclesia sancti Loi coram summo altari.

Januarii. f. 20. *Fabiani et sebastiani.*
Effam eland soror.
Soror Catherina Dendi. Laica, 1639. [This appears to be the latest entry.]

Februarii. e. 16. Juliane uirginis.
Joana Iud soror.
Anna Martina soror, 1629. iacet in choro inferiori sororum ulissiponæ.

Februarii. g. 18.
Dñs dauid turson sacerdos.
1574. Joanna Damster Manra Soror. obiit Mechliniæ et ibi sepulta est apud fratres Augustinenses. De ea vide plura in registro nostro

Aprilis. d. 12.
Henricus Chicheley archiepiscopus cantuariensis qui hic fecit primam professionem. 1443.

May. e. 4.
1535. D. Richardus Raynold sacerdos qui mortem sustinuit apud Tyburne propter catholicam fidem. Martir. [the last word in a later hand].

Julii. f. 14.
Isabella ffyshborn. Soror.
1496. Isabella Marchall. Soror.
1594. Francisca Shelly. Soror. iacet apud Carmelitas excalsūs Ulissiponæ.

Julii. A. 23. *Natalis sancte birgitte.*
Thomas Jañ Episcopus Norwicensis A° do¹. 1500.
Soror Margerie Harte. Ulissiponæ 1628.

Augusti. e. 31. Cuthberge uirginis.
Dñs Henricus rex anglie quintus: fundator huius monasterii primus. Obiit Anno dñi 1422.

Septembris. g. 9. Gorgonii martiris.
Thomas Rasche ffrater laicus.
Dñs Clemens Maydeston. diaconus 1456.

[Probably Clement Maydeston, author of *Directorium Sacerdotum* and other works. Bishop Clifford's registers show that he was ordained sub-deacon and deacon in 1410, and priest in 1412.
The following extract from cap. x of the Constitutions of St. Bridget (Brit. Mus., Add. MS. 5208, fo. 8 b.) shows that one holding the office of "diaconus" at Syon might be a priest in order:—

"Sorores erunt sexaginta et non plures que clericos habebunt qui quotidie de tempore missam et officium quod habetur in ecclesiis cathedralibus illarum terrarum in quibus huiusmodi monasteria sunt decantabunt. . . . . Ipsi quidem sacerdotes debent esse tredecim iuxta numerum tredecim apostolorum. quorum Paulus tertius decimus non minimum laborem sustinuit. Deinde quattuor diaconi *qui etiam sacerdotes possunt esse si volunt* et ipsi figuram habent quattuor precipuorum doctorum. Ambrosii. Augustini. Gregorii et Ieronimi."]

Septembris. g. 16. *Edithe uirginis.*
Agnes ffogge. Soror. 1479.
D. Richardus Whitford. Sacerdos.[1]
D. Thomas Hardingus. Sacre theologie professor. benefactor, 1572.

Nouembris. f. 17. *Hugonis episcopi et confessoris.*
Regina Maria que restaurauit monasterium et religionem nostram post schisma et fuit noua fundatrix et restauratrix eorundem.
Eodem die obijt Reginaldus Polus Cardinalis et legatus a latere/ qui et reconsiliauit totum regnum nostrum Anglie ad unitatem ecclesie catholice/ et constituit nouam incorporacionem de religiosis personis que superstites fuerunt prius ante dissolucionem pertinentibus ad istum nostrum monasterium, 1558°.

Decembris. A. 31. *Siluestri pape* [the last word erased and subsequently restored].
Eodem die Dñs Henricus ffitzhugh. qui primo hunc ordinem adduxit in angliam. Obijt a° dni. 1426.

Fo. 70. *Nomina specialium benefactorum et amicorum.*
Dñs Henricus ffitzhugh dedit dominium et manerium de Henton ut patet in principio huius martilogij ca° ij°.
Ricardus Clyfforde episcopus londoñ. Ad valorem. x. li.
Henricus Chicheley archiepiscopus cantuariensis. Ad valorem. xx. li.
Rogerus Walden. episcopus Londoñ.
Johannes dux Bedfordie. Ad valorem. xx. li.

---

[1] Probably the uncle of our Richard Whytford.

Dōpn' Ioh. london. Reclusus Westmoñ.
Thomas Langley episcopus dunelmensis. xx li.
Margareta ducissa Clarencie. cc. li.
[and others, in all 88 names.]

Fo. 72. A form of bidding prayer for the soul of Thomas Jañ, archdeacon of Essex, commencing " Orate fratres presentes et futuri specialiter pro anima literatissimi iustissimique viri Thome Jañ decretorum doctoris. Archidiaconi Essex' ac ecclesie cathedralis sancti Pauli londoñ. canonici Residenciarii. . ."

[several blank leaves.]

Fo. 77 a-188 a. *Incipit martilogium : per anni circulum.*
This is the Martyrology which Richard Whytford has translated. The original text has received many additions and corrections. In some cases the correction has been written on a slip of paper and pasted in, and in other cases the erasure of the former writing has been so complete that it is not possible to determine the original reading.

In the upper and lower margins have been added in a later hand short passages to be read *in capitulo, e.g.* :—

> Jan. 1. In clericis tonsura quoddam signum est quod in corpore signatur. sed in animo agitur : scilicet ut hoc signo in religione vicia resecentur : et criminibus carnis nostre quasi crinibus exuamur : atque inde renouatis sensibus ut comis rudibus enitescamus. expoliantes nos : iuxta apostolum veterem hominem cum actibus suis. et induentes nouum hominem qui renouatur in agnitione dei. Tu autem domine miserere nostri. Deo gratias.
>
> Mar. 1. Tam doctrina quam vita : clarere debet ecclesiasticus doctor. Nam doctrina sine vita arrogantem reddit : vita sine doctrina inutilem facit.

The course of the Martyrology is interrupted at fo. 94, 95 by two leaves containing the *Preces in capitulo*, which are evidently placed here as being almost exactly in the middle of the book.

At the end of the Martyrologium on fo. 188 :—*Absolucio ffratrum die Canonizacionis beate Birgitte.*

> Auctoritate eciam dei patris omnipotentis et domini nostri ihesu christi. et beatorum petri et pauli apostolorum. et auctoritate michi in

hac parte indulta. ego concedo tibi persistenti in sinceritate fidei catholice. unitate sancte romane ecclesie. ac obediencia et deuocione romani pontificis plenam remissionem omnium peccatorum tuorum de quibus corde contritus es et ore confessus. In nomine patris et filii et spiritus sancti. Amen.

Fo. 188. b. *Preces in capitulo* repeated.

Fo. 189. *Sepultura fratrum iuxta gerras.*[1]

24 names follow.

Sepultura fratrum prope murum.

24 names.

Fo. 190. b. *Sepultura sororum iuxta Januam earum.*

6 names.

Fo. 191 a–192 a. *Sepultura sororum iuxta gerras*[1].

42 names.

Sepultura sororum prope murum.

42 names.

The last entries are :—

Johanna Russhe soror. An° do¹. 1557, 20 die decemb⁷ obijt.

Maria Neuel. soror. An⁰ do¹ 1558 17 die [erasure] obiit hic in Syon.

The reading of the Martyrologium in capitulo. It has been already mentioned that the Martyrologium was read in cathedral and monastic churches, where Sarum use was followed, at the conclusion of prime, when the clergy went in procession to the Chapter House.[2] At Syon the usual custom was not literally followed, for on fo. 13 of A, we have the direction "*Martilogium legatur post* de profundis." This service known as *De Profundis* was peculiar to the Brigettine rule, and consisted of a recitation of the Psalm *De Profundis* followed by a collect at a grave kept always open. This service, according to cap. xxiv of the rule of St. Saviour, was to be said after tierce,[3] and consequently the

---

[1] *Gerra* . . . . in plurali vero adhuc aliud significat. nam gerre rarū dicuntur sepes ferreæ circa altaria et choros. Balbi (Joannis de Janua) *Catholicon, s. v.*

[2] An account of the service *in capitulo* will be found in Dr. Todd's Introduction to *The Book of Obits and Martyrology of Christ Church, Dublin* (Irish Archæological Society), 1844, pp. lxxxvii–xcii.

[3] Cf. *The Myroure of oure Ladye* (E.E.T.S.), p. 142.

Martyrology at Syon could not have been read at the end of prime as it was elsewhere.

The printed Sarum Breviaries, which were intended for use in parish churches, take no direct notice of the reading of the Martyrologium and the service *in capitulo*. Reference is made to it incidentally in the rubrics in Commemoratione Defunctorum (*Breviarum ad usum Sarum*, ed. Procter and Wordsworth, III. 986), and also in the rubrics relating to prime for Maundy Thursday and Good Friday (*Ib.* I. dcclxxxiv, dccxciv).[1] There are similar incidental allusions to the reading of the Martyrology in the York Breviary (ed. Lawley, vol. i. 287, 406; vol. ii. 667).

In the Hereford Breviary, as I am informed by the Rev. W. Howard Frere, the reading of the Martyrology is referred to at the end of prime:—"*Lecto Martilogio sequitur* ℣. Preciosa." But the expression "*ubi vero martilogium non habetur*" implies that the reading of it was not universally enforced.

The following account of the service *in capitulo* at the end of prime is extracted from a MS. "Portiforium ad usum Sarum," of the fifteenth century in the possession of the writer of this Introduction.[2] The book was written for use in the diocese of Norwich, as is shown by the entry in the Calendar on Sept. 24. "Dedicacio ecclesie cathedralis Norwicensis. ix lecciones."

Hiis dictis eant processionaliter clerici in capitulum. et sit ibi quidam de prima forma scilicet puer indutus superpelliceo paratus ad legendum leccionem de martilogio absque Iube domine *sed pronunciando primo numerum nonarum. Iduum uel calendarum. et etatem lune quales erunt in crastino secundum quod dies uidebitur exigere et finiatur leccio sine.* Tu autem. hoc modo. Et aliorum plurimorum sanctorum martirum confessorum atque uirginum.

Finita leccione. si quis obitus fuerit pronuncietur post predictam clausulam. scilicet. Et aliorum. *et cetera et legatur per omnia sicut predicta leccio uidelicet hoc modo.* Eodem die obiit. N. de w. qui fuit decanus istius ecclesie *uel* cancellarius *uel huiusmodi* qui legauit C.

---

[1] A MS. Sarum Portiforium in my possession, which appears to have belonged to the parish of Shillington, Beds., has a rubric in the Sanctorale before the feast of St. Matthias giving directions for the reading of the Martiloge in leap year which are almost identical with the extract from an Ordinale printed in the Notes of this volume, p. 212.

[2] Mr. Christopher Wordsworth has called my attention to a rubric in the printed Sarum Antiphoner of 1520, which is similar to that of the MS. Portiforium.

libras ad emendacionem operis sancte marie et C. marcas ad usum canonicorum et uicariorum. *Si uero plures fuerint obitus hoc modo legantur.* Eodem die obierunt. *et cetera.* *Tunc sacerdos post ipsum lectorem stans dicat sine nota.* Anima eius. *uel.* Anime eorum et anime omnium fidelium defunctorum. *et cetera.* ℞. Amen.

Deinde dicat sacerdos. Preciosa est in conspectu. ℞. Mors sanctorum eius.

Deinde dicat sacerdos. sine Dominus uobiscum. *et sine* Oremus *hanc oracionem.*

Sancta maria mater domini nostri ihesu christi atque omnes sancti iusti et electi dei intercedant et orent pro nobis peccatoribus a[d] dominum deum nostrum. ut nos mereamur ab eo adiuuari et saluari. qui in trinitate perfecta uiuit et regnat deus per omnia secula seculorum. ℞. Amen.

Postea sacerdos dicat sic. Deus in adiutorium meum intende. Domine ad adiuuandum me festina *et dicatur tribus uicibus* Gloria patri. Sicut erat. Kyrieleyson. Christeleyson. Kyrieleyson. Pater noster. et ne nos inducas. Sed libera. Et ueniat super nos misericordia tua domine. Salutare tuum secundum eloquium. Et respice in seruos tuos et in opera tua. Et dirige filios eorum. Et sit splendor domini dei nostri. super nos. Et opus manuum tuarum dirige super nos et opus manuum nostrarum dirige.

Hec sequens oracio dicitur in festis dupplicibus et quocienscumque chorus regitur extra ebdomadam pasche et sine. Dominus uobiscum. *sed cum.* Oremus.

Oracio.

Omnipotens sempiterne deus dirige actus nostros in beneplacito tuo. ut in nomine dilecti filii tui mereamur bonis operibus habundare. Qui tecum uiuit et regnat in unitate spiritus sancti deus per omnia secula seculorum. ℞. Amen. Dominus uobiscum. Benedicamus.

In omnibus aliis festis sine regimine chori et in feriis per totum annum preterquam a cena domini usque ad octavam pasche dicitur hec oracio sine Dominus uobiscum *sed cum* Oremus.

Oracio.

Dirigere et sanctificare et regere dignare domine deus quesumus corda et corpora nostra in lege tua et in operibus mandatorum tuorum. ut hic et ineternum te auxiliante sani et salui esse mereamur. Per dominum nostrum ihesum christum. filium tuum. Qui tecum. *et finiatur cum* Dominus uobiscum. *et cum* Benedicamus domino.

Hijs itaque peractis. puer lector legat aliam leccionem de ome[liis] *et de libro theologorum quam cum.* Jube domine. *incipiat et eandem cum.* Tu autem. *terminat.*

Sacerdos autem dicat benediccionem scilicet quando chorus regitur simpliciter. Ille nos benedicat qui sine fine uiuit et regnat.

In dupplicibus festis in capitulo et in xl^a ad collacionem dicitur ista benediccio. scilicet. Omnipotens deus sua gracia nos benedicat.

Sacerdos uero dicta benediccione ante leccionem in loco suo se reponat et

hec omnia in capitulo dicantur omnibus clericis interim stantibus et exinde sedere tenentur usque post lectam tabulam puer uero finita leccione a pulpito descendat et tabulam legat.
  Et quandocunque dicitur Psalmus. Ad le leuaui. *ad matutinas. tunc ad primam dicitur Psalmus.* Leuaui oculos meos. *stando sine nota* cum. Gloria patri. *et.* Sicut erat. *Sequitur.* Kyrieleyson. Christeleyson. Pater noster. Et ne nos. Sed libera. Ostende nobis domine misericordiam tuam. Et salutare tuum da nobis. Saluos fac seruos tuos et ancillas tuas. Deus meus sperantes in te. Mitte eis domine auxilium de sancto. Et de syon tuere illos. Esto eis domine turris fortitudinis. A facie inimici. Nichil proficiat inimicus in eis. Et filius iniquitatis non apponat nocere eis. Domine exaudi oracionem meam. Et clamor meus ad te ueniat. Dominus uobiscum. Et cum. Oremus.

Oracio.

Adesto domine supplicacionibus nostris. et uiam famulorum tuorum in salutis tue prosperitate dispone: ut inter omnes uie et uite huius uarietates tuo semper protegantur auxilio.

Alia Oracio.

Omnipotens sempiterne deus salus eterna credencium. exaudi nos pro famulis tuis pro quibus misericordie tue imploramus auxilium: ut reddita sibi sanitane[1] graciarum tibi in ecclesia tua referant acciones. Per christum dominum. R̃. Amen.
  Et utraque dicatur sub uno. Per christum. *Excellencior persona dicat.* Benedicite. *Chorus.* Dominus. *Sacerdos.* In nomine patris et filii et spiritus sancti. R̃. Amen.
  Et sic unusquisque muniat se signo crucis et ita recedant in chorum processionaliter.

Description of " The Martiloge in englysshe after the vse of the chirche of salisbury/ 't as it is redde in Syon/ with addicyons." Printed at London by Wynkyn de Worde, Feb. 15, 1526.

The book is a small quarto consisting of 144 leaves. The first two leaves are unnumbered and without signature, the former of them having a woodcut of St. Bridget, with the title above it, whilst the other leaf has the preface in larger type than the rest of the book.

The numbered leaves are in 35 gatherings of 4 each (except the last, kk, which has 6), with signatures a–z, 't, ꝯ, aa–kk.

There are a few mistakes in the numbering of the leaves, fo.

---
[1] *sic* for sanitate.

xcviii, c, and cxli are wrongly numbered xcvii, xcix, and cxxxix, respectively. The last leaf is unnumbered.

The pages are of 32 lines, and the printed page measures 152 mm. by 97 mm. (excluding the head lines). The preface is in larger type, 29 lines to the page, and the size of the printed page is 160 mm. by 95 mm.

The woodcut of St. Bridget on the first leaf (see the facsimile) represents her seated at a desk writing her revelations at the dictation of an angel. Above there is a representation of the Holy Trinity and of the Nativity. Below her kneel a brother and a sister of the order founded by her. Behind her are placed the staff and scrip as symbols of her pilgrimage to Rome; and the crown and arms mark her rank as Princess of Nericia in the kingdom of Sweden.

This woodcut, of which a facsimile is given in this reprint, was used not only by Wynkyn de Worde, but also in same year (1526) by R. Pynson (three times in the same book) for the *Pilgrimage of Perfection*. It was also used by Richard Fawkes in his edition of *The Myroure of oure Ladye*, 1530, and by Robert Redman in *The Pype/ or Tonne/ of the lyfe of Perfection*, 1532, and elsewhere.

The copies of this book which have come under our notice are the following:—

1. BRITISH MUSEUM. [C. 25. c. (4)] A fine and perfect copy.
2. BODLEIAN LIBRARY, OXFORD. [Douce Ww. 113.] A perfect copy.
3. LAMBETH LIBRARY. [xxxv. 2. 7.] This copy wants the first two leaves, but is interesting as being in its original binding of stamped leather. On one side are panels with figures of SS. George, Barbara, Michael and Catharine, and on the other the arms and supporters of Henry VIII, with the legend:—laudate dominum de terra dracones et omnes abyssi. G.R.
4. CATHEDRAL LIBRARY, LINCOLN. [Rr. 4. 26.] This copy wants the last leaf.
5. HUTH LIBRARY. See *Catalogue of the Huth Library*, vol. iii, p. 924. A perfect copy.

6. STONYHURST COLLEGE. See F. H. Dickinson's *List of Service Books*, 1850, p. 15.
7. ARCHBISHOP MARSH'S LIBRARY, DUBLIN. To the Rev. Christopher Wordsworth we are indebted for knowledge of this copy.

(Information as to the existence of other copies will be welcome.)

The present reprint. In reprinting the *Martiloge*, an endeavour has been made to reproduce as closely as possible the peculiarities of the old print, and with this object the contractions have not been expanded. No alteration has been consciously made even in the punctuation, except in a few cases, where in the original print a full stop was left out at the end of a line from want of space, although the next line commenced with a capital letter. As the present print does not reproduce the old one line for line, and the break no longer comes at the end of a line, the stop has usually been supplied. In order to save space the marginal notes have been indented into the text of the reprint. The use of Roman type instead of the black letter of Wynkyn de Worde has of course entirely changed the typography of the book. In some few cases a difficulty has occurred in finding exact equivalents for the marks of contraction in the original. It will be noticed that occasionally the marks of contraction are not used in the conventional manner. In these matters the original has been strictly followed. The contractions in the old print were often determined by the desire of the compositor to compress his matter into one line. Consequently, in our reprint the contractions appear to be used capriciously, as the reason for their use is not apparent without consulting the original text.

The number of typographical errors in Wynkyn de Worde's print does not appear to be large. They have not been corrected in the reprint, but have been marked with an obelus (†) to assure the reader that the text has been reproduced, and that the mistake has not been made in the process of reprinting.

The same mark has also been placed against some of the proper names, which differ in their spelling from that used in other Martyrologies, and in such cases the word is generally referred to in the Notes. In the use of capitals for the proper names, the old printer has been very irregular. Usually his names of persons have capitals, but the names of places begin with small letters. It will, however, be noticed that at the commencement of the book many of the names of places have capitals. When the names of persons begin with *z*, the want of a capital *z* in his fount has compelled Wynkyn de Worde to use a small letter. A small initial *w* is also often used, and the capital *w* which sometimes occurs is in reality only a small *w* belonging to a larger fount.

The book has been reprinted from a transcript made by the Rev. F. Procter from the copy preserved in the Cathedral Library at Lincoln, which was lent for the purpose by the Dean and Chapter. The proofs have been read by Mr. Procter, and compared with this copy; and they have also been compared by his co-editor with the copy of the same edition in the British Museum.

The Editors desire to express their thanks to many who have helped in the production of this book. In the first place, thanks are due to the Dean and Chapter of Lincoln for placing their copy of the Martiloge at the disposal of Mr. Procter for making a transcript, and for the subsequent correction of the proofs. Acknowledgments are also due for facilities and courteous assistance afforded at the British Museum, and in the Library of Lambeth Palace. From several members of the Council of the Henry Bradshaw Society, much help has been received in elucidating obscure and difficult matters. The Rev. Canon Cooke (Chairman), Dr. J. Wickham Legg, Rev. F. E. Warren, Mr. W. H. St. John Hope, have contributed from their stores of knowledge; and especial thanks are due to the Rev. Christopher Wordsworth, Prebendary of Lincoln, who has taken the greatest interest in this work. To him the Society is indebted for the

Index Sanctorum which he has compiled, and also for his kindness in reading the proofs of all the sheets as they appeared, and for many valuable suggestions with which he has enriched the edition.

In conclusion, it should be added that although Mr. Procter has kindly read the proofs of the Notes, Indexes, and Introduction, he is not responsible for the opinions expressed in them, nor for the many errors which it is feared may be found.

E. S. D.

March 22nd, 1893.

TABLE OF CONTENTS.

Introduction :—   PAGE.

    The Martyrology   v

    R. Whytford's Addicyons   xii

    British Saints in the Martiloge   xiv

    Richard Whytford   xxi

    Richard Whytford as a translator xxiii

    The MS. Martyrologium of Syon Monastery   xxv

    The reading of the Martyrologium in capitulo xxxii

    Description of " The Martiloge in englysshe after the vse of the chirche

        of salisbury/ and as it is redde in Syon/ with addicyons." Printed

        at London by Wynkyn de Worde in 1526 xxxv

    The present reprint xxxvii

THE MARTILOGE, 1526   ...   1

Notes   205

Index Sanctorum   237

Glossarial Index of Names of Places   279

Glossary of obsolete or unusual words   285

Appendix :—

    Extracts relating to English Saints in the Canterbury Martyrology ... 287

THE
MARTILOGE

TRANSLATED INTO ENGLISH

BY

RICHARD WHYTFORD

WITH ADDITIONS.

1526.

¶ The Martiloge in englysshe after the vse of the chirche of Salisbury, & as it is redde in Syon, with addicyons.

⁋ Vnto the deuoute reders/ Rychard whytford preest and professed broder of Syon/ in our lorde god and moost swete sauyour Iesu Salutacyon,

Many deuoute persones/ specyally religyous/ whan they done sende forthe werkes of theyr owne makynge/ theyr owne gaderynge/ or translacyon/ done vse customably to reteyne (of mekenes) theyr names: whiche thynge I do not discōmende/ but rather do I prayse them therin: notwithstandynge I beseche you good deuout reders/ take none occasyon in me/ though I do contrary/ that is to saye/ though I (knowyng that my poore labour and doynge in suche thynges/ is no thynge worthy prayse: ⁊ also that myne own conscyence doth not requyre ony maner thanke prayse/ or other tēporall or worldly rewarde but onely doth desyre the spirytuall profyte of the reders or herers) though I saye/ do set forthe my name vnto euery thynge that I sende forth/ not (as I sayd for ambicyon/ our lorde vnto wytnes) but rather to expowne and offre my selfe vnto iust correccyon: wher vnto I do in moost humble maner submyt my selfe. And also an other cause why I do so set forth my name/ is that I haue herde of dyuerse werkes that bē foūde in prynt as faderles childer without auctours/ that bē not onely yᵉ lesse regarded bycause they ben without auctours/ but also ben suspected/ as not holdyng ⁊ kepyng yᵉ ryght path of christianite. I wold therfore none other pson shold be reproued ne blamed for my dede/ but rather that I shold my selfe (as the cōmune puerbe sayth) drynke suche as I brue. Trustynge therfore in your charite/ that ye wyll ascrybe applye/ ⁊ take all thynge vnto yᵉ best/ we haue sent forth this martiloge/ whiche we dyd translate out of latyn in to englysshe/ for the edificacyon of certayn religyous psones vnlerned/ that dayly dyd rede the same martiloge in latyn/ not vnderstādynge what they redde. And the addicyons for theyr more edificacyon/ we gadered out of the sanctiloge/ legendaurea/ catalogo sācto%/ the cronycles of Antonine/ ⁊ of saynt Vincēt/ ⁊ other dyuers auctours. I beseche you of your christyan fauour ⁊ charitable prayer. I shall humbly beseche our lorde that all you/ accordynge vnto the very purpose ⁊ effecte of our mynde may profyte in the redynge hereof. Valete.

⁋ Our lord god ⁊ moost swete sauyour Iesu sende vs all his mercy ⁊ grace. Amen.

⁋ The sayd wretche of Syon
Rychard whytford.

[⁋ The Martiloge was gadred ⁊ ordeyned to be redde [*fo. i.* by the holy doctour saynt Ierome/ ⁊ is contynued in the chirche/ that where all the sayntes may not (for theyr multytude) be syngulerly serued w*t* offyce/ they sholde at y*e* leest vpon theyr dayes/ knowen ouer euen/ haue a memory/ or breue remembraūce/ wherby euery persone moued in grace accordynge vnto theyr deuocyon may worshyp them. The maner of redynge foloweth.

⁋ Here begynneth the Martyloge after the vse of the chirche of Salysbury/ and as it is redde in Syon/ with addycyons.

TO morowe the fyrst day of Ianuary shall be y*e* feest of the circūcysyon of our lord ⁊ sauyour Chryst Iesu/ wherin he fyrst shed his precyous blode for our redempcyon. At rome the feest of sayt Almache a martyr that prechynge vnto y*e* people/ sayd vnto them in this maner. This daye (sayd he) is the octaue/ or eyght daye of y*e* byrth of our sauyour/ wherfore ye people cease ⁊ put awaye your superstycyous†/ your false religyon/ ⁊ your worshyppynge of ydolles/ and leue also your vnlawfull games. For the whiche wordes he was forthwith put to deth by y*e* cōmaundement of the Mayre ⁊ chefe offycer. At rome also the feest of .lx. soudyours or men of warre/ that for Chryst were put to deth by y*e* emperour Diocleciane. At rome also the feest of saynt Martyne a virgyn/ that vnder y*e* emperour Alexander was put to many dyuerse turmentes/ ⁊ at the last heded. At the cyte of spolete/ the [feest of saynt Concorde a martyr/ [*fo. i. b.* that in y*e* tyme of Antonyne the emperour/ was fyrst beten w*t* staues/ than hanged on a gybet/ ⁊ after taken in to pryson a longe tyme fast fettred/ ⁊ so pyned ⁊ nere famysshed/ where notw*t*standynge he was conforted by aūgels/ ⁊ at the last he ended his martyrdome slayne by the swerde. In Cesary the chefe cyte of Capadoce/ the deposicyon of saynt Basyle a bysshop/ whose chefe feest is kepte the .xiiij. daye of Iune. In Affryke the feest of saynt Fulgence bysshop of y*e* chirche of ruspence/ that for the fayth of Chryst/ ⁊ for his noble doctryne/ was exiled a longe tyme : but at y*e* last he returned vnto his chirche ⁊ there honourable in lyuyng/ ⁊ diligent in prechynge he made a holy ende. In the terrytory or fraūchest of Lyons the feest of saynt Augend an abbot/ whose lyfe full of vertue ⁊ myracles/ was grete lyght and good example vnto y*e* people. In Alexander y*e* feest of saynt Eufrosyne a virgyn.

IANVARY. 3

¶ Addycyons.

Gregori⁹. ¶ The feest also of another saynt Fulgence/ that was bysshop of Vtruculane/ a man of grete holynes/ that by myracle was delyuered from yᵉ cruelty of yᵉ kynge of Gotes. The feest also of saynt Odyle a holy abbot ⁊ of many myracles/ moche liberal in almes/ pyteous ⁊ mercyful in all correccyon/ yᵗ whan he was chalenged ⁊ rebuked for prodygalite in expences/ ⁊ as remysse ⁊ negligent in correccyon/ he answered/ sayenge/ that yf he sholde be dampned/ he had leuer it were for mercy thā for rygour. The feest also of many other holy sayntes/ martyrs/ cōfessours ⁊ virgyns. This last clause/ of many other sayntes .⁊c. must euer be redde last.

¶ To morowe.

[¶ The seconde daye of Ianuary. At the cyte of Antio- [*fo. ii.* che yᵉ passyon of blessed saynt Ysidour a bysshop ⁊ martyr. In Thomis a cyte of pont/ the feest of saynt Arge saynt Marcesset ⁊ saynt Marcellyne/ all thre breder ⁊ chylder of age/ yᵗ were taken amonge soudyours that were vnder the capytayne ⁊ prynce Licyne/ ⁊ bycause they were founde of Chrystes fayth/ they were fyrst beten ⁊ turmented nere vnto deth/ ⁊ after taken in to pryson/ ⁊ there almoost famysshed/ ⁊ at the last they were drowned in the see. In the cyte of Thebaida the feest of saynt Machary an abbot. The feest also of saȳt Syridion a bysshop/ ⁊ the octaue of saynt Steuen/ ⁊ the feest of saynt Barbariā a confessour. At the towne of Syluiake/ the feest of saynt Odilion a holy abbot/ that was a pyteous man and of hygh perfeccyon. ¶ Addycyons.

¶ The feest also of an other saȳt Machary a preest of egypt/ of many myracles that amonge other restored a woman vnto her owne fourme/ yᵗ was wytched by nigromancy lyke vnto a beest. The feest also of many other holy sayntes/ martyrs/ cōfessours/ ⁊ virgyns.

¶ To morowe.

¶ The thyrde day of Ianuary. At rome in appia strete the feest of saynt Anthery the pope/ yᵗ whan he had well ruled yᵉ chirche of Chryst .xii. yeres/ suffred deth ⁊ martyrdome vnder yᵉ emperour Maximyan/ ⁊ was buryed in the cimitery of saynt Calixt. In the cyte of Aulane yᵉ feest of saynt Peter/ yᵗ for Chryst folowynge his mayster suffred the deth of the crosse. At ellespont the feest of saynt Ciryke/ saynt Prime ⁊ saynt Theogene. At Paryse the feest of saynt Genofeue a virgyn of

A 2

noble vertue/ and consecrate by saynt Germayne. [The octaue also of saynt Iohñ the euangelyst. [*fo. ii. b.*

¶ Addycyons.

¶ At Padwey the feest of saynt Daniel a deacon and martyr/ whose holy body was there foūde many yeres after his deth by reuelacyon made vnto a blynde woman y^t therby was restored to syght. The feest also of many other holy sayntes/ marP. confes. ꝛ virgyns.

¶ To morowe.

¶ The fourth day of Ianuary/ ye feest of saynt Tyte discyple vnto saynt Paule the apostle/ ꝛ of hym made preest ꝛ bysshop of cretens/ that faythfully fulfyllyng the office of prechynge/ made a blessed ende/ ꝛ was buryed in the same chirche. In affryke the feest of saynt Aquilyne/ saynt Gemyne/ saynt Eugence/ saynt Martiniane/ saynt Quintyne/ saynt Theodour/ and saynt Tryphon all martyrs/ whose noble actes ꝛ dedes ben wryten in theyr legendes. At Rome the feest of saynt Priske a preest/ saynt Priscillyane a clerke/ and saynt Benedicte a virgyn/ y^t all togyder accomplisshed theyr martyrdome by the swerde in the tyme of the emperour Iulyane. At rome also ye feest of saynt Dafrose/ wyfe vnto saynt Fabyane the martyr/ after whose deth she was fyrst exiled/ ꝛ after by ye mayre called prynce heded. In bonony ye feest of saynt Hermete/ saȳt Aggey/ ꝛ saynt Key martyrs/ ꝛ the octaue of ye Innocentes.

¶ Addycyons.

¶ The feest also of saynt Rigobert archebysshop of remens/ a man of noble blode/ ꝛ frō his youth of synguler sanctite/ had in moche honour ꝛ drede/ ꝛ yet more beloued of all persones. At cyzyke in hellespont ye feest of saynt Theogenes a martyr/ y^t was takē ꝛ brought vnto a company of soudyours/ where he confessynge [Chryst/ was beten w^t flayles/ tyll .xviii. of [*fo. iii.* them were fatigate ꝛ weryed/ than was he put in prison ꝛ there nayled fast vnto a stocke/ whome our sauyour with a grete multytude conforted w^t loude voyce/ so that all ye people myght here: yet after was he cast in to the see where in his drownynge was suche a sodeyn lyght ꝛ splendour/ that all the people were stryken blynde/ ꝛ thereby all cōuerted/ ꝛ honourably dyd bury his holy body cast upon the land by ye wawes. The feest also of many other holy sayntes martyrs/ cōfes. ꝛ virgyns.

¶ To morowe.

¶ The fyfth day of Ianuary. At rome ye feest of saynt Thelesfory the pope/ that was the seuenth pope after saynt

Peter/ ƚ a noble martyr. At antioche the feest of saynt Symeon a monke/ whose lyfe and conuersacyon was meruaylous holy. At westmynster yᵉ feest of saȳt Edwarde kynge ƚ cōfessour. The octaue also of saynt Thomas of Caūterbury. And yᵉ euen of yᵉ epyphany. ⁋ Addycyons.

⁋ The feest also of two sayntes yᵗ were kẏnesmen vnto our sauyour Chryst/ whose names be not rehersed but that in the tyme of yᵉ emperour Domiciane that slewe and put to deth all persones of the blode ƚ kynne of Dauyd/ these twayne were brought vnto hym/ ƚ whan he had examined them of Chryst/ he toke theyr sayenge as folysshenes/ ƚ so suffred them to departe ƚ they contynued in the chirche profytynge in the same vnto the tyme of the emperour Traianus/ ƚ bycause theyr daye is vnknowen as well as theyr names/ I put them here in yᵉ feest of our sauyour. The feest also of many other holy sayntes mart̃. cōfessours ƚ virg.

⁋ To morowe.

[⁋ The syxth day of Ianuary. The epyphany of [*fo. iii. b.* our sauyour/ in the whiche daye he was honoured of the thre kynges with gyftes of mystery/ ƚ in the whiche day he accomplysshed in hymselfe the hygh offyce of our saluacyon/ the sacred foūtayne of baptym/ receyuynge yᵉ same of holy saynt Iohn̄ his precursor ƚ foregoer. And in yᵉ whiche daye also he turned water into wyne at yᵉ maryage in the cyte of Cane in yᵉ coūtree of Galile. In the terrytory of Remens the feest of saynt Macrea a virgyn/ that by the mayre called rikciouare was cast hedlonge into a grete fyre/ ƚ therin remayned a long tyme wᵗout hurt/ after she was kept longe in a foule stynkynge prison/ ƚ there nerehande famysshed/ than were her brestes or pappes kytte away/ ƚ she after rolled naked vpon hote syndres ƚ brennynge coles/ ƚ there in prayer she yelded the spiryte. At the cite of Redomist̄ the feest of saynt Melane a bysshop ƚ confessour of grete vertue and many myracles.

Nota.
A ₽rytory
is alone to
saye as a
fraūchest.

⁋ Addicyons.

⁋ The feest also of yᵉ sayd .iii. kynges/ called of Coleyn̄ that in theyr homage dyd offre vnto our sauyour golde/ sence/ ƚ myrre : at whiche tyme after dyuerse auctours/ saynt Iasper called also Gaspar was of yᵉ age of .lx. yeres/ saynt Balthazar of .xl. yeres/ ƚ saynt Melchior .xx. that whan they came home in to theyr owne coūtrees by an other waye (as is sayd in the gospell) they lefte ƚ forsoke all gentilite ƚ lyued a holy lyfe/ yet styll vnbaptysed vnto yᵉ tyme yᵗ after yᵉ deth of Chryst saynt Thomas the apostle came in to ynde/ of whome they receyued yᵉ holy sacrament of baptym ꝛ of cōfyrmacyon/ ꝛ were made wt hym prechers of the fayth/ ꝛ therin they dyed/ whose holy bodyes were translate [by the emperour Constantyne in [*fo. iiii.* to yᵉ cite of constantynople. And after they were trāslated agayne by saynt Eustorge bysshop of Myllen. And now they lye at Coleyn. The feest also of many other holy sayntes martyrs/ confessours and virgyns.

¶ To morowe.

¶ The .vij. day of Ianuary. The relation of tydỹges of the chylde our sauyour Iesu in egypte. And yᵉ feest of saynt Luciane bysshop of antioche/ that was a famous man of grete lernyng ꝛ eloquence/ ꝛ for yᵉ fayth of Chryst he was put to deth in the cite of Nicodemeṭ by the persecucyon of yᵉ emperour Maximiane/ ꝛ buryed at helionopleṭ in bithynie. At antioche the feest of saynt Clere a deacon/ that for Chryst was .vij. tymes racked and put to many turmentes/ famysshed in pryson/ and at the last heded. In the cite of Heraclea the feest of saynt Felix and saynt Ianuary.

¶ Addicyons.

¶ The feest also of saynt Siricius pope/ that among other noble actes dyd make an ordynaūce ꝛ constytucyon/ that no preest sholde saye masse but in places or awters halowed by a bysshop. The feest also of saynt zozyme pope also/ that was a man of grete vertue/ ꝛ vnto poore people very liberall ꝛ moche beneficyall/ ꝛ ordeyned that preestes sholde kepe no tauernes ne sell mete or drynke. The feest also of saynt Simplyće/ the nexte pope after saynt Hilarye/ a grete holy man/ and he ordeyned that no man of the chirche sholde receyue his habyte of a ley man. The feest also of many other holy sayntes/ martyrs/ confessours and virgyns.

¶ To morowe.

¶ The .viij. daye of Ianuary. At campane in naples [the feest of saỹt Seueryne a bysshop ꝛ cōfessour/ that was [*fo. iiii. b.* broder vnto saynt Victoryne yᵉ martyr/ ꝛ a man of grete holynes. At beluake the feest of saỹt Luciane a bysshop/ saynt Maximian a preest/ ꝛ saynt Iulyan a deacon all martyrs by the swerde. The feest also of saynt Eugenian a martyr. At augustndune the feest of saynt Eugenian a bysshop. In greke land the feest of saynt Timothie a martyr.

¶ Addicyons.

¶ In englonde the feest of saynt Wolsyn a bysshop and

cōfessour/ borne of noble blode in ye cite of London/ ⁊ for bycause he was all gyuen vnto vertue in youthe/ his frendes put hym in to ye abbey of westmynster/ where after he was abbot/ ⁊ after that bysshop of shyrborne a man of harde lyfe/ grete pfeccion ⁊ many myracles. The feest also of an other saynt Scueryne an abbot of lyfe aūgelicall/ that had the spiryte of pphecy/ ⁊ by ye grace of his presence/ euery cite where he came was preserued from ye barbarous infydeles that destroyed many coūtrees. The feest also of saȳt Erhard bysshop of ratisponens/ a man of moche pyte vnto the poore ⁊ of notable vertue. The feest also of many other holy sayntes/ martyrs/ confessours and virgyns.

⁋ To morowe.

⁋ The .ix. day of Ianuary. At antioche ye feest of saȳt Iulian an abbot of a .M. monkes/ ⁊ of his wyfe saynt Basilysse a holy virgyn/ for they departed by one assent virgyns bothe in to religyon/ ⁊ she dyed ⁊ all her virgyns before of whome she was abbesse/ ⁊ he after was takē in the tyme of the emperours Dioclecian ⁊ Maximian ⁊ put to meruayllous turmentes ⁊ cruell deth ⁊ al his monkes ⁊ many y^t fledde vnto hym from [the horryble persecucyon/ among whome was saynt Antonyne/ [*fo. v.* saynt Anastase/ ⁊ a chylde called saynt Celsus w^t his moder ⁊ many other all brent. In affryke the feest of saynt Reuocate/ saynt Firmyn/ with other thre persones all martyrs. The feest also of saynt Pascasia a virgyn and martyr. In wentane the translacyon of saynt Nidoke a confessour. In Cesariens the feest of saynt Marciane a virgyn and martyr.

⁋ Addicyons.

⁋ The feest also of saynt Marcellyne bysshop of aconitane†/ an honourable man of holy lyf/ that whan he was seke ⁊ myght not go/ and the cite was all on fyre lyke hooly to haue ben lost/ he cōmaūded to set hym in a chayre before the fyre/ ⁊ so it ceased ⁊ dyd no hurte. In englonde ye feest of saynt Adriane/ borne in affryke ⁊ abbot of veridiane/ that for his grete fame ⁊ synguler vertue was sent in to englonde w^t saynt Theodore that was prymate of englonde nexte after saynt Augustyn/ ⁊ saynt Adriane abbot of Caūterbury/ ⁊ there lyued a holy lyf .xl. yeres in grete labours ⁊ prechynge ⁊ dyd many grete myracles bothe in his lyfe ⁊ after. The feest also of many other holy sayntes/ martyrs/ confessours and virgyns.

¶ To morowe.

¶ The .x. daye of Ianuary. In cipris y̆ᵉ feest of saynt Nichanour/ one of the .vij. deacons yᵗ were in the fyrst begy̆nynge of yᵉ chirche/ a man of grete ⁊ meruaylous vertue ⁊ grace of fayth. In the cite of thebaida yᵉ feest of saynt Paule the fyrst heremyte/ whose blessed soule saynt Antony sawe cōuayde ⁊ caryed in to heuen by yᵉ quere ⁊ celestyall company of aūgels/ apostles ⁊ other sayntes. At Rome the feest of saynt Melchiades the [pope/ a man of grete vertue and holynes.   [fo. v. b.
¶ Addicyons.

¶ The feest also of another saynt Paule/ whose syrname was symple/ that fyndynge his wyfe wᵗ aduoutry/ forsoke her ⁊ went in to wyldernes/ ⁊ was discyple vnto saynt Antony/ ⁊ he was after his name very symple ⁊ meke ⁊ synguler in the vertue of obedyence/ he cured many psones by myracle where saynt Antony fayled/ he knewe yᵉ secrete thoughtes of many persones/ ⁊ had very many other graces. At bituricens yᵉ feest of saynt wylliam a bysshop ⁊ cōfessour/ a man of noble blode/ ⁊ of grete myracles ⁊ synguler sctīte. The feest also of many other holy. saȳtes/ mar./ ǫfes. ⁊ virg.

¶ To morowe.

¶ The .xj. daye of Ianuary. In affryke/ the feest of saynt Saluert/ at whose obit saynt Augustyn preched vnto yᵉ people of cartage. In Alexander yᵉ feest of saynt Peter/ saynt Seuere/ ⁊ saynt Lucius all confessours whose actes ben notable.

a. l. leonce

¶ Addicyons.

¶ The feest also of saynt Ygyn pope ⁊ martyr/ that in the psecucyons of yᵉ emperour Seuere suffred moche trouble/ ⁊ at the last was put to deth/ he made many good ordynaūces/ for he diuyded yᵉ degrees of yᵉ clergy ⁊ ordeyned yᵗ euery psone shold in his baptym at yᵉ lest haue one godfader ⁊ one godmoder: ⁊ in cōfirmacyon one godfader or one godmod/ wᵗ many other. The feest also of many other holy sayntes/ marť. cōfes. ⁊ virg.

¶ To morowe.

¶ The .xij. day of Ianuary. In achaia yᵉ feest of saȳt Sataryt a martyr/ that by yᵉ sygne of yᵉ crosse ⁊ a blast of his mouth/ dyd ouerthrowe ⁊ cast down an ydoll/ for yᵉ whiche dede he was forthwᵗ heded. In maturi[tane at casaryt yᵉ feest [fo. vi.

IANVARY.

of saynt Archade a martyr/ a noble man of byrth/ but more noble in vertu ⁊ myracles. At nicomede the feest of saynt Pastor ⁊ saynt Victor. ❡ Addicyons.

❡ In englond ye feest of saynt Alrede an abbot/ whose face beynge a chylde in his cradell/ was seen bryght shynynge w^t beames y^t gaue shadowe as the sonne/ ⁊ he was a man of very grete pacyence ⁊ many myracles. In englonde also ye feest of saynt Benedict a syrname bysshop an abbot/ that
Nota. buylded ye monasteryes vpon ye waters of were ⁊ tyne/ ⁊ he was .v. tymes at Rome/ frō whens he brought ye chefe syngynge man of Rome to teche his monkes/ and so brought he fyrst prycksonge in to englonde/ he brought also thens many royall bokes. And he fyrst brought in to englonde makers of glaswyndowes/ ⁊ of stone wyndowes barred. And he brought vp of a chylde the grete clerke of englonde called saynt Bede/ that is comynly named the venerable or worshypfull Bede. The feest also of many other holy sayntes/ martyrs/ cōfessours ⁊ virg.

❡ To morowe.

The .xiij. day of Ianuary. At rome in lauicane strete the feest of .xl. soudyours/ that in the psecucyon of ye emperour Galien were put to dethe for Chryst. At pictauis the feest of saynt Hylary a bysshop ⁊ cōfessour/ that for Chryst was exiled iiij. yeres in to the lande of frige/ where amonge many other grete myracles he reysed a persone from deth. At the chefe cite of reme/ ye feest of saynt Remyge a bysshop of synguler vertue/ whome for his grete fame ⁊ strōge fayth the frensshe men haue in grete honour ⁊ worshyp. The octaue also of the epyphany. ❡ Addicyons.

[❡ At the castell of grauion the feest of saynt Vincent [*fo. vi. b.* a holy man/ ⁊ had reuelacyon of aungels/ but fyrst he was a pagan ⁊ cōuerted by saynt Gregory nazanzene whose feest (after some bokes) is also this same daye. The feest also of saȳt Fyrme a martyr/ whose holy body was foūde by myracle in ye cite of ambience/ in the translacyon wherof/ ye frost ⁊ yse was in Ianuary turned into hete ⁊ pleasaūt weder as somer/ so y^t the bare trees sodeynly florysshed ⁊ brought forth fruyte/ wherby seke psones were cured. In wales the feest of saȳt Kentegerne/ that was goten his moder wyst not how/ whan/ nor by whome/ yet was she a holy woman/ ⁊ moche loued our lady. Whan the people perceyued she was with childe/ she was (after the lawe than vsed) cast downe hedlonge from the heyght of a rocke/ and yet scaped vnhurte/ than was she put in to ye see alone in a leder bote/ ⁊ without sayle or ore/ ⁊ came in to Yreland ⁊ there forthw^t

trauayled/ whiche an holy heremyte sawe in spiryte/ ꝧ was cōmaunded to brynge vp the chylde/ ꝧ with hym in youth he reysed two deed persones/ ꝧ dyd many myracles in scotlonde/ englonde/ ꝧ wales/ where he was accompanyed wᵗ saynt Dauid ꝧ was there abbot of .ix.c.lxv. monkes/ ꝧ yet he was before a bysshop in englonde of meruaylous hygh perfeccyon. The feest also of saynt Longyse a confessour. And of many other holy sayntes/ marṫ. cōfes. ꝧ virg.

⁋ To morowe.

⁋ The .xiiij. day of Ianuary. At nole a cite of cāpeyn the feest of saynt Felix a cōfessour/ yᵗ as saynt Paulyne wryteth after many turmentes ꝧ longe imprisonmēt was delyuered by an aūgell. The feest also of an other saynt Felix/ naturall broder vnto the same/ ꝧ a preest [and martyr. The [fo. vii. trāslacyon also of saynt Fayth a virgyn. And the feest of saynt Eufrase a bysshop. And of saynt Clere a deacon : and of saynt Ponciane. ⁋ Addicyons.
⁋ The feest also of saynt Timothy bysshop of alexander. And of an other saynt Felix/ yᵗ after hath an other daye festyuale. The feest also of many other holy sayntes/ martyrs/ confessours/ and virgyns.

⁋ To morowe.

⁋ The .xv. day of Ianuary the feest of sayntes Abacuke ꝧ Micheas yᵉ pphetes/ whose holy bodyes were foūde by diuyne reuelacyon/ in yᵉ tyme of yᵉ emperour Archadius. In egypte the feest of saynt Machary an abbot/ that was discyple vnto saȳt Antony/ a man of grete fame ꝧ myracles. The feest also of saȳt Ysydour an honourable man/ of holy lyuyng/ grete fayth/ and wonderous in myracles. In auerne the feest of saynt Bonyte a bysshop ꝧ cōfessour/ whose lyfe by synguler vertue was vnto the people a lanterne of lyght. In yᵉ terrytory of andogauence† the feest of saynt Maure an abbot/ ꝧ discyple vnto saynt Benet/ yᵗ by his maysters cōmaūdement went vpon the water/ ꝧ toke out of the same a chylde called saynt Placidus/ yᵗ was in peryll. The feest also of saynt Maulean an abbot of grete holynes and vertue. ⁋ Addicyons.
⁋ In yrelande the feest of saynt Dorythy/ that by an other name is called also saynt Sythe/ yᵗ was of grete blode/ ꝧ whan she sholde haue ben maryed vnto a gentyle/ she flede vnto a monastery of virgyns/ where yᵉ deuyll appered vnto her/ ꝧ whan he coude not psuade nor entreate her to leue her purpose/ he

thretened her/ but all she despysynge toke yͤ nexte morowe ye habyte [and was after abbesse of holy lyfe ⁊ many [*fo. vii. b.* myracles/ she moche loued pouerte/ in so moche yᵗ whan golde ⁊ ryches was offred vnto her/ she cast it from her with disdayne/ ⁊ called for water to wasshe her handes bycause she had touched that fylthy mucke ⁊ dungue of the erth. The feest also of an other saynt Micheas a prophete also/ that was of yͤ cite of morast/ of whome saynt Ierome wryteth. The feest also of many other holy sayntes/ martyrs/ confessours/ and virgyns.

¶ To morowe.

¶ The .xvj. day of Ianuary. At rome in salary strete the feest of saynt Marcell pope/ yᵗ by the iudge Maximian was for Chrystes fayth set to be comun herde ⁊ to kepe swyne ⁊ beestes/ wherein as a bondman he contynued many yeres/ weryng harde here/ and doynge grete pennūce/ wherin he dyed. In the cite of aurelatens† ye feest of saynte Honorate a confessour/ whose lyfe in doctryne and myracles was very honourable. In odoberg yͤ feest of saynt Ticiane a bysshop ⁊ cōfessour. In the monastery of patron the feest of saȳt Furcey a cōfessour/ yᵗ oftētymes was inrapt ⁊ had meruaylous vysyons ⁊ dredefull reuelacyons. At Rome the feest of saynt Pricill† a virgyn of synguler sanctite ⁊ holynes. ¶ Addicyons.

¶ The feest also of an other saynt Marcell bysshop of anticyrane/ of whom saynt Ierome wryteth. And yͤ feest of saynt Felix bysshop of tubabocens/ ⁊ a martyr. And of an other saȳt Honorate bysshop of ambianens a man of grete miracles/ whan one tyme in his masse he sholde after the pax haue receyued yͤ sacrament/ he sawe the ryght hande of Chryst take the hoste frō his hande ⁊ put it in his mouth/ ⁊ so he was cōmuned of [Chryst hymselfe. The feest also of the thyrd saynt [*fo. viii.* Honorate an abbot of .cc. mōkes/ a man of strayte dyete ⁊ precyse in silence. The feest also of saȳt Melance a bysshop of grete mekenes/ ⁊ for Chryst he suffred exyle ⁊ moche trouble. And yͤ feest of saynt Faust yᵗ fyrst was an abbot/ ⁊ after a bysshop/ a holy man and a grete clerke. The feest also of saynt Sigybert yᵗ was a kyng of englonde/ ⁊ by enemyes chased into fraūce/ where he receyued the fayth of Chryst ⁊ was baptysed/ ⁊ restored vnto his kyngdome/ where he set vp scoles of holy scripture/ and after resygned his crowne to a kynnesman/ ⁊ was a monke of hygh pfeccyon/ ⁊ at yͤ last he was martyred for the faythe. The feest also of saynt Henry that was borne in yͤ north partyes of englonde of noble blode/ ⁊ whan he sholde haue ben maryed/ he had reuelacyon to go in to yͤ yle of coket besyde northūberlond/ where he lyued a strayte lyfe/ and had many· reuelacions/ and dyd grete myracles. The feest also of many other holy sayntes/ martyrs/ confes. and virg.

⁋ To morowe.

⁋ The .xvij. daye of Ianuary. In thebaida the feest of saynt Antony/ whose holy body was foūde by reuelacyon in the tyme of y⁶ emperour Iustiniane/ ⁊ was brought in to alexander/ ⁊ there buryed in y⁶ chirche of saynt Iohñ baptist. At lynguon y⁶ feest of saynt Sewsyppe/ saynt Helewsyppe/ and saynt Melewsyppe all breder ⁊ martyrs/ that in the tyme of y⁶ emperour Aureliane were put to deth/ ⁊ with them saynt Leonyll theyr graūdmoder/ ⁊ saynt Ionyll/ saynt Neon/ and saynt Theon. In biturica the feest of saynt Sulpyce a martyr/ whose holy lyfe ⁊ precyous deth ben gretly cōmended by many gloryous myracles. [⁋ Addicyons. [*fo. viii. b.*

⁋ The feest also of saynt Andoke and saynt Benigne preestes ⁊ martyrs/ yᵗ were discyples vnto saynt Policarpe a bysshop ⁊ discyple vnto saynt Iohñ y⁶ euangelyst/ ⁊ these two preestes cōuerted many coūtrees/ ⁊ dyd grete miracles/ ⁊ at the last were put to deth/ ⁊ wᵗ them saynt Tyrs/ wᵗ other psones many. The feest also of many other holy sayntes/ marř. confes. ⁊ virg.

⁋ To morowe.

⁋ The .xviij. day of Ianuary. The feest of saynt Peter called cathedra/ that is to saye/ his chayre or trone wherein he was fyrst stalled at rome. The feest also of saynt Prisce a virgyn and martyr. At pont the feest of saynt Moyses ⁊ saynt Ammon that were lectours in order/ but fyrst men of warre/ where they were accused ⁊ boyled in lede/ and caste in to a grete fyre ⁊ brent. At wyllenchester the deposicyon of saynt Vulstane a bysshop ⁊ confessour. In the monastery of turon the feest of saynt Leonard†/ yᵗ forsoke his kynne ⁊ coūtree ⁊ bare in hymselfe y⁶ crosse of Chryst/ ⁊ in y⁶ same monastery enclosed hymselfe as an ancre in a very narowe place or sell. ⁋ Addicyons.

Lectoris. In y⁶ holy sacramēt of preesthode ben vij. orders of y⁶ whiche lector is one.

⁋ The feest also of sayt Deicolus an abbot of englond that was fyrst discyple vnto saynt Colūbane/ ⁊ after he buylded a monastery ⁊ was abbot of hygh perfeccyon/ a well sprange sodeynly where he set his staffe/ and he reysed a deed corps/ with many other notable myracles. The translacyon also of saynt Lucye vnto venyse/ the yere of our lorde M. xl. And the feest of many other holy sayntes/ martyrs/ confes. ⁊ virgyns.

⁋ To morowe.

⁋ The .xix. daye of Ianuary. At smyrme the feest of [saynt Germanyke a martyr/ that vnder the tyraūtes Marke/ [fo. ix. Antony ⁊ Luce awreyle iudges/ was put to wylde beestes to be deuoured/ ⁊ so had the crowne of martyrdome. At spolete in ye time of ye emperour Antonyne the feest of saynt Ponciane a martyr/ that by a cruel iudge was fyrst scourged/ than caused to walke upon hote coles barefote/ after hanged vpon a racke full of hokes y^t rent all his flesshe/ ⁊ yet put agayne in pryson/ where he was cōforted by aūgels/ ⁊ at ye last after many turmentes he was slayne by the swerde. In the fraūchest of dorkasyn the feest of saynt Lānomyare a preest. And ye translacyon of saynt Branwallatour a bysshop and cōfessour. The feest also of saynt Vulstane bysshop of worcester/ a man of synguler sanctite. ⁋ Addicyons.

⁋ The feest also of saynt Bassiane bysshop of landenst that was borne of pagans and sent to rome to study/ where he receyued baptym/ ⁊ by reuelacyō was sent to rauen/ and after made bysshop of landenst/ a man of hygh v̄tue ⁊ many myracles/ he buryed sayt Ambrose. The feest also of many other holy sayn. m̄. cō. ⁊ v̄g.

⁋ To morowe.

⁋ The .xx. day of Ianuary. At rome the feest of saynt Fabiane pope/ that whan he had ruled ye chirche .xiiij. yeres/ was in the tyme of Decius ye emperour put to martyrdom/ ⁊ buryed in the chircheyerde of saynt Calixt. At kathacūbe the feest of saynt Sebastian a martyr/ that was chefe capyteyn w^t the emperour Dioclecian/ ⁊ brought forth as a prisoner w^t a tytle/ that is to say/ a paper vpon his heed/ to declare y^t he was a true chrystian/ ⁊ so he was boūde vnto a stake in ye myddle of the felde for the soudyours to shote at/ ⁊ yet at ye last [they [fo. ix. b bette hym to deth w^t clubbes. In cornel strete the feest of saynt Marius ⁊ of his wife saynt Martha/ ⁊ of theyr two sones saynt Audifax ⁊ Abacuke/ al borne in perse of noble lignage/ ⁊ all came to rome in pilgrymage in ye tyme of ye grete pryce Claudi^9/ where they were put to many turmentes/ fyrst beten w^t staues/ than racked ⁊ torne w^t hokes/ theyr handes cut of/ cast in ye fyre/ and Martha was slayne in a bath/ ⁊ all the other heded and theyr bodyes brent in the fyre.
⁋ Addicyons.

⁋ In yrelonde ye feest of saynt Fekyne/ of the kynges blode/ whose byrth was before shewed by reuelacyon and after he was an abbot of hygh perfeccyon/ he heled yͤ blynde ⁊ defe so borne/ lepres ⁊ palseys/ ⁊ reysed thre psones to lyfe/ wᵗ many other myracles. The feest also of many other holy sayntes/ marͬ. confes. ⁊ virg.

⁋ To morowe.

⁋ The .xxj. day of Ianuary. The feest of saynt Publy the second bysshop of athens after saynt Denyse/ a noble man of lernẏge ⁊ vertue/ ⁊ for Chryst a martyr. At rome yᵉ feest of saẏt Agnes a virgyn/ yᵗ by Symphroniane yᵉ mayre was cast in to a grete fyre/ whiche by her prayer was quēched/ ⁊ she after heded. In spayn at terascone yᵉ feest of saynt Fructuous a bisshop/ saẏt Augurre ⁊ saynt Euloge bothe deacons/ yᵗ in the tyme of Galiene yᵉ emperour were prisoned/ ⁊ after boūden ⁊ cast in to a grete fyre whiche brēned theyr bondes and loused them wᵗout grefe: than all they layd theyr handes in crossewyse eche ouer other/ ⁊ prayed our lorde they myght be cōsumed wᵗ the fyre/ and so they were. At trecas the feest of saynt Patroclus a martyr. ⁋ Addicyons.

[⁋ At cesare palestyne the feest of saynt Thotist/ [*fo. x.* saynt Dompne/ saẏt Theotigne/ ⁊ saẏt Agapy al bisshops. And yᵉ feest of many other holy sayn. mar. cͅfes. ⁊ virg.

⁋ To morowe.

⁋ The .xxij. daye of Ianuary. The feest of saynt Tymothe disciple vnto saynt Paule/ whome he made bisshop of ephesy/ ⁊ after many grete turmentes he had the crowne of martyrdome. In spayne at valentyne yᵉ feest of saynt Vincent a deacon/ yᵗ vnder the iudge Daciane in the tyme of yᵉ emperour Diocleciane and Maximiane suffred meruaylous ⁊ many cruell turmentes ⁊ therby had yᵉ triūphe ⁊ noble victory of martyrdom. At rome the feest of saynt Anastace a monke ⁊ martyr that in cesary palestyne by the perses suffred his passyon by many turmētes/ ⁊ at the last heded/ ⁊ wᵗ hym also .lxx. psones. At ebredune yᵉ feest of an other saynt Vincēt/ saynt Oronce ⁊ saynt Victor all holy martyrs. ⁋ Addicyons.

⁋ The feest also of saynt Potite a martyr. And of an other saynt Anastace yᵗ was yᵉ popes notary in rome/ And he forsoke his office and was a monke of suppentona/ where he was after abbot of hygh perfeccyon/ and had reuelacion of his deth. The feest also of many other holy sayntes/ martyrs/ cōfessours/ ⁊ virgyns.

⁋ To morowe.

⁋ The .xxiij. day of Ianuary. At philyppes the feest of saynt Parmene/ one of y^e .vij. fyrst deacons/ ꝛ baptysed of ye discyples of Chryst/ ꝛ by ye grace of prechynge he dyd moche pfyte/ ꝛ at last he obteyned ye glory of martyrdome. At rome the feest of saynt Emerenciane a virgyn/ y^t as she was in prayer at the tumbe of saynt Agnes/ ꝛ there coūseyled other psones to forsake theyr [lawe of gentylite/ ꝛ bad ye christyans [*fo. x. b.* beware of them she was taken ꝛ stoned to deth/ ꝛ with her suffred also saynt Machare for ye same cause. In maritymy at genecesary the feest of saynt Seueriane/ ꝛ of his wyfe saynt Aquila/ that for Chryst were brent. At ye cite of antinoñ† the feest of saynt Askle a martyr/ y^t for Chryst was hāged ꝛ racked/ ꝛ his body ꝛ rybbes beten w^t fyre hote plates/ w^t many turmentes/ ꝛ at the last drowned in a flode.

⁋ Addicyons.

⁋ This day after some auctours ben remembred the feestes of certayne sayntes of ye olde testament/ y^t is to saye/ of our fyrst parentes saynt Adam ꝛ saynt Eue/ saynt Abel ꝛ saynt Seth/ saynt Enos and saynt Caynan/ saynt Malaliel ꝛ saynt Iared/ saynt Enock and saynt Mathusale. At tolete the feest of saynt Nedolfons† a bysshop of famous lyfe ꝛ grete doctryne. And ye feest of many other holy sayntes/ marꝛ./ confes. ꝛ virg.

⁋ To morowe.

⁋ The .xxiiij. daye of Ianuary. At antioche ye feest of saynt Babyll/ y^t in the psecucyon of the emperour Decius suffred oftentymes many turmentes/ ꝛ yet dyed in pryson. And .iij. chylder (as is sayd) suffred passion and deth w^t hym/ that is to saye/ saynt Vrbane/ saynt Prelidane ꝛ saynt Epolon. In cesary at geneot ye feest of saynt Mardon/ saynt Muson/ saynt Eugen ꝛ saynt Marcel† all martyrs/ that were for Chryst brent/ ꝛ the asshes cast in a ryuer. The feest also of saynt Codoke ꝛ saynt Tymothe.

⁋ Addicyons.

⁋ The feest also of sayt Modest a cōfessour/ a famous man of singuler doctryne/ ꝛ he confoūded the heretyte Marcion. The feest also of saynt Musan a preest ꝛ cōfessour of grete lernynge also/ and he made many bo[kes one specyally [*fo. xi.* agaynst the heretyke Taciane and his secte or company called Eucratykes. The feest also of many other holy sayntes/ martyrs/ cōfes. ꝛ virg.

⁋ To morowe.

⁋ The .xxv. daye of Ianuary. the cōuersyon of saynte Paule/ yᵗ gracyously happed in the seconde yere after the ascencyon of our lorde Iesu. At Damaske the feest of saynt Ananye that baptysed the same holy apostle saynt Paule. At auerne the feest of saynt Proiect† and saynt Amaryne† martyrs/ that were put to deth by yᵉ states of the same cite. At gauale yᵉ feest of saynt Seueryane a bysshop of.grete holynes ⁊ doctryne. At lucas castell the feest of saynt Lyuence a confessour.
⁋ Addicyons.

⁋ At lyons in fraūce yᵉ feest of saynt Pagate a preest ⁊ confessour/ ⁊ of saynt Vect a confessour/ yᵗ in the persecucyon of yᵉ emperour Antonyn/ wᵗ many other psones nere innumerable of yᵉ same cite/ were put to deth for Chryst. The feest also of saynt Alcippiade a martyr/ yᵗ was of strayte abstynence/ ⁊ that also whan he was in prison/ wherfore reuelacyon was shewed vnto saȳt Attale a prisoner also with hym ⁊ martyr/ that his felowe dyd not well in yᵗ strayte abstynence/ ⁊ so he was refourmed/ ⁊ they bothe togyder martyred. The feest also of many other holy sayntes/ marṫ. confes. ⁊ virg.

⁋ To morowe.

⁋ The .xxvj. daye of Ianuary. At smyrme the feest of saynt Policarpe a bysshop/ yᵗ was discyple vnto saynt Iohn̄ the euangelyst/ ⁊ by hym made prymate of all asye/ ⁊ after he was accused vnto the prynces Marke Antonyn ⁊ Lucius aurel/ ⁊ put to deth by yᵉ fyre brent. And wᵗ hym .xij. other psones also yᵗ came wᵗ hym from [philadolph†. The feest also [*fo. xi. b.* of saynt Theogenes ⁊ other .xxxvj. persones/ yᵗ all togyder were put to deth by the emperour Lyzyne.
⁋ Addicyons.

⁋ The feest also of saynt Ionas the pphete yᵗ as a fygure of Chryst was .iij. dayes in yᵉ bely of a whale/ and that preched vnto the cite of Niniue/ ⁊ he is one of the .xij.
Eccl'i. xlix. prophetes nombred in scrypture. The feest also of many other holy sayntes/ martyrs/ cōfes. ⁊ virgyns.

⁋ To morowe.

⁋ The .xxvij. day of Ianuary. the feest of saynt Iohn̄ crisostom bysshop of constantynople/ one of the .iiij. doctours of the grekes/ that by his profoūde doctryne ⁊ holy example of

lyfe/ dyd moche pfyte the religyon of Chryst. The feest also of saynt Marius abbot of bobacens/ whose holy lyfe wryteth ye holy fader saynt Dyname. In bethleem Iude ye feest of saynt Paula a notable woman/ whose holy lyfe saynt Ierom wryteth ꝫ therin testifyeth y^t she was crowned w^t longe martyrdom. In affryke the feest of saynt Auite a martyr. At cenomañ. the feest of saynt Iulian that was the fyrst bysshop of ye cite/ ꝫ he was the same Symon leprose w^t whome our sauyour dyned/ whan Mary mawdeleyn was couerted. The feest also of saynt Iohñ an abbot of meruaylous sanctite and hygh perfeccyon.
℣ Addicyons.
℣ The feest also of an other saynt Iulian/ and of his wyfe saynt Castell/ whose legend is redde in ye frater. And this is he vnto whome the people praye for good herborowe or lodgyge. The feest also of ye thyrde saynt Iulian a man of noble blode/ and of his seruaūt saynt Fereole bothe martyrs. The feest also of ye fourth sayt Iulian a martyr also y^t was put to dethe in ye tyme of [the emperour Dioclecian. And ye feest of [*fo. xii*. saynt Paule the pope/ a man of pfoūde mekenes/ ꝫ very pyteous ꝫ mercyfull/ ꝫ a grete defender of the chirche/ for often tymes he wrote sharpe lettres vnto ye emperours Costantyne ꝫ Leo/ ꝫ refourmed theyr errours/ ꝫ he fyrst ordeyned that diuyne seruyce ꝫ the houres in lent/ all saue complyn/ sholde be done before none/ with many other notable actes ꝫ grete myracles. The feest also of saynt Adiute abbot of carnotens/ called now portese/ a man of hygh pfeccyon/ ꝫ had reuelacyon of his deth ꝫ dyd many myracles/ bothe in his lyfe ꝫ after. And ye feest of many other holy sayntes/ mar. confes. ꝫ virg.

℣ To morowe.

℣ The .xxviij. daye of Ianuary. At rome the seconde feest of saynt Agnes. In apollonia the feest of saynt Lewce/ saynt Tricet ꝫ saynt Galenice all martyrs/ y^t in the tyme of the emperour Decius were put to deth ꝫ heded. In alexander ye feest of saynt Ciryll bysshop of the same/ a noble doctour/ ꝫ a grete defender of Chrystes chirche. In the monastery of reomens the feest of saynt Iohñ a preest of holy couersacyon. And the feest of saynt Charles the emperour/ called Charlemayne that wanne the holy lande and dyd grete myracles.
℣ Addicyons.
℣ The feest also of saynt Iulian a confessour/ whose syrname was sabba an heremyte of holy lyfe ꝫ moche applyed to contemplacyon/ ꝫ he had the spiryte of prophecy. The feest also of an other saynt Iulian a cofessour also/ that was a man of grete wytte ꝫ hygh lernynge/ bothe in greke ꝫ latyn/ ꝫ very eloquent/

and he wrote many noble werkes/ ꝛ was a grete almes man. In ye territory of trecacyne/ the feest of saynt Fabian a [martyr. The feest also of an other saynt Ciryll bisshop of [*fo. xii. b.* Ierusalē/ ꝛ he was a grete clerke ꝛ famylyer with saynt Ierome/ ꝛ wrote many of his myracles/ ꝛ buried hym. Here ben remembred (after some auctours) certayne holy faders of the olde testament/ saynt Noe that made the shyppe ꝛ therin was saued whan all ye worlde (except ye shyppe) was drowned. Saynt Sem also ꝛ saynt Arphaxat/ saynt Sale ꝛ saȳt Heber/ saȳt Falek ꝛ saynt Rewe/ saynt Saruke ꝛ saynt Nachor/ saynt Thare ꝛ saynt Aram. And ye feest of many o.ꝛč.

⁋ To morowe.

⁋ The .xxix. day of Ianuary. At rome in numentane strete ye feest of saynt Papie ꝛ saȳt Maure soudyours that for the cōfessyon of Chryst were put to many turmentes by the mayre Laodice/ knocked on the mouth with stones tyll theyr tethe fell out/ ꝛ than after hard prison/ beten w^t staues ꝛ with plūmettes of lede vnto deth. At treuer ye feest of saynt Valery a bisshop ꝛ discyple vnto saynt Peter. In the territory of trecas ye feest of saynt Salunianet/ that for Chryst was heded by ye emperour Iulian. The feest also of saynt Gyld a holy man.

⁋ Addicyons.

⁋ In the cite of mutyne the feest of saynt Geminian a noble man borne/ ꝛ from youth gyuen all to vertue/ and so bysshop of the same cite/ ꝛ of many grete myracles ꝛ hygh pfeccion. The feest also of many other .ꝛč.

⁋ To morowe.

⁋ The .xxx. day of Ianuary. At antioche the passyon of saynt Ypolite a martyr/ y^t fyrst was somewhat deceyued by a sysmatyke ꝛ false heretyke called Innouatet/ but after by the grace of god he was refourmed ꝛ dyd returne vnto ye charite of Chrystes chirche/ in ye whi[che for the same he nobly [*fo. xiii.* suffred deth. At Ierusalem ye feest of saynt Mathye a bysshop/ of whome ben wryten many meruaylous actes/ ꝛ grete turmentes/ and yet notwithstandynge he dyed in the peace of Chryst. The feest also of saynt Flauian a martyr. In the territory of paryse the feest of saynt Batyld a quene.

⁋ Addicẏons.

⁋ The trāslacyon of saynt Marke ye euāgelyst/ whan his holy body was brought from alexander vnto Venyse/ in ye tyme of the emperour Leo/ ꝛ the duke of Venyse was than Iustiniane.

the yere of our lorde .cccc.lxv. where were done many myracles.
The feest also of many other holy sayntes/ martyrs/ confes. ⁊
virg.

⁋ To morowe.

⁋ The .xxxj. daye of Ianuary. In alexander the feest of
saynt Metran a martyr/ that in the same cite was put to many
turmētes/ his lymmes broken/ his eyes put out/ ⁊ at the last
stoned to deth. In yᵉ same cite also the feest of saynt Saturnyn/
saynt Tyrce ⁊ saynt Victor. And the passyon of saynt Cyre⁺ ⁊
saynt Iohn̄ martyrs. In yᵉ monastery of malbody yᵉ feest of
saynt Aldegunde a holy virgyn.

⁋ Addicyons.

⁋ In alexander yᵉ feest of saynt Apollony a confessour a
man of grete lernyng/ yᵗ wrote agaynst yᵉ heretykes called
cataphriges/ ⁊ confounded theyr opynyons. At ephesum the
feest of saynt Policrate bisshop of yᵉ same cite/ a noble man of
doctryne and holy lyfe/ of whome Eusebius wryteth. The feest
also of many other .⁊c.

⁋ To morowe.

Februaſ.
THe fyrste daye of February. the feest of saynt
Ignace a bysshop ⁊ martyr/ that after saynt
Peter was yᵉ thyrde bysshop of antioche/ a man of
pro[foūde doctryne ⁊ a grete precher/ yᵗ in the [*fo. xiii. b.*
persecucyon of yᵉ emperour Traianus was as a prisoner boūden
⁊ brought to rome/ where in presence of the emperour ⁊ the
senate he was put to meruaylous turmētes/ and at the last he was
cast vnto wode ⁊ rampynge lyons/ ⁊ of them deuoured. At
smyrne the feest of saynt Pion a martyr/ that for Chryst was
put in prison/ where by his holy exhortacyons he conforted many
persones/ ⁊ made them stronge in herte ⁊ redy to martyrdome/
⁊ he was put to many varyaūt turmentes/ ⁊ at the last nayled
fast vnto a table ⁊ so hanged ouer a grete fyre vnto deth/ wᵗ
whome were put to deth .xv. other persones. The feest also of
saynt Effrem a deacon of yᵉ chirche of edissen. At tricas the
feest of saynt Paule a bysshop/ whose lyfe by many grete vertues
was laudable/ ⁊ his deth by myracles moche cōmended. In
Scotlonde the feest of saynt Brigide/ called comynly saynt Bryde/
whose lyfe in vertue ⁊ myracles was very famous. The feest also
of saynt Pollicarpe ⁊ saynt Seueryne bothe bysshops.

⁋ Addicyons.

⁋ The feest also of saynt Seuer/ that whan he was a poore
symple man vnlerned/ was chosen bysshop of rauen by myracle

of a fyry pyller ꝛ bryght beme that descended from heuen ꝛ remayned vpon hym/ forthw{t} after whiche eleccyon he was lerned in all y{e} offyce of a bysshop/ ꝛ eloquent in prechynge/ he moche edifyed by holy lyf ꝛ many miracles. The feest also of an other saynt Seuere/ borne in the same cite/ a preest of hygh perfeccyon ꝛ grete myracles/ amonge whiche he reysed one psone to lyf/ of whose fame ye emperour Maximian heryng/ sent for hym/ ꝛ bycause he wold not do sacrefyce vnto the ydolles/ he caused hym to be heded/ [whose soule in the syght [*fo. xiiii.* of the people was caryed bytwene two aungels in to heuen. The feest also of the thyrde saynt Seuere/ whose syrname was symple/ a preest ꝛ cōfessour/ borne in aquyne of noble lygnage/ a man of hygh doctryne/ ꝛ made many werkes/ he was discyple vnto saȳt Martyn/ whose lyfe he wrote/ ꝛ folowed the same in vertue and myracles. The feest also of many other holy sayntes/ martyrs/ confes. ꝛ virg.

⁋ To morowe.

⁋ The seconde daye of February. the purificacyon of our lady saynt Mary/ ꝛ y{e} oblacyon of our sauyour Iesu in the temple/ accordynge vnto the lawe of Moyses whome Symeon takynge in armes sayd. Nūc dimittis seruū tuū dñe. ꝛc̃. by the visyon of whose beauty ꝛ bryghtnes all this worlde is illumyned ꝛ lyghtned/ ꝛ vnto ryght fayth of saluacyon repared. At cesary the feest of saynt Cornelius/ whome saȳt Peter baptysed that in the same cite was bysshop/ ꝛ of grete holynes. At rome in salary strete the feest of saynt Apropinian that was a gentyle/ ꝛ beyng in the company of saynt Sysyn a deacon/ herde a voyce frō heuen sayenge vnto the saued soules these wordes of the gospel. Venite bñdicti p̃ris mei. ꝛc̃. that is saye/ come ye blessed chylder of my fader/ ꝛ receyue the realme or kyngdome of heuen/ prepared ꝛ ordeyned for you from y{e} begȳnyng of the worlde/ by the whiche voyce he was cōuerted ꝛ baptysed/ ꝛ after for the confessyon of Chryst he was heded. At rome also the feest of saynt Fortunate/ saynt Feliciane/ saynt Fyrme/ ꝛ saynt Cādidus. At orliaūce the feest of saynt Frustole a bysshop. At doroberne the feest of saynt Laurence an archebysshop.

⁋ Addicyons.

[⁋ The feest also of saȳt Heraclyte a cōfessour/ [*fo. xiiii. b.*
              of grete lernyng/ ꝛ made many werkes/ of whome
lit. v. ca. Eusebius wryteth. And the feest also of saynt
xxvij.   Maximus a grete clerke also/ of whome is wryten in
              y{e} same place. The feest also of many other holy
sayntes/ mar. cōf. ꝛ virg.

❡ To morowe.

❡ The thyrde day of February. in sebasten the feest of saynt Blase a bisshop/ that werkyng many myracles was taken by ye iudge Agricolaus ⁊ beten/ scourged ⁊ hanged on a racke/ ⁊ there his flesshe torne w^t hokes/ ⁊ yet put longe in pryson/ ⁊ after cast in to a stynkynge podell or lake/ ⁊ at ye last he was heded/ ⁊ with hym were slayne two yonge men/ ⁊ .vij. women y^t gadred his blode as relykes from the groūde. In affryke the feest of saynt Celeryne a deacon/ ⁊ of saynt Laurence/ saynt Ignace/ and of a woman called also saynt Celeryne martyrs/ of whose martyrdome saynt Cipriane wryteth a pystle. At nice the feest of saynt Triphon a martyr/ y^t was put to deth in the tyme of ye emperour Decius. At wapyng ye feest of saynt Tygryde ⁊ saynt Remedy bothe bysshops/ ⁊ the feest also of saynt warburge a virgyn.

❡ Addicyons.

❡ At alexander the feest of saynt Iohn̄ bysshop ⁊ patriarke of the same cite/ that for his pite ⁊ large almes was called by syrname ye almeser/ a noble man borne ⁊ of grete lernyng/ holy of lyf ⁊ of many myracles. At nouariens the feest of saynt Gaudence bysshop of the same cite/ y^t was disciple ⁊ scrybe vnto saynt Martyn and after his mayster of lyfe ⁊ myracles. The feest also of many other holy sayntes/ martyrs/ cōfes. ⁊ virg.

❡ To morowe.

❡ The fourth daye of February. in egypt at thymus [the feest of saynt Sylet a bysshop/ that in the same cite [*fo. xv.* (as the story ecclesiastyke sheweth) was put to deth/ ⁊ w^t hym the capytaynes owne chylder/ ⁊ other chrystyans innumerable. At rome in ye market place ye passyon of saynt Aquilyne/ saynt Gemyne/ saynt Gelas/ saynt Magnus/ ⁊ saynt Donate martyrs. At trecas the feest of saynt Auentyne a bysshop ⁊ cōfessour. The feest also of saynt walburge a virgyn/ ⁊ of saynt Gylbert a cōfessour. At glocester the feest of saynt Eldade.

❡ Addicyons.

❡ The feest also of saynt Symeon the holy prophete that in ye presentacyon of our sauyour toke hym in his armes/ sayenge Nūc dimit. ⁊c̄. The feest also of saynt Phyllorony/ y^t beholdynge ye cōstancy of saynt Sylet/ and the cruelty of the iudge/ openly reproued hym/ for the whiche he was put to the same deth. The feest also of many other holy sayntes/ mart̄. confes. ⁊ virg.

⁋ To morowe.

⁋ The fyfth daye of February. in cicyle at cathenens the feest of saynt Agast virgyn ⁊ martyr/ that suffred for Chryst many meruaylous and cruell turmentes/ strokes/ buffets/ imprisonment/ rackyng/ scourgyng/ her māmelles or pappes kytte frō her body/ tumbled ⁊ turned naked vpon hote syndres ⁊ brennynge coles/ ⁊ at the last vnder yᵉ iudge Quinciane she was slayne in pryson. At vien the feest of saynt Adiutt a bysshop ⁊ cōfessour/ by whose wysdome ⁊ doctryne the frensshe countree was preserued from arryanes heresyes.

⁋ Addicyons.

⁋ The feest also of saynt Ingemyne bisshop of sabionens/ a holy man ⁊ of grete cōstancy. The feest also of saynt Albuyne bysshop of brixinens/ a famous man of [many myracles. [*fo. xv. b.* Here ben remēbred certayne sayntes of yᵉ olde testament/ the hygh patriarke ⁊ preest saynt Abraham/ vnto whome was made the fyrst expresse promesse of our sauyour ⁊ saluacyon. saynt Sare his wyfe. saynt Melchisedek preest ⁊ kyng of Ierusalem after whose order Chryst in scripture is called a preest sayenge the prophete. Tu es sacerdos ineternū scᵭm ordinem melchisedech. Saynt Lot neuewe ⁊ broders sone vnto Abraham. Saynt Ysaac the patriarke sone ⁊ heyre vnto Abraham/ that was borne whan his fader was of yᵉ age of .C. yeres/ ⁊ his moder Sara .lxxx. Saynt Rebecca his wyfe/ sayt Iacob theyr sone/ sayt Rachel ⁊ saynt Lia his wyues/ ⁊ the .xij. patriarkes his sones/ of whome came all the .xij. tribes ⁊ chylder of israel/ whose names ben these. Ruben/ Symeon/ Leui/ Iudas/ Isachar/ zabulon/ Gad/ Aser/ Dan/ Neptalim/ Ioseph/ and Beniamyn. saynt Ioseph is more specially named/ bycause he was sold in to egypt ⁊ ruled all yᵉ londe/ ⁊ brought thyder his fader/ breder ⁊ al his kynne/ whose lignage was brought thens by myracle ouer the reed see. ⁊ᴄ. Saynt Effraim ⁊ saynt Manasses sones vnto Ioseph/ all these ben here remēbred. And yᵉ feest also of many other holy sayntes. ⁊ᴄ.

⁋ To morowe.

⁋ The .vj. daye of February. At cesare capadoce/ the feest of saynt Dorothe a virgyn ⁊ martyr/ yᵗ was put to meruaylous paynes/ she was closed in an huge instrumēt of metall made lyke a hors/ all full of pryckes and hote as fyre/ after scourged ⁊ her flesshe rent/ ⁊ at the last heded/ by whose example ⁊ exhortacyon a scoler called Theophilus was cōuerted to Chryst/ ⁊ forthwith he was turmented in the same hors/ ⁊ after lyke [wyse [*fo. xvi.*

heded. At auerne the feest of saynt Antolian a martyr. The feest also of saynt Vedast called comynly in englysshe saynt Sawster†/ bysshop of traiectens/ ꝛ of saynt Amand a bysshop also/ ꝛ bothe gloryous/ ꝛ of many myracles. The feest also of saynt Sotheris a virgyn. ¶ Addicyons.

¶ At alexander the feest of an other saynt Dorothe of noble blode/ that made vnto Chryst yᵉ vowe of chastite ꝛ in the persecucyon of yᵉ tyraūt Maxime yᵗ compelled men to worshyp ydolles/ ꝛ women to breke chastyte/ this holy virgyn fledde in to wyldernes/ ꝛ there dyed in the peace of Chryst/ by yᵉ example of whome/ many other virgyns dyd the same/ ꝛ so preserued theyr virginite. In yrelond yᵉ feest of saynt Mele/ saynt Melke and saynt Munyse bysshops/ ꝛ of seynt Ryoke an abbot/ ꝛ all foure breder ꝛ neuewes vnto saynt Patryke by his syster saynt Darerke/ all men of synguler sanctite ꝛ grete myracles. In yrelond also yᵉ feest of saynt Fynian an abbot/ of grete byrth ꝛ more holynes. The feest also of many other holy sayntes/ mar. cōf. ꝛ virg.

¶ To morowe.

¶ The .vij. daye of February. In brytayne at august the feest of saynt Agyl† a martyr ꝛ a bysshop. · The feest also of saynt Moyses a bysshop yᵗ fyrst lyued in desert ꝛ there shewed many tokens of hygh vertue by many myracles. And after he went abrode ꝛ cōuerted vnto Cryst a grete multytude ꝛ coūtrees of the sarasyns and was theyr bysshop/ and by example ꝛ grete myracles and prechynge he moche edyfyed.

¶ Addicyons.

¶ The feest also of an other saynt Moyses an abbot in the desert of syth a holy fader/ of whome is wryten [in [*fo. xvi. b.* vitas patrū. The feest also of saynt Richard a cōfessour/ that was a kynge of englonde/ ꝛ for grete deuocyon he lefte his kyngdome ꝛ went in pylgrymage to rome with his two sones saynt wyllybald and saynt wenebald/ ꝛ as he returned he dyed in yᵉ cite of luke/ ꝛ his sones came home/ ꝛ one was a bysshop/ ꝛ yᵉ other an abbot. And theyr sister the kynges doughter saynt walpurge was an abbesse/ and all of grete holynes ꝛ many myracles. At papye yᵉ feest of saynt Syre a bysshop of singuler sanctite ꝛ many myracles. And yᵉ feest of many other holy sayntes/ martyrs/ confes. ꝛ virg.

¶ To morowe.

¶ The .viij. day of February. at armeny the lesse/ the feest of saȳt Denyse/ saȳt Emilian/ and saȳt Sebastian. At alexander the feest of saynt Coynt a virgyn ⁊ martyr/ that bycause she wolde not worshyp ydolles was drawen by yᵉ heles or feet thrugh yᵉ cite/ ⁊ so they brake her bones ⁊ tare her flesshe tyll she dyed. In lusytane at corduba yᵉ feest of saẏt Salomon a martyr. At rome the feest of saynt Paule a bysshop/ ⁊ yᵉ feest of saẏt Lucius ⁊ saynt Ciriake. ℂ Addicyons.

℃ The feest also of saynt Serapion/ that with saynt Coynt was put to deth/ ⁊ so were many other psones for the persecucyon was so cruell than in alexander yᵗ fewe chrystyans myght escape. The feest also of many other holy sayntes/ martyrs/ confessours/ ⁊ virg.

℃ To morowe.

℃ The .ix. daye of February. at alexander the passyon of saynt Apolyne a virgyn/ whose persecutours fyrst knocked out her tethe/ and after bycause she wold not worshyp theyr ydols/ she was brent/ wylfully goyng her selfe in to the fyre. In cipris the feest of saynt Am[monye and saynt Alexander. [fo. xvii. In rone the feest of saynt Ausbert bysshop of the same cite/ of grete holynes. ℂ Addicyons.

℃ In englond the feest of saynt Theliaus/ that is called saynt Elios/ ⁊ yᵉ comyn people done call hym saynt Eliud/ a noble man borne/ ⁊ from youth applyed vnto vertue/ ⁊ whan he was lerned in scripture/ he herd yᵉ fame of saynt Paulyn in wales/ ⁊ thyder comyng he foūde there saynt Dauid/ ⁊ they twayne lyued ogyder as breder: in theyr tyme the pictes hethen men entred englonde ⁊ destroyed many places ⁊ slewe moche people/ ⁊ a prynce ⁊ capytayne of them went in to wales/ yᵗ by this holy saynt was coūerted/ ⁊ he had reuelacyon to go wᵗ saynt Dauid ⁊ saynt Paterne vnto Ierusalem/ where they all thre preched in yᵗ tongue that before they neuer knewe/ as the apostles/ ⁊ in all languages/ ⁊ dyd there ⁊ by the waye many grete myracles/ ⁊ whan they came home/ saynt Dauid was archebysshop of wales/ ⁊ this saynt a bysshop/ ⁊ whan he was deed thre coūtrees dyd cōtend ⁊ stryue for his body/ ⁊ at yᵉ last by coūseyle they fell all vnto prayer/ ⁊ cōmytted the iudgement vnto almighty god ⁊ our sauyour Iesu/ ⁊ on yᵉ morowe after they foūde there thre bodyes/ all ⁊ eueryche so lyke vnto other/ that no difference myght be noted/ wherfore euery of the thre coūtrees praysynge god toke one body/ one of them lyeth at landaf/ the seconde at kayrmyrthyn/ ⁊ the thyrde in west wales. The feest also of many other holy. ⁊c.

FEBRUARY.

⁋ To morowe.

⁋ The .x. daye of February. at rome the feest of saynt zotyke/ saynt Hyerenet/ sayt Iacynct/ ⁊ saynt Amance all martyrs. In the eest coūtree the feest of saynt So[theris [*fo. xvii. b.* a virgyn/ y^t after many varyaūt turmentes accomplysshed her martyrdome by the swerde. At rome also in lauican strete the feest of .x. soudyours. At ye castell of cassyn the feest of saynt Scolastica a virgyn/ ⁊ sister vnto saynt Benet. In the territory of rone ye feest of saynt Austrobert a virgyn/ ⁊ ye feest of saynt Merpwyn a virgyn/ ⁊ ye translacyon of saynt Gertrude virgyn ⁊ martyr. ⁋ Addicyons.

⁋ The feest also of saynt Apy a confessour and a grete clerke/ that wrote many werkes/ ⁊ in the cōfessyon of Chrystes faythe very famous. And the feest of saynt Sext a cōfessour also/ ⁊ of hygh doctryne/ that made a noble treatyse of the resurreccyon of Chryst/ ⁊ of ye generall resurreccyon. And ye feest also of saynt Arabiane a cōfessour/ ⁊ a lerned man also/ that confoūded many heretykes/ of whome saynt Eusebius wryteth. The feest also of many other holy sayntes/ mar. cōf. ⁊ virg.

⁋ To morowe.

⁋ The .xj. day of February. at lyons the feest of saynt Desyre a bysshop ⁊ cōfessour/ ⁊ of saynt Ponce a martyr. At castelnaūt the feest of saynt Seueryne/ abbot of aganens/ by whose prayer ye noble kynge Clodoueus was cured of a grete sekenes. At alexander the feest of sayt Eufras a virgyn/ y^t in her monastery was by synguler vertue/ grete abstinēce ⁊ many myracles moche famous ⁊ honourable.

⁋ Addicyons.

⁋ In alexander the feest of saynt Leonides a martyr that was naturall fader vnto ye grete clerke Orygene that than beynge of ye age of .xvij. yeres wrote a pystle vnto his fader a prysoner/ wyllyng him to be cōstaūt in ye fayth/ for ye whiche he gladly toke his deth/ heded with a swerde. The feest also of saynt Māmy a quene [⁊ moder vnto the emperour Alexander/ [*fo. xviii.* y^t was cōuerted by the same grete clerke Orygene/ ⁊ by her owne sone ye sayd emperour put to deth for Chryst. The feest also of many other holy sayntes/ mart. confes. ⁊ virg.

⁋ To morowe.

⁋ The .xij. daye of February. At hylpanet the feest of saynt Eulale a virgyn/ y^t was put to deth in barcinon by y^e

emperour Dioclecian. In affryke ye feest of saynt Saturnyn a preest/ saynt Datyue/ saynt Felix/ saynt Apely/ w^t many other all martyrs/ that by ye procōsull Auolyn† were put to deth. At alexander ye feest of saynt Modest and saynt Ammony bothe chylder. The feest also of saynt Machary/ saynt Ruffyne/ ⁊ saynt Iust. ⁋ Addicyons.

⁋ At cesary capadoce the feest of saŷt Firmiliane bysshop of ye same cite/ ⁊ discyple vnto ye grete clerke Origene/ ⁊ the feest of saynt Theodour ⁊ saynt Anthinodour naturall breder ⁊ disciples also vnto ye same Origene/ that for theyr grete lernynge ⁊ synguler vertue were cōpelled in theyr yonge age bothe to be bysshops. The feest also of many other holy sayntes/ mart̄.⁊c.

⁋ To morowe.

⁋ The .xiij. day of February. the translacyon of saynt Edward kynge ⁊ cōfessour/ whose holy body was taken vp by prouydence of god ⁊ his owne reuelacyon/ ⁊ by ye ayde of his owne broder kynge Etheldrede/ w^t the bysshops ⁊ clergye/ ⁊ all the nobles of englond/ ⁊ shryned w^t grete honour/ ⁊ set amonge other holy relykes. At antioche the feest of ye holy pphete saynt Agabus/ of whome saŷt Luke wryteth in ye actes of ye apostles. At mylen in armenye the feest of saynt Poliact a martyr/ whose name by interpretacyon is prayenge/ or he [that [*fo. xviii. b.* prayeth. In the cite of andegaue the feest of saŷt Lizyne/ a man of grete grauite and synguler sanctite. In brytayne the feest of saynt Ermenyld a virgyn of noble blode.

⁋ Addicyons.

⁋ At rauen the feest of saynt Fuske a virgyn of grete blode/ that in ye age of .xv. yeres was baptysed by the meanes of her nourysshe or brynger vp. saynt Maure that w^t her was put to dethe by the accusacyon of her owne fader. At graūtmoūt the feest of saynt Sephan† an abbot/ a noble man borne/ of synguler vertue ⁊ many wonderous myracles. The feest also of an other saynt Stephan an abbot also/ that (as saynt Gregory wryteth) was of grete ⁊ hygh vertue/ but synguler in pacience. The feest also of saynt Castor/ of noble byrth and an abbot in desert/ by whose prayer a shyppe was saued/ ⁊ the psones refourmed ⁊ made pyteous/ with many other myracles. The feest also of saŷt Hyldebert bysshop of myldynens/ a man of synguler pfeccyon/ y^t besyde many other grete myracles/ reysed one psone to lyfe. The feest also of saynt Iulian/ ⁊ of many other holy sayntes/ martyrs/ confessours and virgyns.

¶ To morowe.

¶ The .xiiij. day of February. At rome yᵉ feest of saynt Valentyn a preest ⁊ martyr/ a man of many myracles specyally in curynge of the seke/ ⁊ he was of grete lernyng ⁊ stronge fayth/ for the which he suffred many turmentes/ in the tyme of the emperour Claude /⁊ at the last heded. At Rome also the feest of saynt Vitale/ saynt Felycule ⁊ saynt zenon all martyrs. At interam the feest an other saynt Valentyne a bysshop ⁊ martyr/ that after longe imprisonment ⁊ many turmētes was heded. At alexander yᵉ feest of saynt Basse/ saynt [Antony ⁊ saynt [*fo. xix.* Protholyke all martyrs/ yᵗ for Chryst were drowned in yᵉ see. The feest also of saynt Ciryon a preest/ ⁊ of saynt Moyses/ saynt Bassimiane ⁊ saynt Agathon that were brent/ ⁊ of saynt Denyse ⁊ saynt Ammon yᵗ were heded.
¶ Addicyons.

¶ At alexander the feest of saynt Syre a martyr/ that bycause he wold not do sacrefyce vnto yᵉ ydolles/ was stryken in yᵉ bely wᵗ a swerde/ ⁊ so yᵉ martyr of Chryst. In yᵉ same alexander the feest of saynt Cheramon bysshop of nicopole ⁊ a martyr/ and of his wyfe/ ⁊ many other psones/ that in yᵉ persecucyon of Decius yᵉ emperour were murthered ⁊ pryuely slayne. And the feest of many other holy sayntes/ martyrs/ confes. ⁊ virg.

¶ To morowe.

¶ The .xv. daye of February. At rome yᵉ feest of saynt Craton a martyr/ yᵗ was cōuerted by saynt Valentyne and soone after bothe he ⁊ his wyfe ⁊ all his houshold were put to deth. In bryxe the feest of saynt Faustyne ⁊ saynt Iouite a deacon martyrs. In fraūce at vasion the feest of saynt Quinyde a bysshop/ whose precyous deth by many myracles is proued acceptable vnto our lorde. At interampnis the feest of saynt Agapes a virgyn. At antioche the feest of saynt Ioseppe a deacon. ¶ Addicyons.

¶ The feest also of saynt Calocery yᵗ was put to deth with saynt Faustyne ⁊ saynt Iouite. The feest also of a certayne holy matrone/ ⁊ of her two doughters virgyns/ whose names be vnknowen/ yᵗ in ye persecucyon of ye emperours Dioclecian ⁊ Maximian were put to deth for Chryst. And the feest of many other holy .⁊c̄.

¶ To morowe.

¶ The .xvj. daye of February. the feest of saynt Hone[simus/ of whome saynt Paule wryteth vnto Philemon/ ⁊ he [*fo. xix. b.* was bisshop of ephesios/ where saỹt Paule lefte hym wᵗ grete charge to preche/ than was he accused ⁊ brought to rome ⁊ there stoned to deth/ whose holy body was brought by his discyples where he was bysshop. At cume the feest of saynt Iulian virgyn and martyr/ that suffred many turmentes/ ⁊ kepte open batayle with the fende/ ⁊ was cast in to a grete fyre/ ⁊ after boyled in a potte/ and at the last heded.

¶ Addicyons.

¶ The feest also of saynt Honest a martyr/ ⁊ of saynt Adaucte yᵗ was duke of a cite in fryge land/ ⁊ in yᵉ persecucyon of Dioclecian/ whan he ⁊ his cite all chrystyans were desyred to do sacrefice/ ⁊ they all denyed/ the cite was set on fyre/ ⁊ all the people nere innumerable brent. In alexander the feest of many martyrs/ yᵗ in yᵉ same psecucyon were put to deth by many varyaūt ⁊ moost cruel turmentes. And yᵉ feest of many other .⁊c̃.

¶ To morowe.

¶ The .xvij. daye of February. In egypte the feest of saynt Iulian a martyr/ ⁊ of other psones yᵗ with hym were put to deth for Chryst .v. M. In babilon a cite of perse the feest of saynt Policron a bysshop ⁊ martyr/ yᵗ in the presence of yᵉ emperour Decius dyed in prayer. At corduba yᵉ passyon of saynt Donate/ saynt Secundian/ saynt Romule/ wᵗ other .viij. C. and .vj. martyrs. In scotlond yᵉ feest of saynt Finian a preest ⁊ cōfessour of singuler ṽtue. In teruens yᵉ feest of saynt Syluyne bysshop of tolane. At cleremoūt the trāslacyon of saynt Luuiane a confessour.

¶ Addicyons.

¶ At cawsyne yᵉ feest of saynt Sauyne bysshop of the same cite/ yᵗ by an enemy dranke poyson/ by yᵉ whiche [drynke [*fo. xx.* yᵉ same enemy beynge in an other coūtree ferre thens/ was forthwᵗ intoxicate ⁊ poysoned to deth/ as though he hymselfe had dronke the poyson/ ⁊ the bysshop was not hurt therby The feest also of many . ⁊c̃.

¶ To morowe.

¶ The .xviij. day of February. the receyuyng of saynt Edwarde kynge ⁊ martyr in to sephton frō perham. And the

FEBRVARY.

feest of saynt Symeon a bysshop ⁊ martyr/ ⁊ nere kynsman vnto our sauyour Chryst/ for he was sone vnto Cleophas y^t was broder vnto Ioseph/ ⁊ he was nexte after saynt Iames called Chrystes broder bysshop of Ierusalem/ ⁊ in ye psecucyon of Traianus after many varyaūt turmentes he was crucyfyed/ ⁊ so valyaūtly he toke his deth/ that the selfe iudge ⁊ all the people had meruayle/ to se a man of y^t age of .Cxx. yeres suffre so strongly the paynes of ye crosse. At hoste the feest of saynt Maximus/ saynt Claudius/ ⁊ saynt Prepedīge wyfe vnto saynt Claudius/ w^t two of theyr sones/ all martyrs/ of noble byrth/ ⁊ exiled for Chryst by the emperour Dioclecian/ ⁊ after put to deth by ye fyre. In affryke the feest of saynt Rutyle/ saynt Syluane ⁊ saynt Maximiane.

¶ Addicyons.

¶ In englond ye feest of saynt Eudelme a holy virgyn. At alexander ye feest of saynt Phyle/ saynt Hesychius saynt Pachomius ⁊ saynt Theodour/ all bysshops of egypt ⁊ martyrs/ put to deth in the psecucyon of Dioclecian. The feest also of saynt Pānucius a bysshop of egypt/ that was put to deth by the emperour Maximiane. And the feest of many other holy sayntes ⁊c.

¶ To morowe.

¶ The .xix. day of February. the feest of saynt Gabine a preest ⁊ martyr/ y^t by the emperour Dioclecian was [put [*fo. xx. b.* to deth by many cruel turmentes. In affryke the feest of saynt Publy/ saynt Iulian/ ⁊ saynt Marcell.

¶ Addicyons.

¶ In germany the feest of saynt Gall a preest ⁊ cōfessour. In ye coūtree of ybery the feest of a holy woman of
lib. .x. whome Eusebius wryteth/ y^t was taken prysoner out of christianite/ ⁊ thyder brought ⁊ kept as a thrall or bonde woman/ by whome yet at ye last all ye coūtree was cōuerted vnto Chryst/ notw^{t}standyng her name is not expressed. The feest also of many other holy .⁊c.

¶ To morowe.

¶ The .xx. daye of February. At tyre ye feest of a grete multitude of martyrs/ whose nōbre passyng mannes wytte/ is onely reserued vnto ye knowlege of god/ whiche multytude by the emperour Dioclecian were put to deth by diuerse turmentes/ scourgynge/ hangyng/ rackynge/ terynge w^t hokes/ ⁊ at the last brent in fyre/ of ye whiche multytude these were chefe/ saynt Ciran saynt Siluan/ saynt Pelewse/ ⁊ saynt Line a bysshop and saynt zenoby a preest. In the yle of cipres the feest of saynt Potamye/ and saynt Nemesye. In almayne the feest of saynt Gasly† a preest ⁊ cōfessour. At rome yᵉ feest of saynt Gayus/ saynt Victor/ ⁊ saynt Pakamye.†

℣ Addicyons.

℣ The feest also of saynt Eukare bysshop of orliaūce/ and a man of grete holynes. In englonge† the feest of saynt wolryke a preest/ borne .viij. myles frō bristowe that in youth was very wylde ⁊ a grete hunter/ ⁊ yet after he closed hymselfe as an ancre/ ⁊ was of hygh perfeccyon/ ⁊ many myracles. In yrelonde the feest of saynt Bolke/ yᵗ was borne in englonde/ of noble blode/ whose moder after the deth of her housbonde went in [to [*fo. xxi.* yrelonde beynge wᵗ chylde ⁊ there dyed/ ⁊ was buryed/ whome her owne natural broder saynt Patryke reysed by prayer/ ⁊ forthwᵗ she trauayled ⁊ was soūdly deliuered of this holy saynt/ ⁊ after he was of hygh perfeccyon/ ⁊ many grete myracles. The feest also of many other holy sayntes/ martyrs/ confes. and virg.

℣ To morowe.

℣ The .xxj. day of February. At scicilie† yᵉ feest of .lxxix. holy martyrs/ that vnder yᵉ emperour Dioclecian/ by dyuerse cruell turmentes/ receyued of Chryst for yᵉ cōfessyon of his name yᵉ crowne of perpetuall glory. In affryke at adrumete yᵉ feest of saynt Verole/ saynt Secūdyn/ saynt Scrule/ ⁊ .xx. other psones all martyrs. ℣ Addicyons.

℣ At rome yᵉ feest of saynt Symake pope/ that made Gloria in excelsis/ ⁊ ordered yᵉ same to be songe or sayd euery sondaye ⁊ feestfull day at masse. At his eleccyon was a sysme/ but he obteyned ⁊ was of holy lyf ⁊ many myracles. The feest also of many other holy. ⁊c.

℣ To morowe.

℣ The .xxij. daye of February. At antioche the stallacion or tronizacyon of saynt Peter called cathedra sctī Petri. And yᵉ feest of sayt Papie bysshop of ierapole/ yᵗ was discyple vnto saynt Iohñ the euangelyst/ ⁊ scole felowe wᵗ saynt Policarpe. The feest also of saynt Aristion/ one of the .lxxij. disciples of Chryst. At alexander the feest of saynt Abily bysshop of yᵉ same/ ⁊ the second after saynt Marke/ ⁊ well ruled his chirche in vertue ⁊ good example .xiij. yeres. The feest also of saynt Tecla a virgyn. ℣ Addicyons.

℣ At tornate the feest of saynt Piaton a preest ⁊ martyr/ borne at Rome ⁊ sent wᵗ saynt Denyse in to fraūce/ [where

after he had conuerted moche people/ he was heded [*fo. xxi. b.*
in the persecucyon of the emperour Domiciane whose deed body
toke vp the heed in his owne armes and bare it more than two
myles/ by the whiche myracle moo than .M. gentyles were
cōuerted. The feest also of many other holy sayntes/ mart̃.
confes. ꝛ virg.

⁋ To morowe.

⁋ The .xxiij. day of February. At siryne yᵉ feest of saȳt
Seueret̃ a monke ꝛ martyr/ yᵗ by the emperour Maximian was
heded for chryst. The feest also of .lxxij. martyrs that in the
same cite were put to deth. And yᵉ feest of saynt Policarpe a
preest ꝛ confessour/ that wᵗ saynt Sebastian cōuerted many
persones/ and by his holy exhortacyons conforted them vnto
martyrdome. ⁋ Addicyons.
⁋ The feest also of saȳt Modest bisshop of treuer. And of
saynt Pion an abbot/ of whome is wryten in vitas patrū. The
feest also of saynt Apelles/ yᵗ was a smyth by occupacyon/ vnto
whome the deuyl appered lyke a woman of singuler beaute/
whome he stroke on yᵉ face wᵗ the hote yren yᵗ he wrought/ ꝛ
he lyued many yeres without ony fode but onely yᵉ holy sacrament whiche he receyued euery sonday/ ꝛ he was taught by an
aūgell/ ꝛ preched ꝛ moche edifyed/ ꝛ he knewe the preuy vyces
or vertues of his breder/ wᵗ many other notable thynges. The
feest also of many other holy sayn. ꝛc̃.

⁋ To morowe.

⁋ The .xxiiij. day of February. the feest of saynt Mathye
the apostle/ that after yᵉ ascencion of our sauyour was chosen
by lotte ꝛ by grace of yᵉ holy ghost/ by the other .xj. apostles/
in yᵉ place ꝛ rome of Judas yᵉ traytour/ ꝛ he preched the gospell
in the londe of iudee.
[⁋ The feest also of the inuencyon of saynt Iohñ [*fo. xxii.*
baptystes heed/ that was foūde in the tyme of the prynce
Marcian/ by yᵉ reuelacyon of yᵉ same holy saynt Iohñ that was
made vnto two monkes. In cesary the feest of saȳt Serge a
martyr/ whose noble gestes ben wryten in the legend. In
englond the feest of saynt Athelbert/ the fyrst chrysten kynge
of this realme.

⁋ A canon or rule for the redynge of this Martiloge in the
lepe yere.

For the lepe yere.

⁋ In euery lepe yere this lettre .ff. in the kalender is twyse nombred for two dyuerse dayes/ and euer vpon the latter daye is saynt Mathyes daye/ and therfore ye must begyn your Martiloge on y{e} fyrst f. the .xxiiij. daye thus.

⁋ The feest also of y{e} inuencyon .&c. at this marke ✠ And the nexte daye after rede of saynt Mathye/ vnto the same marke/ & than your addicyons as folowe.

⁋ Addicyons.

⁋ The feest also of saynt Gerard bysshop of Pānony/ promoted therunto for his sanctite by saynt Stephen kynge of hungary/ & there as he preched he was put to deth by infydeles. The feest also of an other saynt Gerard a cōfessour & bysshop of luke/ & of meruaylous sanctite/ & many myracles. The feest also of saynt Serene a monke & martyr/ that by the emperour Maximian was put to deth for Chryst. And the feest of an other saynt Serene an abbot of synguler graces/ specyally in the vertue of chastite. And the feest of many other holy sayntes/ martyrs/ confessours & virgyns.

⁋ To morowe.

⁋ The .xxv. daye of February. In egypte the feest of [saynt Victoryne & saynt Victor/ saynt Nicofore & [*fo. xxii. b.* saȳt Claudiane/ saynt Dioscour/ saynt Serapion/ & saynt Papy/ y{t} by y{e} emperour Numeriane were put to many varyaunt & moost cruell turmentes & vnto dyuerse dethes. At rome the inuencyon of saynt Paules heed the apostle.

⁋ Addicyons.

⁋ The y{e}† feest also of saynt Walpurge a virgyn. The feest also of saynt Piamon a preest in y{e} deserte of sythe that by the reuelacyon of an aūgell knewe his breders synnes/ & refourmed them to penaunce & forgyuenes. And y{e} feest of saynt Beniamyn an olde fader/ y{t} dwelled in wyldernes/ and beynge seke hymselfe/ so that he myght not go/ he heled all maner of persones y{t} were brought vnto hym of all maner of sekenes. The feest also of many other holy sayntes/ mart͛. cōfes. & virg.

⁋ To morowe.

⁋ The .xxvj. daye of February. In pergenpamphyle the feest of saynt Nestour a bysshop/ that in y{e} persecucyon of y{e} emperour Decius was racked & put to many cruell turmentes/ whiche w{t} a stronge hert & noble courage he susteyned for

FEBRVARY.

Chryst/ ꝫ at yᵉ last as a noble chāpion he folowynge his mayster Chryst/ dyed vpon the crosse. In alexander the feest of saynt Alexander/ that was a sage fader of profoūde doctryne. And in a generall sene of .cccxviij. bysshops ꝫ reuerende faders of yᵉ chirche/ he cōdempned for euer/ ꝫ cursed solempnely the grete heretyke Arrius ꝫ all his secte ꝫ opinyons with many other noble actes. The feest also of saynt Fortunate/ saynt Felix/ wᵗ other xxvij. holy martyrs. ❡ Addicyons.

❡ The feest also of saȳt Syre/ saȳt Paule/ saynt Isay that all togyder mette at a water banke/ ꝫ all purpo[synge [*fo. xxiii.*] one thynge/ ꝫ yet none knewe of an other/ ꝫ all they went to vysyte a holy fader saynt Anub/ ꝫ were caryed all ouer that water by myracle/ ꝫ eueryche of them had a singuler reuelacyon of yᵉ same saynt Anub ꝫ he had reuelacyon of them ꝫ theyr thoughtes/ ꝫ in yᵉ mornyng after he dyed amonge them/ ꝫ they after/ all full of sctīte ꝫ pfeccyon. The feest also of many oth. ꝫc.

❡ To morowe.

❡ The xxvij. day of February. In alexander the passyon of saynt Iulian a martyr/ yᵗ was seke of yᵉ gowte not able to go/ ꝫ therfore he was brought before the iudge on horsbacke/ with his seruaūt saynt Euno/ by whome they were iudged to be caryed thrugh the cite vpon mules/ ꝫ in the syght of yᵉ people to be scourged in dyuerse stretes/ ꝫ theyr flesshe was rent ꝫ torne wᵗ hokes/ tyll by suche turmentes they were deed. In spayne in the cite of hyspale the feest of saynt Leandre a bysshop ꝫ cōfessour/ by whose prechynge/ wysdome and doctryne/ all the gotes wᵗ theyr kynge saynt Recared were conuerted from yᵉ wycked heresye of Arrius. At lyons yᵉ feest of saynt Baldomere/ at whose tombe ben done many grete myracles. In alexander the feest of saynt Abundance/ and of saynt Fortunion. ❡ Addicyons.

❡ At cesary capadoce yᵉ feest of saynt Honoryne a holy virgyn/ yᵗ after many straūge turmentes was slayne by the swerde/ ꝫ with her were put to deth saynt Kalixt ꝫ saynt Trist bothe virgyns/ yᵗ by her were cōuerted vnto Chrystes fayth. The feest of many other .ꝫc.

❡ To morowe.

❡ The .xxviij. daye of February. In the terrytory of lyons the feest of saynt Romane/ fyrst an heremyte/ ꝫ [after [*fo. xxiii. b.*] an abbot/ euer of holy cōuersacyon ꝫ famous in myracles. The feest also of saynt Machare/ saynt Rufyne/ saynt Iust/ ꝫ saynt

MARTILO.

Theophyle. In englonde at worcester the feest of saynt Oswalde an archebysshop of moche vertue.

⁋ Addicyons.

⁋ In yrelonde yᵉ feest of saynt Ayd. At Rome the feest of saynt Iohn̄ a monke of hygh perfeccyon/ yᵗ was closed in a strayte sell/ ⁊ foūde of almes by his owne fader ⁊ moder/ but vnknowen vnto them/ vnto the tyme of his deth. The feest also of an other saynt Iohn̄ an abbot in sythe/ that whan an heremyte came to vysyte hym/ that there had dwelled .xl. yeres/ ⁊ saynt Iohn̄ axed hym of his moost pfeccyon. He answered/ yᵉ sonne (sayd he) sawe me neuer ete ne drynke. Ne me (sayd saynt Iohn̄) angry/ wrothe/ or dyspleased. Hereof is wrytē in vitas patrū. The feest also of yᵉ thyrde saynt Iohn̄ an abbot also of yᵉ desert of yᵉ hygher thebaydes that thre yeres contynually prayed euer standynge/ ⁊ neuer dyd he syt nor lye/ ne neuer ete ne dranke/ but yᵗ euery sondaye he receyued the body of our lorde/ after he went forth to preche by the reuelacyon of an āugell by whome he was euery sonday refresshed at his sell. Of hym is also wryten in vitas patrū. The feest also of yᵉ fourth saynt Iohn̄/ wryten of in vitas patrū also a gracyous man/ ⁊ vnto all persones moche cōfortable and of grete myracles. The translacyon also of our holy fader saynt Augustyne/ from hypponens vnto papye/ solempnly done by kynge Luprand/ kynge of longobardynes/ in the yere of our lord .vij. c. xviij. ⁊ after his deth .CC. and .lxxx. yeres/ at whiche translacyon were done many grete myracles. The feest also of many other holy sayntes/ martyrs/ confessours ⁊ virg.

[⁋ To morowe. [fo. xxiiii.

Marche.

THe fyrst day of Marche. at rome yᵉ feest of ccxij. martyrs/ whome yᵉ emperour Claudius fyrst condempned chrystyans/ ⁊ for theyr punysshement he set them to labour ⁊ to dygge sondes for yᵉ cite/ ⁊ after syth they wolde not forsake Chryst/ they were teyed without salary gate in a playne/ to be shotte at by the soudyours/ ⁊ so put to deth. In cartage yᵉ feest of saynt Donate a martyr/ that by the iudge Vrsace/ ⁊ the tribune Marcelline was there put to deth. In andegaue the feest of saynt Albyne a bysshop ⁊ confessour/ a famous man of synguler sanctite. At massylye the feest of saynt Heremete and saynt Adrian. The feest also of saynt Leo a martyr/ of many myracles. In brytayne now wales/ the feest of saynt Dauid an archebysshop and confessour/ a man of many graces ⁊ notable vertues. In peruse yᵉ feest of saynt Erculaue† a bysshop.

¶ Addicyons.

¶ In sythe yᵉ feest of saynt Sare an holy abbesse/ yᵗ in youth was moche tempted wᵗ lechery/ but so by contynuall prayer she resysted/ that yᵉ deuyll appered vnto her ⁊ sayd/ yᵘ hast vaynquysshed ⁊ ouercome me. Nay sayd she/ my lorde god ⁊ sauyour Chryst/ ⁊ not I hath vaynquysshed ⁊ confounded the/ ⁊ than she went in to desert/ ⁊ there was an abbesse of blessed lyfe .lx. yeres. The feest also of saynt Syncletyke an abbesse also in yᵉ same wyldernes/ of whome is wryten in vitas patrū. The feest also of many other holy sayntes/ mart̄. ⁊c.

¶ To morowe.

¶ The seconde day of Marche. at rome in latyn strete the feest of saynt Iouyne ⁊ saynt Basylewe martyrs that were put to deth by yᵉ emperours Galiene ⁊ Va[leriane. At [*fo. xxiiii. b.* rome also yᵉ feest of many martyrs vnnombred/ that by yᵉ emperour alexander were put to deth by many turmentes. In englond at lychefelde yᵉ feest of saynt Chadde a bysshop ⁊ confessour/ whose lyfe of meruaylous vertue sayt Bede wryteth. The feest also of saynt Lucius a bisshop/ saynt Absolon and saynt Lorget confessours.

¶ Addicyons.

¶ The feest also of sayt Cedde yᵗ was naturall broder vnto saynt Chadde a bysshop also ⁊ a cōfessour of synguler vertue ⁊ many myracles. The feest also of saynt Symplice pope ⁊ martyr. In ytaly yᵉ feest of .CCCC. martyrs that were put to deth by yᵉ longobardes. In affryke the feest of many bysshops/ prelates ⁊ clerkes that in the tyme of the emperour Iustinian were put to deth by the wandales. In englonde yᵉ feest of saynt Wyllyam a preest of grete fame in vertue ⁊ myracles that flourysshed in the tyme of the emperour Henry yᵉ thyrde. And the feest of many other holy sayntes .⁊c.

¶ To morowe.

¶ The thyrde day of Marche. at cesary palestyne the feest of saynt Maryne/ a man of warre/ yᵗ confessynge the name of Chryst boldly/ was heded in the persecucyon of the emperour Valeriane/ by whose constancy saynt Astecet a senatour cōfessed hymselfe a chrystyan also/ ⁊ lapped the holy corps in his senatours cloke/ to haue buryed it wᵗ due honour/ for the whiche he was forthwᵗ put to the same deth. In galace at legionens yᵉ feest of saynt Enutheret ⁊ saynt Seledon yᵗ were there soudyours/ ⁊ put to many turmentes/ ⁊ after brought to **calagurryn**/ ⁊ there receyued the crowne ⁊ palme of martyrdome. The feest also of saynt wynewale a bysshop.

⁋ Addicyons.

[⁋ In almayne at bamberge the feest of saynt [*fo. xxv.* Kunegund a virgyn/ ⁊ wyfe vnto saynt Henry ye emperour and yet bothe by one assent kepynge purite lyued virgyns/ notw^{t}standynge/ she by the malyce of ye deuyll ⁊ enuyous suspicyon was accused of incontynency/ but she for her purgacyon went barefoted thrugh a grete fyre of grete length/ ⁊ vpon coles ⁊ glowȳge hote yren w^{t}out blemysshe or noyaunce/ ⁊ so was declared. The feest also of many other holy sayntes/ mar. cōf. ⁊ virg.

⁋ To morowe.

⁋ The .iiij. day of Marche. at rome in appia strete the feest of saynt Luke pope ⁊ martyr/ y^t in the psecucyon of ye emperours Valeriane ⁊ Galiene was fyrst put to exile for Chryst/ ⁊ after by dyuyne reuelacyon he was called home vnto his chirche/ ⁊ there heded. At Rome also in ye same strete ye feest of .ix. C. martyrs/ that in ye same psecucyon were put to deth/ ⁊ buryed in ye cimytery of saynt Cicilyes. The feest also of saynt Gay and saynt Palatyne† that were drowned in the see/ ⁊ with them xxvij. other persones all martyrs.

⁋ Addicyons.

⁋ At nicomede ye feest of saynt Adrian/ that after many affliccyons was there put to deth/ ⁊ w^t him .xxiij. other persones all martyrs. The feest also of saynt Tabite/ y^t in ye grete monastery of thebaydes was holden ⁊ supposed a fole ⁊ drabbe of kechyn/ of whome was reuelacyon made vnto saynt Piery/ whiche knowen she fledde in to desert.⁊ The feest also of many other .⁊c.

⁋ To morowe.

⁋ The .v. day of Marche. At antioche ye feest of saynt Foke a martyr/ y^t suffred many affliccyons ⁊ open batayle w^t the deuyll in ye syght of ye people/ wherof they [speke [*fo. xxv. b.* vnto this daye. The feest also of saynt Eusebius saynt Palatyne†/ ⁊ .xj. other martyrs. In yrelonde the feest of saynt Ciaue a bysshop and confessour.

⁋ Addicyons.

⁋ The feest also of saynt Quiryake a bysshop ⁊ martyr/ that was ye same Iudas y^t was cōpelled by saynt Elene to fynde the holy crosse/ ⁊ after his baptym he was bisshop of Ierusalem/ ⁊ put to deth for ye fayth of the crosse. At palestyne ye feest of saynt Theophile bysshop of ye same cite/ of whome saynt

Ierome wryteth grete prayse. And yͤ feest of an other saynt Theophyle bysshop of alexander/ a man of excellent doctryne/ that confoūded many heresyes/ ꝛ wrote many werkes agaynst them. In cornwell yͤ feest of saynt Pyrane/ called also saynt Keran/ borne of the nobles of yrelonde in the tyme of saynt Patryke/ a man of hygh pfeccyon ꝛ very many myracles/ ꝛ had visyon of aūgels/ ꝛ lyued meruaylously longe without sekenes or disease. The feest also of many other holy sayntes/ mar. cōf. ꝛ virg.

⁋ To morowe.

⁋ The .vj. day of Marche. At nicomede yͤ feest of saȳt Victor ꝛ saynt Victoryne/ yᵗ by the space of thre yeres were with saynt Claudiane ꝛ saynt Basse his wyfe/ in grete affliccyon/ ꝛ at the last they dyed in pryson. At tolete yͤ deposycyon of saynt Iulian a bysshop/ yᵗ there is had in grete honour.

⁋ Addicyons.

⁋ At terdon the feest of saynt Marcian a bysshop and martyr/ yᵗ by aūgels was brought out of pryson for yͤ conforte of saynt Secūde/ whiche saynt Secūde was ledde by an aūgell/ after yᵗ vnto hym in yͤ same prison/ ꝛ brought hym the sacrament of Chrystes body before his martyrdome. In englond the feest of saynt Kyne[burge/ doughter vnto kynge Penda/ [*fo. xxvi.* ꝛ wyfe vnto the kyng of the marches/ ꝛ after an holy abbesse. And the feest also of her syster Kenyswyde a virgyn/ yᵗ after her succeded abbesse. And yͤ feest also of theyr kynswoman saynt Tybbe a virgyn/ ꝛ all thre of synguler sanctite ꝛ grete myracles. And yͤ feest of many otħ. ꝛc.

⁋ To morowe.

⁋ The .vij. day of Marche. At mauritane amonge yͤ tyburbitans yͤ feest of ₁yͤ holy women saȳt Perpetua ꝛ saynt Felicite martyrs/ ꝛ of saynt Reuocate and saynt Saturnyne/ that wᵗ them by the prynce Seuere were put to deth all deuoured wᵗ wylde beestes/ ꝛ the feest of saynt Secūdole that was taken with them/ but he dyed in pryson/ and so with them a martyr.

⁋ Addicyons.

⁋ The feest also of saynt Thomas of aquyne/ a noble man borne/ ꝛ yet more noble in vertue ꝛ myracles/ ꝛ yᵗ amonge holy sayntes was of excellent lernynge/ and amonge lerned men of synguler sanctite. The feest also of saynt Satyre/ broder vnto saȳt Saturnyne/ ꝛ (after some auctours) put to deth wᵗ his broder ꝛ his felowes. In the monastery of saynt Paule vpon yͤ water of tyne in englonde/ yͤ feest of saynt Esterwyne abbot of the same/ ꝛ a man of grete pfeccyon. And ye feest of many other holy sayntes/ marꝭ. cōfes. ꝛ virg.

¶ To morowe.

¶ The .viij. day of Marche. At antion yᵉ feest of saynt Philomont ꝛ saynt Apollyn a deacon/ yᵗ bycause they wolde not do sacrefice vnto the ydolles/ were thrylled or bored thrugh the heles vnder yᵉ ancles/ ꝛ so drawen by cordes thrugh yᵉ cite/ ꝛ at yᵉ last slayne by yᵉ swerde. In the same cite yᵉ feest of saynt Ariane/ saynt Theo[tyke/ ꝛ of other thre psones [*fo. xxvi. b.* all martyrs/ yᵗ after many horryble turmentes were drowned in yᵉ see/ whose holy bodyes were brought to londe by a delfyne. At cartage the feest of saynt Ponce a deacon/ ꝛ of saynt Cirprianet a bysshop ꝛ his companyon in all troubles/ of whose lyfe/ noble actes and passion he made a notable boke/ ꝛ after for Chryst suffred gloryous martyrdom. In brytayne yᵉ feest of saẏt Felix a bysshop ꝛ cōfessour.

¶ Addicyons.

¶ In yrelonde the feest of saynt Fenan a bysshop/ of whome saẏt Patryke pphecyed .vj. score yeres before he was borne/ shewynge yᵗ suche a man of his name ꝛ maner/ shold be in his rome archebysshop of yrelonde/ and so he was/ ꝛ of lyke holynes and myracles. The feest also of many other holy sayntes/ mar. cōf. ꝛ virg.

¶ To morowe.

¶ The .ix. day of Marche. At nice yᵉ feest of saẏt Gregory a bysshop/ ꝛ broder vnto saẏt Basyle bysshop of cesariens/ a man of grete fame/ synguler doctryne/ goodly eloquence/ ꝛ of hygh pfeccyon. At barcinon the feest of saynt Pacian/ yᵗ dyed in the tyme of prynce Theodos. At sebasten the feest of .xl. martyrs all famous men of warre.

¶ Addicyons.

¶ In the regyon of galace the feest of saynt Phyllorrony a preest of meruaylous abstinence/ ꝛ of cōtynuall labours/ ꝛ oftentymes had open batayle wᵗ euyll spirytes/ ꝛ yet was of grete cōtemplacion. The feest also of saynt Gadane/ a man of harde lyuyng/ for he neuer lay in hous ne couerture/ but alwaye in yᵉ open ayre ꝛ weder. The feest also of many other holy sayntes .ꝛc.

⁋ To morowe.

⁋ The .x. day of Marche. At apamia the feest of saynt [Alexander/ ꝧ saynt Gay martyrs/ that (as saynt [*fo. xxvii.* Apolinar bysshop of Ierapolitan wryteth in his boke agaynst the catafryges) were put to deth in ye persecucyon of Antonyn vere. In perse ye feest of .xlij. martyrs. At parys ye feest of saynt Dorothene an abbot/ ꝧ discyple vnto saynt Germayn the bysshop. The feest also of saynt Atale an abbot ꝧ discyple vnto saynt Colūbane. And ye feest of saynt Agathe/ saynt Gorgon and saynt Fyrme. ⁋ Addicyons.

⁋ The feest also of saynt Syluia a virgyn/ that was doughter vnto ye mayre of alexander/ ꝧ of grete doctryne/ ꝧ very eloquent/ ꝧ spent ye nyghtes hooly in redȳge of holy scripture/ ꝧ the daye in prayer ꝧ cōtemplacyon content w^t lytell slepe ꝧ small fedynge/ ꝧ she lyued in ye wyldernes of the thebaides .lx. yeres/ ꝧ neuer laye in bedde ne strawe/ but vpon the bare erth. The feest also of many other holy sayntes/ mart̃. confes. ꝧ virg.

⁋ To morowe.

⁋ The .xj. day of Marche. At sebasten in ye lesse armenye the feest of .xl. martyrs men of warre/ y^t by kynge Lucyne had many turmentes/ ꝧ at ye last theyr thyes ꝧ legges were broken/ ꝧ so ended theyr martyrdome/ ye capytaynes and moost noble men of them were saynt Cirion ꝧ saynt Candidus.
⁋ Addicyons.

⁋ In the marches of englond the feest of saynt Paule bysshop of leonens/ y^t whan he was a nouyce droue before hym a flocke of byrdes that destroyed the corne/ ꝧ brought them vnto his abbot to be punysshed. And after he cōmaunded the see to remoue a myle backe/ ꝧ to leue all ye lande vnto the monastery/ ꝧ so it yet remayneth/ w^t many other grete myracles. At cartage ye feest of saynt Hyrade/ saynt zozime/ saynt Alexander/ saynt [Candidus/ saynt Piperion/ ꝧ other [*fo. xxvii. b.* xx. psones all martyrs. In fraunce the feest of saynt Gūpert bysshop of herbipole/ y^t for his holynes ꝧ hygh vertue/ was compelled agaynst his wyll to be a bysshop/ ꝧ he lyued but a smal tyme after. The feest also of many other ho. ꝧc.

⁋ To morowe.

⁋ The .xij. day of Marche. At rome the feest of saynt Gregory the pope/ ꝧ one of the .iiij. doctours/ called also the apostle of englond/ bycause he sent saynt Augustyne in to

englonde/ by whome the people there were cōuerted. At
nicomede yͤ passyon of saynt Peter a martyr/ yᵗ was seruaūt ꝯ
of yͤ chambre wᵗ the prynce Dioclecian/ ꝯ whan he sawe the
cruelte of his prynce vnto the chrystyans/ he boldly reproued hym/
for yͤ whiche he was hanged by the heles ꝯ scourged/ ꝯ his
flesshe rent ꝯ toren/ ꝯ than vynegre ꝯ salte cast therupon/ ꝯ
after he was broyled vpon the coles/ ꝯ so made the hoste ꝯ
sacrefyce of Chryst. At the same cite the feest also of saynt
Eddune a preest wᵗ other .vij. martyrs/ yᵗ vnto yͤ terrour ꝯ
fere of the people were put to deth eche after other. The feest
also of saynt Alphege bysshop of wentane ꝯ a confessour.
  ¶ Addicyons.
  ¶ At rome the feest of saynt Peter a deacon/ ꝯ disciple
vnto saynt Gregory. The feest also of saynt Sysyn a monke of
grete vertue/ but synguler in chastite/ so yᵗ he neuer knewe
differēce bytwene man kynde ꝯ women. In the desert of
thebaydes yͤ feest of saynt Diocles/ yᵗ was fyrst a seculer
philosopher of grete lernyng/ ꝯ after of strayte ꝯ harde lyuyng
closed in a caue many yeres vnto yͤ ende of his lyf. And yͤ
feest of many oth. ꝯc.

  ¶ To morowe.

  ¶ The .xiij. daye of Marche. At nicomede the feest of
[saynt Macedon a preest/ saynt Patryke/ ꝯ saynt [fo. xxviii.
Modest martyrs. At nice the feest of saynt Thensete/ saȳt
Horre/ saynt Theodour/ saȳt Nympodour/ saȳt Marke/ ꝯ saynt
Arabye martyrs/ all brent. At thebaydes yͤ feest of saynt
Eufrase a virgyn.   ¶ Addicyons.
  ¶ The feest also of saynt Capithon a cōfessour/ that in youth
was a stronge thefe/ ꝯ after went in to wyldernes/ ꝯ there for
his penaunce he enclosed hymselfe in a denne .l. yeres/ ꝯ neuer
came in to yͤ company of people. The feest also of saynt Amata
a virgyn ꝯ an abbesse of .lx. virgyns in yͤ desert of thebaides/ a
woman of hygh pfeccion/ ꝯ in yͤ age of .lxxx. yeres she before
her systers not feynynge seke ne dyseased/ made her redy to be
buryed/ ꝯ whan she came vnto yͤ sepulcre/ she yelded her
spiryte. The feest also of many other holy sayntes .ꝯc.

  ¶ To morowe.

  ¶ The .xiiij. day of Marche. At rome the feest of .xlix.
martyrs/ that were baptyzed of saynt Peter/ whyle he was in
pryson in the kepynge Mamurtyne wᵗ his coapostle and felowe
saynt Paule/ where they were kepte .ix. monethes/ but these holy

sayntes were put to deth by the tyranny ⁊ swerde of the cruel emperour Nero. In affryke the feest of saynt Peter a martyr. And the feest of saynt Eufrose a bysshop ⁊ confessour.
⁋ Addicyons.
⁋ In egypte yᵉ feest of saynt Punyfyke/ an honourable preest ⁊ abbot of many monkes/ ⁊ of hygh pfeccion ⁊ many myracles/ yᵗ in his age wyllynge to auoyde yᵉ fame ⁊ prayse of the worlde/ fledde pryuely in a seculer habyte vnto an other abbey in desert/ of more strayter lyuynge/ ⁊ there he remayned many dayes/ layenge styll before ye gates/ desyryng to be receyued/ but they [longe deferred bycause of his age/ yet at yᵉ last by [*fo. xxviii. b.* his importunite/ they toke hym/ ⁊ there he dyd the moost vyle labours in yᵉ hous/ ⁊ oft he wold ryse in yᵉ nyght to do certayn labours necessary/ bycause no man shold knowe the doer. Than his owne monastery fell in dekey/ ⁊ the breder went abrode to seke hym/ ⁊ whan he at yᵉ last was founde/ he returned home/ ⁊ there ended his lyf. The feest also of many other holy sayntes .⁊c̄.

⁋ To morowe.

⁋ The .xv. day of Marche. in cesary Capadoce yᵉ passyon of saynt Longyne/ that perced ⁊ opened the syde of our sauyour wᵗ a spere/ as in his legende is wryten. The translacyon also of saynt Leodegare a bysshop ⁊ martyr. At yᵉ cite of thessolonyke the feest of saynt Macronet̄ a martyr/ a woman of grete cōscyence/ that confessyng euer the name of Chryst/ was beten to deth wᵗ staues. The feest also of saynt Iames ⁊ saynt Luke/ bothe bysshops.   ⁋ Addicyons.
⁋ In sythe the feest of saynt Theremon an abbot/ of hygh pfeccyon. At pamphilye yᵉ feest of saynt Arteby a bysshop/ that was an hcremyte/ ⁊ by violence was made bysshop of yᵉ sayd cite/ ⁊ well ⁊ holyly ruled his flocke/ ⁊ there lyeth buryed. In ytaly yᵉ feest of saynt Habetdeū/ bysshop of lunens ⁊ a martyr/ yᵗ after exyle ⁊ many troubles was heded by yᵉ wādales. The feest also of many other holy sayntes/ marī. confes. ⁊ virg.

⁋ To morowe.

⁋ The .xvj. day of Marche. at aquiley yᵉ feest of saynt Hyllary a bysshop/ ⁊ saynt Taciane a deacon/ yᵗ were hanged on a gybet/ ⁊ by many other turmētes put to deth/ ⁊ wᵗ them were also martyred saynt Felix/ saynt Large/ ⁊ saynt Denyse. At rome the passyon of saynt [Ciriake a deacon/ that [*fo. xxix.* after longe imprysonmēt was taken out ⁊ hote pytche wᵗ sulphure pored vpon hym/ than was he racked ꝑ his mēbres stretched wᵗ cordes/ ꝑ at the last by the cōmaūdement of the tyraūt Maximian he was heded/ ꝑ wᵗ hym were put to deth saynt Large ꝑ saynt Smaragdus/ with .xx. other psones/ whose seconde feest is kepte the .viij. daye of August. whan they were translated and tombed or shryned by saynt Marcel pope. At auerne yᵉ feest of saynt Patrike a bysshop ꝑ confessour.

⁋ Addicyons.

⁋ In yrelonde yᵉ feest of saynt Fynan a bysshop of synguler sanctite/ he reysed thre psones from deth/ wᵗ many famous myracles. In scotlond yᵉ feest of saynt Abbane/ called also saynt Kyryne/ whose syrname was Boniface/ and therfore of many called saynt Boniface/ borne in yᵉ coūtree of galilee at bethsayda/ ꝑ by nacyon a iewe/ ꝑ ordered a bysshop by saynt Iohñ patriarke of Ierusalē/ ꝑ after he was a grete pylgrym vnto all the places where Chryst had ben/ ꝑ than to Rome by reuelacyon/ ꝑ from thens to scotlond/ where he cōuerted the kynge ꝑ the coūtree/ ꝑ after he went in to yᵉ out yles/ where he buylded .C. chirches/ ꝑ cōuerted of the people vnto Chryst .xxxvj. M. ꝑ reysed .vij. psones frō deth/ ꝑ he made yᵉ defe to here/ the blynde to se/ yᵉ lame to go/ and he cast out wycked spirytes/ wᵗ many other myracles/ ꝑ he lyued vnto the age of .C. yeres ꝑ moo. The feest also of many other holy sayntes/ marṫ. ꝇc.

⁋ To morowe.

⁋ The .xvij. daye of Marche. In scotlonde the feest of saynt Patrike bysshop ꝑ confessour/ that fyrst preched there Christes fayth. At nicomede yᵉ feest of saynt Eugene/ saynt Pāphilian/ saynt Castor/ ꝑ saynt Serene. [The feest [*fo. xxix. b.* also of saynt witburge a virgyn. In the monastery of nūgell the feest of saynt Geretrude a virgyn and martyr.

⁋ Addicyons.

⁋ At alexander the feest of saynt Ambrose a deacon of the same cite ꝑ chefe chirche/ ꝑ a notable man of hygh vertue. The feest of saynt Cassiadour/ yᵗ was chaūceler vnto the kynge of ytaly/ ꝑ after a senatour of rome ꝑ all he forsoke ꝑ was a monke of grete holynes ꝑ excellent lernyng/ ꝑ wrote many werkes vnto the edifycacyon of Christes chirche/ ꝑ after his deth he dyd many myracles. The feest also of many other holy sayn. ꝇc.

⁋ To morowe.

⁋ The .xviij. daye of Marche. In englond the feest of saynt Edward kynge ꝑ martyr/ sone ꝑ heyre vnto the noble

kynge Edgare/ that was a grete founder of monasteryes/ whiche
sayd kynge Edward as a true professour of Chrystes fayth/ was
martyred by the psecucyon of his stepdame/ ꝛ of certayne lordes
of her counseyle/ wherby he was ioyned vnto yᵉ college ꝛ company of holy sayntes in heuen/ as playnly is declared by
many grete miracles dayly shewed at his tombe. The feest
also of saynt Alexander a bysshop/ yᵗ for deuocyon wente from
capadoce his owne cite vnto Ierusalem/ where by diuyne
reuelacyon he toke vpon hym yᵉ cure ꝛ gouernaūce of yᵉ cite/ ꝛ
after in his olde age he was brought prysoner vnto cesary/ where
for the fayth of Chryst he was put to deth by the persecucyon
of the emperour Decius. ⁋ Addicyons.

⁋ The feest also of saynt Frygdiane bysshop of lucane ꝛ a
cōfessour/ of hygh pfeccyon. And one of yᵉ feestes of saynt
Ancelme. The feest also of saynt Geremare an abbot/ borne of
grete kynne/ ꝛ after the deth of his pa[rentes he solde [fo. xxx.
all his londes ꝛ goodes ꝛ dystrybuted vnto the poore/ ꝛ after
was made abbot by saynt Audowene/ ꝛ yet remoued thens by
the enuy of his monkes/ but he after buylded an other monastery
by the shewyng of an aūgell/ ꝛ therin serued god vnto yᵉ
ende of his lyfe. The feest also of many other holy sayn. ꝛc.

⁋ To morowe.

⁋ The .xix. day of Marche. the feest of saynt Iohn̄/ a man
of grete pfeccion/ yᵗ borne in syria came in to ytaly ꝛ there
in the towne of penarens buylded a monastery ꝛ therin remayned all his lyfe/ wᵗ other religyous breder/ ꝛ dyd many
miracles. At suretyke yᵉ feest of saynt Quynt/ saynt Quyntyll/
saynt Quartyll/ saynt Marcyll/ wᵗ other .ix. all martyrs. At
bryxe the feest of saynt Coloteryt a martyr. And the feest of
saynt Ioseph the holy virgyn ꝛ spouse of our blessed lady
ꝛ euer virgyn Mary/ that also was nouryssher ꝛ bringer vp
of our sauyour Chryst. The feest also of saynt Theodour a
bysshop/ saynt Appolon/ saynt Leonce/ and saynt Florence.
The trāslacyon also of saẏt Mary mawdeleyn.
⁋ Addicyons.

⁋ The feest also of saynt Remachlewe a bysshop/ that of
humylite resygned his bysshopryke ꝛ was a poore monke ꝛ a
nouyce ꝛ moost lowly in obedience/ ꝛ lyued euer as a discyple/
notwᵗstandynge yᵗ before he was a bysshop. The feest also of
many other holy saynꝑ. ꝛc.

⁋ To morowe.

⁋ The .xx. day of Marche. In englonde y̆ᵉ feest of saȳt Cutbert/ that of an ancre was made bisshop of lyndisfarnēs/ a man of grete age ⁊ synguler sanctite/ wᵗ many grete myracles/ whiche thynge his holy body doth testyfye/ that yet remayneth vncorrupted. In asya yᵉ [feest of saynt Archyppe/ [fo. xxx. b. that was disciple vnto saynt Paule/ ⁊ his contynual companyon in prechynge ⁊ in Chrystes warre/ of whome he wryteth vnto the colosenses. In syre the feest of saynt Paule/ saynt Cyryll/ saynt Eugene/ ⁊ other .iiij. psones all martyrs. In the fraūchyse of rone yᵉ feest of saynt Vlfran a confessour ⁊ bysshop.

⁋ Addicyons.

⁋ At the monastery of crispinens yᵉ feest of saynt Landelme a cōfessour/ yᵗ fyrst was in youth a stronge thefe ⁊ a robber/ ⁊ after cōuerted by saynt Ausbert bysshop of cameracēs/ ⁊ after that he was discyple vnto saynt Martyne/ ⁊ he foūded two monasteryes/ ⁊ was abbot in the sayd crispinens/ of holy lyfe ⁊ many myracles/ in whose tyme many famous psones came to religion out of englonde/ scotlond/ and other partyes/ amonge whome was saȳt Gyslen an abbot/ saynt Maldegare a duke ⁊ saynt Valdetrude his wyf/ ⁊ her sister saynt Aldegūde/ ⁊ saȳt Trude/ wᵗ many other/ whose feestes be vnknowen. The feest also of many other holy .⁊c̃.

⁋ To morowe.

⁋ The .xxj. day of Marche. At yᵉ cāstell of cassyne the feest of the holy fader saynt Benedict/ called saynt Benet an abbot/ ⁊ fyrst foūder of yᵉ blacke monkes/ whose holy lyfe full of vertue and myracles/ saynt Gregory wryteth. In alexander the feest of saynt Serapion an ancre/ ⁊ a man of synguler vertue. In the terrytory of lyons yᵉ feest of saynt Lupycyne an abbot/ whose gracyous ⁊ holy lyfe was by many myracles moche famous. ⁋ Addicyons.

⁋ At rome the feest of saynt Benet yᵉ pope/ that from youth was of synguler vertue/ ⁊ so encreaced ⁊ grewe therin that he was worthy yᵗ dignite/ he was of pro[foūde mekenes/ [fo. xxvi. very pyteous ⁊ lyberall. The feest also of the thyrde saynt Benet a monke of campane .xl. myles from rome/ that was sore vexed by infydeles yᵗ set fyre vpon his sell/ but it wolde not bren/ than they hete an ouen fyre hote/ ⁊ put hȳ closed therin all nyght ⁊ on yᵉ morowe they foūde hym in helth/
iij. di. ca. ⁊ his clothes vntouched/ of hym wryteth saynt
xviij. Gregory. The feest also of many other holy sayntes/ mar. confes. ⁊ virg.

⁋ To morowe.

⁋ The .xxij. daye of Marche. At septimane in byterne the feest of saynt Affrodose a bysshop ⁊ cōfessour/ ⁊ the feest of saynt Paule/ y^t was ordered ⁊ made bysshop of narbonens by ye apostle Paule/ where after many gloryous actes ⁊ grete myracles/ he rested in our lorde.
⁋ Addicyons.

⁋ The feest also of saynt Berno abbot of cluniacens/ ⁊ the fyrst foūder of y^t religyon/ a holy man of hygh perfeccyon/ ⁊ many myracles/ y^t before his deth resygned his rome vnto his owne discyple ⁊ monke saynt Odo/ and so dyed an obedyenser in the peace of Chryst. The feest also of many other holy sayntes/ mar. cōf. ⁊ virg.

⁋ To morowe.

⁋ The .xxiij. daye of Marche. In affryke the feest of saynt Victoriane/ ⁊ of two natural breder called bothe by one name/ saynt Frumence/ that (as saynt Victor bysshop of affricane wryteth) were put to many grete turmentes by ye kynge Honoryke for Chrystes fayth. In antioche ye feest of saynt Theodour a preest. In cesare the feest of saynt Iulian.
⁋ Addicyons.

⁋ In affryke the feest of .xij. infantes yonge persones that in the persecucyon of the wandales/ bycause they wolde not by ony psuasyon or entreates forsake chryst [they were [*fo. xxxi. b.* scourged to deth/ by the example of whome two ryche marchaūtes called bothe saynt Frumence by one name/ and .v. religyous psones/ saynt Liberate abbot of cartage/ saynt Boniface a deacon/ saynt Rustyke a subdeacon/ ⁊ saynt Rogate ⁊ saynt Maximus monkes/ were all put to deth for ye cōfessyon of Chryst. In affryke also the feest of an other saynt Liberate w^t his wyfe ⁊ two chylder/ ⁊ saynt Crescence a preest/ w^t an other chylde of vij. yeres olde/ y^t in the persecucyon of the arryanes were all put to deth for Chryst. The feest also of many other holy sayntes/ mar. cōf. ⁊ virg.

⁋ To morowe.

⁋ The .xxiiij. daye of Marche. The grete hygh and solempne feest called ye souper of our lorde ⁊ sauyour Iesu/ wherin he consecrate ye sacrament of his owne precyous body ⁊ blode/ ⁊ therw^t cōmuned his apostles ⁊ wasshed theyr fete. At Rome ye passion of saȳt Pigmeny a bysshop/ y^t was mayster ⁊

brynger vp of Iulian the apostata/ that after forsoke ⁊ renyed
Chryst ⁊ his fayth/ ⁊ was a cruell tyraūt ⁊ persecutour therof/ ⁊
so in the cite of tyberym he put to deth his owne mayster the
foresayd saynt Pigmeny. In mauritane the feest of saynt
Romule/ saynt Secundole/ naturall breder ⁊ martyrs. At syre
yᵉ feest of saynt Agapite a cōfessour of holy lyfe.

❧ Addicyons.

❧ In affryke the feest of saynt Murite a martyr/ yᵗ by a
renegate whome he before had baptized was put to deth/ wᵗ
many other bothe of yᵉ clergy ⁊ comyn people. In englond at
the monastery of barkynge the feest of saynt Hyldelyth a
virgyn/ ⁊ nexte abbesse after saynt Ethelburge/ a woman of
synguler graces (as saynt Bede wryteth) and of many myracles/
⁊ put to deth ⁊ [brent with all her systers/ ⁊ the hole [*fo. xxxii.*
monastery by the danes yᵗ slewe saynt Edmonde. The feest
also of saynt Sebba a kynge of englond/ yᵗ gyuen or applyed all
to vertue of youth/ wolde haue resygned ⁊ left his crowne for to
haue ben a religyous man/ but the quene his wyfe wolde not
consent therunto/ tyll after whan he had chylder/ ⁊ had reygned
xxx. yeres/ than she assented/ ⁊ he was a monke consecrate by
yᵉ bysshop of london/ ⁊ was of synguler perfeccyon ⁊ many
myracles. The feest also of saynt Mackartyne/ yᵗ came wᵗ
saynt Patryke from ytaly vnto yrelonde/ ⁊ was cōtynually
accōpanyed wᵗ hȳ/ ⁊ euery where famous of holy lyf ⁊ grete
myracles. The feest also of many other holy .⁊c.

❧ To morowe.

❧ The .xxv. daye of Marche. yᵉ hygh ⁊ solempne feest
called good fryday/ in yᵉ whiche daye our sauyour Iesu the
lambe of god was offred in sacrefyce for yᵉ saluacyon of the
worlde/ ⁊ so enhaūced ⁊ exalted on yᵉ crosse/ he by moost
paynfull ⁊ moost shamefull deth temporal redemed vs from deth
eternall ⁊ everlastynge. In nazareth at galilee the annunciacyon
of our blessed lady saynt Mary/ where (after yᵉ byleue of our
moost true fayth) the aūgell Gabriell saluted ⁊ grette her/ yᵗ
was predestynate ⁊ ordeyned to chylde ⁊ brynge forth yᵉ redemer
of the worlde our swete sauyour Chryst Iesu/ she notwᵗstandynge
euer remaynynge a virgyn moost pure/ moost clene/ immaculate
⁊ vndefouled. At siryne the passyon of saynt Hyren a bysshop/
that in the tyme of the emperour Maximus/ after longe prison ⁊
many cruell turmentes was heded. At rome yᵉ feest of saynt
Ciryne a martyr/ yᵗ by the kyng Claudius was spoyled of all his
goodes/ ⁊ than after hard pryson ⁊ many [affliccyons [*fo. xxxii. b.*
⁊ turmentes slayne by the swerde. At nicomede the feest of saynt

Theole/ called also saynt Dule a virgyn/ y^t was bond mayde
vnto a man of warre/ ꝯ slayne for ye defence of her chastite. In
the yle of andro the feest of saynt Hermeland an abbot/ whose
holy lyf and conuersacyon is euydent by many myracles.
¶ Addicyons.

¶ All though saynt Gabriell the archaūgell hath no ꝑpre ne
specyall daye festyuall/ yet is he of many persones more deuoutly
and singulerly honoured as this daye/ bycause that on ye same
daye he brought ye moost ioyfull message of our saluacyon.
The feest also of saȳt Dysmas the thefe that was hanged vpon
the ryght hande of Chryst/ ꝯ he is a cōfessour ꝯ not a martyr/
bycause he was put to deth by deseruynge for his owne synnes ꝯ
euyll dedes/ ꝯ not for ye fayth of Chryst. The feest also of
many other holy sayntes/ mar. cōf. ꝯ virg.

¶ To morowe.

¶ The .xxvj. daye of Marche. the holy ꝯ solempne saterdaye/
in the whiche our lorde ꝯ sauyour Iesu after his deth/ repaused
and rested in his sepulcre/ therby shewynge ꝯ assurynge vs/ y^t
yf we dye well/ we shall haue rest euerlastȳge
in our soules. At pentapolym in libia the feest
of saynt Theodour a bysshop/ saynt Hyreney a
deacon/ saynt Serapion and saynt Ammony bothe
lectours in order. At rome in lauicane strete the
feest of saynt Castole a martyr/ y^t (as is wryten in
the werkes of saȳt Sebastyan) was thre tymes
hanged ꝯ euer taken downe ꝯ newly examyned/ ꝯ
whan by no meanes he wolde forsake Chryst/ but
rather w^t more constancy cōfessed his name/ he
was buryed quycke ꝯ moche sonde ꝯ grauell cast
vpon hym. At smyrme the [feest of [*fo. xxxiii.*
saynt Montane a preest/ ꝯ saynt Maximian†/ y^t bothe togyder
were drowned in the see/ ꝯ so martyrs.

Note.
In the holy
sacrament of
presthode bē
vii. orders.
i. Lector.
ii. Hostiarie.
iii. Exorcist.
iiii. Colet.
v. subdeacon.
vi. Deacon.
vii. Preest.

¶ Addicyons.

¶ In yrelond ye feest of saynt Fynchell an abbot/ borne
there of blode royall/ ꝯ euer frō youth gyuen to vertue and so
contynued in many myracles. The feest also of saynt Peter a
bysshop ꝯ confessour. At Rome ye feest of saynt Quiryne a
martyr. y^t after some auctours hath his solempnite ꝯ chefe feest
the .xix. day of Ianuary w^t saynt Mari⁹ ꝯ his felowes. The
feest also of many .ꝛc.

¶ To morowe.

¶ The .xxvij. daye of Marche. the gloryous resurreccyon of our lord ꝛ sauyour Iesu Chryst/ and the noble victory of his triumphe/ wherby he ouercame yᵉ deuyl ꝛ brake vp the gates ꝛ clausures of hell/ ꝛ therby also shewed playnly vnto vs example of our resurreccyon bothe in soule ꝛ body/ how yᵗ in tyme to come we shall also aryse/ ꝛ as his propre membres folowe hym our heed vnto Ioye ꝛ blysse euerlastyng. In egypt yᵉ feest of saynt Johñ an holy heremyte/ yᵗ amonge other
Nota.   many myracles ꝛ tokens of vertue/ shewed by yᵉ spiryte of pphecy vnto yᵉ moost chrysten emperour Theodosius how he sholde haue the victory of yᵉ tyraūt his enemy. In the fraūchest of aspane the feest of saynt Euthery that was bysshop of Tourney. At Pamont the feest of saynt Alexander a martyr of grete constancy.
¶ Addicyons.

¶ The feest also of sayt Ioseph ab arymathy/ that buryed yᵉ body of our sauyour/ ꝛ therfore was by yᵉ iewes put in pryson/ to the entent that after yᵉ feest of pace he sholde be put to deth/ vnto whome Chryst apperynge conuayed ꝛ brought hym vnto his owne hous at ary[mathy/ ꝛ after that he was bap- [*fo. xxxiii. b.* tized by the apostles/ ꝛ preched wᵗ them/ ꝛ in prechynge he was taken ꝛ closed vp in a wall/ where whan yᵉ emperours destroyed Ierusalē/ he was foūde in good helth ꝛ went forth to preche agayne/ ꝛ therin dyed wᵗout other martyrdom. The feest also of sayt Nicodeme that halpe Ioseph to bury Chryst/ ꝛ therfore the iewes dyd bete and stryke hym wᵗ staues/ ꝛ lefte hym for deed/ but saynt Gamaliell brought hym to his hous ꝛ kepte hȳ many dayes ꝛ at the last he buryed hym in his owne tombe/ where after he hymselfe ꝛ saynt Steuen were buryed. The feest also of saynt Mary Iacobi/ moder vnto saynt Iames the lesse/ ꝛ syster vnto our blessed lady/ that wᵗ her was at yᵉ deth of our sauyour/ ꝛ wᵗ Mary mawdeleyn went to anoynt hym in the sepulcre. The feest also of her syster saynt Mary Salome/ moder vnto saynt Iames yᵉ more ꝛ vnto saynt Iohñ the euangelyst/ that wᵗ the other two Maryes was also diligēt to anoynt our lord. And whan she herde yᵗ her sone saynt Iohñ was taken at rome/ she came thyder/ but than was he exiled/ ꝛ she returned vnto the cite of campane/ where she dyed/ ꝛ laye in a denne or caue many yeres/ tyll by the reuelacyons of saynt Iames her sone/ her holy body was foūde smellynge all swete as roses/ ꝛ there is honourably shryned/ where almyghty god shewed many grete myracles. The feest also of saynt Rupert bysshop fyrst of warmaciens/ ꝛ after of saltzpurge/ a man of the blode royall of fraūce/ ꝛ of hygh pfeccyon ꝛ many grete myracles. And yᵉ feest of saynt Virgyl y⁴ after hỹ was bysshop there/ ꝯ a sure folower of his steppes ꝯ sanctite. The feest also of many other holy sayn. ꝫc̃.

⁋ To morowe.

[⁋ The .xxviij. day of Marche. At cesare pales- [*fo. xxxiiii.* tyne the feest of saynt Pryske/ saynt Malcus ꝯ saỹt Alexander martyrs/ y⁴ in the psecucyon of yᵉ emperour Valeriane were so hote kendled wᵗ the feruour of Chrystes fayth that wylfully they reproued the iudge of his cruell tyranny agaynst the seruaūtes of Chryst/ for yᵉ whiche the same iudge caused them to be deuoured wᵗ wylde beestes. At cabilonens yᵉ feest of saynt Gūdran a kyng that so feruently applied hymselfe vnto the werkes of mercy ꝯ vnto spirytuall exercyse/ that he left ꝯ forsoke all tēporall estate/ ꝯ gaue all his tresour ꝯ goodes vnto the chirche ꝯ vnto yᵉ poore people/ ꝯ was of hygh perfeccyon. At tharse yᵉ feest of saynt Castor/ ꝯ saynt Dorothey.

⁋ Addicyons.

⁋ The feest also of saynt Iohñ/ whose syrname was called obedience/ for his synguler pfeccyon in yᵗ vertue with other/ ꝯ a man also of many myracles. The feest also of saynt Syxt a pope/ ꝯ of many other holy .ꝫc̃.

⁋ To morowe.

⁋ The .xxix. day of Marche. In affryke yᵉ feest of saỹt Armogaste/ saynt Archymyne/ ꝯ saynt Satyre cōfessours/ yᵗ in yᵉ psecucyon of yᵉ wandales vnder kyng Geseryke/ susteyned ꝯ suffred many grete troubles for yᵉ cōfessyon of Chryst/ ꝯ therin ended theyr lyues by martyrdome. At nicodemet the feest of saynt Pastor/ and of saynt Victoryn. And the deposycyon of saynt Eustace abbot of luxaniens†/ and fader of .vj. C. monkes/ and a man of synguler vertue/ and many myracles.

⁋ Addicyons.

⁋ The feest also of saynt Or an heremyte of synguler sanctite/ yᵗ by the space of thre yeres was fedde wᵗout ony bodyly fode. In englond yᵉ feest of saynt Gūdlewse [a kynge of the south parte of englond/ ꝯ a kynges sone euer [*fo. xxxiiii. b.* moche desyrous of spirytuall exercyse ꝯ encreace of pfeccyon/ so yᵗ an aūgell appered vnto hym ꝯ shewed hym a place on a hyll after his mynde ꝯ desire/ where he sholde do seruyce vnto almyghty god/ wherfore he fortwᵗ resygned his crowne ꝯ realme vnto his sone/ ꝯ on yᵗ hyll buylded a chirche/ ꝯ therin lyued a pfyte lyfe full of myracles. The feest also of many other holy .ꝫc̃.

MARTILO.

¶ To morowe.

¶ The .xxx. day of Marche. At rome in appia strete ye passyon of saynt Quiryne/ ⁊ of saynt Trybune martyrs/ y^t vnder ye emperour Valerian were put to many turmētes/ theyr tongues kytte/ hāged vpon gybettes theyr handes ⁊ fete stryken of/ ⁊ at the last ended theyr gloryous martyrdom by the swerde. In thessalonyke the feest of saynt Dōnyne/ saynt Philopole/ and saynt Achayce. At the castell of syluanectence ye feest of saynt Rewle a bisshop ⁊ cōfessour. At orliaūce ye feest of saynt Pastor bysshop of palatyne.
¶ Addicyons.

¶ The feest also of saynt Secunde/ a man of warre/ y^t was cōuerted vnto Chrystes fayth by an aūgell/ ⁊ after his baptym he was cōmuned by ye aūgell/ ⁊ than after many meruaylous turmentes he was put to deth but his holy body was buryed by aūgelles. The feest also of saynt Mamertyn an abbot/ y^t was a pagan/ ⁊ cōuerted by reuelacyon ⁊ myracle/ ⁊ baptized of saynt German/ ⁊ after hym abbot of synguler pfeccyon ⁊ many myracles. The feest also of many other holy sa .⁊c.

¶ To morowe.

¶ The .xxxj. daye of Marche. the feest of saynt Amos the pphete/ that by the cruell kynge Ozie was bored thrugh the temples of the heed/ ⁊ so put to deth/ notw^t[standyng [*fo. xxxv.* he was not fully deed/ vnto ye tyme he came vnto his coūtree where he was buryed. At Rome the feest of saynt Balbyne a virgyn/ ⁊ doughter vnto saȳt Quiryne the martyr/ y^t after ye course of this lyf spent in grete holynes/ was buryed in appia strete besyde her sayd fader. In affryke the feest of saynt Diodole ⁊ saynt Anesye martyrs. At the monastery of fontanellence the feest of saynt wandrigesyle ⁊ saynt Ausbert/ whan theyr holy bodyes were translated vnto ye chirche of saynt Peter ye apostle/ w^t grete solempnite ⁊ moche Ioyfull honour.
¶ Addicyons.

¶ The feest also of saynt Hugh bysshop of granopole/ of whome his moder whā he was in her wombe/ had a reuelacyon/ ⁊ he was after of grete holynes ⁊ many myracles. And after some auctours he was a monke of the charterhous/ ⁊ one of the fyrst foūders ⁊ begynners of ye ordre. The feest also of saynt Amos an abbot in ye desert of sythe/ ⁊ fader of .M. ⁊ .v.C. monkes/ the moost holy ⁊ pfyte cōgregacion y^t we rede of. The feest also of saynt Amony an abbot of ye inward ⁊ depe desert of nitrea/ ⁊ the feest of his two naturall breder/ saynt Euseby ⁊

saynt Eutymy/ yᵗ with hym were monkes/ ꝛ so also his spūall breder/ ꝛ of the thyrde broder a bysshop vnnamed. And of many other holy sayntes .ꝛc̓.

¶ Apryle.

¶ To morowe.

Apryll. The fyrst daye of Apryll. At rome the passyon of saynt Theodour/ syster vnto the noble martyr saynt Heremete/ a holy woman/ ꝛ put to dethe by the prynce Aurelian/ ꝛ buryed in salary strete besyde her sayd broder. The feest also of saynt Venance a bysshop ꝛ martyr. In egypt the feest of saynt Victor ꝛ of saynt [Steuen/ ꝛ the deposicyon of saynt Valery an abbot. [*fo. xxxv. b.*
¶ Addicyons.
¶ The feest also of saynt Hugh a mōke/ whome saynt Bernard made abbot of boneuale/ a man of hygh vertue ꝛ grete myracles. The feest also of saȳt Deodorike a bysshop/ that was cosyn vnto yᵉ emperour Othon/ a man of synguler deuocyon vnto relykes/ so yᵗ he gadered in to his chirche the relykes of xx. sayntes/ where he after was buryed/ ꝛ sheweth many myracles. The feest also of many other holy sayntes/ mar. cōf. ꝛ virg.

¶ To morowe.

¶ The seconde daye of Apryll. At cesare capadoce the passyon of saynt Theodose a virgyn ꝛ martyr/ yᵗ in the last dayes of the emperour Dioclecian offred her selfe wylfully amonge other christyans yᵗ were taken/ and was put to many turmentes/ racked/ drowned in the water/ ꝛ cast vnto wylde wode beestes/ wᵗ other paynes/ ꝛ yet after all ouercome ꝛ vaynquysshed/ she was heded. At lyons yᵉ feest of saynt Nicesy yᵉ bisshop there whose lyfe and also deth was by holynes ꝛ myracles moche laudable ꝛ gloryous. The feest also of saynt Eustace abbot of luxoniens. At palestyne the feest of saynt Mary egypcyake/ so called bycause she was borne in egypt/ yᵗ from thens came vnto the cite of alexander/ ꝛ there from the age of .xij. yeres vnto xxix. she lyued all in fylthy lechery a comyn woman/ than came she vnto Ierusalem to se the holy crosse/ but Chryst wolde not suffre her to come in to the temple/ than she loked by ꝛ sawe an ymage of our blessed lady/ before whiche she kneled/ ꝛ wᵗ depe cōtrycyon ꝛ plenteous teres wepyng besought her of helpe ꝛ socour/ ꝛ than she entred in to the temple ꝛ honoured yͤ holy crosse wᵗ grete reuerēce ⁊ [depe deuocyon/ [*fo. xxxvi.* mekely besechynge forgyuenes ⁊ mercy/ ⁊ forthwᵗ as she went out/ a voyce frō heuen spake vnto her/ sayenge. Mary/ go in to yͤ wyldernes ouer ⁊ beyonde the water of Iordane/ ⁊ there yᵘ shalt obteyne saluacion. wherunto she obeyed ⁊ there lyued xvij. yeres wᵗ two loues and a halfe of brede/ ⁊ after she lyued xxx. yeres by herbes ⁊ rotes/ where than saynt zosymas foūde her/ of whome she was purely ⁊ hooly confessed/ ⁊ vpon sherthursdaye next she went drye foted ouer yͤ water of Iordane vnto his monastery/ ⁊ there of hym receyued the sacrament of Chrystes body/ ⁊ so returned in to the same wyldernes/ ⁊ there forthwᵗ yelded her spiryte vnto almyghty god/ whose holy body the same holy fader foūde a yere after hole ⁊ vncorrupted/ vnto whome came a lyon ⁊ made yͤ graue/ wherin he buryed her.

¶ Addicyons.

¶ The feest also of saynt Dydake bysshop of oxforde†/ that was mayster vnto saÿt Dominyke/ ⁊ a grete precher/ ⁊ cōuerted many heretykes in the coūtree of albigens/ ⁊ after came home ⁊ there lyeth ful of myracles. The feest also of many other holy sayntes/ marͬ. ⁊c.

¶ To morowe.

¶ The thyrde day of Apryl. In syth at thomis yͤ feest of saynt Euagrye a bysshop/ ⁊ of saynt Benygne. At thessalonyke yͤ passyon of saynt Agapis a virgyn/ ⁊ of saynt Chionye a virgyn also/ yᵗ bothe togyder suffred many affliccyons by the emperour Dioclecian/ ⁊ after all they were cast in to a grete fyre/ but no thynge greued wᵗall/ tyll they prayed our lorde to take them by yᵗ martyrdom/ ⁊ so he dyd. At tawromeny in cicile yͤ feest of saynt Pācrace. In englond yͤ feest of saynt Richard bysshop of chechester.

¶ Addicyons.

[¶ The feest also of an other saynt Euagrye a [*fo. xxxvi. b.* preest of grete doctryne/ ⁊ made many werkes/ ⁊ was of holy lyfe ⁊ many myracles. The feest also of saynt Florence bysshop of argentyne/ a man of gloryous lyfe ⁊ hygh pfeccyon. And yͤ feest also of many other holy sayñ .⁊c.

¶ To morowe.

¶ The .iiij. day of Apryll. At mylen the deposicyon of saynt Ambrose bysshop ⁊ cōfessour/ by whose dilygēce ⁊ labouryous prechyng (besyde his other noble actes of hygh doctryne/ holy lyf ⁊ many myracles) all ytaly was cōuerted from the false opinyons ꝑ wycked heresyes of yᵉ cursed arryens. At hyspale the deposicyon of saynt Isydour a bysshop.

⁋ Addicyons.

⁋ In englonde the feest of saynt Tiernake yᵗ was of the kynges blode of yrelond/ ꝑ in yᵉ tyme of warre was taken a childe ꝑ brought in to englond ꝑ sold as a bond man/ whome for his fauour ꝑ beauty yᵉ kyng bought ꝑ layde hym in his owne chambre/ ꝑ euery nyght the bedde where he lay semed to be all on fyre/ whiche perceyuynge the quene/ caused hym to lye in bedde wᵗ her two sones/ ꝑ on yᵉ morowe after they were foūde bothe deed/ but by his prayers they were reysed/ ꝑ than the kyng made hym free/ ꝑ foūde hym to scole tyll he was a bysshop/ than after yᵉ kynges deth he went to rome/ in whiche iourney (besyde other myracles) he reysed .ix. psones to lyfe/ ꝑ whan he came home in to englond he reysed yᵉ yonge kynges wyfe ꝑ sacred her a holy virgyn/ ꝑ an other man that longe had been deed/ wᵗ many other grete myracles. The feest also of many other .ꝛc̃.

⁋ To morowe.

⁋ The .v. day of Apryll. In egypt yᵉ feest of saynt Nichandre/ ꝑ of saynt Appolon martyrs. At thessalonyke [the feest of saynt Hyrene a virgyn/ that by yᵉ erle [fo. xxxvii. Sysynny was slayne wᵗ an arowe of his owne shotynge/ by whose tyranny ꝑ false accusacyons her two systers saynt Agapes and saynt Chyon yᵗ before ben spoken of were put to deth. At lice in cesary yᵉ feest of saynt Amphian ꝑ of saynt Marcian.

⁋ Addicyons

⁋ The feest also of saynt Vincent/ a man of grete holynes/ ꝑ of hygh doctryne/ ꝑ of the ordre of saynt Dominyke. The feest also of saynt Bene an abbot in desert/ yᵗ (as saÿt Ierom wryteth) neuer sware ne lyed/ ne neuer was wroth/ ne neuer ydle/ ꝑ of moost pfoūde mekenes/ ꝑ dyd many myracles. The feest also of ma .ꝛc̃.

⁋ To morowe.

⁋ The .vj. day of Apryl. at rome yᵉ feest of saynt Syxt pope ꝑ martyr/ yᵗ in the tyme of the emperour Adriane gladly suffred deth for Chryst. In macedony the feest of saynt Tymothy/ and of saynt Diogenes. ⁋ Addicyons.

⁋ The feest also of saÿt Theodour bysshop of ancyran a holy ꝑ grete lerned man/ and made many werkes agaynst heresyes/ specially agaynst yᵉ heretyke Nestor. At antioche yᵉ feest of an other sa͡yt Theodour a preest yᵗ also was a man of hygh doctryne ⁊ noble eloquence. ⁊ made .xv. bokes agaynst yᵉ heretykes called appolynaryes ⁊ anomeyes. The feest also of many other .⁊c.

⁋ To morowe.

⁋ The .vij. daye of Apryll. In affryke yᵉ feest of saynt Epiphan a bisshop/ saynt Donate/ ⁊ other .xiij. psones all martyrs. The feest also of sa͡yt Iesyppe/ a grete holy man/ yᵗ was nere the tyme of yᵉ apostles/ ⁊ wrote all the actes of the prelates ⁊ faders of the chirche/ from the passyon of Chryst vnto his tyme/ that lyke as he [folowed theyr holy lyfe [*fo. xxxvii. b.* ⁊ cōuersacyon/ so by his wrytynge other psones myght lerne the same. In alexander the feest of saynt Peluse a preest of grete holynes. ⁋ Addicyons.

⁋ In englonde yᵉ feest of saynt Bernake a gentylman of grete possessyons/ whiche all he solde ⁊ went on pylgrymage to rome/ where ⁊ by the waye he dyd many myracles/ ⁊ whan he came in to englonde agayne/ he was of grete fame ⁊ moche magnifyed/ whiche to declyne and auoyde/ he fledde pryuely in to south wales/ where he was assayled wᵗ the tētacyon ⁊ persecucyon of a lady in lyke maner as Ioseph in egypt/ but with grace he vaynquysshed ⁊ was of hygh pfeccyon/ many myracles/ ⁊ had reuelacyons ⁊ also vysyons of aūgels. The feest also of many other holy sayntes .⁊c.

⁋ To morowe.

⁋ The .viij. daye of Apryll. At corynth yᵉ feest of saynt Denyse a bysshop/ by whose lernynge ⁊ gracyous sermons in the tyme of Marke/ Antony and Luke aurell emperours many persones were gretly edifyed/ ⁊ yet many ben edyfyed/ ⁊ instructed vnto this tyme. At turynet the feest of saynt Perpetuus/ a man of meruaylous sanctite.
⁋ Addicyons.

⁋ The feest also of saynt Pitrion an abbot in thebaide that was discyple vnto saynt Antony/ a man of grete grace in helyng of seke psones/ ⁊ in auoydyng of euyll spirytes/ ⁊ had meruaylous knowlege of them where ⁊ in whome they dwelled/ ⁊ he wold ofte saye yᵗ a persone shold neuer chace ⁊ auoyde wycked spirytes/ tyll he fyrst auoyded ⁊ chaced awaye his owne synnes/ ⁊ that who so euer wolde vaynquysshe his owne vyces shold soone vaynquysshe all euyll spirytes/ he was al[so of [*fo. xxxviii.* precyse abstinence and many myracles. The feest also of many other holy sayntes/ mar. confes. ⁊ virg.

⁋ To morowe.

⁋ The .ix. day of Apryll. the feest of saynt Prokor/ one of the .vij. fyrst ⁊ chefe deacons/ a famous man/ that in antioche was put to martyrdom. In syryne yͤ feest of .vij. holy virgyns/ that by theyr precyous ⁊ paynfull deth bought the herytage of blysse euerlastynge. ⁋ Addicyons.
⁋ The feest also of saynt Dioscour an abbot of .C. monkes/ ⁊ a man of singuler sanctite. In yͤ desert of nitrea the feest of saȳt Ierony/ yᵗ was discyple vnto saȳt Antony/ a man of moost pſoūde mekenes/ ⁊ there dyed in yͤ age of .C. ⁊ .x. yeres. The feest also of many other .⁊ͨ.

⁋ To morowe.

⁋ The .x. day of Apryll. the feest of saynt Ezechiel the pphete/ a martyr of yͤ olde testament/ yᵗ was slayne by a iudge of the chylder of israell in babylon/ ⁊ was buryed in yͤ sepulcre of Sem ⁊ Arphaxat. At rome yͤ feest of many martyrs yᵗ were baptized of pope Alexander/ ⁊ by the tyraūt Aurelian they were put in to the see in an olde shyppe/ ⁊ theyr neckes teyed vnto grete stones and the shyppe bored/ ⁊ so all drowned. At alexander yͤ feest of saynt Appolon a preest/ ⁊ with hym other fyue persones martyrs. ⁋ Addicyons.
⁋ The feest also of saynt Diogenes an ancre/ yᵗ was discyple vnto saynt Antony in the desert of nitrie/ ⁊ by his holy worde moche edifyed many psones. The feest also of saynt Iulius called by syrname Aphrycan/ a grete wryter of storyes/ ⁊ restored many errours ⁊ contrauersyes in the gospell/ specyally in Mathewe and Luke. And the feest of many other holy sayntes .⁊ͨ.

[⁋ To morowe.   [*fo. xxxviii. b.*

⁋ The .xj. daye of Apryll. the feest of saynt Leo yͤ pope in whose tyme was the sene ⁊ generall coūseyle of calcedonens. In crete at gortyn the feest of saynt Phylyp a bysshop/ yᵗ in yͤ tyme of Antonyn vere ⁊ Lucy auriell emperours/ was a man of grete fame/ ⁊ honourable in all vertue ⁊ doctryne. In dalmatyke at saloma the feest of saȳt Domion a bysshop/ ⁊ of .viij. men of warre all martyrs. At nicomede the feest of saynt Eustorge a preest. In brytayne the feest of saynt Guthlake a confessour.
⁋ Addicyons.
⁋ At turon the feest of saynt Agryke an abbot of grete holynes. At lyons the feest of saynt Fiagry a bysshop. The feest also of saȳt Archiloke/ called also Archilawe bysshop of

mesopotamy/ a man of honourable cōuersacyon/ ꝛ of grete lernyng/ yᵗ made a boke agaynst yᵉ manyches/ ꝛ disputed yᵉ same wᵗ an heretyke/ with many other noble actes. The feest also of many other ho. ꝛc.

⁌ To morowe.

⁌ The .xij. day of Apryll. At rome in aurely strete the feest of saynt Iuly the pope/ yᵗ in the tyme of Cōstance the emperour was exiled in grete trouble yᵉ space of .x. monethes/ after whose deth he was brought agayne to rome wᵗ grete glory ꝛ ioyfull triūphe/ ꝛ there dyed in the peace of Chryst. The feest also of saynt zenon/ bysshop of veronens/ yᵗ in the tyme of strayte ꝛ cruell psecucyon ruled his chirche wᵗ meruaylous wysdom ꝛ in the tyme of Galiene the emperour he suffred deth for yᵉ same. At wapyng yᵉ feest of saẏt Cōstantyn a bysshop.
⁌ Addicyons.

⁌ At alexander yᵉ feest of saynt Agryppe called by syrname Castor/ a cōfessour/ ꝛ a man of p̃foūde doctryne/ [that [*fo. xxxix.* confoūded ꝛ improued .iiij. c. ꝛ .xxiiij. bokes/ yᵗ the heretyke Basilides wrote vpon the gospelles cōtrary. vnto yᵉ fayth ꝛ vnto the determynacyon of yᵉ chirche/ ꝛ he made a boke agaynst them/ ꝛ therin in a style moost eloquent he defended ꝛ declared the true fayth/ and he was a notable man of holy lyfe ꝛ good example. The feest also of many other holy sayntes/ mar. confes .ꝛc.

⁌ To morowe.

⁌ The .xiij. day of Apryll. In asya at pergamū the feest of saynt Carpe a bysshop/ ꝛ of saynt Papyre a deacon ꝛ of yᵉ vertuous matrone saynt Agathonyke/ ꝛ of many women that with her were put to deth by yᵉ emperours Antonyne vere ꝛ Aurely comedy/ wᵗ the whiche women saynt Iustyne also was put to deth/ a man of grete lernynge ꝛ eloquence/ ꝛ toke grete labours for yᵉ religyon of Chryst. In spayne the feest of saynt Erminygyld a kyng/ yᵗ for Chrystes fayth after many afficcyons was knocked on yᵉ heed wᵗ an axe/ ꝛ so chaūged his tēporall realme for yᵉ kyngdom of heuen. The feest also of saynt Eufeme a virgyn ꝛ martyr called Effam.
⁌ Addicyons.

⁌ In wales at breknoke the feest of saynt Caradoke/ a man of noble blode/ ꝛ fyrst a courtyer ꝛ a galaūt/ but after he forsoke yᵉ worlde ꝛ was a preest of holy lyfe/ ꝛ had reuelacyon of aūgels ꝛ open cōflict wᵗ the deuyll ꝛ dyd many grete myracles

The feest also of sayt Atyke bysshop of cōstantynople/ a man of grete lernyng/ that made a boke of fayth ꝫ of virgynite vnto ye doughters of ye emperour Archady/ in ye whiche boke he also confoūded ye heresyes of Nestorye/ ꝫ was of noble fame ꝫ many myracles. The feest also of many other ho. ꝫc̄.

⁋ To morowe.

[⁋ The .xiiij. day of Apryl. At rome in appia [*fo. xxxix. b.* strete the feest of saynt Tiburce/ saynt Valeriane ꝫ Maximy all martyrs. At alexander ye feest of saynt Fronton an abbot of grete fame ꝫ holynes. At interamnis the feest of saynt Procule a martyr. The feest also of saynt Dōnyne a virgyn/ ꝫ w^t her many other virgyns all martyrs.
⁋ Addicyons.
⁋ The feest also of sayt Bacchyle bysshop of corynthy a man of synguler sanctite ꝫ grete lernynge. The feest also of saynt Fetyke bysshop of aduens/ a man also of notable lernynge/ ꝫ made a boke agaynst the heretyke Nouaciane/ w^t many other profytable werkes/ ꝫ was of hygh pfeccion ꝫ holynes. The feest also of many .ꝫc̄.

⁋ To morowe.

⁋ The .xv. day of Apryl. In perse at corduba the feest of saynt Olympiade/ and of saynt Maximy martyrs/ that were noble men of byrth/ and for Chrystes fayth they suffred by Decius ye emperour many turmentes ꝫ at the last they were knocked on y^t hedes w^t butchers axes like beestes/ ꝫ so accōplysshed theyr martyrdom. In ytaly the feest of saynt Maro/ saynt Euticete/ and saynt Victoryne martyrs/ y^t were fyrst exiled in to the yle of ponciane/ where they cōuerted many psones/ ꝫ after by prynce Nerue they were by many varyaunt turmentes put to deth. ⁋ Addicyons.
⁋ The feest also of saynt Paterne/ borne of ye noble blode of englond/ ꝫ of youth applyed all to vertue/ y^t with saynt Dauid went vnto Ierusalē/ where he receyued sodeynly ye grace of tōgues to speke in euery lāguage/ where also he dyd many myracles/ ꝫ was there made bysshop by ye handes of ye patriarke/ ꝫ after came in to englond where he had the reuelacyon of aūgels/ ꝫ rey[sed two persones to lyf/ w^t many other [*fo. xl.* grete myracles. In englond also at norwyche ye feest of saynt wylliam of whome his moder had reuelacion whan he was in her wombe/ he was of poore byrth/ ꝫ a childe set vnto a crafte in norwyche/ where certayn iewes that tyme dwellyng stale hym

vpon a good fryday/ ꝉ with meruaylous turmentes they crucy-
fyed hym in the age of .xij. yeres/ ꝉ after by reuelacyon he was
founde/ ꝉ dyd many myracles/ ꝉ so he dyd in his lyfe before he
was .vij. yeres olde. The feest also of many other holy .ꝉc̃.

¶ To morowe.

¶ The .xvj. day of Apryll. At corynthe yᵉ feest of saynt
Calixt ꝉ of saynt Carisy/ wᵗ other .vij. psones all drowned in the
see. In cesaraugust yᵉ feest of .xviij. martyrs that is to saye/
saynt Quintilian/ saynt Cassian/ saynt Matutyn/ saynt Publy/
saynt Vrbane/ saynt Marciall/ saynt Fauster/ saynt Successe/
saynt Felix/ saynt Ianuary/ saynt Primityue/ saynt Euote/ saynt
Cecilian/ saynt Optate/ saynt frōton/ saynt Lupert/ saynt
Apodeme/ ꝉ saynt Iuly/ that by yᵉ president of spayne Daciane
were put to deth by moost greuous turmentes for yᵉ gloryous
name of Chryst. ¶ Addicyons.
¶ In egypte yᵉ feest of saynt Pholcas bysshop of tampnis a
noble man borne ꝉ of grete possessions ꝉ ryches ꝉ all he lefte to
serue god/ ꝉ was of grete lernyng ꝉ very eloquent/ ꝉ he made
a boke of yᵉ laude of holy martyrs/ wherin he prophecyed of his
owne martyrdom. ꝉ so was he put to deth in the psecucyon of
Maximian the emperour. The feest also of saynt Gēnand
bysshop of cōstantinople/ a man of quycke vnderstandyng/ ꝉ of
eloquence/ ꝉ he expowned the boke of Daniel thrugh/ with many
other werkes/ ꝉ was also of synguler san[ctite. The [fo. xl. b.
feest also of many other holy sayntes .ꝉc̃.

¶ To morowe.

¶ The .xvij. day of Apryll. In affryke yᵉ feest of saynt
Mappalyke a martyr/ yᵗ (as saynt Ciprian wryteth) was put to
deth wᵗ many other psones. At antioche yᵉ feest of saynt Peter
a deacon/ ꝉ of saynt Hermogeny. In the eest countree yᵉ feest
of saynt Nicofore/ yᵗ vnder Valerian ꝉ Galiene yᵉ emperours was
put to deth for Chryst. At corduba the feest of saynt Hely a
preest/ ꝉ of saynt Paule ꝉ saynt Isidour monkes. At rome yᵉ
feest of saynt Anicete pope ꝉ martyr.
¶ Addicyons.
¶ The feest also of saynt Heleny an abbot/ yᵗ in desert dyd
many myracles/ ꝉ in disputyng longe tyme wᵗ an heretyke he
entred a grete fyre in yᵉ quarel of his fayth and remayned therin
a longe season wᵗout hurte or blemysshe/ wherby the heretyke
was confoūded/ he had also reuelacyon of aūgelles. The feest
also of an other saynt Paule an abbot in libia/ ꝉ fader of .v.C.
monkes ꝉ of hygh pfeccyon. The feest also of many other .ꝉc̃.

¶ To morowe.

¶ The .xviij. day of Apryll. In naples at messany the feest of saynt Euletherṫ a bysshop/ and of saynt Anthye his moder/ a man he was of hygh pfeccyon ꝯ a martyr/ yᵗ by prynce Adriane was put to many cruell turmentes/ he was cast vpon a bedde of yren full of pryckes/ ꝯ than lyke saynt Laurēce layd vpon a hote gyrdyron/ after that he was put in to a potte boylynge wᵗ oyle/ pytche/ rosyne ꝯ brymstone/ ꝯ yet after cast vnto wylde wode beestes/ ꝯ euer he remayned vnhurt/ ꝯ at the last he was heded wᵗ his sayd moder. At rome the feest of saynt Appolon a senatour/ yᵗ by his owne seruaūt was accused vnto prynce Comod⁹ for a christyan [and brought before the senate/ [*fo. xli.* where he redde openly a boke yᵗ he had made of the prayse ꝯ poyntes of Chrystes fayth ꝯ religion/ for the whiche by yᵉ iudgement of the same senate he was heded. At corduba yᵉ feest of saynt Perfyte a preest ꝯ martyr. The feest also of saẏt Lafreane an abbot. ¶ Addicyons.

¶ The feest also of saẏt Apollon an abbot of .v.C. monkes/ yᵗ for more pfeccyon dwelled in a caue or den/ nere vnto hermepole/ where our sauyour Chryst appered vnto hym ꝯ badde hym put his hande in his owne bosom/ ꝯ pull out what he foūde ꝯ holde fast/ ꝯ he pulled out a fende a deuyll : yᵗ fende sayd Chryst is yᵉ spiryte of pryde/ wherwith yᵘ hast ben sore assayled/ ꝯ for yᵉ auoydaūce wherof yᵘ hast so longe ꝯ cōtinually prayed/ thou hast now vaynquysshed hym/ do wᵗ hym what yᵘ wylt for yᵘ art now delyuered of hym/ ꝯ than the holy fader cast hym in a quyksand/ ꝯ lowly thanked our lord/ and so he returned to his monastery/ where he fedde a hole coūtree .iiij. monethes wᵗ the vytayle yᵗ was scant able ꝯ sufficyent for his breder by theyr custome one day/ ꝯ many other grete myracles he dyd. The feest also of yᵉ thyrde saẏt Appolon a cōfessour/ a holy man ꝯ of grete charite to seke psones. The feest also of many oth. ꝯc.

¶ To morowe.

¶ The .xix. daye of Apryll. the feest of saynt Thimon/ one of the .vij. fyrst deacons/ yᵗ was a doctour of Chrystes fayth at beron/ ꝯ goynge about to preche yᵉ worde of god/ he came to corynth/ where by malyce of the iewes ꝯ of the grekes he was cast in to a grete fyre/ but no hurte had/ than was he nayled vnto the crosse lyke vnto his mayster Chryst/ ꝯ so ended his martyrdome. The feest also of saẏt Alphege an archebysshop ꝯ mar[tyr. At mylytane in armeny the feest of saynt [*fo. xli. b.* Hermogenis/ saynt Gayus/ saynt Expedite/ saẏt Aristonyke saynt Rufe/ ⁊ saynt Galathe al martyrs. At cantiliber the passyon of saynt Vincent a martyr. In y*e* suburbes of hamonens y*e* feest of sa*ȳ*t Cosmare a bysshop ⁊ cōfessour of synguler vertue ⁊ holynes. ❡ Addicyons.

❡ The feest also of saynt Fronton an abbot/ ⁊ fader of .lx. monkes y*t* lyued in desert/ ⁊ neuer made puysyon of ony sode for the next daye/ but euer abode y*e* ordynaūce of god/ ⁊ yet they neuer wanted/ for an aūgell warned the ryche men of the cytees by course to visyte them w*t* sode. The feest also of saynt Leo the .x. pope of y*t* name a man of synguler pyte vnto the poore. And the feest of saynt Tymon bysshop of vesegoryne in araby/ where he for Chryst was put to martyrdome. The feest also of many other holy sayntes/ mar*ȓ*. confes. and virg.

❡ To morowe.

❡ The .xx. daye of Apryll. at rome y*e* feest of saynt Victor the .xv. pope after sa*ȳ*t Peter/ ⁊ .x. yeres he moche edifyed y*e* chirche of Chryst/ ⁊ than by prynce Seuere put to deth. At rome also y*e* feest of saynt Sulpice/ sa*ȳ*t Publy ⁊ saynt Seruulanc† martyrs/ y*t* were cōuerted by the prechynge ⁊ myracles of saynt Domicill y*e* virgyn/ ⁊ after bycause they wold not do sacrefyce vnto y*e* ydolles/ they were by the mayre Aniane all heded. In fraūce at bredunens† the feest of saynt Marcell a cōfessour/ ⁊ bisshop of the same cite/ y*t* by diuyne reuelacyon came from affrike vnto the moūtaynes of ytaly w*t* his disciples ⁊ companyons saynt Vincent ⁊ saynt Domnion/ where by his holy worde ⁊ myracles he cōuerted the moost parte of y*t* coūtree.

❡ Addicyons.

❡ The feest also of an other saynt Victor bisshop of car[tage/ a holy man ⁊ of pfoūde doctryne/ y*t* wrote a boke agaynst [*fo. xlii.* y*e* heresyes ⁊ opinyons of y*e* grete heretyke Arrius/ w*t* many other good werkes vnto y*e* edificacyon of Chrystes fayth. The feest also of many other holy . ⁊c.

❡ To morowe.

❡ The .xxj. day of Apryl. In perse y*e* feest of saynt Symeon a bysshop ⁊ martyr/ y*t* by kyng Sapour of perse was taken/ ⁊ confessynge w*t* lowde voyce the name of Chryst he was put in harde prison/ ⁊ w*t* hym .C. other psones/ some preestes/ ⁊ other of dyuerse orders/ ⁊ at y*e* last after many turmentes he ⁊ they al were heded/ w*t* whome also were put to deth certayne noble persones saynt Vskazand/ saynt Abdell/ saynt Ananye/ ⁊ saynt Publy w*t* his doughter a holy sacred virgin. At alexander ye feest of saynt Arator a preest/ saynt Fortune/ saȳt Felix/ saynt Syluy ꝯ saynt Vitale all martyrs/ ꝯ dyed in prison. The deposicyon also of saynt Ancelme an archebysshop of Caūterbury. ⁋ Addicyons.

⁋ The feest also of saynt Gulphyle the fyrst bysshop ꝯ apostle of the people called gothes/ y^t by his holy lyfe/ grete myracles ꝯ dilygent prechynge/ conuerted them vnto Chryst/ and he fyrst ordeyned lettres ꝯ the wrytynge of theyr speche/ for before they had no wrytyng but all by hert/ and he translated the byble in to theyr moder tongue and commune language. The feest also of saynt Gemyne bysshop of nisebene/ a man of grete lernynge for his age/ ꝯ of synguler sanctite. The feest also of many other holy sayntes/ mart̃. confes. ꝯ virg.

⁋ Note here how dilygent holy faders were to trās̄late holy scripture l to the moder tōgue and cōmune language.

⁋ To morowe.

⁋ The .xxij. day of Apryll. At rome in appia strete the feest of saynt Gay pope/ y^t after he had ben pope .xj. yeres .vij. monethes and .xij. dayes/ was put to martyr[dom by [*fo. xlii. b.* the prynce Dioclecian. In perse ye feest of many martyrs vnnamed/ y^t were put to deth by ye tyraūt kynge Sapour/ amonge whome these were knowen saynt Melesy a bysshop/ saynt Accepsymy a bysshop with his preest saynt Iames/ saynt Marcias ꝯ saynt Bitro bothe bysshops w^t .CC. psones of theyr clergy/ ꝯ with .l. monkes/ and many sacred virgyns/ amonge whome saynt Tarbua a quene ꝯ syster vnto ye bysshop saynt Symeon/ w^t her bondmayd/ were kytte thrugh the bodyes w^t a sawe. At corduba ye feest of saynt Permenye/ saynt Helymen ꝯ saynt Schrysotele preestes/ ꝯ of saynt Luke ꝯ saynt Mycy deacons/ al martyrs/ of whose triūphe ꝯ noble victory is wryten in ye legend ꝯ passyon of saynt Laurence. At lyons the feest of saynt Epypode a martyr/ y^t by the persecucyon of Antonyne vere/ was after many turmentes heded. The feest also of saynt Sother pope ꝯ martyr. And ye inuencyon of saynt Denyse ꝯ his felowes. ⁋ Addicyons.

⁋ The feest also of saynt Oportune a virgyn/ ꝯ an abbesse/ of many grete graces/ specially in curyng of seke psones. At rome ye feest of an other saȳt Gay a preest ꝯ cōfessour/ a man of grete holynes ꝯ of excellēt doctryne that confoūded ꝯ destroyed many heresyes. The feest also of saynt Leo ye fyrst pope of y^t name/ y^t cōdempned many heretikes/ ꝯ wrote agaynst them many werkes by ye reuelacyon ꝯ instruccyon of saynt Peter/ ꝯ where he had stryken of his owne hand/ bycause it was occasyon of tēptacyon vnto a frayle woman/ it was agayn restored by the myracle of our blessed lady/ ꝛ he after of more hygh pfeccyō ꝛ many myracles. The feest also of saynt Agapite yᵉ fyrst pope of yᵗ name/ yᵗ fyrst ordered yᵗ euery sonday sholde be p̄cessyon/ ꝛ he was of grete họ[lynes ꝛ many [*fo. xliii.* myracles. The feest also of many. ꝛc.

¶ To morowe.

¶ The .xxiij. daye of Apryll. In perse at dyospole the passyon of sayt George a martyr/ whose gestes (as vn to grete parte) ben nōbred amonge yᵉ apocriphase/ notwithstandynge his noble martyrdom is had in yᵉ chirche in solempne honour ꝛ deuout reuerence/ specyally in englonde. In frāuce at valence yᵉ feest of saynt Felix a preest/ ꝛ of sayt Fortunate ꝛ saynt Achilley deacons/ that whan they had cōuerted the moost parte of yᵉ cite vnto Chryst/ were taken/ imprysoned/ scourged/ theyr legges ꝛ thyes broken/ ꝛ all theyr membres ꝛ hole body stretched vpon a rote or turnyng whele/ hanged on a gybet ouer a grete smoke/ and at the last ended theyr martyrdom by the swerde. In the castell of syluanect the feest of saynt Rule/ a bysshop ꝛ cōfessour. At bruce the feest of saynt Adhelbert a bisshop ꝛ martyr of hygh perfeccyon.

Apocripha ben called suche storyes or writynges as ben of no sure grounde ne of certayn auctoryte/ ꝛ therfore ben not accepted for verey trouth/ all though they may sōtyme be wryten/ spoken ꝛ byleued without offence.

¶ Addicyons.

¶ The feest also of saynt Leomya bysshop/ꝛ of saynt Malachy yᵉ prophete. In egypte yᵉ feest of saynt Heraclide a cōfessour/ yᵗ was disciple vnto saynt Isidour/ ꝛ by hym brought vnto the desert of thebaydes/ ꝛ there cōmitted disciple vnto saynt Dorothey yᵉ holy abbot wᵗ whome he lyued many yeres/ ꝛ after hym he occupyed his rome ꝛ place/ ꝛ wente aboute vnto many solytary persones/ ꝛ wrote a boke of theyr lyues/ ꝛ so after many myracles and grete holynes he departed vnto our lorde. The feest also of many other holy sayntes. ꝛc.

¶ To morowe.

¶ The .xxiiij. day of Apryll. In frāuce at lyons yᵉ feest of saynt Alexander a martyr/ yᵗ in the psecucyon of Antonyne vere was so rent ꝛ torne in his body wᵗ hokes yᵗ [his [*fo. xliii. b.* rybbes opened ꝛ his bowelles came out/ ꝛ after all he was (as his mayster) put vpon the crosse where he yelded his holy spiryte/ ꝛ wᵗ hym were put to deth also .xxxiiij. other psones.

In brytayn yᵉ feest of saynt Mellyte a bysshop ⁊ confessour.
At hylyber the feest of saynt Gregory a bysshop ⁊ confessour.
The feest also of saynt Crowne a virgyn. ⁋ Addicyons.
⁋ The feest of saynt Egbert yᵗ was borne in englonde ⁊
spent his lyf hooly in other londes in prechyng ⁊ pylgrymage.
And yᵉ feest of saynt wylfryde archebysshop of yorke/ borne in
englonde of yᵉ blode royall. At whose byrth was seen a pyller
of fyre/ so yᵗ all the hous semed on fyre/ he was euer vertuous
from youth/ ⁊ so contynued in singuler perfeccion ⁊ many
myracles. The inuencion also of saynt Yue. At blese yᵉ feest
of saynt Deodate an abbot. At reme the feest of saynt
Boue/ ⁊ saynt Dode bothe virgyns. And yᵉ feest also of many
oth. ⁊c.

⁋ To morowe.

⁋ The .xxv. day of Apryll. At rome is the grete letany ⁊
pcessyon vnto yᵉ chirche of saynt Peter. At alexander the
feest of saynt Marke yᵉ euangelyst/ yᵗ was discyple vnto saynt
Peter/ and his interpretour/ yᵗ required instaūtly by many
peticyons of yᵉ chrystyans/ wrote the gospell ⁊ lyfe of Iesu/ ⁊
whan they had receyued ⁊ admytted yᵉ same gospell/ he went
in to egypt/ ⁊ he fyrst preched Chrystes fayth in alexander/ ⁊
there he ordeyned a chirche/ ⁊ than was he taken by the
infydeles ⁊ put to many cruell turmentes/ in yᵉ whiche he had
cōfort by yᵉ reuelacyons of aūgels/ ⁊ after of our sauyour hym-
selfe/ by whome he was called vnto yᵉ kyngdome celestyall the
viij. yere of Nero the emperour. At syracusane the feest of
saynt Euody ⁊ saynt Hermogenis.
⁋ Addicyons.
[⁋ The feest also of saynt Adelbert a bysshop ⁊ a [fo. xliiii.
martyr/ that was a noble man borne and all applyed vnto vertu/
⁊ brought vp in lernynge wᵗ the archebisshop of paryhenopole/
after whose deth he was called vnto yᵉ emperours courte ⁊ made
a knyght/ but after by diuyne reuelacyon he was called agayn
to religyon ⁊ was bysshop of prage/ a holy man ⁊ diligent in
prechynge/ specially vnto yᵉ infydeles/ of whome by yᵉ last he
was put to martyrdom. The feest also of many other . ⁊c.

⁋ To morowe.

⁋ The .xxvj. daye of Apryll. At rome the feest of saynt
Clete yᵉ seconde pope after saynt Peter/ yᵗ after he had ruled ⁊
gouerned the chirche .xij. yeres/ was in yᵉ persecucyon of yᵉ
emperour Domician put to martyrdom. At rome also the feest

of saynt Marcellyne a bysshop/ that whan he had wel gouerned his chirche .ix. yeres ꝛ .iiij. monethes/ was in the psecucyon of yᵉ emperour Dioclecian put to deth/ ꝛ wᵗ hym saynt Claudy/ saynt Ciryne ꝛ saynt Antonyn. In yᵗ tyme was a grete psecucyon/ so yᵗ in one moneth .xvij. M. chrystyans were put vnto martyrdome. In the fraūchest of pontyne at the monastery of Centule the feest of saynt Rychary a preest ꝛ confessour.

⁋ Addicyons.

⁋ In the yle of sardyny yᵉ feest of saynt Lucifere bysshop of calaritane/ yᵗ wrote a boke agaynst yᵉ heresy of Arrius/ ꝛ sent the same boke vnto the emperour Constance yᵗ was of the same opinyon/ by whome he was put in exile/ after whose deth he moche edyfyed yᵉ chirche of Chryst/ of whome saynt Ierome wryteth. The feest also of many other holy sayntes/ mar. cōf. ꝛ virg.

⁋ To morowe.

[⁋ The .xxvij. day of Apryl. At rome the [*fo. xliiii. b.* deposicyon of saynt Anastace the pope/ of whome saynt Ierom reuerently sayth/ the worlde was not worthy to haue his lyf ony longe tyme. At nicomede the feest of saynt Anchymy a bysshop ꝛ martyr/ yᵗ in the psecucyon of Dioclecian (as is wryten in the story ecclesiastyke) was heded/ ꝛ with hym yᵉ moost parte of all his flocke ꝛ cure was put to deth/ some heded/ some maymed/ some brent/ some manacled ꝛ cast in to the see/ ꝛ some slayne by many other cruell turmentes. In sicilie† at tharse yᵉ feest of saynt Castor ꝛ of saynt Stephan martyrs.

⁋ Addicyons.

⁋ At altyne the feest of saynt Liberall a confessour of hygh perfeccyon/ ꝛ had reuelacyon of aūgels. At ciuilitane yᵉ feest of saynt Pule a lector in ordre/ yᵗ in the psecucyon of Dioclecian ꝛ Maximian the emperours suffred passyon for Chryst. The feest also of saynt Ancare a man of meruaylous sanctite. And the feest of many other holy sayntes/ martyrs/ confessours ꝛ virgyns.

⁋ To morowe.

⁋ The .xxviij. day of Apryll. At rauen yᵉ feest of saynt Vitale a martyr/ yᵗ bycause he buryed wᵗ due reuerence the holy body of saynt Vrsylyne/ was taken by the tribune Paulyn/ ꝛ after rackynge ꝛ many turmentes he was buryed quycke. At alexander yᵉ feest of saȳt Theodour a virgyn/ yᵗ bycause she wold not do sacrefyce vnto the ydolles/ was sent to yᵉ bordelhous/ from whens saynt Didymus inflambed wᵗ heuenly zele/ rauysshed her by violence ꝛ strength/ and after wᵗ her was put to martyr-

dome. The feest also of saynt Affrodose/ saynt Carilyppe/ saynt Agapy/ ꝫ saynt Euseby all martyrs. At padway† the feest of saynt Palion† a martyr.
[⁋ Addicyons. [fo. xlv.

⁋ The feest also of saynt Valeriane/ wyfe vnto saynt Vitale/ that after she had sought her sayd housbonde was in her returne taken by ye infydeles ꝫ put to deth. At treuer the feest of saynt Latrocinian a martyr/ that borne in spayne came in to fraūce/ ꝫ there sowed ye sede of Chryst/ ꝫ was there put therfore to deth by ye tyraūt Maximian/ ꝫ in ye tyme of ye emperour Theodosius/ ye fyrst of y^t name. The feest also of many other holy .ꝛc̄.

⁋ To morowe.

⁋ The .xxix. day of Apryl. At paphū the feest of saynt Tite disciple vnto saynt Paule/ whome oft he remembreth in his epystles/ callyng hym his moost dere broder ꝫ felowe in ye seruice ꝫ bondage of god. In numyde at a vyllage nere vnto circen ye feest of saynt Agapite ꝫ saynt Secūdyne bysshops ꝫ martyrs/ y^t in the psecucyon of the emperour Valerian/ were after many turmentes put to dethe/ ꝫ w^t them also suffred deth saynt Emilian a man of warre/ saynt Tercull ꝫ saynt Antony virgyns/ ꝫ a woman vnnamed w^t her two chylder twyndles. At myllen ye feest of saynt Peter a martyr/ one of the ordre of freres prechers. In Brytayne the translacyon of saynt Edmonde kynge and martyr. ⁋ Addicyons.

⁋ The feest also of saynt wylfryde the yonger/ y^t was also archebysshop of yorke. The feest also of saynt Torpede a martyr/ ꝫ of saynt Leo a bisshop in grece/ of synguler holy lyfe/ ꝫ of grete myracles/ ꝫ in his deth many moo. The feest also of saȳt Robert/ y^t was fyrst foūder of ye order of cirstercienst/ called the whyte monkes he was before abbot of ye monastery of molysme/ ꝫ bycause he wold lyue a more harde lyf/ he toke .xxj. of his [moost holy monkes/ ꝫ went [fo. xlv. b. vnto a wyldernes called cisterciū/ where by the auctorite of ye archebysshop of lyons/ ꝫ of the bysshop of cabilony/ ꝫ by ye helpe of the duke of burgoyn called Odo/ he buylded a monastery ꝫ there began the sayd ordre of whyte monkes/ ꝫ after he refourned† his owne monastery vnto the same pfeccion ꝫ many other monasteryes ꝫ was of many grete myracles. The feest also of saynt Marian a lay broder ꝫ a monke of biturience y^t was a herdman ꝫ kepte the beestes of ye monastery/ ꝫ he saued a wylde bore from hunters that chased hym/ ꝫ euer after he folowed the holy man all his lyfe as a tame dogge. The feest also of many other holy sayntes/ marṫ. confes. ꝫ virgyns.

MARTILO.

⁋ To morowe.

⁋ The .xxx. daye of Apryll. At lambesitane the feest of saynt Mariane a lectour in ordre/ and saynt Iames a deacon/ that were put in pryson ꝧ there cōforted by diuyne reuelacyon/ ꝧ than after many cruell turmentes they were slayne by the swerde/ ꝧ wᵗ them many other chrystyans. At sanctonas the feest of saynt Eutrope a martyr/ whome saynt Clement the pope made a bysshop/ ꝧ than sent hym in to fraūce/ where he coūerted moche people/ ꝧ dyd many myracles/ and after for the fayth of Chryst he was heded. In englonde at london the deposicyon of saynt Erkenwald bysshop of yᵉ same cite/ a cōfessour of grete holynes/ in lyf ꝧ myracles moche famous ꝧ honourable.

⁋ Addicyons.

⁋ The feest also of saÿt zozimas an abbot in yᵉ partyes of palestyne nere vnto egipte/ a man of hygh pfeccyon and a grete labourer in sekyng of straūge places ꝧ vnused desertes/ in whiche serche and labours he founde saynt Mary egypciake/ ꝧ buryed her as on her day is [shewed/ ꝧ after he returned vnto [*fo. xlvi.* his monastery/ where he remayned in moost holy lyfe and grete myracles. The feest also of many other holy sayntes/ marꝫ. ꝧc.

⁋ May.

⁋ To morowe.

May. THe fyrst daye of May. In egypte the feest of the prophete Ieremy a martyr of yᵉ olde testament that of the people was murthered wᵗ stones cast vpon hÿ in a grete hepe/ ꝧ so dyed at a place called taphnas. The feest also of yᵉ holy apostles saynt Phylip ꝧ saynt Iames/ whiche saynt Phylip after he had conuerted nere all the londe of sythe/ was put to dethe in asia at ierapole/ ꝧ saÿt Iames called yᵉ broder of our sauyour Iesu/ was cast downe heedlonge from an hygh place nere vnto the temple in Ierusalem/ ꝧ so his necke broken/ ꝧ he there buryed. In fraūce in yᵉ fraūchest of viuariens yᵉ feest of saynt Andeole a subdeacon/ whome saynt Policarpe sent from the eest partyes in to fraūce with dyuerse other felowes to preche yᵉ fayth/ whiche whan yᵉ emperour Seuery had perceyued/ he caused hym to be takē ꝧ cruelly to be beten wᵗ thorny busshes ꝧ breres/ ꝧ so put hym in harde prison/ ꝧ at the last after moche afflyccyon he was sawed ouerthwarte yᵉ heed in crosse wyse wᵗ a sawe of harde wode/ ꝧ so ended his martyrdom. At sedunens yᵉ feest of saynt Sygismund the kyng. At austrace yᵉ feest of saynt Orient a bysshop ꝧ cōfessour of holy lyfe ꝧ synguler vertues/ ꝧ therafter made a gloryous ende. At antysiodour yͤ feest of saynt Amatour a bysshop ⁊ cōfessour. In brytayne yͤ feest of saynt Thoremyny a bysshop. ❡ Addicyons.

❡ The feest also of saynt Barucke yͤ prophete/ yᵗ was disciple ⁊ scrybe vnto the sayd prophete Ieremy. The [feest also of sayͭ Walburge called also sayͭ Gauburge ⁊ [*fo. xlvi. b.* some psones call her saynt walpurge/ a virgyn ⁊ an abbesse/ borne in englond/ ⁊ of singuler sanctite ⁊ grete myracles. The feest also of saynt Magnus kynge of norwey/ that was of hygh ⁊ meruaylous pfeccyon in all his lyfe/ whose soule at his dethe was seen by vysyon caryed and conueyed by aūgels in to heuen. The feest also of many other holy sayntes/ mar. cōf. ⁊ virg.

❡ To morowe.

❡ The seconde daye of May. the feest of saynt Athanasius bysshop of alexander a cōfessour/ that made the psalme Quicūqȝ vult. wᵗ many other notable werkes vnto the cōfusyon ⁊ destruccyon of heresyes/ for yͤ whiche he suffred meruaylous psecucyon/ for the worlde nerehand hooly coniured/ agreed ⁊ consented vnto his deth/ with dyuerse realmes/ kyngdomes ⁊ coūtrees/ pryncꝭ ⁊ lordes/ ⁊ the vnyuersall people were moued agaynst hym/ ⁊ men of warre were layd in wayte for hym/ and moost furyous agaynst hym were the grete heretykes called arrians/ ⁊ full hardly he escaped/ but euer he fledde/ dryuen from place to place all yͤ worlde ouer/ ⁊ yet in no place coude he be sure/ notwᵗstandyng god euer preserued hym for the encreace ⁊ cōtynuaūce of the fayth/ ⁊ the erudicyon of many psones/ ⁊ so at yͤ last after many victoryes of pacyence/ he rested in the peace of Chryst/ vnder the reygne of yͤ emperours Valentynian ⁊ Valent/ whan he had ben preest .xlvj. yeres. The feest also of saynt Saturnyne ⁊ saynt Neopole martyrs/ that were murthered in pryson. ❡ Addicyons.

❡ At taruis the feest of saynt Florens a bysshop/ ⁊ of saynt Vindemiale a noble precher/ and of synguler san[ctite [*fo. xlvii.* ⁊ many myracles. The feest also of saynt Sycare a martyr. And of many other holy sayntes/ marͭ. ⁊c̃.

❡ To morowe.

❡ The thyrde day of May. At Ierusalem the inuencyon of yͤ holy crosse/ foūde by saynt Elene quene ⁊ moder vnto yͤ emperour Cōstantyne. At rome in numentan strete the passyon of saynt Alexander pope/ and of saynt Euence ⁊ saynt Theodole preestes/ that al were put to many greuous turmentes/ ⁊ at the last heded. The feest also of saynt Iuuenall a bysshop ⁊ cōfessour. ℭ Addicyons.

ℭ The feest also of saynt Sophrony a cōfessour/ a man of grete lernyng bothe in greke ⁊ latyn/ ⁊ made many noble nokest/ ⁊ trāslated out of latyn in to greke yᵉ psalter ⁊ the prophetes/ after yᵉ same copye yᵗ saynt Ierom made ⁊ had translated them out of ebrewe in to latyn/ ⁊ after he went in to wyldernes/ ⁊ there lyued as an heremyte in holy cōtemplacyon all his lyfe. The feest also of many other holy sayntes/ marṛ. confes. ⁊ virg.

ℭ To morowe.

ℭ The .iiij. day of May. In palestyn at gaze yᵉ feest of saynt Syluane bysshop of yᵉ same cite/ yᵗ in the persecucyon of yᵉ emperour Dioclecian was put to deth wᵗ many other martyrs. At Ierusalem the passyon of saynt Quiriake a bysshop/ that was the same Iudas yᵗ by saynt Elene foūde ⁊ shewed the holy crosse/ ⁊ after he was put to deth for the fayth of yᵉ same by yᵉ emperour Iulian. In fauence at metall yᵉ feest of .xl. martyrs all heded for Chryst. At nicomede yᵉ feest of yᵉ holy woman saynt Antonye a martyr/ yᵗ was hanged by one of her armes thre dayes/ ⁊ after kept in pryson two yeres/ ⁊ thā after many meruaylous turmētes she was brent. [At oricoripens [*fo. xlvii. b.* yᵉ feest of saynt Floriane a martyr/ that was tyed by the necke vnto a mylstone/ ⁊ so cast in to yᵉ water of anyse. At antisiodour yᵉ feest of saynt Coreode a deacon.

ℭ Addicyons.

ℭ At Ierusalem the feest of saynt Amony/ yᵗ by saynt Quiriake was cōuerted/ ⁊ wᵗ hym put to deth. And yᵉ feest also of saynt Anne moder vnto yᵉ same saynt Quiriake. The feest also of the holy virgyn saynt Heryne/ doughter vnto yᵉ emperour Lycyne/ yᵗ in the age of .vj. yeres was for her beauty enclosed by her sayd fader in a toure/ wᵗ other .xiij. virgyns/ ⁊ neuer sawe man/ but onely her techer ⁊ scolemayster/ ⁊ whan she was .xij. yeres of age/ after a reuelacyon she forsoke the ydolles ⁊ made her prayer vnto Chryst/ whiche sent an aūgell that taught her his fayth/ ⁊ brought a preest vnto her by whome she was baptyzed/ whiche thynge whan her fader knewe/ he put her to meruaylous turmētes in the whiche he hymselfe was slayne/ whome she by prayer reysed from deth/ ⁊ cōuerted hym ⁊ her moder also/ than his broder this virgyns vncle toke her ⁊ put her to cruell turmētes/ in yᵉ whiche he also was slayne. After whome his sone ⁊ eyre put her to newe paynes meruaylous/ ⁊ he also slayne by the same/ by the whiche .xxxviij. M. persones were cōuerted/ ⁊ wᵗ her sayd fader ⁊ moder baptized. After this an other kynge deuysed newe terryble turmentes/ whiche whan she w^tout hurte had vaynquisshed/ he was couerted/ ℄ after hym an other kynge was baptized w^t all his realme/ ℄ many dyuerse coūtrees she conuerted/ ℄ at the last she was enclosed in a caue of stone lyke a sepulcre/ ℄ there dyed/ ℄ is accounted for a martyr. The feest also of .xl. martyrs y^t were put to deth at the castell of lauryake. [And the feest [*fo. xlviii.* of other .xl. martyrs/ y^t were rude labouryng men/ ℄ in the tyme of saynt Gregory ye fyrst pope of that name/ were by the longoberdes put to deth for Chryst. The feest also of saȳt Monica moder vnto saȳt Augustyn. And the feest of many other holy sayn. ℄c.

℄ To morowe.

℄ The .v. daye of May. the ascencyon of our lord ℄ sauyour Iesu Chryst/ in the whiche daye (his apostles beholdynge w^t clere ℄ open syght) he (as a victoryous champyon after his gloryous resurreccyon) dyd ascende aboue all heuens/ ℄ so opened vnto vs ye gate of euerlastynge lyfe. At alexander the feest of saynt Eutheme a deacon that dyed in pryson. At thessalonyke ye feest of saynt Hyren/ saynt Peregryne/ ℄ saȳt Heren martyrs that were brent. In fraūce at arelatens ye feest of saȳt Hyllary bysshop ℄ cōfessour/ a famous man of synguler vertue. At vien the feest of saȳt Nicete a bysshop of grete holynes. At antisiodour ye feest of saȳt Iouinian a martyr and a lector in ordre. The translacyon also of saynt Audoen/ done by saynt Ausbert a bisshop/ by the whiche translacyon he was made hole of a grete brennynge feuer.

℄ Addicyons.

℄ The feest also of saynt Gotard a bysshop ℄ cōfessour a man of grete fame/ ℄ fyrst he was an abbot/ ℄ after by ye emperour Henry he was pmoted to be a bysshop whiche he toke by the reuelacyon of our lady/ ℄ was therin of holy lyfe ℄ many myracles. The feest also of saynt Fortunate a bysshop ℄ cōfessour/ ℄ of saynt Triphon a chylde ℄ a martyr of grete myracles. The feest also of saynt Appolyn a confessour ℄ an abbot. And the feest of many other holy sayntes/ mar. confes. ℄ virg.

℄ To morowe.

[℄ The .vj. daye of May. The feest of saynt Iohn [*fo. xlviii. b.* the euangelyst/ called portlatyn/ bycause he was as that daye by the cōmaundement of ye emperour Domician brought to rome from Ephese where he was in exile/ ℄ in the presence of the senate he was put in to a tonne of boylynge oyle before the gate called portlatyn/ but bycause he escaped wtout hurte or noyaūce/ the people made a feest/ whiche yet is kepte solempne vnto this daye. At antioche the feest of saynt Euod/ yt (as saynt Ignacius wryteth) was the fyrst bysshop of that cite ordeyned by the apostles/ ⁊ in the same he suffred martyrdom for Chrystes fayth. The feest also of saynt Lucius/ the fyrst bysshop of cyrenen/ instytuted also ⁊ ordeyned by ye apostles/ whome saȳt Luke remembreth in the actes of ye apostles. In affryke the feest of saynt Helyodour and saynt Venust/ with other martyrs in nombre .lxxv. ¶ Addicyons.

¶ The feest also of the grete clerke ⁊ noble lerned man saynt Iohn damascene/ that fyrst was a iewe/ ⁊ after conuerted in youth beynge euer a virgyn/ ⁊ whan he was in religyon/ he had synguler deuocyon vnto our blessed lady/ and wrote many werkes of her laude ⁊ prayse/ ⁊ whan his hande was cutte of/ he was sory ⁊ complayned vnto her yt he coude no more wryte of her. She than brought vnto hym ye same drye hande that longe tyme had hanged vpon a wall ⁊ was wydred/ ⁊ she ioyned it vnto his arme/ ⁊ he was all hole/ ⁊ after he wrote many werkes of diuinite/ ⁊ was of holy lyfe ⁊ grete myracles. The feest also of saȳt Victorian/ ⁊ of many other holy sayntes/ martyrs/ cōfes. ⁊ virgyns.

¶ To morowe.

¶ The .vij. daye of May. At teracyne in campane the [feest of saynt Domicyll a virgyn ⁊ martyr/ that was [*fo. xlix.* of noble byrth/ nece vnto the cōsull Flauius clement/ ⁊ she was veyled ⁊ consecrate by saynt Clement ye pope/ ⁊ after she was for Chryst put to exile in to the yle of ponce/ wt many other holy v̥gyns/ where they suffred many affliccyons/ ⁊ at ye last whan she had by her holy doctryne ⁊ myracles conuerted many persones/ she was brent/ ⁊ wt her two holy virgyns her cōpanyons saynt Eufrosyn and saynt Theodour. The feest also of saynt Iuuenall a martyr. At nicomede the passyon of saynt Flauy/ saynt August/ ⁊ saynt Austustyn† all breder ⁊ martyrs. The deposicyon also of saynt Iohn beuerley archebysshop of yorke.
¶ Addicyons.

¶ The same daye is also a feest ioyntly of saynt Stephan and saynt Laurence/ bycause yt by the emperour Theodosius ye yonger/ theyr two bodyes were ioyned bothe togyder/ ⁊ so shryned at rome by myracle. The apparicyon also of saynt Mychaell/ ⁊ the feest of saynt Raphaell ye archaūgell/ yt is the sure helper ⁊ socourer of all seke ⁊ trauaylyng psones. The feest also of saynt Letarde bysshop of saynt Martyns in london/

yt was goostly fader vnto quene Bert doughter vnto ye kynge of fraūce ꝛ wyfe vnto kynge Ethelbert of englonde/ a deuoute lady ꝛ faythfull/ yt by the coūseyle of the sayd bysshop/ had all her seruaūtes ꝛ houshold chrysten persones/ all though ye londe than was hethen/ ꝛ all they herd masse ꝛ goddes seruyce at saynt Martyns before sayd/ where the sayd bysshop by his holy prechynge ꝛ grete myracles cōuerted many persones vnto Chryst. The feest also of saȳt Serenyke a cōfessour. ꝛ of many other holy .ꝛc.

⁋ To morowe.

⁋ The .viij. daye of May. At mylen the feest of saynt [Victor/ that was baptized in youth/ ꝛ euer a true [*fo. xlix. b.* chrystyan/ ꝛ beynge a soudyour in the emperours warres whan he was cōmaūded to do sacrefice vnto ye ydolles he vtterly despysed them/ for ye whiche he was scourged/ ꝛ than boylynge lede pored vpon his body/ ꝛ after many other paynes suffred wtout grefe/ he was at the last heded. In egypte ye feest of saynt Stephan ꝛ saynt Victor. The feest also of saynt Ellad a bysshop. In the golden moūt the dedicacyon of saynt Mychaelles chirche the archaūgell. ⁋ Addicyons.

⁋ In yrelond ye feest of saynt Catald a bysshop/ of many notable myracles/ whose heed as soone as he was borne/ fell by chaunce vpon a marble stone/ and entred therinto as though it had been waxe/ and the prynt of his foreheed remayned there for euer/ whiche marble was in ye playne felde/ ꝛ the water yt by the rayne fell in to that holowe prynt/ dyd hele all maner of sekenes or sores/ whose moder for payne of trauaylynge there dyed/ ꝛ the chylde arose vpon his fete ꝛ toke her in his armes/ ꝛ therwt she reuyued ꝛ was all hole. He reysed also thre other psones from deth/ ꝛ dyd many myracles/ ꝛ cōuerted many vnto Chrystes fayth. The feest also of saynt Indrake a kynge of yrelond/ yt forsoke all his royalty ꝛ went to rome wt his syster saynt Dominyke/ wt dyuerse other/ yt al togyder lyued a priuate lyf full of sctīte ꝛ myracles/ ꝛ at the last martyred for chrystes fayth. The feest also of many other holy sayn .ꝛc.

⁋ To morowe.

⁋ The .ix. daye of May. the translacyon of saynt Andrewe the apostle/ whan his holy body/ wt the bones of saynt Luke the euangelyst/ ꝛ the bones of saynt Thymothe disciple vnto saynt Paule/ were brought out of [akaia vnto cōstantinople by [*fo. l.* ye emperour Constantyne. At rome the feest of saynt Hermen/ whome the apostle Paule remembreth in his epystle vnto the romaynes a holy man ꝉ of hygh perfeccion. At nazant the feest of saynt Gregory a bysshop/ called by syrname diuync for his grete ꝉ noble lernynge/ vnto whome saynt Ierom was dyscyple/ ꝉ wryteth of hym/ yᵗ whan he had by techynge made many clerkes/ ꝉ by prechynge moche edifyed/ he resigned his bysshopryche/ ꝉ lyued yᵉ resydue of all his lyfe in religyous exercyse as a monke in prayer ꝉ cōtemplacyon. The translacyon also of saynt Nicolas bysshop ꝉ cōfessour from myrre vnto barum. In perse yᵉ feest of .cccx. holy martyrs. In the castell of wyndocyn yᵉ deposicyon of saynt Bertyne a cōfessour.

⁋ Addicyons.

⁋ The translacyon also of saynt Ierom/ that two tymes was translate/ fyrst by saynt Cirill on trinite sondaye/ whose holy body was than foūde hole/ ꝉ of meruaylous odour ꝉ swete smell/ by yᵉ whiche .xvj. blynde psones were restored vnto syght/ ꝉ thre psones delyuered from deuyls. And yᵉ sone of a poore wydowe was there in yᵉ prece ꝉ thronge of people murthered to deth whome she cast in to the graue where yᵉ body of saynt Ierom had ben/ ꝉ forthwith he arose all hole/ whiche thynge perceyuynge a housband man yᵗ thre dayes before had buryed his sone/ ranne ꝉ brought hym thyder and layd hym in the same graue/ ꝉ he anone receyued lyfe/ ꝉ went forth all hole. Many other myracles were done in yᵗ translacyon/ ꝉ yet notwᵗstandyng his holy body on the morowe after was foūde agayn in the same graue/ ꝉ cōmaūdement gyuen by his owne reuelacion there to rest a tyme/ ꝉ so it dyd vnto yᵗ by his owne re[uelacyon also it was after trāslated vnto rome/ [fo. l. b. where it remayneth in yᵉ chirche of saynt Mary the more. At veron yᵉ feest of saynt Metron a confessour/ yᵗ for a trespace fettred hymselfe wᵗ a locke ꝉ cast the key into yᵉ see hauynge token by reuelacyon/ that whan yᵗ key were foūde his synne shold clerely be forgyuen/ whiche key a lytell before his deth was foūde in yᵉ bely of a fysshe and soone after he departed vnto our lorde. The feest also of many other holy sayntes/ marꝑ. confes. ꝉ virg.

⁋ To morowe.

⁋ The .x. daye of May. the feest of saynt Iob the holy pacyent ꝓphete. At rome in latyn strete yᵉ feest of saynt Gordian/ yᵗ after many longe turmētes was heded/ ꝉ with hym saynt Epimache/ bothe martyrs under Iulian the emperour. At rome also the feest of saynt Calipode a preest/ yᵗ by yᵉ emperour Alexander was put to deth/ ꝉ his body cast in yᵉ water of tyber/ ꝉ wᵗ hym suffred deth saynt Palmacy consull of rome/ wᵗ his wyfe ꝉ chylder/ ꝉ of his housholde .xlij. persones/

after them was put to deth also saẏt Symplice a noble senatour
⁊ all theyr hedes were set vp at dyuerse gates of rome for
example vnto yᵉ chrystyans. In rome also in latyn strete at a
place called yᵉ hondred halles yᵉ feest of saynt Quart ⁊ saynt
Quint martyrs. ❡ Addicyons.

❡ In yrelond the feest of saynt Congall a holy abbot/ whose
byrthe was shewed by reuelacyon vnto saynt Patryke .lx. yeres
before ⁊ vnto an other holy bysshop many years before/ at
whose baptym sprange a well/ ⁊ a blynde preest was restored
vnto syght/ ⁊ after he grewe to hygh perfeccyon/ ⁊ he reysed
x. or .xij. psones vnto lyfe/ ⁊ had reuelacyons/ ⁊ was of many
grete ⁊ wonderous myracles. The feest also of saynt william
[borne in englond/ a holy man ⁊ of grete myracles. And [fo. li.
yᵉ feest of saynt Maturyn a cfessour. ⁊ of many oth.⁊c.

❡ To morowe

❡ The .xj. day of May. At rome in salary strete yᵉ feest of
saynt Authymet a preest ⁊ martyr/ a noble precher ⁊ of many
myracles/ yᵗ whan he was for chryst cast in to the water of
tyber/ he was brought agayne by an aūgell vnto his own chirche
⁊ there preched/ and after was taken agayne ⁊ heded. At
vien the feest of saynt Mamert a bysshop ⁊ cōfessour/ yᵗ for
the seacynge of a grete plage/ ordeyned yᵉ solempne letany to
be songe before the ascencyon. In brytayne the feest of saynt
Fremund kynge therof ⁊ martyr. The feest also of saynt
Maiole abbot of syluinyake/ ⁊ yᵉ feest of saẏt Montane.
❡ Addicyons.

❡ At lyngon yᵉ feest of saynt Gengolfe a holy cōfessour and
of grete myracles/ yᵗ was slayne by a clerke yᵗ kept his wyfe in
auoutry/ whiche wyfe vsed moche to scorne the myracles ⁊
to mocke yᵉ holynes of her sayd housbonde/ in vengeaūce
wherof euery fryday (for on that day he was slayne) at euery
worde she spake came out of her mouth a stynkynge breth/
that nerehande poysoned yᵉ people in her presence/ a grete
example for mockers of holy psones. At tergest yᵉ feest of
saynt Pryme a preest/ ⁊ of saynt Marke a deacon yᵗ by the
emperour Adriane were put to cruell martyrdom/ ⁊ with them
saynt Iason ⁊ saynt Celian/ that by them were cōuerted. The
feest also of many other holy sayntes.⁊c.

❡ To morowe.

❡ The .xij. day of May. at rome in ardiatyn strete the
feest of saynt Neyre ⁊ saynt Achyll martyrs/ yᵗ were baptyzed

of saynt Peter/ ͺ for Chryst were put to exile [in to the [*fo. li. b.*
yle of ponce/ and after many cruel turmentes they were heded.
At rome also in aurell strete the feest of saynt Pancras a
martyr/ yᵗ in the age of .xiiij. yeres was put to many turmentes
by the emperour Dioclecian/ ͺ at yᵉ last heded. The feest also
of saynt Denyse yᵗ was naturall fader vnto the sayd saynt
Pancras/ ͺ a man of synguler vertue. At cipres yᵉ feest of
saynt Epiphan bysshop of salamyne.

⁋ Addicyons.

⁋ The feest also of saynt Philyp yᵉ fyrst chrysten emperour/
ͺ of his sone saynt Philyp also ͺ emperour/ whiche bothe
emperours were conuerted vnto Chryst by saynt Ponce ͺ
baptized/ ͺ after they bothe were martyred by the emperour
Decius/ yᵗ was theyr seruaunt ͺ by false traytory put them
bothe to dethe. The feest also of many other holy sayntes/
mart̄. confes. ͺ virg.

⁋ To morowe

⁋ The .xiij. daye of May. The feest of our lady called
sancte marie ad martyres .i. saynt Mary at the martyrs/ whiche
is the dedicacyon of a chirche that saynt Bonyface yᵉ pope
halowed in the worshyp of our lady ͺ of all martyrs. The feest
also of saynt Muce a preest that was put to many turmentes/
fyrst at amphyble/ ͺ after at byzance where he was heded. The
feest also of saynt Seruace a confessour/ ͺ bysshop of tungrens.
For whose meryte ͺ holynes to be knowen/ it pleased ged to
shewe this myracle/ yᵗ whan hard frost ͺ snowe couered all the
coūtree/ his graue was neuer wete ne ouerflowed ne hydde/ tyll
suche tyme as the citezyns had buylded a chirche ouer it/ ͺ
many myracles were done therin.

⁋ Addicyons.

⁋ The feest also of saynt Boniface/ the fyrst pope of yᵗ
name/ for whose eleccyon was a sysme/ but he obtey[ned [*fo. lii.*
and well ruled/ he ordeyned that no woman shold handle the
chalys ne corporas/ and that no bond man shold be 'preest/ wᵗ
many other good statutes/ ͺ he was called the mekest man vpon
erth/ and moost pyteous. The feest also of an other saynt Boniface yᵉ fourth pope of yᵗ name/ ͺ he ordeyned that yᵉ chefe sete
ͺ chirche of christianite shold be at rome/ for before it was at
constantynople/ ͺ he obteyned of yᵉ emperour Foke yᵉ temple
in rome called Panteon/ yᵗ was of all ydolles/ ͺ he made it the
chirche of all halowes/ ͺ ordeyned yᵗ feest/ with many other good
statutes. The feest also of saȳt Hyllary an abbot/ yᵗ in the age
of .xiij. yeres forsoke the worlde/ ͺ was brought by an aūgell

vnto an hyll called moūt emyle/ where at .xx. yeres of age he buylded a chirche/ ꝧ put out a deuyll frō a noble man/ yᵗ after wᵗ hym was a monke/ ꝧ there he lyued tyl he was of the age of lxxxij. yeres/ than by reuelacyon of an aūgel he made his owne graue thre dayes before his deth/ ꝧ so departed full of myracles. The feest also of saynt Onesymy a confessour. In yrelond the feest of saynt Maeldoke a cōfessour/ ꝧ the deposicyon of saynt Marcellian a cōfessour. And the feest of many other holy sayn. ꝧc̃.

☛ To morowe.

☛ The .xiiij. daye of May. In fraūce at cymele yᵉ feest of saynt Ponce a martyr/ yᵗ by his holy prechynge and wyse doctryne cōuerted two of the emperours sones/ ꝧ after by the emperours Valerian ꝧ Galiene he was put to martyrdome. In syre the feest of saynt Victor a martyr/ ꝧ of an other mānes wyf called saynt Crowne that beholdynge yᵉ constancy of saynt Victor in his turmentes/ praysed hym ꝧ blessed hym: ꝧ forthwᵗ she sawe two crownes comyng downe frō heuen/ one sent vnto [saynt Victor/ ꝧ the other vnto her selfe/ whiche vision [*fo. lii. b.* she openly shewed before all the people/ for the whiche she was sawed in sonder betwyxt two stockes/ ꝧ saynt Victor was heded. The feest also of saynt Pachomy yᵗ in egypte buylded many monasteryes/ ꝧ wrote a rule vnto his monkes yᵗ he lerned by the reuelacyon ꝧ endytyng of an aūgell/ ꝧ he was a grete precher ꝧ of many myracles. The feest also of saynt Boniface a martyr yᵗ in tharse was put to deth/ but he was buried in rome. At the monastery of fomanelꝷ yᵉ deposicion of saynt Herymbert bysshop of tolosane. ☛ Addicyons.

☛ The feest also of an other saynt Boniface a bysshop that in his chyldhode dyd many myracles/ ꝧ after he was bisshop many moo/ ꝧ he was a grete almes man. The feest also of saynt Felix and saynt Fortunate martyrs ꝧ naturall breder/ ꝧ bothe heded togyder. At muthon the feest of saynt Barbary a martyr/ yᵗ was a noble duke/ ꝧ by the emperour Iulian put to many cruel turmentes/ in yᵉ whiche he cōuerted many psones/ specyally a duke called saynt Backe/ and two knyghtes/ saynt Almache ꝧ saȳt Denyse/ yᵗ all were heded before hym/ ꝧ he last. The feest also of an other saynt Pachomy a monke of sythe/ a holy man. The feest also of saȳt Theodour an abbot/ ꝧ of saynt Orosiens an abbot also ꝧ bothe discyples vnto saynt Pachomy. In yrelond yᵉ feest of saynt Cartake a bysshop/ of whome was had reuelacyon before his byrth/ ꝧ in his chyldhode he dyd many myracles/ ꝧ cured many persones of all maner diseases/ ꝧ reysed thre persones to lyfe/ after he was a bysshop he went in to an other coūtre/ ꝫ wᵗ hym .viij. c. ꝫ .xl. monkes/ whiche he brought thrugh a grete water/ that by his blessyngc was dyuyded/ ꝫ they went [ouer drye foted/ in maner of [*fo. liii.* the chylder of israell. The feest also of many other holy sayntes/ mar. cōf. ꝫ virg.

¶ To morowe.

¶ The .xv. day of May. At rome yᵉ feest of saynt Tor quate/ saynt Thesifon/ saynt Secūde/ saynt Iudalecet/ sayni Cecily/ saȳt Esicy ꝫ saynt Eufrasc/ yᵗ all togyder at rome were made bysshops by yᵉ apostles/ ꝫ all sent in to spayne to preche/ where whan they had cōuerted in dyuerse citees people innumerable/ they were diuyded/ ꝫ dyed all cōfessours in dyuerse places. In the yle of chire the feest of saynt Ysydour a martyr/ in whose chirche remayneth yᵉ same pyt wherin he was drowned/ by yᵉ water wherof many psones ben cured. At lamosate yᵉ passyon of saynt Peter ꝫ saynt Andrewe martyrs/ ꝫ yᵉ feest of saynt Paule a martyr/ ꝫ of a holy woman called saynt Denyse.

¶ Addicyons.

¶ This daye after some auctours is remembred the feest of pentecost/ ꝫ of the trinite. In englond yᵉ feest of saynt Brithyne/ yᵗ was deacon vnto saynt Iohn of beuerley/ by hym he was made abbot of beuerley/ whiche monastery the same saynt Iohn founded/ ꝫ therin lyeth shryned/ ꝫ with hym this holy saynt his disciple. The feest also of saynt Sophy/ a man of many myracles. And yᵉ feest of many other holy sayntes/ mar. ꝫc.

¶ To morowe.

¶ The .xvj. daye of May. In the prouynce of ysawry the feest of saynt Aquilyn ꝫ saynt Victoryan/ whose holy actes ben cōteyned in the legend. At antisiodour the feest of saynt Peregryne/ yᵗ was the fyrst bysshop of yᵉ cite/ ꝫ there for Chrystes fayth was heded. In the terrytory of Iuliens the feest of saynt Maxima a virgyn of holy lyfe. In yrelonde the feest of saynt Brendane a [preest and an abbot/ of many [*fo. liii. b.* grete myracles. **¶ Addicyons.**

¶ The feest also of saynt Vbald a bysshop. In yrelond the feest of saynt Carantoke/ yᵗ is also called saynt Ceruach/ a kȳges sone of englond/ applyed al vnto vertue from youth/ ꝫ whan his fader waxed aged/ he wolde haue resygned his crowne vnto hym as his heyre/ he than stale away pryuely/ ꝫ chaūged clothynge with a poore begger/ ꝫ therin made his prayer vnto our lorde to guyde ꝛ directe hym wheder he wolde/ forhwᵗt came an aūgell in lykenes of a doue/ ꝛ ledde hym vnto a solytary place/ where he lyued in grete holynes/ after the same aūgell in yᵉ same lykenes brought hym in to yrelonde to visyte saynt Patryke/ ꝛ from thens vnto many places/ where euer he did grete myracles/ ꝛ moche edifyed the fayth/ wherin he dyed full blessedly. The feest also of saynt Fidele/ a man of synguler sanctite. And the feest of many other holy sayntes/ mart. ꝛc.

¶ To morowe.

¶ The .xvij. daye of May. At tuscia the feast of saynt Torpete a martyr/ yᵗ was a grete offycer wᵗ Nero the emperour/ ꝛ whan he knewe he was a chrystyan/ he caused hym to be scourged ꝛ put vnto wylde beestes/ ꝛ many turmentes/ ꝛ at the last to be heded. His daye of deposicyon is the .xxix. daye of Apryll/ ꝛ yet ordered by the chirche to be kept as this day. At niuedune yᵉ feest of saynt Eracly/ saynt Paule/ saynt Aquilyn/ and of other twayne vnnamed psones. The translacyon also of saynt Bernard.

¶ Addicyons.

¶ At papie the feest ꝛ translacyon of saynt Syre bysshop of the same cite/ in whiche translacyon were reysed many deed psones/ the blynd restored to syght/ the [dombe ꝛ defe/ [fo. liiii. halte ꝛ lame cured/ ꝛ many other myracles were than shewed. The feest also of saynt Felix ꝛ saynt Fortunate martyrs. And of many other hol. ꝛc.

¶ To morowe.

¶ The .xviij. day of May. In egypt the feest of saynt Dioscour a lector in order/ yᵗ was put to many turmentes/ his nayles were dygged from his fyngers ꝛ toos/ his body enflambed with boylynge oyle/ in yᵉ whiche flambe came downe a lyght frō heuen that vnto hym was moche cōfortable/ ꝛ vnto his turmentours so ferefull/ that they fell downe as deed/ ꝛ at the last he was brent to deth wᵗ hote plates of yren. The traslacyon also of saynt Elene quene and empresse. The feest also of saynt Felix a bysshop ꝛ martyr/ that was put to deth by the emperour Maximian at the cite of spelatens.

¶ Addicyons.

¶ The feest also of saynt Mary/ whome saynt Dioscour toke by violence from certayne infydeles yᵗ wolde haue deuoured her. The feest also of the holy prophete Sophonie. At cameryn yᵉ feest of saynt venaūce a martyr/ that by the emperour Decius suffred many turmentes/ ꝯ at the last was slayne by the swerde. The feest also of many other holy sayntes/ mar. cōf. ꝯ virg.

⁌ To morowe.

⁌ The .xix. daye of May. At rome in appia strete the feest of saynt Kalocery/ that was chamberlayn wᵗ the emperour Decius/ ꝯ of saynt Perthemy capytayne of his garde/ bothe enukes ꝯ martyrs/ that bycause they wolde not do sacrefyce vnto the ydolles/ were bothe togyder put to deth. In englond at caūterbury yᵉ feest of saȳt Dunstane an archebysshop of many grete graces and a grete foūder of monasteryes/ ꝯ by his hygh do[ctryne ꝯ synguler vertues he moche honoured yᵉ [fo. liiii. b. chirche of englond/ he dyed in grete age/ ꝯ was buryed at Chrystes chirche/ where he doth many myracles. At rome yᵉ feest of saynt Potencian a virgyn/ yᵗ for Chryst suffred many affliccyons ꝯ troubles/ ꝯ was very diligent to bury the bodyes of holy martyrs/ ꝯ a grete almes woman. The feest also of saȳt Prudent†/ naturall broder vnto the same virgyn/ ꝯ he was discyple vnto the apostles/ ꝯ baptized of them/ and so folowed truly theyr doctryne. ⁌ Addicyons.

⁌ In alexander the feest of saȳt Iohñ a martyr/ that was fyrst a pagan named Neamy/ ꝯ a duke vnder the emperour Maximian/ by whome he was cōmaūded to pursue the christen people/ after the maner of saynt Paule/ in the whiche persecucyon Chryst ouerthrewe hym as he dyd Paule ꝯ cōuerted hym/ ꝯ after he pursued the infydeles ꝯ destroyed many of them/ at yᵉ last he was taken ꝯ put to many varyaūt turmentes/ in yᵉ whiche he conuerted many psones/ ꝯ dyd grete myracles/ whose holy body was translate frō alexander vnto constantynople/ ꝯ frō thens to venyse. The feest also of saynt Celestyne the fyrst pope of yᵗ name/ that ordeyned a verse to be sayd with the offyce of yᵉ masse/ ꝯ in a sene he condempned many heresyes/ ꝯ there cōfirmed as our true fayth/ that in Chryst was one psone ꝯ two natures/ ꝯ that our blessed lady sholde be called ꝯ byleued yᵉ very moder of god/ wᵗ many other holy statutes. The feest also of an other Celestyn/ the .v. pope of that name/ yᵗ was a holy heremyte/ ꝯ whan yᵉ see of rome ꝯ the papalite had ben voyde two yeres ꝯ more/ he was electe agaynst his wyll/ ꝯ was of holy lyfe. The feest also of the thyrde saynt Celestyn a monke/ yᵗ (as saynt [Vincēt wryteth) was a man of singuler sanctite. [fo. lv. The feest also of saynt Yue a preest of hygh pfeccyon ꝯ many myracles/ yᵗ ofte was visyted of aūgels/ ꝯ he fedde a grete multytude of people wᵗ one lofe of brede/ ꝯ had reuelacyon of his

deth/ with many other notable myracles.   The feest also of many
other holy sayntes .℔,

⁋ To morowe.

⁋ The .xx. day of May. At rome in salary strete yᵉ feest of
saynt Basyll a virgyn ⁊ martyr/ called also saȳt Babyll/ of noble
byrthe ⁊ despoused by her frendes vnto a noble man/ whome for
Chryst she forsoke/ for the whiche after many turmētes she was
slayne by yᵉ swerde. In fraūce at nemause yᵉ feest of saynt
Bawdell a martyr/ yᵗ for yᵉ fayth was put to many turmentes.
At bituryke yᵉ feest of saȳt Austregyll a bysshop ⁊ cōfessour.
In englond the feest of saynt Adelbert kyng of yᵉ same and a
martyr/ whose holy body lyeth at herford/ ⁊ his heed at westmynster.   ⁋ Addicyons.
⁋ The feest also of saynt Eustache ⁊ of his wyfe saȳt Theo-
phist/ ⁊ of saynt Agabite ⁊ saȳt Theophist theyr sones/ whiche
saynt Eustache was a noble ⁊ chefe capytayne vnder the
emperour Traianus/ ⁊ as vpon a daye he hunted a wylde hart/
our sauyour Chryst appered vnto hym bytwene the hornes of yᵉ
hart/ ⁊ so conuerted hym/ ⁊ baptized hym ⁊ his wyfe ⁊ chylder/
⁊ shewed hym he sholde be assayled ryght sore by tentacyon/ ⁊
so he was. For he lost all his seruaūtes by pestilence/ ⁊ all his
goodes robbed by theues/ ⁊ his wyfe was taken from hym by
force/ ⁊ bothe his sones in his syght borne away wᵗ wylde beestes/
⁊ he (as Iob) left alone/ ⁊ fayne to kepe beestes in grete pouerte
a longe tyme/ yet at the last god restored hym agayn vnto his
[wyfe/ chylder/ goodes ⁊ honours/ ⁊ after yᵗ all they [*fo. lv. b.*
togyder were put to martyrdom by the emperour Hardrian.† The
feest also of saynt Bernardyn a gray frere of grete lernynge/ ⁊ he
buylded frō yᵉ groūde moo than fyfty monasteryes/ ⁊ many mo
he reformed. The feest also of his discyple saynt Iohn̄ capistrane
a holy man ⁊ of many myracles. The feest also of many other .℔.

⁋ To morowe.

⁋ The .xxj. daye of May. In mauritane at cesariens the
feest of saynt Thimothe/ and of saynt Pole ⁊ saynt Euthyke a
deacon/ all martyrs/ put to dethe for prechynge the fayth. At
cesary capadoce the feest of saynt Poliacte/ saynt Victor ⁊ saynt
Donate. At corduba the feest of saynt Secūdyne a martyr.
In brytayn at fynthall† the feest of saynt Godryke a confessour.
            ⁋ Addicyons.
⁋ The feest also of saynt Constantyne the emperour/ that
endowed the chirche wᵗ large possessyons/ ⁊ ordeyned yᵗ for

euer ye pope shold be in honour aboue all prynces/ ⁊ all the worlde subiect vnto hym/ of whose cōuercyon ⁊ noble actes is largly wryten in the lyfe of saynt Syluester. The feest also of saynt Hospice/ y^t for pſecsyon enclosed hymselfe in yren as though he had ben a prysoner/ ⁊ there he kepte grete abstynence/ and had the spiryte of prophecy/ and dyd many myracles. The feest also of many other holy sayntes/ mar. cōf. ⁊ virg.

⁋ To morowe.

⁋ The .xxij. day of May. In affryke the feest of saynt Cascet ⁊ saynt Emile (as sayt Cipriane wryteth in his boke of the fall of martyrs) were put to martyrdom by the fyre. At corsite ye feest of saynt Iule a virgin y^t was martyred by the passyon of ye crosse. At antisiodour the [feest of saynt [*fo. lvi.* Elene a virgyn. At rome ye feest of saynt Sawstynet ⁊ saynt Tymothe. ⁋ Addicyons.

⁋ The feest also of saynt Auson a bysshop ⁊ martyr/ y^t was slayne by the wandales. And ye feest of saynt Romane a monke/ y^t was abbot vnto saynt Benet/ ⁊ fyrst clothed hym in the habyte of that religyon. The feest also of many other holy sayntes/ marṫ. confes. ⁊ virg.

⁋ To morowe.

⁋ The .xxiij. day of May. at lyngon ye passyon of saynt Desyre a bysshop ⁊ martyr/ y^t for the rest of his flocke ⁊ people offred hymselfe vnto ye wandales/ ⁊ by them was put to deth w^t many of his owne goostly chylder. · At spane the feest of saynt Thyket/ and of saynt Basile bysshops.
⁋ Addicyons.

⁋ At lyons in fraūce ye feest of an other saynt Desyre a bysshop also ⁊ a martyr/ a man of gloryous fame ⁊ notable myracles. At nicomede ye feest of saynt Theopompe a bysshop ⁊ martyr/ y^t by the emperour Dioclecian was put to many turmentes/ ⁊ sore assayled of a wytche or nygromancer/ whome he cōuerted ⁊ baptized/ ⁊ named hym Seneses/ y^t with hym was put to martyrdom. The feest also of saynt Antidy a bysshop ⁊ martyr of grete holynes/ he sawe in vision an euyl spiryte shewe vnto his prynce ⁊ vnto the other cōpany of deuylles how he had brought the pope vnto a deedly synne/ wherabout he had laboured many yeres/ than this holy saynt charged the same spiryte in ye vertue of Chryst to brynge hym to rome/ where he refourmed the pope vnto penaunce/ ⁊ than returned vpon ye same deuyll/ and after was he martyred by the waudaies. The feest also of many other holy sayntes/ marṫ. ⁊c̀.

MAY.

¶ To morowe.

[¶ The .xxiiij. day of May. At antioche yᵉ feest [fo. lvi. b of saynt Manahen a noble doctour and a prophete of the newe testament. The feest also of saynt Ioane yᵗ was wyfe vnto Chusi Herodes proctour/ that sent vnto her husbond (as is remembred in yᵉ gospell) that he sholde not medle agaynst Chryst. At rome the feest of saynt Vincent a martyr. In fraunce at nāmetc† the feest of saynt Donacian ꝛ saynt Rogacian martyrs/ yᵗ for Chrystes fayth were hardly imprisoned/ ꝛ after hanged on a gybet/ ꝛ theyr flesshe torne wᵗ hokes/ ꝛ prycked in yᵉ body with launces/ ꝛ at the last heded. At hystre the feest of saynt zoell/ saynt Seruyle/ saynt Felix/ saȳt Syluane and saynt Dyod† all martyrs. The translacyon also of saynt Dominyke confessour. ¶ Addicyons.

¶ At rome yᵉ feest of saynt Anolyne/ keper of yᵉ pryson vnder Almachius/ yᵗ whan saynt Vrban was cōmytted vnto his warde/ was by hym conuerted wᵗ other thre grete capytaynes/ ꝛ all there in prison baptized/ ꝛ on the nexte morowe whan the mater was knowen/ they were all put to martyrdom. The feest also of many other holy sayntes/ martyrs/ confes. and virgyns.

¶ To morowe.

¶ The .xxv. day of May. At rome in numentanes strete yᵉ feest of saynt Vrbane pope ꝛ martyr/ by whose holy prechyng ꝛ doctryne moche people was cōuerted/ ꝛ many in the psecucyon of the emperour Alexander put to martyrdom. At mylen yᵉ feest of saynt Denyse a bysshop ꝛ confessour/ yᵗ in the cite of capadoce was iudged to exyle/ ꝛ yet dyed there/ ꝛ there was buryed/ whose holy relykes were preserued by saynt Basyle the bysshop/ ꝛ after by saynt Ambrose they were translated ꝛ shryned. In mafiaen† at dorostre yᵉ feest of saynt Passe[crate/ saynt Valencion/ ꝛ of other two holy psones all martyrs [fo. lvii. togyder. In the fraūchest of trecassyn yᵉ feest of saynt Leo a cōfessour. In brytayne at yᵉ monastery of mildunens yᵉ feest of saynt Aldelme a bysshop ꝛ confessour. The translacyon also of saynt Fraūcys a confessour/ ꝛ fyrst begynner of the ordre of freres minors. ¶ Addicyons.

¶ The feest also of saynt Nicete a martyr/ slayne by yᵉ gothes/ whose holy body was foūde by yᵉ ledyng of a sterre/ ꝛ dyd grete myracles. At florence yᵉ feest of saynt zenobe bysshop therof/ a holy man/ he reysed two persones vnto lyfe/ wᵗ many other myracles/ ꝛ at his trāslacion whan his body by chaūcc touched a drye tree in the wynter/ sodeynly it brought

MARTILO. F

forth fresshe floures ⁊ fruyte. The feest also of saynt Muce an abbot/ yᵗ fyrst was a pagan/ and by reuelacyon was conuerted/ ⁊ of hygh pfeccyon/ he neuer toke fode but vpon yᵉ sondaye ⁊ that was sent frō god by an aūgell/ he reysed many deed psones/ ⁊ saued many soules in dyuerse ferre coūtrees/ for in a moment in a twynklynge of an eye/ he coude be in ferre countrees where he wolde. The feest also of an other saynt Muce a confessour ⁊ a monke/ yᵗ before had be maryed/ ⁊ he was synguler in obedience for whan his abbot badde hym cast his owne childe in to a grete ryuer/ forthwᵗ he so

Note wel dyd/ but the chylde was saued by yᵉ other
yᵉ meryte monkes/ in whiche dede (as by reuelacyon was
of pure ⁊ shewed vnto yᵉ abbot) he was of lyke meryte wᵗ
symple Abraham. The same daye was the fyrst institucyon
obedience. of the feest of corpus christi/ ordeyned by pope

Vrbane the fourth/ in the yere of our lord .M. cc. lxiij. The occasyon wherof was this myracle. A good ⁊ deuoute preest was moche tempted wᵗ the doubte of that [sacrament. And vpon a daye whan he was at masse/ [*fo. lvii. b.* a lytell before the cōmunyon or receyuynge/ in the brekyng of the hoste/ sodeynly ranne out quycke ⁊ fresshe blode/ wherwᵗ the corporas was all wete ⁊ blody/ ⁊ so yet remayneth vnto this daye/ for no water ne lycour coude wasshe it/ ⁊ it is now amonge the relykes at viterbe/ by yᵉ occasyon (as is sayd) therof/ ⁊ for yᵉ synguler deuocyon of yᵗ sacrament/ the sayd pope ordeyned yᵉ sayd feest to be kepte for euer the next thursdaye after trinite sonday/ which was than yᵉ .xxv. day of May. The feest also of many other holy sayntes/ marᵗ. ⁊c̃.

⁌ To morowe.

⁌ The .xxvj. daye of May. At rome the feest of saynt Eleuthery pope ⁊ martyr. In atens the feest of saynt Quadrate/ yᵗ was discyple vnto the apostles/ ⁊ in the persecucyon of the emperour Adrian whan yᵉ chrysten people for fere were fledde ⁊ dispersed/ he wysely gadered them togyder/ and by his holy lyf ⁊ doctryne he fedde them goostly/ ⁊ made a boke of yᵉ defence of chrystes religyō. At rome yᵉ feest of saȳt Symniter† a priest ⁊ of .xxij. holy persones all martyrs togyder. The feest also of an other saynt Quadrate a martyr/ in whose solēnite saynt Augustynes sermons were foūde. At tudertusce the feest of saynt Felicissimus/ saynt Eracly ⁊ saynt Paulyne. In the terrytory of antisiodour yᵉ passyon of saynt Priske a martyr/ wᵗ whome were put to deth grete multytudes of chrystyans. In englond the feest of saynt

Augustyn a bysshop ⁊ cōfessour/ y^t is called the apostle of englond/ bycause he was sent thyder by saynt Gregory · the pope/ ⁊ he fyrst preched ye gospel ⁊ fayth of Chryst vnto y^t people. In ye same yle of englond ye deposicyon of saynt Bede/ called ye worshypfull [preest ⁊ most holy doctour of [*fo. lviii.* englond/ whose holsom doctryne is vniuersally knowen/ ⁊ his lyfe ⁊ merytes done openly appere by his bokes ⁊ myracles/ he dyed in the age of .lxxxx. yeres/ the same daye y^t he desyred/ that is to saye/ the ascencyon daye of our sauyour/ the yere of his incarnacyon .vij. C. xxxj. ⁊ after the deth of saynt Gregory C. xxj. yeres. ⁋ Addicyons.

⁋ The feest also of saynt Hyldēt a bysshop of grete merytes/ he reysed a childe that dyed vnbaptized/ ⁊ gaue hym y^t sacrament/ namyng hym Adelbert/ which after was translate ⁊ shryned w^t hym/ bothe togyder holy sayntes. The feest also of saynt Iohn the fyrst pope of that name. And the feest of saynt Theodour ⁊ saynt Agapite bothe cōsulles of rome/ and of an other saynt Agapite a noble man also of rome/ all martyrs put to deth by the emperour Theodoryke/ y^t was of the secte of arrianes heretykes. The feest also of an other saynt Iohn the second pope of y^t name/ a holy man/ that condempned ye patriarke of Ierusalem y^t was an arriane ⁊ many other of that secte. The feest also of the thyrde saynt Iohñ the thyrde pope of y^t name/ that dyd grete honour vnto sayntes/ ⁊ buylded many chirches/ and was a grete almes man/ and of many myracles. The feest also of many other holy sayntes/ mar. cōf. ⁊ virg.

⁋ To morowe.

⁋ The .xxvij. day of May. In marsia at doroscorens† the feest of saynt Iule a martyr/ that was an aūcyent man of warre/ ⁊ bycause he despised ye ydolles ⁊ cōfessed Chryst/ he was heded. In fraūce at arawsyke the feest of saȳt Eutrope a bysshop/ whose lyfe ⁊ myracles wrote saynt Vere ⁊ eloquently described them. In the terrytory of adartens ye feest of saynt Ranulph a mar[tyr/ of synguler perfeccyon ⁊ many [*fo. lviii. b.* grete notable myracles. ⁋ Addicyons.

⁋ At rauen the feest of saynt Sȳmachy/ a noble man of rome/ ⁊ of his sone in lawe saynt Boece/ y^t was also called saynt Seueryne/ bothe martyrs put to deth by the emperour Theodoryke the heretyke. The feest also of saȳt Maxence an abbot of hygh merytes/ he was fedde by aūgels/ ⁊ reysed deed persones w^t many other myracles. At rome ye feest of saynt Sȳmetre a preest/ y^t by the emperour Antonyn was put to *martyrdom/ w^t .xxij. other holy chrystyans. The feest also of many .⁊c.

⁋ To morowe.

⁋ The .xxviij. daye of May. At rome the feest of saynt Iohñ the pope/ that (as saynt Gregory wryteth) was longe in pryson/ ⁊ at yᵉ last put to cruell martyrdom wᵗ many other chrystyans. At parys yᵉ feest of saynt Germayn a cōfessour ⁊ bysshop of the same cite/ whose holy life ⁊ myracles saynt Fortunate a preest wryteth in a style moche eloquent. At sardyn yᵉ feest of saynt Emyly/ saynt Felix/ saynt Priamy ⁊ saynt Luciane. At carnot the feest of saynt Charāny a martyr. The translacyon also of our holy moder saynt Birgyt.

⁋ Addicyons.

⁋ At lyons the feest of saynt Wylliam a cōfessour/ that was duke of aquyne ⁊ of puynce/ ⁊ a noble capytayne for vnder yᵉ frensshe kyng Charles he obteyned a grete victory of the sarasyns. For the good spede wherof he foūded in lyons two monasteryes/ one of mōkes/ wherin he hȳselfe was after enclosed/ ⁊ yᵉ other of virgyns/ wherin his two systers were enclosed/ ⁊ he was euer a lay broder most lowly in obedience/ ⁊ had no preemynence/ but dyd the moost vyle ⁊ cōmun seruyce of ony [other/ notwithstandyng his fore estate/ ⁊ that [*fo. lix.* he was foūder/ ⁊ he was of many myracles/ ⁊ had yᵉ spiryte of prophecy. The feest also of saynt Lamfranke an archebysshop/ a man also of noble byrthe/ ⁊ a grete clerke/ ⁊ all he forsoke and was a monke in a poore monastery/ whome for his sanctite/ duke Wyllyam of normandy called to haue rule of a monastery of his foūdacyon/ ⁊ after whan yᵉ same duke wylliam was kynge of englond by conquest/ he cōpelled the sayd fader by yᵉ popes lettres to be archebysshop of Caūterbury/ wherin he had moche trouble ⁊ grete labours/ but euer he contynued a holy lyfe full of myracles. The feest also of many other holy sayntes/ martyrs/ confes. and virgyns.

⁋ To morowe.

⁋ The .xxix. day of May. In ysawre at yconiū yᵉ feest of saynt Canon ⁊ of his sone/ yᵗ by the emperour Aurelian were cast vpon hote syndres/ ⁊ after vpon a gredyren wᵗ hote coles/ ⁊ oyle cast ther vpon/ after they were fryed in a panne/ ⁊ than hanged vpon a gybet/ ⁊ yet agayne put vnto the fyre/ ⁊ at the last theyr fyngers ⁊ handes were beten vpon stythes wᵗ hamers/ vnto the tyme they yelded the spirytes vnto our lord. The feest also of saynt Sysynny ⁊ saynt Alexander martyrs/ yᵗ by the psecucyon of gentyles in yᵉ partyes of ananyuc† (as saynt Paulyn wryteth) receyued yᵉ crowne of martyrdom. At treuer yᵉ feest of saynt Maximus a bisshop ⁊ confessour/ yᵗ with honour ⁊ gladnes receyued saynt Athanasius yᵉ bysshop/ whan he fledde the psecucyon of Constance yᵉ emperour. At rome in aurell strete the feest of saynt Rustyke†. And in tyburtyne strete at rome also/ yᵉ feest of .vij. natural breder/ all there put to cruel martyrdom togyder.

⁜ Addicyons.

[⁜ The feest also of saynt Martyry a lector in order/ [*fo. lix. b.* ⁊ a martyr put to deth with yᵉ foresayd saynt Sysynny ⁊ saynt Alexander. The translacyon also of saynt Nicolas frō mirrea vnto venys/ wherin were shewed many grete myracles. And wᵗ the same body yᵉ same tyme were translate the body of saynt Theodour/ that was also bysshop of myrre before saȳt Nicolas/ ⁊ a martyr. And the body also of an other saynt Nicolas that was godfader ⁊ vncle vnto this saynt Nicolas/ ⁊ the nexte bysshop saue one before hym/ a man of grete holynes and many myracles/ ⁊ had yᵉ spiryte of prophecy. The feest also of many other holy sayntes/ mar. cōf. ⁊ virg.

⁜ To morowe.

⁜ The .xxx. daye of May. At rome in aurell strete the feest of saynt Felix pope/ yᵗ after he had wel ruled .v. yeres was by yᵉ emperour Claudius put to martyrdom. In yᵉ toures of sardyne yᵉ feest of saynt Gabyn ⁊ saynt Crispol martyrs. The feest also of saynt Hutbert a bysshop ⁊ confessour.

⁜ Addicyons.

⁜ In antioche yᵉ feest of saȳt Ysyce ⁊ of saynt Palatyn martyrs/ yᵗ for Christes fayth were put there to many cruell turmentes. The feest also of many other ho. ⁊c̄.

⁜ To morowe.

⁜ The .xxxj. day of May. At rome yᵉ feest of saynt Pernell a virgyn of grete holynes ⁊ many myracles/ specyally in yᵉ curyng of seke psones/ whome an erle desyred vnto his wyfe/ ⁊ she in thre dayes had for respyte of answere/ gaue her hooly to watche/ fastynge/ and prayer/ ⁊ on yᵉ thyrde daye she was cōmuned/ ʼt so yelded her spiryte by feruent loue vnto Chryst her spouse. At aquiley yᵉ feest of saynt Cance ⁊ saynt Canciane breder/ ⁊ of saȳt Cancianyll theyr syster a virgyn/ all mar[tyrs/ [*fo. lx.* they were of the kynges blode of assisiour†/ ⁊ for Chryst they were all heeded togyder/ and with them saynt Prothe theyr scolemayster. At the toures of sardyne the feest of saynt Crescenciane a martyr. ⁜ Addicyons.

⁜ The feest also of saynt Theodosy a cōfessour ⁊ emperour/ yᵗ moche multyplyed the religyon of Chryst/ ⁊ destroyed all

ydolatry/ ꝛ vaynquysshed his enemyes more by fastyng/ prayer
ꝛ almes/ than by ony hoost or army/ ꝛ he was very deuoute/ for
by his mocyon the pope Damasus caused saynt Ierom to ordre
yᵉ seruyce of the chirche as now it is songe ꝛ sayd/ whiche before
was neuer so vsed/ and he was singuler in mekenes ꝛ obedience.
For whan saynt Ambrose for a trespace suspended hym/ ꝛ pro-
hibyt hym the chirche tyll he wolde do open penaūce/ he lowly
toke his penaunce ꝛ openly before all yᵉ people
note how accomplysshed it wᵗ profoūde mekenes ꝛ depe
the emperour contricion/ ꝛ moche praysed saynt Ambrose of
dyd open indifferent iustyce/ ꝛ many notable actes he dyd
penaunce. and myracles. The feest also of saynt Lybertyne
an abbot that was discyple vnto saynt Honorate/ ꝛ
for yᵉ loue of his mayster after his deth he bare euer vpon hym as
a relyke one of his maysters sockes/ whiche he layd vpō a deed
chylde ꝛ made his prayers/ ꝛ forthwᵗ the childe arose hole/ he
was of profoūde mekenes/ ꝛ of aūgelycall pacyence/
j. dia. ca. ij. of whome saynt Gregory wryteth. The feest also
of many other holy sayntes/ mar. cōf. ꝛ virg.

⁋ Iune.

⁋ To morowe.

THe fyrst day of Iune. at rome the feest of saynt
Iune. Nicomede a preest ꝛ martyr. In palestyne at
cesare the feest of saynt Pamphyly a preest/ yᵗ in
yᵉ per[secucyon of Maximiane yᵉ emperour was put to [fo. lx. b.
martyrdom/ of whose lyf Eusebius bisshop of cesare made thre
bokes. And saynt Ierom sayth yᵗ he foūde certayn volumes ꝛ
bokes of his owne hande wrytynge/ whiche he kept wᵗ more Ioy
ꝛ pleasure ꝛ for greter tresour than the hole rychesse of Crese/
whiche was yᵉ rychest man of the worlde. At augustudune the
feest of saynt Reuereane a bysshop/ ꝛ of saynt Paule a preest ꝛ
martyrs/ yᵗ by yᵉ prynce Aurelian were put to martyrdom/ ꝛ
with them .x. other chrystyans. In the monastery of lirinens the
feest of saȳt Caprase an abbot. At treuer yᵉ feest of saynt
Symeon a cōfessour. At rome the feest of saynt Vincent a
martyr. ⁋ Addicyons.

⁋ In englonde at ewsam the feest of saynt wystane a kyng of
the same realme ꝛ a martyr/ yᵗ trayterly was slayne by a tyraunt
yᵗ vnlawfully wolde haue maryed his moder/ entendyng to put
hym also frō his crowne/ whiche tyraūt fell madde forthwᵗ whan
he had slayne his kynge/ whose holynes was shewed openly/ for
a pyller of meruaylous bryghtnes stretched in lengthe streyght

vp from the place of his martyrdom vnto heuen/ ꝧ so remayned xxx. dayes contynually. And euery yere yᵉ same daye the same heres yᵗ the tyraūt plucked from his heed dyd growe there all fresshe and newe amonge the grasse/ so fast yᵗ no man coude pull them out ne yet breke them/ ꝧ euer on the morowe after they vanysshed/ ꝧ many other myracles our lord wrought for hym. The feest also of saynt Quence. At rome the feest of saynt Iomny an abbot. And of many other holy . ꝇc̃.

℟ To morowe.

℟ The second daye of Iune. At rome the feest of saynt Marcellyne a preest/ ꝧ of saȳt Peter an exorcist in order [martyrs/ that by the iudge Seren were put in prison where [*fo. lxi.* they conuerted many psones/ ꝧ after were put to many cruell turmentes/ ꝧ at yᵉ last heded. In fraūce at lyons the feest of saynt Fotyne bisshop of yᵉ same cite and of saynt zachary a
preest/ saynt Saynt a deacon/ saynt Epagate/ saynt
Saynt a name.   Mature/ saynt Attalus/ saynt Albyne ꝧ saynt Geate†/
wᵗ other .xl. chrystyans/ all (as the story ecclesiastyke sheweth) put to deth togyder/ ꝧ of the same company was yᵉ holy virgyn saynt Blandyne that was put to grete affliccyons ꝧ many assayles by flatery ꝧ fayre speche the space of thre dayes/ ꝧ whan by no meanes she wold forsake Chryst/ she was on the fourth daye cruelly scourged/ ꝧ than broyled after the maner of saynt Laurence/ with many other varyaūt turmentes/ ꝧ at the last slayne by the swerde.

℟ Addicyons.

℟ The feest also of saynt Odo/ chylde vnto yᵉ infydeles that came in to englond wᵗ Hyngware/ but he in youth forsoke his parentes ꝧ kynne/ ꝧ receyued Chrystes religyon/ ꝧ was a doctour ꝧ precher of his fayth/ ꝧ than bysshop of salysbury/ ꝧ after archebysshop of caūterbury/ ꝧ boldly rebuked yᵉ kyng ꝧ refourmed hym of many errours/ specyally of auoutry/ ꝧ he was of many myracles. The feest also of many other holy sayntes .ꝇc̃.

℟ To morowe.

℟ The thyrde daye of Iune. In campane the feest of saynt Herasmus a bisshop ꝧ martyr/ yᵗ fyrst by yᵉ emperour Dioclecian was beten with staues ꝧ with plummettes of lede/ ꝧ after rosyne/ brymstone/ pytche/ lede/ waxe ꝧ oyle were all boyled togyder ꝧ cast vpon his body/ ꝧ than was he put to many other varyaūt ꝧ horryble turmentes/ whiche all in Chryst he vaynquysshed. [And after that he was presented vnto the Emperour [*fo. lxi. b.*

Maximian/ ꝥ there put newly vnto vnspekable tyrannous turmentes/ ꝥ at the last by yᵉ callyng of our lorde Iesu he rendred his spiryte vnto his handes. In arecy at tuscia the feest of saynt Pergentyne/ and of saynt Laurentyne breder ꝥ martyrs/ yᵗ by the emperour Decius were in theyr yonge age put to meruaylous turmentes/ ꝥ at the last slayne by the swerde. At corduba the feest of saynt Isake a monke/ yᵗ in the age of xxvij. yeres/ was for Chryst martyred by yᵉ swerde. In the terrytory of orlyaūce yᵉ feest of saynt Lyphard a preest and confessour. ⁋ Addicyons.

⁋ At lyons the feest of saynt Fotyne a martyr/ that in the age of .lxxxx. yeres by his owne desyre of god/ suffred cruell martyrdom. The feest also of saynt Nicolas a confessour/ whose syrname was pylgrym/ yᵗ so was called bycause yᵗ from grekelond where he was borne he came in pylgrymage vnto Rauen a lytell frō rome/ berynge by all yᵉ waye a crosse of wode vpon his backe bare foted ꝥ bare heded/ wᵗ symple ꝥ bare clothes/ ꝥ wᵗ the same crosse he went aboute the cite/ ꝥ gadered the chylder of yᵉ cite aboute hym/ by the meanes of apples fygges ꝥ suche fruyte as was gyuen hym/ ꝥ euer he sange Kyrieleyson/ ꝥ the chylder euer repeted yᵉ same/ ꝥ he neuer ete ne dranke tyll nyght/ ꝥ than but a lytell brede and water/ and so he cōtynued vnto his deth/ at whose buryall many were heled of dyuerse infyrmytees by touchynge of yᵉ sayd crosse/ ꝥ euer at his tombe ben contynuall myracles. At antioche the feest of saynt Ysake a preest of the same chirche/ a man of grete lernynge ꝥ more holynes. In the partyes of syre the feest of an other saynt Ysake a confessour of holy lyf ꝥ grete [myracles/ ꝥ had ⌈fo. lxii. the spiryte of prophecy. In yrelond yᵉ feest of saynt Keynyne an abbot/ yᵗ founde two women newly heded by theues ꝥ robbers/ ꝥ he set the heedes vnto yᵉ bodyes/ ꝥ they arose all hole/ ꝥ a man lykewyse that was slayne by many cruell woūdes/ with many other myracles/ he had also yᵉ spiryte of prophecy. The feest also of many other holy sayntes/ mar. cōf. ꝥ virg.

⁋ To morowe.

⁋ The fourth day of Iune. In sythe† at ylliricū yᵉ feest of saynt Quiryne a bysshop/ that for yᵉ fayth (as Prudence wryteth) was tyed vnto a mylstone/ ꝥ cast in to a flode/ where notwᵗ-standyng he flowed ꝥ preched vnto the chrystyans yᵗ stode vpon the londe/ ꝥ moche cōforted them vnto martyrdom/ ꝥ after by his owne prayer he drowned. At niuedune yᵉ feest of saynt zotyke/ saynt Attale ꝥ sayt Eutyke martyrs. The deposicyon also of saynt Patryke† a confessour.

⁋ Addicyons.
⁋ The feest also of .xliiij. martyrs/ y^t by saynt Syryke ꝛ saynt Iulite were cōuerted/ ꝛ put to martyrdom by ye emperour Alexander. The feest also of many oth. ꝛc.

⁋ To morowe.

⁋ The .v. daye of Iune. the feest of saynt Boniface a martyr/ y^t in ye cite of tharsum was put to martyrdom by ye emperours Dioclecian ꝛ Maximian/ but his holy body was buryed at rome in latyn strete/ this holy saynt was in youth drowned many yeres in the stynkynge synne of lechery/ but after by the inspiracyon of grace/ he was contryte ꝛ toke grete penaunce/ ꝛ had y^t synne in abhomynacyon/ ꝛ for ye loue of Chryst he wylfully went to deth and suffred cruell martyrdom. The feest also of an other saynt Boniface a bysshop ꝛ martyr/ borne in englond/ from whens he went in to fryse [londe to [*fo. lxii. b.* preche ye fayth of Chryst/ where whan he had cōuerted moche people/ he was put to martyrdome/ ꝛ with hym saỹt Eobanket a bysshop/ with many other persones. ⁋ Addicyons.
⁋ At coleyn the feest of saynt Seueryne bisshop of the same cite/ of whom was had reuelacion after his deth. In egypt the feest of saynt Marciane/ saynt Nitrand ꝛ saynt Appolyne martyrs. At cartage the feest of the thyrde saynt Boniface/ bysshop of the same cite ꝛ a confessour of grete doctryne ꝛ synguler vertue. The feest also of many other holy sayntes/ mart. confes. ꝛ virg.

⁋ To morowe.

⁋ The .vj. day of Iune. the feest of saynt Philyp/ one of ye fyrst .vij. deacons/ a man of notable vertue ꝛ grete wonderous myracles/ that dyed at cesary capadoce/ ꝛ there lyeth buryed w^t his two doughters/ y^t in ye newe lawe were pphetes. In the londe of cecilet at tharsum the feest of .xx. martyrs/ that by ye emperours Dioclecian ꝛ Maximian were put to deth by many cruell turmentes. At rome the feest of saynt Arthemy that was heded/ and of his wyfe saynt Candida ꝛ his doughter saynt Paulyne/ y^t were bothe after hym stoned to deth. At niuedune the feest of saynt Amance ꝛ saynt Alexander.
⁋ Addicyons.
⁋ The feest also of saynt Vincent and saynt Benigne martyrs/ that in theyr passyon cōuerted many psones of the whiche .vj.c. were put to deth w^t saynt Benigne ꝛ many multytudes after cōuerted by saynt Vincent. The feest also of saynt

Goodwale a bisshop/ borne of yͤ noble blode of englonde/ that for synguler pfeccyon resygned his mytre/ and dwelled vpon a desolate rocke/ where he buylded a monastery/ ꝛ by miracle had there [a well of quycke water/ ꝛ there he gadered [*fo. lxiii.* C.lxxxviij. monkes/ ꝛ bycause the rome was lytell/ he went vnto the see at the lowest ebbe ꝛ charged the see in the name of our lorde it shold kepe that place ꝛ neuer flowe nerer the monastery/ ꝛ so had yᵗ groūde for euer/ he heled the seke/ reysed yͤ deed/ with many other myracles/ ꝛ had reuelaciōs of aūgels. The feest also of many other. ꝛc̃.

⁋ To morowe.

⁋ The .vij. day of Iune. at constantynople the feest of saynt Paule/ bysshop of the same cite/ that by yͤ emperour Constancius was exiled vnto cucusse/ where by the treason of the heretykes called arrianes/ he was murthered. At corduba the feest of saynt Peter a preest saynt Auens ꝛ saynt Ieremy/ with other thre psones martyrs. The translacyon also of saynt Wolston bysshop of worcester/ a man of synguler sanctite.
⁋ Addicyons.
⁋ The translacyon also of saynt Seruace/ yᵗ was trāslated thre tymes/ ꝛ in euery trāslacyon grete myracles were shewed. In yrelond the feest of saynt Colman a bysshop/ of whome was made reuelacyon vnto saynt Patryke .xxx. yeres before his byrthe/ a holy man/ he reysed a kynge yᵗ was slayne by his enemyes/ ꝛ a kynges sone yᵗ was deed/ ꝛ his owne syster yᵗ was slayne by robbers ꝛ theues/ ꝛ a virgyn also that was deuoured by a water dragon/ wᵗ many other grete myracles. In englond the feest of saynt Robert/ borne in yͤ dioces of yorke/ ꝛ toke the habyte of yͤ religyon in yͤ monastery of wyteby/ ꝛ after he was abbot of saynt Maryes of yorke/ ꝛ he buylded a monastery in northumberlond and was of grete sanctite ꝛ many myracles. The feest also of many other holy sayntes/ marṫ. confes. ꝛ virg.

[⁋ To morowe. [*fo. lxiii. b.*

⁋ The .viij. day of Iune. In fraūce at swesion yͤ feest of saynt Medard bysshop of nouiomēs/ a man of grete merytes/ as well appered at his deth/ for yͤ heuen opened in the syght of all yͤ people/ ꝛ celestyall lyghtes appered ꝛ went before hym bryght shynynge vnto blysse. The feest also of his naturall broder saynt Gyldarde/ bysshop of rone/ that (as holy chirche recordeth) were bothe borne of one moder vpon one day/ ꝛ toke holy orders bothe in one daye/ ꝛ were deed ꝛ buryed bothe in one day. At senon the feest of saynt Eraclius a bysshop ⁊ confessour. At sardyne yᵉ feest of saynt Salustian. Acṫ corduba the feest of saynt Habūde a preest ⁊ martyr. ❡ Addicyons.

❡ In englonde the feest of saynt Wylliam bysshop of yorke/ a noble man of byrthe/ but moche more noble of holynes/ synguler vertue ⁊ many myracles. The feest also of many other holy sayntes/ marṙ. confes. ⁊ virg.

❡ To morowe.

❡ The .ix. daye of Iune. At rome in the moūt of Sely the feest of saynt Pryme ⁊ saynt Feliciane martyrs/ yᵗ were put to deth by the tyranny of yᵉ emperours Dioclecian ⁊ Maximian/ wherby after many variaūt turmentes they were slayne by the swerde. In fraūce at agēno the passyon of saynt Vincent a deacon ⁊ martyr. In scotlond the feest of saynt Colūbaneṫ a preest ⁊ confessour of meruaylous ⁊ singuler vertue. At nice yᵉ feest of saynt Diomede. In yᵉ monastery of saynt Germane the dedicacyon of saynt Peters chapell. In englonde the translacyon of saynt Edmūde archebysshop of caūterbury.

❡ Addicyons.

❡ The feest also of saynt Onofre an heremyte/ that in [egypte serued god in desert .lx. yeres .xxx. wherof [*fo. lxiiii.* he lyued by fruyte/ herbes ⁊ rotes/ ⁊ the other .xxx. by the fedyng of aūgels wᵗout ony other erthly fode/ ⁊ euery sondaye he was cōmuned receyuyng yᵉ sacrament of chrystes body by yᵉ mynistery of yᵉ same aūgels/ by whome at his deth he was buryed/ ⁊ his soule conueyed vnto blysse. The feest also of saynt Maximian a bysshop of hygh perfeccyon and many grete myracles. The feest also of many other holy sayntes/ marṙ. confes. ⁊ virg.

❡ To morowe.

❡ The .x. day of Iune. At rome in aurely strete yᵉ feest of saynt Basilyde/ saynt Tripode/ ⁊ saynt Amandaleṫ martyrs/ that by the mayre Plato at yᵉ cōmaūdement of the emperour Aurelian were put to deth/ ⁊ wᵗ them .xx. other holy martyrs. At Rome also in salary strete yᵉ feest of saȳt Getuly a noble man/ of grete lernyng/ that was put to martyrdom wᵗ his felowes saynt Cereall/ saynt Amance ⁊ saynt Primytyue/ yᵗ by the emperour Adriane after many turmētes were brent. At nicomede the feest of saynt Zachary. At antisiodour the feest of saynt Censure a bysshop ⁊ confessour. At parys yᵉ feest of saynt Ytamarṫ a bysshop and confessour.

⁋ Addicyons.

⁋ In aquens the feest of saynt Maximyne/ one of the .lxxij disciples/ vnto whome saynt Peter cōmytted his doughter Mary magdalene/ lyke as Chryst cōmytted his moder vnto saynt Iohn/ whiche bothe togyder w^t his felowe saynt Cedony/ ⁊ her broder saynt Lazare ⁊ her syster saynt Martha w^t her mayde saynt Marcill/ were by the psecucyon of the iewes put all in a shyppe without takelynge/ ⁊ they aryued at massely/ where Mary preched ⁊ cōuerted all the people/ ⁊ Lazar was [theyr bysshop/ ⁊ this holy saynt Maximyne was bysshop of [*fo. lxiiii. b.* aquence .xl. yeres/ ⁊ he mynistred ye sacramentes vnto his sayd doughter Mary at her deth/ and honourably buryed her in his owne chirche/ where .v. yeres after he was buryed hymselfe besyde her/ all full of sanctite ãd grete myracles. In englond the feest of saynt Yue an archebysshop/ that was borne in perse/ a kӯges sone ⁊ a quenes/ ⁊ after many labours he came in to englond/ ⁊ dwelled in a village besyde hūtyngton .viij. myle from ramesey/ called slepe/ now called saynt Yues/ where his holy body was foūde by reuelacyon/ ⁊ there shewed grete myracles. In scotlond the feest of saynt Margarete/ quene of the same/ ⁊ doughter vnto saynt Edmūdes broder called Edward/ y^t maryed the emperours doughter/ and by her had this doughter/ whome he maryed vnto the kynge of scotlond/ where she refourmed the fayth of Chryst/ ⁊ was of hygh pfeccyon ⁊ many myracles. The feest also of many oth. ⁊c.

⁋ To morowe.

⁋ The .xj. day of Iune. the feest of saynt Barnabe the apostle/ that was ye apostle of cipres/ ⁊ assigned felowe with saynt Paule to preche vnto the gentyles/ whose holy body was founde by his owne reuelacyon in the tyme of ye emperour zenon. In aquiley ye feest of saynt Felix ⁊ saynt Fortunate breder/ that by the psecucyon of ye emperours Dioclecian ⁊ Maximian were racked ⁊ hote flambynge lampes ⁊ cressettes put to theyr bodyes/ whiche by ye myght of god were sodeynly quenched/ than hote boylӯg lede was cast vpon theyr wombes/ ⁊ at the last after many turmentes they were heded/ and so ended theyr martyrdom in Chrystes cōfessyon.

⁋ Addicyons.

[⁋ The feest also of sayt Onophry an heremite [*fo. lxv.* of hygh perfeccyon. And ye feest also of saynt Timothy an heremyte of egypt/ y^t for a grete synne cōmytted/ dyd grete penaūce .xxx. yeres/ fedde onely w^t dates ⁊ water/ ⁊ he had many conflyctes w^t the deuyll/ ⁊ euer grete cōforte by y^e

reuelacion of aūgels. The feest also of saynt Iohñ/ saynt Andrewe/ saynt Tadye ꝸ saynt Philyp .iiij. holy faders/ that lyued .l. yeres in the wyldernes of egypte by fruyte onely/ excepte yᵗ euery sondaye a lofe of brede was brought vnto euery of them by an aungell/ whiche holy aūgell brought vnto them the reuerend fader saynt Pannucius/ ꝸ than for the tyme of his presence they had .v. loues euery sondaye/ men all of grete myracles. The feest also of many other holy sayntes .ꝸc̃.

To morowe.

⁋ The .xij. day of Iune. at mylen yᵉ feest of saȳt Nazary a martyr/ that in yᵉ psecucyon of yᵉ tyraūt Nero was put to many affliccions/ at yᵉ last by the iudge Anolyne he was famysshed in prison/ ꝸ his seruaūt saynt Celse whome he had brought vp of a chylde was heded/ whose holy bodyes (as saynt Paulyn wryteth) were foūde of saynt Ambrose by reuelacyon. At mylen also yᵉ feest of saynt Basilidis/ saynt Ciryne/ ꝸ saynt Nabour martyrs. In fryselond yᵉ feest of saynt Adulph† a holy cōfessour of many myracles. ⁋ Addicyons.

⁋ In yᵉ moūt of soract yᵉ feest of saynt Nonos a monke ꝸ proctour of yᵉ same monastery/ a man of synguler pacyence/ ꝸ by his prayer in yᵉ nyght he remoued a grete rocke that was noyous vnto the monastery/ he multiplyed oyle by his prayer/ wᵗ many other myracles ꝸ signes of sanctite. The feest also of many other holy .ꝸc̃.

⁋ To morowe.

[⁋ The .xiij. day of Iune. At rome in ardiatyne [*fo. lxv. b.* strete the feest of saynt Felicule a virgyn ꝸ martyr/ yᵗ bycause she denyed maryage ꝸ wolde not do sacrefyce vnto the ydolles/ was put in harde pryson ꝸ there well nere famysshed/ after hanged vpon a gybet/ scourged/ ꝸ after many other cruell turmentes she was drowned. The translacyon also of saynt Bartholomewe yᵉ apostle. At corduba the feest of saynt Fandil a preest/ yᵗ after many turmētes was heded. At padue yᵉ feest of saȳt Antony a preest ꝸ confessour of saynt Augustynes rule/ ꝸ after of saynt Fraūcys rule/ ꝸ euer moche famous in reguler obseruaūce. In affrike yᵉ feest of saynt Luciane ꝸ of saynt Crescenciane cōfessours. ⁋ Addicyons.

⁋ The trāslacyon of the grete saynt Antony the heremyte/ wherof was reuelacyon made vnto yᵉ emperour Constantyne/ wherby he sent out messengers to seke yᵉ blessed body/ and anone in theyr iourney a sterre apperynge went forth cōtynually before them/ ⁊ with that sterre was also the aūgell Gabriell/ by whome yᵉ sayd reuelacyon was made/ ⁊ by whome the sayd messengers were brought vnto the place from whens wᵗ due honour they brought his sayd holy corps/ in whiche trāslacyon were done many grete myracles. The feest also of many other holy sayntes/ marṫ. confes. ⁊ virg.

¶ To morowe.

¶ The .xiiij. daye of Iune. the feest of the holy pphete Helisey/ that (as saynt Ierom wryteth) lyeth buryed in samary at palestyne/ where also lyeth the prophete Abdye. In cesare at capadoce the feest of saynt Basyle a bysshop/ yᵗ in the tyme of the emperour Valent was excellent famous in doctryne/ vertue/ wysdome ⁊ myracles. In the terrytory of swessy the feest of saynt Ru[fyne and saynt Valery/ that by the [*fo. lxvi*. mayre Rykciouare were put to cruell turmentes/ ⁊ at the last heded. The feest also of saynt Quinciane a preest and martyr.
¶ Addicyons.
¶ One of the feestes also of sa\u0233t Brandane/ that was borne in englond/ ⁊ an abbot in yrelond of .iij. M. monkes/ a holy fader ⁊ gretely exercysed ⁊ laboured in pylgrymages/ after the whiche he was made a bysshop in yrelond/ ⁊ euer of synguler sanctite. The feest also of many other holy sayntes/ martyrs/ confes. ⁊ virgyns.

¶ To morowe.

¶ The .xv. day of Iune. In sicilie the feest of sa\u0233t Vite saynt Modest ⁊ saynt Crescence martyrs/ that by the emperour Dioclecian were put in a potte of boylynge lede/ but no thynge noyed wᵗall/ than were they put to wylde beestes/ but they wold not touche them. And at the last they were hanged all in a racke vnto deth. At beneuent yᵉ feest of saynt Mercury a martyr. In messy at dorostore the feest of saynt Esichy a man of warre yᵗ was accused wᵗ saynt Iule/ ⁊ by yᵉ presydent Maximy put to deth. In englonde the deposicyon of saynt Eadburge a holy ⁊ blessed virgyn. ¶ Addicyons.
¶ The feest also of saynt Honorate bysshop of ambian a holy man of hygh merytes. On a tyme whan he came in his masse vnto the cōmunyon/ our sauyour appered vnto hym ⁊ gaue hym yᵉ sacrament wᵗ his owne handes. The feest also of many other holy sayntes .⁊c̃.

¶ To morowe.

¶ The .xvj. day of Iune. In fraūce at vesucet the feest of saynt Fereole a preest/ ⁊ of saynt Ferrucion a deacon bothe martyrs/ y^t were sent by saynt Hyren ye bysshop to preche the fayth/ for the whiche they were taken/ ⁊ [by iudge [*fo. lxvi. b.* Claudius after many turmentes slayne by ye swerde. At antioche ye feest of saynt Cirice ⁊ his moder saynt Iulite/ that after many cruell turmentes were heded. At lyons the deposicyon of saynt Aureliane bysshop of arelatens. At manuetet ye feest of saynt Symylyane a bysshop ⁊ cōfessour. At cisceter the translacyon of saynt Rycharde a bysshop and a confessour. ¶ Addicyons.
¶ The feest also of saynt Lupe a bysshop ⁊ confessour. The feest also of saynt Aury ⁊ of his syster a holy virgyn saȳt Iustyne bothe martyrs. At roūcyuale ye feest of saynt Rowlande a knyght that slewe a gyaūt of the myght ⁊ strength of xl. men/ ⁊ after he ⁊ w^t hym saynt Olyuer/ w^t many other knightes ⁊ men of warre that in batayle for the fayth of Chryst vnder Charlemayne were slayne by treason/ ⁊ forthwith his soule ⁊ all his company were seen caryed vnto heuen by aūgels. The feest also of many other holy sayntes/ mar. cōf. ⁊ virg.

¶ To morowe.

¶ The xvij. daye of Iune. At rome the feest of .cc. lxij. martyrs/ that were buryed in olde salary strete/ at the hyll fote called the gourde. In the terrytory of bitury the feest of saynt Gūdulf a bysshop ⁊ confessour. At orlyaūce the feest of saynt Anytet a preest. The feest also of saynt wolmare a man of meruaylous sanctite/ and perfyte in religyon. In brytayn the feest of saynt Botulfe an abbot. ¶ Addicyons.
¶ In tusce the feest of saynt Hymere a bysshop of synguler vertue ⁊ grete myracles. The feest also of saynt Elizabeth of sconanget a holy virgyn and a relygyous woman of the same monastery/ of hygh perfeccyon as in her lyfe more largely appereth. In yrelond the feest [of saynt Molyng/ a [*fo. lxvii.* bysshop of synguler sanctite/ ⁊ had reuelacyon of aūgels/ ⁊ he reysed a kynges sone to lyfe and cured the blynde ⁊ defe/ dombe ⁊ lame/ lepres ⁊ dyuerse infyrmytees/ ⁊ many grete myracles. The feest also of the holy matrone saynt Sophie/ that is to saye in englysshe Wysdome/ ⁊ of her thre doughters saynt Fayth/ saynt Hope ⁊ saynt Charite virgyns/ all borne in grece/ ⁊ came in pylgrymage to rome/ where ye virgyns cōfessed ye fayth of

Chryst/ for the whiche by many varyaūt turmentes they were put to deth/ ⁊ yᵉ moder desyred of god she might dye wᵗ them/ ⁊ so in prayer vpō theyr graue she yelded her soule vnto our sauyour. The feest also of many other holy sayntes/ marṫ. ⁊c̃.

⁌ To morowe.

⁌ The .xviij. day of Iune. At rome in ardiatyne strete the feest of saynt Marke ⁊ saynt Marcell† breder ⁊ martyrs/ yᵗ by duke Fabiane were boūde ⁊ layd vpryght ⁊ pricked in the soles of the fete wᵗ elsyns/ ⁊ at yᵉ last they were slayne wᵗ speres. In spayne at malact the feest of saynt Cyriake/ ⁊ of saynt Paule a virgyn/ bothe martyrs/ that after many turmentes were murthered in sond ⁊ stones. In alexander the passyon of saynt Maryne a virgyn ⁊ martyr. In the terrytory of zenon the feest of saynt Fortunate a bysshop and confessour. ⁌ Addicyons.

⁌ The feest also of saȳt Macra a virgyn ⁊ martyr. In the puynce of valery yᵉ feest of saynt Martyry a cōfessour/ a famous man of sanctite ⁊ myracles/ yᵗ amonge other made a sygne of the crosse ouer a cake that was couered wᵗ asshes ⁊ coles/ ⁊ whan yᵉ cake was baken yᵉ crosse apered thervpon. The feest also of many otħ. ⁊c̃.

⁌ To morowe.

[⁌ The .xix. day of Iune. At mylen yᵉ feest of [fo. lxvii. b. saynt Geruase ⁊ saynt Prothase breder ⁊ martyrs/ yᵗ were after many turmentes put to dethe by duke Astasy/ whose holy bodyes saynt Ambrose foūde as hole in yᵉ graue ⁊ vncorrupte/ as though they had newly ben slayne the same daye. At rauen the feest of saynt Vrcissyne a martyr/ that by the iudge Paulyne after many turmentes was heded/ and so accomplysshed his martyrdome. ⁌ Addicyons.

⁌ The feest also of saȳt Romwald a holy abbot of grete myracles. The feest also of saynt Dace bysshop of mylen/ yᵗ in his iourney toward cōstantynople was wylfully lodged in a hous yᵗ was occupyed wᵗ wycked spirytes/ whiche aboute mydnyght made a crye lyke vnto swyne ⁊ other beestes/ vnto whome yᵉ holy bysshop sayd/ full well were you serued/ that beynge aūgels of beauty wolde not be content excepte by your pryde ye myght be equall with god/ ⁊ now therfore ye be lyke beestes/ auoyd I charge you amōge beestes/ ⁊ so was the hous safe for euer. The feest also of many other .⁊c̃.

⁋ To morowe.

⁋ The .xx. day of Iune. At rome the feest of saynt Syueret pope ⁊ martyr. At rome also yᵉ deposicyon of saynt Nouate broder vnto saynt Tymothe/ ⁊ bothe disciples vnto yᵉ apostles/ ⁊ the holy virgyns saynt Potenciane ⁊ saynt Praxede were theyr systers. At thomis yᵉ feest of saynt Paule ⁊ saynt Ciriake. The translacyon also of saynt Edwarde kynge and martyr. And the feest of saynt Iouyne a preest ⁊ confessour of grete holynes. ⁋ Addicyons.

⁋ The feest also of saynt Iohñ and saynt Benet monkes/ that were grete prechers/ and conuerted a kynge [and [*fo. lxviii.* his realme/ ⁊ after were martyred by theues/ whose holy bodyes wrought grete myracles. The feest also of saynt Abagare a confessour/ and kynge of edysse vnto whome our sauyour wrote an epystle/ and therwᵗ sent hym the very ymage of his owne face/ ⁊ after his resurreccion he sent the apostle Tade to teche hym the fayth ⁊ baptyse hym ⁊ all his people. The feest also of many other holy sayntes/ martyrs/ confes. and virg.

⁋ To morowe.

⁋ The .xxj. daye of Iune. In sicilie at siracusane the feest of saynt Rufyne ⁊ saȳt Marce martyrs. In cesare capadoce at palestyne yᵉ feest of saynt Eusebius a bysshop/ a grete clerke ⁊ a wryter of storyes. At rome the feest of saynt Demetria a virgyn/ that in examinacion before Iulian the apostata yelded her spiryte vnto her spouse Iesu. In the frauchest of madriacens the feest of saynt Lewfryde a cōfessour/ yᵗ amonge other myracles/ caused by prayer a well to sprynge out of a baren drye groūde. In affryke the feest of saynt Quiriake ⁊ saynt Apollinare. The translacyon also of saynt Warburge a virgyn. ⁋ Addicyons.

⁋ The feest also of saynt Albane a bysshop/ ⁊ of saynt Vrs ⁊ saynt Dominyke/ that all togyder suffred martyrdom for the fayth of Chryst. In englond the feest of saynt Cassiane a c̦fessour. And of many other holy . ⁊c̄.

⁋ To morowe.

⁋ The .xxij. day of Iune. In brytayne yᵉ feest of saynt Albane a martyr/ that in the tyme of yᵉ emperour Dioclecian after many turmētes/ suffred at verolanet deth heded by the swerde/ ⁊ with hym was a soudyour put to deth bycause he refused to do yᵉ execucyon vpon hym. At nole in campane yᵉ

MARTILO. G

feest of saynt Paulyne a bysshop [⁊ cōfessour/ a [*fo. lxviii. b.* famous man (as saynt Gregory wryteth in his dialoges) not onely in lernyng ⁊ holynes/ but also in myracles/ specyally in expellyng of euyll spirytes. The feest also of saynt Cōsorce a virgyn. And the deposicyon of saynt Nice/ bysshop of the cite of romaciane. ⁋ Addicyons.

⁋ In alexander the feest of saynt Acace ⁊ saȳt Heliade two noble capytaynes/ yᵗ with theyr host of .x.M. men were by an aūgell cōuerted vnto Chrystes fayth/ ⁊ after grete vyctory had ouer theyr enemyes/ they were all togyder put to martyrdom by the emperours Adriane ⁊ Antony. The feest also of saynt Peter bysshop of tarentase/ a holy man of grete myracles. The decollacyon also of saynt wenefrede whan her heed was stryken of ⁊ she agayn reysed to lyfe. The feest also of saynt Hyldegard a virgyn/ that in the age of .v. yeres entred religyon/ ⁊ therin cōtynued a strayte ⁊ holy lyf/ ⁊ was abbesse/ ⁊ had the spiryte of prophecy. And all though she were vnlerned (for more she coude not but her psalter ⁊ seruyce) yet was she oftentymes rapte in spiryte and so enfourmed ⁊ taught by our lord/ that she caused many bokes of hygh diuinite to be wrytē as she spake them/ whiche bokes ⁊ werkes were all approued by the pope Eugene in a generall cōuseyle/ ⁊ he wrote vnto her dyuerse lettres/ ⁊ so dyd other two popes after hym/ with many bysshops/ ⁊ the holy fader also saynt Barnard wrote vnto her/ ⁊ she was of hygh pfeccyon and many myracles bothe in her lyfe ⁊ after. The feest also of many other holy sayntes/ marṛ. confes. ⁊ virg.

⁋ To morowe.

⁋ The .xxiij. daye of Iune. The vigyll of saynt Iohn baptist. The feest also of saynt Iohñ a preest/ yᵗ by Iu[lian the apostata at rome in salary strete was brought before the [*fo. lxix.* ydoll of the sonne/ ⁊ bycause he wolde not do sacrefyce thervnto/ he was heded. In tusce at vtryne the feest of saynt Felix a preest ⁊ martyr/ yᵗ by yᵉ mayre Tracius was beten vpon yᵉ mouth wᵗ stones/ bycause he confessed Chryst/ tyll he was deed.

Saynt Audre.
In brytayn the feest of saynt Etheldrede a virgyn ⁊ quene/ whose holy body .xj. yeres after her buryall was foūde hole ⁊ vncorrupte.

⁋ Addicyons.

⁋ The feest also of saynt Iulian a martyr/ that in the age of xviij. yeres suffred many turmentes for Chrystes fayth/ ⁊ at the last he was knytte in a sacke full of serpentes ⁊ sond ⁊ so cast in to the see/ whose holy body was cast vpon the londe ⁊ foūde by myracle. The feest also of saynt Marie of cegnies/ that in yᵉ age of .xij. yeres was maryed cōtrary her wyll/ notw'standyng yet she lyued so holy a lyfe/ that by her example ꝯ mocyon her housbond made a vowe of chastite/ ꝯ she lyued sole a meruaylous strayte lyfe/ ꝯ had reuelacyons/ ꝯ was often visyted with aūgels/ ꝯ by our blessed lady/ saynt Iohn̄ the euangelyst/ wᵗ other yᵗ were seen aboute her at her deth/ ꝯ after her deth they mette her wᵗ a multitude of aūgels ꝯ cōuayed her soule vnto blysse. In the terrytory of leodicens .vj. myles from yᵉ cite/ nere vnto a monastery of virgyns called erkenrode yᵉ feest of saȳt Elizabeth a virgyn/ of meruaylous holynes and hygh pfeccyon/ she was enrapt .vij. tymes euery day/ ꝯ yᵗ in a synguler ꝯ meruaylous maner/ ꝯ had the woūdes of Chryst in her hādes/ fete ꝯ syde/ after yᵉ same maner ꝯ quantite as he had ꝯ suffred in maner lyke turmentes in euery parte of her body/ ꝯ was of many myracles. The feest also of many other holy sayntes/ marꝑ. ꝯc.

[ꝯ To morowe.   [*fo. lxix. b.*

ꝯ The .xxiiij. day of Iune. the natiuite of saynt Iohn̄ baptist the precursor ꝯ fore messenger of our sauyour/ of whome he sayd amonge the childer of women goten by the sede of man/ none was borne of more sanctite ꝯ auctorite than Iohn̄ baptist. In yᵉ terrytory of parys in cristoyle strete the passyon of saynt Agohard ꝯ saynt Gylbert/ wᵗ other chrystyans in maner vnnombrable. At austudune† yᵉ deposycyon of saynt Symplicy a bysshop ꝯ confessour.   ꝯ Addicyons.

ꝯ In englond the feest of saynt Bartholomewe borne in the north partyes ꝯ a monke of duram/ that in his chyldhode had reuelacyons/ ꝯ after he reysed two persones from deth/ with many other grete myracles. At rome the feest of saynt Lucey a virgyn/ ꝯ of saynt Aucy† a kynge bothe martyrs togyder/ whiche sayd kyng in his warres toke the sayd virgyn prysoner/ and for her beauty he wolde haue had her vnto paramour/ and so mysused her/ she coūseyled hym nay/ for I haue (sayd she) a spouse ꝯ housbond that wyll reuenge yᵗ vylany ꝯ enormite/ by whiche wordes he restrayned his appetyte/ ꝯ was affrayd to touche her/ ꝯ suffred her to lyue after her owne maner of Chrystes lawe/ ꝯ so holy her lyfe was/ that by her example he was cōuerted/ ꝯ by her monycyon had by reuelacyon he forsoke his kyngdom ꝯ went wᵗ her to rome/ where they bothe togyder for yᵉ cōfessyon of Chryst were put to deth by yᵉ swerde. Here is also remembred the feest of two holy faders of the olde testament saynt Ezechye ꝯ saynt Iosye bothe kynges of Icrusalem. The feest also of many oth. ꝯc.

⁋ To morowe.

⁋ The .xxv. day of Iune. at puricoroea⁺ yᵉ feest of saynt [Sosipater discyple vnto the apostle Paule. In alexander [*fo. lxx.* the feest of saynt Gallicane a martyr/ yᵗ was a noble warryour/ ⁊ for his victoryous dedes of armes he was in grete fauour with the emperour Constancy/ ⁊ there was he conuerted vnto Chrystes fayth by saynt Constance the emperours doughter/ ⁊ by yᵉ coūseyle of the holy martyrs Iohñ ⁊ Paule/ than he left yᵉ worlde ⁊ was of suche pfeccyon that many psones came from dyuerse coūtrees by the fame yᵗ spredde of hym/ to se ⁊ lerne at hym/ ⁊ moche they meruayled to se hym that was somtyme a cōsull of rome ⁊ of so noble blode/ now to knele ⁊ wasshe poore mennes fete/ couer theyr table/ dresse theyr mete/ ⁊ gyue them water vnto theyr handes/ ⁊ so mynyster vnto them/ specyally vnto yᵉ seke in all thynges/ as though he had ben theyr bond seruaūt but moche more were they edifyed/ to se whan he was accused his grete constaūce vnto yᵉ fayth of Chryst/ for the whiche he gladly suffred dethe/ vnder Iulian the apostata slayne by yᵉ swerde. At rome the feest of saynt Luce a virgyn ⁊ martyr/ and with her xxij. other virgyns. At glocester in englonde the feest of saynt Keneburge a virgyn and a martyr of synguler sanctite.

⁋ Addicyons.

⁋ At venys the inuencyon of saynt Marke the euangelyst/ whan his holy body was foūde by reuelacyon/ in the whiche grete myracles were shewed. The feest also of saynt Prosper a bysshop/ ⁊ a man of grete lernynge/ ⁊ wrote many werkes/ ⁊ cōfoūded many heretykes/ whose holy body .xxxiiij. yeres after his dethe was translated by reuelacyon. In englond the feest of saynt Amphybale a martyr/ yᵗ conuerted saynt Albane yᵉ fyrst martyr of englond/ ⁊ after many yeres he was [put to [*fo. lxx. b.* deth/ ⁊ with hym .M. chrystyans/ whose holy body was foūde after by yᵉ reuelacyon of saynt Albane. In englond also the feest of saynt Milburge a virgyn that was a kynges doughter/ ⁊ syster vnto saynt Mildrede/ ⁊ she was of hygh pfeccyon ⁊ many myracles. The feest also of many other holy sayntes/ marᵗ. ⁊c.

⁋ To morowe.

⁋ The .xxvj. daye of Iune. At rome the feest of saynt Iohñ ⁊ saȳt Paule martyrs/ yᵗ were grete offycers wᵗ saynt Constance yᵉ emperours doughter/ ⁊ by yᵉ tyraūt Iulian receyued the palme of martyrdom slayne by yᵉ swerde. At trientyne⁺ the feest of saȳt Vigily a bysshop ⁊ martyr/ that by the consull Iustilocon⁺ was stoned to deth. In the fraunchest of pictauens the feest of

IVNE.

saynt Maxence a famous man of many myracles. At valenciane the feest of saynt Saluy a martyr and bysshop of ewgolysme. The feest also of saynt Perseuerande a holy virgyn.
⁋ Addicyons.
⁋ The feest also of an other saynt Vigily a bysshop also ⁊ a martyr/ ⁊ a man of grete almes ⁊ pyte/ ⁊ whā he had buylded a chirche ⁊ an hospytall/ he was by a tyraūt put to martyrdom/ whose holy body forthw^t after his deth dyd grete myracles. The feest also of ye thyrde saynt Vigily pope ⁊ martyr/ that in his begynnynge was ambicyous/ but after he was cōtryte/ he was a grete post of ye chirche/ ⁊ in a generall sene cōdempned many heretikes/ ⁊ for the fayth suffred deth. The feest also of the fourth saynt Vigily a deacon/ ⁊ a monke of hygh pfeccyon. The feest also of many other holy . ⁊c.

⁋ To morowe.

⁋ The .xxvij. day of Iune. At galace the feest of saynt Crescent discyple vnto saynt Paule/ and he preched in fraūce/ ⁊ after returned agayn to galace where he had [chefe [*fo. lxxi.* cure/ ⁊ there by his holy conuersacyon he moche edifyed vnto ye ende of his lyfe. In ytaly at tyburtyne the feest of saynt Symphorose/ w^t her .vij. sones/ saynt Crescent/ saynt Iulian/ saynt Nemele/ saynt Primytyue/ saynt Iustyne/ saynt Stacte/ ⁊ saynt Eugyn/ all martyrs/ whiche holy moder confortynge her chylder to dye for Chryst by meruaylous wordes ⁊ grete constancy/ was fyrst put vnto turment/ beten/ scourged/ racked/ ⁊ after many variaūt affliccyons she was tyed vnto a mylstone ⁊ so drowned/ and her sones eche after other put to meruaylous paynes ⁊ deth/ whiche ioyfully they toke for Chryst. At corduba the feest of saynt zoyle a martyr/ whose holy lyfe after longe tyme was foūde by reuelacyon made vnto saynt Agapy bysshop of the same cite. At glassenbury the translacyon of saȳt Bemonus† a confessour. ⁋ Addicyons.
⁋ The feest also of an other saynt zoyle a preest of holy lyfe/ that by the reuelacyon of saynt Grisogone knewe before the daye of his deth. The feest also of saynt Benygne a confessour. And of many other holy saynt̄ .⁊c.

⁋ To morowe.

⁋ The .xxviij. daye of Iune. the vigyll of the apostles Peter ⁊ Paule. And ye feest of saynt Leo pope ⁊ doctour. At lyons in fraunce the feest of saynt Hyrene bysshop ⁊ martyr/ that (as saynt Ierom wryteth) was discyple vnto saȳt Policarpe/ ⁊ nere vnto the tyme of Chrystes dyscyples/ whiche saynt Hyrene was put to martyrdom by the emperour Seuere/ ꝓ with hym nerehand all the people of his cite. At alexander the feest of saynt Plutarke/ saynt Serene/ saynt Heraclide/ saynt Heroys/ saynt Potānant ꝓ saynt Marcell/ all martyrs/ ꝓ with them other thre psones. The chefe of these mar[tyrs was the holy [*fo. lxxi. b.* virgyn saynt Potānant/ that for the custody of her virgynite suffred many harde and meruaylous batayles/ ꝓ after for Chryst innumerable turmentes/ suche as neuer before were seen ne herde of/ ꝓ after all she was brent. ❡ Addicyons.

❡ The feest also of an other sayt Leo/ that was thyrde pope of that name/ at whose entre was herde yᵉ voyce of an aungell/ ꝓ yet notwᵗstandynge he was after yᵗ by fals accusacyon taken/ ꝓ his eyes put out ꝓ his tongue kytte/ ꝓ so nere deed put in to a monastery/ where the same nyght he was restored as well vnto pfyte helth as vnto his speche ꝓ syght/ ꝓ after contynued pope many yeres in holy lyfe/ synguler perfeccyon ꝓ myracles. The feest also of many other holy sayntes/ marꝑ. ꝓc.

❡ To morowe.

❡ The .xxix. day of Iune. At rome yᵉ feest of yᵉ apostles Peter ꝓ Paule/ that bothe in one day were put to deth by the tyraunt Nero whan Baske ꝓ Tuske were consulles. Saynt Peter lyeth buryed nere vnto the strete triumphall/ where he is honoured of all chrystyans/ ꝓ saynt Paule in lyke honour lyeth in ostiens strete. At yᵉ castell of argentomate the feest of saynt Marcell a martyr/ ꝓ with hȳ was put to deth saynt Anastace a man of warre. In the terrytory of senony the feest of saynt Benedicte a holy blessed virgyn of many myracles.

❡ Addicyons.

❡ The feest also of saynt Casse a bysshop of holy lyfe/ of whome sayt Gregory wryteth in his dialoges And the feest of sayt Beate a virgyn of grete merytes. The feest also of many other holy sayntes/ mar. cōf. ꝓ virg.

❡ To morowe.

❡ The .xxx. daye of Iune. the cōmemoracyon of saynt [Paule/ that wᵗ saynt Peter was crucifyed/ ꝓ yet he [*fo. lxxii.* ended his martyrdom by yᵉ swerde/ so that (as saynt Augustyn wryteth) they dyed bothe in one day ꝓ one tyme ꝓ not as some heretykes done saye at dyuerse tymes or dyuerse dayes. At rome also the feest of yᵉ holy woman saynt Lucyne/ that was discyple vnto yᵉ apostles. In lemonigat the feest of saynt

Marciall a bysshop ꝛ martyr/ yᵗ was discyple vnto our lorde/ ꝛ wᵗ hym saynt Alpymany ꝛ saȳt Stratocliane two honourable preestes ꝛ of holy lyfe/ noble fame ꝛ grete myracles. In ytaly yᵉ feest of saynt Corsite a preest/ ꝛ saynt Leo a deacon. In the terrytory of viuariens the feest of saynt Ostiane a preest ꝛ martyr. ☛ Addicyons.

☛ The feest also of an other saynt Lucyne a holy matrone of grete almes ꝛ moche charite vnto all chrystyans/ for the whiche the emperour Maximian put her vnto exile ꝛ vnto many affliccyons/ ꝛ so vnto yᵉ palme of martyrdom. The feest also of many other holy .ꝛc̗.

☛ Iuly.

☛ To morowe.

Iuly. THe fyrst day of Iuly. In the moūt of hor yᵉ feest ꝛ deposicyon of saynt Aaron/ the fyrst preest of the olde lawe/ that was cōsecrate by Moyses. In the terrytory of lyons the deposicyon of saynt Domiciane an abbot/ that fyrst in those partyes exercysed yᵉ lyfe of heremytes/ ꝛ he gadered many breder vnto the same p̃feccyon/ ꝛ so contynued famous in vertue ꝛ gloryous in myracles. At engolysme the feest of saynt Eparchy a monke ꝛ confessour. In the fraūchest of cenomānyke the feest of saynt Carylef a preest. In yᵉ terrytory of remens the feest of saynt Theodoryke a cōfessour/ ꝛ the octaue of saynt Iohñ baptist. ☛ Addicyons.

[☛ The feest also of Mary the prophetysse/ syster [fo. lxxii. b. vnto Moyses ꝛ Aaron/ that as Moyses was guyder of the men ꝛ amonge yᵉ childer of israell/ so was she of the women. The feest also of saynt Eleazar preest and sone vnto Aaron ꝛ his successour/ and the feest of saynt Phynees his sone ꝛ successour. In englond the feest of saynt Aaron ꝛ saynt Iule martyrs/ yᵗ in the passyon of saynt Albane were cōuerted/ ꝛ this day wᵗ many other chrystyans put to dethe. The feest also of saynt Theobald a confessour/ that was a noble man ꝛ of grete rychesse/ ꝛ all forsoke for Chryst/ ꝛ lyued an heremyte of singuler sanctite and many myracles. The feest also of saynt Pambo an abbot vnlerned/ ꝛ he came vnto a clerke purposynge to lerne a psalme to serue god wᵗ/ ꝛ the clerke was than in redynge this psalme Dixi custodiā vias meas vt nō delinquā in lingua mea. The holy fader axed hym the sentence of that verse/ ꝛ he answered thus it is to meane. I haue made sure p̃messe that I wyll kepe well ꝛ take good hede vnto my wayes ꝛ passage of my lyf/ so yᵗ by no meanes I offende or faute in my tongue or speche. And therwᵗ he departed ꝛ wolde lerne no more/ halfe a yere after yᵉ clerke axed why he wold not lerne ferther/ and he answered/ I haue not yet (sayd he) truly fulfilled that lesson. This holy fader by chaunce sawe a comyn woman apparayle her selfe/ wherw^t he bytterly wept/ ⁊ whan the cause was axed he answered/ two thynges (sayd he) done cause me to wepe/ one for the soule of this woman/ the other/ that I was neuer so diligēt to please god/ as she is to please the worlde. He was also of grete abstinence/ ⁊ synguler in sylence. The feest also of saynt Leonore a bysshop ⁊ cōfessour. And of many other holy sayntes/ mart̃. ⁊c̃.

[❡ To morowe. [*fo. lxxiii.*

❡ The second day of Iuly. At rome in auriel strete the feest of saynt Processe ⁊ saynt Martiniane martyrs/ y^t were baptized of saynt Peter/ and by the tyraūt Nero they were knocked vpon the mouth w^t stones for ye confessynge of Chryst/ than hāged vpon gybettes/ racked/ scourged/ enflambed w^t fyre/ cast vnto scorpyons ⁊ venymous serpentes/ ⁊ after all turmentes slayne by the swerde. The feest also of thre men of warre that were put to deth w^t saynt Paule ye apostle. The feest also of saynt Aristion/ saynt Crescenciane/ saynt Ewticiane/ saynt Vrbane/ saynt Vran†/ saynt Vitale/ saynt Iust/ saynt Felicissym/ saynt Felix/ ⁊ the holy women saynt Marcy ⁊ saynt Symphorose martyrs/ all put to deth togyder in campane. At turon the feest of saynt Monegunde a virgyn. In englonde at wynchester ye deposicyon of saynt Swythune a preest of hygh perfeccyon/ whose holy body was founde by reuelacyon/ ⁊ therby many people cured/ ⁊ grete myracles done/ not onely there but also in dyuerse partes of englonde. The feest also of our blessed lady saynt Mary called ye visitacyon. ❡ Addicyons.

❡ At landaf in wales the feest of saynt Ondoce a bysshop of grete sanctite ⁊ many myracles/ amonge whiche is notable/ that whan he sholde drynke ⁊ lacked a cuppe/ he fourmed the fashon of a goblet of butter that stode before hy̅/ ⁊ therein he dranke/ ⁊ after it so remayned ⁊ semed all gold/ ⁊ so yet it doth/ ⁊ is there reserued as a holy relyke. The feest also of many other holy .⁊c̃.

❡ To morowe.

❡ The thyrde day of Iuly. In mesopotamye at edisse the translacyon of the holy apostle saynt Thomas. At [geneocesarepont ye feest of saynt Gregory bysshop ⁊ confessour [*fo. lxxiii. b.* of synguler vertue/ ⁊ gloryous in myracles/ y^t amonge other in buylding of a chirche/ where a grete hyll was noyous thervnto/ he by prayer remoued the hyll. At clusyne the feest of say̅t

IVLY.

Hyreney a deacon/ ꝥ of the noble matrone saynt Mustiole/ yᵗ by the prince Aurelian were bothe togyder put to martyrdom. In syre at laodice yᵉ feest of saynt Anathole a bisshop of famous doctryne/ ꝥ made many werkes/ not onely of philosophy/ but also of good religyon. At alexander the feest of saynt Triphon/ ꝥ with hym other .xij. chrystyans all martyrs. At cōstantynople the feest of saynt Euloge a confessour of hygh merytes.

⁋ Addicyons.

⁋ The feest also of another saynt Gregory bysshop of lingoniens/ yᵗ fyrst was a maryed man/ ꝥ after of high pfeccyon ꝥ grete myracles/ ꝥ had reuelaciōs/ at whose deth heuē was seen open/ ꝥ he therinto receyued. The feest also of saynt Heliodour a bysshop/ yᵗ by the reuelacyon of an augell cōuerted in his prechyng a grete coūtre/ he had also the spiryte of prophecy/ ꝥ was of grete myracles. The feest also of saynt Lanfranke an abbot ꝥ confessour/ a man of grete lernynge/ yᵗ in the presence of the pope cofoūded an heretyke/ he had also the spiryte of prophecy/ ꝥ was of many myracles. The feest also of many other holy sayntes/ marꝰ. confes. ꝥ virg.

⁋ To morowe.

⁋ The .iiij. day of Iuly. yᵉ feest of yᵉ holy pphete saynt Osee. At turon yᵉ trāslacion of saynt Martyn bysshop ꝥ cōfessour/ in the whiche daye also he was electe ꝥ cōsecrate bysshop. In affryke the feest of saynt Iocūdiane a martyr. In smyrme yᵉ feest of saȳt Innocent ꝥ saynt Sebaste/ wᵗ other .xxx. chrystyans all martyrs. In the [terrytory of byture the feest of [*fo. lxxiiii.* saynt Laureane a martyr/ whose holy heed was brought in to spayne vnto yᵉ cite of hyspale. The deposicyon also of saynt Vldaryke called also Odalryke a bysshop ꝥ cōfessour. In yᵉ hygh monastery of villaren/ the comynge ꝥ solempne receyuynge of the relykes of saynt Policarpe/ saynt Sebastiane/ saynt Vrbane/ ꝥ saynt Quiryne all martyrs. ⁋ Addicyons.

⁋ Here is remembred yᵉ feest of all the .xij. prophetes/ but specially of the holy pphete Aggey. At orlyauce yᵉ feest of saynt Argentary a monke/ that amonge other signes of sanctite reysed a man frō deth/ as saynt Gregory wryteth in his dialoges. The feest also of ma. ꝥc.

lib. iij.
ca. xvij

⁋ To morowe.

⁋ The .v. day of Iuly. In syre yᵉ feest of saynt Domicy a martyr of hygh meryte as his dayly myracles done shewe. At rome yᵉ feest of yᵉ reuerend matrone saynt zoe/ that bycause she praysed the vertue of saynt Peter was put in harde prison/ ⁊ after many cruell turmentes she was hanged wᵗ her owne heere/ ⁊ a grete stynkynge smoke made vnder her/ ⁊ so put to martyrdom. The feest also of saynt Modwen a holy virgin of hygh perfeccyon ⁊ grete myracles. ℂ Addicyons.

ℂ The feest also of the grete clerke saynt Ancelme that was borne in englond/ ⁊ buryed in london. The feest also of an other saynt Ancelme borne in burgoyne/ a bysshop of grete doctryne/ ⁊ made many werkes/ ⁊ was of many myracles. The feest also of saynt Hugh abbot of cluniacence/ of whome beyng in his moders wombe reuelacyon was made vnto a preest that sayd masse for her/ ⁊ he after was a monke ⁊ had reuelacyons/ ⁊ he sawe our blessed lady dryue ⁊ chace awaye the deuyll [from his monastery/ at whose deth she was seen/ and [*fo. lxxiiii. b.* with her saynt Martyn/ saynt Benet/ wᵗ other sayntes ⁊ aūgels innumerable/ that amonge them caryed his soule vnto blysse. The same daye a lytell before a holy abbot sawe in reuelacyon two beddes made in heuē/ ⁊ whan he axed for whome they were/ the aungels answered/ the one is for saynt Hugh/ ⁊ the other for saynt Ancelme archebysshop of caūterbury. The feest also of saynt Hugh de sctō Victore/ a confessour/ ⁊ a synguler man of lernyng/ that wrote many werkes of grete edificacyon/ ⁊ was of synguler sanctite ⁊ many myracles. The feest also of many other holy sayntes/ marť. ⁊c.

ℂ To morowe.

ℂ The .vj. day of Iuly. In yᵉ iewry the feest of the prophete Esai/ that by the iewes was sawed in sonder in two partes/ and was buryed vnder rogelles oke. The octaue also of the apostles/ ⁊ it is noted/ yᵗ saynt Paule came the same daye fyrst to rome/ in the seconde yere of the cruell tyraūt Nero the emperour. At rome the feest of saynt Tranquillyne a martyr/ yᵗ bycause he praysed the vertue of saynt Paule/ was stoned to deth. In the fraūchest of machiens the feest of saynt Goar a preest ⁊ cōfessour. In englond yᵉ feest of saynt Sexburge a virgyn/ that was syster vnto saynt Etheldrede called saȳt Audre.

ℂ Addicyons.

ℂ The feest also of saynt Kenfrede a deacon ⁊ cōfessour. In the prouynce of valery the feest of saynt Valence a preest/ of
dia. iij. grete fame and many myracles/ of whome saynt
ca. xij. Gregory wryteth in his dialoges. The feest also of many other holy sayntes/ martyrs/ confes. ⁊ virg.

¶ To morowe.

¶ The .vij. day of Iuly. at alexander the feest of saynt [Panten/ a man of vertue ⁊ maner of lyuynge like vnto [*fo. lxxv.* the apostles/ yᵗ for the feruent deuocyon of prechyng went in to the vttermest angyles ⁊ costes of yᵉ eest partyes/ ⁊ cōuerted moche people. At rome yᵉ feest of saynt Nicostrate/ saynt Claudy/ saynt Castar†/ saynt Victoryne/ ⁊saynt Symphoriane/ all martyrs/ that by the iudge Fabiane were sore laboured by the space of thre dayes to forsake Chryst/ ⁊ whā by no meanes he coude haue his purpose/ he cast them all in to yᵉ see. The feest also of saynt Hedde a cōfessour of many myracles. The feest also of saynt Ethelburge/ called saynt Alborowe a holy virgyn/ ⁊ syster vnto saynt Etheldrede .i. Audre.
¶ Addicyons.
¶ The feest also of saynt Nicostrate a martyr/ yᵗ was housbond vnto saynt zoe. The feest also of saȳt Erkengode a virgin/ ⁊ syster vnto saȳt Sexburge/ bothe borne in englonde in kent/ ⁊ she in youth went in to fraūce to be religious (as many gentyles dyd in those dayes) where she lyued a holy lyfe/ and had reuelacyon of her deth/ whose soule was seen openly of many persones cōuayde and caryed in to heuen. The feest also of saynt Grymbald an holy abbot/ yᵗ came out of fraūce to haue the gouernaunce of the monastery of hyde in englond/ nere vnto wynchester/ where he lyeth full of sanctite ⁊ myracles. The feest also of many other holy saynt̄ .⁊c̄.

· ¶ To morowe.

¶ The .viij. daye of Iuly. In the lesse asie the feest of saynt Aquile ⁊ of his wyfe saynt Priscill/ of whome is remem- braūce in the actes of yᵉ apostles. In palestyne the feest of saynt Procope a martyr/ that was brought prisoner
a towne from sanctipole† vnto cesare/ ⁊ there for Chryst by duke Fabian put to deth. The feest also of saynt Ci[liane a martyr. In yᵉ monastery of [*fo. lxxv. b.* wentane the deposicyon of saynt Grūbald a preest ⁊ monke. The feest also of saynt Kyliane/ saynt Colonare† ⁊ saynt Conace† martyrs/ and of saynt Neote a cōfessour. The translacyon also of the holy virgyn saynt Wydburge. ¶ Addicyons.
¶ The feest also of saynt Ciliane a bysshop/ saynt Colonate a preest/ ⁊ saȳt Romane a deacon/ yᵗ by a woman were mur- thered/ whose holy bodyes were foūde by reuelacyon/ ⁊ dyd grete myracles. The feest also of saynt Norbert a bysshop/ a noble man borne/ ⁊ all he forsoke ⁊ was a preest/ ⁊ buylded a

monastery ⁊ began therin a newe religyon of saynt Augustynes order ⁊ was abbot/ after he was made an archebysshop/ ⁊ euer of synguler sanctite ⁊ grete myracles. The feest also of saynt Paule a martyr/ borne in cōstantynople of noble lignage/ ⁊ a duke vnder yᵉ emperour Cōstantyne yᵉ heretyke that bycause he rebuked his heresyes put hym to deth by many turmentes/ whose holy body many yeres after was foūde by reuelacyon/ and dyd grete myracles. The feest also of saynt Iulian a martyr. And of many other holy sayntes/ martyrs/ confessours ⁊ virgyns.

⁋ To morowe.

⁋ The .ix. day of Iuly. at rome in a place where a drop of water cōtynually welleth out/ yᵉ feest of saynt zenon a martyr/ ⁊ with hym .x.M.cciij. moo holy martyrs. The feest also of saynt Ciryll a bysshop ⁊ martyr/ that was cast in to a grete fyre/ ⁊ came out therof after lōge tyme wᵗout noyaūce/ by whiche myracle the iudge for that tyme delyuered hym/ but whan after he herde of his cōtynuall prechynge/ he toke him agayne ⁊ heded hym. At tyre the feest of saynt Anathole a virgyn/ that [after many turmentes was slayne by the swerde/ ⁊ wᵗ [fo. lxxvi. her was heded also saynt Audax. At marcull† yᵉ feest of saynt Brythe† a bysshop ⁊ confessour/ that by his holy lyfe ⁊ prechynge cōuerted moche people/ ⁊ suffred many afflicions/ wherin euer he was cōforted/ somtyme by saynt Peter/ ⁊ somtyme by aūgelles and sayntes.   ⁋ Addicyons.
⁋ The feest also of an other saÿt Ciryl a deacon ⁊ martyr/ yᵗ by yᵉ emperour Cōstance after many turmentes was put to deth/ ⁊ the pagans of cruelty ete his herte and lyuer/ for whiche some of them lost theyr tethe/ ⁊ of some theyr tongues rotted/ ⁊ of some the eyes stert out of theyr hedes. The feest also of saynt zenon an abbot of the desert of thebayde/ where he lyued a holy lyf ⁊ had reuelacyons of aūgels. The feest also of many oth. ⁊c̃.

⁋ To morowe.

⁋ The .x. daye of Iuly. at rome the feest of .vij. breder martyrs/ ⁊ sones vnto saynt Felicite/ yᵗ by the emperour Antonyn were put to dethe/ the fyrst saynt Ianuary was scourged ⁊ racked ⁊ beten to deth wᵗ plūmettes/ ⁊ saynt Felix ⁊ saynt Philip were knocked in the heed wᵗ clubbes. The fourth saynt Syluane was cast downe hedlonge frō a toure toppe/ ⁊ so his necke broken. The other thre saynt Alexander/ saynt Vitale ⁊ saynt Marciall were heded. In affryke the feest of saÿt Ianuary saynt Maryne/ saynt Nabor ⁊ saynt Felix martyrs all heded. At rome yᵉ feest

IVLY.

of saynt Rufyne ⁊ saynt Secūde virgyns/ yᵗ in the psecucyon of yᵉ emperour Valeriane were martyred by the swerde.
❧ Addicyons.

❧ The feest also of saynt Amalberge a virgyn/ ⁊ yᵉ feest of saynt Paterniane a bysshop ⁊ cōfessour/ yᵗ fyrst was an abbot in palestyne/ from whens he wente wᵗ all his [monkes [*fo. lxxvi. b.* by the reuelacyon of the archaūgell Gabryell in to egypte/ where he had many reuelacyons ⁊ many open conflictes wᵗ yᵉ deuyll/ ⁊ knowlege of his deth .xxx. dayes before. The feest also of many other ho. ⁊c̃.

❧ To morowe.

❧ The .xj. day of Iuly. the translacyon of saynt Benet the abbot. In yᵉ lesse armeny at nicopole yᵉ feest of saynt Ianuary ⁊ saynt Pelage martyrs/ that were torne wᵗ hokes ⁊ cast vpon hote syndres/ ⁊ so by .iiij. dayes put to many turmentes ⁊ to deth. At mauritane cesariens yᵉ feest of saynt Marciane a virgyn ⁊ martyr. In the terrytory of senon the feest of saynt Sydron a martyr. In the fraunchest of pictauens the feest of saynt Sabyne. ❧ Addicyons.

❧ The feest also of saynt Pituouse pope/ yᵗ by a reuelacyon shewed vnto saynt Herme/ ordeyned eester day to be kepte alway vpon the sondaye/ wᵗ many other good statutes/ ⁊ after in the psecucyon of yᵉ emperours Antonyne ⁊ Marke he was put to martyrdom. At constantynople yᵉ feest of saynt Ewloge a martyr/ yᵗ was there put to deth/ wᵗ other thre persones. The feest also of an other saȳt Ewloge/ yᵗ by reuelacyō knewe yᵉ thoughtes ⁊ preuy synnes of many psones/ wherby he reuoked ⁊ wᵗdrewe them from vnworthy cōmunion/ ⁊ refourmed theyr fautes/ ⁊ he was of many myracles. At parys yᵉ feest of saȳt Albyne a cōfessour. And of many other .⁊c̃.

❧ To morowe.

❧ The .xij. day of Iuly. In cipris yᵉ feest of saynt Nason/ one of Chrystes dyscyples. In aquiley the feest of saynt Ermagory a bysshop/ yᵗ was discyple vnto saynt Marke yᵉ euangelyst a grete precher/ ⁊ cōuerted many coūtrees by his sanctite ⁊ myracles/ ⁊ at yᵉ last was by [many turmentes put to [*fo. lxxvii.* deth/ ⁊ with hym his archedeacon saynt Fortunate. In cesary the feest of saynt Clyset† a confessour. ❧ Addicyons.

❧ The feest also of saynt Anaclete pope/ that ordeyned by decre that preestes shold be had in honour aboue seculer psones. The feest also of saynt Nabor ⁊ saynt Felix martyrs/ yᵗ by yᵉ emperour Maximian/ after many turmentes were heded. The feest also of many oth. &c.

⁋ To morowe.

⁋ The .xiij. day of Iuly. the feest of saynt Ioell ⁊ saȳt Esdre yᵉ prophetes. In macedony yᵉ feest of saynt Syle discyple vnto the apostles/ ⁊ one of the fyrst yᵗ by them was assigned to preche/ wherin he had grete ⁊ synguler grace/ ⁊ toke grete labours wᵗ dylygence/ ⁊ so rested in our lord. In affryke yᶜ feest of saynt Eugene bysshop of cartage/ a famous man ⁊ a martyr. And the feest of saynt Salutary an archedeacon/ ⁊ saȳt Murite an offycer wᵗ the sayd bisshop/ that wᵗ hym were put to deth ⁊ wᵗ them other psones vnto the nombre of .v.C. of dyuerse degrees ⁊ age/ as wel childer as men/ that were put to many varyaūt turmentes/ ⁊ thre tymes examyned them in the same turmentes/ after exile/ for yᵉ whiche they obteyned a synguler laude ⁊ prayse of cōstancy ⁊ perseuerauce. In the lesse brytayn yᵉ feest of saynt Thuran/ a bysshop ⁊ cōfessour of meruaylous playne maners/ symple and innocent. In englond the feest of saynt Mildrede a virgyn of grete holynes. ⁋ Addicyons.

⁋ Here ben remembred the feestes of certayne faders of the olde testament/ saynt zorobabell duke ⁊ prynce of the trybe of Iude. Saynt Iesus ioiedeke†/ that in his tyme was yᵉ hygh preest of the iewes. Saynt Neemie [the prophete. In [*fo. lxxvii. b.* englond the feest of saynt Iuthware a virgyn/ that by her stepmoder was falsly accused vnto her owne broder of fornicacyon/ for the whiche in a fury he stroke of her heed/ whiche heed she her self toke vp before hym ⁊ all his people/ and there sprange vp a well ⁊ a grene tree growyng therby/ than bare she her heed in to the chirche/ were after were shewed many grete myracles. The feest also of many other holy .&c.

⁋ To morowe.

⁋ The .xiiij. day of Iuly. At pont yᵉ feest of saynt Foke bysshop of synopole†/ that by the emperour Traianus was imprysoned ⁊ strayned wᵗ bandes/ ⁊ after many other turmentes/ he was fettred/ ⁊ so cast in to a grete fyre ⁊ brent. At alexander yᵉ feest of saynt Eracle a bysshop of so grete a name
a wryter ⁊ fame/ that (as Affrycane the historiagraph†
of storyes writeth) he hymselfe wᵗ many other persones came from dyuerse ferre coūtrees to se hym and speke with hym. In fraūce at lyons the deposicyon of saynt Iust ⁊ saynt Amyke. The feest also of saȳt Phocate a bysshop/ ⁊ of saynt Donate a martyr of singuler pacyence.

¶ Addicyons.

¶ The feest also of saynt Henry ye emperour/ a man of hygh pfeccion ⁊ many myracles/ ⁊ euer he lyued a clene virgyn with his wyfe saynt Cūgund a virgyn also whome notw^tstādyng by false accusacyon he suspected of aduoutry/ but she for ye declaracyon of her virgynite went .xv. steppes vpon fyrehote yren w^tout noyaunce. The feest also of many other holy sayntes/ marť. ⁊c̑.

¶ To morowe.

¶ The .xv. daye of Iuly. At misybbet the feest of saynt Iames a bisshop of synguler vertue ⁊ notable lernyng that was one of the doctours y^t in the psecucyon of the [em- [*fo. lxxviii.* perour Maximus at the grete coūseyle of nice/ dyd by diuyne disputacyon cōfoūde ⁊ cōdempne ye dampnable opinion ⁊ peruerse heresy of the grete heretyke Arrius. At rome in a gate ye feest of saynt Eutrope/ saynt zosymy ⁊ saynt Bonose all naturall systers ⁊ martyrs. At cartage the feest of saynt Catulyne a deacon/ saynt Ianuary his felowe/ ⁊ of ye holy women saynt Florēce saynt Iule ⁊ saynt Iuste/ all martyrs togyder/ ⁊ buryed in saynt Faustes chirche. At alexander the feest of saynt Philip/ saynt zenon ⁊ saynt Narsey/ w^t .x. yonge infantes al martyrs. The trāslacion also of sayt Swythune a bysshop of synguler vertue ⁊ many myracles/ whiche dayly ben shewed at his tombe. In englonde the feest of saynt Deusdedit/ y^t is to say/ saynt godgaue the syxth archebysshop of caūterbury after saynt Augustyne a holy man. ¶ Addicyons.

¶ This daye also is remembred ye diuisyon ⁊ insonder departynge of the .xij. apostles in to the worlde abrode to preche ye fayth of Chryst. The feest also of the .lxxij. disciples/ wherin they ben all togyder honoured. The feest also of saynt Quiryke a childe of the age of .iij. yeres/ ⁊ of his moder saynt Iulit/ that by the emperour Alexander were put to martyrdome. The feest also of many other holy sayntes/ martyrs/ cōfes. ⁊ virgyns.

¶ To morowe.

¶ The .xvj. daye of Iuly. In syre at antioche the feest of saynt Eustache a bysshop ⁊ cōfessour/ y^t by the emperour Constantyne was for Chryst put to exile in to intrapolet in trace/ ⁊ there rested in our lord. At oste ye feest of saynt Hyllaryne a monke ⁊ martyr/ that in the persecucyon of ye emperour Iulian the apostata/ bycause he wolde not do sacrefyce vnto the ydolles/ was beten [with clubbes to deth. [*fo. lxxviii. b.*

¶ Addicyons.

¶ The feest also of saynt Leo ye fourth pope of y^t name that moche edifyed the fayth of Chryst/ in whose tyme englond was fyrst vnder one kyng/ called kyng Aldulf that went in pylgrymage vnto rome/ ꝛ he than graūted the Peter pens/ that yet in englond ben payd. The feest also of many other holy sayntes/ marꝛ. confes. ꝛc.

¶ To morowe.

¶ The .xvij. day of Iuly. In cartage the feest of saynt Sperate/ saynt Nartaby/ saynt Betury/ saynt Felix/ saynt Stytyny†/ saynt Aquilyne/ saynt Letace/ saynt Ianuary/ ꝛ of ye holy women also saynt Generose/ saȳt Bessia/ saȳt Donate ꝛ saynt Secūde all martyrs togyder/ that by the mayre of stillicitane† were after many turmentes all put vpon ye crosse as Chryst theyr mayster/ but there coude they not dye/ ꝛ therfore they were taken downe ꝛ heded. In englond the passyon of saynt Kenelme kynge and martyr. At rome the feest of saynt Alexy a confessour. ¶ Addicyons.

¶ The feest also of saynt Maryne a virgyn/ that was a monke in ye clothynge of a man/ ꝛ that was accused of fornicacyon ꝛ getynge of a chylde by a yonge woman/ for the whiche she suffred moche affliccyon in moost high pacyence. The feest also of ye holy woman saynt Theodour/ y^t was maryed vnto a vertuous man/ ꝛ bycause she was yonge ꝛ of excellent beauty/ she was sore assayled of an other vngracyous man/ y^t at the last deceyued ꝛ brought her vnto auoutry/ for ye whiche one acte she toke suche cōtricyon ꝛ repentaūce/ y^t she stale away from her housbond in his clothynge vnto a monastery and there was a monke of grete penaūce ꝛ hygh pfeccyon ꝛ many myracles/ whome the deuyll so enuyed [that he caused a woman [*fo. lxxix.* goten w^t chylde to accuse her therof/ for the whiche .vij. yeres she lay at ye monastery gate ꝛ nourysshed the chylde w^t cowes mylke/ ꝛ in the meane tyme many open batayles had she w^t the deuyll. At the ende of whiche .vij. yeres the abbot for pite toke her agayne ꝛ her childe w^t her/ where she lyued holyly two yeres/ ꝛ than enclosed her selfe ꝛ the chylde also as an ancre/ whome whan she had brought vp ꝛ clothed a monke/ she blessedly departed/ ꝛ thā was foūde a woman/ vnto whome her owne housbond was brought by reuelacyon/ ꝛ in ye same sell a monke/ ended his lyfe in hygh pfeccyon/ ꝛ the chylde was after abbot of the monastery. The feest also of many other holy sayn. ꝛc.

¶ To morowe.

¶ The .xviij. daye of Iuly. At cartage ye feest of saynt Gūdene a holy woman ⁊ a martyr/ yt by the iudge Rufyne was iiij. tymes racked/ ⁊ her flesshe torne wt hokes/ ⁊ at ye last slayne by the swerde. At dorostre ye feest of saynt Emyliane a confessour. The feest also of saynt Aquilyne a bysshop. At wentane ye feest of saynt Eadburge a virgyn. The feest also of saȳt Arnulph a martyr. And of saynt Symphorose a matrone wt her seuen sones all martyrs/ of meruayllous pacyence and gloryous triumphe. ¶ Addicyons.
¶ The feest also of saynt Rophyle a bysshop of holy lyf and many myracles/ ⁊ had knowlege by reuelacyon of his deth day. The feest also of saynt Filiaster a preest ⁊ a noble precher/ that by his holynes ⁊ myracles cōuerted moche people/ bothe of the iewes ⁊ gentyles/ ⁊ reuoked also many from the heresy of the arrianes. The feest also of many other holy sayntes/ mar. cōf. ⁊ virg.

¶ To morowe.

[¶ The .xix. day of Iuly. the feest of saynt [*fo. lxxix. b.* Epafre/ that by saȳt Paule was made bysshop of colose/ where for the defence of his flocke he receyued the palme of martyrdom. At thebaydes the feest of the holy fader saynt Arseny/ that (as is wryten in ye collacyons of ye olde faders) had cōtynually a sudary to wype the aboūdaūce of his flowynge teres. In spayne at hyspale ye passion of saynt Iustyn ⁊ saynt Rufyne virgyns/ that by the mayre Diogemant were racked ⁊ theyr flesshe torne wt hokes/ ⁊ so put in to prison/ where saynt Iustyne dyed ⁊ saynt Rufyne was heded. ¶ Addicyons.
¶ In the monastery of saynt Peter at prenestyne the feest of an holy abbot whose name we can not fynde/ yt brought vp a discyple vnto hygh pfeccyon/ that euery daye wrought vpon the makynge of his owne graue/ vnto whome the abbot gaue cōmaūdement yt he sholde bury hym in that graue. The discyple answered that he sholde dye soone after hȳ/ ⁊ there was not space for bothe. The abbot sayd yes/ it shall serue vs bothe. so whan anone after the abbot he was brought deed vnto the graue/ one of his felowes pccyuynge there was not space/ sayd/ here is not rome sufficyent. The deed corps answered ⁊ sayd yes/ ⁊ therwt turned vpon the one syde/ ⁊ so the other corps was layd therby/ where ben done many myracles. The feest also of many .⁊c.

⁋ To morowe.

⁋ The .xx. day of Iuly. yᵉ feest of saynt Ioseph/ whose symamᴇ was iust or ryghtwyse/ one of yᵉ discyples of Chryst/ ⁊ a grete precher/ ⁊ had moche persecucyon/ he dranke poyson after some auctours as dyd saȳt Iohñ without noyaūce. In damaske the feest of saynt Sabyne/ saynt Maximy/ saynt Iulian/ saynt Macroʟy/ [saynt Cassy/ ⁊ of the holy women [*fo. lxxx.* saynt Paule ⁊ saynt Cassye/ wᵗ other .x. psones all martyrs togyder. In the fraūchest of bononye yᵉ feest of Vlmare a confessour. In antioche the feest of saynt Margarete a virgyn ⁊ martyr/ yᵗ suffred passyon vnder iudge Olibry. ⁋ Addicyons.
⁋ At corduba the feest of saynt Paule a deacon ⁊ martyr. In englonde at glocester the feest of saynt Aryld a virgyn and martyr. In the monastery of the same glocester the feest of saynt Modmund a martyr. The feest also of many other holy sayntes/ marẽ. confes. ⁊ virg.

⁋ To morowe.

⁋ The .xxj. day of Iuly. the feest of saynt Daniell the prophete. At rome yᵉ feest of saynt Praxede a virgyn of pure chastite/ cōtynuall exercyse/ ⁊ of grete lernyng/ yᵗ lyeth buryed in salary strete besyde her syster saȳt Potenciane. In fraūce at massyle the feest of saynt Victor a martyr/ yᵗ was a man of warre/ ⁊ bycause he wolde not fyght agaynst chrystyans/ nor yet do sacrefyce vnto the ydolles/ he was put in a paynful pryson/ where he had conforte ⁊ visitacyon of aūgels/ ⁊ after he was put to many varyaūt turmentes/ ⁊ at the last he was cast bytwene two mylstones/ ⁊ so crusshed ⁊ brused to deth/ ⁊ with hym saynt Alexander/ saynt Feliciane/ ⁊ saynt Longyne men of warre also/ were put to dethe. At trecas the feest of saynt Iule a virgyn ⁊ martyr. ⁋ Addicyons.
⁋ The feest also of an other saynt Daniell an abbot of egypte/ of hygh pfeccion ⁊ many myracles/ of whome is wryten in vitas patrum. At rome the feest of saynt Acoucy that was keper of saynt Peters chirche a very meke. man ⁊ of grete grauite/ that cured a seke mayde [by the reuelacyon [*fo. lxxx. b.* of saynt Peter/ wᵗ many other myracles. The feest also of many other holy saynẽ. mar. ⁊c̃.

⁋ To morowe.

⁋ The .xxij. day of Iuly. the deposicyon of saynt Mary magdalene/ vnto whome our sauyour after his resurreccyon fyrst appered/ wherof she brought the fyrst tydynges ⁊ knowlege vnto yᵉ apostles/ ⁊ after she preched ⁊ cōuerted moche people/ dyd many myracles/ ⁊ lyued alone in desert/ ⁊ after all she was a whyle conuersaūt wᵗ saynt Maximy bisshop of aquens/ in whose chirche after she had receyued the sacramentes/ she in prayer yelded her spiryte/ where he buryed her in a reuerend tombe/ ⁊ after made a goodly chirche ouer the same/ where after he was buryed hymselfe. The feest also of saynt Wandregesyle a cōfessour. In syret at galast yᵉ feest of saynt Plato a martyr/ of holy lyf ⁊ myracles. The feest also of saȳt Synticen a virgyn/ whome saynt Paule remēbreth in his epystles/ ⁊ she lyeth buryed at phylypes.   ☙ Addicyons.

☙ The feest also of an other saynt wandregesyle/ that was a maryed man ⁊ a duke of noble blode/ ⁊ for deuocyon he pswaded his wyfe to kepe her virgynite/ by yᵉ whiche she was pfessed in to religyon/ ⁊ he a monke/ ⁊ after abbot of grete holynes. The feest also of saynt Meneley a confessour. And of many other holy sa. ⁊c̃.

☙ To morowe.

☙ The .xxiij. day of Iuly. the feest of saynt Apolynare a bysshop/ cōsecrate by saynt Peter/ ⁊ sent vnto rauen to preche/ where for Chryst he was put to deth by many cruell turmentes. At rome yᵉ deposicyon of our holy moder saynt Birgit.
☙ Addicyons.

☙ The feest also of another saynt Apolynare/ bysshop [of Ierusalemt ⁊ a cōfessour/ a man of synguler vertue [fo. lxxxi. and notable doctryne/ that (as saynt Ierom writeth) made many pfytable werkes/ specyally agaynst heretykes. The feest also of many other holy saynt. ⁊c̃.

☙ To morowe.

☙ The .xxiiij. day of Iuly. At rome in tiburtyne strete the feest of saynt Vincent a martyr. In spayne at emerite yᵉ feest of saynt Victor a man of warre/ that wᵗ his two breder saynt Sterkace ⁊ saynt Antiogene by dyuerse grete turmentes were put vnto martyrdom. In ytaly at tyre yᵉ feest of saȳt Chrystyne a virgyn ⁊ martyr/ that by two iudges was put to meruaylous turmentes/ ⁊ the thyrde iudge kytte her tongue ⁊ bounde her vnto a stake ⁊ let yᵉ archers shote her to deth with arowes. The feest also of saynt Nicete ⁊ saynt Aquile virgyns ⁊ martyrs/ yᵗ were conuerted by saynt Chrystofre/ and for Chryst heded. At amitermyn the feest of .lxxxiij. sowdyours. The vigyll also of saynt Iames yᵉ apostle.

⁋ Addicyons.

⁋ The feest also of saynt Vrsysyne/ ⁊ of saynt Panace bothe bysshops. The feest also of saynt Vince a confessour. And the feest also of many other holy saynt̃. ⁊c.

⁋ To morowe.

⁋ The .xxv. day of Iuly. the feest of saynt Iames the apostle/ broder vnto saynt Iohñ the euāgelyst/ y{t} was heded by kyng Herode/ whose holy bones were trāslated out of Ierusalem in to spayne/ ⁊ there ben had in grete reuerēce. In syret at samon y{e} feest of saynt Chrystofre a martyr/ that was beten with roddes/ racked/ ⁊ his flesshe torne ⁊ rent w{t} hokes/ ⁊ so cast hedlonge in to a grete fyre/ ⁊ all by the myght of Chryst he vaynquysshed/ than was he shotte full of arowes/ ⁊ at the [last heded. At bartimont the feest of saynt Cucu- [*fo. lxxxi. b.* phate a martyr/ that by thre iudges eche after other was put to many varyaūt turmentes/ ⁊ at the last slayne by y{e} swerde. In fraunce at parys the translacyon of saynt German a bysshop ⁊ cōfessour. At cenoman y{e} translacyon of saynt Iulian a bysshop also ⁊ cōfessour/ of synguler sanctite. ⁋ Addicyons.

⁋ The feest also of saynt Iosye a martyr/ that was a scrybe amonge the iewes/ ⁊ in y{e} passyon of saynt Iames he fyrst put the corde about his necke/ but forthw{t} he was by hym conuerted ⁊ baptized/ ⁊ w{t} hym put to deth. The feest also of saȳt Nemesy a noble man/ that herynge y{e} fame ⁊ myracles of saynt Stephan y{e} pope brought vnto hym his blynde doughter saynt Lucill/ whome the pope baptized/ ⁊ therby restored her syght ⁊ forthw{t} her sayd fader was cōuerted ⁊ baptized/ ⁊ after they bothe cōuerted many other psones/ ⁊ at y{e} last by y{e} emperours Valerian ⁊ Galiene they bothe togyder were put to deth. The feest also of saynt Iudoke a kynges sone of englond/ that for Chryst forsoke all. the worlde ⁊ went in pilgrimage/ ⁊ was a holy heremyte and dyed in the fraūchest of pontyne. The feest also of many other holy sayntes/ martyrs/ cōfes. ⁊ virgyns.

⁋ To morowe.

⁋ The .xxvj. day of Iuly. the feest of saynt Erast that by saȳt Paule was made bysshop of philypes/ where he was put to martyrdome. At rome the feest of saynt Iacinct a martyr/ y{t} was cast in to a grete fyre/ ⁊ there remayned a longe tyme w{t}out noyaunce/ ⁊ than in to a ryuer/ ⁊ there lykewyse/ at the last by y{e} consull Leonce he was slayne by y{e} swerde. At rome also in latyn strete the feest of saynt Symphrony/ saynt Olympy/ saynt [Theodole ⁊ saynt Exsuper/ that (as is wryten in the [*fo. lxxxii.* gestes of saynt Stephan) were all brent. The feest also of saynt Anne moder vnto our blessed lady/ borne in bethleem. The feest also of saynt Pastour a preest and confessour.

¶ Addicyons.

¶ This daye is also honoured the feest of saynt Ioachym housbond vnto saÿt Anne/ ⁊ fader vnto our blessed lady/ bycause the very daye of his deposicyon can not be knowen. The feest also of many other holy .⁊c.

¶ To morowe.

¶ The .xxvij. day of Iuly. at ephesum ye feest of saynt Maximyan/ saynt Malcus/ saynt Martynian/ saynt Denyse/ saynt Iohn̄/ saynt Serapion ⁊ saynt Cōstantyne all martyrs/ called the .vij. slepers/ that fledde the psecucyon of ye emperour Decius/ ⁊ hyd themselfe in a caue in the mout of cellion/ where they rested .ccclxxij. yeres/ vnto the tyme of ye emperour Theodosy/ whan there was a grete heresy of the generall resurreccyon/ for ye wytnes ⁊ profe wherof to be shewed in themselfe they all arose as though they had slept but one nyght/ ⁊ whā they had shewed themselfe ⁊ the cause of theyr rysynge/ they forthwᵗ rested agayne in our lorde. At nicomede ye feest of saynt Hermolay a preest/ saynt Hernempy ⁊ saynt Hermogiate† breder ⁊ martyrs/ that by the emperour Maximian after many turmētes were heded. In sicilie ye feest of saynt Symeon a monke. At antisiodour the feest of saynt Ewthery a bysshop and confessour. ¶ Addicyons.

¶ The feest also of saynt Santuly a preest of singuler sanctite/ he made oyle of water/ ⁊ fedde many labourers .x. dayes wᵗ one lofe of brede/ ⁊ euer more remayned than was in the begynnynge/ he also offred hym[selfe to be heded for an [*fo. lxxxii. b.* other man/ but his arme yᵗ shold haue stryken hym/ stode starke ⁊ myght not bowe/ tyll he had promysed neuer after to hurt ony chrystyan/ by the whiche myracle many were cōuerted/ ⁊ many chrystyans delyuered frō deth. The feest also of many .⁊c.

¶ To morowe.

¶ The .xxviij. day of Iuly. at nicomede ye feest of saÿt Pantaleon a martyr/ that by ye emperour Maximian was racked ⁊ hote oyle cast vpō his naked body/ with other many cruell turmentes/ in ye whiche he had consolacyon by ye presence ⁊ syght of our sauyour Iesu/ ⁊ at the last he was slayne by the

swerde. In yᵉ lesse brytayne at the monastery of dole the feest of saynt Sampson a bysshop ⁊ cōfessour. In fraūce at lyons the feest of saynt Peregryne a preest/ a famous man of many myracles. The feest also of saynt Victor ⁊ of saynt Innocent bothe popes and martyrs. At mylen the feest of saynt Nazary/ ⁊ of saȳt Celse a childe/ both martyrs. ¶ Addicyons.
¶ The feest also of saynt Vrse a cōfessour/ ⁊ the feest of saynt Redempte bysshop of serentyne/ a man of meruaylous sanctite/ ⁊ had the spiryte of pphecy/ ⁊ was moche
lib. iij. ca. famylyer wᵗ saynt Gregory the pope ⁊ doctour/ of
xxxviii. whome he wryteth in his dialoges. The feest also of many other holy sayntes/ martyrs/ confes. ⁊ virg.

¶ To morowe.

¶ The .xxix. day of Iuly. At rome in aurele strete the feest of saynt Felix pope/ that by the emperour Cōstantyne was deposed/ ⁊ after slayne by yᵉ swerde. At rome also in portunens strete the feest of saynt Symplicy ⁊ saynt Faustyne breder ⁊ martyrs/ yᵗ by the emperour Dioclecian after many turmētes were heded/ ⁊ theyr [syster saynt Betrice was murthéred [*fo. lxxxiii.* in prison. At trecas yᵉ feest of saynt Lupe a cōfessour/ that wᵗ saynt German came in to brytayne/ where he lyued .lij. yeres in holy cōuersacyon. The feest also of saȳt Martha syster vnto Mary magdalene/ borne at bethany/ ⁊ buryed in tarastont in a forest of her owne. ¶ Addicyons.
¶ The feest also of saȳt Marcill/ seruaūt ⁊ bondmayd vnto saynt Martha/ that contynued wᵗ her maystresse durynge her lyfe/ ⁊ after wrote her legende/ ⁊ than she went in to sclauony/ where she cōuerted moche people and .x. yeres after her maystres she departed vnto our lorde/ whose holy body lyeth besyde the body of Mary magdalene. The feest also of saynt Flore ⁊ saynt Lucil virgyns/ borne in rome ⁊ there religyous nūnes/ that in the psecucyon of the barbaries were taken by kyng Eugene/ yᵗ for theyr beauty wold haue mysused them/ but at yᵉ last they cōuerted hym/ ⁊ by suche reuelacyon as was made vnto them by an aūgell of theyr martyrdom/ he was also so enflambed/ yᵗ he forsoke his kyngdom ⁊ went wᵗ them to rome/ where he was baptized and with them put to martyrdom/ by whose example all these psones folowynge/ yᵗ is to saye/ saynt Antony/ saynt Theodour/ saynt Denyse/ saȳt Appollony/ saȳt Campany/ saynt Pioly/ saynt Corsy/ saȳt Corygenes/ saynt Pake/ saynt Saturne/ saynt Victor/ and .ix. mo persones vnnamed/ were all cōuerted/ ⁊ there wᵗ them heded. The feest also of many other holy sayntes .⁊c.

IVLY.

¶ To morowe.

¶ The .xxx. daye of Iuly. At rome ye feest of saynt Abdon ⁊ saynt Sēnen martyrs/ that by ye emperour Decius were brought in cheynes frō corduba vnto rome where after many cruell turmentes they were slayne [by the swerde. [*fo. lxxxiii. b.* In affryke at lucernary ye feest of saynt Maxima/ saynt Donatill/ ⁊ saynt Secūde virgyns ⁊ martyrs/ that in the psecucyon of ye emperour Galiene were cōstrayned after ye example of theyr spouse Iesu to drynke eysell ⁊ gall/ than were they scourged naked/ racked/ ⁊ theyr lymes strayned w^t cordes/ cast vpon a gredyren ⁊ broyled/ put vnto wode wyld beestes/ ⁊ yet at the last slayne by the swerde/ ⁊ so receyued ye palme of martyrdom. The feest also of saynt Vrsy a bisshop ⁊ cōfessour. At caūterbury the feest of saynt Tadwyne a bysshop ⁊ cōfessour. The feest also of saynt Speciouse a monke ⁊ disciple vnto sayt Benet/ a noble man borne ⁊ of grete possessyons/ whiche all he distrybuted vnto the poore/ ⁊ w^t his broder saynt Gregory went vnto religyon/ whiche sayd broder sawe his soule cōueyed by aūgels in to heuē. The feest also of many other ho .⁊c.

¶ To morowe.

¶ The .xxxj. day of Iuly. In cesare ye passyon of saynt Fabiane a martyr/ that bycause he refused to bere the baner of honour before the mayre vnto the sacrefyce of ydolles/ was .iij tymes examined by dyuerse turmentes/ ⁊ at the last heded. At rauen ye deposicyon of saynt German/ bysshop of antisiodour/ a noble man borne/ ⁊ more noble in vertue ⁊ myracles. At synade the feest of saynt Demotrice/ saynt Secūde/ ⁊ saynt Denyse. And the feest also of saynt Neoche† a preest ⁊ confessour. ¶ Addicyons.

¶ The feest also of saynt Fantyne a cōfessour/ of whome before he was conceyued/ reuelacyon was made vnto his parentes than beynge gentyles/ ⁊ after at .xij. yeres of age/ accordynge vnto ye same reuelacyon/ he conuerted his sayd fader ⁊ moder/ ⁊ conforted them vnto [martyrdom/ wher vnto he [*fo. lxxxiiii.* ordered hymselfe w^t them/ but an aūgell delyuered hym/ for the more edificacyon of the fayth. For by his holy lyfe ⁊ grete myracles/ he cōuerted many coūtrees/ ⁊ in ye age of .xxxiij. yeres he departed/ vpon whose holy body descended a lyght frō heuen/ so that he lay vnburyed .xxx. dayes/ ⁊ his body w^tout ony sygne of corrupcyon of a meruaylous swete odour/ ⁊ after out of his sepulcre oyle stylled of excellēt vertue. In englond the feest of saynt Wolfade ⁊ saynt Rufyne breder ⁊ martyrs/ ⁊ sones vnto kyng Wolfere kynge of the marches by his quene saynt Ermenyld/ whiche kyng was a christyan/ ⁊ after by wycked coūseyle he was a renegate ⁊ apostata/ whose two sayd childer in huntyng of a hart were brought vnto saynt Chadde bisshop of lychefelde/ ⁊ by hym instructed in ye fayth ⁊ baptized. For euer they were gyuen to vertue/ whiche thyng whā theyr fader knewe/ he slewe them with his owne handes/ but after by the counseyle of his holy quene/ he toke repentaūce ⁊ went vnto saynt Chadde/ ⁊ there forsoke his apostasy/ ⁊ was confessed and dyd penaūce/ ⁊ made a blessed ende. The feest also of many other holy sayntes/ martyrs/ confes. ⁊ virg.

❡ August.

❡ To morowe.

August. THe fyrst day of August. the feest of the holy machabies. At rome ye feest of saynt Peter ad vincula. In ytaly the feest of saynt Eusebius bysshop of vercell/ a man of excellent doctryne/ that by the emperour Cōstantyne was exyled fyrst in to sythopole/ and after vnto capadoce/ and yet euer he returned vnto his owne chirche/ ⁊ at the last by the psecucyon of ye heretykes called arrianes he was put to martyrdome. At [rome [*fo. lxxxiiii. b.* also the passyon of saynt Fayth/ saynt Hope/ and saynt Charite virgyns ⁊ martyrs/ and of theyr blessed moder saynt Sapience/ that by the prince Adriane all togyder receyued the crowne of martyrdom. At rome also in latyn strete ye feest of saynt Bone a preest/ saynt Faust ⁊ saynt Maure all martyrs togyder/ and (as is wryten in the actes of saynt Stephan the pope) seuen other persones suffred deth with them. In spayne at gerūd the feest of saynt Felix a martyr/ y^t by the iudge Daciane after many turmentes was racked/ and his flesshe torne ⁊ rent frō the bones tyll he was deed. In araby at philadelphe ye feest of say͂t Cirill/ saynt Aquil/ saynt Peter/ saynt Domician/ saynt Rufy ⁊ saynt Medardt/ all martyrs in one daye. In ye terrytory of parys the feest of saynt Iustyne a martyr. In ye fraūchest of lysyn ye feest of saynt Nemesy a cōfessour. In englond at wynchester the deposicyon of saynt Adelwold a bysshop ⁊ confessour/ ⁊ a founder of many monasteryes. ❡ Addicyons.

❡ The feest also of saynt Salomon/ sone vnto kynge Dauid/ y^t after his grete synnes ⁊ ydolatry came vnto grete repentaūce/ and for a notable penaūce/ he caused hymselfe to be drawen as a thefe or traytour thrugh ye stretes of Ierusalem vnto ye solempne temple that he hȳselfe had made/ ⁊ there he brought forth .vij. roddes ⁊ charged .iiij. offycers of yᵉ lawe to bete hym wᵗ those roddes as longe as they might last/ whiche to do they refused/ sayenge they wold not lay violent hādes vpon the oynted man of our lord. Than he hymselfe syttyng as kyng in iudge-mēt/ fyrst deposed ⁊ put downe hymselfe from his kyngdom/ ⁊ than he bette hymselfe naked wᵗ the sayd roddes tyll they were spent/ ⁊ after wᵗ [lowde voyce he sayd. Christus [*fo lxxxv*. purgauit pctā illius et exaltauit ineternū cornu eius: ⁊ dedit illi thronū regni et sedē glorie israel. That is to saye. Chryst hath purged ⁊ clensed his synnes/⁊ hath exalted his power for euer/ ⁊ he hath gyuen vnto hym the trone of his kyngdom/ ⁊ the sete or restynge place of the glory of israell. The feest also of saynt Iesus syrake a pphete of grete sanctite ⁊ wysdom/ ⁊ a doctour of the lawe ⁊ ruler of yᵉ people/ borne in Ierusalem/ ⁊ he made the boke called in scripture ecclesiasticus. The feest also of saynt Mary a virgyn/ whose syrname was consolatryce or conforter/ a mayde of hygh perfeccyon ⁊ many myracles/ ⁊ lyeth at verona where she was borne. The feest also of saynt Iust a martyr/ yᵗ was sone vnto saȳt Iustyne and had many reuelacions/ ⁊ after he was heded/ his tongue spake/ wᵗ many other myracles. In englond at lyncolne yᵉ feest of saynt Hugh a chylde/ yᵗ by the iewes that tyme there dwellyng/ was stolen ⁊ put vnto all yᵉ paynes of Chryst ⁊ crucyfyed/ whose holy body wolde not abyde in the erth/ ne in the water/ ne ony where be hydde vnto yᵉ tyme it was foūde ⁊ knowen/ ⁊ they expelled. In englonde also the feest of saynt Kenede that was lame borne/ ⁊ therfore he was cast in to a ryuer/ whiche ryuer caryed hym in to yᵉ see/ ⁊ yᵉ see cast hym vpon a roche in to an ylelonde/ where he was fedde ⁊ brought vp by an aūgel/ ⁊ he was of singuler holynes ⁊ many wonderous myracles/ ⁊ in yᵉ tyme of saynt Dauid. The feest also of saynt Exsup a bisshop ⁊ cōfessour that cured yᵉ blynde ⁊ lame/ expelled euyll spirytes/ wᵗ many other grete myracles. The feest also of saynt Iosaphat the kynges sone of ynde/ whose legende is of a grete length/ ⁊ full of notable myracles. The feest also [of many [*fo. lxxxv. b.* other holy sayntes/ martyrs/ confes. ⁊ virg.

⁋ To morrowe.

⁋ The seconde day of August. at rome in the cimitery of saynt Calixt yᵉ feest of saynt Stephan yᵉ pope ⁊ martyr/ that in the psecucion of yᵉ emperour Valeriane/ for the desyre of martyrdom/ sayd masse openly/ in yᵉ whiche masse as he sate in his trone/ he was heded. In yᵉ prouynce of birynet at nice the feest of saynt Theodour a matrone/ ⁊ of her sone saynt

Euody/ that after many cruell turmentes/ was w^t her sone ꝛ other two of his breder ꝛ her sones also/ cast al togyder in to a grete fyre ꝛ brent. In englond the inuencyon of the holy body of saynt Albane the fyrst martyr of the same realme.

❡ Addicyons.

❡ At rome the feest of an other saynt Stephan the seconde pope of that name/ a confessour/ y^t valyaūtly dyd defende the right of the chirche/ ꝛ was a man of hygh pfeccyon. The feest also of the thyrde saynt Stephan the thyrd pope of that name/ a grete lerned man/ that by vertue ꝛ good example moche edyfyed ye chirche of Chryst. The feest also of many other holy sayntes .ꝛc.

❡ To morowe.

❡ The thyrde day of August. at Ierusalem the inuencyon of saynt Stephan ye fyrst martyr/ ꝛ of saynt Gamaliel/ saynt Nicodeme/ ꝛ saynt Abibon/ whose holy bodyes in ye tyme of prynce Honory were foūde by a reuelacyon/ shewed vnto saynt Luciane a preest/ y^t wrote ꝛ publysshed the story therof vnto many nacyons for ye edifycacyon of Chrystes chirche. At cōstantynople the feest of saynt Hermell a martyr.

❡ Addicyons.

❡ In englond at yorke ye feest of saynt wallene/ called also saynt Walthef/ sone vnto the erle of huntyngton/ [that [*fo. lxxxvi.* forsoke all his enherytaūce ꝛ was a monke of holy cōuersacyon ꝛ grete myracles. The feest also of saŷt Eufrony a confessour/ ꝛ of saynt Stephan an holy heremyte/ that amonge other had in synguler maner the spiryte of coūseyle ꝛ cōsolacyon/ so y^t no psone went frō hym in heuynes or discōforte/ ꝛ he was euer seke and full of sores/ ꝛ yet of meruaylous pacyence. The feest also of many other holy sayntes/ marꝛ. confes. ꝛ virg.

❡ To morowe.

❡ The .iiij. day of August. the feest of saynt Aristarke discyple vnto saynt Paule. At rome in latyn strete the passyon of saynt Tranquilyne a martyr/ y^t by the emperour Aureliane was scourged/ beten w^t staues/ put in harde pryson/ and there well nere famysshed/ brent vpon ye rybbes with hote plates ꝛ lampes/ racked/ the flesshe torne w^t hokes/ the senous of al his lŷmes kytte insonder/ ꝛ after all heded.

❡ Addicyons.

❡ The feest also of saynt Iustyne a preest/ that with saynt Syxt ꝛ saynt Laurence diuyded the goodes of ye chirche vnto the poore/ ꝛ the next yere after theyr deth he was accused vnto the emperour Decius/ ꝛ put to martyrdom by many cruell turmentes. The feest also of saynt Tertulyne a martyr/ ꝛ of saynt Lugyde an holy abbot. And yᵉ feest also of many other holy sayn.ꝛc.

❡ To morowe.

❡ The .v. day of August. In the puynce of rece at augustane yᵉ feest of saynt Affra a martyr/ that fyrst was an vnclene ꝛ comyn woman/ ꝛ after by saynt Narcisse the bysshop she ꝛ all her housholde were co̅uerted and baptized/ ꝛ wᵗ feruent desyre went vnto martyrdom/ ꝛ was brent in a grete fyre. In englonde yᵉ feest of saynt Oswald kynge ꝛ martyr/ whose actes ꝛ holy life saȳt [Bede the reuerend clerke doth [*fo. lxxxvi. b.* wryte in yᵉ cronycles of englonde. In augustudune the feest of saynt Cassiane a bisshop ꝛ co̅fessour. At cathalamnis† the feest of saynt Neminyne† a bysshop. At lornon† yᵉ deposicyon of saynt Dominyke a co̅fessour/ that by the auctorite of yᵉ pope for the zele ꝛ loue yᵗ he had vnto Chrystes fayth/ ꝛ for yᵉ destruccyon of certayne heresyes yᵗ were in his tyme/ began fyrst yᵉ order of freres prechers/ called comynly the blacke freres.

❡ Addicyons.

❡ In englonde at douer the feest of saynt Thomas a monke/ that for the ryght of the chirche was there put to deth by frensshemen that came to inuade the realme or kyngdom/ at whose sepulcre ben shewed many myracles. At rome yᵉ feest of our lady/ called yᵉ feest of saȳt Mary at the snowe/ bycause the fyrst chirche of our lady in rome was buylded by a reuelacyon/ ꝛ a myracle of snowe yᵗ fell there in grete quantite the .v. day of August. The feest also of saynt Emygdy a bysshop ꝛ martyr/ ꝛ a grete precher/ that co̅uerted coūtrees/ cytees/ ꝛ moche people vnto Chryst/ ꝛ was of many myracles. The feest also of saynt Meny a co̅fessour ꝛ bysshop/ co̅scrate by saȳt Peter the apostle/ that co̅uerted moche people ꝛ dyd grete myracles. The feest also of saȳt Yon a martyr/ that after he was deed/ bare his owne heed a myle. The feest also of saynt Ioh̅n a holy heremyte. At augustane yᵉ feest of saynt Quiryake/ saynt Large/ saynt Crescenciane/ saynt Diomade/ saynt Caryke/ saynt Philadelphe/ saynt Agapa/ saynt Peter/ with other .xvij. persones all martyrs/ heded for the fayth. The feest also of many other holy sayntes/ marṫ. ꝛc.

❡ To morowe.

❡ The .vj. day of August. the transfyguracyon of our [lorde ꝛ sauyour Iesu. At rome in appia strete yᵉ feest of [*fo. lxxxvii.*

saynt Syxt a bysshop ℞ martyr. At rome also in yᵉ cimitery of saynt Pretexate the feest of saynt Felicissimy ℞ saynt Agapite martyrs/ yᵗ were deacons vnto the sayd saynt Sixt/ ℞ by yᵉ emperour Decius heded wᵗ hym/ ℞ the feest of saynt Ianuary/ saynt Magn⁹/ saynt Vincent ℞ saynt Stephan subdeacons/ that (as is wryten in the boke of yᵉ gestes of popes ℞ bysshops) were that tyme also wᵗ them heded. And (as saynt Cipriane wryteth) saynt Quarte was put to deth wᵗ the same company. In spayne at complute the feest of saynt Iust ℞ saynt Pastor breder/ that beynge childer in the scole/ ℞ herynge of the rewarde of martyrdome/ sodeynly cast downe theyr bokes ℞ ran wᵗ gladnes vnto yᵉ emperour Daciane ℞ there cōfessed Chryst/ whome yᵉ emperour put vnto many turmētes/ wherin they as yf they had ben men of grauite/ eche conforted other/ ℞ after all by the cōmune hangman they were put to deth.
⁋ Addicyons.

⁋ At rome the feest of an other saynt Sixt the thyrde pope of yᵉ name/ that was a grete clerke ℞ cōdempned many heretykes/ he buylded many chirches ℞ well ordered them/ ℞ he was a grete almesman/ and of many myracles. The feest also of many other holy sayn .℞c.

⁋ To morowe.

⁋ The .vij. daye of August. In arece at tusce yᵉ feest of saynt Donate a martyr ℞ bysshop/ that by yᵉ emperour Iulian (as saynt Gregory wryteth) suffred grete psecucyon/ ℞ vpon a tyme whan he was at masse the paganes brake the chalys in peces/ whiche by prayer he restored hole agayne wᵗout ony effusyon of yᵉ sacramēt. At rome the feest of saynt Peter ℞ saynt Iulian/ with [other .xviij. martyrs. At [*fo. lxxxvii. b.* mylen the feest of saynt Faustyne/ that by the emperour Aurelius comodus was put to deth. ⁋ Addicyons.

⁋ The feest also of an other saynt Donate a bysshop ℞ cōfessour/ that wᵗ his walkynge staffe slewe a dragon/ whose body .viij. yoke of oxen coude scant drawe vnto the fyre/ wᵗ many other grete myracles. The feest also of many other holy sayntes/ martyrs/ cōfes. and virg.

⁋ To morowe.

⁋ The .viij. daye of August. At rome in ostience strete the feest of saynt Ciriake a deacon/ saynt Large ℞ saȳt Smaragde/ wᵗ other .xx. psones put to martyrdom by the emperour Dioclecian. In fraūce at nyennaț ye feest of saynt Seuere/ that after many labours ꝼ grete dylygence of prechynge came vnto ye same cite/ where he cōuerted the multytude therof/ ꝼ so rested in our lorde. ¶ Addicyons.

¶ At rome the feest of saynt Hormysdy pope/ that fyrst ordeyned psalmes to be songe in dyuyne seruyce/ ꝼ he cōdempned the heresy of euticiane/ and was a man of grete pyte/ ꝼ moost lyberall in almes. The feest also of an other saynt Hormysdy a martyr/ y^t by the kynge of perse was put to dethe. The translacyon also of saynt Quiryke a bysshop ꝼ martyr. And ye feest of many .ꝼc̃.

¶ To morowe.

¶ The .ix. day of August. the vigyll of saynt Laurēce. In tuscia at colen the feest of saynt Secūdiane/ saynt Marcelliane ꝼ saynt Veriane martyrs/ y^t by the iudge Promote vnder the emperour Decius were scourged/ racked/ theyr flesshe torne w^t hokes/ ꝼ hote flambes of fyre put vnto ye woūdes/ ꝼ at ye last slayne by ye swerde. At rome ye feest of saynt Romane a martyr/ that was a [man of warre vnder the em- [*fo. lxxxviii.* perour Decius/ ꝼ conuerted by saynt Laurence/ ꝼ desyred of him to be baptized for the whiche he was put to many turmentes/ and at the last heded. ¶ Addicyons.

¶ The feest also of saynt Fyrmy ꝼ saynt Rustyke martyrs/ that by meruaylous many turmentes were put to deth/ whose holy bodyes were buryed by aūgels/ ꝼ after foūde by reuelacyon/ ꝼ than lost agayne in ye persecucyon of Chrystes people/ ꝼ yet after by ye prayer of saynt Mary cōsolatrice the virgyn/ they were founde agayne vnto the grete cōforte of chrystyans. The feest also of many other holy sayntes/ marṫ. confes. ꝼ virg.

¶ To morowe.

¶ The .x. daye of August. At rome in tyburtyne strete the feest of saynt Laurence a martyr/ that by ye emperour Decius was put in hard prison/ scourged/ racked/ his flesshe torne ꝼ enflambed w^t fyry plates/ ꝼ at ye last sprad vpon a gredyren w^t coles ꝼ so broyled vnto deth. At rome also the feest of .clxv. soudyours all martyrs. ¶ Addicyons.

¶ The feest also of saynt Hope/ y^t buylded ye monastery of capłet/ ꝼ there was abbot/ but by ye space of .xl. yeres he was blynde/ than appered an aūgell vnto hym ꝼ restored his syght/ ꝼ cōmaunded hym to preche vnto the monasteryes aboute hym/

and so he dyd as the aūgell taught hym/ and after .xv. dayes he returned vnto his owne monastery/ ⁊ there called all his breder togyder ⁊ before them he receyued the sacramentes of yᵉ chirche ⁊ when they were syngyng he departed vnto our lord and all they sawe euydently his soule in symilytude of a doue departe and go streyght in to heuen. The feest also of many other holy sayntes/ mart̃. confes. ⁊ virg.

[¶ To morowe. [*fo. lxxxviii. b.*

¶ The .xj. day of August. At rome bytween two laureres the passyon of saynt Tyburce a martyr/ yᵗ by the iudge Fabiane was cōpelled to walke vpon hote coles ⁊ synders/ ⁊ so after many affliccyons he was heded. At rome also yᵉ feest of saynt Susan a virgin ⁊ martyr of noble blode/ nece vnto saynt Gay the pope/ ⁊ by the emperour Dioclecian she was put to deth/ heded by yᵉ swerde. At camberake the feest of saynt Gangeryke† a bysshop and cōfessour. At the castell of ebroas the feest of saynt Tawryne a bysshop and confessour. ¶ Addicyons. ¶ The feest also of the crowne of our sauyour/ the one halfe wherof Charlemayne brought frō cōstantinople vnto parys/ at yᵉ departure ⁊ diuisyon wherof yᵉ same crowne flourysshed ⁊ brought forthe grene leues and fresshe floures/ of the wuiche† leues ⁊ floures the sayd kyng Charles fylled both his gloues/ ⁊ reserued them for relykes. And of the people yᵗ were present .ccc. ⁊ moo were heled of dyuerse sekenes by yᵉ odour ⁊ smell that came therfrō/ wᵗ many other grete miracles. The feest also of saynt Cromacy/ fader vnto saynt Tyburce the martyr/ yᵗ by the emperours Dioclecian ⁊ Maximian were put to deth/ ⁊ wᵗ hym a M. ⁊ .cccc. other psones. The feest also of an other saynt Cromacy/ a bysshop of grete lernyng/ vnto whome saynt Ierom dedicate many werkes/ ⁊ sent hym pystles/ ⁊ receyued many of hỹ. The feest also of the .vij. slepers/ that is to saye/ whan they arose/ ⁊ forthwith after dyed. For yᵉ other feest in Iuly was whā they slept. The feest also of many .⁊c̃.

¶ To morowe.

¶ The .xij. day of August. In cicilie at cathyne yᵉ feest [of saynt Ewple a deacon/ that by the emperours [*fo. lxxxix.* Dioclecian ⁊ Maximian after many turmētes was slayne by the swerde. At augustane the feest of saynt Hyllary moder vnto saynt Affra/ that as she was in prayer at the graue of her sayd doughter/ was taken/ ⁊ wᵗ her yᵉ holy women saynt Digne/ saynt

Ewmeny/ and saynt Ewprepy/ and all brought vnto the iudge/ whiche cast them all in to a grete fyre ⁊ brent them. At rome yᵉ feest of saynt Quiriake/ saynt Large/ ⁊ saynt Crescenciane ⁊ of the holy women saynt Menye ⁊ saynt Iulian/ wᵗ many other chrystyans/ that by the mayre Pertinace were all put to deth togyder. At salary† yᵉ feest of saynt Graciane†/ ⁊ of saynt Felicissima a virgyn/ bothe martyrs/ yᵗ for the confessyon of Chryst were knocked vpon the mouth wᵗ stones/ ⁊ after many other turmētes put to deth by yᵉ swerde. In syre yᵉ feest of saynt Machare ⁊ saynt Iuliane cōfessours. At assyse the feest of saynt Clare a holy virgyn. The feest also of saynt Ethelwold a cōfessour of many merytes.   ¶ Addicyons.

¶ At reatyne yᵉ feest of saynt Probe/ bysshop of yᵉ same cite/ a man of singuler vertue/ that in the houre of dethe was brought vnto blysse by saynt Ewlethery† ⁊ saynt Iuuenall martyrs/ with other aūgels ⁊ sayntes. At rome yᵉ feest of saynt Romula a virgyn of synguler pacyence/ moost hygh obedience/ ⁊ of strayte sylence/ moche ⁊ in maner cōtynually occupyed in prayer/ yᵗ was taken wᵗ the palsey/ ⁊ so lay many yeres lame/ but neuer impacyent/ ne neuer lefte therfore prayer/ whose soule was caryed vnto blysse wᵗ a quere celestyal moost swetely syngyng. The feest also of many other ho.⁊c.

¶ To morowe.

¶ The .xiij. daye of August. At rome the feest of saynt [Ypolity a martyr/ that by the mayre Valeriane [*fo. lxxxix. b.* was tyed by yᵉ fete vnto wylde horses/ ⁊ so drawen thrugh busshes ⁊ breres tyll he was deed/ with whome .xviij. persones of his houshold were put to deth/ besyde his nurse saynt Concorde/ yᵗ before hym was beten to deth with plūmettes. At forcill the feest of saynt Cassiane a martyr/ that bycause he wolde not do sacrefyce vnto yᵉ ydolles/ was iudged to dye/ ⁊ for his mere payne/ he was delyuered vnto certayn of his owne scolers/ whome before he had corrected for theyr defautes/ ⁊ they by many ⁊ greuous turmentes put hym to martyrdom. At pictauy the feest of saynt Radegūd a quene/ whose lyfe by many myracles was in grete fame.   ¶ Addicyons.

¶ The feest also of an other saynt Ypolity bysshop of aphricane/ a man of noble doctryne/ ⁊ made many profytable werkes/ and was of notable vertue ⁊ many myracles. The feest also of an other saynt Cassiane/ called also saynt Iohn̄ cassiane the heremyte/ that wrote the collacyons of the olde faders in egypte/ ⁊ theyr rules ⁊ maners/ wᵗ many other noble werkes/ vnto the grete edificacion of yᵉ chirche. The feest also of many oth. ⁊c.

THE MARTILOGE.

⁋ To morowe.

⁋ The .xiiij. day of August. The vigyl of ye assumpcyon of our lady. At rome in appia stretc ye feest of saynt Euseby a preest ͛ cōfessour/ that by ye emperour Cōstancy was put to many affliccyons/ ͛ at the last he was closed in a cabon within his owne hous/ ͛ there dyed. ⁋ Addicyons.

⁋ The feest also of saynt Hely the holy prophete/ y^t as this day was raptc ͛ taken lyuynge in to paradyse/ where he so remayneth w^t Enoke/ vnto a lytel before y^e [general [fo. xc. iudgement/ at whiche tyme they shall come in to the erth/ ͛ here haue cōflicte w^t Antechryst/ whome he shall put to deth/ but after notw^{t}standyng they shall by ye power of god be reysed agayne vnto lyfc/ ͛ vaynquysshe ͛ confoūde hȳ. The feest also of many oth. ͛c.

⁋ To morowe.

⁋ The .xv. daye of August. the deposicyon of ye moder of god our lady saynt Mary/ whome our moder ye chirche byleueth without ony doubte to be deed/ accordyng vnto the cōdicyon of our nature/ but where y^t honourable temple of her sayd body/ by the diuyne counseyle ͛ ordynaūce of god was layde/ or where now it resteth or remayneth/ the olde chirche wolde no thynge determyne/ but rather let the mater hange in doubte ͛ suspence/ than ony thynge to wryte or teche w^{t}out auctoritc/ vnto suche tyme it myght please our lord god ferther to shewe therin/ wherypon it pleased his goodnes syth y^t tyme to shewe by reuelacyon vnto dyuerse psones/ whiche our sayd moder ye chirche hath approued ͛ so now doth hold ͛ teche/ that her holy body is with her blessed soule in blysse gloryfyed/ ͛ therfore is this feest now called ye assumpcyon. At rome in appia strete the feest of saynt Tarsycy a colet in order/ that bycause he wolde not shewe the sacrament of Chrystes body vnto the paganes that they myght haue had it in derysyon/ was beten with staues ͛ stones vnto deth. ⁋ Addicyons.

⁋ The feest also of saynt Euseby a bysshop/ a man of notable doctryne/ y^t wrote many storyes ͛ other profytable werkes. The feest also of an other saynt Euseby an abbot/ and discyple vnto saynt Ierom/ a noble man borne/ ͛ went in pilgrymage vnto ye holy lond/ where [he foūde saȳt [fo. xc. b. Ierom at bethleem/ ͛ than he forsoke all the worlde ͛ was w^t hym a mōke/ ͛ after abbot/ ͛ euer of synguler sanctite/ ͛ had reuelacyons/ ͛ was of many myracles. The feest also of many other holy . ͛c.

¶ To morowe.

¶ The .xvj. day of August. In bytyny at nice the feest of saynt Vrsacy a confessour/ that fyrst was a man of warre vnder y⁰ tyraūt Luciane/ ꝛ after he lyued as an heremyte solytary/ ꝛ amonge other many grete myracles he slewe a grete horryble dragon. At metēs y⁰ feest of saȳt Arnuff a bysshop/ that lyued as an heremyte in synguler sanctite ꝛ many myracles. At rome y⁰ feest of saynt Serene a noble matrone/ wyfe vnto the emperour Dioclecian. ¶ Addicyons.

¶ The feest also of saynt Artemye a virgyn ꝛ martyr that was doughter vnto y⁰ sayd emperour Dioclecian by his wyfe the same matrone saynt Serene/ whiche sayd virgyn after y⁰ deth of her fader was put to deth by her owne broder. The feest also of saynt Franbold a bysshop ꝛ cōfessour. And the feest also of many oth. ꝛc̃.

¶ To morowe.

¶ The .xvij. day of August. In affrike y⁰ feest of saynt Liberate an abbot/ saynt Boniface a deacon/ saȳt Seuy† ꝛ saynt Rustyke bothe subdeacons/ saynt Rogate ꝛ saynt Septimy monkes/ ꝛ saynt Maximy a childe all martyrs/ that in the psecucyon of the wandales were by kynge Huneryke put to martyrdome. In capadoce at cesary the feest of saynt Māmete a martyr/ that by the cōmaūdement of Valeriane the emperour was by the mayre Alexander put to dethe. The octaue also of saynt Laurence. ¶ Addicyons.

¶ The feest also of saynt Tharcill/ aunt vnto saȳt Gre[gory the pope/ a holy woman/ that by saynt Felix [*fo. xci.* had reuelacyon of her deth/ at the whiche our sauyour Iesu came visybly vnto her/ vnto whome she yelded her spiryte/ ꝛ whan her body was wasshen they foūde her knees and elbowes as harde as the camelles knees by longe vse of knelynge ꝛ prostracyons. The feest also of many other holy sayntes/ martyrs/ confes. and virg.

¶ To morowe.

¶ The .xviij. day of August. At preuestyn† .xxxiij. myle from rome y⁰ feest of saynt Agapite a martyr/ yᵗ moche desyred martyrdom/ ꝛ in the age of .xv. yeres he was brought vnto the emperour Valeriane/ ꝛ by y⁰ mayre Antiocus he was scourged wᵗ senous/ racked/ ꝛ after many cruell turmentes/ slayne by the swerde. At rome the feest of saynt Crispe ꝛ saynt Iohñ bothe

MARTILO. I

preestes/ that in the psecucion of the emperour Dioclecian were very dilygent in buryenge ye bodyes of holy martyrs/ wherby they ben taken as of lyke merites w^t them. At rome also in lauicane strete ye feest of saŷt Elene moder vnto the emperour Cōstantyne. The feest also of saynt Pontyne a holy cōfessour.
ℂ Addicyons.

ℂ The feest also of saynt Fyacre a cōfessour/ borne of ye noble blode of yrelonde/ y^t forsoke all the worlde ⁊ went in to fraūce/ ⁊ there was an heremyte of hygh perfeccyon ⁊ many myracles. In yrelonde the feest of saynt Daygens a cōfessour/ that in his childhode dyd many myracles/ ⁊ after he reysed .xiij. psones vnto lyf/ w^t many other notable actes/ ⁊ dyed in the age of .cxl. yeres full of sanctite ⁊ pfeccyon. The feest also of many .⁊c.

ℂ To morowe.

ℂ The .xix. dye of August. the feest of saynt Magnus ⁊ saynt Andrewe martyrs/ y^t with .MM.v.C.xcviij. [other [*fo. xci. b.* persones of theyr company were put to deth for the cōfessyon of Chryst. In the fraūchest of sigesteryke the feest of saynt Donate a preest/ that frō youth was endowed with many grete graces/ ⁊ euer he lyued ye strayte lyf of heremytes. At rome ye feest of saynt Iule a martyr/ that was a senatour/ ⁊ by the emperour Comodus beten to deth w^t battes. In ye terrytory of bituriens the feest of saynt Mariane a holy confessour.
ℂ Addicyons.

ℂ The feest also of saynt Lewys a bysshop/ that was sone ⁊ heyre vnto kyng Charles of fraūce/ ⁊ forsoke all worldly pompe/ ⁊ was a frere of saynt Fraūcys order ⁊ after an heremite/ ⁊ whan he was preest he was by reuelacyon made a bysshop/ ⁊ euer of hygh pfeccyon ⁊ many myracles. The feest also of many other holy .⁊c.

ℂ To morowe.

ℂ The .xx. day of August. the feest of saynt Samuell the prophete/ whose holy bones (as saynt Ierom wryteth) were translate by the emperour Archady from ye iury vnto tracy. The feest also of saŷt Porphiry/ mayster ⁊ techer vnto saynt Agapite. In the yle of nere† the feest of saynt Phylibert an abbot/ y^t was fyrst a temporall knyght/ ⁊ after gaue hymselfe hooly vnto Chryst/ ⁊ was a grete foūder of monasteryes/ ⁊ of hygh pfeccyon. At corduba the feest of saynt Leouigylde ⁊ saynt Crystouer mōkes ⁊ martyrs/ y^t were heded/ ⁊ theyr

AVGVST.

bodyes brent. The feest also of saynt Bernard a cōfessour and abbot of clareuale. ℂ Addicyons.

ℂ The feest also of saynt Oswyne a kynge of englond that for ye welth of his people/ wylfully put hymselfe in the handes of his enemyes/ ℔ with hym was put to deth a noble knyght y^t wolde in no wyse byde behynde [his mayster. The [*fo. xcii.* feest also of saynt Credane an abbot ℔ of saynt Samuell a preest/ that was a grete clerke/ ℔ made many werkes/ specyally agaynst heretykes. The feest also of saynt Leoncy ℔ saynt Carpofore martyrs/ that by the iudge Lisye were put to deth by many greuous turmētes. The feest also of saynt Hely the hygh preest ℔ iudge of israell/ ℔ mayster vnto the sayd prophete Samuell. The feest also of many other .℔c.

ℂ To morowe.

ℂ The .xxj. day of August. In the terrytory of gaualitan the passion of saynt Priuate a bysshop ℔ martyr/ y^t in the psecucyon of the emperours Valerian ℔ Galien was put to martyrdom. The feest also of saynt Bonosy ℔ saynt Maximian martyrs/ whose actes ben wryten at length in the legende. At salon the feest of saynt Anastace a martyr/ that by the emperour Aurely was put to deth. The feest also of saynt Quadrate a bisshop and confessour. ℂ Addicyons.

ℂ In yrelonde the feest of saynt Moghtewe an abbot that in youth beyng a pagan dyd myracles/ ℔ after by reuelacion he went to rome/ where he was instructed in the fayth ℔ baptized/ ℔ than returned in to yrelonde where he cōuerted moche people/ ℔ he reysed thre persones vnto lyfe/ of the whiche psones one had ben deed .vij. dayes/ ℔ an other thre dayes. The feest also of saȳt Tymothe bysshop of Alexander/ ℔ of saynt Protery a preest both martyrs/ y^t by the heretyke Dioscour were put to martyrdome. The feest also of many other .℔c.

ℂ To morowe.

ℂ The .xxij. daye of August. At rome in ostience strete the feest of saynt Tymothe a martyr/ that bycause he wold not do sacrefyce vnto ye ydolles/ was thre tymes [scourged/ [*fo. xcii. b.* ℔ after many other turmentes heded. At augustudune the feest of saynt Symphoriane a martyr/ that by ye emperour Aurely was put to many turmentes/ ℔ at ye last heded. In a gate of rome ye feest of saynt Marcial/ saynt Eputet†/ saynt Saturnyne/ saȳt Aprile ℔ saynt Felix martyrs ℔ pylgrymes/ w^t

I 2

many other of theyr company/ all put to deth. At rome also in auriell strete the feest of saynt Antonyne a martyr/ that by the iudge Vitelly was heded. The octaue also of our lady.

⁋ Addicyons.

⁋ At rome also the feest of saynt Muse a virgyn/ vnto whome in yonge age appered our blessed lady w^t many virgyns of her age/ ꝛ axed her wheder she wold go w^t them/ ꝛ the virgyn answered/ she wolde gladly/ vnto whome our lady sayd/ ꝛ this daye .xxx. dayes y^u shalte be with them/ at whiche daye our lady came vnto her agayn/ than beynge sore seke ꝛ sayd/ come your waye doughter/ ꝛ she w^t lowde voyce ꝛ grete gladnes answered/ I come/ ꝛ therw^t expyred/ ꝛ so a virgyn was ioyned vnto ye celestyall virgyns. The feest also of ma .ꝛc.

⁋ To morowe.

⁋ The .xxiij. day of August. At antioche ye feest of say͂t Donate/ saynt Restitute/ saynt Valeriane/ saynt Fructuous/ w^t other .xij. all martyrs. In lice at egea ye feest of saynt Claude/ saynt Austere†/ saynt Neon/ ꝛ of ye holy women saynt Dominyne ꝛ saynt Theonyll all martyrs/ that by the mayre Lisy were put to deth by many grete ꝛ varyaūt turmentes. In a gate of rome the feest of saynt Ypolite/ saynt Quiriake ꝛ saynt Akchyl.† The feest also of saynt Zache/ that was the fourth bysshop of Ierusalem after saynt Iames. At alexander ye feest of saynt Theon a bysshop. At remens the feest of [saynt [fo. xciii. Timothe ꝛ say͂t Appollinare martyrs. At lyons in fraūce the feest of saynt Minerue ꝛ saynt Eleazare/ with .viij. of theyr chylder/ all martyrs. The vigyl also of saynt Bartholomewe.

⁋ Addicyons.

⁋ The feest also of an other saynt Zache/ that was the fyrst bysshop of antioche after saynt Peter/ whome he hymselfe consecrate whan he went to rome after Symon magus ye heretyke. The feest also of an other say͂t Theon an abbot in sythe of .iij.M. monkes/ a grete lerned man in dyuerse languages/ ꝛ of y^t pfeccyon/ that in .xxx. yeres he neuer sware othe/ ne made ony lye/ nor yet spake ony voyd or ydle worde/ nor at ony tyme was wroth or impacyent/ ꝛ his sayenge was oftentymes/ that no thyng is more peryllous vnto a religyous persone/ than to kepe preuy from his souerayne his dedes or thoughtes. In yrelond ye feest of saynt Eugene/ fyrst an abbot/ ꝛ after made a bisshop by reuelacyon/ ꝛ euer of hygh pfeccyon/ he had reuelacyon of aūgels/ ꝛ was of many myracles. The feest also of many other .ꝛc.

AVGVST.

⁋ To morowe.

⁋ The .xxiiij. day of August. the feest of saynt Bartholomewe the apostle/ that in ynde for prechynge Chryst was heded/ whose holy body was buryed in the yle of lyppary/ ꝭ after translated vnto beneuent/ where it is had in grete honour ꝭ reuerence. The feest also of .ccc. martyrs/ that by the emperours Valeriane ꝭ Galiene after many cruel turmētes were cast in to a lyme kylne ꝭ therof were they named the whyte lumpe or whyte hepe of martyrs. In normandy at rone ye feest of saynt Audoene a cōfessour/ that despysed moche ye pompe of the worlde/ and yet by force he was made bisshop. In yrelond at nyuerne ye feest of saynt Patryke an abbot [and of [fo. xciii. b. saynt Gyldard a cōfessour. ⁋ Addicyons.

⁋ The feest also of saynt Polymy a kyng of ynde/ that was cōuerted by saynt Bartholomewe/ ꝭ made there a bysshop/ ꝭ well he gouerned his chirche .xx. yeres/ ꝭ than was buryed at the fete of his maister. In the yle of same the feest of saynt Gregory/ saynt Theodour/ ꝭ saynt Leo cōfessours/ y^t were seculer knightes/ ꝭ oftentymes by grete desyre they offred themselfe wylfully vnto martyrdom/ but for theyr honour they were exyled in to ye sayd yle/ where they serued god in extreme penaūce ꝭ contynuall prayers/ ꝭ all dyed vpon one daye after whose deth many grete myracles were shewed. The feest also of saynt Sydon a bysshop/ of grete lernynge/ ꝭ made many bokes. The feest also of an other saynt Patryke an holy abbot. At cesaraugust the feest of martyrs nerehande innumerable/ that by the treason of the mayre Daciane were put to deth. The feest also of many other holy sayntes/ marṫ. confes. ꝭ virg.

⁋ To morowe.

⁋ The .xxv. day of August. At rome the feest of saynt Euseby/ saynt Poncianc/ saynt Vincent ꝭ saynt Peregryne all martyrs/ that by ye emperour Comody were hanged on gybettes/ strayned with cordes/ scourged/ racked/ ꝭ hote flambes applyed vnto theyr naked bodyes/ ꝭ at the last in a fury they were beten to deth w^t plūmettes of lede. At rome the feest of saynt Denyse† a martyr/ y^t by the emperour Dioclecian was scourged and racked/ ꝭ his flesshe torne w^t hokes/ ꝭ hote lampes applyed vnto his body/ ꝭ euer in all his turmentes he cryed w^t lowde voyce/ there is no kynge but Chryst/ for whose loue I gladly suffre/ ꝭ though ye wolde slee me a thousand tymes/ yet shall ye neuer take hym frō my [herte/ ꝭ at ye last he was [fo. xciiii. heded. The feest also of saynt Genesy/ a grete offycer in arelatēs/ ⁊ bycause he wold not punysshe chrystyans/ he was forthwith heded/ ⁊ so a martyr baptized in his owne blode. At ytalyke the feest of saynt Geronce a confessour and bysshop.

⁋ Addicyons.

⁋ One of the feestes also of saynt Tyte dyscyple vnto saynt Paule the apostle/ vnto whome he wrote one of his epystles red in yᵉ chirche. The feest also of an other saynt Tyte a bysshop of synguler doctryne/ that wrote many werkes agaynst here- tykes/ specially agaynst yᵉ manyches. The feest also of saynt Seuery an abbot of notable lyfe ⁊ many myracles. The feest also of saynt Seruane a kȳges sone ⁊ broder vnto saynt Clare/ yᵗ for the loue of Chryst forsoke all his enherytaūce/ ⁊ by the reuelacyon of an aūgell went vnto Ierusalem/ ⁊ from thens vnto rome/ where he was cōsecrate a bisshop/ ⁊ euery where he was euer famous in vertue ⁊ myracles. The feest also of saynt Ebbe an abbesse/ a holy virgyn/ borne in englond/ ⁊ syster vnto kynge oswy kyng of northumberlond/ a womā of notable vertue ⁊ many myracles. The feest also of an other saynt Ebbe/ a woman also of synguler sanctite/ ⁊ of noble progenye also. And the feest also of saynt Hunegūde a virgyn. In cartage yᵉ feest of saynt Lowys kynge of fraūce. In englond at yorke yᵉ feest of saynt Edburt kyng of northumberlond/ that forsoke yᵉ worlde ⁊ was a monke of hygh perfeccyon. The feest also of many other holy sayn̄. ⁊c.

⁋ To morowe.

⁋ The .xxvj. day of August. At rome the feest of saynt Zepheryne pope/ ⁊ of saynt Hyren ⁊ saynt Habūd martyrs/ that ben remembred in the lyf ⁊ passyon of saynt [Lau- [*fo. xciiii. b.* rence. In ytaly at the castel of victymyle yᵉ feest of saynt Secūde a noble man/ ⁊ one of the capytaynes of the legyon of thebeys. At pergamy the feest of saynt Alexander/ a capytayne also of the same legyon/ yᵗ for his meruaylous cōstancy was heded. In the terrytory of lemonicens† the feest of saynt Arecly† a preest ⁊ cōfessour. ⁋ Addicyons.

⁋ In englond the feest of saynt Brigwyne bysshop of caūterbury/ a man of synguler sanctite ⁊ many grete myracles/ of noble byrth/ sone vnto the kyng of kent. The feest also of saynt Elewthery a bisshop of notable vertue ⁊ many myracles. And yᵉ feest of many oth̄. ⁊c.

⁋ To morowe.

⁋ The .xxvij. day of August. At capua yᵉ feest of saynt Rufe a martyr/ a noble man borne/ ⁊ discyple vnto saȳt

AVGVST. 135

Appollinare/ that was discyple vnto yͤ apostle Peter At thomys the feest of saynt Marcellyne a noble capytayne/ ⁊ of his wyfe saynt Mānea/ saynt Iohn̄/ saynt Serapion and saynt Peter all martyrs togyder. The feest also of saynt Aurely/ saȳt Felix/ ⁊ of the holy woman saynt Nataly ⁊ saȳt Liliose all martyrs. And the feest of saynt George a deacon ⁊ a mōke of meruaylous abstynence/ that went in pylgrymage frō Ierusalem vnto corduba/ wᵗ certayn psones of noble lignage borne in the same cite/ where accordynge vnto a reuelacyon shewed vnto hym/ he receyued that before he had lōge desyred/ the crowne of martyrdom/ slayne by yͤ swerde. At arelatens yͤ feest of saynt Cesary a bysshop/ of meruaylous vertue ⁊ synguler pyte. At augustudune the feest of saynt Fiagry† a bysshop and confessour. ⁋ Addicyons.

⁋ The feest also of saȳt Pelagy a martyr/ borne of no[ble lignage/ that after the desece of his parentes/ solde his [*fo. xcv.* londes ⁊ gaue all vnto the poore/ ⁊ whan the persecucyon of the emperour Numeriane was in moost fury ⁊ violent/ he wylfully offred hymselfe vnto yͤ iudge ⁊ cōfessed the name of Chryst/ for the whiche after many meruaylous turmētes he was heded. At rome the feest of an other saynt Pelagy the fyrst pope of yᵗ name a noble man/ ⁊ a grete correcter of heretikes. The feest also of the thyrde saynt Pelagy the second pope of that name/ a pyteous man ⁊ moche deuoute/ that ordeyned all the prefaces yᵗ ben sayd in the masse/ except the preface of our lady/ whiche saynt Gregory his nexte successour added. In denmarke the feest of saȳt Anastasy a martyr. And the feest of many other holy saynȶ. ⁊c.

⁋ To morowe.

⁋ The .xxviij. day of August. At rome yͤ feest of saynt Ermete a martyr/ that was a noble man borne/ ⁊ (as is wryten in yͤ lyfe of saynt Alexander yͤ pope) he was longe kept in harde prison/ ⁊ after slayne by yͤ swerde. The feest also of saynt Iulian a martyr/ that in a grete psecucyon of chrystyans/ fledde frō rome/ more by coūseyle of saȳt Ferreole than of his owne mynde/ ⁊ came vnto auerne/ where by treason for Chrystes faȳth his throte was kytte/ and he so a martyr. At cōstantynople yͤ feest of saynt Alexander pope ⁊ cōfessour of grete fame ⁊ glory/ by whose vertue ⁊ holy prayer the grete heretyke Arrius was condempned. In affryke the feest of saynt Augustyne bysshop ⁊ confessour/ that fyrst was translated vnto sardyne/ ⁊ after by yͤ kyng of longobardynes vnto ticyne/ where he was honourably shryned. At sanctonas the feest of saynt Iulian† a bysshop ⁊ confessour.

❡ Addicyons.

[❡ The feest also of saynt Daniell the holy pro-[*fo. xcv. b.* phete/ ⁊ of saynt Susan/ whome he delyuered from the deedly accusacyon of ye false iudges. The feest also of ma. ⁊c.

❡ To morowe.

❡ The .xxix. daye of August. The decollacion of saynt Iohñ baptist/ not that he as this day was heded (for as the gospell recordeth/ he was heded aboute eester) but that the chirche doth now worshyp his sayd decollacyon/ bycause his heed was foūde the seconde tyme as this day/ ⁊ in edyssa shryned with grete honour/ by reason wherof it sholde be called rather the feest of the inuencyon therof. At rome the feest of saynt Sabyne a matrone of noble estate/ that by the emperour Adriane was put to martyrdom by ye swerde. In the fraūchest of trecassyne ye feest of saȳt Sabyn a virgyn/ that toke grete labours in pilgrymage/ ⁊ was moche holy ⁊ famous in myracles. At parys ye feest of saynt Meryke a preest ⁊ mōke. The feest also of saynt Cādida a virgyn. ❡ Addicyons.

❡ The feest also of saynt Sauynyane a martyr/ that was a pagan ⁊ cōuerted by an aūgell/ and after many grete myracles/ he was for Chryst heded/ ⁊ forthw^t he toke vp his owne heed ⁊ bare it a certayne space/ where he was buryed/ after whose departyng his sister saȳt Sauyne than also a pagan ⁊ a virgyn/ made instaunt prayer vnto ye ydolles for her sayd broder/ vnto whome appered an aūgel/ ⁊ shewed her where he was/ wherby she was also cōuerted ⁊ went vnto rome/ where she was baptized/ ⁊ after many myracles ⁊ holy lyfe/ she dyed at the sepulcre of her broder/ the same day of his deposicyon/ ⁊ her mayde w^t her a virgyn also/ ⁊ bothe buryed by hȳ. The feest also of an other saynt Sabyne [a virgyn ⁊ martyr/ that bycause she [*fo. xcvi.* ꝫadered ye relykes of saynt Serapy/ notw^tstandyng that she was of noble byrth/ yet was she put to deth by many cruell turmentes. The feest also of saynt Edwold/ broder vnto saynt Edmūde kyng ⁊ martyr/ y^t after the deth of his broder was required to reigne kyng as his heyre/ whiche for Chryst he forsoke/ ⁊ by an aūgell he was brought vnto desert ⁊ there was an heremite of hygh ꝑfeccyon ⁊ many myracles/ but many mo myracles were done at his sepulcre after his deth. The feest also of many oth. ⁊c.

❡ To morowe.

❡ The .xxx. daye of August. At rome in ostience strete the feest of saynt Felix a preest ⁊ martyr/ y^t by the emperours

AVGVST.

Dioclecian ⁊ Maximian was hanged ⁊ racked/ ⁊ at the last heded/ ⁊ with hym also cōfessynge Chryst was heded saynt Adauct/ that is to saye added/ eched or ioyned/ so called bycause his owne name was vnknowen. At rome also yᵉ feest of saynt Gaudence a virgyn. In the fraūchest of meldence yᵉ feest of saynt Agily a confessour. ¶ Addicyons.

¶ The feest also of saȳt Terēciane ⁊ saynt Flacke martyrs/ whiche saynt Flacke was bysshop of yᵉ ydolles/ ⁊ brought vnto saȳt Terenciane an ydoll/ whervpon he blewe ⁊ brake it/ ⁊ the same blast overcast yᵉ bysshop/ ⁊ stroke him blynde/ than the iudge Leciane after many turmētes kytte his tongue/ wherby yᵉ iudge hymselfe was dombe/ ⁊ the saynt spake/ ⁊ at yᵉ last yᵉ iudge was so vexed with his turmentes yᵗ he dyed/ after whiche saynt Flacke was cōuerted ⁊ baptized/ ⁊ so they bothe togyder heded. At ambience yᵉ feest of saynt Fyrmyne bysshop of yᵉ same/ a noble man borne/ but moche more noble in vertue ⁊ myracles. The feest also of many .⁊c̃.

[¶ To morowe.   [*fo. xcvi. b.*

¶ The .xxxj. day of August. At treuere yᵉ feest of saynt Paulyne a bysshop ⁊ cōfessour/ that by the emperour Constantyne was exiled ⁊ dryuen wᵗ moche affliccyon from place to place/ tyl at the last he dyed in fryselond.† At atens the feest of saynt Aristidy a grete clerke/ that made many werkes/ ⁊ in open disputacyon before the emperour Adriane he proued by good lernyng/ reason and auctorite/ that our sauyour Iesus was very god. At antisiodour the feest of saynt Optate a bysshop ⁊ cōfessour. The feest also of saȳt Eilady† a bysshop. In brytayne at the monastery of glastingens yᵉ feest of saynt Aidane a bysshop ⁊ cōfessour/ whose soule saynt Curtbert† sawe caryed and cōueyed by aungels vnto blysse. The feest also of saynt Cutburge a virgyn.   ¶ Addicyons.

¶ At nole the feest of saynt Felix a preest ⁊ cōfessour/ of many myracles. In englonde yᵉ feest of saȳt Eanswyde a virgyn/ yᵗ was yᵉ kynges doughter of kent/ whome the kynge of northumberlond desyred vnto wyfe/ but she for yᵉ loue of Chryst forsoke all the worlde/ ⁊ caused her fader to buylde a monastery/ wherin she was professed and lyued a holy life full of myracles. The feest also of many other holy sayntes/ mart̃. confes. ⁊ virg.

⁋ September.

⁋ To morowe.

September. THe fyrst day of September. The feest oı saynt Iesu naue/ called also Iosue/ that nexte after Moyses was capytayne ⁊ duke of yᵉ chylder of israel/ ⁊ the feest of saynt Gedeon the prophete. The feest also of saynt Anne the prophetisse/ of whose sanctite yᵉ holy gospell maketh mencyon. In atens the feest of saynt [Gyles an abbot/ moche honourable ⁊ famous of holy [fo. xcvii. lyf ⁊ many myracles/ at whose deth dyuerse persones herde a melody of aūgelles that caryed his soule vnto blysse. At capua in aquary strete yᵉ feest of saynt Priske a martyr/ yᵗ was an olde discyple of Chryst. At remys the feest of saynt Syxt a bysshop ⁊ cōfessour. At senon the feest of saynt Lupe a bysshop ⁊ cōfessour/ that for a specyall token of our lord/ had a precyous stone sent in to the chalys as he was at masse. At cenoman yᵉ feest of saynt Victor a bysshop ⁊ cōfessour of grete holynes.

⁋ Addicyons.

⁋ The feest also of saynt Calef/ one of yᵉ .xij. that were sent by Moyses to serche the lond of pmyssyon/ ⁊ therfore he onely ⁊ an other of all that came out of egypte entred thervnto. the feest also of saynt Raabe yᵉ comyn woman/ that lodged ⁊ saued the same serchers. The feest also of saynt Othoniel the fyrst iudge of israel after Iosue/ ⁊ of saynt Haiot the second iudge/ ⁊ of saynt Delbora yᵉ prophetisse/ that wᵗ her housbond Baracke was the thyrde iudge/ ⁊ of ſaȳt Gedeon the .iiij. iudge ⁊ of saynt Thola the .v. iudge/ ⁊ of saynt Iabyr the .vj. iudge/ ⁊ of saynt Iepte the .vij. iudge/ ⁊ of saynt Abesan the .viij. iudge/ ⁊ of saynt Hailon the .ix. iudge/ ⁊ of saynt Abdon the .x. iudge/ ⁊ of saynt Sampson the .xj. iudge/ ⁊ Iosue before named was the .xij. ⁊ fyrst in order ⁊ honour. The feest also of saynt Rutte the holy wydowe. The feest also of .xij. martyrs all naturall breder/ whiche ben put in the kalender of rome ⁊ there solemply serued. The feest also of saȳt Viuard a bysshop ⁊ of his dyscyple saynt Berkar a martyr ⁊ an abbot/ yᵗ by one of his owne mōkes for doyng of due correccyon was murthered/ out of whose tombe floweth oyle that [cureth many [fo. xcvii. b. psones. The feest also of saynt Agyly an abbot/ borne of noble lignage/ a grete precher/ ⁊ cōuerted moche people/ ⁊ had reuelacyon of his deth/ ⁊ was of many myracles. At ambianens the feest of saynt Honorate a bysshop ⁊ confessour. And of many other . ⁊c.

SEPTEMBER.

⁋ To morowe.

⁋ The second day of September. In fraūce at lyons the feest of saynt Iust a bysshop ⁊ cōfessour/ that lyued in desert in suche pfeccyon/ that his lyfe was accoūted next vnto aūgels/ whose holy relykes with ye relykes also of his seruaūt saynt Viatour were foūde by reuelacyon. At lyons also ye feest of saynt Helpedy a bysshop ⁊ cōfessour. At apamya ye feest of saynt Antonyn a martyr. ⁋ Addicyons.
⁋ The feest also of saȳt Mederike an abbot/ that was of noble byrth/ ⁊ forsoke the worlde ⁊ went vnto relygyon/ wherin he lyued in high pfeccyon/ ⁊ was of many myracles. The feest also of an other saynt Helpedy an abbot/ of notable abstynence/ for of .xxv. yeres he neuer toke bodyly fode but twyse in the weke/ and was contynuall in prayer. The feest also of saynt Cosman a confessour/ of hygh perfeccyon/ lyuynge euer in desert. The feest also of saynt Mansuete a bysshop and cōfessour. And the feest also of many other holy saynt̃. ⁊c.

⁋ To morowe.

⁋ The thyrde day of September. the eleccyon ⁊ ordynacion of saynt Gregory pope/ ⁊ one of y^e .iiij. doctours. The feest also of ye holy womā saȳt Pheben/ of whome the apostle Paule wryteth vnto ye romaynes. At rome the passion of saynt Seraphy a virgyn ⁊ martyr/ that by ye prȳce Adriane was delyuered vnto certayn yonge men to be corrupted : but whā they neyther coude moue [her mynde/ ne yet defoule [*fo. xcviii.* her body/ she was than enflambed w^t brennynge oyle ⁊ pytche/ ⁊ after scourged ⁊ racked/ ⁊ after many other turmentes heded/ ⁊ so accōplysshed her martyrdom the .xxix. day of Iuly/ notw^tstandynge/ bycause her holy body was not foūde vnto this daye/ therfore her sayd passyon is here festyuate. At capua the feest of saynt Antonyn a martyr/ y^t in .the age of xx. yeres was put to deth/ ⁊ ye feest also of saynt Aristey a bisshop ⁊ martyr/ that w^t hȳ was put to deth ⁊ bothe theyr gestes wryten in one boke. At tull ye feest of saynt Mansuete a bysshop. ⁋ Addicyons.
⁋ The feest also of saynt Effam ⁊ saynt Dorothy/ naturall systers/ ⁊ of saynt Tecla ⁊ saynt Erasma/ naturall systers also/ and vnto them cosyn germaynes/ breders childer/ all. iiij. virgyns ⁊ martyrs/ y^t by the accusacyon of theyr owne kyn were put vnto meruaylous cruell turmentes/ ⁊ after all the fader of two the fyrst ⁊ vncle vnto ye other/ slewe them all w^t his owne handes. The feest also of saynt Antidy a bysshop ⁊ martyr that

was put to deth by yᵉ wandales/ ⁊ lyeth at turon/ it is specyally noted in his lyf/ that he had power ouer wycked spirytes/ ⁊ so had the deuyll subiecte/ that he caused hym to cary hym where he wolde lyke a beest/ as a horse or a mule/ with many other myracles. The feest also of many other holy sayntes/ marṛ/ cōfes. ⁊c.

⁋ To morowe.

⁋ The .iiij. day of September. the feest of saynt Moyses yᵉ pphete/ ⁊ leder of yᵉ childer of israell out of egipt. In galace at auchyre† the feest of saynt Rufyne/ saynt Syluane/ ⁊ saynt Vytalicy/ all chylder ⁊ martyrs. At cabilon yᵉ feest of saynt Marcell a martyr/ yᵗ by the president Priske was desyred vnto a solempne feest of the [ydolles/ wheder whan he [fo. xcviii. b. came/ he defyed bothe the mete ⁊ yᵉ ydolles/ ⁊ with grete boldnes reproued theyr foly/ for yᵉ whiche the sayd president deuysed for hym a newe turment of cruell vengeaūce/ ⁊ caused hym to be set fast in yᵉ erth ouer yᵉ gyrdell/ so yᵗ he myght bowe no waye/ where he cōtynued in yᵉ laude of Chryst thre dayes/ ⁊ so departed. The feest also of saynt Magnus/ saynt Chaste ⁊ saynt Maximy. And the translacyon of saynt Cutbert/ and of saynt Byryne/ bothe bysshops of synguler sanctite.

⁋ Addicyons.

⁋ The feest also of saynt Priske/ a man of synguler deuocyon ⁊ grete lernynge/ yᵗ ordered many lessons ⁊ respondes for yᵉ feestfull dayes/ ⁊ made many good werkes. The feest also of saynt Maryne/ yᵗ fyrst was a mason/ ⁊ laboured moche for poore psones/ ⁊ after he gaue hymselfe to lernyng ⁊ was a grete precher/ ⁊ cōuerted many gentyles/ ⁊ so was made a deacon in order/ and than he buylded many monasteryes ⁊ chirches/ ⁊ well ordered them/ ⁊ was of many myracles. The feest also of many other holy sayntes/ marṛ. confes. and virg.

⁋ To morowe.

⁋ The .v. day of September. At rome yᵉ feest of saynt Victoryn a martyr/ yᵗ was a famous man of vertue ⁊ myracles/ so yᵗ by the hole assent of the people/ he was electe bysshop of amyterne/ ⁊ soone after he was accused for a christyan vnto yᵉ emperour Nerue/ ⁊ after many turmētes he was hāged by yᵉ heles his heed downwarde ouer a stynkynge dyche full of carayne ⁊ brymstone/ ⁊ there henge thre dayes in yᵉ cōfession of Chryst ⁊ so departed. In a gate of rome the feest of saynt Herculiane. At capua the feest of saynt Quynt/ saynt Arconcy ⁊ saynt

SEPTEMBER.

Donate martyrs. In yᵉ fraūchest of ter[uernens yᵉ feest [*fo. xcix.* of saynt Bertyne an abbot ꝛ cōfessour.   ⁋ Addicyons.
⁋ The feest also of an other saȳt Victoryne a cōfessour that was a gentyle ꝛ a grete lerned man/ scolemayster vnto saynt Ierom/ ꝛ in his age he was cōuerted vnto Chryst/ ꝛ made many pſytable werkes/ ꝛ moche edyfyed the chirche. The feest also of saynt Gondegrand a martyr. And the feest of many other holy sayntes .ꝛc.

⁋ To morowe.

⁋ The .vj. day of Septēber. the feest of saynt zachary the pphete/ that in his age came from caldey vnto his owne coūtree/ ꝛ there was buryed nere vnto yᵉ pphete Agge. In affryke the feest of saynt Donaciane/ saynt Presydy/ saynt Mansuete/ saynt Germane and saynt Fuscole/ all cōfessours ꝛ bisshops/ that notwᵗstandyng were put to many turmētes/ racked/ scourged ꝛ beten with staues/ ꝛ after put vnto exyle/ from whiche company was taken saynt Lety/ a noble man of excellent doctryne/ yᵗ after longe ꝛ harde prison ꝛ many turmentes was brent/ ꝛ so a martyr. In capadoce at reatyne the feest of saynt Cokcydy a deacon. At rome yᵉ feest of saynt Eluthery a bysshop and confessour.   ⁋ Addicyons.
⁋ The feest also of saȳt zachary a preest of yᵉ olde lawe that was slayne by kynge Ioas/ of yᵉ whiche zachary our sauyour maketh mencyon in the gospel. The feest also of saynt Onesyphour discyple vnto saynt Paule yᵉ apostle. In yrelond yᵉ feest of saynt Maculyne a kȳges sone/ by whose sanctite a chylde spake in his moders wombe/ a man also of many other myracles. The feest also of many other holy sayntes/ marꝛ/ confes. ꝛ virg.

Math.
xxiij.

⁋ To morowe.

[⁋ The .vij. daye of September. At nicomede [*fo. xcix. b.* the feest of saynt Iohn̄ a martyr/ yᵗ by zele of Chryst tare ꝛ rent a boke of the emperours lawe/ wherin were wryten certayne decrees agaynst chrystyans. For the whiche dede the emperours Dioclecian ꝛ Maximian than bydynge in yᵉ same cite/ put hym in a fury vnto many varyaūt ꝛ moost cruell turmentes/ whiche he suffred vnto deth with moost mylde and pacyent behauyour. At orlyaūce the deposicyon of saȳt Eurcy a cōfessour/ that (as is wryten in his legend) was the fyrst subdeacon of the chirche of rome/ ꝛ after by a myracle in a sygne of a doue/ he was electe bisshop of the same cite. In the terrytory of augustudune y̆ᵉ feest of saynt Regyne a virgyn ⁊ martyr/ that by the consull Olybry was racked ⁊ enflambed with lampes/ ⁊ after many greuous turmentes heded. In the fraūchest of parys yᵉ feest of saȳt Clodoald a preest/ borne of noble blode/ but more noble in vertue ⁊ good maners.   ⁋ Addicyons.

⁋ One of yᵉ feestes also of saynt Dūstane archebysshop of caūterbury. In englond at durham yᵉ feest of saynt Alkūde a cōfessour ⁊ bisshop/ that longe after his deth was trāslated by reuelacyon/ ⁊ in his trāslacyon were many myracles shewed. The feest also of many ot. ⁊c.

⁋ To morowe.

⁋ The .viij. day of September. The feest of our lady called the nautiuite/ or of her byrth/ whiche before was shewed ⁊ prophecyed/ ⁊ how of her virgynall wombe (she euer immaculate) sholde procede the sauyour of yᵉ worlde/ ⁊ how she also sholde be yᵉ ppetuall patronysse of all mankynde. At nicomede yᵉ feest of saynt Adriane a martyr/ wᵗ other .xxiij. persones/ that by yᵉ emperour Dioclecian after many turmentes/ had theyr thyes ⁊ [lȳmes broken/ ⁊ so put to deth. In alexander [*fo. c.* yᵉ feest of saynt Ammon/ saynt Theophily ⁊ saynt Neothery/ wᵗ .xxij. moo/ all martyrs. At antioche yᵉ feest of saynt Tymothe ⁊ saynt Faustyne.   ⁋ Addicyons.

⁋ The feest also of an other saynt Adriane yᵉ fyrst pope of that name/ a grete buylder ⁊ reparer of chirches ⁊ monasteryes/ ⁊ he kept a generall coūseyle or sene at cōstantynople/ with many other noble actes/ ⁊ was of hygh perfeccyon. The feest also of saynt Corbiniane a bysshop of holy lyfe ⁊ many myracles. And the feest of many other holy sayntes/ martyrs/ confes. ⁊ virgyns.

⁋ To morowe.

⁋ The .ix. day of September. At nicomede the passion of saynt Dorothy ⁊ saynt Gorgony/ that rebuked the emperour Dioclecian vnto his owne face/ for yᵉ tyrāny he vsed vnto chrystyans/ for yᵉ which they were racked/ scourged/ ⁊ theyr flesshe rent wᵗ hokes/ than were theyr wombes or belyes flayne the skynne of/ ⁊ salt/ vynegre ⁊ gall put thervpon/ ⁊ so were they sprad vpon a gredyren wᵗ hote coles ⁊ broyled/ ⁊ after many moo turmentes/ they were hāged by the neckes as theues ⁊ so accomplysshed theyr martyrdom. And in a whyle after yᵉ body of saynt Gorgony was trāslate vnto rome

SEPTEMBER.

⁊ there lyeth in latyn strete. At sabyn .xxx. myles from rome yᵉ feest of saynt Iacinct/ saynt Alexander ⁊ saynt Tyburce. In yᵉ fraūchest of taruernens yᵉ feest of saynt Audomare a bysshop ⁊ cōfessour. In scotlond yᵉ feest of saynt Querany an abbot. The feest also of saynt Modwen a virgyn.

❡ Addicyons.

❡ In yrelond the feest of saynt Osman a virgyn/ that was a kȳges doughter/ borne of pagans/ ⁊ yet heryng of Chryst/ she forsoke her parentes/ ⁊ with one mayde [she [fo. c. b. fledde in to wyldernes/ where she cōtynued a holy lyfe all full of myracles. The feest also of an other saȳt Dorothy an abbot in egypte/ a man of meruaylous strayte lyf ⁊ grete holynes. The feest also of saȳt Sergy the pope/ yᵗ amonge other of his nobles actes/ ordeyned agnus dei .iij. tymes to be songe or sayd in yᵉ masse. he foūde also at rome by reuelacion a porcyon of yᵉ holy crosse/ ⁊ had many other reuelacyons/ ⁊ was of synguler sanctite. In englonde at barkyng the feest of saynt wolsyld a virgyn/ yᵗ was abbesse bothe of barkynge ⁊ horton/ whome kyng Edgare wolde haue maryed by force/ but she escaped by myracle/ ⁊ was of many myracles/ ⁊ had also the spiryte of prophecy. The feest also of many other holy sayntes/ marṫ. confes. and virg.

❡ To morowe.

❡ The .x. day of September. At rome the feest of saȳt Hyllary the pope. In affryke the feest of saynt Nemesiane/ saynt Felix ⁊ saynt Lucy all bysshops. The feest also of saynt Felix/ saynt Luthy/ saynt Poliane/ saynt Victor/ saynt Iadery/ ⁊ saynt Datyue/ yᵗ in the persecucyon of Decius ⁊ Valeriane yᵉ emperours/ after many affliccyons were kepte in fettres as prysoners/ ⁊ so caused to dygge ⁊ myne stones/ ⁊ therin contynued as bondmen all theyr lyues/ vnto whome saynt Cipriane wrote a pystle/ yᵗ remayneth yet amonge his werkes. In calcidony the feest of saynt Sosteny ⁊ saynt Victor that by the consull Priske were hardly prisoned/ ⁊ cast vnto wylde beestes/ with many other affliccyons/ ⁊ at the last a voyce frō heuen called them as they were in prayer/ ⁊ therwᵗ they gladly yelded theyr spiryte. The feest also of saȳt Brydhestane a bysshop ⁊ cōfessour/ ⁊ of saynt Denyse ⁊ saynt Ammon cōfessours. At wynche[ster the translacyon of saynt [fo. ci. Adelwold a bysshop. And the translacyon also of saynt Augustyne the apostle of englond with certayne of his felowes and company. ❡ Addicyons.

❡ In yrelonde yᵉ feest of saynt Fynan/ called also saynt wynyn a bisshop ⁊ cōfessour/ of whome saynt Patrike dyd prophecy/ accordynge vnto the whiche he was of synguler sanctite ꝛ many myracles/ amōge which is notable y{t} he reysed thre psones vnto lyfe/ one of y{e} whiche persones had ben deed thre dayes. The feest also of saynt Hereodardet/ bysshop of tungrens and a martyr. And the feest of many other holy sayntes/ marꝭ. ꝛc.

℺ To morowe.

℺ The .xj. daye of September. At rome in olde salary strete the feest of saynt Prothe ꝛ saynt Iacinct/ enukes vnto y{e} emperour Galiene/ y{t} whan they were knowen for christyans/ were now compelled/ now entreated to do sacrefyce vnto y{e} ydolles/ but in no wyse wolde they consent therto/ for the whiche after many turmentes they were heded. At tarente y{e} feest of sayt Peter archebisshop of y{e} same. At lyons the deposicyon of saynt Pacience a bysshop ꝛ cōfessour.
℺ Addicyons.
℺ The feest also of saynt Hely an abbot in the desert of egypt/ that by his holy coūseyle gadered in to one monastery ccc. virgyns/ of y{e} whiche he was fader ꝛ gouernour in grete holynes ꝛ hygh perfeccion. The feest also of an other saynt Hely an abbot also nere the same partyes/ that was discyple vnto saynt Antony/ and a man of synguler sanctite. The feest also of saynt Venery an abbot in the yle of palmary/ that was also discyple vnto saynt Antony/ a man of strayte lyfe and many myracles. The feest also of an other saynt Venery a [monke of the monastery of saynt Benet/ that for [*fo. ci. b.* pfeccyon went from thens in to wyldernes w{t} onely thre loues of brede/ wherby he lyued there foure yeres/ and after many yeres by herbes/ fruytes/ and rotes. The feest also of many other holy sayntes/ marꝭ. confes. ꝛc.

℺ To morowe.

℺ The .xij. day of September. At ticyne y{e} feest of sayt Syre ꝛ saynt Euence/ discyples vnto sayt Hermagory ꝛ by hym sent thyder to preche/ where by theyr vertue ꝛ myracles they fyrst conuerted that cite/ ꝛ also moche edyfyed the other citees y{t} before were cōuerted/ ꝛ there they were bothe bysshops/ of holy lyfe ꝛ hygh perfeccyon. At lyons the deposycyon of saynt Sacerdos/ in englysshe saynt preest. ℺ Addicyons.
℺ The translacyon also of the foresayd saynt Hermagory. And the feest of an other saynt Euence/ borne of y{e} noble

SEPTEMBER. 145

blode of spayne/ ꝛ a man of grete lernynge ꝛ holy cōuersacyon. At nicomede yᵉ feest of saynt Nicete a martyr/ yᵗ by his owne fader kynge of the same lond/ was put to many cruell turmētes/ wherin he dyd grete myracles/ ꝛ cōuerted many psones. The feest also of saynt Bone/ called also saynt Cordimūde/ a virgyn of yᵉ noble blode of egypte/ yᵗ beynge a gentyle whan she herde of our sauyour/ forsoke many noble maryages/ ꝛ wylfully chase ꝛ elected hym vnto her spouse/ for whose loue she stale pryuely vnto a monastery of virgyns/ where she was baptized ꝛ toke yᵉ holy habyte/ ꝛ so contynued a holy lyfe full of myracles. In yrelond yᵉ feest of saynt Albey a bysshop ꝛ cōfessour/ of synguler pfeccyon ꝛ many myracles. The feest also of many other holy .⁊c.

¶ To morowe.

¶ The .xiij. day of September. In egipt at alexander [the feest of saẏt Phylyp/ that was fader vnto the holy [*fo. cii.* virgyn saynt Eugene/ a noble man ꝛ a capytayne of yᵉ cite/ whiche rome ꝛ all yᵉ worlde he forsoke for Chryst/ ꝛ was after a bysshop/ whiche thynge knowen yᵉ emperours Volusian ꝛ Galiene caused yᵉ mayre Perhēny to put hym vnto dethe by the swerde. The feest also of saynt Amaty a preest ꝛ abbot of yᵉ monastery of romaryke/ a man of meruaylous abstynence/ ꝛ lyued as an heremyte in hygh pfeccyon wᵗ many myracles. At andegaue yᵉ feest of saynt Mauryly a bysshop ꝛ cōfessour. At turon the feest of saynt Lidor a bysshop also ꝛ confessour.

¶ Addicyons.

¶ In grece yᵉ feest of saynt Ligour a martyr/ the daye of whose deth ꝛ passyon was shewed by reuelacyon/ ꝛ proued by myracle. The feest also of saynt Maximy a bisshop ꝛ cōfessour. And yᵉ feest of many other holy .⁊c.

¶ To morowe.

¶ The .xiiij. day of September. the exaltacyon of the crosse/ whan the emperour Eracly brought it frō perse vnto Ierusalem. A porcyon of the whiche crosse foūde in yᵉ sextry at rome by pope Sergius/ is brought forth as this daye yerely ꝛ honoured of the people. At rome in appia strete the feest of saynt Cornelius pope ꝛ martyr/ that by the emperour Decius was put to exyle/ ꝛ yet reuoked/ ꝛ after many turmentes heded/ ꝛ wᵗ hym .xx. other psones/ amonge whome was also heded saẏt Cereall a man of warre/ and his wyfe saynt Salust/ whome saẏt Cornely had baptized. In affryke yᵉ feest of saynt Cipriane a bisshop/ yᵗ
MARTILO. K

by the prynce Valeriane was fyrst exyled/ ⁊ after reuoked/ and vj. myles from cartage at the see syde/ he was heded/ wᵗ whome were put also to deth saynt Victor and saynt Crescenciane [and the holy women saynt Rosula and saynt General all [*fo. cii. b.* martyrs. ¶ Addicyons.

¶ The feest also of the holy fader of the olde testament saynt Toby. And of yᵉ famous wydowe saynt Iudith that for the delyueraūce of yᵉ people of god/ put herselfe in grete daūger/ ⁊ yet by the helpe of our lord she slewe Oliferne ⁊ spedde her holy purpose. The feest also of yᵉ holy wydowe ⁊ quene saynt Ruth. And of saynt Hester a quene also. The feest also of many other holy saī. ⁊c.

¶ To morowe.

¶ The .xv. day of September. At rome in numentane strete yᵉ feest of saynt Nicomede a preest ⁊ martyr/ that by yᵉ emperour Domiciane required to do sacrefyce vnto yᵉ ydolles/ sayd he wolde do sacrefyce onely vnto our lorde god/ for the whiche he was beten to deth wᵗ plūmettes of lede. In the fraūchest of cabilonens the feest of saynt Valerian a martyr/ that by the mayre Priske was racked ⁊ his flesshe rent wᵗ hokes/ ⁊ after many other greuous turmentes wherin he was constaunt/ he was slayne by the swerde. At tull the feest of saynt Apry a bysshop ⁊ cōfessour. At carneto yᵉ feest of saynt Leopite a bysshop and cōfessour. And the octaue of our blessed lady.

¶ Addicyons.

¶ The feest also of saynt Aycard an holy abbot. In the prouynce of Valery the feest of two holy monkes martyrs/ whose names ben vnknowen/ yᵗ by the longobardes were hanged/ after whose deth theyr soules sange swete psalmody/ soo that the sayd longobardes were affrayde/ ⁊ all the other chrystyans prysoners moche conforted therby. The feest also of many other ho. ⁊c.

¶ To morowe.

¶ The .xvj. day of September. At calcidony the feest [of saynt Eufemia/ called comynly saynt Effam a virgyn ⁊ martyr/ [*fo. ciii.* that by the proconsull Priske was after longe ⁊ hard prison/ scourged/ racked in an instrument full of wheles/ cast boūden in to a grete fyre/ pressed wᵗ grete knotty rough stones/ cast to wylde beestes/ scourged agayn wᵗ thorny busshes tyll the skyn was rent ⁊ the flesshe/ ⁊ put in to a fryenge potte of boylynge oyle/ ⁊ yet agayne cast vnto wylde rauenous beestes/ whiche

SEPTEMBER.

turmētes all she bare ⁊ suffred as no thinge noyed by them/ and at the last in the cōfessyon of Chryst/ she myldly rendred her spirite. At rome the feest of ye noble matrone saynt Lucy/ ⁊ of saỹt Geminiane/ bothe martyrs togyder/ that by ye emperour Dioclecian after many varyaūt turmentes were put to deth by ye swerde. At wynchester† ye feest of saynt Edythe a holy virgyn.
❧ Addicyons.

❧ The feest also of saynt Mynyane a bysshop/ y^t was a kynges sone of the north partyes of englond/ and for Chryst he forsoke ye worlde ⁊ went to rome/ where he was in grete fauour w^t the pope/ ⁊ whan he was suffycyently lerned in Chrystes doctryne/ he was made bysshop/ ⁊ so returned in to englonde/ where he cōuerted moche people/ buylded many chirches ⁊ monasteryes/ and was of synguler sanctite ⁊ many myracles. The feest also of many other holy sayntes/ marṫ. ⁊ċ.

❧ To morowe.

❧ The .xvij. day of September. At rome in tyburtyne strete ye feest of saynt Iustyne a preest ⁊ cōfessour/ that bydynge constaūtly in the confession of Chryst escaped the psecucyon of thre emperours/ Decius/ Gally/ and Volusiane. At rome also the feest of saynt Narcisse and saynt Crescencianet martyrs. At leodike ye feest of saynt [Lambert [fo. ciii. b. bysshop of tungren/ an innocent man of profoūde mekenes/ ⁊ put to martyrdom by the treason of wycked psones. In brytayn ye feest of saynt Socrates ⁊ saynt Stephan. At niuedune the feest of saynt Valeriane/ saynt Macryne/ ⁊ saynt Gordiane martyrs. At corduba ye feest of saynt Emiliane a deacon/ ⁊ of saynt Ieremy bothe martyrs heded. The feest also of saynt Flocell/ a holy man ⁊ martyr. ❧ Addicyons.

❧ The feest also of saynt Cerbony a bysshop ⁊ confessour/ ⁊ of saynt Gengulfy a cōfessour. The translacyon also of saynt Tharrasy a confessour. And the feest also of many other holy sayntes/ martyrs/ confes. ⁊ virg.

❧ To morowe.

❧ The .xviij. day of September. the feest of saynt Metody bysshop of olympylet/ ⁊ after bysshop of tyre/ that in grece (as saynt Ierom wryteth) in the cite of calcydy was by ye emperour Dioclecian put to martyrdom. At vien ye feest of saynt Ferreoly a noble capitayn/ that after hard imprisonment ⁊ many turmentes was heded/ ⁊ so the martyr of Chryst.

K 2

⁋ Addicyons.

⁋ The feest also of saynt Victor a martyr/ y^t was thre dayes in a hote fourneys/ ꝛ other thre dayes he hāged by the helcs/ ꝛ there flayne quycke/ ꝛ at ye last after many cruell turmentes he was heded/ in whose passyon were done many myracles. And ye holy woman saynt Stephane was there cōuerted/ ꝛ w^t hym put to deth. The feest also of many other holy sayntes/ mar. cō. ꝛc.

⁋ To morowe.

⁋ The .xix. day of September. In naples at campane the feest of sayͦt Ianuary bysshop of beneuentane. And of saynt Festy ꝛ saynt Proculy deacons/ saynt Desyre saynt Ewtyke ꝛ saynt Acute/ y^t by the emperour Dio[clecian were in the [fo. ciiii. cite of pluteolane† after many turmentes heded. In palestyne ye feest of saynt Peley and saynt Nyle bysshops/ that in a grete psecucyon w^t many chrystyans were brent. At nuceria the feest of saynt Felix/ ꝛ of the holy woman saynt Cōstance/ y^t by Nero the emperour, were put to martyrdom. In ye terrytory of lyngonyke ye feest of saynt Signy a preest/ ꝛ of saynt Genony a martyr. At turon ye feest of saynt Eustache a bysshop of synguler vertue.   ⁋ Addicyons.

⁋ The feest also of saynt Goeryke/ that was a noble knyght/ ꝛ sodeynly stryken blynde/ ꝛ yet after restored to syght by the reuelacyon of an aūgell/ ꝛ made a bysshop. The feest also of saynt Theodour archebisshop of caūterbury/ that by the pope was sent in to englonde to instructe ye people/ where he ordeyned many scoles/ both of the greke ꝛ latyn tongue/ ꝛ by his holy lyfe ꝛ grete myracles/ moche edyfyed the chirche of Chryst. The feest also of many other holy sayntes/ marꝛ. ꝛc.

⁋ To morowe.

⁋ The .xx. day of Septēber. In cizyke ye feest of saynt Fawste a virgyn/ that vnder ye emperour Maximian by the iudge Eiulasy was put to the bordell hous to be defouled/ but she was preserued by an aūgell/ than he hanged her ꝛ racked her/ ꝛ at the last kytte her thrugh the myddle w^t a sawe/ in ye whiche passyon beholdyng her cōstancy/ the same iudge was cōuerted ꝛ baptized ꝛ with her put to deth. At corduba ye feest of saynt Eulogy a preest ꝛ martyr. In fryselonde† the feest of saynt Denyse and saynt Priuate martyrs. The vigil also of saynt Mathewe the apostle.   ⁋ Addicyons.

⁋ At rome ye feest of saynt Agapite pope ꝛ martyr. At

the monastery of cassyne the feest of saynt Speciouse a [monke and disciple vnto saynt Benet/ whose soule his owne [*fo. ciiii. b.* naturall broder saynt Gregory yt with hym had forsaken the honour ⁊ rychesse of ye worlde/ ⁊ was also a monke/ sawe cōuayed ⁊ caryed in to heuen by aūgels. The feest also of many other holy payntes/ mar℞. ⁊c.

Greg. iiij. dial. ca. ix.

¶ To morowe.

¶ The .xxj. day of September. the feest of the apostle ⁊ euangelyst saynt Mathewe/ that preched in ynde/ ⁊ was there put vnto martyrdom/ whose gospell wryten in ebrewe was foūde by his owne reuelacyon/ in ye tyme of the emperour zenon. In the village of clawde .xx. myles from rome/ the passyon of saynt Alexander a bysshop/ that by the emperour Antonyne was boūden ⁊ beten/ racked/ brenned wt lampes/ his flesshe torne wt hokes/ cast vnto wyld beestes/ ⁊ after in to a flambyng fourneys/ and at the last after all turmentes/ he was slayne by the swerde. At rome the feest of saynt Pamphily a martyr/ ⁊ of saȳt Laude a bysshop ⁊ cōfessour. ¶ Addicyons.

¶ The feest also of saynt Ephigene a virgyn/ the kynges doughter of egypte/ and discyple vnto saynt Mathewe/ ⁊ by hym consecrate ⁊ veyled/ whome kynge Hyrtacus wolde haue maryed/ as appereth in the legende of her mayster ye sayd apostle/ after whose deth she was abbesse ⁊ moder of .cc. virgyns/ ⁊ euer of synguler perfeccyon/ ⁊ so rested in ye peace of Chryst. The feest also of many other holy payntes/ mar℞. confes. ⁊c.

¶ To morowe.

¶ The .xxij. day of Septēber. In fraūce at sedune the feest of saynt Mawrice/ saynt Exsuper/ saynt Cādydy/ saynt Victor ⁊ saynt Innocent/ wt theyr felowes of the legyon of thebeys .vj.M.vj.C.lxvj. all martyrs/ that [by the [*fo. cv.* emperour Maximian were put to martyrdom. At bauary ye feest of saynt Hamptran a bysshop ⁊ martyr/ that was full of pyte/ so that whan a certayn man of his knowlege had cōmytted fornycacyon/ by drede wherof he was nere in despeyre/ the bysshop caused hym to lay the synne vnto his charge/ ⁊ so for the delyueraūce of his frende/ he put hymself in peryll of deth. In the fraūchest of pictauens ye feest of saynt Florence a preest ⁊ cōfessour. In ye terrytory of byturiens ye feest of saynt Syluane a bysshop ⁊ confessour/ of hygh perfeccyon ⁊ notable myracles. ¶ Addicyons.

¶ The feest also of an other saȳt Syluane an abbot of the

wyldernes of sythe/ of whome is wryten in vitas patrū. The feest also of saynt Ionas a preest ꝫ martyr that came wᵗ saynt Denyse in to fraūce/ ꝫ there besyde parys he was heded/ and he forthwᵗ toke vp his owne heed ꝫ bare it a myle thens/ where now by many myracles he is had in grete honour ꝫ reuerence. The feest also of saynt Sanctyny a bisshop ꝫ cōfessour/ that toke orders of saynt Denyse/ ꝫ so went towarde rome/ in yᵉ which iourney he reysed his felowe saynt Antonyne that many dayes had layne buryed in a dunghyll/ ꝫ so they both togyder went to rome/ ꝫ after his cōfirmacyon they returned in to fraūce/ where they bothe preched/ ꝫ whan he was deed/ saynt Antonyne succeded hym/ ꝫ bothe full of sanctite ꝫ myracles. The feest also of many other holy sayntes/ marṫ. confes. and virg.

⁋ To morowe.

⁋ The .xxiij. daye of Septēber. In campany the feest of saynt Sosy a deacon of the chirche of mesennate/ frō whose heed as he redde the gospell/ saynt Ianuary yᵉ bysshop sawe a fyre flambe ꝫ streme in grete hyghnes [by the whiche [*fo. cv. b.* token he prophecyed yᵗ his sayd deacon sholde be a martyr/ ꝫ so he was heded in yᵉ age of .xxx. yeres wᵗ the same bysshop. The feest also of saȳt Tecla a virgyn/ that was cast dyuers tymes in to grete flambyng fyres/ put vnto wylde beestes/ with many other cruell turmentes/ whiche she by yᵉ myght of god vaynquysshed/ and came vnto the cite of selewce/ where she gretely edifyed Chrystes chirche/ ꝫ there rested in the peace of chryst. In the terrytory of abrynce the feest of saynt Patryne a bysshop ꝫ cōfessour. At rome yᵉ feest of saynt Lybery a bysshop. ⁋ Addicyons.

⁋ The feest also of saȳt Lyne pope ꝫ martyr. And the feest of saynt Constancy a cōfessour/ a man of grete notable mekenes/ so that whan a rude psone in dyspleasure called hym wretche/ he lowly thanked hym/ that he wᵗout flatery shewed hym yᵗ he perceyued for trouth. The feest also of an other saynt Constancy bysshop of aquine/ a holy man of many myracles/ ꝫ had the spiryte of prophecy. The feest also of saynt Salaberge an abbesse/ of noble kynne/ borne blynde/ yᵗ by the prayers of saȳt Eustace was rendred vnto syght/ ꝫ after by her frendes compelled to mary an erle/ by whome she had fyue chylder/ ꝫ at the last by grete labour she obteyned of her housbonde yᵉ consent of chastite/ ꝫ than she buylded a large monastery/ wherin she was abbesse of .ccc. systers professed/ ꝫ was of hygh pfeccyon ꝫ many myracles. The feest also of many other holy sayntes .ꝫc.

¶ To morowe.

¶ The .xxiiij. day of Septēber. the cōcepcyon of saynt Iohn baptist. At augustudune yͤ feest of saȳt Andoche a preest/ saynt Tyrcy a deacon/ ꝗ saynt Felix/ that by the holy bysshop saȳt Policarpe were sent in to fraūce [to preche/ where [*fo. cvi.* by the tyraūt Aureliane they were taken/ prysoned/ hanged an hole day by the handes/ cast in to a grete fyre/ and at the last after many other turmentes/ theyr neckes were broken with leuers/ and so martyrs. ¶ Addicyons.
¶ The feest also of .xlix. martyrs/ that were taken wᵗ saynt Effam ꝗ kepte in pryson vnto this daye/ ꝗ so put to martyrdom. The feest also of saȳt Geremare an abbot of hygh pfeccyon/ that by aūgels had many reuelacions. The feest also of saynt Solempny a bysshop ꝗ cōfessour. And yͤ feest of many other holy sayntes .ꝗc.

¶ To morowe.

¶ The .xxv. daye of Septēber. the feest of saynt Cleophas/ one of the discyples of Chryst/ that (as is sayd) was put to deth in the castell of emaus/ and there honourably buryed/ where after the resurreccyon he had knowlege of Chryst in yͤ brekynge of brede. At ambianens the feest of saynt Firmyne a bysshop ꝗ martyr/ yᵗ by the mayre Rictiouare after many turmentes was heded. At lyons yͤ deposicyon of saynt Lupe a bysshop ꝗ an ancre. The feest also of saynt Herculan/ that is remembred in the passyon of saynt Alexander. At antisiodour the feest of saynt Annary† a bysshop and cōfessour. At blese the feest of saynt Solempny a bysshop. ¶ Addicyons.
¶ In englond at yͤ monastery of iarewe vpon the water of tyne yͤ feest of saynt Golfryde abbot of the same/ that in age resygned his rome ꝗ went to rome/ in the whiche iourney he dyed/ at whose sepulcre ben many grete myracles. In yrelonde the feest of saynt Barry a bysshop/ that spake in his moders wombe/ ꝗ after had many reuelacyons of aūgelles/ ꝗ dyd grete myracles. [The feest also of many other sayntes/ mar. [*fo. cvi. b.* cō. ꝗc.

¶ To morowe.

¶ The .xxvj. daye of September. the feest of saynt Ciprian a bysshop/ ꝗ of saȳt Iustyne a virgyn bothe martyrs/ whiche saynt Ciprian beynge a pagan/ put the sayd virgyn to moche trouble/ ꝗ wold by wytchecrafte haue made her madde/ but she at y̅e̅ last cōuerted hym/ ꝫ he was a bysshop/ ꝫ bycause he was a man of notable doctryne/ he moche edifyed y̅e̅ chirche of Chryst/ for the whiche they bothe after in one day suffred martyrdom/ whose holy bodyes were brought vnto rome. At albane the feest of saynt Senatour. At rome the feest of saynt Euseby. ⁋ Addicyons.

⁋ In yrelond the feest of saynt Colmauell an abbot/ y̅t̅ whan his moder trauayled of hym/ dyd myracles/ ꝫ euer so contynued in werkynge myracles/ tyll he was abbot/ and than of moo myracles ꝫ synguler sanctite. The feest also of many other holy sayntes/ marꝝ. ꝫc̃.

⁋ To morowe.

⁋ The .xxvij. day of September. At ege y̅e̅ feest of say̅t̅ Cosmas ꝫ of saynt Damiane martyrs/ that in the persecucyon of Dioclecian were fettred ꝫ put in pryson/ ꝫ after cast in to y̅e̅ see/ ꝫ than in to a hote fyre/ after that crucyfyed/ stoned/ set as a butte to shote therat/ w̅t̅ many other turmentes/ whiche all vay̅n̅quysshed/ they were at the last heded. It is also supposed ꝫ wryten/ y̅t̅ other .iij. of theyr naturall breder/ saynt Antymy/ say̅t̅ Leoncy/ ꝫ saynt Ewprepy suffred passyon and deth w them. At corduba the feest of saynt Adulphe ꝫ of saynt Iohn̅. martyrs and breder. At the castell of persewdon† the feest of saynt Florentyne/ that in company w̅t̅ saynt Hyllary was taken ꝫ his tongue kytte/ ꝫ slayne after [by the swerde/ ꝫ so [fo. cvii. wanne the palme of martyrdom. ⁋ Addicyons.

⁋ The feest also of saynt Surane an abbot ꝫ martyr/ that by y̅e̅ longoberdes was put to deth/ in whose martyrdom the erth quaked ꝫ shoke. The feest also of saynt Iust a deacon ꝫ martyr/ a man of synguler sanctite/ y̅t̅ by the longoberdes also was heded/ ꝫ he that stroke of his heed/ was before his company stryken to deth by a wycked spyryte. The feest also of many other holy .ꝫc̃.

⁋ To morowe.

⁋ The .xxviij. day of September. At tolose the feest of saynt Exsupery a bysshop ꝫ cōfessour/ of whome saynt Ierom sheweth/ y̅t̅ he was vnto hymselfe very hard ꝫ scarce/ ꝫ vnto nedy psones very liberall. At rome y̅e̅ feest of saynt Stakty. At iāne the feest of saynt Salomon a bysshop ꝫ confessour. ⁋ Addicyons.

⁋ The feest also of saynt Olaty† a martyr/ y̅t̅ was kyng of norwey/ and beynge a pagan he dyd moche hurt in englond ꝫ in fraūce vnto the chrysten people/ ꝝ yet at yᵉ last beynge in normandy he was cōuerted/ and in rone baptized/ ꝝ so returned in to his owne lande/ where by his prechynge ꝝ holy lyfe he cōuerted moche people/ ꝝ at yᵉ last he was by treason put to martyrdom. In yrelond yᵉ feest of saynt Fors a bysshop of grete holynes/ ꝝ had reuelacyon of aungels/ and (as Bede wryteth) he after longe sekenes departed this lyfe/ ꝝ than he sawe ꝝ perceyued a grete disputacyon ꝝ cōtencyon bytwene the aūgels ꝝ dampned spirites for his soule/ but at the last the good aungels brought his soule vnto the body agayne/ ꝝ so reysed hym frō deth/ ꝝ after he lyued many yeres in grete perfeccyon/ ꝝ cōuerted moche people ꝝ dyd many myracles. The feest also of saynt wyncesse [a martyr/ yᵗ was duke of beame [*fo. cvii. b.* ꝝ forsoke all worldly honour for the seruice of Chryst/ ꝝ at yᵉ last he was put to dethe by the emperour Harry/ at the translacyon of whose blessed body were shewed many grete myracles. The feest also of saynt Maximy a martyr. And of many other holy sayntes/ martyrs/ confes. and virg.

⁋ To morowe.

⁋ The .xxix. day of September. In the moūt of gargane the rcuerend memory of saynt Mychaell the archaūgell/ where a chirche of hym is cōsecrate/ that is but of poore buyldyng/ yet notwᵗstandyng it is adourned wᵗ many grete vertues. In trace the feest of saynt Ewtyke/ saynt Plantḟ/ ꝝ of the holy woman saynt Ercley. At antisiodour the feest of saynt Fraterny a bysshop and confessour. ⁋ Addicyons.
⁋ The feest also of saynt Theophany a cōfessour/ that was erle of centuncellēs/ a man of grete pyte ꝝ a grete almes man/ in token of whose sanctite whan he sholde departe this lyfe/ he pphecyed that fayre weder shold immedyatly after his deth folowe the tempest yᵗ was than vehement/ ꝝ where many yeres his fete ꝝ legges were sore ꝝ stynkyng by sekenes/ anone after his deth they were all hole ꝝ of swete smell/ and whan a stone sholde be layde vpon his graue/ ꝝ the erth styrred for yᵉ same/ there came out an odour ꝝ smell of meruaylous swetenes. The feest also of many other holy sayn. ꝝc̃.

⁋ To morowe.

⁋ The .xxx. daye of September. In fraūce at yᵉ castell of salodourṭ the passion of saynt Victor/ ꝝ of saynt Vrsy martyrs/ of the legyon of thebeyes/ that were put vnto meruaylous cruell turmentes/ in yᵉ whiche a heuenly lyght descendynge shone vpon them so bryghtly/ yt [all the mynistres fell [*fo. cviii.* therby flatte vnto ye groūde/ ꝉ the martyrs were therby delyuered of theyr turmentes ꝉ set on fote. After they were cast in to a grete fyre/ but no thynge noyed therby/ ꝉ at the last they were slayne by ye swerde. At bethleem iude the deposicyon of saynt Ierom a preest ꝉ one of the .iiij. doctours/ that translated out of ebrewe ꝉ other tongues in to latyn/ all holy scripture/ ꝉ made many noble werkes/ ꝉ dyed in ye age of xcviij. yeres ꝉ .vj. monethes. At placence the feest of saynt Antonyne a cōfessour. The dedicacion also of the chirche of salisbury. ❡ Addicyons.

❡ The feest also of saynt Honory archebysshop of caūterbury/ that was discyple vnto sayt Gregory/ a man of grete lernynge/ synguler sanctite ꝉ grete myracles. The feest also of saynt Ceran a bysshop. And of many other holy sayntes/ martyrs/ confessours ꝉ virgyns.

❡ October.

❡ To morowe.

October. THe fyrst daye of October. the feest of saynt Arthy† a martyr/ wt whom were put to deth v.C. and .iiij. martyrs. At thomys the feest of saynt Priske saynt Crescence ꝉ saynt Euagry. In the puynce of lusitame† at olisepon the feest of saynt Verissimy/ ꝉ of his two systers saynt Maxima ꝉ saynt Iulia. At tourney the passion of saynt Plato† a preest ꝉ martyr/ that was put to deth in fraūce/ wt the company that were sent wt saynt Denyse. The feest also of saynt Germayn a cōfessour ꝉ bysshop of antisiodour. And of saynt Remygy a cōfessour ꝉ bysshop ɔf remens. And of saynt Vedasty a confessour also ꝉ bysshop/ bothe of atrebacens ꝉ of cameracens. In the graūd port† ye fcest of saynt Bauon a cōfessour. And the feest also of saynt Melour a martyr/ [that was sone vnto ye duke of [*fo. cviii. b.* cornwell. The dedicacion also of sayt Paules at london.

❡ Addicyons.

❡ Here ben remembred certayne of the sayntes of the olde testamēt. The feest of saynt Mathathy duke ꝉ capytayne of the iewes/ whose noble actes ben remembred in scripture. The feest also of his sone ꝉ successour Iudās machabeus hygh preest ꝉ duke also of ye iewes. And of saynt Ionathas his broder ꝉ successour/ preest ꝉ duke in lyke maner. And of saynt Symon machaby theyr broder ꝉ lyke successour also. And of his sone and successour saynt Iohn machaby. The

feest also of sayt Symon hygh preest/ that was sone vnto saynt
Ony/ a noble man/ as appereth in scripture. And
of his sone ꝛ successour saynt Onyas/ a noble
man also/ as appereth in the seconde boke of the
machabeys. And yᵉ feest of saynt Eleazary a
martyr of the old testament in the tyme of the
machabeys/ as appereth in yᵉ second boke. The
feest also of saynt Piatour a preest/ yᵗ with saynt Denyse came
in to fraūce/ where he was put to martyrdom. The feest also
of many other holy sayntes. ꝛc.

Eccli. v.

Machabeoꝛ. ij.

¶ To morowe.

¶ The seconde day of October. At nycomede the feest of
saynt Elewthery a martyr/ that by the emperour Dioclecian/
after many varyaūt and cruell turmentes was brent/ wᵗ whome
were put to deth martyrs innumerable/ some drowned in the
see/ some heded ꝛ slayne by the swerde/ some brent ꝛ by other
turmentes martyred. In yᵉ terrytory òf atrebatens yᵉ passyon
of saynt Leodegare bysshop of augustudune/ that by Ebrony
stewarde of yᵉ kynges hous was by many turmentes put to deth.
The feest also of saynt Seueryne a confessour. And the
deposicyon of saynt Thomas bysshop of [herford.   [*fo. cix.*
¶ Addicyons.
¶ The feest also of saynt Geryne a martyr/ that with
saynt Leodegar was put to deth. The feest also of sayt Antony
a mōke of saynt Gregories monastery in rome a man of notable
vertue and grete compunccyon/ vnto whose spirytuall cōforte a
voyce spake frō heuen two tymes a lytell before his dethe/ at
whose sepulcre ben many grete myracles. The feest also of
many oth. ꝛc.

¶ To morowe.

¶ The thyrde day of October. the feest of sayt Denyse a
bysshop ꝛ martyr/ a grete lerned man ꝛ a noble precher/ yᵗ (as
saynt Aristidy wryteth in his boke of Chrystes religyon) was by
grete cruelty put to deth. Amonge the olde saxons yᵉ feest of
saynt Ewald/ ꝛ of an other saynt Ewald bothe of one name ꝛ
bothe preestes/ that for prechynge yᵉ fayth amonge them/ were
put to deth vpon whose holy bodyes a grete lyght from heuen
appered ꝛ shone in yᵉ nyght a longe tyme/ declaryng vnto the
faythfull people what they were/ ꝛ of how grete merytes. At
rome at the capped bere the feest of saynt Candydy a martyr.

¶ Addicyons.

¶ At rome the feest of saynt Meroly a monke of saynt Gregoryes monastery/ a man of grete compunccyon ⁊ contynuall in prayer/ vnto whome a lytell before his deth appered in visyon a crowne or garlond descẽdyng from heuen ⁊ closynge his heed/ ⁊ forthw^t after he fell seke ⁊ departed. And .xiij. yeres after whan a deuoute abbot wolde haue made his sepulcre where he laye/ a meruaylous swete smell came out of his graue declarynge his sanctite. The feest also of many other .⁊c.

¶ To morowe.

¶ The .iiij. day of October. At corynth ye feest of saynt [Cryspy and saynt Gay/ of whome saynt Paule wrote [*fo. cix. b.* vnto the corynthes. In egipt ye feest of saynt Marke ⁊ saynt Marciane breder ⁊ martyrs/ with whome were put to deth martyrs innumerable/ bothe men ⁊ womẽ of grete glory ⁊ holynes/ of ye whiche some were scourged and beten to deth/ some racked/ some brent/ some drowned in the see/ some heded/ some famysshed/ ⁊ many were hanged/ partly by ye neckes ⁊ parte by ye heles ⁊ so by varyaũt turmentes all obteyned the crowne of martyrdom. In fraũce at parys ye feest of saynt Aurey a virgyn. The feest also of saynt Fraũcys a confessour that next vnto the apostles was the moost precyse and strayte folower of the lyfe of the gospell. And he wrote a rule of moost hygh perfeccion/ whiche of very mekenes he called the rule of freres mynours/ he toke vpon hym for Chryst many grete bodyly labours/ ⁊ many spirytual troubles/ ⁊ before his deth he was notably marked with the ymage ⁊ woundes of our sauyour/ in whose peace he departed full of myracles.

¶ Addicyons.

¶ The feest also of saynt Aniane a bysshop ⁊ dyscyple vnto saynt Marke/ a noble man borne ⁊ of large possessyons/ whiche by chaũce he lost hooly/ ⁊ came vnto suche pouerty/ y^t he was fayne for his lyuynge to do seruyce vnto a poore cobler in alexander/ wheder whan saynt Marke came his shoo rent/ in ye mendyng wherof saynt Aniane hurt his fynger/ whiche by say͠t Marke was cured/ ⁊ he coũerted ⁊ ordered there bysshop/ ⁊ contynued in hygh perfeccyon ⁊ many myracles. The feest also of saynt Petrony bysshop of bonony/ electe by reuelacyon/ a noble man of the emperours blode/ a charytable man and a grete buylder ⁊ reparer of chirches. [The feest also of saynt [*fo. cx.* Amelie ⁊ of saynt Amyke/ that of dyuerse parentes of noble blode were borne bothe in one nyght/ ⁊ bothe from theyr countrees sent by theyr frendes vnto rome to be baptized/ in ye whiche

OCTOBER. 157

iourney they mette by chaūce at lucane/ ꝗ so lyke were they of face/ stature ꝗ all other membres/ that no psone coude discerne ꝗ knowe the one from the other/ wherby they fell in amyte ꝗ loued as breder/ ꝗ after many troubles taken for Chryst/ they were bothe togyder slayne in batayle for his fayth/ ꝗ they were buryed in dyuers chirches/ but that notwᵗstandynge theyr bodyes on yᵉ morowe after were foūde bothe togyder. These .ij. knyghtes ꝗ martyrs ben called in englysshe syr Amyas ꝗ syr Amylyon/ and theyr story wryten at length. The feest also of many other holy sayntes/ marͬ/ confes. ꝗ virg.

⁋ To morowe.

⁋ The .v. daye of October. In sicilie the feest of saynt Placydy ꝗ saynt Ewtyke martyrs/ ꝗ with them .xxx. other holy martyrs. In ewmeny yᵉ feest of saynt Tharsy a bysshop/ yᵗ in smyrme was put to deth. In fraunce at valence the feest of saynt Appollinare a bysshop/ whose lyfe by synguler sanctite was famous/ and his deth by many myracles laudable. At antisiodour yᵉ deposicyon of saynt Firmate a deacon/ ꝗ of his syster saẏt Flauiane a holy virgyn.   ⁋ Addicyons.

⁋ At rome the feest of saynt Gale a wydowe/ borne of noble blode/ and of grete rychesse/ that after the deth of her housbond/ notwᵗstandyng her state/ youth/ beauty/ ꝗ possessyons/ enclosed her selfe ꝑfessed in yᵉ monastery of saynt Peter/ where she lyued in hygh perfeccyon/ ꝗ had by saynt Peter reuelacyon of her deth. The feest also of many other holy sayntes/ marͬ/ confes. ꝗ virg.

[⁋ To morowe.   [*fo. cx. b.*

⁋ The .vj. day of October. At capua the feest of saynt Marcell/ saynt Casty/ saynt Emyly/ ꝗ saynt Saturne all martyrs. The feest also of saynt Sagary a bysshop ꝗ martyr/ that was one of the olde discyples of saynt Paule. At agen yᵉ feest of saynt Fayth a virgyn ꝗ martyr/ by whose holy example saynt Caprase was cōforted to martyrdom. The feest also of saynt Rogate a confessour.   ⁋ Addicyons.

⁋ At rome yᵉ feest of saynt Euseby pope. In burgoyne the feest of saynt Gungulf a holy martyr. And the feest also of many other holy sayntes/ marͬ. confes. ꝗ virg.

⁋ To morowe.

⁋ The .vij. day of October. At rome in appia strete the deposicyon of saẏt Marke the fyrst pope of that name. The

feest also of saynt Marcell ꝛ saȳt Apuley/ that by the doctryne
of saynt Peter were coūerted from yᵉ heresy of Symon magus/
and after for Chrystes fayth they bothe togyder by Aureliane
the consull were put to deth ꝛ buryed not ferre from rome. In
the prouince of auguste at eufratesi† the feest of saynt Bachy ꝛ
saynt Sergy/ that in the tyme of the emperour Maximian were
put to many turmentes/ racked/ scourged/ and so saȳt Bachy
was beten to deth/ ꝛ saynt Sergy heded. In the same prouince
the feest of saynt Iulia a virgyn ꝛ martyr/ that by yᵉ mayre
Marcian was put to deth. The feest also of saynt Osythe a
virgyn ꝛ martyr/ that by yᵉ danes was heded/ ꝛ she forthwᵗ toke
vp her owne heed ꝛ bare it vnto yᵉ place where she wolde be
buryed. The canonizacyon also of our holy moder saȳt Birgit.

⁋ Addicyons.

⁋ The feest also of saynt Iustyne a virgyn ꝛ martyr/
[that was a kynges doughter/ ꝛ by her faders successour [*fo. cxi.*
put to martyrdom. The feest also of an other saȳt Marke the
second pope of that name/ that ordeyned yᵉ crede to be songe or
sayd euery sonday/ ꝛ in yᵉ feestes also of the apostles. The
feest also of ye thyrde saynt Marke a cōfessour ꝛ an heremyte/
that bycause he wrote yᵉ lyues of many heremites he had for his
syrname wryter/ ꝛ so was called Marke wryter/ he was of
synguler pfeccyon/ for whan his moder wold nedely se hym than
beynge in religyon/ he by the cōmaūdemēt of his souerayne went
vnto her clothed in a sacke/ ꝛ his face all soyled wᵗ dust ꝛ sote/
and yet he wynked bycause he wolde not se her/ all though he
were seen of her. The feest also of many other holy sayntes/
marꝛ. confes. ꝛc.

⁋ To morowe.

⁋ The .viij. day of October. the feest of saȳt Symeon that in
Chrystes presentacyon toke hym in his armes ꝛ sayd Nūc
dimittis seruū tuū dñe .ꝛc. At thessolonieyt the feest of saynt
Demetry a martyr. In the terrytory of lyons yᵉ feest of saynt
Benedicte a virgyn ꝛ martyr. At hyspale the feest of saynt
Peter a martyr. At Ierusalem the feest of the holy woman
saynt Pelage/ that was called a grete synner ꝛ wretche. In
brytayne the feest of saynt Yue a confessour of synguler sanctite.

⁋ Addicyons.

⁋ The feest also of saynt Margarete a virgyn/ yᵗ was of so
notable beauty/ yᵗ her frendes wold suffre no man but by
synguler fauour to look vpon her. And she after was called
broder Pellagy/ for yᵉ same nyght that she by compulsyon of
her frendes was maryed/ she stale away in a mānes clothynge/

OCTOBER. 159

⁊ was a mōke of so hygh pſeccyon/ that his abbot dyd cōmytte vnto his gouer[naūce a monastery of virgyns/ in the [*fo. cxi.* ⅅ whiche one dyd fornicacyon/ ⁊ imputed the chylde vnto Pellagy/ for yᵉ whiche she was put to prison/ ⁊ shamefull rebuke many yeres/ tyll she sawe she must depart this lyf/ ⁊ than she shewed the trouth what she was/ ⁊ frō whens she came/ ⁊ so wᵗ grete mournyng ⁊ lamentacyon she was buryed in the monastery of virgyns. The feest also of saynt Thays/ that many yeres was a comyn woman of suche beauty yᵗ many men solde theyr londes ⁊ spent theyr goodes vpon her/ ⁊ many were sore wounded/ ⁊ grete blodeshed done for her sake/ wherof herynge the holy abbot saynt Pānucy/ toke seculer aray ⁊ went vnto her/ ⁊ by grace conuerted her/ ⁊ aftes thre yeres penaūce/ she lyued in a monastery of virgyns a whyle/ ⁊ so made a holy ende. The feest also of saynt Reparate a virgyn ⁊ martyr/ that by Decius the emperour was racked/ her flesshe rent wᵗ hokes/ ⁊ her body sprynkeled wᵗ boylynge lede/ than was she broyled lyke vnto saȳt Laurence/ her brestes and rybbes brent wᵗ fyry plates/ ⁊ than scourged wᵗ thorny busshes/ her woūdes rubbed with vynegre/ salt ⁊ aqua vite/ ⁊ at yᵉ last after all turmentes she was heded/ whose soule was openly seen flye in to heuen lyke a doue. The feest also of saynt Keyna/ called also saynt Keynwir a virgyn/ ⁊ doughter vnto saynt Breghan kynge of breknoke in wales/ whiche had .xij. sones and .xij. doughters all holy sayntes one of yᵉ whiche doughter was moder vnto saynt Dauid/ ⁊ this virgyn an other/ that was shewed by reuelacyon before her byrth/ ⁊ after forsoke her kynne and coūtree/ ⁊ dwelled in a desert full of venymous serpentes/ whiche by her prayers were turned al in to stones that yet vnto this daye done kepe the fourme ⁊ fashon [of yᵉ same serpentes/ where she cōtynued in hygh [*fo. cxii.* pſeccyon ⁊ many myracles. The feest also of many otħ.⁊c.

⁋ To morowe.

⁋ The .ix. day of October. the feest of yᵉ holy patriarke saynt Abraham. At parys the feest of saynt Denyse a bysshop/ saynt Rustyke a preest/ ⁊ saynt Elewthery a deacon/ that by the pope were sent to cōuerte fraūce/ ⁊ whan in the sayd cite they had done theyr offyce with dilygence/ at the last they were taken/ ⁊ by the mayre Fescēny put to deth all by the swerde. At iule the feest of saynt Dompnyne a martyr/ that in the pſecucion of the emperour Maximian wolde haue fled/ but whan he was pursued ⁊ taken/ he boldly confessed Chryst/ ⁊ gladly toke his deth by yᵉ swerde. The feest also of saȳt Gysleny a confessour. ⁋ Addicyons.

⁋ In englond at caūterbury the feest of saynt Aymon

archedeacon of the same/ a man of grete abstynence/ a notable clerke ⁊ a noble precher/ yᵗ in a certayne nyght whan he studyed to preche on the morowe after of the incarnacyon of our sauyour/ yᵉ deuyll appered vnto hỹ in a terryble lykenes/ ⁊ he lyfte vp his ryght hande to blesse hym/ whiche the deuyll helde fast/ than he lyfte vp the other hande/ ⁊ that also yᵉ deuyl helde fast than he spytte in his face ⁊ sayd/ the crosse is in my herte/ I defye the/ wherwᵗ yᵉ deuyll departed/ but he called hym agayne ⁊ charged hym to shewe vnto hym why he so dyd/ ⁊ he sayd/ to haue letted the of thy sermon/ for no thynge so greueth vs as yᵉ incarnacyon of Chryst. And after he lyued in hygh perfeccyon ⁊ many myracles. The feest also of many other holy sayntes/ marṝ. ⁊c.

¶ To morowe.

¶ The .x. daye of October. At crete the feest of saynt [Pyncty a bysshop of grete lernynge/ so that in his [fo. cxii. b. lernynge we may se his ymage as though it were in a glasse. At agryppyny the feest of saynt Gereon a martyr/ that by syrname was called mallose/with whome in the persecucyon of yᵉ emperour Maximian .cccxviij. martyrs wylfully layde downe theyr hedes wᵗ all pacyence to receyue the palme of martyrdom. In the terrytory of the same cite the feest of saynt Victor a martyr/ ⁊ with hym were put to deth .xviij. persones. The feest also of saynt Cassy ⁊ saỹt Florence martyrs/ with whome were put to dethe many other martyrs. In englond the feest of saynt Paulyne a cōfessour ⁊ archebysshop of yorke. The feest also of saynt Ewbrache a confessour.   ¶ Addicyons.

¶ The feest also of saynt Cerbony a bysshop of many myracles/ ⁊ had the spyryte of prophecy. The feest also of saỹt Gerald a cōfessour of hygh pfeccyon/ of whome his parētes had reuelacyon before he was goten/ ⁊ he spake in his moders wombe/ ⁊ after dyd many grete miracles. The feest also of saynt Piery a preest/ a grete lerned man of notable eloquence and synguler sanctite. The feest also of many other holy sayntes/ marṝ. ⁊c.

¶ To morowe.

¶ The .xj. day of October. At tharsum the chefe cite of cicilye† the feest of saynt Tharake/ saynt Proby/ ⁊ saỹt Andronyke martyrs/ that in the persecucyon of yᵉ emperour Dioclecian were kepte longe in hard pryson/ ⁊ thre tymes put vnto moost cruell turmētes/ ⁊ so obteyned the palme of martyrdom. In the fraūchest of vulcasyne the passyon of saynt

Nigasy a preest/ with his felowes saynt Quiryne/ saynt Skumculy/ ꝛ the holy virgyn saynt Pience/ all martyrs/ that were of ye com[pany sent with saynt Denyse in to fraūce. [*fo. cxiii.* In scotlond the feest of saynt Canuke an abbot. At vrs† the feest of saynt Firmyne a bysshop ꝛ cōfessour. The feest also of saynt Ethelburge a virgyn. At redon the feest of saynt Melan a cōfessour. The translacyon also of our holy fader saynt Augustyne/ y^t is to saye/ whan Lynthbrand the kynge of longoberdynes brought his holy body w^t moche honour from sardyne vnto his owne cite. ⁋ Addicyons.

⁋ The feest also of saynt Ewstache an abbot/ and of an other saynt Ewstache bysshop of antioche/. a noble lerned man/ ꝛ made many werkes/ specially agaynst the heresyes of Arrius/ for ye whiche he suffred grete psecucyon/ ꝛ was put to exyle. The feest also of many .ꝛc.

⁋ To morowe.

⁋ The .xij. daye of October. At rauen in lawrentyne strete the feest of saynt Edisty a martyr. In affrike the feest of saynt Cipriane ꝛ saȳt Felix preestes ꝛ martyrs of whose company were .iiij.M.ix.C.lxxvj. holy sayntes/ some cōfessours/ some martyrs/ ꝛ all by kyng Huneryke put to. exyle in a waste wyldernes/ where many dyed/ many were put to deth by cruell turmentes/ the chefe of whome were bisshops/ preestes ꝛ deacons with other psones of the clergy/ ꝛ suche faythfull persones as vnto them resorted. In syre the feest of saynt Ewstace a preest. In brytayn the deposicyon of saynt Wylfryde a bysshop ꝛ cōfessour. At byturyke ye feest of saynt Epion a preest ꝛ cōfessour.   ⁋ Addicyons.

⁋ In englond the feest of saynt Edwyne kyng of northumberlond/ ꝛ housbond vnto saynt Ethelburge the virgyn/ by whom he was conuerted vnto Chrystes fayth/ ꝛ after a holy man/ ꝛ of many myracles/ and by [treason put to [*fo. cxiii. b.* martyrdom. The feest also of saȳt Marcell a bysshop ꝛ martyr. And ye feest of many other .ꝛc.

⁋ To morowe.

⁋ The .xiij. day of October. At troades ye feest of saynt Carpe/ discyple vnto saynt Paule. In spayne at corduba the passyon of saynt Fausty/ saynt Ianuary ꝛ saȳt Marciall martyrs/ that fyrst were racked/ ꝛ than the browes ouer theyr eyes were flayne/ theyr eares and noses kytte/ theyr ouer tethe knocked out/ ꝛ at the last after many cruell turmentes they

MARTILO.   L were brent. At antioche the feest of saynt Theophily/ the syxth bysshop there after saynt Peter. At turon the feest of saynt wynance an abbot. In the more brytayne the translacyon of saynt Edwarde kynge ͫ cōfessour. The feest also of saynt Marcell/ saynt Adriane/ saynt Marke/ ͫ saynt Gyrald all confessours. ⁋ Addicyons.

⁋ The feest also of an other saynt Theophily a confessour/ that forsakynge his baptym/ made thervpon an obligacyon vnto the deuyll/ but by the helpe ͫ myracle of our blessed lady he was reconsyled/ ͫ made vnto her this sequens Aue maria. wherein is mencyon made of hymselfe by name. The feest also of many other ho. ͫc̷.

⁋ To morowe.

⁋ The .xiiij. daye of October. At rome in aurell strete the feest of saynt Calixt pope ͫ martyr/ y^t by the emperour Alexander was kepte longe in harde pryson ͫ nere famysshed/ ͫ euery day scourged ͫ beten w^t staues/ ͫ at the last after many turmentes he was cast downe hedlonge from the hyghest toure of ye same pryson/ ͫ so ended his martyrdom. At tubertyn† ye feest of saynt Fortunate a bysshop of many synguler vertues/ specyally in chasynge awaye of wycked spirytes. The feest also of [saynt Saturnyne and of saynt Lupe confessours. [fo. cxiiii. ⁋ Addicyons.

⁋ The feest also of saynt Gawdrysyue a virgyn/ of noble byrth ͫ synguler beauty/ for ye whiche vnto ye cōseruacyon of her virgynite/ she prayed vnto our sauyour that she myght lose all y^t beauty of body ͫ be defourme ͫ so she was/ vnto the tyme she was professed in relygyon/ ͫ than fortw^t her beauty was rendred agayne more goodly than before. And after she was abbesse/ ͫ cuer of hygh pfeccyon ͫ many myracles. The feest also of saynt Gaudency a bysshop ͫ martyr/ a man of notable doctryne/ wherby he conuerted moche people/ but many moo by his holy lyf ͫ myracles. The feest also of an other saynt Fortunate/ an eloquent man of grete lernynge/ y^t wrote the lyfe of saynt Martyne/ ͫ made many werkes/ specyally many of ye ympnes y^t ben songe ͫ sayd in the chirche/ ͫ was also of hygh pfeccyon ͫ many myracles. In fraūce at lyons the feest of saynt Iust bysshop of ye same cite/ a man of synguler vertue/ ͫ had the spirite of pphecy. The feest also of many other . ͫc̷.

⁋ To morowe.

⁋ The .xv. day of October. At colen agryppyne ye feest oɪ ccc. martyrs of ye legyon of thebeys. At rome in aurel strete

OCTOBER.

yᵉ feest of saynt Fortunate. In fraūce at lyons the feest of saynt Antioche a bysshop. In the terrytory of remens yᵉ feest of saynt Basoly a cōfessour/ ꝯ of saynt Vlfran an archebysshop ꝯ cōfessour. At capua yᵉ feest of saynt Lufyle ꝯ saȳt Fortunate.

⁋ Addicyons.

⁋ The feest also of saynt Placidia a virgyn/ doughter vnto yᵉ emperour Valentiniane by his wyfe saynt Eudox/ doughter vnto the emperour Theodosy/ whiche holy virgyn by reuelacyons had in youth/ forsoke her [frendes ꝯ pompe of the [*fo. cxiiii. b.* worlde/ ꝯ serued god in pouerty and penaunce/ ꝯ was of notable vertue ꝯ many myracles. One of the feestes also of saynt Leonard. And the feest of many other holy sayntes/ martyrs/ confes. ꝯc̄.

⁋ To morowe.

⁋ The .xvj. daye of October. In yᵉ moūt of tumbe the reuerend memory of saynt Michaell the archaungell. In affrike the feest of .cc.lxx. martyrs. And the feest of saynt Marciane ꝯ saynt Satirian breder/ with other two also of theyr breder/ all martyrs/ that were scourged/ racked/ theyr flesshe rent wᵗ hokes vnto the bones ꝯ so were they turmented euery day by day/ of a longe tyme/ ꝯ euer on yᵉ morowe they were foūde hole agayn ꝯ without hurt or blemysshe/ tyll at the last they were tyed vnto the tayles of cartes/ ꝯ so drawen thrugh bushes/ breres ꝯ thornes vnto deth. The feest also of saȳt Maxima a virgyn/ that with them was put to deth. In the fraūchest of bituricens yᵉ feest of saynt Ambrose bysshop of caturicence/ ꝯ the feest of saynt Saturnyne ꝯ saynt Nery/ with other psones .ccclxxv. all martyrs. In suenuy† the feest of saynt Gall a preest ꝯ cōfessour.

⁋ Addicyons.

⁋ The feest also of saȳt Magnobone a bysshop/ of grete pfeccion ꝯ many myracles. The feest also of an other saynt Ambrose a confessour/ ꝯ discyple vnto saynt Dydymy/ a grete lerned man/ and made many werkes/ whome saynt Ierom putteth by name amonge yᵉ noble lerned men. The feest also of saȳt Bercare an abbot that was slayne by one of his owne monkes/ bycause he rebuked his synne/ which mōke forthwᵗ fell madde in furye posseded of a spiryte/ ꝯ whan the abbot was buryed/ oyle stylled out of his graue/ wherby seke per[sones were cured. The feest also of many other .ꝯc̄. [*fo. cxv.*

⁋ To morowe.

⁋ The .xvij. day of October. At antioche yᵉ feest of saȳt Heron/ discyple vnto saynt Ignacy the martyr/ ꝯ his successour/

as well in his bysshopryche as in holy lyfe and good edifycacyon of his flocke/ for the whiche lyke vnto his mayster he was put to martyrdom. At aurasyke the feest of saynt Florentyne a bysshop ⁊ cōfessour of synguler vertue. In the terrytory of nyuernens the feest of saynt Vincent a cōfessour. And the trāslacyon of saynt Awdre a virgyn ⁊ a quene. The feest also of saȳt Victor/ saynt Alexander/ and saynt Mariane confes.
☙ Addicyons.
☙ At rome the feest of saynt Priuate a martyr/ y^t was a man of warre ⁊ conuerted by saynt Calixt the pope/ with whome by the emperour Alexander he was put to deth. In englond at ramsey the feest of saynt Etheldrede ⁊ saynt Ethelbryght martyrs ⁊ breder/ borne of noble blode/ neuewes vnto kynge Ercombert/ whiche were murthered by a wycked tyraūt/ ⁊ after by ye myracle of a bright piller of fire they were foūde/ ⁊ at theyr tombe many myracles. The feest also of many oth. ⁊c.

☙ To morowe.

☙ The .xviij. day of October. The feest of saynt Luke the euangelyst/ that in the age of .lxxiij. yeres dyed in bythynye/ whose holy bones in the .xx. yere of ye emperour Cōstantyne were translate in to the cite of cōstantynople. The feest also of saynt Esclepiady/ bysshop of antiochene ⁊ a martyr/ that by the emperour Decius with many other chrystyans was put to martyrdom. At rome ye feest of saynt Triphonia/ wyfe vnto ye emperour Decius. In the terrytory of beluacens the feest of [saynt Iust ⁊ saynt Iustyniane martyrs/ and of saynt [*fo. cxv. b.* Alexander and saynt Victor confessours.   ☙ Addicyons.
☙ At andegaue the feest of saynt Erblandy an abbot. At tarentasiens the feest of saynt Peter bysshop of the same cite/ a man of notable vertue/ the fame wherof spryngynge vnto lausemy/ thre certayne men wrongfully imprysoned/ made theyr prayers vnto hym for theyr delyueraūce/ vnto whome forthw^t he appered ⁊ losed them/ ⁊ brought them thrugh the myddle of the kepers vnperceyued/ and so delyuered them. After he was called in to englond by kynge Henry/ in ye whiche iourney he delyuered a mayde from daūger that was bewytched/ with many other grete myracles. The feest also of many other holy sayntes/ mart. confes .⁊c.

☙ To morowe.

☙ The .xix. day of October. At senon the feest of saynt Sauinian a bysshop/ ⁊ of saynt Potencian his felowe bothe mar-

tyrs/ yᵗ were sent vnto yᵉ same cite to preche yᵉ fayth/ where for
the same they suffred deth. In egypt at alexander the feest of
saynt Tholonyt a martyr/ that by yᵉ emperour Antonyne
pyteously by many turmentes was put to deth/ wᵗ whome saÿt
Lucy also suffred martyrdom. In syre at antioche yᵉ feest of
saynt Beronyke/ ⁊ of yᵉ holy woman saynt Pelage bothe martyrs
togyder/ ⁊ with them .xlix. other chrystyans. The feest also of
saynt Frediswyde a virgyn. At puteole the feest of saÿt Proculy/
⁊ of his moder saynt Nice bothe martyrs togyder.
⁋ Addicyons.
⁋ In yrelond yᵉ feest of saynt Ethebyne/ yᵗ was borne in
englond ⁊ nourysshed/ where he had reuelacyons ⁊ sawe our
sauyour in lykenes of a lepre/ ⁊ after he went [in to [*fo. cxvi.*
yrelond/ where he lyued a holy lyfe/ full of myracles. The feest
also of many other holy sayntes .⁊c.

⁋ To morowe.

⁋ The .xx. day of October. In the prouynce of auiens the
feest of saynt Maximy a deacon ⁊ a martyr/ yᵗ wylfully shewed
hymselfe vnto his pursewers/ of whome he was racked/ scourged
⁊ beten wᵗ battes/ ⁊ after many turmentes he was murthered in
sond ⁊ stones. In fraūce at agen yᵉ feest of saynt Caprasy a
martyr/ yᵗ for drede fledde the psecucyons of chrystyans/ ⁊ hyd
hymselfe a certayne tyme/ but after he wylfully shewed hÿselfe/
⁊ boldly for Chryst suffred deth. The feest also of saynt Astrobert a virgyn. At colen yᵉ feest of saynt Martha ⁊ saynt Saule
virgyns ⁊ martyrs/ wᵗ whome many other psones were put to
deth. The receyuynge also of yᵉ relykes of saynt George a
deacon ⁊ of saynt Aurely martyrs. The dedicacyon of the
chirche of syon. ⁋ Addicyons.
⁋ In englonde the feest of saynt Akke a bysshop/ that was
discyple vnto saynt Wylfryde ⁊ his successour/ a holy man/ ⁊ had
many reuelacyons ⁊ the spiryte of pphecy/ ⁊ dyd many myracles
in his lyfe/ and yet many moo after his deth. The feest also of
many other .⁊c.

⁋ To morowe.

⁋ The .xxj. day of October. At nicomede yᵉ feest of saÿt
Dacy/ saynt zoticy ⁊ saÿt Gay/ wᵗ other .xij. soudyours all
martyrs togyder. At colen the passyon of the .xj.M. virgyns.
The feest also of saynt Hyllarion a monke/ whose holy lyfe saynt
Ierom wryteth. At hoste yᵉ feest of saynt Austere a preest/ yᵗ
is remembred in the legend and passyon of saynt Calixt the pope.

The feest also of saÿt Viatour/ seruaūt vnto saÿt Iust bysshop of lyons. [At burdegale the feest of saÿt Seueryne a [*fo. cxvi. b.* bysshop. At the monastery of fontanell the feest of saynt Condedy a confessour of many merytes. ¶ Addicyons.

¶ In englond yᵉ ordynacyon of saynt Dunstane/ archebysshop of caūterbury. The feest also of saynt Recticy bysshop of augustudunens/ a man of notable doctryne as saynt Ierom wryteth/ and made many profytable werkes/ and was of synguler sanctite. The feest also of many other holy sayntes/ martyrs/ confes. ⁊ virg

¶ To morowe.

¶ The .xxij. day of October. At adrianopole in trace yᵉ feest of saynt Philyp a bysshop/ saynt Euseby ⁊ saynt Ermete all martyrs. The feest also of saynt Marke/ a noble man borne ⁊ of grete lernynge/ yᵗ of the gentyles was the fyrst bysshop of Ierusalem/ ⁊ in a whyle after put to martyrdom. The feest also of saynt Salomee/ that (as is redde in the gospell) was dylygent aboute the sepulture of our sauyoure. The feest also of saynt Mellon archebysshop of rone. At oska the feest of saynt Mimilon† and saynt Ewlodie virgyns ⁊ martyrs/ that after longe pryson ⁊ many turmentes were heded. ¶ Addicyons.

¶ The feest also of saynt Melane a matrone/ borne in rome of noble lignage/ ⁊ for deuocyon went vnto Ierusalem/ in the whiche iourney she vysyted in desert the holy faders saÿt Pambo/ saynt Serapion/ saynt Ysydour ⁊ other/ ⁊ for them suffred grete persecucyon/ ⁊ wᵗ saynt Rufyne ⁊ saynt Aquila she came vnto Ierusalē/ where she buylded a monastery of virgyns/ and ruled there in nombre fyfty/ ⁊ dyd there many noble dedes/ ⁊ so rested in our lorde. The feest also of an other saynt Melane a matrone also/ vnto whome she was graūd[moder/ for she was [*fo. cxvii.* her sones doughter/ and her goddoughter/⁊ was maryed vnto a noble man by whome she had two sones/ whiche departed bothe vnto god/ ⁊ she than wᵗ grete instaūce cōuerted her housbonde vnto relygyon/ ⁊ so she buylded a monastery of .xl. virgyns/ ⁊ he an other of .xxx. mōkes/ where they lyued in hygh perfeccyon. The feest also of many other holy sayn .⁊c.

¶ To morowe.

¶ The .xxiij. daye of October. In syre at antioche the feest of saynt Theodour a preest/ that in yᵉ psecucyon of the emperour Iulian yᵉ apostata was racked ⁊ enflambed with hote lampes/ ⁊ after many other turmentes slayne by the swerde. In spayne the feest of saynt Scruand/ ⁊ saynt German/ that after grete labours/ hard imprysonment/ rackynge ⁊ other turmentes were heded/ ⁊ saynt German was buryed at emerite/ ⁊ saynt Seruand at hyspale. In normandy at rone the deposicyon of saynt Romayn archebysshop ⁊ cōfessour. In yᵉ fraūchest of pictauens the feest of saynt Benet a cōfessour. The feest also of saynt Elflede a virgyn. At colen the feest of saynt Seueryne a bysshop ⁊ confessour. ¶ Addicyons.

¶ In the fraūchest of ambianēs the feest of saynt Graciane a martyr/ that in goynge to deth prycked downe his staffe in the grounde/ whiche forthwᵗ flourysshed ⁊ bare grene leues ⁊ nuttes/ ⁊ euery yere the same day ⁊ houre it bereth rype nuttes. The feest also of an other saynt Seueryne a martyr/ called also saȳt Boece/ a noble man borne/ ⁊ a grete clerke of notable eloquence/ ⁊ made many werkes/ ⁊ was of synguler vertue/ ⁊ for Chryst suffred grete persecucyon and dethe. The feest also of many other holy sayntes/ mart̃/ confes. ⁊ virg.

[¶ To morowe. [fo. cxvii. b.

¶ The .xxiiij. daye of October. In napules at venyset the feest of saynt Felix a bysshop/ saynt Audacty ⁊ saȳt Ianuary preestes/ saynt Fortunate ⁊ saynt Septimy lectours in order all martyrs/ yᵗ by the emperour Dioclecian after many turmentes were put to deth by the swerde/ amonge whome saynt Felix the sayd bysshop was moost notable/ a fader of .lvj. yeres ⁊ a clene virgyn. In the monastery of vertane yᵉ feest of saynt Martyne an abbot. The feest also of saynt Vitale a holy confessour.
¶ Addicyons.

¶ In englonde the feest of saynt Maglour/ called also saynt Maiour a bysshop/ yᵗ resigned his dignite ⁊ was a monke in desert ⁊ a fader of religyon/ of hygh perfeccyon ⁊ many myracles/ and had also reuelacyon of his deth by an aūgell. The feest also of an other saynt Maiour a martyr/ that by the wandales after many cruell turmentes was put to deth by the swerde. The feest also of many other holy sayntes/ mart̃. confes. ⁊ virg.

¶ To morowe.

¶ The .xxv. day of October. At rome the feest of .xlvij. martyrs men of warre/ that all togyder were baptized by saynt Denyse the pope/ ⁊ forthwᵗ by the emperour Claudy they were heded/ and buryed in salary stretc/ where also were buryed other martyrs .cxxj. of yᵉ whiche saynt Theodosi/ saynt Lucy/ saynt Marke ⁊ saynt Peter were chefe capitaynes. At petragoryke the feest of saynt Frontony a bisshop/ cōsecrate in rome by saynt Peter/ with saynt George a preest/ that by the staffe of saynt Peter was before reysed from deth/ ꝯ by him assigned as felowe wᵗ saynt Frontony to cōuerte the sayd cite/ where whan they had truly accomplysshed theyr [offyce by [*fo. cxviii*]. holy lyfe ꝯ many myracles/ the sayd bysshop rested in Chryst. At swesyon the feest of saynt Crispyn ꝯ saynt Crispinian/ that in the persecucyon of the emperour Dioclecian after many cruell turmentes were slayne by yᵉ swerde. At florence yᵉ passyon of saynt Mineate/ that by the prynce Decius was put to deth. At gauale the feest of saynt Hyllary a bysshop ꝯ cōfessour. At rome in salary strete the feest of saynt Crisant/ ꝯ of the holy virgyn saynt Daria bothe martyrs togyder. In englond yᵉ feest of saynt Iohñ beuerlake a bysshop and confessour.

¶ Addicyons.

¶ The feest also of saynt Demetry a martyr/ borne of noble lignage/ ꝯ beynge a seculer knyght he conuerted many psones vnto Chryst/ for yᵉ whiche he was taken ꝯ by the emperour Maximian put to many turmētes in the whiche he dyd many myracles ꝯ conuerted moche people/ ꝯ at yᵉ last was slayne by the swerde. The feest also of many other holy sayntes/ marꝑ. confes. ꝯc.

¶ To morowe.

¶ The .xxvj. day of October. In affrike yᵉ feest of saȳt Rogacian a preest/ ꝯ of saȳt Felicissimy bothe martyrs that in the pscucyon of the emperours Decius ꝯ Valerian were put to deth/ of whome saȳt Cipriane wryteth in his epystles vnto the confessours. At narbone the feest of saynt Rustyke a bysshop and confessour. ¶ Addicyons.

¶ The feest also of saynt Florēce a bysshop ꝯ cōfessour. At rome yᵉ feest of saynt Euarysty pope ꝯ martyr/ that was a iewe borne/ ꝯ cōuerted in youth/ ꝯ made many profytable ordynaūces in the chirche/ ꝯ at yᵉ last in the persecucion of the emperour Traianus he was put to martyrdom. The feest also of many other holy saī. ꝯc.

[¶ To morowe.   [*fo. cxviii. b.*

¶ The .xxvij. day of October. In spayne at habull the passion of saynt Vincent/ ꝯ of yᵉ holy women saynt Sabyne ꝯ saynt Aristea† all martyrs/ yᵗ by the mayre Dacian were racked and so strayned ꝯ stretched/ that all the ioyntes of theyr bodyes were losed from theyr places/ ꝯ at the last theyr braynes knocked out wᵗ battes. At tylecastell the feest of saynt Florence a martyr. The vigyll also of the apostles Symon and Iude. ⁋ Addicyons.

⁋ The feest also of saynt Frumence a bysshop/ yᵗ in his chyldhode lefte yᵉ cite of rome/ ꝝ went in to yᵉ moost desolate desert of ynde/ where by his holy lyf he cōuerted moche people/ ꝝ was theyr bysshop perseueraūt in the same ꝝ prechyng vnto his deth. The feest also of saynt Abbany a kynges sone of yrelond/ yᵗ forsakynge all the pompe of the worlde/ entred religyon/ wherin he lyued so perfytly/ that he heled yᵉ lepre ꝝ lame/ blynde ꝝ defe/ reysed the deed/ with many other myracles/ ꝝ had visytacyon of aūgels ꝝ reuelacyon of his deth. The feest also of many other holy sayntes/ mart̃. confes. ꝝ virg.

⁋ To morowe.

⁋ The .xxviij. day of October. the feest of the apostles saynt Symon/ called by syrname canany/ yᵗ fyrst preched in egipt/ ꝝ of saynt Tadey/ called also saynt Iude that fyrst preched in mesopotamy/ ꝝ after they bothe mette in perse/ where they conuerted a multytude of people nerehand innumerable vnto the fayth/ ꝝ at the last were put to deth for the same. At rome the feest of saynt Ciryll/ doughter vnto yᵉ emperour Decius/ yᵗ by the prȳce Claudy was slayne by the swerde. At melde the feest of saynt Pharao/ bysshop of ambianens and a [cōfessour. At parys the translacyon of saynt Geneuefe [*fo. cxix.* a virgyn/ and the feest of saynt Felix a martyr.

⁋ Addicyons.

⁋ At babylon the feest of saȳt Abdy/ discyple vnto the apostles Symon ꝝ Iude/ and by them made bysshop of babilon/ where he well ruled and moche edifyed the chirche of Chryst/ and dyed a confessour. The feest also of many other holy sayntes/ martyrs/ confes. ꝝ virg.

⁋ To morowe.

⁋ The .xxix. day of October. At Ierusalem the feest of saynt Narcisse/ that (as yᵉ story ecclesiastyke recordeth) was notably perfyte in fayth ꝝ pacyence. At sydon the feest of saȳt zenoby a preest/ yᵗ in the fury of yᵉ grete psecucyon was put to martyrdom. In yᵉ puince of lucane the feest of saȳt Iacynct/ saynt Quintyn/ saȳt Felician ꝝ saynt Lucy martyrs.

⁋ Addicyons.

⁋ In englond the feest of saynt Elflede a virgyn/ of noble byrth/ at whose byrth were shewen heuēly tokens. And she was

after abbesse of rumsey/ ⁊ of holy lyf and many myracles.
The feest also of saynt Iohn̄ bysshop of augustudunēs/ a man
of many myracles/ specyally in curȳg of seke psones. The
feest also of many oth .⁊c.

℃ To morowe.

℃ The .xxx. day of October. In affryke the feest of .cc.
and .xxx. martyrs. At tyngentyne the passyon of saynt
Marcell a capytayne of .C. soudyours/ yᵗ by the iudge Agricolane
was heded. In antioche the feest of saynt Serapion a bysshop/
a man of notable doctryne. The feest also of saȳt Germayn
bysshop of capuane/ whose blessed soule the reuerend fader
saynt Benet sawe conuayed by aungels in to heuen. The
ordynacyon also of saynt Swythune a bysshop. At tolose the
feest of saynt [Saturnyne a confessour. [*fo. cxix. b.*
℃ Addicyons.
℃ The feest also of saynt Leoncy a cōfessour/ that was
cōuerted by saynt Cesary the martyr. The feest also of saynt
Lucane a martyr/ that after he was heded/ bare his owne heed
a myle vnto the place where he wolde be buryed. The feest
also of many other holy sayn. ⁊c.

℃ To morowe.

℃ The .xxxj. day of October. the vigyl of all halowes. At
rome the feest of saynt Nemesy a deacon/ and of his doughter
saynt Lucyll/ that by the emperours Valeriane ⁊ Galiene after
many turmētes were heded/ the day of whose passyon ⁊ deth/
is the .xxv. day of August but bycause that pope Sixt dyd as
this day translate theyr holy bodyes in to appia strete/ therfore
he ordeyned theyr feest this day. In fraūce at vermendens the
feest of saynt Quintyne a martyr/ that by yᵉ emperour
Maximian was put to deth/ whose holy body .lv. yeres after
was foūde by the reuelacyon of an aungell. ℃ Addicyons.
℃ At rome yᵉ feest of saynt Nataly a cōfessour/ that for
ambycyon ⁊ couetyse was a renegate ⁊ made bysshop of certayn
heretykes/ but after he was cōuerted ⁊ recōsyled by reuelacyon/
⁊ forsoke yᵉ fals errours ⁊ vayngloryous honour/ ⁊ dyd grete
penaūce/ ⁊ was of hygh perfeccyon ⁊ many myracles. The
feest also of saynt Foyllane/ borne of the noble blode of
yrelond/ that forsoke all honour to serue god/ ⁊ was a bysshop/
⁊ than called after yᵉ maner of Abraham in to fraūce/ where he
receyued the crowne of martyrdom/ whose holy body was
founde by the reuelacyon of an aūgell at the prayer of saynt

Gertrude/ w^t whome he was before in company. The feest also
of many other holy sayntes/ mar͡t.⁊c̃.

[☞ To morowe. [*fo. cxx.*

Nouēber.   THe fyrst day of Nouember, the feest of all
sayntes/ that fyrst was ordeyned by pope
Boniface in the honour of our lady ⁊ of all
martyrs onely. But after pope Gregory decreed and deter-
myned that the same feest the same daye sholde solempnly be
kepte for euer in the honour of all halowes ⁊ sayntes. At the
castell of diuyon the feest of saynt Benigne a preest ⁊ martyr/
y^t by saynt Policarpe was sent in to fraūce to preche/ where by
ye erle Terenciane after many turmētes his necke was broken
with an yren barre/ ⁊ his body woūded w^t a spere. In campane
at terracyne ye feest of saynt Cesary a deacon ⁊ martyr/ y^t
after longe pryson ⁊ many turmētes was by ye emperour Claudy
put in to a sacke w^t saynt Iulian a preest ⁊ cast in to the see/ ⁊
so they bothe togyder martyrs. At parys ye feest of saynt
Marcell a bysshop/ chosen for his singuler sanctite and grete
myracles/ for somtyme he chaunged water in to wyne/ somtyme
in to baume/ with many other signes of holynes. At tyburtyne
the feest of saynt Seueryne a monke. At baiocas ye feest of
saynt Vigour a bysshop. In the fraūchest of wastinens the feest
of saynt Maturyne a cōfessour. The feest also of saynt Mary
a virgin ⁊ martyr/ that was scourged/ racked/ ⁊ her flesshe rent
w^t hokes/ ⁊ so ended her martyrdom. At pictauy ye feest of
saynt Hyllary a cōfessour.   ☞ Addicyons.

☞ In spayne the feest of saynt Iuuency a preest/ and a man
of notable doctryne/ y^t made the .iiij. euangelystes in verses/
with many other pfytable werkes. In syre at laodyce the feest
of saynt Apollynare/ bysshop of the same cite/ a man also of
grete lernynge ⁊ synguler sanctite/ that made many werkes/
specyally agaynst here[tykes. The feest also of many [*fo. cxx. b.*
other holy sayntes. ⁊c̃.

☞ To morowe.

☞ The seconde daye of Nouember. The feest of saynt
Victoryne bysshop of pitabion/ that (as saynt Ierom wryteth)
after grete labours in prechynge and moche edificacyon was
crowned w^t martyrdom. At rome the feest of saynt Eustace a
martyr/ ⁊ of saȳt Theospis his wyfe/ with theyr sone saynt

Agapy/ ⁊ theyr doughter saynt Theospita all martyrs togyder/ put to deth by yᵉ emperour Adriane/ whose very daye of passyon was yesterdaye all halowen daye/ but bycause of yᵗ solēnite they ben here remēbred/ ⁊ theyr actes moche notable ⁊ meruaylous. At laudice† the feest of saynt Theodourt a bysshop/ of notable vertue/ ⁊ moche eloquēt in p̄chynge. The feest also of saȳt Ambrose/ abbot of agunens/ a famous man of holy lyfe ⁊ many myracles. The cōmemoracyon also and remembraunce of all soules. ⁌ Addicyons.

⁌ The feest also of saynt Iust a martyr/ that was cast in to the see/ but after yᵉ holy body was cast vnto londe ⁊ foūde by reuelacyon. The feest also of saynt Eustoche a virgyn ⁊ martyr/ put to deth by yᵉ emperour Iulian. And yᵉ feest of an other saynt Eustoche a virgyn/ discyple vnto saȳt Ierom/ vnder whose obedience she lyued with her moder saynt Paule/ yᵗ buylded at bethleem a monastery/ where after the deth of her moder she was abbesse of .l. virgyns/ vnto whome saȳt Ierom wrote a rule. The feest also of saynt Alcyndyne/ saynt Pygasy/ ⁊ saynt Anepothyst martyrs/ yᵗ by the kyng of perse were scourged/ soden ⁊ broyled/ in whose passyon saȳt Antonyne was cōuerted/ ⁊ forthwᵗ before them put to deth/ ⁊ they all were cast in to the see/ where the same [saynt Antonyne with an aungell [fo. cxxi. came vnto them and brought them safe to lond/ where they cōuerted .xxviij. persones/ that forthwᵗ with them were put to deth. In yrelonde the feest of saynt Malachy a bysshop of grete holynes ⁊ many myracles/ whose legende saynt Barnard wryteth. In yrelond also the feest of saynt Herke a bysshop/ yᵗ was a gentyle of grete iustyce ⁊ good lyuyng/ ⁊ was cōuerted by reuelacyon/ ⁊ sacred bysshop by saynt Patrike/ ⁊ after of hygh p̄feccyon/ ⁊ had yᵉ spiryte of prophecy/ ⁊ reysed a persone vnto lyfe/ wᵗ other many grete myracles. The feest also of many oth.⁊c̃.

⁌ To morowe.

⁌ The thyrde daye of Nouember. The feest of saynt Quarte/ discyple vnto yᵉ apostles. In capadoce at cesary the feest of saynt Germane/ saynt Theopholy/ saynt Sesary ⁊ saȳt Vitale/ martyrs all togyder put to deth in the persecucyon of the emperour Daciane. At cesaraugust the feest of martyrs vnnombrable/ that by Dacian yᵉ presydent of spayne were put to deth. The trāslacyon also of saynt Edythe a virgyn. And the deposycyon of saynt Parmyn a bysshop/ ⁊ of saynt Hukbert a confessour. At carboyle the feest of saynt Gwenady an abbot and cōfessour. And of saynt Wenefrede a virgyn and martyr.

NOVEMBER.

¶ Addicyons.

¶ The feest also of saynt Kenelme/ ̄t of saynt Alpayde a virgyn/ of poore byrth/ ̄t a keper of beestes in yᵉ felde/ yet obteyned she of our lorde yᵉ clere vnderstandynge of holy scripture/ ̄t the spirite of coūseyle/ wᵗ meruaylous prudence/ yet was she euer seke in body ̄t neuer hole/ ̄t lyued many yeres wᵗout ony fode/ but onely the sacrament of Chrystes body/ ̄t many tymes was she rapte into heuen/ hell ̄t purgatory/ as by syght in her soule [and vnderstandynge of the ioye ̄t payne/ [*fo. cxxi. b.* she had also yᵉ spiryte of prophecy/ ̄t was of many myracles. In englond yᵉ feest of saynt Clitanke a martyr/ a kynges sone of strayte iustyce/ a louer of peace/ ̄t of pure chastite/ ̄t of strayte ̄t perfyte lyfe/ yᵗ was cruelly slayne by a fals traytour/ at whose deth were shewed many myracles and at his tombe after many moo. In englond also the feest of saynt Rūwold the kynges sone of northumberlond/ that forthwᵗ whan he was borne/ cryed wᵗ lowde voyce sayeng thre tymes togyder these wordes. I am a chrystyan/ ̄t than required the sacrament of baptym ̄t after to haue masse ̄t was cōmuned/ ̄t than he made a noble sermon wᵗ meruaylous good eloquence/ ̄t lyued thre dayes/ ̄t so departed ̄t lyeth in buckyngham ful of myracles. The feest also of many other holy saynt̄ .̄tc̄.

¶ To morowe.

¶ The .iiij. day of Nouēber. In alexander the feest of saynt Hyery a preest/ a noble lerned doctour/ of holy lyf and many myracles. In normandy at rone the feest of saynt Amance a bysshop of grete fame in lyfe ̄t myracles. In yᵉ fraunchest of vilcasyne yᵉ feest of saynt Clare a preest ̄t cōfessour. At augustudune the feest of saynt Proculy a bysshop. In englonde at wynchester yᵉ feest of saynt Brinstane a bysshop of holy lyfe ̄t many myracles.   ¶ Addicyons.

¶ The feest also of an other saÿt Clare a martyr/ borne in englond at orchester/ of noble parētes/ whome wᵗ all worldly pompe he forsoke and wente in to normandy/ where he lyued a solytary lyfe in desert/ ̄t cured yᵉ seke/ reysed the deed/ ̄t dyd many myracles. At the last yᵉ deuyll enflambed a grete lady in concupyscence of hym/ whome (as Ioseph) he fledde and auoyded in to a ferre [countree/ wherwith she was kendled in a [*fo. cxxii.* fury/ ̄t sent after hym ̄t heded hym/ ̄t he forthwᵗ toke vp his owne heed ̄t bare it vnto a monastery yᵗ he before had buylded hÿselfe/ where he lyeth full of myracles. The feest also of saynt Vitale ̄t saynt Agricola martyrs/ whose holy bodyes saynt Ambrose dyd translate/ ̄t wrote also yᵉ legend of theyr passion. The feest also of many other. ̄tc̄.

⁋ To morowe.

⁋ The .v. daye of Nouember, the feest of saynt zacary the pphete/ fader vnder saynt Iohn baptist. In campane at teracyne the feest of saynt Felix a preest/ and of saynt Euseby a monke bothe martyrs/ that conuerted moche people/ for the whiche they were bothe togyder heded. In the terrytory of orlyaūce ye feest of saynt Lety a preest. In the fraūchest of lyngon at the monastery of clareuale the feest of saynt Malachy a bysshop ⁊ confessour.   ⁋ Addicyons.
⁋ The feest also of saynt Elyzabeth/ wyfe vnto saynt zacary and moder vnto saynt Iohn̄ baptist. The feest also of an other saynt zacary the pope/ a man of synguler vertue ⁊ notable doctryne/ bothe in ye greke ⁊ latyn tongue/ that ordeyned that gossyppes sholde not mary togyder/ ne the chylder by them baptized vnto theyr owne chylder/ w^t many other good statutes ⁊ decrees. The feest also of many other holy sayntes/ mar̄. ⁊c̄.

⁋ To morowe.

⁋ The .vj. day of Nouember. In affryke at tonyse the feest of saynt Felix/ at whose buryall saynt Augustyn preched ⁊ expowned a psalme vnto ye people. The feest also of saynt Leonard a cōfessour ⁊ an abbot. In ye eest countree at theopole the feest of .x. martyrs/ that were slayne by the sarasyns. In fryselonde† the feest of saynt [Actike. At redon the [*fo. cxxii. b.* feest of saynt Melane a cōfessour.   ⁋ Addicyons.
⁋ In englond ye feest of saynt Yltute/ cosyn vnto kyng Arthur ⁊ a seculer knyght/ that forsoke all ye worldly pompe ⁊ was a religyous man/ of hygh perfeccyon ⁊ many myracles. The feest also of an other saynt Felix a monke/ that cōmaūded a serpent to kepe his gardyn wherby a thefe was taken and refourmed. The feest also of many other holy sayntes/ mar̄. confes. ⁊ virg.

⁋ To morowe.

⁋ The .vij. day of Nouember. In alexander the feest of saynt Achyl a bysshop/ a noble man of notable doctryne ⁊ holy lyfe. In ytaly at perusyne the feest of saynt Herculane a bysshop/ a martyr slayne by ye swerde/ whose holy body (as saynt Gregory wryteth) was foūde .xl. dayes after his dethe as hole w^{t}out wēme/ as though no swerde ne wepen had touched hym. At abbiens† the feest of saȳt Amarance a martyr/ that lyeth buryed in the same cite. In fryselond yͤ deposicyon of saynt wylibrorde a bysshop ⁊ cōfessour. ❡ Addicyons.

❡ The feest also of saynt Prosdocymy a bysshop/ that was a noble man borne of the grekes/ ⁊ came wᵗ saynt Marke the euangelyst ⁊ with saynt Appolinare vnto saynt Peter/ of whome he was cōsecrate/ and after he preched ⁊ cōuerted many kynges ⁊ realmes/ and dyd grete myracles/ ⁊ he lyued vnto the age of .cxiiij. yeres of the whiche he was bysshop .xciij. yeres/ a moneth ⁊ .xv. dayes/ and lyeth full of dayly myracles at patauie where he was bysshop. The feest also of many oth. ⁊c̃.

❡ To morowe.

❡ The .viij. daye of Nouember. At rome in lauycane strete the passyon of saynt Clawdy/ saynt Nicostrate ⁊ [of [*fo. cxxiii.* other thre persones all martyrs/ yᵗ by the emperour Dioclecian were scourged wᵗ scorpyons/ ⁊ after many other turmentes cast in to yᵉ see. At rome also in yᵉ same strete yᵉ feest of saynt Seuere/ saynt Seueriane/ saynt Capaforet ⁊ saynt Victoryne martyrs/ that by yᵉ emperour Dioclecian were beten to deth with plūmettes of lede/ ⁊ bycause theyr names that tyme were vnknowē they were called the .iiij. crowned martyrs/ tyll after theyr names were shewed by reuelacyon. ❡ Addicyons.

❡ In cornwell the feest of saynt Keby a bysshop/ borne of the blode royall/ ⁊ for that he was elected to be kyng of that coūtree/ but he forsoke all the worlde for yᵉ loue of Chryst/ ⁊ toke the holy habyte of relygyon/ wherin he cōtynued in hygh perfeccyon and many myracles. The feest also of many other holy sayntes/ marᵗ. ⁊c̃.

❡ To morowe.

❡ The .ix. day of Nouember. At amase a cite of yᵉ marmaritanes the feest of saynt Theodour a martyr/ that by the emperours Maximy ⁊ Maximian was scourged ⁊ so put in hard pryson/ where our sauyour appered vnto hym ⁊ cōforted hym/ than was he hanged ⁊ racked/ ⁊ his flesshe so rent ⁊ torne with hokes/ yᵗ his bowelles myght be seen/ ⁊ at the last he was brent. At byturyke the feest of saynt Vrsycyne a cōfessour ⁊ bysshop of yᵉ same cite/ consecrate at rome by yᵉ successours of the apostles. At verdune the feest of saynt Vycony a cōfessour. The deposicyon also of saynt Theodour bysshop/ bysshop of lyons. ❡ Addicyons.

❡ The feest also of an other saynt Theodour a martyr that was a knyght/ ⁊ slewe a dragon after suche maner as is sayd of saȳt George/ ꝧ whan he was knowen [for a christyan/ [*fo. cxiii. b*. he was by the emperour Lycyne after many turmentes put vpon yᵉ crosse lyke vnto his mayster Chryst/ where he henge thre dayes/ and whan he was taken downe/ he was quycke lyuyng ꝧ without ony wounde or hurte/ where he conuerted .xxviij. soudyours/ that before hym were put to deth/ ꝧ he at the last heded. The feest also of many other holy sayntᵱ. ꝦƐ.

℃ To morowe.

℃ The .x. day of Nouēber. the feest of saynt Martyne pope/ that by the emperour Constantyne the heretyke was iudged vnto exile in to the puynce of lyce/ where in the cite of cerson he lyeth full of myracles. In the terrytory of agathen the feest of saynt Tybery/ saynt Modest ꝧ saynt Florence/ that by the emperour Dioclecian were all togyder by dyuerse turmentes put to martyrdom. At antioche the feest of saynt Demetry a bysshop saynt Aniane a deacon and saynt Eustoche all martyrs/ with whome were put to dethe .xx. other psones. The deposicyon also of saȳt Iust archebysshop of yorke.† At orlyaūce the feest of saynt Monytour a bysshop ꝧ confessour.

. ℃ Addicyons.

℃ The feest also of saynt Tryphon a martyr that by the emperour Decius was put to many turmētes/ in whose passyon/ saynt Respicy ꝧ the holy virgyn saynt Nympha were conuerted/ ꝧ bothe wᵗ hym put to deth all heded. The feest also of saynt Theodour a martyr/ that by the emperour Iulian the apostata was put to deth. And yᵉ feest of an other saynt Theodour a bysshop ꝧ cōfessour/ of hygh pfeccyon. At rauen yᵉ feest of saynt Proby bysshop of yᵉ same cite/ a goodly man of fauour ꝧ persone/ an eloquent precher/ ꝧ of many grete graces specyally in the curynge of all maner dyseases/ he also [expelled [*fo. cxxiiii*. wycked spirytes/ ꝧ had reuelacyon of aūgels and lyeth in the same cite full of dayly myracles. The feest also of many other holy sayntes/ marᵱ. confes. ꝦƐ.

℃ To morowe.

℃ The .xj. day of Nouēber. At turon the feest of saynt Martyn/ bysshop of yᵉ same/ a man of notable vertues that reysed thre psones vnto lyfe/ with many other famous myracles. In fryselonde† at sythe† the passyon of saynt Men a martyr/ that in the psecucyon of yᵉ emperour Dioclecian fled in to wyldernes/ but after he boldly came forth ꝧ cōfessed the name of Chryst/ for yᵉ whiche after many turmentes he was slayne by yᵉ swerde. At lyons ye feest of saynt Seueriane a bisshop/ famous in vertue ⁊ myracles. ⁋ Addicyons.

⁋ The feest also of an other saynt Men a confessour/ y^t lyued in desert/ vnto whome beres and wylde beestes were subiecte ⁊ obedient/ ⁊ he knewe the thoughtes ⁊ preuy synnes of many psones and refourmed them/ of whome also saynt Gregory wryteth in his dialoges. In fraunce at gaualytane the feest of saynt Verany a bysshop/ borne of noble blode/ ⁊ forsoke the worlde and went in pylgrymage in to many coūtrees/ where euer he dyd many myracles/ at whose buryall ye pall wherwith his holy corps was couered/ sodeynly arose as quycke ⁊ went before ye people ouer a grete ryuer/ whiche they passed all drye foted vnto a chirche of our lady that he hȳselfe had buylded/ where he lyeth gloryous in myracles. The feest also of many other holy saī. ⁊c.

lib. iij. ca. xxvj.

⁋ To morowe.

⁋ The .xij. day of Nouember. In the prouynce of terraconens at tyrason ye feest of saynt Emiliane a preest ⁊ cōfessour/ whose meruaylous lyfe saynt Brawly bys[shop of [*fo. cxxiiii. b.* cesaraugust doth wryte at length. At agryppe the deposicyon of saynt Cūbert a bisshop ⁊ martyr. In the fraūchest of senonyke ye feest of saȳt Patryne a martyr. At ye castell of melidune ye feest of saynt Leo a cōfessour/ of many grete merytes.

⁋ Addicyons.

⁋ The feest also of saynt Achie the pphete/ that was in the tyme of Salomon/ ⁊ of his sone Ieroboam. At rome the feest of saynt Martyne the fyrst pope of that name ⁊ a martyr/ y^t in a generall coūseyle condempned the patriarke of constantinople for an heretyke/ for the whiche he was by the emperour Cōstantyne fyrst put vnto exile/ and after to deth. The feest also of saynt Hor an abbot of the desert of egipt/ a man of notable perfeccyon/ for he neuer made lye/ ne neuer sware othe/ ne neuer cursed or spake euyll worde/ ⁊ he was precyse in sylence/ for he neuer spake w^tout grete necessite/ he lyued thre yeres fedde onely by aungels/ ⁊ was lerned w^tout study by myracle/ ⁊ he coūerted moche people/ and dyd many myracles. The feest also of many other holy. ⁊c.

⁋ To morowe.

⁋ The .xiij. daye of Nouēber. At rauen ye feest of saynt Valentyne/ saynt Solutour/ ⁊ saynt Victor martyrs. At aquis
MARTILO.   M

the feest of saynt Demetry a martyr. In affryke the feest of saynt Archady/ saynt Paskasy/ saynt Proby ⁊ saynt Ewticiane all martyrs/ that for the reprouynge of the heresy of Arrius/ were after exile and many turmentes put to deth. At turon the deposicyon of saynt Brice bysshop ⁊ confessour/ that was discyple vnto saynt Martyn ⁊ his successour. At tholete ye feest of saynt Eugene a bysshop and confessour. In the monastery of malbody the feest of saynt Aldegunde a virgyn. At parys the feest of saynt Gundulfe a bysshop ⁊ [con- [*fo. cxxv.* fessour. ⁋ Addicyons.

⁋ The feest also of saynt Homobone a cōfessour/ ⁊ the feest also of the fyfty wyse maysters y^t disputed w^t saynt Katheryne/ ⁊ by her coūerted/ were by ye tyraūt Maxence put to martyrdome. The feest also of many other .⁊c.

⁋ To morowe.

⁋ The .xiiij. day of Nouember. In trace at eracle the feest of saynt Clementyne/ saynt Theodoce/ and saynt Philomon. In alexander the feest of saynt Serapion/ that in the psecucyon of ye emperour Decius was put vnto suche turmentes/ that all his ioyntes were losed eche from other/ ⁊ he cast downe an hyll hedlonge/ ⁊ so the martyr of Chryst. The trāslacyon also of saynt Erkenwald a bysshop ⁊ cōfessour. ⁋ Addicyons.

⁋ At trecasyne the feest of saynt Venerand a martyr/ a pagan borne of noble lignage/ ⁊ cōuerted in youth by an aūgell/ ⁊ baptized by our sauyour Chryst hymselfe ⁊ euer of holy lyfe ⁊ many myracles/ that by the emperour Aurelian after many turmētes wherin he cōuerted moche people/ was heded/ whose deed body toke vp the heed ⁊ bare it a grete space/ where he lyeth full of myracles. The feest also of an other saynt Venerand a virgyn ⁊ martyr/ ⁊ one of the .xiiij. peticioners/ that in the age of .xxx. yeres preched the worde of god ⁊ conuerted moche people/ ⁊ whan she came to rome/ there she was scourged ⁊ racked/ ⁊ than nayled hādes ⁊ fete vnto a stocke layeng vpryght ⁊ a grete stone layd vpon her/ ⁊ than she was losed ⁊ cast in to a panne full of oyle/ pytche/ water ⁊ brymstone/ ⁊ fyre made thervnder/ sethynge by .vij. dayes contynually/ in the whiche passyon she conuerted moche people/ ⁊ was delyuered w^{t}out hurt/ ⁊ than she cōuerted a kyng ⁊ all his subiectes [and at the last after many other turmētes wherin she conuerted [*fo. cxxv. b.* ix.C.xc. persones/ she was heded. In south wales the feest of saynt Dubrice bysshop of landaf/ ⁊ after archebysshop of all englonde ⁊ wales/ that was in the tyme of kynge Arthur/ whose moder whan he was in her wombe/ was by her owne fader a kyng of wales put in to a narowe vessell/ ⁊ cast dyuerse tymes in to a flode/ ⁊ euer the vessell came to lond agayn/ than was she bounde ⁊ cast in to a grete fyre/ wherin she remayned all nyght/ ⁊ therin was delyuered of this childe/ ⁊ gaue hym sowke in the myddle of the fyre w^tout noyaūce/ whiche chylde forthw^t dyd myracles/ ⁊ after in his holy lyfe many moo. In yrelond ye feest of saynt Constant an abbot/ ⁊ the feest of saynt Laurence a kynges sone of yrelond and a bysshop/ of many myracles/ whiche he dyd not onely in yrelond/ but also in englond ⁊ wales/ ⁊ moost of all in normandy/ specyally at his translacyon/ for there he lyeth full of dayly myracles. The feest also of many other holy sayntes/ marṫ. ⁊c.

℣ To morowe.

℣ The .xv. day of Nouember. In campane at nole the feest of saynt Felix a bysshop ⁊ martyr/ that from ye age of xv. yeres was euer full of myracles/ ⁊ was put to deth by the presydent Marcian/ with other .xxx. martyrs. In the fraūchest of parys the feest of saynt Eugeny a martyr. The feest also of saynt Macute a bysshop and cōfessour. In the lesse brytayn the feest of an other saynt Macute a bysshop also and confessour.
℣ Addicyons.
℣ The feest also of an other saynt Eugeny/ bysshop of cesarience/ discyple vnto the grete clerke Origene. And (as saynt Ierom wryteth) he was also of synguler ⁊ [not- [*fo. cxxvi.* able doctryne. The feest also of many other ho. ⁊c.

℣ To morowe.

℣ The .xvj. day of Nouember. At lyons ye feest of saynt Ewtheret a bysshop ⁊ cōfessour/ that fyrst was a senatour ⁊ forsoke ye worlde ⁊ entred religyon/ ⁊ after he closed hymselfe in a strayte narowe caue/ from whens he was called by reuelacion to be bysshop of the sayd cite. At pontinyake the deposicyon of saynt Edmund archebysshop of caūterbury. ℣ Addicyons.
℣ At altyne the feest of saynt Fidence a bysshop ⁊ martyr/ that by ye emperour Maximian after many cruell turmentes was put to martyrdome. The feest also of many other holy sayntes/ martyrs/ confes. and virg.

℣ To morowe.

℣ The .xvij. day of Nouember. In alexander ye feest of saynt Denyse a bysshop ⁊ martyr/ y^t by the emperours Valerian

and Galien was by many turmentes put to deth. At corduba the passyon of saynt Acyldy†/ ⁊ of the holy woman saýt Victoria bothe martyrs togyder/ in the cōmendacyon of whose precyous deth/ euery yere on the daye of theyr passyon/ swete ⁊ fresshe roses done sprynge by myracle. At orlyaūce yᵉ feest of saynt Aniane a bysshop and confessour/ of many gloryous myracles. The feest also of saynt Gergery† bysshop of turon. In englonde the feest of saynt Hugh bysshop of lyncolne/ whose holy lyfe ⁊ godly behauyour is shewed by myracle. ⁋ Addicyons.
⁋ In yrelond the feest of saynt Hylde a virgyn and an abbesse of high pfeccyon ⁊ many myracles. In spayne the feest of an other saynt Gergery bysshop of librens/ a grete lerned man/ ⁊ made many profytable werkes for the edificacyon of Chrystes chirche/ and was of no[table vertue and many [fo. cxxvi. b. myracles. The feest also of many other holy sayntes/ martyrs/ cōfessours ⁊ virgyns.

⁋ To morowe.

⁋ The .xviij. daye of Nouēber. At antioche the feest of saynt Roman a martyr/ that by the emperour Dioclecian bycause he resysted a tyraūt that wold haue brent a chirche/ was after many turmentes put to dethe/ wᵗ whome saýt Barala a chylde was also put to martyrdom. In the same cite the feest of saynt Esychy a man of warre/ that herynge a crye that euery man shold do sacrefyce vnto the ydolles/ cast away his armure ⁊ cōfessed the name of Chryst/ for the whiche a grete stone was tyed at his ryght arme/ ⁊ he so cast in a ryuer. At turon the feest of saynt Odo an abbot. The octaue also of saynt Martyne. And yᵉ feest after some bokes of saýt Hyld the abbesse/ of whome was redde yesterdaye. ⁋ Addicyons.
⁋ In yrelond the feest of saynt Roman a bysshop/ that dyd myracles in his moders wombe/ ⁊ after in his lyf many moo/ ⁊ was of hygh pfeccyon. The feest also of saynt Aude a virgyn. And of saynt Gelagy† yᵉ fyrst pope of that name/ a grete lerned man/ that condempned ⁊ destroyed the werkes ⁊ bokes of yᵉ heretykes called maniches/ ⁊ made many good werkes hymselfe/ ⁊ many prayers ⁊ ympnes/ ⁊ also the cotidiane preface yᵗ dayly is songe ⁊ sayd in the masse/ with many other notable actes. At lucane yᵉ feest of saynt Phridiane bysshop of the same cite/ that amonge other grete myracles (as saynt
iij. dialo. Gregory wryteth) cōmaūded the flode that was
ca. ix. lyke to have drowned the cite/ to folowe hym two myles from yᵉ cite/ ⁊ there to kepe that course for euer/ ⁊ so it doth vnto this day. The feest also of many other .⁊c.

[⊞ To morowe. [*fo. cxxvii.*

⊞ The .xix. day of Nouember. At rome in appia strete the feest of saynt Maximy a bysshop ꝫ martyr/ that in the psecucyon of the emperour Maximian was put to deth/ ꝫ lyeth buryed by saȳt Sixt. At rome also yᵉ feest of saynt Pocianet pope ꝫ martyr. At agenst the feest of saynt Crispyne a bysshop ꝫ martyr heded. At vien the feest of saynt Seueryne/ saynt Exsuper and saynt Feliciane martyrs/ whose holy bodyes many yeres after theyr deth were foūde by theyr owne reuelacyon/ and translated by yᵉ bysshop of the same cite wᵗ due honour. The feest also of saynt Faust a deacon ꝫ martyr heded. The feest also of saynt Symplicy a holy bysshop/ and of saynt Elizabeth a gloryous matrone. ⊞ Addicyons.

⊞ The feest also of saynt Elizabeth of vngary/ called comynly hongry/ notwᵗstandyng some bokes haue her feest as yesterday the .xviij. daye of this moneth. The feest also of many other holy sayntes/ mar. cfes. ꝫ virg.

⊞ To morowe.

⊞ The .xx. day of Nouēber. At rome the feest of saynt Ponciane pope ꝫ martyr/ that in the psecucyon of the emperour Maximian was brought vnto sardyny/ ꝫ wᵗ hym saynt Ypolite a preest/ where they bothe togyder were put to dethe/ beten wᵗ clubbes/ but his holy body was after foūde by the reuelacyon of saynt Fabiane yᵉ pope/ ꝫ buryed in the cimitery of saynt Calixt. At cabilon the feest of saynt Syluere a bysshop of grete vertue ꝫ many myracles. In cicyll at messane yᵉ feest of saynt Ampely ꝫ saynt Gay. At tauryn yᵉ feest of saynt Octauy/ saynt Solutaryt ꝫ saynt Aduentour. In englonde the feest of saynt Edmund kyng ꝫ martyr/ that by the [kyng [*fo. cxxvii. b.* ꝫ tyraūt Hyngware ꝫ certayne danes that with hym inuaded the realme/ was taken ꝫ boūden vnto a tree/ scourged naked/ ꝫ than shotte full of arowes/ ꝫ at the last heded. ⊞ Addicyons.

⊞ The feest also of saynt Maxence a virgyn ꝫ martyr that was a kynges doughter/ ꝫ forsoke yᵉ worlde/ ꝫ after by a tyraunt that wolde by force haue maryed her/ she was heded/ ꝫ forthwᵗ she toke vp her owne heed ꝫ bare it a grete space where she lyeth full of myracles. The feest also of saynt Barbens an old man that was her seruaunt/ ꝫ of saynt Rosebe a virgyn her mayde/ yᵗ bothe were put to deth wᵗ theyr maystres. The feest also of saynt Stephan a preest of hygh pfeccyon ꝫ many myracles/ ꝫ the feest of saynt Antipa a preest ꝫ martyr. At edysse the feest of saynt Samon ꝫ saynt Gury martyrs/ that by yᵉ emperour Dioclecian were put to deth for prechyng the fayth. The feest also of many oth. ⁊c̃.

⁋ To morowe.

⁋ The .xxj. day of Nouember. the feest of saynt Rufy/ of whome yᵉ apostle Paule wryteth vnto yᵉ romaynes. At neoconens the feest of saynt Mary a virgyn ⁊ martyr/ that by the emperour Adrian was after many turmentes put to deth. In the prouynce of hystrie the passyon of saynt Mawre a martyr. At hoste yᵉ feest of saȳt Demetry ⁊ saynt Honory. The feest also of saynt Colūbane an abbot/ ⁊ the presentacyon of our blessed lady.   ⁋ Addicyons.

⁋ The feest also of an other saynt Colūbane/ that was kynsman ⁊ discyple vnto the sayd abbot. The feest also of saynt Paciane a bysshop of synguler puryte ⁊ hygh vertue/ ⁊ a grete lerned man/ that wrote many profytable werkes/ specyally agaynst the heretykes called [nouacianes/ of whom [*fo. cxxviii*. saynt Ierome wryteth. The feest also of many other holy sayntes/ mar..çfes. ⁊ virg.

⁋ To morowe.

⁋ The .xxij. daye of Nouēber. At rome yᵉ feest of saynt Cicily a virgyn ⁊ martyr/ yᵗ cōuerted her owne spouse saynt Valerian ⁊ his broder saynt Tiburce/ ⁊ hertned them vnto martyrdom/ ⁊ after was herselfe vnder the emperours Marke and Cōmody put to cruell ⁊ meruaylous turmentes/ ⁊ at the last slayne by the swerde. At rome also yᵉ feest of saynt Mawre a martyr/ that by the mayre Celeryne was put to martyrdom. At augustudune the feest of saynt Pragmas a bysshop ⁊ cōfessour of notable sanctite.   ⁋ Addicyons.

⁋ The feest also of saynt Medrysyne a virgyn/ moche gloryous in myracles. At altynens the feest of saynt Theonyst a bysshop/ saynt Tabra ⁊ saȳt Tabrate deacons ⁊ all martyrs togyder/ yᵗ by yᵉ emperour Theodosy were put to deth. The feest also of many other .⁊c̃.

⁋ To morowe.

⁋ The .xxiij. day of Nouember. the feest of saynt Clement the fourth pope after saynt Peter/ that in yᵉ persecucion of the emperour Traianus was cast in to the see/ ⁊ so ended his martyrdome. The feest also of saynt Felicite/ that by the emperour Antonyne after yͤ martyrdom of her .vij. sones was heded. In ytaly the feest of saynt Colūbane/ a foūder of many monasteryes. In the fraūchest of hyspane⸶ the feest of saynt Trudony a preest ⁊ confessour. At parys the feest of saynt Seueryne a solytary monke. At emeryte the feest of saynt Lucrecye a virgyn. ❡ Addicyons.

❡ At alexander the feest of saynt Faustyne quene and empresse/ a martyr/ cōuerted by saȳt Katheryne/ ⁊ put [to deth by her owne housbond yͤ emperour Maxcens. [*fo. cxxviii. b.* The feest also of an other saynt Clement/ a senatour of rome ⁊ vncle vnto the sayd pope/ ⁊ conuerted by saynt Peter/ ⁊ after a bysshop in fraunce/ where by his holy lyfe/ prechyng ⁊ myracles he cōuerted a hole cite/ with many other notable actes. The feest also of saȳt Traianus/ that by the prayers of saynt Gregory was saued. The feest also of many other holy sayntes/ mart. ⁊c.

❡ To morowe.

❡ The .xxiiij. daye of Nouember. At rome the feest of saynt Grysogon a martyr/ that by the emperour Dioclecian after many turmentes was heded/ ⁊ his holy body cast in to yͤ see. At rome also yͤ feest of saynt Crescenciane a martyr/ of whome is wryten in yͤ passyon of saynt Marcell the pope. In the castel of blaue the feest of saynt Romane a preest ⁊ cōfessour/ whose sanctite is declared by dayly myracles. At corduba yͤ feest of saynt Floure a virgyn/ ⁊ of saynt Mary a virgyn also/ that bothe togyder after many turmētes/ were put to deth by the swerde. In tusce at peruse the feest of saynt Felicissimy a confessour.

❡ Addicyons.

❡ At alexander the feest of saȳt Porphurie with .cc. of his scruaūtes ⁊ soudyours/ yᵗ was conuerted by saynt Katheryne/ 't bycause he buryed the quene saynt Faustyne/ he with his were put to martyrdom. In yrelond the feest of saynt Kenan a bysshop/ borne there of yͤ kynges blode/ ⁊ in youth whan he sholde haue ben slayne he was delyuered by an aungell/ ⁊ after he had many reuelacyons of aungels/ ⁊ was of synguler sanctite/ ⁊ he reysed thre persones vnto lyfe. And by his prayer a woman yᵗ by yͤ space of thre yeres had borne styll in her wombe two chylder/ was soūdly delyuered/ wᵗ many [other grete myracles. The feest also of saynt Flauian ā⸶ [*fo. cxxix.* bysshop. And of many other holy sayntes/ mar. cōf. ⁊c.

❡ To morowe.

❡ The .xxv. day of Nouember. the feest of saynt Peter bysshop of alexander/ ⁊ a martyr/ a man of notable doctryne/ yᵗ by the iudge Maximyne was heded/ ⁊ with hym were put to deth bysshops of egipte ⁊ other of the clergy ⁊ of the leyfeet vnto the nombre of .vj.C. and .lx. persones. At antioche ye feest of saynt Herasmus a gloryous martyr. At alexander ye passyon of saynt Katheryne a virgyn ⁊ martyr/ that by ye emperour Maxence after many cruell turmentes was heded/ whose holy body was cōuayed ⁊ caryed by aūgels vnto the moūt of synai/ where it lyeth full of dayly grete myracles.   ❡ Addicyons.

❡ At cesaraugust the feest of saynt Marcury a martyr that was chefe capitayne w^t the emperour Decius/ ⁊ was cōuerted by an aūgell. And whā he was knowen for a chrystyan/ he was put to dethe by meruaylous cruell turmentes/ in whose passion moche people was cōuerted. The feest also of saynt Mercuriall bysshop of liuience. And of many other holy sayntes/ mar. cōf. ⁊c.

❡ To morowe.

❡ The .xxvj. daye of Nouēber. the feest of saynt Lyne the fyrst pope after saȳt Peter/ that whan he had well gouerned ye chirche .xij. yeres/ was put to martyrdom and buryed in vaticanes strete. At alexander ye feest of saynt Faust a preest/ saynt Dius ⁊ saynt Ammony all martyrs/ that w^t saynt Peter bysshop of the same cyte were by the tyraūt Maximian put to martyrdom. At augustudune the feest of saȳt Amatour a bysshop. In the monastery of wendoper the feest of saynt Leonard [a [*fo. cxxix. b.* confessour.   ❡ Addicyons.

❡ The feest also of saynt Basoly a cōfessour/ of synguler sanctite. At edysse the feest of saynt Peter a bysshop of notable vertue/ ⁊ a grete lerned man/ ⁊ made many werkes moche edificatyue vnto Chrystes chirche/ and was also a grete precher and fedde many soules. The feest also of many other holy sayntes/ mart. confes. ⁊c.

❡ To morowe.

❡ The .xxvij. daye of Nouēber. At bonony the feest of saynt Agricola a martyr/ y^t was lyke vnto Chryst crucyfyed/ ⁊ of his seruaūt saynt Vitale/ that bycause he wolde not forsake his mayster ⁊ his fayth/ was before hym put to deth by many turmentes. In fraūce at regens ye feest of saynt Maximy a confessour/ y^t frō youth was of notable vertue/ ⁊ than abbot of lyrynens/ ⁊ after bysshop of regens/ a man of many grete myracles.   ❡ Addicyons.

❡ In perse ye feest of saynt Peter whose syrname was

intercyse/ borne of the kynges blode/ but of chrysten parentes/ ⁊ he in youth baptized/ whiche thynge whan the kyng knewe/ he caused hȳ by moost horryble cruelty to be kytte every membre frō other one by one. The feest also of saȳt Iosaphat a kynges sone/ yᵗ was discyple vnto saynt Barlaame/ by whome he was baptized ⁊ with whome he lyued in desert a holy lyſ full of myracles. The feest also of many other holy sayntes .⁊c̃.

¶ To morowe

¶ The .xxviij. day of Nouember. At corynth yᵉ feest of saynt Sostones† discyple vnto saynt Paule/ of whome he maketh mencyon in his epystle vnto the corynthes. In affryke yᵉ feest of saynt Papyne ⁊ saynt Mansuete bysshops ⁊ martyrs/ that in the persecucyon of yᵉ wandales were enflambed wᵗ hote yren plates/ ⁊ by many [other turmentes put to deth. At [*fo. cxxx.* rome the feest of saynt Rufy a martyr/ that by the emperour Dioclecian was put to deth with all his hole housholde/ and so all martyrs.   ¶ Addicyons.

¶ At rome the feest of saynt Gregory yᵉ second pope of that name/ a grete lerned man ⁊ very eloquent/ and a grete impugner ⁊ confoūder of heretykes/ ⁊ he cursed the emperour Leo/ bycause he destroyed the ymage of Chryst/ of our lady/ ⁊ of other sayntes/ wᵗ many other notable actes. At rome also the feest of an other saynt Gregory yᵉ thyrde pope of that name/ ⁊ successour vnto the other/ a man also of excellent doctryne/ bothe in the greke ⁊ latyn tongue/ of singuler vertue/ ⁊ of grete pite vnto the poore/ ⁊ a bolde man/ for he wᵗout drede cōfyrmed the curse of yᵉ sayd emperour Leo/ ⁊ ouer that for his obstinacy he put hym and all his successours from all preuyleges/ profytes/ dominion/ lordshyp or gouernaunce in rome/ ytaly ⁊ spayne for euer. The feest also of many other holy sayntes/ marť. confes. ⁊ virgyns.

¶ To morowe.

¶ The .xxix. day of Nouember. the vigyl of saynt Andrewe the apostle. At rome in salary strete the feest of saynt Saturnyne/ ⁊ of saȳt Sisynny a deacon ⁊ bothe martyrs/ yᵗ by the prynce Maximian were kepte longe in harde pryson/ ⁊ after scourged/ beten wᵗ staues/ racked/ and theyr ioyntes strayned wᵗ cordes/ enflambed wᵗ fyry plates/ ⁊ at yᵉ last after many moo turmentes heded. At tolose the feest of saynt Saturnyne a bysshop ⁊ martyr/ that was cast downe from the hyghest toure of the cite/ ⁊ so martyred.

⁋ Addicyons.

⁋ In egypte the feest of saynt Amos/ that maryed by his frendes/ persuaded his wyfe to kepe virginite/ ⁊ so [they lyued togyder virgyns .xviij. yeres/ and after her deth he [*fo. cxxx. b.* went in to desert/ ⁊ was an abbot of hygh perfeccyon ⁊ many myracles. The feest also of saynt Panucy an abbot of ye wyldernes of heracly/ that axed .iij. tymes of our lord/ what persones were of lyke meryte vnto hym/ ⁊ he had answere/ a mynstrell/ a mayre of a cite/ ⁊ a marchaūt/ whiche psones all thre left ye worlde ⁊ went with hym in to desert/ where they all lyued in hygh perfeccyon/ ⁊ at his deth his soule in open syght was caryed by aungelles in to blysse. The feest also of many other holy sayntes/ martyrs/ confes. ⁊ virgyns,

⁋ To morowe

⁋ The .xxx. day of Nouēber. In achaya at patras the feest of saynt Andrewe ye apostle/ that after he had preched in sythe/ came vnto the sayd cite/ where by ye proconsull Egeas after many turmentes he was hanged vpon the crosse/ where vpon he remayned quycke two dayes/ prechynge styll vnto ye people. At sanctonas the feest of saynt Trophianet/ a man of meruaylous perfeccyon/ whiche is playnly shewed by dayly myracles. The passion also of saynt Iustyne a gloryous martyr.

⁋ Addicyons.

⁋ The feest also of saynt Nathanaell/ one of the .lxxij. discyples/ whome our sauyour called a very israelyte/ that is to saye/ a very true ⁊ faythfull chylde of israell. The feest also of an other sayt Nathanael an heremyte that was sore vexed by ye deuyll ⁊ had many illusyons and tētacyons/ whiche by the helpe of grace he ouercame/ and was of notable perfeccyon. Also here is remembraunce made of the aduent and comynge of our sauyour Chryst Iesu. And the feest also of many other holy sayntes/ martyrs/ confessours/ and virgyns.

[⁋ To morowe. [*fo. cxxxi.*

Decēber.   THe fyrst daye of December. At rome the feest of saynt Crysant ⁊ of sayt Daria a virgyn/ bothe martyrs/ that by the emperour Numerary after many turmentes/ were murthered in sonde ⁊ grauell. At rome also ye feest of saynt Dyodour a preest/ ⁊ of saynt Marian a deacon/ that with many other psones were by the same emperour put to martyrdom. At magonce

DECEMBER.

the feest of saynt Albane a martyr. At nouiome yᵉ feest of saynt Eligy a bysshop ⁊ confessour/ gloryous in holy lyfe ⁊ myracles. The feest also of saynt Natale a matrone/ that was wyfe vnto saynt Adrian the martyr. At naryne the feest of saynt Proculy a preest/ ⁊ of saynt Mawre/ a martyr of gloryous triumphe. ¶ Addicyons.

¶ The feest also of saynt Diodory a bysshop ⁊ confessour/ ⁊ of grete lernynge/ ⁊ made many werkes. The feest also of saynt Ansan/ ⁊ of his godmoder saÿt Maxima a virgyn/ bothe martyrs/ that by his fader a noble man of rome were brought vnto yᵉ emperours Dioclecian ⁊ Maximian/ where she was beten to deth wᵗ staues/ ⁊ he heded. The feest also of many other holy .⁊c̃.

¶ To morowe.

¶ The seconde day of Deceber. the feest of saynt Vere ⁊ saynt Secury breder/ yᵗ in affryke were put to martyrdom. At rome the feest of saynt Viuyane a holy woman ⁊ a martyr/ that by yᵉ emperour Iulian yᵉ apostata was beten to deth with plūmettes of lede. ¶ Addicyons.

¶ The feest also of saynt Peter archebysshop of rauen electe by reuelacyon/ a man of notable doctryne/ by whose epystle the heretyke Ewtices was cōdempned [he was so [*fo. cxxxi. b.* eloquent in speche/ that he was called by syrname chrisologus/ that is to saye/ golden speech or vtteraunce/ ⁊ he had reuelacyon ⁊ knowlege of his deth by an aungell/ and was of many myracles. The feest also of many other holy sayntes/ mart̃. confes. ⁊ virg.

¶ To morowe.

¶ The thyrde daye of December. At rome the feest of saynt Clawdy a noble man/ ⁊ a chefe offycer/ ⁊ a martyr/ that was tyed vnto a grete stone ⁊ cast in to the see. And than his wyfe saynt Hyllary wᵗ theyr two sones saynt Iason ⁊ saÿt Mawre/ and .lxx. of his soudyours and seruaūtes/ all togyder by yᵉ emperour Numerian heded. At tynge yᵉ passyon of saynt Cassiane a martyr/ that was a iudge ⁊ persecutour of chrysten people many yeres/ ⁊ at the last cōuerted by dyuyne inspiracyon ⁊ by grudge or remorce of conscyence/ ⁊ after receyued gladly suche iudgemēt of martyrdom as he before had gyuen. At wynchester the feest of saynt Byryne a bysshop and confessour. ¶ Addicyons.

¶ The feest also of saynt Lucy a kynge of englonde/ yᵗ was

baptized by saynt Tymothe discyple vnto saynt Paule/ ⁊ after in his realme he cōuerted moche people and at the last he resygned his crowne/ ⁊ lyued a holy pryuate lyfe/ by ye example wherof many psones were brought vnto hygh pfeccyon/ ⁊ notwithstandynge the grete persecucyon of chrystyans/ yet dyed he in peace a cōfessour. The feest also of many other holy saynt̃. ⁊c̃.

¶ To morowe.

¶ The .iiij. day of December. At pont the feest of saynt Melecy a bysshop ⁊ confessour/ of grete lernynge ⁊ notable vertue. At nicomede the passyon of saynt Barbara a virgyn. At alexander the feest of saynt Clement a [preest/ a [*fo. cxxxii*. famous man of lernynge in scripture. In the fraunchest of bituricens the feest of saynt Gignauy an abbot/ of hygh pfeccyon.
¶ Addicyons.
¶ The feest also of an other saynt Melecy a bysshop/ y^t for his notable vertue ⁊ doctryne was electe bysshop of antioche/ but after he was put out by ye heretykes called arrianes/ ⁊ than he lyued w^t saynt Euseby in hygh pfeccion ⁊ many myracles. At bituricens ye feest of sayt Saryne an abbot. And the feest also of many other .⁊c̃.

¶ To morowe.

¶ The .v. day of December. In affrike at colen thebestyne ye feest of saynt Crispyne a virgyn ⁊ martyr/ that bycause she wold not do sacrefyce vnto ye ydolles/ was by the procōsull Anolyne vnder the emperours Dioclecian ⁊ Maximian heded. In ytaly ye feest of saynt Dalmatyke a martyr. At treuer the feest of saynt Niceny† a bisshop ⁊ cōfessour. At tagora the feest of saynt Iuly/ ⁊ of the blessed woman saynt Potamie. The feest also of saynt Saby a confessour and an abbot.
¶ Addicyons.
¶ At nyce the feest of saynt Basse a bysshop ⁊ martyr/ that after many cruell turmentes was set standynge vpon a stocke/ ⁊ two nayles of yren made of his owne lengthe were dryuen through out his body from his sholders on eyther syde downe through his fete in to the stocke/ and there so he dyed. In wales at the mynster of saynt Dauid the feest of saynt Iustiniane a bysshop ⁊ martyr/ borne of the noble blode of the lesse brytayne/ and for Chryst he forsoke his countree and kynne/ ⁊ was ledde by an aũgell in to many coũtrees/ where he euer dyd many myracles/ ⁊ at the last he came vnto saynt Dauid and was his dayly ghostly

DECEMBER.

fader/ where [his own seruaūtes bycause he rebuked [*fo. cxxxii. b.* theyr synnes stroke of his heed/ where forthwith sprange a well/ ⁊ the decd body toke vp the heed ⁊ bare it ouer the see/ ⁊ the people folowed as though it had ben the drye londe vnto they came where now he lyeth full of myracles. The feest also of many other holy sayntes/ marť. ⁊c̃.

℟ To morowe.

℟ The .vj. daye of December. the feest of saynt Nicolas bysshop of myrre in the countree of lycie/ a man of synguler sanctite and many notable myracles/ among whiche is chefely remembred how beynge in a countree ferre of/ he appered by vysyon vnto the emperour Constantyne/ ⁊ by warnynge ⁊ thretenynge he withdrewe his dyspleasure and sentence agaynst certayne persones that wrongfully were iudged vnto deth. In affryke the feest of yᵉ holy women saynt Denyse/ saynt Datyue/ ⁊ saynt Leoncy. And of saynt Cercy† a monke saynt Emilian ⁊ saynt Boniface/ with other three persones all martyrs/ put to dethe at one tyme by moost cruell turmentes.

℟ Addicyons.

℟ The feest also of an other saynt Nicolas yᵉ fyrst pope of that name/ a grete and bolde defender of the chirche for he cursed the emperour of constantinople/ bycause he enterprysed and medled with yᵉ correccyon and punysshement of the clergy. And he cursed the kynge of fraūce/ bycause he helde a concubyne besyde his wyfe whiche sayd kynge was compelled to come hymselfe vnto the same pope at rome to be assoyled. The feest also of many other holy sayntes/ martyrs/ cōfes. ⁊ virg.

℟ To morowe.

℟ The .vij. daye of December. In alexander the feest of saynt Agathon a martyr/ yᵗ beynge a man of warre [with the emperour Decius/ grudged ⁊ spake agaynst the [*fo. cxxxiii.* cruelty that was done vnto the christen people/ for the whiche he was heded. At sanctonas yᵉ feest of saŷt Martyne an abbot/ at whose tombe ben dayly myracles. In the fraunchest of meldinens† the feest of saynt Fare a virgyn. The ordynacyon also ⁊ consecracyon of saynt Ambrose bysshop ⁊ confessour. And the octaue of saynt Andrewe. ℟ Addicyons.

℟ In yrelonde the feest of saynt Boecy a bysshop and confessour/ that reysed a kynge of englonde from deth and a kynges doughter of yrelond/ with many other persones/ and other grete myracles in many dyuerse countrees. And had the spiryte of prophecy and reuelacyon of his deth. The feest also of saynt Agathon an abbot/ that bycause he wolde precysely kepe sylence/ bare a stone contynually thre yeres in his mouth/ and he neuer slepte or wente to reste wrothe or dyspleased with ony persone. For a wrathfull persone (sayd he) all though he reysed deed bodyes and dyd myracles/ yet doth he no thynge please god. And he oft sayd/ that a religyous persone sholde euer contynue as he began the fyrst daye of his entre/ and in no wyse trust vnto hymselfe/ for selfe trust (sayd he) is the moder of passyons and trouble. The feest also of saynt Genebawde bysshop of laudunens/ and of his sone saynt Latry bysshop also of the same cite and his successour. The feest also of many other holy sayntes/ mart. confes. ℞ virg.

¶ To morowe.

¶ The .viij. day of December. The concepcyon of our lady saynt Mary the moder of god. At rome the feest of saynt Ewtician pope and martyr/ that after he had ruled the chirche one yere/ was by the emperour Au[relian put to [fo. cxxxiii. b. martyrdom/ and buryed in the cymitery of saynt Calixt. In alexander the feest of saynt Machary a martyr/ that by the emperour Decius bycause he wold not forsake Chryst/ was brent. In the frauchest of dymens the deposycyon of saynt Leonard a confessour of notable vertue.   ¶ Addicyons.

¶ The feest also of saynt Romaryke an abbot of hygh perfeccyon/ whose soule was seen passe in to heuen by a clowde. The feest also of sayt zenon a bysshop/ a man of noble doctryne/ and made many werkes/ ℞ was of many myracles. The feest also of an other saynt Ewtician a cōfessour. The feest also of many other holy .℞c.

¶ To morowe.

¶ The .ix. daye of December. The feest of saynt Leocade a virgyn/ that in the cite of tolete was put in prison by Decius the presydent of spayne/ wherin whan she herde of the passyon of the holy woman saynt Ewlaly with other martyrs/ she kneled to praye/ ℞ in that prayer she expyred. The feest also of saynt Cipriane abbot of petragoryke a man of synguler sanctite ℞ many myracles. The translacyon also of saynt Sebastian a martyr/ and of saynt Gregory pope.   ¶ Addicyons.

¶ The feest also of saynt Proculy a bysshop and confessour/ that in the persecucyon of the emperour Maximian wylfully offred hymselfe vnto martyrdom. And bycause the iudge supposed and thought he had doted for age/ he delyuered hym/ for yᵉ whiche he made grete sorowe and mournynge/ than he preched boldly ⁊ conuerted moche people/ ⁊ dyd many myracles. The feest also of saynt Syre a bysshop and confessour/ a man of grete lernynge/ and conuerted many coūtrees/ ⁊ was [of many myracles. The feest also of many [*fo. cxxxiiii.* other holy sayntes/ martyrs/ confessours/ and virgyns.

¶ To morowe.

¶ The .x. day of December. At hyspolitane the feest of saynt Capoforyt a preest/ and of saynt Habundy a deacon/ that in the persecucyon of yᵉ emperour Dioclecian were beten with staues/ nere famysshed in prison/ racked/ and after many other turmentes at the last heded. In spayne at emeryte the passyon of saynt Ewlale a virgyn and martyr/ that by the mayre Daciane after many cruell paynes was racked/ and her flesshe torne with hokes/ and than two grete fyres made on euery syde/ ⁊ so by long space she was consumed vnto deth. In the same cite the feest of saynt Iulia a virgyn and martyr/ cosyne germayne vnto the sayd virgyn/ and felowe with her in all her paynes/ and with gladde mynde receyued with her the crowne of martyrdom. The feest also of saynt Melchyady pope ⁊ martyr. ¶ Addicyons.
¶ The feest also of saynt Erynbald a iudge/ that vnto iustyce had synguler zele/ in soo moche that whan his systers sone had rauysshed a virgyn/ he beynge vpon his deth bedde/ iudged hym vnto dethe/ but the offycers for fauoure suffred hym to escape/ after the yonge man supposyng his vncle had forgoten the mater/ came to vysyte hym/ whome he secretly called vnto hym/ and with a knyfe kytte his throte/ for the whiche dede his ghostly fader called hym an homycyde/ ⁊ wolde not mynystre vnto hym the sacrament of Chrystes body/ vnto the whiche he answered/ that he dyd that dede without ony malyce for the zele of iustyce/ ⁊ so was it there shewed by reuelacyon/ and he receyued [the sacrament by myracle without ony [*fo. cxxxiiii. b.* mānes hande and so departed. The feest also of many other holy . ⁊c̃.

¶ To morowe.

¶ The .xj. day of December. At rome the feest of saynt Damasy pope. The feest also of saynt Traso a martyr/ that by the emperour Maximian was put to martyrdom with saynt Ponciane and saynt Pretaxate. At beamet the feest of saynt

Gencian and saynt Fustinianȝ martyrs/ that were bounden vnto a post/ and iuce of herbes with vynegre ⁊ peper blowen in to theyr eares and nosethrylles/ and theyr hedes nayled vnto the post with hote fyry nayles/ theyr eyes put out/ and theyr bodyes shotte full of arowes/ and after all these ⁊ many other cruell paynes/ they were heded/ with whome saynt Victoryke theyr host that lodged them was put to martyrdome. In spayne the feest of saynt Ewtyke a noble man/ and of synguler vertue.
℣ Addicyons.
℣ The feest also of saynt Sauyne bysshop of placentyne/ a man of synguler sanctite/ that by reuelacyon dyd translate the body of saynt Antonyne. The ryuer also of pade by his commaūdement wente backe from the chirche londes in to the canell/ ⁊ neuer after noyed ne hurte ony parte of ye same londes/ with many other notable myracles. The feest also of many other ho. ⁊c.

℣ To morowe.

℣ The .xij. daye of December. At narbon the feest of saynt Paule a confessour/ that by the apostle Paule was consecrate bysshop of the same cite/ and after he wente with hym in to spayne to preche/ where the apostle lefte hym/ and he there dyd grete dilygence/ and by his holy lyfe and myracles he coūerted moche peo[ple. At alexander the feest of [*fo. cxxxv.* saynt Ammonary ⁊ saynt Mercury/ with other two all foure holy women and martyrs/ that after many cruell and newfounde turmentes were slayne by ye swerde. The feest also of sayͭ Hermogenes/ saynt Donate/ and of other .xxij. persones all martyrs. In the fraūchest of niuiacens ye feest of saynt Waleryke a preest and confessour. ℣ Addicyons.
℣ The feest also of sayͭ Ewstrace a martyr/ that was a duke and chefe capitayne vnder the emperours Dioclecian and Maximiane/ ⁊ was taken at satale where he was put to meruaylous turmentes and passion/ in the whiche saynt Ewgene a grete offycer was coūerted/ and than were they bothe togyder nayled vnto a blocke/ and so caryed vnto auare/ where they were put to newe passyon/ in the whiche saynt Auxence/ saynt Mardary/ and saynt Oresty/ with many other persones were coūerted/ ⁊ all togyder put to deth. At alexander the feest of saynt Epimachy/ and saynt Alexander martyrs. In yrelonde the feest of saynt Fynany an abbot/ in whose concepcyon his moder had of hym a reuelacyon/ he cast a water lyke a mere in to the see/ and where it was he buylded a monastery/ and he ordeyned in an other monastery .iij. M. monkes. And he reysed

v. persones from deth/ and turned water in to wyne/ with many other myracles/ that he dyd as well in englonde and wales as in yrelonde/ ꝛ had also reuelacyon of his deth. The feest also of many other holy .ꝛc̃.

⁋ To morowe.

⁋ The .xiij. day of December. In sicilie at syracusane the feest of saynt Luce a virgyn and martyr/ that in the persecucyon of the emperour Dioclecian was fyrst [cōmytted by [*fo. cxxv. b.* the iudge Pascasy vnto the cōmune bawdes to haue ben defouled/ but whan they pulled her forthe/ she (by the vertue of Chryst) stode immouable as an hyll/ than they tyed cordes and ropes vnto her/ and put to grete strengthe of men and many yokes of oxen/ but no thynge for them all she remoued or stered/ than made they a grete fyre aboute her where she stode/ and cast therin pytche and rosyne/ and cast vpon her body boylynge lede and oyle/ and at the last after many turmentes/ they put a swerde in to her bowelles/ and so she ended her martyrdom. The feest also of saȳt Awthebert/ bysshop of camber. The deposicyon also of saynt Iudoke a confessour of synguler sanctite. ⁋ Addicyons.

⁋ In yrelonde the feest of saynt Columby an abbot/ borne of noble lignage/ and forsoke the worlde to serue god in religyon/ wherin he was of hygh perfeccyon/ ꝛ a grete founder of monasteryes/ he put in two monasteryes thre hondred monkes/ he reysed also from deth a kynges sone of englonde and his doughter/ and conuerted hym and all his people/ and many myracles he dyd in ytaly and in other regyons/ and he was caryed by aūgels from a ferre countree vnto the deth of saynt Fynane/ with many other notable actes. The feest also of many other holy sayntes/ martyrs/ cōfes. ꝛ virg.

⁋ To morowe.

⁋ The .xiiij. daye of December. In cypris the feest of saynt Spiridion a bysshop/ one of the confessours that by the emperour Maximiane were put to many turmentes/ after whiche he put out theyr ryght eyes/ ꝛ kytte of theyr lefte thūmes/ and so condempned them vnto exyle/ where this holy saynt lyued in hygh per[feccyon and many myracles. At [*fo. cxxxvi.* alexander the feest of saynt Heron/ saynt Arseny/ saynt Ysidour/ and a childe called saynt Dioscour/ that by myracle was delyuered for that tyme/ where the other after many turmentes were brent. At antioche the feest of saynt Drusy/

saynt zosymy/ and saynt Theodour all martyrs. At reame the feest of saynt Nicasy a bysshop and martyr/ and of his syster saynt Ewtropie. The deposicyon also of sayt Attyke a monke. The feest also of saynt Lothary an abbot/ of high perfeccyon and many myracles. ⁋ Addicyons.

⁋ The feest also of saynt Agnelly an abbot of synguler sanctite ꝛ many myracles/ whose holy body lyeth in naples in grete honour and glorye. The feest also of many other holy sayntes/ martyrs/ confes. ꝛ virgyns.

⁋ To morowe.

⁋ The .xv. daye of December. In affryke the feest of saynt Valerian a bysshop and confessour/ that in ye age of .lxxx. yeres was for the defence of the chyrche put out of his cite/ and strayte cōmaundement gyuen that no persone sholde take hym vnto lodgynge/ ne yet suffre hym to lodge vpon theyr grounde/ so was he compelled to byde contynually vnto his dethe in the hye wayes and stretes. In the terrytory of orlyaunce the feest of saynt Maximyne an holy abbot/ of synguler perfeccyon and many myracles. ⁋ Addicyons.

⁋ The feest also of saynt Theodour bisshop of tarcens a noble lerned man and made many werkes/ and specyally vpon Paules epystles/ of whose vertue saynt Ierome wryteth. The feest also of many other holy sayntes/ martyrs/ confessours and virgyns.

[⁋ To morowe.   [*fo. cxxxvi. b.*

⁋ The .xvj. daye of December. the feest of thre stryplynges/ saynt Ananie/ saynt Azary/ and saynt Misael that were put in to the flambynge fourneys/ where they remayned without noyaūce/ whose holy bodyes done lye at babylon in a caue. At tuscia ye feest of saynt Barbara a virgyn and martyr/ that in ye persecucyon of the emperour Maximyane was nere famysshed in harde pryson/ scourged/ racked/ hote lampes put vnto her body/ her pappes kytte from her brest/ with many other meruaylous turmentes/ and after all slayne by the swerde. At rauen ye feest of saynt Valentyne/ saynt Vanaly† and saynt Agricoly.
⁋ Addicyons.

⁋ At treuer the feest of saynt Prisciliane bysshop of bapyll and a martyr/ a noble lerned man/ and made many werkes/ and (as saynt Ierome wryteth) he was put to martyrdom by a tyraūt called Maximian/ that was a capitayne w^t the emperour Theodosy the fyrst. The feest also of many other holy sayntes/ mart. ꝛc.

⁋ To morowe.

⁋ The .xvij. day of December. the trāslacyon of saynt Ignacy a bysshop ꝫ martyr/ brought from rome vnto antioche/ where he lyeth without dampnytyke gate in the cymiterye of the same chyrche. The feest also of saynt Lazare/ whome (as the gospell testyfyeth) our sauyour reysed from deth. The feest also of his syster saynt Martha/ in the worshyp of whome a fayre chirche is buylded at bethany/ anenst yᵉ hous where they dwelled. In the eest partyes at elewteropole the feest of fyfty martyrs/ that were put to deth by yᵉ sarasyns. ⁋ Addicyons.

[⁋ At gaze the feest of saynt Floriane/ saynt [*fo. cxxxvii.* Kalanyke and of .xl. other persones all martyrs. The feest also of many other holy sayntes/ martyrs/ confes. ꝫ virgyns.

⁋ To morowe.

⁋ The .xviij. daye of December. At philyppes in macedony the feest of saynt Ruf/ ꝫ of saynt zosymy martyrs/ that were of yᵉ fyrst sorte of discyples/ by whome the chirche of Chryst was founded/ of whose martyrdome saynt Policarpe wryteth in his epystle vnto the phylipens. In affryke the passyon of saynt Moysety a martyr. At turon the feest of saynt Cancianet̄ the fyrst bysshop of the same cite/ and sente thyder from rome/ where he dyd many myracles/ and gretely edifyed the chirche of Chryst. ⁋ Addicyons.

⁋ At toletane the feest of saynt Hyldefons/ bysshop of the same cite/ a man of synguler deuocyon vnto our lady/ for the whiche he ordeyned a feest of her to be kepte in his chirche before Chrystmas/ in the whiche she appered vnto hym/ and brought hym a whyte stole and a chayre/ whiche yet vnto this day ben there reserued for holy relykes. The feest also of many other holy .ꝫc̃.

⁋ To morowe.

⁋ The .xix. daye of December. In egypte the feest of saynt Nemesy a martyr/ that by the iudge Emyliane after many turmētes was brent amonge theues and robbers. At nice the feest of saynt Darius a martyr. At antisiodour the feest of saynt Gregory a bysshop ꝫ confessour. ⁋ Addicyons.

⁋ In yrelonde the feest of saynt Samdyne a virgyn/ borne of noble blode/ and by her frendes maryed/ but for the desyre of virginite she was delyuered from her spouse by myracle/ and so entred religyon/ wherein she [came to hygh [*fo. cxxxvii. b.*

perfeccyon ⁊ was abbesse/ a grete almes woman and very pyteous/ and many persones she delyuered from shame and rebuke/ many also from pryson by myracle/ and by her prayer she remoued a chirche/ with many other notable actes. The feest also of many other holy sayntes/ martyrs/ confes. ⁊ virgyns.

⁋ To morowe.

⁋ The .xx. day of December. At alexander the feest of saynt Ammony/ saynt zenony/ saynt Tholomy/ saynt Iugeny†/ and saynt Theophyly all martyrs/ that for confortynge a martyr that faynted in his turmentes/ were all taken/ and after greuous turmentes put to deth. In trace at gelduba the feest of saynt Iuly a martyr. At amphitre ye feest of saynt Liberate/ ⁊ the vigyll of saynt Thomas. ⁋ Addicyons.

⁋ At cesaree palestyne the feest of saynt Gelasy bysshop of the same cite/ a man of notable doctryne/ and made many werkes/ and was of synguler sanctite ⁊ many myracles. The feest also of many other holy .⁊c.

⁋ To morowe.

⁋ The .xxj. daye of December. the feest of saynt Thomas the apostle/ that preched vnto the parthes ⁊ medes/ and after in ynde he was put to martyrdome/ after the whiche many yeres he was translate vnto the cite of edisse. In tuscie the feest of saynt Iohn/ and of saynt Festy. The feest also of saynt Ewyne a quene. In englonde within the frauchest of oxford/ at betony the deposicyon of saynt Berenwald preest ⁊ martyr.
⁋ Addicyons.
⁋ The feest also of saynt Denyse a bysshop and discyple vnto the sayd apostle saynt Thomas/ whome he couerted with saynt Pelagia his spouse that was the [kynges [*fo. cxxxviii.* doughter/ whome the apostle consecrate a virgyn/ and made her an abbesse/ whiche after the deth of her sayd spouse was desyred vnto maryage of a noble man/ vnto whome bycause she wolde not consent/ she was heded and buryed in the same sepulcre with her spouse. The feest also of many other holy sayn. ⁊c.

⁋ To morowe.

⁋ The .xxij. daye of December. At rome in lauycane strete bytwene the laureres the feest of .xx. martyrs/ that in ye persecucyon of yᵉ emperour Dioclecian were put to deth all togyder. At alexander the feest of saynt Chiridon a martyr/ that bycause he wold not do sacrefyce vnto the ydolles/ was prycked in the bely and body with nalles and botkyns tyll he was deed. At antioche the feest of saynt Basyley/ saynt Dewtrey†/ saȳt Honorate ⁊ saynt Flour martyrs. The feest also of saȳt Theosie† a virgyn. ℂ Addicyons.

ℂ The feest also of saynt Theotimy bysshop of cireney a noble lerned man/ and made many pfytable werkes and was of holy lyfe ⁊ many myracles. The feest also of many other holy sayntes/ martyrs/ confes. ⁊ virg.

ℂ To morowe.

ℂ The .xxiij. daye of December. At nicomede the feest of xx. martyrs/ that in yᵉ persecucyon of the emperour Dioclecian were by moost cruell turniētes put to deth. At rome the feest of saynt Victor a virgyn and martyr that in the persecucyon of the emperour Dioclecian bycause she wolde not mary a pagan/ ne yet do sacrefyce vnto the ydolles/ was put to cruell passyon/ in yᵉ whiche she conuerted many virgyns and other persones/ and dyd grete myracles/ and after all she was thrast vnto the herte with a swerde. At rome also the feest of [saynt Seruuly/ that (as saȳt Gregory wryteth) was euer from [*fo. cxxxviii. b.* youth seke of the palsey/ and yet of synguler sanctite and many myracles. At nicomede the feest of .xxxv. martyrs. At rome the feest of .viij. C. ⁊ .xxx. martyrs. The deposicyon also of saynt Gyldebert a kynge. ℂ Addicyons.

ℂ The feest also of saynt Amphilacy bysshop of ycony a man of notable vertue and grete lernynge/ and made many werkes moche profytable vnto Chrystes fayth amonge whiche werkes/ one he wrote vnto saynt Ierome of the holy ghost/ he was also of many myracles. The feest also of many other holy sayntes/ mart̃. ⁊c.

ℂ To morowe.

ℂ The .xxiiij. day of December. the vigyl of the byrth of Chryst. In syre at antioche the feest of .xl. virgyns and martyrs/ that in the persecucyon of the emperour Daciane were all togyder put to martyrdom. In tuscia at spolete the feest of saynt Gregory a preest ⁊ martyr/ that in the persecucyon of yᵉ emperour Dioclecian was beten with staues/ racked/ and after broyled/ and than prycked all ouer the body/ specyally in his knees with botkyns/ his rybbes brent with hote lampes/ ⁊ at the last after all turmētes he was heded. At tripole the feest of saynt Lucian/ a holy confessour. ⁋ Addicyons.

⁋ The feest also of saynt Abdi the prophete/ that was the thyrde capitayne that came from kynge Acab vnto the prophete Hely/ which saynt Abdi hydde a hondred prophetes from the cursed quene Iezabell y^t slewe and destroyed ye prophetes of god/ for the whiche dede almyghty god made him a pphete/ whose wyfe and chylder after his deth were releued by ye prophete Eli[zey/ by whose prayer she fylled many [*fo. cxxxix.* vesselles of oyle out of one lytell vessell/ and so she payde her dettes and saued her childer/ and after these two prophetes were buryed bothe togyder/ where after was buryed also saynt Iohn baptist. The feest also of ye prophete Naū. And of many other holy sayntes/ mart̃. confes. t̃ virg.

⁋ To morowe.

⁋ The .xxv. daye of December. At bethleem iude the nativite and byrth of our lorde t̃ sauyour Iesu Chryst the essenciall sone of almyghty god/ t̃ the naturall sone of our blessed lady saynt Mary euer moost pure t̃ immaculate virgyn/ whiche blessed byrth was in the .xlij. yere of the emperour Augustus/ t̃ the very true tyme named and appoynted by the prophecy of Daniell/ as appereth in the .ix. chapytre of his boke. The yere also of a notable date amonge the iewes called olympiades .C.lxxx. and .xiij. The yere also from the foundacyon t̃ buyldynge of Rome .vij.C. and .lij. And the yere from the begynnynge of the worlde .v.M.C.lxxix. The feest also of saynt Anastas a virgyn and martyr/ that by the emperour Dioclecian was brought vnto the yle of palmary/ where after longe imprysonment t̃ many turmentes she was brent/ with whome were put to deth by varyaūt turmentes .CC. men/ and .vij.C. women. At rome in the cimitery of saynt Aproniane the feest of saynt Ewgeny a virgyn and martyr/ a woman of notable myracles/ and an abbesse of many virgyns/ that by the emperour Galiene after many turmentes was slayne by the swerde.

⁋ Addicyons.

⁋ The deposicyon also of saynt Luciane a preest/ that translated the holy bodyes of saynt Steuen/ saynt Nicodeme/ saynt Gamaliel and saynt Abibon/ and wrote [also [*fo. cxxxix. b.* the story of the reuelacyon. The feest also of many other holy sayntes/ martyrs/ confessours/ t̃ virgyns.

⁋ To morowe.

⁋ The .xxvj. daye of December. At Ierusalem ye feest of

saynt Stephan the fyrst martyr/ that in the same yere of the
ascencyon of our sauyour was by the iewes stoned vnto deth/
whose holy body in ye tyme of prynce Honory was founde by
reuelacyon. At rome in appia strete ye deposicyon of Denyse
pope/ a noble man of doctryne and holynes. At rome also the
feest of saynt Maryne a martyr/ that was a noble capytayne
vnder the emperour Marciane/ ⁊ by hym put to martyrdom.
℣ Addicyons.
℣ The feest also of two monkes/ whose names be not shewed/
that by the infydeles in a fury and rage were put to cruell
martyrdom. The feest also of many other holy sayntes/ martyrs/
confessours/ and virgyns.

℣ To morowe.

℣ The .xxvij. day of December. At ephesy the feest of
saynt Iohñ the euangelyst/ that was exyled in to the yle of
pathmos/ where by diuyne reuelacion he wrote the apocalypse/
and after returned in to asia/ where he wrote his gospell of our
sauyour/ and founded there many chyrches and gouerned many
persones/ and so he perseuered vnto the reygne of the emperour
Traianus/ and than he departed in the age of .lxxx. and .xix.
yeres/ ⁊ in the yere of our lord after his passyon .lxviij. and was
buryed nere vnto the sayd cite. At alexander the feest of saynt
Maximy a bysshop of notable vertue in the confessyon of Chryst.
℣ Addicyons.
℣ The feest also of an other saynt Maximy bysshop of
[tawrinens/ a man of notable doctryne/ and made many [*fo. cxl.*
Omelyes/ that is to saye sermons/ and many werkes of grete
eloquence moche edifycatyue and profytable vnto the chyrche
of Chryst. The feest also of many other holy sayntes/ martyrs/
confessours/ ⁊ virgyns.

℣ To morowe.

℣ The .xxviij. day of December. At bethleem the feest of
the Innocentes/ that for Chryst were slayne by Herode. In galas
at anchyr the feest of saynt Ewticy a preest/ and saynt Domiciane a deacon. ℣ Addicyons.
℣ The feest also of an other saynt Ewticy an abbot of hygh
perfeccyon/ that notwithstandynge dyd no myracles in his lyfe/
but after his deth very many. The feest also of saynt Florens a
cõfessour/ that was felowe vnto the sayd abbot/ and after his
eleccyon he remayned alone/ vnto whome came a bere and
mekely dyd hym seruyce/ and kepte his shepe/ and euer at the

due houre cōmaunded he brought them home. And he dyd many myracles in his lyfe and moo after. The feest also of saynt Alphege archebysshop of caūterbury/ that before was elect by reuelacyon bysshop of wynchester whiche reuelacyon was shewed vnto saynt Dunstane vnto whome was also shewed that he shold be his successour/ and so he was. And after he was by the danes put to moost cruell martyrdom/ ⁊ was buryed at london/ where his holy body .x. yeres after was foūde in the same state and maner/ and the flesshe and blode as grene and fresshe as the same daye he was slayne/ and euer full of myracles. The feest also of many other holy sayntes/ martyrs/ confessours/ and virgyns.

⁋ To morowe.

[⁋ The .xxix. day of December. At Ierusalem [*fo. cxl. b.* the feest of saynt Dauid kynge and prophete. At arelate yᵉ feest of saynt Trophyne†/ of whome the apostle Paule wryteth vnto his discyple Tymothe/ and whome he consecrate bysshop of the same cite/ by whose holy lyfe/ doctryne and myracles/ all fraunce (as saynt zozymy the pope wryteth) was gretely edifyed. In the fraūchest of oxforde† the feest of saynt Ebrulfe an abbot and martyr/ that for defendynge the lybertees of his chyrche was in the chyrche slayne with swerdes. At Ierusalem the feest of saynt Melane a sacred nonne. ⁋ Addicyons.

⁋ Here ben remēbred certayne faders of the olde testament. At bethleem the feest of saynt Iesse/ that by an other name was also called Ysai/ fader vnto saynt Dauid the prophete/ and a man of noble blode ⁊ holy conuersacyon. The feest also of saynt Nathan/ that in the tyme of Dauid ⁊ Salomon was the prophete of god. The feest also of an other saynt Dauid a monke ⁊ confessour/ that many yeres was a robber and capitayne of .xxx. theues/ but after he toke grete compunccyon ⁊ contricyon ⁊ entred religyon/ wherin he lyued a strayte and holy lyfe/ and at the last he had reuelacyon by an aūgell yᵗ all his synnes were forgyuen/ ⁊ he was than of many grete myracles. The passion also of saȳt Thomas archebysshop of caūterbury. The feest also of saȳt Vrsyne a bysshop. And of many other holy saynt̄. ⁊c̄.

⁋ To morowe.

⁋ The .xxx. daye of December. At spolete the feest of saynt Sabyne a bysshop/ saynt Exsuperance/ ⁊ saynt Marcell deacons/ saynt Venustiane and his wyfe and chylder all martyrs/ that by the emperour Maximian [were put to deth by [*fo. cxli.*

DECEMBER.

many varyaūt ℟ cruell turmentes. At alexander the feest of saynt Mansuete a martyr/ wᵗ other .x. persones put to dethe with hym. At rome the feest of saynt Felix a bysshop. At turon the feest of saynt Perpetuy a bysshop/ that honourably buylded yᵉ chyrche of saynt Martyne bysshop and confessour.
¶ Addicyons.
¶ In englonde the feest of saynt Ewgynet bysshop of worcester/ where he was borne of the kynges blode/ a man of synguler sanctite ℟ many myracles. The feest also of saynt Liberall a bysshop and martyr/ that for his notable vertue was made deacon in the age of .xvj. yeres/ at .xviij. preest/ and at xx. bysshop of cānens/ a grete precher/ by fame wherof the emperour Hadrian sent for hym vnto rome/ where he was put vnto meruaylous turmentes/ in the whiche moche people was conuerted/ and saynt Cerbery was put to dethe with hym/ ℟ his owne moder saynt Euanthe that folowed hym vnto rome was heded with her sone. The feest also of an other saynt Felix the thyrde pope of yᵗ name/ a grete confounder of heretykes/ and he ordeyned that chirches sholde not be cōsecrate of ony other but a bysshop/ with many other good statutes. The feest also of many other holy sayntes/ martyrs/ confes. ℟ virg.

¶ To morowe.

¶ The .xxxj. day of Decēber. At rome the feest of saynt Siluester pope/ whose actes ben wrytē at more length in the legende. At senon the feest of saynt Sabiane and saynt Potenciane a bysshop/ and bothe martyrs/ that were sente by the pope vnto the moder chyrche of the same cite to preche/ where they were put to martyrdome. In the same cite also the feest of saynt Colūbynet [a virgyn/ that by the prynce [fo. cxli. b. Aureliane was cast in to a fyre/ ℟ after many other turmentes at the last slayne by the swerde. At reciar the feest of saynt Hermete an exorcist in order/ of hygh perfeccyon. ¶ Addicyons.
¶ The feest also of saynt Barbaciane a preest and confessour/ that with saȳt Tymothe came to rome where they dyd soo many myracles/ that by the fame therof saynt Gall the empresse whose syrname was Placida moder vnto the emperour Valentiniane/ came to rome to se them/ but whan she came saynt Tymothe was deed/ and saynt Barbaciane had enclosed hymselfe in a lytell sell/ where he dyd many notable myracles/ ℟ in a whyle he also departed/ whome yᵉ sayd empresse buryed with grete honour/ where he lyeth full of dayly myracles. The feest also of saȳt Odilion an abbot/ that was a knyghtes sone/ and lame borne of all his lȳmes but after he was cured by a myracle of

our lady/ and was a monke of the monastery of cluniacens/ where after he was abbot/ and euer of holy lyf ⁊ many grete myracles. And he fyrst ordeyned ye seruyce of all soules nexte after all halowes/ and cōmaūded the same feest to be kepte solemply through out all his order/ with many other noble actes/ whose blessed soule after his deth was seen lyke vnto an aūgell/ and his holy body there buryed/ where he remayneth full of grete ⁊ many myracles. The feest also of many other holy sayntes/ martyrs/ confessours/. and virgyns.

℞ Deo gratias.

℞ Praye for the wretche of syon your moost vnworthy broder Rychard whytford.

℞ [Thus endeth the Martiloge with the Addicyons [*fo. cxlii.*
Imprynted at London in Fletestrete at the sygne
of the sonne/ by Wynkyn de worde. The yere
of our lorde god .M.CCCCC.xxvj. the
xv. daye of February.

NOTES.

EXPLANATION OF ABBREVIATIONS, AND TITLES OF EDITIONS REFERRED TO IN THE NOTES.

A. MS. Martyrologium formerly belonging to Syon Monastery. (British Museum, Add. MS. 22,285.)

Aberd. Martyrology for the use of the Church of Aberdeen, of which extracts relating to Scottish Saints are printed in *Proceedings of the Society of Antiquaries of Scotland*, Vol. II., p. 256.

Ado. *Martyrologium Adonis*. . . . Ab Heriberto Rosweido. . . . recensitum. Nunc ope codicum Bibliothecæ Vaticanæ recognitum et Adnotationibus illustratum opera et studio Dominici Georgii. . . . . Romæ, 1745.

C. *The Book of Obits and Martyrology of the Cathedral Church of the Holy Trinity, commonly called Christ Church, Dublin* (Irish Archæological Society), 1844.

Cat. Sanct. *Catalogus Sanctorum* . . . *editus a Reverendissimo in christo patre domino Petro de Natalibus de venetiis dei gratia episcopo Equilino*. Lugduni, 1508.

D. Martyrologium in *Missale Drummondiense*, edited by Rev. G. H. Forbes. Burntisland, 1882.

H. Martyrologium in MS. Breviarium ad usum Sarum (lettered *Missale*) (Brit. Mus. Harleian MS. 2,785). The Martyrology extends from Nov. 28 to June 17 inclusive.

N. L. A. *Nova Legenda Anglie* [J. Capgrave]. Londonias in domo Winandi de Worde, 1516.

R. *Martyrologium Romanum*. . . . Gregorii xiii. Pon. Max. Iussu editum. . . accesserunt Notationes. . . auctore Cæsare Baronio. Romæ, 1586.

R. 1564. *Martyrologium secundum morem Romanæ Ecclesiæ*. Venetiis. 1564 [an un-reformed Roman Martyrology.]

U. *Usuardi Martyrologium*. Opera et studio J. B. Sollerii. Printed in *Acta Sanctorum*, Junii, Tom. vi. Parisiis et Romæ, 1866.

U-Auct. refers to the *Auctaria* in the above edition, in which will be found various readings and local additions adopted in Martyrologies based upon Usuard.

*** The principal aim of the following notes is to show the variations of Richard Whytford's English version from the MS. Syon Martyrologium (A). No complete collation with other MSS. and editions has been attempted. Some variants are given to illustrate the irregularities of mediæval martyrologies, whilst others will enable the reader to judge whether the errors which occur should be charged to the translator or his original. Aberd. C. and D. have only been referred to for the Scottish and Irish Saints.

p. 1. l. 32. *The addicyons for theyr more edificacyon/ we gadered out of the sanctiloge/ legendaurea/ catalogo sanctorum/ the cronycles of Antonine/ and of saynt Vincent.* The *Sanctiloge* is probably not the *Sanctilogium Britannicum* of John of Tinmouth, of which a MS. may be seen in the British Museum (Cottonian MS. Tiberius, E. 1); but is more likely to be the *Sanctilogium Salvatoris* of which a copy in two volumes had been presented to Syon Monastery by the Duchess of Clarence. This gift is recorded in a valuable MS. now preserved in Corpus Christi College, Cambridge, which gives a catalogue of the Library of Syon Monastery (fo. 43. b).

The *legendaurea* or *Legenda Aurea* is a name commonly given to the *Legenda Sanctorum* compiled by Jacobus de Voragine, O.S.D., archbishop of Genoa (1292-1298). Its immense popularity is attested by the number of editions which issued from the continental presses at the close of the fifteenth and beginning of the sixteenth centuries. It was translated into most European languages with local additions. Of these vernacular versions one of the most interesting is the *Golden Legende* which was printed by Caxton about 1484, and afterwards by Wynkyn de Worde and Julian Notary. There were at least six copies of the *Legenda Aurea* in the Library of Syon.

The *Catalogus Sanctorum* compiled by Petrus de Natalibus, bishop of Equilio (1370-1400), had a popularity almost equalling that of the last mentioned work, and many editions issued from the early presses of Lyons and elsewhere. Syon Monastery possessed a copy.

The cronicles of Antonine and of saynt Vincent apparently refer to the *Liber Cronicarum* or *Historiale* of St. Antonino, archbishop of Florence (1448-1459), and to the *Speculum Historiale* of Vincentius, all of which are found in the Syon catalogue.

Jan. 1. l. 8. *superstycyous* probably for superstycyons, *your false religyon* being added by the translator as an explanation. Cessate a supersticionibus idolorum. A.

l. 10. *was forthwith put to deth* . . . a gladiatoribus occisus est. A. Richard Whytford has omitted the gladiators. *The Roman Martyrologe* (S. Omers, 1667) renders the passage: "was killed by the Gladiators or Fencers at sharp."

l. 11. *the feest of .lx. soudyours.* corone militum triginta A. H. U. R.

l. 29. *Augend.* augendi A. H. Eugendi U. R.

Jan. 2. l. 3. *Marcesse.* Narcissi A. H. U. R.

l. 5. *taken amonge soudyours.* . . . Qui sub licinio principe. inter thrones comprehensi. cum nollent militare. cesi ad mortem. et diu in carcere macerati. atque in mare mersi. martirium consummauerunt. A.

l. 9. *In the cyte of Thebaida.* In thebayda A. In Thebaide U.

l. 11. *Barbariā.* barbaciani A.

l. 12. *Siluiake.* siluiacum A. siluiniacum H. (Souvigny).

Jan. 4. l. 6. *Eugence.* eugenii. A.
  l. 15. *Key.* agaii A. gaii H. caii R. Gai U.
Jan. 6. l. 16. *At the cite of Redomis.* Redonis A. H. U. Rhedonis R. (Redoni, Rennes).
  H. adds : In britannia ciuitate cancia monasterio sancti petri apostoli. deposicio sancti adriani abbatis. . . . The *Martiloge* has this St. Adrian in the Addicyons (l. 9) to Jan. 9.
Jan. 7. l. 1. *The relation of tydyges.* . . . . . Relacio pueri ihu ex egypto A.
  l. 6. *Nicodeme.* Nichomedie A. Nicomediæ U.
  l. 7. *helionople.* helyonopoli A. helenopoli. H. Helenopoli U. R. Ado.
Jan. 8. l. 1. *At campane in naples.* Neapoli campanie A.
  l. 7. *Eugenian a bysshop.* eugenionii episcopi A. H. Eugenionis U-Auct. The name has been confused with that of Eugenian the martyr already commemorated.
Jan. 9. l. 11. *In affryke the feest of saynt Reuocate/ saynt Firmyn.* In affrica : sanctorum reuocati et firmi. A. Ad siniam sanctorum natalis renouati fortunati et firmini. H. Apud Smyrnam sanctorum Vitalis Reuocati et Fortunati. U. R.
  l. 12. *In wentane the translacyon of saynt Nidoke.* In wintonia sancti iudoci. A. (H. om.) In the MS. the word might easily be read nidoci, but Iudocus, a royal hermit, is probably intended. His Deposition is noticed on Dec. 13. Cf. July 25, Add.
  l. 13. *In Cesariens.* In mauritania cesariensi. A. H. U.
  Add. l. 1. *aconitane* for anconitane. Ancona.
  Add. l. 6. *Abbot of veridiane.* A mistake for Nirida near Naples (see Bede, *H. E.* iv, 1).

Jan. 11. l. 2. *Saluer.* saluii A. H. U. R.
  Add. l. 1. *saynt Ygyn.* To the text of A. has been added in a later hand : Rome: sancti ignii pape et martyris. The name is elsewhere written Iginus, Iginius, Higinus, and Higinius.

Jan. 12. l. 2. *Satary.* satiri A. H. Satyri. U. R.
  l. 4. *In maturitane at casary.* In cesarea mauritanie. A. H.
  Add. l. 5. *saynt Benedict a syrname bysshop,* i.e. S. Benedict by surname Biscop. On the use of *a* as a preposition, see Murray's *New English Dictionary, sub voce* A. St. Benedict is omitted by A., but in a seventeenth century hand there has been added : In Anglia S. Benedicti abatis. H has : Apud monasterium beati petri quod nuncupatur pirumpe deposicio benedicti abbatis. St. Benedict was the founder of St. Peter's, Wearmouth. Pirumpe appears elsewhere under the forms Piremuthe, and Wirimunda, which are disguises of the familiar Wearmouth. The Anglo-Saxon W (p) and the thorn letter (þ) are often mistaken for P by later transcribers. In this way Wareham has been transformed into Perham on Feb. 18 (p. 23).

Jan. 13. l. 6. *At the chefe cite of reme.* Remis metropoli. A. H.
Add. l. 1. *At the castell of grauion the feest of saynt Vincent.* In *Cat. Sanct.* the name of the saint is Viuentius. It is also there recorded that he was converted by St. George, and that he died "apud castrum grauiorem," but that his body was afterwards translated "in montem verriacum : ut dicit frater vincentius." In monte Verziaco, sancti Viuentii confessori. U-Auct. Grauio Castellum, near Poitiers.
Add. l. 9. *Kentegerne.* For the story in full see *N. L. A.* fo. ccvii. b.

Jan. 14. l. 3. *many turmentes.* cocleis ac testulis vinctus superpositus iaceret. A.
l. 8. *Ponciane.* A. H. omit. Apud Spoletum passio sancti Ponciani. U-Auct.

Jan. 15. l. 7. *In auerne.* avernis. A. Arvernis R. U.
l. 9. *andogauence.* andegauensi. A. (Angers.)
l. 13. *Maulean.* maulii A. (H. om.)
Add. l. 1. *saynt Dorythy/ that by an other name is called also saynt Sythe.* The story of this saint agrees with that of St. Ita, Yta or Mida in Boll. *Acta Sanctorum,* Jan. 15. St. Ita occurs in D. (Jan. 16).
l. 12. *Micheas of ye cite of morast, i.e.,* Micah the Morasthite (Jer. xxvi, 18 ; Micah i, 1). This is the prophet already mentioned with Habakkuk at the beginning of this day. The "other saynt Micheas" should be Micaiah the son of Imlah (1 K. xxii, 8). Cf. *Cat. Sanct.* ii, 76-78.

Jan. 16. l. 2. *Maximian.* maximiano A (in margin : maxentio) Maximino Ado. U.
l. 6. *aurelatens.* Apud aurelatensem ciuitatem A. Apud arelatem H. U. Arelate R.
l. 7. *odoberg.* odobergia A. Opitergii R. U-Auct. Cf. *Cat. Sanct.* ii, 89.
l. 8. *Ticiane.* riciani A. Titiani. U-Auct. R.
l. 9. *patron.* perrona A. pariona H. Peronæ R. Parrona U.
l. 11. *Pricill.* priscille A. H. U-Auct.
Add. l. 1. *Marcell.* The compiler has taken the accounts of Marcellus and the five saints which follow from *Cat. Sanct.* ii, 84.

Jan. 17. l. 4. *At lynguon.* Lingonis A. H. Langres.
l. 5. *Sewsyppe Helewsyppe and Melewsyppe.* Seusippi alasippi et melasippi A. over erasure. Speusippi Eleusippi et Meleusippi R. Speusippi Elasippi et Melasippi. U.
l. 9. *Theon.* A om.

Jan. 18. l. 6. *boyled in lede* . . . . primo ad metalla deputati : nouissime igni traditi sunt. A.
l. 8. *At wyllenchester* . . . *saynt Vulstane.* A. H. omit. Apparently this is a blundered duplicate of "Wulstanus episcopus Wigorniensis" commemorated on the following day.
l. 10. *Leonard.* Leobardi A. H. U-Auct.

Jan. 19. l. 1. *At smyrme.* In Smirma A. H. In Smirna U. Smyrnæ R.
l. 10. *In the fraūchest of dorkasyn.* In pago dorcasino A. Pagus Durocassinus, a district N. of Chartres.
l. 11. *Lānomyare.* Launoniaricus abbas carnotensis. *Cat. Sanct.* ii. 104.

Jan. 20. l. 16. *slayne in a bath.* in nimpha necata. A. H. Nympha on the Via Cornelia, about thirteen miles from Rome.

Jan. 22. l. 7. *At Rome.* Rome ad aquas salinas. A.

Jan. 23. l. 9. *In maritymy at genecesary.* In mauritania ciuitate geneocesarea A. In maritania ciuitate gneocesarea H. In Mauritania ciuitate Cneocæsarea U.
l. 11. *antinoñ* for antinoū. Antinoum A.
A. adds in later hand: Item sancte osburge virginis apud ciuitatem Couentrie in Anglia.

Jan. 23. Add. l. 6. *Nedolfons* for Ildefonso. Toleti sancti Ildefonsi episcopi R.

Jan. 24. l. 6. *In cesary at geneo.* Geneocesarea ciuitate A. Neocæsareæ R.
l. 7. *Marcel.* mecelli A. Metelli U. R.
l. 9. *codoke.* cadoci A. U-Auct. (H. om.)
Add. l. 6. *Eucratykes* for Encratites.

Jan. 25. l. 5. *Proiect.* preiecti A. H. Præjecti. U. Projecti R.
l. 5. *Amaryne.* marini A. (altered from amarini) H. R. Amarini U. Martini R. 1564.

Jan. 26. l. 6. *philadolph.* philadelphia A. U. philadelfa. H.

Jan. 27. l. 11. *the same Symon leprose w' whome our sauyour dyned/ whan Mary mawdeleyn was coūerted.* A. H. omit. Julianus Cenomanensis episcopus fuit. Hic simon ille leprosus fuisse dicitur: quem dominus a lepra sanauit: et qui eum ad conuiuandum inuitauit. *Cat. Sanct.* iii. 35.

Jan. 28. l. 3. *Trice.* tirci A. Thyrsi U. R.
l. 8. *saynt Charles the emperour called Charlemayne.* Not in A. or H., but in several martyrologies given in U-Auct., *e.g.*, Karoli Magni regis et imperatoris Romanorum. Christianæ fidei propugnatoris constantissimi.

Jan. 29. l. 8. *Saluniane.* sabiniani A. U. R. sabini H.
l. 9. *Iulian.* aureliano A. H. U. R.

Jan. 30. l. 3. *Innouate.* qui nouati scismate A. innouati H. Nouatiani. R. 1564. Nouati Ado. U. R.

Jan. 31. l. 5. *Cyre.* tyri A. (H. om.) Cyri. R. U-Auct.
l. 7. *Aldegunde.* Aldegundis is commemorated on Jan. 30 in Ado. and U.

Feb. 1. l. 8. *and of them deuoured.* eorum que dentibus perforatus. hostia christi efficitur. A.
l. 20. *Seueryne.* seueri A. Severiani U-Auct.

Feb. 2. l. 9. *Apropinian.* approniani A. over an erasure. Aproniani U. R.
l. 18. *Fyrme.* sirini. A. Firmi. U. R.
l. 19. *Frustole.* frustoli A. folcoli. H. R. 1564. Fusculi U. Flosculi R.
l. 19. *At doroberne.* dorobernie A. H.
Richard Whytford was unable to recognize Canterbury under the form Dorobernia. At Nov. 10 he confuses Dorobernensis with Eboracensis, and makes St. Just an archbishop of York.

Feb. 4. l. 2. and Add. l. 4. *Syle* for *Fyle.* filee A. philee H. Fileæ U. Phileæ R. After filee A. adds: et philoronii tribuni. But in Whytford's *Martiloge* St. Phyllorony is placed in the Addicyons.
l. 5. *At Rome in the market place.* Romæ foro simphronii. A.
l. 9. *At glocester the feest of saynt Eldade.* A. and H. omit. Probably St. Aldate, in whose honour churches are dedicated in Oxford and Gloucester.

Feb. 5. l. 1. *In cicyle at cathenens.* Apud siciliam ciuitate cathenensium A.
l. 2. *Agas.* agathe A. Agathæ R. U. Agas was the popular form of Agatha. "Agas; nomen proprium. agatha vel agathes." *Catholicum Anglicum* (E. E. T. S.) p. 4. An inventory of relics at Reading Abbey has the entry: "Item a bone of saynt Agas." (*Letters relating to the Suppression of Monasteries*, Camden Society, p. 227.) The MS. English Prymer at St. John's College, Cambridge (ed. by H. Littlehales, 1891) has on Feb. 5, "seynt agace." But Caxton's *Golden Legend*, Marshall's *Goodly Prymer*, 1535, and *The Prymer in Englyshe*, 1538, have "agathe." In the following century the English version of the *Roman Martyrologe*, S. Omers, 1667, has "Agatha." In the case of proper names we often see this return to the original Latin. Thus Ponce Pilate of our early creeds has gone back to Pontius Pilate.
l. 7. *Adiut.* auiti A. H. U.
Add. l. 1. *Ingemyne* and all the saints in the Addicyons on this day are from *Cat. Sanct.* iii. 85–95.

Feb. 6. l. 3. *she was closed in an huge instrumēt of metall made lyke a hors/ all full of pryckes and hote as fyre/* This is the translator's expansion of "equuleo uexata" A.
l. 6. *a scoler.* scolasticus A. H. U.
l. 10. *Sawster* for *Fawster.* In the city of London we have the church of St. Vedast *alias* Foster.
l. 10. *traiectens.* atrebatensium A. (over an erasure).
Add. l. 7. *Mele.* Mel. C. D.

Feb. 7. l. 1. *In brytayne at august.* In britanniis ciuitate augusta. A. H. U. Augusta is supposed to be London.
l. 2. *Agyl.* auguli A. H. U. R.

NOTES.

Feb. 8. l. 3. *Coynt.* corinthe A. compte. H. Cointhæ. Ado. Cointæ. R.

Feb. 9. l. 2. *Apolyne.* apolonie A. Apolloniæ. U. R.
    Add. l. 1. *Theliaus.* Cf. *N. L. A.* fo. cclxxx. b. Also known as St. Teilo.

Feb. 10. l. 2. *Hyerene.* hi renei A. H. Irenæi R. Hirenæi U.
    l. 9. St. Merpwyn and St. Gertrude are not in H.
    l. 10. *martyr.* A. om.

Feb. 11. l. 2. *Desyre.* desiderii A. U. R.
    l. 3. *At castelnaūt.* Castro nantonensi A. U.
    l. 5. *Eufras.* eufrosine A. Eufrasiæ U.

Feb. 12. l. 1. *At hylpane.* In hispaniis A. U.
    l. 4. *·Apely.* Apelii A. H. Ampelii R. (Feb. 11).
    l. 5. *Auolyn.* anolino A. U. R. annolino H.

Feb. 13. l. 1. *the translacyon of saynt Edward kynge and confessour.* The context shews that Edward the Martyr is intended. This account of St. Edward may perhaps be peculiar to the Syon Martyrology. It would have been specially suited for Shaftesbury, where the relics of St. Edward, King and Martyr, were preserved. The Latin version is as follows :—Translacio sancti edwardi regis et martiris. Cuius sacratissimum corpus dei gracia preueniente. et eiusdem sancti martiris monitu et reuelacione. fratrisque sui regis ethelredi imperio : a sanctissimis pontificibus. et terre optimatibus. de tumulo sublimiter eleuatum. in locello ad hoc digniter preparato : in sancta sanctorum cum aliis sanctorum reliquiis. honorifice positum est. A. (H. om.)
    l. 8. *At mylen in armenye.* In militana ciuitate armenie A.
    Add. l. 5. *Sephan* for *Stephan.*

Feb. 14. l. 7. *At interam.* interamnis A. Interamna, now Terni.
    l. 12. *Bassimiane.* bassimiani A. H. Bassiani U. R.

Feb. 17. l. 5. *At corduba.* cordubam A. concordiam H. U. Concordiæ R.
    l. 8. *In teruens ye feest of saynt Syluyne bysshop of tolane.* In pago taruenensi : sancti silvini tolosane civitatis episcopi. A.
    l. 10. *Luuiane.* lupiani. A. H. U-Auct.
    Add. l. 1. *At cawsyne.* Sabini episcopi Camisinæ civitatis U-Auct. This saint is also commemorated on Feb. 9 in other martyrologies : Apud Canusium civitatem Apuliæ, depositio beati Sabini episcopi et confessoris. The principal church at Canosa is dedicated under the title of San Sabino.

Feb. 18. l. 1. *the receyuyng of saynt Edwarde kynge 't martyr in to sephton frō perham.* Aduentus sancti edwardi regis et martiris de perham in sephtoniam. A. (H. om.). The places here mentioned are now known as Wareham (Cf. Notes, Jan. 12, Add.) and Shaftesbury.
    l. 11. *Prepedīge.* prepedigne. A. U.
    Add. l. 1. *Eudelme.* ethelina. (Harl. MS., 1260).

Feb. 20. l. 7. *Ciran.* tyrannius A. tyranno H. Tyrannio U. R.
l. 10. *Gasly.* galli A. H. The name has already been correctly given in the Addicyons of the previous day, with the variation of "germany" instead of "almayne" (Alemannia).
l. 11. *Pakamye.* pantamie A. Potamii U. (H. om.)
Add. l. 1. *Eukare.* Eucherius, bishop of Orleans, c. 717–738 (Gams, *Series Episcoporum*, 1873, p. 593).
l. 2. *englonge* for *englonde.*

Feb. 21. l. 1. *At scicilie.* Apud siciliam A. H.
l. 5. *Serule.* Seruuli. A. H. U. R.

Feb. 22. Add. l. 1. *tornate* for *tornace.* Tornacum, Tournai.

Feb. 23. l. 1. *At siryne.* apud sirmiam. A. apud sirmium H. U. R.
l. 2. *Seuere.* sereni A. over erasure. seueri H. Sineri U. Sireni R.

Feb. 24. l. 9. *In cesary.* In cesarea capadocie A.
l. 13. *A canon or rule for the redynge of this Martiloge in the lepe yere.* With this we may compare the following passage which has been noticed by Rev. W. H. Frere in a Sarum Ordinale in the British Museum (Arundel MS. 130, fo. 64):—

De modo legendi lectionem de martilogio in anno bisextali (*sic*) in festo sancti mathie apostoli et in precedente die.

Notandum est quod in anno bisextali hoc modo legatur lectio de martilegio in [die iij a] cathedra sancti Petri.

vj° Kalend' Marcii luna N. Inuentio capitis precursoris domini tempore Marciani principis quum precursor idem duobus monachis primum eiusdem capud ubi relatum [celatum?] iacet reuelauit. In cesaria capadocie sancti Georgii [Sergii?] martiris cuius gesta preclarissima habentur. Et aliorum plurimorum sanctorum martirum confessorum atque uirginum.

Et tunc in die iij [iiij?] a cathedra sancti petri hoc modo legatur lectio de Martilegio.

vj° Kalend' Marcii luna N. Natiuitas beati Mathie apostoli post ascensionem domini qui apostolis sorte electus est apud Iudeam euangelium christi predicauit in hoc siquidem die carnee habitacionis ergastulo delutus [solutus?] in celestis regie aulam letantibus angelis feliciter est susceptus. Et cetera. Et aliorum plurimorum ut supra.

Feb. 27. l. 5. *upon mules.* camelis A. H. U. R.
l. 13. *In alexander.* The name of a saint here seems to be converted into a place. Item alexandri abundancii et sancti fortunionis. A. Item sanctorum alexandri abundii et fortuionis. H. Romæ natalis sanctorum martyrum Alexandri, Abundii, Antigoni, et Fortunati. R.

Feb. 28. l. 5. *saynt Oswalde.* In H. placed at the beginning of the day, with a long account of him.
Add. l. 1. *Ayd.* Aidus or Aidanus. *N. L. A.*

NOTES. 213

March 1. l. 2. *ccxii.* ducentorum sexaginta A. (over an erasure) U.
l. 14. *Erculaue* for *Erculane.* Erculani A. In ciuitate Perusii translatio corporis sancti Herculani. U-Auct.¹

March 2. l. 9. *Lorge.* largii A. lorgii H. R. U-Auct.

March 3. l. 4. *Astece.* asterii A. H. U. R.
  l. 8. *Enuthere.* Enutherii (altered to emitherii). A. Emitherii. H. U. Hemeterii. R.
    Seledon. celedonii. A. H. U. Cheledonii. R.
  l. 11. *wynewale.* wynewaloei. A. (H. om.) Winwaloci. U-Auct.

March 4. l. 7. *saynt Gay and saynt Palatyne.* sancti gaii palatini. A. H. Caii palatini. U. R. An adjective has here given birth to a new saint.

March 5. l. 4. *saynt Eusebius saynt Palatyne.* sancti eusebii palatini. A. H. U. R. Cf. March 4. l. 7.
  l. 5. *saynt Ciaue.* sancti ciaui (or ciani) A. H. om. Ciaran D. Kyriani, Kerani. U-Auct.

March 7. At end A. adds in a late hand: Item sancti thome de alquino.

March 8. l. 1. *Antion.* antionū A. antinoum H. U. R.
  l. 2. *Philomon.* philemonis. A. H. U. R.
  l. 6. *Ariane.* adriani A. H. Arriani U. Hadriani. R. 1564. Ariani R.
  l. 10. *Cirpriane.* cipriani A. H. Cypriani U. R.
  l. 13. *saynt Felix.* Sancti felicis episcopi in monasterio quod rameseya dicitur quiescentis. A. (over an erasure). Sancti felicis orientalium anglorum episcopi et predicatoris qui in monasterio ramesey tumulatur. H.
  Add. l. 1. *Fenan.* Senan. D.

March 10. l. 6. *Dorothene.* dorothonei A. H. Droctovei U. R.
  l. 8. *saynt Agathe.* not in A. Item sancte agape uirginis... H. In Antiochiâ sanctæ agapæ virginis U-Auct.

March 11. l. 2. *Lucyne.* Lucinii A.
  Add. l. 1. *saynt Paule bysshop of leonens.* In the sixth century St. Paul was bishop of the city now known as St. Pol de Léon. He is usually commemorated on March 12.
  l. 9. *Gūpert.* The only name resembling this among the bishops of Wurzburg given by Gams (*Series Episcoporum*, 1873) is Humbert, who is said to have died on March 9, A.D. 842.

March 12. l. 2. *Gregory.* . . gregorii doctoris ac apostoli anglorum et innocencii A. The translator has omitted Innocent, which omission also occurs in other versions of Usuard.
  l. 12. *Eddune.* egduni A. H. U. Egdunii R.
  l. 14. *bysshop of wentane.* wentane ciuitatis episcopi. A. Winchester.

March 13. l. 2. *Patryke* and *Modest.* patricie et modeste. A. H. Patriciæ et Modestæ. R. U.

l. 3. *At nice the feest of saynt Thensete/ saȳt Horre/ saynt Theodour/ saȳt Nympodour/ saȳt Marke/ 't saynt Arabye martyrs.* Nicea ciuitate: sanctorum martirum theusete. horris. theodore. nimpodore. marci. et arabie A.

March 14. l. 1. *xlix martyrs.* quadraginta septem A. H. U. R.

March 15. l. 5. *Macrone.* matrone A. H. U. R.

March 16. Add. l. 1. *Fynan.* leprosus Finan D.

March 17. l. 5. *nūgell.* nimgella A. over an erasure. nimgella H. Niuigella. U. R. Nivelle.

March 18. l. 1. *The feest of saynt Edward.* This long account of St. Edward is perhaps, like that on Feb. 13, peculiar to the Syon Martyrology.

The Latin version is as follows: In prouincia occidentalium saxonum: passio sancti edwardi regis et martiris anglorum. et eximii testis dei: qui christianissimo fundatori monasteriorum edgaro pia proles successit in regno. Quem in primeuo pubescentem. et pubertatis flore regnantem: grauissima fastidientis nouerce. et principum gentis sue persecucio. serenissimum martirem christo confecerat: et beatorum collegio in celis coniunxerat. Qui quam magnificus fulget in astris: ad tumbam ipsius demonstrat nunc operata causa salutis. A. (H. merely has at the end of the day: Eodem die sancti edwardi martiris.)

March 19. l. 5. *At suretyke.* apud sureticum A. surrentum H. Sorrento.

l. 6. *Marcyll.* marcelli. A. Marci. R. U.

l. 7. *Colotery.* caloceri. A. H. U.

l. 11. *Florence.* A. and H. omit.

March 22. l. 1. *At septimane in byterne.* Apud septimaniam in biternis. A. biteris. H. Biterris. U.

l. 2. *Affrodose.* Affrodosii A. following U. Ado om. At end A. adds in a later hand: In affrica: sancti saturnini et aliorum nouem.

March 23. l. 3. *Victor bysshop of affricane.* Victor affricanus episcopus. A.

March 24. l. 8. *In the cite of tyberym.* a quo ipse postea in tyberim pro fide christi necatus est. A. The transformation of the river Tiber into a city is noteworthy.

l. 10. *At syre y* feest of saynt Agapite.* Apud siriam: sancti seleuci. In frygia: sancti agapiti confessoris. A. Here two clauses have been made into one by the omission of the end of the former, and the beginning of the latter. A similar case will be found on June 10.

NOTES. 215

At end A. adds in a later hand: In Suecia natale sancte Catherine virginis diue matris Birgitte filie.
Add. l. 15. *Mackartyne.* Meic Cairthinn D.

March 25. l. 12. *At siryne.* In sirinio. A. H. Apud Sirmium. Ado. Sirmii. R. Sirmium in Illyricum.
l. 18. *Theole.* theole. A. dule. H. Dulæ. U.

March 26. l. 15. *At smyrme.* In smirmia. A. Sirmii. R. In Sirmio. U.
l. 16. *Maximian.* maxime. A. (over an erasure of maximiane). maximi. H. Maximæ. Ado. U. R.
Add. l. 1 *Fynchell.* Sinchell. D.

March 27. l. 12. *In the fraunchest of aspane the feest of saynt Euthery that was bysshop of Tourney.* In pago aspanio : sancti eutherii thuronensis episcopi. A. In pago hascanio sancti eutherii turonensis episcopi et confessoris. H. Eucherii turonensis episcopi. U.
l. 13. *At Pamon.* In pannonia. A. H. U.

March 28. l. 8. *Gūdran.* guntranni. A. Guntramni. U.

March 29. l. 5. *nicodeme.* nichomedia. A.
l. 7. *luxaniens.* luxoniensis A. H. Luxoviensis. U.
Add. l. 3. *Gūdlewse.* Gundleus. *N. L. A.* fo. clxviii.

March 30. l. 2. *saynt Quiryne and saynt Trybune.* beati quirini. tribuni et martiris A. (over an erasure). beati Quirini martiris et tribuni U. A mistake has here occurred not unlike that of "saynt Palatyne" on March 4 and 5.

April 2. l. 7. *Nicesy.* nicesii. A. nicerii. H. Nicetii. U.
l. 10. *saynt Mary egypcyake.* The long account of this saint is in A. but is not in Usuard. H. briefly has : Apud palestinam depositio sancte marie egipciace que peccatrix appellatur.
Add. l. 1. *saynt Dydake bysshop of oxforde.* This anticipation of a see of Oxford is the result of confusing Oxomensis with Oxoniensis, the former being the adjective of Oxoma, Burgo de Osma, in the N. of Spain. Caxton's *Golden Legende* in the life of "Seynt Domynyk" cautiously gives us "the diocise of Oxonyence." The translator of the *Martiloge* finds another use for "oxforde" on Dec. 29 (l. 7), where it represents Oximæ, Exmes in Normandy.

April 4. l. 5. *ye cursed arryens.* The original Latin is not so strong: cuius studio inter cetera doctrine et miraculorum insignia. tempore arriane perfidie. tota ytalia ad catholicam fidem conuersa est. A.
Add. l. 1. *Tiernake.* Tigernach. D.

April 5. l. 1. *Nichandre* and *Appolon.* marciane nicanoris et appolonii. A. meandri nicanoris et appollinii H. Martianæ, Nicanoris et Apollonii. U.

April 5. l. 7. *saynt Marcian.* A. H. omit here. The translator appears to have put in at the end the Marcian which has dropped out of his first clause.

April 6. Add. l. 6. *Appolynaryes and anomeyes.* Apollinarians and Anomeans.

April 7. l. 3. *Iesyppe.* egesippi. A. U.

April 8. l. 5. *At turyne.* Turonis A. U. Tironis. H.
H. adds: Item concessi ammonii et successi.
Add. l. 1. *Pitrion.* Cf. De sancto Pithirione: in *Vitas Patrum*, 1485.

April 9. l. 3. *In syryne.* In syrmio. A. over an erasure. In sirmio. H. U.
H. adds: Item sanctorum fortunati et donati.

April 11. l. 6. *saynt Domion.* Domionis. A. U. Dominionis. H.
H. adds: Turonis agirici abbatis. Lugduno sancti siagri episcopi.
. . . Item fortuna (*sic*) et aliorum quadraginta.
Two of the names, under a slightly different form, will be found in the Addicyons.
Add. l. 2. *saynt Fiagry*, probably for Siagry. Lugduni Siagrii episcopi. U-Auct.
Lugduni sancti Sicarii episcopi et confessoris. Du Saussay. *Mart. Gall.* 1637, i. 203.

April 16. l. 5. *Fauster.* fausti. A. U.

April 18. l. 1. *In naples at messany.* Apud messanam ciuitatem apulie. A.
l. 2. *saynt Eulether.* eleutherii. A. H. U. R.
l. 7. *cast vnto wylde wode beestes.* leonibus proiectus. A. U.
l. 9. *Appolon.* Apollini. A.
l. 15. *Perfyte.* Perfecti. A.

April 19. l. 10. *cantiliber.* cantiliberi. A. Cancoliberi Hispaniæ. Ado. R.
l. 11. *In ye suburbes of hamonens ye feest of saynt Cosmare.* In pago hamonensi: sancti cosmari. episcopi et confessoris A. Cenebio labiis. sancti osmari episcopi. H. Cœnobio Laubiis Usmari episcopi et confessoris. U. In cœnobio Laubiensi sancti Vrsmari. R. Lob in Hainault.
Add. l. 6. *Leo the .x. pope.* Not Leo X. (1513-1521), but St. Leo IX. (1049-1054). Cf. *Cat. Sanct.* iv. 65.

April 20. l. 4. *Seruulane.* seruiliani. A. H. U.
l. 8. *at bredunens.* In ciuitate ebredunensi. A. U.
l. 11. *Domnion.* Domnino. A. U.

April 21. l. 7. *Vskazand.* vstazandis. A. vstaradis H. Ustazadis U. Ustadadis and Ustazadis are among the variants of this name.

April 21. l. 8. *Publy.* pusicius. A. R. Pusitius. U.
  Add. l. 1. *Gulphyle.* Gulphilas (*Cat. Sanct.* xi. 86). Ulphilas.

April 22. l. 8. *Bitro.* Bitro. A. Bicor. Ado. U. R.
  l. 13. *Schrysotele.* chrisoteli A. U. crisoteli. H.
  l. 13. *Mycy.* mucii A. R. Mutii. U.

April 23. l. 15. *Rule.* Reguli. A.
  l. 16. *at bruce.* Brucie. A. In Prusia. R.

April 24. H. adds: Sydrac mysaac et abdenago. Remis ciuitate natalis sanctorum uirginum bone et docle. Ipso die inuencio corporis sancti yuonis episcopi et confessoris. Some of these names are found in the Addicyons.
  Add. l. 9. *Boue.* Bone. R.

April 26. l. 2. *Clete.* cleti. A. R. Anacleti. Ado.

April 27. l. 4. *Anchymy.* anthimi A. H. U. R.
  l. 9. *In sicilie at tharse.* Tarso sicilie A. tharso cilicie. H. Tarso Ciliciæ U.

April 28. l. 3. *Vrsyline.* vrsisini A. urcissini H. Ursicini U. R.
  l. 10. *At padway the feest of saynt Palion a martyr.* In pannonia sancti polionis martyris. A. In Pannonia sancti Pollionis martiris U. R.

April 29. l. 4. *In numyde at a vyllage nere vnto circen.* In numidia apud cyrcensem coloniam A. Cirta.
  l. 8. *Tercull.* terculla A. certula H. Tertulla U. R.
  Add. l. 5. *cirsterciens* for *cisterciens.*
  l. 12. *refourned* for *refourmed.*

May 1. l. 19. *At austrace.* Apud ciuitatem austrasiam A. austiam H. Auscium U. R. Auch.
  l. 22. *Thoremyny.* thoremini. A. corentini. H. In Britannia minori. Corentini episcopi et confessoris. U-Auct.

May 3. Add. l. 2. *nokes* for *bokes.*

May 4. l. 7. *In fauence at metall.* in metallo fauencii A. In metallo Phennensi Palestinæ. R. "At the Metal-mynes of Phennes in Palestin." *The Roman Martyrologe,* S. Omers, 1667.
  l. 11. *At oricoripens.* In oricopensi A. In Noricoripensi H. In Norico Ripensi U. R.
  l. 14. *Corcode.* coreodii A. corcodimi H. Curcodemi U. Curcodomi R.

May 5. H. omits: Ascensio domini.
  l. 6. *Eutheme.* euthemii A. antimi H. Euthymii U. R.

May 7. l. 11. *Austustyn.* augustini A. U.
  Add. l. 7. *saynt Martyns in london.* The translator is probably responsible for this transfer of St. Martin's, Canterbury, to London.
  Letarde. Lethardus *N. L. A.* fo. ccxviii. b.

May 10. H. adds: In pago wastinensi sancti maturini confessoris. Probably this is the saynt Maturyn at the end of the Addicyons.

May 11. l. 2. *Authyme.* anthimi A. H. U.

May 12. Add. l. 3. *Ponce.* Cf. May 14, l. 2.

May 13. l. 6. *amphyble.* amphibuli A. U. amfinubali H. Amphipoli R.

May 14. l. 3. *two of the emperours sones.* duo philippi imperatores A. (over an erasure). duo Philippi Cæsares R. Cf. May 12, Add.
l. 17. *fomanel.* Fontanelle A.
Add. l. 13. *Cartake.* carthachi. D.

May 15. l. 2. *Iudalece.* vidalecii A. Indaletii U. Indaletius. R.
l. 6. *in dyuerse places.* acci. uergii. abule. ursi. heliberi. carcesi. eligurgi. A.
l. 7. *chire.* chiro A. Chio R.
l. 9. *At lamosate.* lamosatum A. Lamasacum. Ado. Lampsaci. U. R.

May 16. l. 5. *In the terrytory of Iuliens.* In pago foro iuliensi. A. Fréjus or Friuli. The martyrologists of France and Italy severally claim St. Maxima for their own Forum Julii.
Add. l. 7. *forhw^t* for *forthw^t*.

May 17. l. 7. *Eracly.* Eraclii A. Eradii R.
l. 8. *The translacyon also of saynt Bernard.* Not in A., but in U-Auct.

May 18. l. 8. *Elene.* Eluine A. Elgivæ U-Auct. St. Elgiva, Queen of Edmund I. and afterwards a nun of Shaftesbury, is commemorated on this day in an old English Calendar: sancte aelfgiue regine (Br. Mus. Cott. MS. Titus D. xxvii, fo. 5).
l. 10. *at the city of spelatens.* apud spelatensem urbem. A. apud spoletanensem urbem H. Spoleti R.

May 19. l. 14. *Prudent.* prudentis A. H. Pudentis. Ado. U. R. Generally identified with the Pudens of 2 Tim. iv, 21.
l. 14. *naturall broder.* patris A.

May 20. l. 8. *Adelbert.* ethelberti A.
Add. l. 14. *Hardrian* for *Hadrian*.

May 21. l. 6. *fynthall.* fyncale A. (H. om.). The ruins of Finchale Priory are about 3½ miles from Durham.

May 22. l. 2. *Casce.* casti A. H. U. R.
l. 2. *in his boke of the fall of martyrs.* in libro de lapsis A. U.
l. 4. *corsite.* apud corsicam A. U.
l. 6. *Sawstyne.* faustini. A. H. R. U-Auct.

May 23. l. 2. *Desyre.* desiderii A. H. U. R.
l. 5. *Thyke.* epictici A. epictati H. Epitacii R.
In a later hand in A. there is added to this day : Eodem die ciuitate roffensi : sancti willelmi martiris (St. William of Perth).

May 24. l. 6. *At rome.* in portu romano A. Porto at the mouth of the Tiber.
l. 7. *nāmete.* namnetis A. U. nannetis H. Nantes.
l. 12. *Dyod.* diodis A. dioclis H. Ado. U. R.

May 25. l. 9. *In mafiaen at dorostre.* Apud mesiam ciuitate dorostro A. Dorostori in Mysia R. Dora in Bulgaria.
l. 12. *mildunens.* meldunensi monasterio A. Malmesbury.

May 26. l. 8. *Symniter.* symmitrii A. Simmitrii U.
l. 11. *At tudertusce.* tudertuscie A. Tuder Tusciæ U. Todi.
l. 25. *C. xxi.* centesimo vicesimo septimo A.

May 27. l. 1. *In marsia at doroscorens.* Apud marsiam ciuitate dorostorensi. A. Apud mesiam ciuitate dorostorensi. H. U.
l. 6. *adartens.* atrebatensi. A. H. Adartensi. U. Adartensis appears to be a variant of Atrebatensis. At Feb. 6 some MSS. describe St. Vedast of Arras as Adartensis.
Add. l. 7. *Symetre.* apparently a repetition of Symmitrius of May 26. l. 8.

May 28. l. 6. *in a style moche eloquent.* ueraci stilo A.
l. 9. Item translacio sancte matris nostre birgitte. A. in later hand.
Add. l. 11. *Lamfranke.* Lamfrancus *N. L. A.*

May 29. l. 2. *Canon.* canonis A. R. 1564. cononis H. U. R.
l. 9. *in the partyes of ananyue.* anaunie partibus A. U. Anaunia, now Val d'Anagna in the Tyrol.
l. 11. *Maximus.* maximi. A. R. 1564. maximini H. U. R.
l. 14. *Rustyke.* restituti. A. H. U. R.

May 30. l. 3. *In ye toures of sardyne.* turribus sardinii A. Torre on the W. coast of Sardinia.
l. 5. *Hutbert.* huberti A. (over an erasure). cuthberti H. Hucberti U. The name appears in other martyrologies as Bucberti, Bucherti, and is by some identified with Hubert of Liége.

May 31. l. 1. *Pernell.* Petronilla A. H. U.
l. 9. *assisiour.* assisiorum A. aniciorum H. U. R.

June 1. l. 14. *Vincent.* vincencii A. uiuencii H. Iuuencii R.
Add. l. 1. *ewsam.* Evesham. The story of St. Wistan is in *N. L. A.*

June 2. l. 7. *saynt Saynt a deacon.* Cf. Sanctus vero re non minus quam nomine, Diaconus. Du Saussay, *Mart. Gall.* i. 324.
l. 8. *Geate.* grate A. H. Ado. U.

June 3. l. 3. *with plummettes of lede.* plumbatis A.

June 4. l. 1. *In sythe.* scithia A. H. Apud Illiricum civitate Sciscia U.
   l. 8. *Patrike.* Petroci A. U-Auct. The name of St. Petrock is preserved at Petroc-stow, now Padstow, and his relics were kept at Bodmin.

June 5. l. 12. *Eobanke.* eobaneo. A. (over an erasure). eubarico H. Eobano. U. R.

June 6. l. 4. *In the londe of cecile at tharsum.* Apud tharsum scilicie A. cicilie H. Apud Tarsum Ciliciæ U.

June 7. l. 5. *Auens.* auencii A. H. Auentii U. Habentii R.

June 8. l. 10. *Ac* for *At.*

June 9. l. 1. *in the moūt of Sely.* in monte celio. A. H. U.
   l. 6. *Colūbane.* columbe A. U. Aberd. corumcille H. St. Columba or Columcill (for the meaning of this latter name see Reeve's *Adamnan's Life of St. Columba*, 1857, pp. lxx, 5).

June 10. l. 2. *Amandale.* madalis A. (over an erasure) H. U. Mandalis Ado.
   l. 10. *At parys ye feest of saynt Ytamar a bysshop and confessour.* Two clauses have here been made into one by omitting the end of the first and the beginning of the second. The Latin is as follows: Parisius sancti landerici episcopi et confessoris. In britannia ciuitate roffensi sancti itamari episcopi et confessoris. A.
   In cathedrali ecclesia Roffensi iacet sanctus Ythomar tercius a sancto iusto eiusdem ciuitatis in miraculis gloriosus. (*Cathalogus sanctorum in Anglia pausantium et oriundorum.* Lambeth MS. 99. fo. 187 b.)

June 12. l. 8. *In fryselond* frigia A. (for frisia).
   Adulph. odulphi A. Apud Trajectum inferius depositio sancti Odolfi, Canonici monasterii sancti Salvatoris. U-Auct. H. omits S. Odulph, and has instead: Aurelianis sancti euurcii episcopi. Alexandrie sancti iohannis elimonis episcopi.

June 15. l. 7. *In messy at dorostore.* Apud messiam ciuitate dorostoro A. mesiam H. Apud Messiam civitate Dorostoro. U.

June 16. l. 1. *vesuce.* vesancium A. Vesuntionem U. Besançon.
   l. 8. *manuete.* namnetis A. U.

June 17. l. 5. *Anyte.* auiti A. H. U. R.
   Add. l. 3. *sconange.* sconangia (*Cat. Sanct.* v. 123). Sconaugia is the usual Latin form of Schönau (in the diocese of Trier).
   l. 5. *Molyng.* Moling D. Moloci. Aberd.

June 18. l. 2. *Marcell.* marcelliani. A. U. R

June 18. l. 6. *were murthered in sond and stones.* lapidibus obruti. A.
l. 8. *In the territory of zenon.* In territorio zeno[nensi *added in later hand*]. A. In territorio Senonensi sancti Fortunati episcopi. Du Saussay, *Mart. Gall.* p. 1135. Cf. U-Auct.

June 19. l. 6. *Vrcissyne.* vrsicini A. U. R.

June 20. l. 1. *Syuere.* siluerii A. R. U-Auct.
l. 6. *The translacyon also of saynt Edwarde.* This is the usual day for the Translation of St. Edward K. M. The Syon Martyrology has already commemorated a translation of St. Edward on Feb. 13, and the bringing of his body from Wareham to Shaftesbury on Feb. 18.

June 21. l. 2. *In cesare capadoce at palestyne.* In cesarea palestine A. (over an erasure). capadocie was apparently the original word after cesarea.
l. 10. *Warburge.* werburge A. St. Werburg of Chester.

June 22. l. 3. *verolane.* uerolamia A. Verolamio U. Verulam, St. Albans.
l. 11. *romaciane.* Baronius in his notes (*Mart. Rom.* Junii 22) identifies Romatiana with Aquileia.

June 23. l. 5. *In tusce at vtrine.* In tuscia ciuitate utrina A. Sutrii in Tuscia R.
l. 6. *Tracius.* Tracius A. Turcius. U. R.

June 24. l. 7. *w^t other chrystyans in maner vnnombrable.* cum aliis innumeris promiscui sexus. A. U.
l. 7. *At austudune.* Augustuduno. A. Augustoduno U. Autun.
Add. l. 4. *Lucey.* Luceia (*Cat. Sanct.* vi, 4). The same Luceia appears in June 25, l. 18, as Luce.

June 25. l. 1. *At puricoroea.* Apud puricoroeam A. Apud Pirriberœam U. At end A. adds in a later hand : Item canonizacio sancte Catherine. beate Birgitte filie virginis in sanctitate vite et miraculis preclare.

June 26. l. 4. *At trientyne.* Apud trientinam urbem. A. (altered by a later hand to tridentinam).
l. 5. *Iustilocon.* sub iustilicone A. sub Stilicone U-Auct.
l. 7. *At valenciane.* In portu valenciano A. In portu valenciano sancti Salvii Engolismæ civitatis episcopi. U-Auct. Valenciennes.

June 27. l. 7. *Nemele.* nemesio. A. U.
l. 8. *Eugyn.* eugenio A.
l. 16. *At glassenbury the translacyon of saynt Bemonus a confessour.* Apud glasconiam : translacio sancti benigni confessoris. A.
Add. l. 3. *Benygne* may be a duplicate notice of St. Benignus of Glastonbury, or St. Benignus, a martyr of Chartres, whose relics were at Utrecht (U-Auct. June 28).

June 28. ll. 9, 11. *Potānan*. potamiena A. over an erasure. Potamiæna U. R.

June 29. l. 6. *castell of argentomate*. castrum argentomatum A. Argentomacum U.
l. 9. *Benedicte*. benedicte A. Beatæ U.
Add. l. 3. *Beate*, apparently a repetition of the above.

June 30. l. 7. *At· lemoniga*. Lemoniga ciuitate A. Lemovicas civitate U. Limoges.
l. 9. *Alpymany and Stratocliane*. alpimano et stratocliano A Alpiniano et Stratocliniano U.
l. 11. *Corsite*. corsiti A. Corsici U.
Ib. *Leo a deacon*. Leonis subdiaconi A. (over an erasure) U.

July 2. l. 10. *saynt Vran*. not in A. U. The name seems to be part of the previous Vrbane repeated in error.

July 3. l. 2. *At geneocesarepont*. apud geneocesaream ponti A. Apud Cneocæsaream Ponti U. At end A. has : Item constantinopoli : sancti eulogii. eufemie. accaci. et demetrii (the last three names in later hand).

July 4. l. 4. *In smyrme*. Apud smirmium. A. Apud Sirmium U.

July 5. l. 3. *bycause she praysed the vertue of saynt Peter*. que dum ad confessionem beati petri apostoli oraret. A. U. Cf. July 6, l. 7.

July 6. l. 7. *bycause he praysed the vertue of saynt Paule/was stoned to deth*. Qui dum ad beati pauli confessionem oraret. tentus a paganis ac lapidatus. martirium consummauit. A. "As he was praying at the Tomb of S. Paul." (*The Roman Martyrologe*, S. Omers, 1667.) Estando este sancto orando junto a las reliquias y sepulchro del Apostol S. Pablo. (*Martyrologio Romano*, Valladolid, 1586.) These two last passages give the correct translation of the word *confessio*, which was misunderstood by Richard Whytford.
l. 8. *In the fraüchest of machiens*. in pago machiensi A. In pago Trevirensi. R.

July 7. l. 6. *Castar*. castorii A. U.
A. adds : Item translacio sancti thome martiris cantuariensis archiepiscopi.

July 8. l. 5. *sanctipole*. scithopoli A. Scitopoli U.
l. 7. *In ye monastery of wentane the deposicyon of saynt Grūbald a preest 't monke*. In wentana ciuitate deposicio sancti grimbaldi presbiteri et monachi A. St. Grymbald of wynchester (July 7. Add.) here reappears as St. Grūbald of wentane.
l. 9. *Kyliane, Colonare and Conace*. St. Kilian is given twice on this day as Ciliane and Kyliane and again a third time as Ciliane in the Addicyons. The spelling of the names of his companions is subject to great variation. Colonari et chonati A. Colmanni et Totmanni U-Auct.

July 8. l. 11. *Wydburge.* wythburge A.
Add. The "addicyons" on this day with the exception of Julian are taken from *Cat. Sanct.* In making them the compiler appears not to have noticed that Ciliane Colonate and Romane had been already given above with slightly different spelling.

July 9. l. 8. *At tyre.* In ciuitate tyro. A. R. 1564. Tyriæ. Ado. Thora R.
l. 10. *At marcull ye feest of saynt Brythe.* Ciuitate martula: sancti bricii. A. Civitate Martula sancti Brictii U.

July 10. l. 6. *cast hedlonge from a toure toppe/ 't so his necke broken.* precipicio interemptus. A.
l. 11. *Valeriane.* valeriani et galieni A.

July 11. Add. l. 1. *Pituouse pope* i.e. Pius I.

July 12. l. 1. *Nason.* nasonis A. Ado. Iasonis R. Mnason. (Acts xxi, 16).
l. 7. *Clyse.* disi A. over an erasure. Dii. Ado. U.

July 13. l. 14. *Thuran.* thuriani A. over an erasure. Turiani U.
Add. l. 3. *Iesus ioiedeke.* Jesus son of Josedek (Ecclus. xlix, 12; 1 Esdr. v, 5).

July 14. l. 2. *synopole.* sinopis A. Synope in Ponto R.
l. 6. *historiagraph.* historiographus. A.
l. 11. *Donate.* A. omits. In Africa, Donati. U-Auct.

July 15. l. 1. *At misybbe.* Nisibi A. U. R.
l. 5. *dyd cõfoũde 't cõdempne ye dampnable opinion and peruerse heresy of the grete heretyke Arrius.* peruersitatem arrii opposicione dampnarunt A.
l. 6. *At rome in a gate.* Rome in portu. A.

July 16. l. 3. *in to intrapole.* in tranopolim A. in Trajanopolim U. R. At end A. adds in later hand: Item translatio Sancti Osmundi Episcopi sarisburiensis. Cf. Notes, Dec. 4.

July 17. l. 1. *In cartage.* In cartagine: natalis sanctorum martirum stillicitanorum A. scillitanorum U.
l. 2. *Nartaby.* nartabi A. Nartali U. R.
l. 3. *Stytyny.* cithini A. U. Cythini R.
l. 5. *the mayre of stillicitane.* sub saturnino prefecto. A. U.

July 19. l. 8. *Diogeman.* diogeniano A.U. R.

July 20. l. 7. *Cassye.* A. om. Cassii U.

July 22. l. 11. *Wandregesyle.* Wandregesili U. Wandragesili A.
l. 11. *In syre at galas.* Ancyra galacie A. Ancira Galaciæ U.

July 23. Add. l. 1. *Apolynare bysshop of Ierusalem.* Apollinaris hieropolitanus episcopus. *Cat. Sanct.* vi, 129. Hierapoli in Asia sancti Apollinaris episcopi R. (Jan. 8).

July 24. l. 11. *At amitermyn.* amiternina ciuitate. A. U. Now San Vittorino, three miles from Aquila in the Abruzzi.

July 25. l. 4. *In syre at samon.* In licia ciuitate samon A. U.
  l. 9. *At bartimon.* ciuitate barcinona. A. U.

July 26. l. 3. *At rome.* rome in portu A. U.

July 27. l. 12. *Hernempy.* hernempi A. U. Hermippi R.
  l. 13. *Hermogiate.* hermogratis A. U. Hermocratis R.

July 29. l. 6. *Betrice.* Beatrix A. U.
  l. 10. *In taraston in a forest of her owne.* apud tarasconam in heremo suo. A.

July 30. l. 3. *corduba.* in corduba ciuitate persarum A.
  l. 12. The word Addicyons has been accidentally omitted before "The feest also of saynt Vrsy," which with all that follows is not in A.

July 31. l. 8. *Neoche.* neothi A. over an erasure. Neoti U-Auct.

Aug. 1. l. 20. *Medard.* menandri A. (over an erasure). U.
  l. 23. *Adelwold.* ethelwoldi A. (over an erasure).
  Add. l. 1. *Salomon.* The story of Solomon's penance is found in *Cat. Sanct.* vii. 6.

Aug. 2. l. 5. *In ye province of biryne at nice.* In prouincia bitinie ciuitate nicea. A. In Provincia Bithinia urbe Niceæ U.
  l. 6. *Theodour.* theodore A. Theodotæ U. R.

Aug. 4. l. 3. *Tranquilyne.* tertulini A. (over an erasure). Tertullini U. R. In the Addicyons l. 5 "Tertulyne" appears under the usual form of the name.

Aug. 5. l. 9. *At cathalamnis.* cathalannis A. for cathalaunis. Catalaunis U.
  l. 10. *Neminyne.* meminii A. Memmii U. R.
  l. 10. *At lornon.* apud bononiam A. U-Auct.
  Add. l. 1. *saynt Thomas.* St. Thomas, a monk of St. Martin's, Dover, murdered by the French in 1295 because he refused to reveal the place where the church treasures had been hidden for safety (see *N. L. A.*).

Aug. 7. A. adds in later hand: Item solemne festum nominis Je su.

Aug. 8. l. 4. *at nyenna.* Apud viennam A. U. At end A. adds in later hand: Item sancte agapes virginis.

Aug. 10. Add. l. 1. *saynt Hope.* Sanctus Spes is placed in *Cat. Sanct.* among those "quorum certa dies celebrationis ignoratur"; and the name of his monastery is given as Cample, about six miles from Nursia (Norcia). Cf. R. (March 28).

Aug. 11. l. 7. *Gangeryke.* gauderici A. (over erasure). Gaugerici. U.
  Add. l. 4. *wuiche* for *whiche.*

Aug. 12. l. 1. *In cicilie at cathyne.* In scicilia ciuitate cathina A.
l. 8. *At rome.* in prefata ciuitate A. U. R., i.e., at Augsburg.
l. 12. *At salary ye feest of saynt Graciane.* urbe falari : passio sanctorum martirum graciliani . . . (the last word over a partial erasure) A. Urbe Falari passio Graciliani U.
l. 17. *Ethelwold.* Edwoldi A.
Add. l. 3. *Ewlethery.* Eleutherius. R. (March 15).

Aug 13. l. 4. *xviij.* decem et nouem. A. U.
l. 6. *At forcill.* forcille A. Forosillæ U. Apud Forum Syllæ R. At end A. adds in later hand : Ipso die : sancti laudulphi.

Aug. 14. At end A. adds in a later hand: In affrica : sancti demetrii.

Aug. 16. l. 2. *Vrsacy.* ursacii A. Ursatii. U. Arsacii R.
l. 3. *Luciane.* licinio A. U. R.
l. 5. *At metēs ye feest of sayt Arnuf.* Apud ciuitatem metensium sancti arnulphi A. Arnulphi U. At end A. adds in a later hand: Lugduni gallie : beati rochi confessoris.

Aug. 17. l. 2. *Seuy.* seruii A. Servii U.
l. 7. *Valeriane.* ualeriano A. Aureliano U. R.

Aug. 18. l. 1. *At preuestyn.* Apud prenestinam ciuitatem A. U.
l. 4. *Valeriane.* aurelii A. Aureliani R.

Aug. 19. *saynt Magnus 't saynt Andrewe.* Natalis sancti magni et sancti andree. A. sancti Magni seu sancti Andreæ. Ado.

Aug. 20. l. 5. *In the yle of nere.* Nerio insula A. Herio insula U. Du Saussay *Mart. Gall.* i. 534. Noirmoutier.

Aug. 22. l. 6. *In a gate of rome.* In portu urbis rome. A. In portu Romano U.
l. 7. *Epute.* epictei A. Epicteti. Ado. U. R.

Aug. 23. l. 3. *In lice at egea.* Apud liciam ciuitate egea A. Apud Lyciam civitate Ægæa U. Ægææ in Cilicia R.
l. 4. *Austere.* asterii. A. U.
l. 6. *In a gate of rome.* In portu urbis rome. A. U.
l. 7. *Akchyl.* archillai A. (over an erasure). Ado. U.
l. 10. *Theon.* thione A. Theonæ U.
Add. l. 10. *no thyng is more peryllous vnto a religyous persone than to kepe preuy from his souerayne his dedes or thoughtes.* At Syon the abbess is frequently spoken of as the *sovereign*, as in the following extract from the Additions to the Rule of St. Saviour and St. Bridget :—" None therfor schal use presumptuously to laughe ouer much or oute of mesure dissolutly, but whan the *souereyne*, or any of the elder sustres begyn to laughe upon any other suster or sustres by wey of recreation, curtesy, wylle, and very loue and charity, that they smyle or laughe agene soberly."
(Aungier's *History of Syon Monastery*, 1840, p. 299.)

Aug. 24. At end A. adds in later hand: In scocia: sancte Ebbe abbatisse.

Aug. 25. l. 3. *hanged on gybettes.* in equuleum leuati. A. U.
l. 7. *Denyse.* genesii A. Ado. U. R.
l. 16. *ytalyke.* Italica, the site of which, five miles from Seville, is now occupied by the poor village of Santi Ponce, which appears to derive its name from a corruption of San Gerontio.

Aug. 26. l. 8. *lemonicens.* lemonicensi or lemouicensi A. ' In territorio Lemovicensi sancti Aredii presbiteri ' is the reading of some MSS. of Usuard, instead of ' Antisiodoro, Eleuterii Episcopi' which is the usual reading of the last clause.
l. 8. *Arecly.* aredii A.

Aug. 27. l. 15. *Fiagry.* fiagrii A. Siagrii. Ado. U. R.

Aug. 28. l. 13. *ticyne.* papiam A. (over an erasure). Ticinum U.
l. 14. *Iulian.* uiuiani A. (over an erasure). Bibiani. Ado. Vibiani. U. Viuiani R.

Aug. 29. l. 12. *Meryke.* mederici A. U.

Aug. 30. l. 5. *Adauct.* Huius nomen ignorantes christiani. adauctum eum appellauerunt : eo quod sancto felici auctus sit ad coronam. A.

Aug. 31. l. 4. *in fryselond.* Apud frigiam. A. U.
l. 9. *Eilady.* euadii A. Elladii U-Auct.
l. 10. *Glastingens.* glastingensis A. Cf. *The Leofric Missal* (Ed. F. E. Warren), where the Kalendar on August 31 has: In glastonia sci. aidani episc. The relics of St. Aidan had been brought to Glastonbury.
l. 11. *Curtbert.* cuthbertus A. At the end of A. a later hand has added : In cancia : sancte eanswide virginis.

Sept. 1. Add. The names of the Judges are found with similar spelling in *Cat. Sanct.* viii, 1–14, as well as in MSS. and early printed editions of the Vulgate.

Sept. 4. l. 2. *In galace at auchyre.* apud anchiram galacie. A. Apud Anciram Galatiæ U.

Sept. 5. l. 8. *In a gate of rome.* rome in portu A. U.
Add. l. 5. *Gondegrand.* Ciuitate Sais sancti Godegranni episcopi et martyris. U-Auct. Ciuitate Sagiensi sancti Godegrandi episcopi et martyris. U-Auct. (Sept. 3).

Sept. 6. l. 10. *Cokcydy.* coccidi A. Cottidi U. R.
Add. l. 6. *Maculyne.* Maculini C. Meic cuilinn D.

Sept. 7. l. 8. *Eurcy.* eurcii A. Euurtii U. Euortii R.

NOTES. 227

Add. l. 1. *One of ye feestes also of saynt Dūstane.* The compiler of the "addicyons" has followed *Cat. Sanct.* viii, 49, in which the day of the death of St. Dunstan is wrongly given as vii. Id. Sept. According to Florence of Worcester (*Chronicon.* ed. Thorpe, i. p. 148) St. Dunstan died on xiv Kal. Junii (May 19) A.D. 988, and he is commemorated on this day in the Sarum, York, Hereford, and other English Calendars, and also in the Martiloge.

Add. l. 2. *At durham ye feest of saynt Alküde.* Alhmundus, bishop of Hexham, died Sept. 7. A.D. 779 (*Chron. Flor. Wigorn.* ed. Thorpe, i, 59).

Sept. 8. l. 11. *Faustyne.* faustini A. Fausti. U. R.

Sept. 9. l. 14. *Querany.* querani A. Kyrani. Aberd. Ciarani D.

l. 15. *Modwen.* modowenne A.

Add. l. 11. *Wolsyld.* Wulfhilda.

Add. l. 12. *horton.* Horton in Dorset, about 6 miles N. of Wimborne. The dedication of Horton Church preserves the name of St. Wolfride or Wulfhild.

Sept. 10. l. 14. *Brydhestane.* brydhestani A. The Winchester Calendar printed in Hampson's *Medii Ævi Kalendarium* from Cottonian MS. Vitell. E xviii. has on Sept. 10 : sancti Fridestani episcopi. In the Chronicle of Florence of Worcester (ed. Thorpe p. 131) we read of : " Vir eximiae sanctitatis Frithestanus Wintoniensis episcopus," who resigned his bishoprick and died in 733.

l. 15. *Denyse.* demesii A. Demetrii U-Auct.

l. 17. *Adelwold.* ethelwoldi A.

Add. l 6. *Hereodarde.* Theodardi martiris episcopi Tungrensis U-Auct. Leodii in Belgia sancti Theodardi episcopi et martyris. R.

Sept. 11. l. 6. *At tarente ye feest of sayt Peter archebisshop of ye same.* Tharentensis archiepiscopi A. It is not easy to identify this St. Peter, unless the notice is intended for St. Peter archbishop of Tarentaise, d. 1171, canonized in 1191, who is commemorated on 22 Jun. Add. l. 5, and also on 18 Oct. Add. l. 2. He is placed in *Cat. Sanct.* among the saints whose day is not known. Gams gives Sept. 14 as the day of his death, and May 10 as the day of his canonization. (*Series Episcoporum,* Ratisbonæ, 1873, p. 829.)

Sept. 13. Add. l. 1. *Ligour.* Sancti Ligorii martiris. Qui in Greciæ partibus ob Christi nomen occisus postmodum Venetias translatus est. Cum vero dies passionis ejus ignoretur, ipse per visum hunc diem designavit. U-Auct.

Add. l. 3. *Maximy.* In territorio Boloniensi, sancti Maximi Regensis episcopi. U-Auct.

Sept. 15. l. 10. *At carneto ye feest of saynt Leopite.* karneto sancti leopiti A Sancti Leobini episcopi carnutensis R. Carnoto sancti Leobini episcopi U.

Add. l. 1. *Aycard.* Aichadri. U-Auct.

Sept. 16. l. 14. *At Wynchester.* wyltonie. A. Wilton, near Salisbury.
Add. l. 1. *Mynyane.* for Ninian. In Scocia Sancti Niniani episcopi et confessoris sepultus apud cathedrale cenobium Candide case. Aberd.

Sept. 17. l. 5. *Crescenciane.* crescencionis A. Crescentionis U.
Add. l. 3 *Tharrasy.* Tarrasis confessoris, cujus corpus juxta Constantinopolim in spelunca reperto . . . . . in urbem prinium regiam deinde Venetias translatum, in monasterio beati zachariæ quiescit. U-Auct. Pilgrims passing through Venice were shewn many relics in the church of San Zacharia. Amongst others we find: Item sotto la confessione della detta chiesia repossa el corpo de s. Tharaso eremi, portado dale parte de Romania (*Viaggio da Venetia al santo Sepulchro, Venetia,* 1524).

Sept. 18. l. 2. *olympyle:* olimpii licie A. (the first word over an erasure). Olimpi Liciæ U.
Add. l. 5. *Stephane.* Stephana, quæ Latine dicitur Corona. U-Auct.

Sept. 19. l. 5. *in the cite of pluteolane.* in ciuitate pluteonana A. Puteolana U.
l. 10. *Signy.* signi A. Sequani. U. Sigonis *seu* Signi. U-Auct.
At end A. adds in a later hand: In cancia: sancti theodori archiepiscopi.

Sept. 20. l. 8. *In fryselonde.* In frigia A. In Phrigia U. In Phrygia. R.

Sept. 21. l. 5. *In the village of clawde.* uia claudia A. U.
Add. l. 1. *Ephigene.* Epigenia. U-Auct.

Sept. 22. l. 6. *Hamptran.* hamptranni A. Emmerammi U.
Add. l. 7. *Sanctyny.* Sanctini episcopi Meldensis U-Auct. Cf. *Cat. Sanct.* viii. 108.

Sept. 23. l. 13. *Lybery a bysshop.* liberii pape et confessoris A. (over an erasure). Romæ sancti Liberii episcopi. U-Auct Romæ depositio sancti Liberi episcopi. (*Vetustius Martyrologium D. Hieronymo tributum.* Lucæ, 1668, p. 852.)

Sept. 24. Add. l. 5. *Solempny.* Item Blesis sancti Solennis. U-Auct. (Sept. 25).

Sept. 25. l. 6. *Rictiouare.* ricciouaro A. Rictiovaro U.
l. 7. *saynt Lupe a bysshop & an ancre.* sancti lupi episcopi ex anacoreta A. (over an erasure). U.
l. 10. *Annary.* Anuarii A. (over an erasure). Aunarii U. R. 1564. Anacharii R.
Add. l. 2. *Golfryde,* i.e. Ceolfrid, Abbot of St. Paul's, Jarrow.
Add. l. 3. *Resigned his rome and went to rome.* Richard Whytford has here (perhaps unconsciously) lapsed into a pun and anticipated Shakespeare's play with the same word:—

"Now is it Rome indeed and room enough."

(*Julius Cæsar,* I, 2.)

A similar use of the word *rome* for an office has already occurred at Sept. 13 :—" Saynt Phylyp . . . a noble man and a capytayne of the cite/ which rome and all the worlde he forsoke for Chryst."

Sept. 26. l. 8. *At albane.* Albanum, probably Albano near Rome, but according to Du Saussay (*Mart. Gall.* ii, 1173) a place bearing the same name near Narbonne.
Add. l. 1. *Colmauell*, i.e. Colmanel or Colman Elo, mentioned in the Life of St. Columba. In Ybernia sancti Colmani confessoris viri Dei inter suos diuinis scripturis eruditissimi. Aberd.

Sept. 27. l. 7. *Antymy.* autimus A. Anthymus U.
l. 10. *At the castell of persewdon.* Castro perseudono A. Castro Pseuduno U. See Notes to editions of Ado and Usuard.

Sept. 28. l. 5. *At iane.* ciuitate ianuis A. U. Genoa.
l. 5. *Salomon* salonis A. U.
Add. l. 1. *Saynt Olaty*, i.e., St. Olave, who, however, is commemorated in the Aberdeen Breviary on March 30 and July 29.
Add. l. 7. *saynt Fors.* Forseus (*Cat. Sanct.* viii, 126). The story is told in Caxton's *Golden Legende* (of the Lyfe of seint Forsyn).
Add. l. 15. *saynt wyncesse duke of beame.* Apud Pragam civitatem Bohemiæ natale sancti Wenceslai ducis et martiris U-Auct. Vinceslaus dux boemiorum. *Cat. Sanct.* viii, 127.

Sept. 29. l. 5. *Plant.* Planti A. Plauti. R.

Sept. 30. l. 2. *Salodour.* salodoro A. Solodoro U. R. Soleure.

Oct. 1. l. 2. *Arthy.* arethe A. Arethæ U. Aretæ R.
l. 5. *in the prouynce of lusitame.* apud prouinciam lusitanam A. Lusitaniam U.
l 5. *olisepon.* olisepona A. U. Lisbon.
l. 7. *Plato.* piatonis A. (over an erasure). U.
l. 12. *In the graud port.* In portu granda. A. for : In portu ganda. (Ghent.)

Oct. 3. l. 10. *at the capped bere.* ad ursum pilleatum A. U.

Oct. 4. Add. l. 1. *Aniane.* Anianus. *Cat. Sanct.* ix, 19.
l. 9. *Petrony bysshop of bonony.* Petronius episcopus bononie. Cat. Sanct. ix, 20.
l. 12. *Amelie* and *Amyke.* Amelius et amicus. *Cat. Sanct.* ix, 21.

Oct. 5. At end A. adds in a later hand :—Rome : sancte babille virginis.
Add. l. 1. *Gale.* Galla. U-Auct.

Oct. 6. l. 2. *Saturne.* saturnini A. U.
l. 3. *Sagary.* beati sagaris martiris. et episcopi laodicensis. A. U.

Oct. 7. l. 7. *In the prouince of auguste at eufratesi.* Apud prouinciam que nuncupatur augusta eufratesia. A. U.

l. 15. *The canonizacyon also of our holy moder sayt Birgit.* A. omits.

Oct. 8. l. 3. *thessoloniey* for *thessalonicy.* apud thessalonicam A. U.

l. 8. *Yue.* iui A. Two Winchester Calendars printed in Hampson's *Medii Ævi Kalendarium* (pp. 431, 444) have on this day: Sancti Iwigii confessoris.

Add. l. 27. *saynt Keyna called also saynt Keynwir.* "Ob hoc enim que prius keyna vocabatur postea britannice keynwiri id est keyn virgo dicta est." *Nova Legenda Anglie,* 1516, fo. cciv. b.

According to the Legend the place to which S. Keyna went was beyond the Severn (vltra sabrinam), and when she first asked for it the king of the country refused her petition because the spot was full of serpents. She, however, persisted in her request and obtained it; and then the story goes on: "Concesso igitur virgini loco ad solitas preces se prostrauit et omnia illa mox genimina viperarum mortificata in lapidum duritiem commutauit. Lapides enim usque hodie imaginem serpentinam exprimunt per campos et vicos quasi arte lathomi sculpterentur."

The like account is given of the origin of the ammonites, which are plentiful in the cliffs of Whitby, where the miracle is attributed to St. Hilda.

l. 28. *saynt Breghan.* braghanus. *N. L. A.*

Oct. 9. l. 7. *At iule.* Apud iuliam uia claudia A. U.

Add. l. 1. *saynt Aymon.* Author of *Summa de Vitiis et Virtutibus.* The account of him is from *Cat. Sanct.* xi, 108.

Oct. 11. l. 2. *cicilye.* cilicie A. Ciliciæ U.

l. 10. *Canuke.* camichi. A. Cainichi U. Cainnich D. Kenneth.

l. 10. *At vrs.* urcia A. Civitate Uzetia U. Uzès near Nîmes. Uzetia has also been identified with the place of the same name in Africa.

Editions of *Martyrologium Romanum* of Gregory XIII read: Uzeciae in Africa. But those, subsequent to the revision of Clement X, read: Ucetiae in Gallia Narbonensi.

l. 13. *Melan.* melani A. Æmiliani U-Auct. (some MSS. read melani).

Oct. 13. l. 5. *ouer teeth.* dentes superiores A.

l. 9. *Wynance.* venancii A (over an erasure). U.

Oct. 14. l. 5. *cast downe hedlonge from the hyghest toure of ye same prison.* per fenestram domus in qua custodiebatur precipitatus. A.

l. 6. *At tubertyn.* Ciuitate tudertina A. Tudertum, Todi.

Oct. 15. l. 5. *saynt Vlfran an archebysshop.* Cf. March 20. St Wulfran, archbishop of Sens, resigned his office and died a monk at Fontanelle, March 20. A.D. 720. (Surius, *De Vitis Sanctorum,* Venetiis, 1581, tom. ii, fo. 91 b.)

NOTES. 231

Oct. 16. l. 9. *vnto the tayles of cartes.* post terga currencium quadrigarum A. U.
l. 14. *In suenuy.* In suevia A. Swabia.

Oct. 18. l. 5. *Esclepiady.* asclepiadis A. U.
l. 9. *Iustyniane.* A. and other martyrologies omit.
Add. l. 2. *At Tarentasiens* . . . *saynt Peter.* St. Peter of Tarentaise is placed by Peter de Natalibus (*Cat. Sanct.* xi, 119) amongst the saints 'quorum certa dies celebrationis ignoratur.' He is also noticed in this Martiloge on June 22 Add. and perhaps on Sept. 11.
l. 3. *vnto lausemy.* lansemia. *Cat. Sanct.* xi, 119.

Oct. 19. l. 5. *Tholony.* tholomei A. Ptolomei. U.
Add. l. 1. *Ethebyne.* Ethbini U-Auct.

Oct. 20. l. 8. *Astrobert.* austroberte A.
l. 12. *The dedicacyon of the chirche of syon.* A. over an erasure: Ipso die festum canonisacionis sancte Birgitte. The Martiloge in English commemorates this canonization on Oct. 7, as do also the two calendars of A.
On Oct. 20 the first calendar has: Festum Dedicacionis Ecclesie de Syon a° x¹ 1588 (in a later hand)—and the second calendar which has the notices of obits: Dedicacio monasterii de Syon. a° x¹ 1488.

Oct. 22. l. 8. *Mimilon.* numilionis A. over an erasure. (originally: mimilonis?) Nunilonis U. R. Milonis. Ado (Add.).

Oct. 23. l. 11. *Elflede* apparently St. Elflede, abbess of Romsey, noticed also on Oct. 29 Add.

Oct. 24. l. 1. *In napules at venyse.* In venisia ciuitate apulie A. In Vesusia civitate Apuliæ U. Venosa.
Add. l. 1. *In englonde the feest of saynt Maglour.* Cf. Vita de sancti Maglorii secundi episcopi Dolensis in Britannia minori. (Surius, *De Vitis Sanctorum*, Venetiis 1581, tom. v. fo. 330.)

Oct. 25. l. 19. *ye feest of saynt Iohn beuerlake.* translaciò. A.

Oct. 27. l. 3. *Aristea.* Cristine A. (over an erasure). Cristetæ U.

Oct. 28. l. 9. *Pharao.* pharaonis A. (over an erasure). Faronis U.

Oct. 29. Add. l 1. *Elflede.* Cf. Oct. 23. l. 11.

Oct. 30. l. 2. *xxx martyrs.* viginti A. U.
l. 3. *Agricolane.* agricolao A. Agricolano. U.

Oct. 31. l. 7. *vermendens.* viromandensi. A. (over an erasure). Virmandensi. U.

Nov. 2. l. 2. *Pitabion.* pitabionensis. A. Ado. U. Pictauiensis R.
The reading of the Roman Martyrology appears to be a conjectural attempt to explain a name which cannot be identified with certainty.
l. 10. *At laudice.* apud laodiciam A. U.
l. 10. *Theodour.* theodoti A. U. R.
Add. l. 16. *Malachy.* Cf. Nov. 5. l. 7.

Nov. 3. l. 3. *Sesary.* cesarii A. U.
l. 8. *Hukbert.* huberti A. (over an erasure) Huberti U-Auct.
l. 9. *carboyle.* carboilum A. Corboilum U-Auct.
l. 9. *Gwenady.* guenadi A. Guinardi. Guinaldi. U-Auct.

Nov. 4. l. 5. *vilcasyne.* vulcasino A. Vilcasino U.
l. 7. *Brinstane.* St. Birstan, bishop of Winchester, d. 934.
Add. l. 2. *orchester.* Orchestria *N.L.A.*
It is not easy to identify Orchester. The suggested substitution of Rochester is a mere guess.

Nov. 5. l. 7. *saynt Malachy*, archbishop of Armagh, died at Clairvaux, on the nones of November (*Cat. Sanct.* x, 27), but according to some on Nov. 2, on which day he is noticed in the Addicyons of R. Whytford.

Nov. 6. l. 6. *In fryselonde.* In frigia A. U.
l. 6. *Actike.* attici A. U.

Nov. 7. l. 6. *At abbiens.* apud albigensem urbem. A. (altered from abbigensem). U.

Nov. 8. l. 2. A. adds in a later hand—simphoriani. castorii. et simplicii. which are also in U.
l. 6. *Capafore.* Carpofori A. U. Carpophori R.

Nov. 9. l. 10. *saynt Theodour bysshop of lyons.* The last three words have no counterpart in A. or U.

Nov. 10. l. 10. *sayt Iust archebysshop of Yorke.* dorobernensis archiepiscopi A. The translator has failed to recognize Canterbury under the form Dorobernia, and has apparently confused Dorobernensis with Eboracensis. Cf. Notes, Feb. 2.

Nov. 11. l. 4. *In fryselonde at sythe.* In scithia metropoli frigie salutarie. A. U. Cotyæi in Phrygia. R.

Nov. 12. l. 4. *At agryppe.* Ciuitate agrippinensi. A. Coloniæ R.
l. 5. *Cubert.* cumberti A. Cuniberti U. R.
l. 6. *At ye castell of meledune.* In oppido Milleduno U. Melun on the Seine.
l. 7. *Leo a cōfessour. alias* Leonius, as in the metrical Martyrology of Wandalbertus:—
 " Leonium Sequanæ recolunt quoque littora sanctum."
  (D'Achery, *Spicilegium*, 1723, tom. ii, p. 55.)

NOTES.   233

Add. l. 2. *of Salomon and of his sone Jeroboam.* The compiler of the Addicyons is responsible for this relationship. The account of Ahijah (Ahias) is probably taken from *Cat. Sanct.* x. 51, where, however, we find : hieroboam *seruus* salomonis.

Nov. 13. l. 3.   *Demetry.* demetrii A.   Mitrii. Ado U. R.

Nov. 14. Add. l. 8. *one of the xiiij. peticioners.* This expression is not found in *Cat. Sanct.* x. 61, from which the rest of the account of St. Veneranda is taken. It recalls the *quatuordecim auxiliatores* of German hagiology, but St Veneranda is not found in the enumeration of their names in *Hortulus anime,* Nurenberge, 1519, fo. cvii. b.

Nov. 16. l. 2.   *Ewthere.* eucherii A. U.

Nov. 17. l. 4. *Acyldy.* aciseli A. (over an erasure). Aciscli. U. Cf. "Corduba Acisclum dabit," Prudentius *Peristephanon,* Hymn. iv. 19.

l. 9.   *Gergery* for *Gregory.*
Add. l. 1. *In yrelond the feest of saynt Hylde.* In Anglia, sanctæ Hildæ abbatissæ, quam omnes qui noverant, ut Beda testatur libro iv, ob insigne pietatis et gratiæ, matrem vocare consueverant. U-Auct. St. Hilda of Whitby is commemorated on this day in the Calendar of the Westminster Missal and in a Durham Calendar [Br. Mus. Harl. MS. 1804], but in the York Calendars on Aug. 25.

Nov. 18. l. 11.   *of whome was redde yesterdaye.* A. om.
Add. l. 4.   *Gelagy* for *Gelasy* (Gelasius I).
Add. l. 9. *At lucane ye feest of saynt Phridiane.* Lucæ in Tuscia translatio sancti Frigdiani episcopi et confessoris. R. This is the Irish St. Finnian, known in Lucca as San Frediano.
Add. l. 11. *the flode that was lyke to have drowned the cite.* The subject of San Frediano turning the course of the river Serchio has been painted by Filippo Lippi and other Italian artists. See illustrations in Miss Stokes' *Six months in the Apennines,* 1892, pp. 41, 80.

Nov. 19. l. 4.   *Pociane.* Ponciani A.
l. 5. *At agens.* Ciuitate astiagensi. A. U. Astiagis, now Ecija in Andalusia.
ib. *Crispyne.* Cipriani A. Crispini U. The Latin text (A.) is here in error. The translator must have had before him a text with the usual reading Crispini. St Crispin is said to have been the first bishop of Ecija.
Add. l. 1.   *Elizabeth* already mentioned in the previous line.

Nov. 20. l. 7.   *Syluere.* siluestri. A. U. R.
l. 10.   *Solutary.* solutoris. A. U. R.

Nov. 22. l. 4.   *Marke.* marci aurelii A.
l. 8.   *Pragmas.* pragmacii A.   Pragmatii U.

Nov. 23. l. 7. *In the fraunchest of hyspane.* In pago haspanio A. Hasbanio U.

Nov. 25. l. 4. *leyfee* a misprint for *leytee.*

Nov. 26. l. 3. *in vaticanes street.* in vaticano A. U.

Nov. 28. l. 2. *Sostones.* sostenis A. (over an erasure) sostenes H. U. Sosthenis R.

Nov. 30. l. 6. *Trophiane.* traiani A. troiani H. U. R.

Dec. 1. l. 4. *Numerary.* numerario A. Numeriano U.

Dec. 4. It is strange that a Martiloge claiming be "after the vse of the chirche of Salisbury" should omit St. Osmund. A. adds in a later hand: Item in anglia. deposicio sancti osmundi episcopi sarisburiensis.
On July 16 the Translation of St. Osmund has been similarly omitted in the Martiloge, although a later hand has added it to A.

Dec. 5. l. 6. *Niceny.* nicecii A. H. U.
Add. l. 6. *saynt Iustiniane a bysshop 't martyr.* The story agrees in most particulars with that of St. Justinian, hermit of Ramsey Island, near St. Davids.

Dec. 6. l. 9. *Cercy.* tercii A. H. U.

Dec. 7. l. 3. The translator has here somewhat departed from his original: Qui cum militaris esset. et prohiberet quosdam volentes illudere mortuis cadaueribus martirum. A.
l. 7. *In the fraunchest of meldinens.* In pago meldicensi. A. H. U.

Dec. 8. l. 8. *In the fraūchest of dymens* in territorio dunensi. A. (H. om.). Diviniensi. U-Auct. Dijon.

Dec. 9. l. 2. *by Decius the presydent of spayne.* a prefecto hispaniarum daciano. A. U.

Dec. 10. l. 1. *At hyspolitane the feest of saynt Capofory* . . . . .
Apud ciuitatem hispolitanam: sanctorum martirum carpofori presbiteri. et habundii diaconi. A. U.

Dec. 11. l. 4. *At beame.* Ciuitate ambianis A. H. U. Amiens.
l. 5. *Fustinian.* fustiani A. fusciani H. U.
l. 6. *iuce of herbes with vynegre 't peper blowen in to theyr eares and nosethrylles.* In horum naribus et auribus iussit iudex tarincas inmitti. A. "Tarincæ, Sudes ferreæ." (Du Cange, *Glossarium Mediæ et Infimae Latinitatis.*)

Dec. 12. l. 6. The translator has omitted—In alexandria: sanctorum martyrum epimachi et alexandri. A. U.
Add. l. 1. *Ewstrace.* eustratius. *Cat. Sanct.* i, 61.
l. 3. *satale.* satalia. *Cat. Sanct. l. c.*
l. 6. *auare.* civitas auraricenorum. *Cat. Sanct. l. c.*
l. 11. *Fynany.* Finnani. Aberd.

Dec. 14. l. 5. *vnto exyle.* per metalla A. U.

Dec. 15. l. 8. *Maximyne.* maximi A. H. maximini U.

Dec. 16. l. 10. *Vanaly.* naualis A. H. R.

Dec. 18. l. 6. *Canciane.* graciani A. H. Gatiani U. R.
Add. l. 3. *he ordeyned a feest of her to be kept in his chirche before Chrystmas.* Reference is here made to Expectatio Beatæ Mariæ, observed in Spain, Dec. 18. Cf. *Cat. Sanct.* i, 76.

Dec. 20. l. 2. *Iugeny.* ingenii A. H. U.
l. 3. *Theophyly.* theophoti A. theophili H. U.
l. 5. *In trace at gelduba.* In tracia ciuitate gelduba. A. U. Du Saussay (*Mart. Gall.* ii, p. 1204) and others consider that Usuard has wrongly placed Gelduba in Thrace, and identify it with Geldub on the Rhine below Cöln.

Dec. 21. l. 5. *The feest also of saynt Ewyne a quene.* Ipso die sancte eluine regine. A. (H. omits). On May 18th, Eluina ('Elene') appears to represent St. Elgiva of Shaftesbury.
l. 6. *In englonde within the fraūchest of oxford/ at betony the deposicyon af saynt Berenwald preest 't martyr.* In britannia territorio oxoniensi vico bentone : deposicio sancti berenwaldi presbiteri et martiris. A. (H. omits). In Leland's *Collectanea* (Hearne's Ed. 1770) vol. III, p. 408, there is an extract " E. libello de Locis, quibus S. in Anglia requiescunt," in the course of which we find " S. Brenwaldus apud Bamptonam." Betony (Bentona) may therefore be probably identified with Bampton, Oxon. Nothing further seems to be known of Berenwald. For the reference to Leland we are indebted to Mr. James Parker of Oxford.

Dec. 22. l. 2. *xx.* triginta A. U.
l. 4. *Chiridon.* chiridionis A. Ischyrionis Ado. Chæremonis R.
l. 7. H. has : ciuitate hostia sanctorum demetrii honorati et flori. Ciuitate antiochia sancti basilii.
l. 8. *Dewtrey.* demetrii A. H. U.
l. 9. *Theosie.* theodosie A. (H. omits). U-Auct.

Dec. 23. l. 13. after *martyrs* A. adds in a later hand : Parisius dedicacio basilice in honore sancte crucis et sancti vincencii.
l. 13. *The deposicyon also of saynt Gyldebert a kynge.* et deposicio domini childeberti regis A.

Dec. 24. l. 3. *in the persecucyon of the emperour Daciane.* sub deciana persecucione A.
l. 6. *Dioclecian.* diocliciani et maximiani. A. U.
l. 7. *specyally in his knees with botkyns.* cardis ferreis in genibus percussus. A.

Dec. 25. l. 8. *a notable date amonge the iewes called olympiades.* The attempt of the translator to explain the word olympiad is rather unfortunate.

Dec. 28. At end A. adds in a later hand—In affrica : sanctorum victoris. castoris. et rogaciani.

Dec. 29. l. 3. *Trophyne.* trophimi A. U.

l. 7. *In the fraūchest of oxforde.* In pago oximensi A. (over an erasure) U. oxiniensi H. Oximum or Oximæ, now Exmes in Normandy, the district round which is known as L'Exmesin.

It is strange to find the passion of St. Thomas of Canterbury omitted from a Martiloge which claims to be "after the vse of the chirche of Salysbury" and relegated to the Addicyons. The omission was probably accidental, for the octave of the festival is given in the usual place on Jan. 5. In A. the entry was carefully scraped out in the time of Henry VIII, but was reinserted apparently in the time of Queen Mary. It now runs :—Cantuarie passio sancti thome archiepiscopi et martiris. Qui ob defensionem libertatis ecclesiastice in cathedrali ecclesia gladio percussus migrauit ad christum.

In H. there is a long eulogy of St. Thomas, which has escaped mutilation, although in the same book the word *papa* has always been carefully erased. The account is as follows :—

Item in britannia ciuitate cantuariensi/ passio beati thome archiepiscopi. qui cum pro libertate ecclesie dei fideliter decertaret/ diutinum exilium in cilicio uigiliis et ieiuniis deuota mente sustinuit. Postmodum paciendi desiderio et amore ouium ad sedem propriam rediens non multum post quattuor militum armatorum temulenta inuasione cum fratres vespertinos ymnos psallerent/ ceruicis et corone diminucione et cerebro cum ense extracto. hostiam deo in ecclesia placentem obtulit. signis et uirtutibus clarus. (Cf. Appendix, p. 291.)

Dec. 30. l. 5. *many varyaūt 't cruell turmentes.* This is a condensed account of details given in A.

Add l. 1. *Ewgyne.* Egwin, bishop of Worcester, d. 717.

Add l. 6. *bysshop of canens.* episcopus cannensis, que ciuitas est apulie (*Cat. Sanct.* ii. 20).

Dec. 31. l. 7. *Colūbyne.* columbe A. (corrected from columbine). H. U.

INDEX NOMINVM SANCTORVM

A

CHRISTOPHORO WORDSWORTH. A.M.
ORDINATVS.

*** In cases where the saints-names as given by Whytford are incorrectly or unusually written, it has been thought desirable to give cross-references to the more ordinary forms as they appear in the index to the " *Vetus Romanum Martyrologium a Baronio desideratum.*" This, together with the Martyrology and Festivals of Ado bishop of Vienne, was provided with an index by Heribert Rosweyd, S.J., of Utrecht in the folio *Martyrologium Romanum* which issued from the Plantin press at Antwerp in 1613.

Aureola.   C. = Confessor.
          M., MM., = martyr, martyres.
Conditio.   Ap. = Apostolus.
          Pr. = Presbyter.

Conditio.   R. = Rex aut Regina.
          V. = Virgo.
          Diac. = diaconus.
          Ep. = Episcopus.

Add. = Whytford's 'Addicyons' ; *al.* = alias ; *v.* = vide.

Aaron, sacerdos ordinis Levitici, [C.], in Monte Hor, 1 Jul.
Aaron, cum S. Albano, in Brit., 1 Jul. Add.
Abacuc, nobilis, M. Romæ, 20 Jan.
Abacuc, *v.* Habacuc.
Abbane (vocatus 'Kyryne'), 16 Mar. Add.
Abbany, filius regis Hiberniæ, 27 Oct. Add.
Abbas quidam in monasterio S. Petri Prænestinensis, 19 Jul. Add.
Abdella, senex M., in Perside, 21 Apr.
Abdias, Ep. C., Babyloniæ, 28 Oct. Add.
Abdias, propheta, 24 Dec. Add.
Abdon, judex, 1 Sep. Add.
Abdon, subregulus M. Romæ, 30 Jul.
Abel, 23 Jan. Add.
Abesan, judex, 1 Sep. Add.
Abgarus, R. C., Edessæ, 20 Jun. Add.
Ahibon, ejus Inventio, Hierosol, 3 Aug.
Abilius, Ep., Alexandriæ, 22 Feb.
Abraham, patriarcha, pater omnium credentium, 9 Oct.
Abraham, 5 Feb. Add.

Absolon, M. (*al.* C.) Cæsareæ in Cappadocia, 2 Mar.
Abundance, Alexandriæ, 27 Feb.
Abundius (' Habund '), M. Romæ, 26 Aug.
Abundius, Diac. M., Spoleti ('at Hyspolitane '), 10 Dec.
Abundus, *v.* Habundus. 8 Jun.
Acacius, miles, Alexandriæ, 22 Jun. Add.
Acatius ('Acute '), M., Puteolis, 19 Sep.
Acepsimas, Ep. M., in Perside, 22 Apr.
Achaicus, Thessalonicæ, 30 Mar.
Achias, propheta, 12 Nov. Add.
Achilleas, Ep., Alexandriæ, 7 Nov.
Achilleus, diac. M., Valentiæ in Galliis, 23 Apr.
Achilleus, eunuchus M. Romæ, 12 Mai.
Achilleus ('Akchyl '), *v.* Archilaus, in Portu Romano, 23 Aug.
Acisclus (' Acyldy '), M., Cordubæ, 17 Nov. (' Acisolenus ' app. in Adonis Martyrol., 18 Nov.), *al.* Ascisclus.
Acontius, Romæ, 21 Jul. Add.
Actike, in Fryselond, *v.* Atticus.
Acute, *v.* Acatius.
Acyldy, *v.* Acisclus.

INDEX SANCTORUM.

Adam (secundum quosdam), 23 Jan. Add.
Adaucte, 16 Feb. Add.
Adauctus, M. Romæ, 30 Aug.
Adelbert, *v.* Ethelbertus, R.C., 24 Feb.
Adelbertus, R.M., in Brit., 20 Mai.
Adelbertus, Ep. Pragensis, M. in Prusia ('at Bruce'), 23 Apr.; *item* 25 Apr. Add.
Adelwoldus, Ep. C., in Anglia, 10 Sep.
Adelwoldus, eius Translatio, Wintoniæ, 1 Aug.
Adiute, Abbas, 27 Jan. Add.
Adjutus, *v.* Avitus, Ep. C.
Adrian, M., 4 Mar. Add.
Adrianus, Cantuar. abbas, 9 Jan. Add.
Adrianus I, papa, 8 Sep. Add.
Adrianus, M. *v.* Hadrianus.
Adrianus, C., 13 Oct.
Adulph, *v.* Odulphus.
Adulphus, M., Cordubæ, 27 Sep.
Adventor, miles Thebanæ legionis, M. Taurini, 20 Nov.
Adventus Saluatoris nostri J.C. 30 Nov. Add.
Aegidius, abbas C., Athenis, *al.* in prov. Narbonensi, 1 Sep.
Aemilianus, M., in Armenia minore, 8 Feb.
Aemilianus, C., Dorostori, 18 Jul.
Aemilianus ('Emilian'), miles M., Cirthæ in Numidia, 29 Apr.
Aemilianus, Diaconus, M., Cordubæ, 17 Sep.
Aemilianus ('Melan'), C. apud Rhedones, 11 Oct.
Aemilianus, Pr. C., Turiasone in Hispania Tarraconensi, 12 Nov.
Aemilianus, medicus C., in Africa, 6 Dec.
Aemilius, M., in Africa, 22 Mai.
Aemilius, M., in Sardinia, 28 Mai.
Aemilius, M., Capuæ, 6 Oct.
Aetherius ('Ewthery'), Ep. C., Antisiodori, 27 Jul.
Afra, M. Augustæ Vindelicorum in Rhætia, 5 Aug. (9 Oct. append. in Adon.)
Affrodose, *v.* Aphrodisius, M.
Affrodose, *v.* Epaphroditus, Ep. C., 'at Septimane in Bytern,' 22 Mar.
Agabite, 20 Mai. Add.
Agabus, proph. apud Antiochiam, 13 Feb.
Agapa, M., 5 Aug. Add.
Agapes, V. M., Interamnæ, 15 Feb.
Agapes, V.M., Thessalonicæ, 3 Apr.
Agapitus, Ep., Synnadæ in Phrygia, 24 Mar.
Agapitus, diac. M. Romæ, Aug.
Agapitus, M. Præneste, 18 Aug.
Agapitus, I., papa, 22 Apr. Add.
Agapitus, consul, M., 26 Mai. Add.
Agapitus, nobilis, M, 26 Mai. Add.
Agapitus, papa, M., Romæ, 20 Sep. Add.
Agapius, M., 28 Apr.

Agapius, filius S. Eustachii, M., Romæ, 2 Nov.
Agapius ('Agapite'), Ep. M., Cirthæ in Numidia, 29 Apr.
Agapy, Ep., 21 Jan. Add.
Agatha ('Agas'), V. M., Catanæ in Sicilia, 5 Feb.
Agathe, cum Gorgonio et Firmo, M., 10 Mar.
Agatho, exorcista M., Alexandriæ, 14 Feb.
Agatho, miles M., Alexandriæ, 7 Dec.
Agathon, abbas, 7 Dec. Add.
Agathonica, M., apud Pergamum Asiæ, 13 Apr.
Aggaeus, M., Bononiæ, 4 Jan.
Aggaeus, propheta, 4 Jul. Add.
Agily, C. in pago Meldensi, 30 Aug.
Agilbertus ('Gylbert'), M., in territorio Parisiensi, 24 Jun.
Agnellus, abbas, 14 Dec. Add.
Agnes, V. M. Romæ, 21 Jan.
Agnes, 2do. Romæ, 28 Jan.
Agyl, *v.* Augulus.
Agoardus, M., Parisiis, 24 Jun.
Agricola, M. Bononiæ in Italia, 27 Nov.
Agricola, cum Valentino et Navali, M., Ravennæ, 16 Dec.
Agricola, M., 4 Nov. Add.
Agryke, abbas, 11 Apr. Add.
Agryppe, cognomine Castor, 12 Apr. Add.
Agyly, abbas, 1 Sep. Add.
Aidanus, Ep. Lindisfarn., C., Glastoniae in Brit., 31 Aug.
Akchyl, *v.* Archelaus.
Akke (Acca), Ep., 20 Oct. Add.
Albina, M., Lugduni, 2 Jun.
Albanus, miles M., Verolami in Britannia, 22 Jun.
Albanus, eius Inventio, 2 Aug.
Albanus, M., Maguntiæ, 1 Dec.
Albanus, Ep. M., 21 Jun. Add.
Albey, Ep. C. 12 Sep. Add.
Albinus, C. 11 Jun. Add.
Albinus, Ep. C., Andegavi, 1 Mar.
Alborowe, *v.* 'Ethelburga' V.
Albucinus, Ep. 5 Feb. Add.
Alcippiade, M. 25 Jan. Add.
Alcyndyne, M. in Perside, 2 Nov. Add.
Aldegunda, V., in Malbodio Hannoniæ monasterio, 30, *al.* 31 Jan.; *item* 13 Nov.
Aldegunde, 20 Mar. Add.
Aldelmus, Ep. in Brit., 25 Mai.
Alexander, M. in Cypro, 9 Feb.
Alexander, Ep., Alexandriæ, 26 Feb.
Alexander, M. Apamiæ, 10 Mar.
Alexander, Ep. M., Caesareæ, 18 Mar.
Alexander, M. in Pannonia, 27 Mar.
Alexander, M. apud Caesaream Palestinæ, 28 Mar.
Alexander, M. Lugduni in Gallia, 24 Apr.
Alexander I, papa M., Romæ, 3 Mai.

Alexander, M. in Anaunia, 29 Mai.
Alexander, M., Novioduni in Galliis, 6 Jun.
Alexander, filius S. Felicitatis, M. Romæ, 10 Jul.
Alexander, miles M., Massiliæ in Gallis, 21 Jul.
Alexander, miles M. dux legionis Thebaeorum, Bergomi, 26 Aug.
Alexander (papa), Ep. C. Constantinopoli, 28 Aug.
Alexander, in Sabinis, 9 Sep.
Alexander, Ep. M., via Claudia, xx° miliario, 21 Sep.
Alexander, C., 17 Oct.
Alexander, C. in territorio Belvacensi, 18 Oct.
Alexander, miles M., 11 Mar. Add.
Alexander, M., Alexandriæ, 12 Dec. Add.
Alexius, C., Romæ, 17 Jul.
Alkunde, Ep. C., 7 Sept. Add.
Almachius, miles M., 14 Mai. Add.
Almachius, M. Romæ, 1 Jan.
Alodia, soror Munilonis, V.M., Oscæ in Hispania, 22 Oct.
Alpadia, V., 3 Nov. Add.
Alphege, Archiep. M., 28 Dec. Add.
Alphege, v. Elphegus, Ep.
Alpinianus ('Alpymany'), Pr., Lemovicis, 30 Jun.
Alrede, abbas, 12 Jan. Add.
Amalberga, V. 10 Jul. Add.
Amandale, M., v. Mandalis.
Amandus, Ep. Trajectensis, C., 6 Feb.
Amandus, eius Commem.. 26 Oct.
Amantius, M. Novioduni in Galliis, 6 Jun.
Amantius, M. Romæ, 10 Feb.
Amantius, M. Romæ, 10 Jun.
Amantius, Ep. C. (apud Ruthenos), in Gallia, 4 Nov.
Amantius, Ep. C.
Amarantus, M. in Albigensi civitate, 7 Nov.
Amaryne, v. Marinus, M.
Amata, V., 13 Mar. Add.
Amator, Ep. C., Augustoduni, 26 Nov.
Amator, Ep. C., Antisiodori, 1 Mai.
Amatus, Pr., Abbas monasterii S. Romerici, 13 Sep.
Ambrose, 17 Mar. Add.
Ambrosius, Ep. C., eius Depositio, Mediolani, 4 Apr.
Ambrosius, eius Ordinatio, Mediolani, 7 Dec.
Ambrosius, abb. Agaunensis, 2 Nov.
Ambrosius, Ep. Caturicensis, in territorio Bituricensi, 16 Oct.
Ambrosius, C., 16 Oct. Add.
Amelie (seu Amilion), miles M., 4 Oct. Add.

Amyke (seu Amyas), 4 Oct. Add.
Ammon, M. Alexandriæ, 8 Sep.
Ammon, miles, M. Alexandriæ, 20 Dec.
Ammonaria, V.M. Alexandriæ, 12 Dec.
Ammonaria altera, M., Alexandriæ, 12 Dec.
Ammonius, miles lector, M. in Ponto, 18 Jan.
Ammonius, infans, Alexandriæ, 12 Feb.
Ammonius, M., in Cypro, 9 Feb.
Ammonius, frater Dionysii, M., Alexandriæ, 14 Feb.
Ammonius, lector apud Pentapolim Libyæ, 26 Mar.
Ammonius, C., 10 Sep.
Ammonius, M. Alexandriæ, 26 Nov.
Ammonius ('Amony'), 4 Mai. Add.
Amony, abbas, 31 Mar. Add.
Amos, propheta, 31 Mar.
Amos, abbas, 31 Mar. Add.
Amos in Egypto, 29 Nov. Add.
Ampelius ('Apely'), M., 12 Feb.
Ampelus, Messaniæ in Sicilia, 20 Nov.
Amphianus, Cæsareæ in Lycia, 5 Apr.
Amphibalus, M., cum S. Albano, 25 Jun. Add.
Amphilacius, Ep., Iconii, 23 Dec. Add.
Amyke, Lugduni, 14 Jul.
Anacharius ('Annary'), Ep. C., Antisiodori, 25 Sep.
Anacletus ('Clete'), papa, M., Romæ, 26 Apr.
Anaclete, papa, 12 Jul. Add.
Ananias, Damasci, 25 Jan.
Ananias, senex M., in Perside, 21 Apr.
Ananias, cum Azaria, &c., 16 Dec.
Anastasia, V. M., 25 Dec.
Anastasius, M., Antiochiæ, 9 Jan.
Anastasius, monach. M. 22 Jan.
Anastasius, papa, Romæ, 27 Apr.
Anastasius, miles, M., 29 Jun.
Anastasius, M., Salonæ, 21 Aug.
Anastace, abbas, 22 Jan. Add.
Anatolia, V. M., 9 Jul.
Anatolius, Ep., Laodiceæ, in Syria, 3 Jul.
Ancare, 27 Apr. Add.
Anceias ('Aucy'), R. M., Romæ, 24 Jun, Add.
Anchymy, v. Anthimus.
Andeolus, subdiac, M., in Galliis, territ. Vivariensi, 1 Mai.
Andochius, pr. M. Augustoduni, 24 Sep.
Andoke, Pr. M., 17 Jan. Add.
Andreas, M., Lampsaci, 15 Mai.
Andreas, cum Magno, M., 19 Aug.
Andreas, Ap. M., 30 Nov.
Andreas, eius Vigilia, 29 Nov.
Andreas, eiusdem Octava, 7 Dec.
Andreas, eius Translatio, Constantinopoli, 9 Mai.
Andreas, in deserto Egypti, 11 Jun. Add. .

Andronicus, M., Tarsi in Cilicia, 11 Oct.
Anepothiste, M., in Perside, 2 Nov. Add.
Anesye, M., in Africa, 31 Mar.
Anianus, diaconus (M.) Antiochiae, 10 Nov.
Anianus, Ep. C., Aurelianis, 17 Nov.
Anianus, discip. S. Marci, Ep., 4 Oct. Add.
Animarum, Omnium Fidelium Defunctorum Commemoratio, 2 Nov.
Anicetus, papa M., Romæ, 16, *al.* 17 Apr.
Anna, mater B., Mariæ, 26 Jul.
Anna, prophetissa, Hierosolymis, 1 Sep.
Anna, mater Cyriaci, 4 Mai. Add.
Annaris, *v.* Anacharius.
Annuntiatio beatissmæ V. Mariæ, 25 Mar.
Anolinus, M., 24 Mai. Add.
Ansanus, M., 1 Dec. Add.
Anselmus ('Ancelme') Archiep., eius Depositio, 21 Apr. Cf. 18 Mar. Add.
Anselmus, natus in Anglia, 5 Jul. Add.
Anselmus, natus in Burgundia, 5 Jul. Add.
Anteros ('Anthery'), papa M., Romæ, 3 Jan.
Anthia, mater Eleutherii, apud Messanam Apuliæ, 18 Apr.
Anthimus, Ep. M., Nicomediæ, 27 Apr.
Anthimus, presb. M., Romæ, 11 Mai.
Anthimus, M., Ægææ, 27 Sep.
Anthinodour, 12 Feb. Add.
Antidy, Ep M., Turonis. 3 Sep. Add.
Antidy, Ep. M., 23 Mai. Add
Antholianus, M., Arvernis in Gallia, 6 F. b.
Antinogenus ('Antiogene'), M., Emeritæ in Hisp., 24 Jul.
Antiochus, Ep., Lugduni, 15 Oct.
Antipas, Pr. M., 20 Nov. Add.
Antonia, V. sacra, M., Cirthæ in Numidia, 29 Apr.
Antonia, M.. Nicomediæ, 4 Mai.
Antoninus, M., Romæ, 26 Apr.
Antoninus, M., Apamiæ, 2 Sep.
Antoninus, carnifex, *v.* Antonius.
Antoninus, puer M., Capuæ, 3 Sep.
Antoninus, C ?, M. ex legione Thebæorum, Placentiæ, 30 Sep.
Antoninus, M. in Perside, 2 Nov. Add.
Antonius ('Antonyne'), Pr. M., Antiochiæ, 9 Jan.
Antonius, M. Alexandriæ, 14 Feb.
Antonius, monachus in Thebaide in Aegypto, 17 Jan.
Antonius, monachus Lusitanus, Pr. C., Patavii, 13 Jun.
Antonius, carnifex M., Romæ, 22 Aug.
Antonius, eremita, ejus Translatio, 13 Jun. Add.
Antonius, M., 29 Jul. Add.
Antonius, monachus, 2 Oct. Add.
Antony, *v.* Antoninus, 2 Sep.
Anyte. *v* Avitus, Ep. C.
Apelles, 23 Feb. Add.

Apely, *v.* Ampelius.
Apostolorum octava, 6 Jul.
Aphrodisius, M., 28 Apr.
Aphrodisius ('Eufrose'), M. in Africa, 14 Mar.
Apodemus, M., Cæsaraugustæ in Hisp., 15, *al.* 16 Apr.
Apollinaris, M, in Africa, 21 Jun.
Apollinaris, Ep. M. Ravennæ, 23 Jul.
Apollinaris, M., Rhemis, 23 Aug.
Apollinaris, Ep. Valentiæ in Gallia, 5 Oct.
Apollinaris, Ep. C., 23 Jul. Add.
Apollinaris, in Syria, 1 Nov. Add.
Appolinus, abbas, C., 5 Mai. Add.
Apollonia ('Apolyne'), V. M., Alexandriæ, 9 Feb.
Apollonius, abbas, 18 Apr. Add.
Apollonius, C., 18 Apr. Add.
Apollonius, M., 29 Jul. Add.
Apollonius, diaconus, M. apud Antinoum in Aegypto, 8 Mar.
Apollonius, Ep. Nicomediæ, 19 Mar.
Apollonius, apud Aegyptum, 5 Apr.
Apollonius, Pr. M., Alexandriæ, 10 Apr.
Apollonius, senator, M. Romæ, 18 Apr.
Apollony, C., 31 Jan. Add.
Apollyn, *v.* Apollonius, diac.
Apollyn, abbas, 5 Mai. Add.
Apolyne, *v.* Apollonia, V. M.
Appolyne, M., in Egypto, 5 Jun. Add.
Appianus, M., Alexandriæ, 30 Dec.
Aprilis, M. in Portu Romano, 22 Aug.
Apro[pi]nianus, commentariensis, M. Romæ, 2 Feb.
Aprus ('Apry'), Ep. C., Tullensis, 15 Sep.
Apuleius, discip. Petri, M., Romæ, 7 Oct. Add.
Apy. C., 10 Feb. Add.
Aquila, vxor Severiani, M., Neocæsareæ in Mauritania, 23 Jan.
Aquila, conjux Priscillæ, 8 Jul.
Aquila, M., Philadelphiæ in Arabia, 1 Aug.
Aquila, V. M., 24 Jul.
Aquilinus, M. in Africa, 4 Jan.
Aquilinus, M. Romæ, 4 Feb.
Aquilinus, M., in Isauria, 15, *al.* 16 Mai.
Aquilinus, M. cum duobus aliis, Novioduni, 17 Mai.
Aquilinus, M. Carthagine, 17 Jul.
Aquilinus, Ep., 18 Jul.
Arabia, M. Nicaeæ, 13 Mar.
Arabiane, C., 10 Feb. Add.
Aram, 28 Jan. Add.
Arator, Pr. M., Alexandriæ, 21 Apr.
Arcadius. nobilis M., Cæsareæ in Mauritania, 12 Jan.
Arcadius, M. in Africa, 12, *al.* 13 Nov.
Archilaus ('Akchyl'), in Portu Romano, 23 Aug.
Archiloke, *al.* Archilawe, Ep., 11 Apr. Add.
Archinimus, C. in Africa, 29 Mar.

Archippus, commilito S. Pauli in Asia, 20 Mar.
Arcontius, M. Capuæ, 5 Sep.
Aredius ('Arecly'), Pr. C., 26 Aug.
Aretas ('Arthy'), M. Romæ, 1 Oct.
Argentarius, monachus, 4 Jul. Add.
Argeus, puer M., Tomis in Ponto, 2 Jan.
Arianus, praeses M., apud Antinoum in Aegypto, 8 Mar.
Aristarchus, discip. S. Pauli, Ep., 4 Aug.
Aristea, v. Christeta, M.
Aristeus, Ep. M., Capuæ, 3 Sep.
Aristides, Athenis, 31 Aug.
Aristion, discip. Christi, 22 Feb.; Salaminæ in Cypro, 22 Feb.
Arist[i]on et alii, MM. in Campania, 2 Jul.
Aristonicus, M., Militanæ in Armenia, 19 Apr.
Armogastes, M., al. in Africa, 29 Mar.
Arnulphus, Ep. C., Metis, in Gallia, 18 Jul.
Arnulphus, Ep. Metensis, 16 Aug.
Arphaxat, 28 Jan. Add.
Arsacius, v. Ursatius.
Arsenius, diac., 19 Jul.
Arsenius, M., Alexandriæ, 14 Dec.
Arteby, Ep., 15 Mar. Add.
Artemia, V. M., 16 Aug. Add.
Artemius, conjux Candidæ, M., Romæ, 6 Jun.
Aryld, V. M., Glocestriæ in Anglia, 20 Jul. Add.
Ascensio Domini, 5 Mai.
Asclas ('Askle') M., apud Antinoum in Aegypto, 23 Jan.
Asclepiades, Ep. M., Antiochiæ, 18 Oct.
Asterius ('Austere'), M., Aegæeæ in Cilicia, 23 Aug.
Asterius ('Astece'), senator, M., Caesareæ Palestinæ, 3 Mar.
Asterius, Pr. M., Ostiæ, 21 Oct.
Astroberta, 20 Oct.
Athanasius, Ep. C., Alexandriæ, 2 Mai.
At[t]ala, abbas in monast. Luxoviensi, 10 Mar.
Attalus, M., 4 Jun.
Attalus, nobilis, M., Lugduni, 2 Jun.
Atticus, in Phrygia, 6 Nov.
Atticus, monachus, 14 Dec.
Atyke, Ep. 13 Apr. Add.
Aucy, v. Anceias.
Auda, V., 18 Nov. Add.
Audactes, Pr. M., Venusiæ in Apulia, 24 Oct.
Audax, M. Tyriæ, 9 Jul.
Audifax, Persa nobilis, M., Romæ, 20 Jan.
Audoënus, Ep. C., Rotomagi, 24 Aug.
Audoënus, eius Translatio, 5 Mai.
Audomarus, Ep. C., in territorio Tarvanensi, 9 Sep.

Audre, v. Audrey, v. Etheldreda.
Aventynus, Ep. C., Trecis, 4 Feb.
Avens, v. Habentius.
Augulus ('Agyl'), Ep. M., Augustæ in Brit., 7 Feb.
Augend, v. Eugendus, abbas.
Augur[r]ius, diac. M. Tarraconæ in Hisp., 21 Jan.
Augustinus, M., Nicomediæ, 7 Mai.
Augustinus, Ep. C., Anglorum Apostolus, Cantuariæ, in Brit., 26 Mai.
Augustinus, eius Translatio, 10 Sep.
Augustinus, Ep. C., in Africa, 28 Aug.
Augustini Translatio per Luithprandum, 11 Oct., 28 Feb. Add.
Augustus, M., Nicomediæ, 7 Mai.
Avitus, M., in Africa, 27 Jan.
Avitus ('Adiut'), Ep. C., Viennæ, 5 Feb.
Avitus ('Anyte'), Pr. C., Aurelianis, 17 Jun.
Aurea, V., Lutetiæ Parisiorum, 4 Oct.
Aureus, M., Moguntiæ, 16 Jun. Add.
Aurelianus, Ep. Arelatensis, eius Depositio Lugduni, 16 Jun.
Aurelius, M., 27 Aug.
Aurelius, eius Reliquiarum receptio, Parisiis, 20 Oct.
Ausbertus, Ep. Rotomagensis, in monast. Fontanella, 9 Feb.
Ausbertus, eius Translatio ad S. Petrum, 31 Mar.
Ausonia, M., Lugduni, 2 Jun.
Ausonius, Ep. M., 22 Mai. Add.
Austere, v. Asterius.
Austregillus, Ep. C., Biturici, 20 Mai.
Austreberta, V., in pago Rotomagensi, 10 Feb.
Austriclinianus ('Stratocliane') Pr. Lemovicis in Gallia, 30 Jun.
Austustyn, v. Augustinus, M. Nicomediæ.
Autberbtus, Ep. C., Cameraci in Gallia, 13 Dec.
Auxentius, M., 12 Dec. Add.
Aycard, abbas, 15 Sept. Add.
Ayd, 28 Feb. Add.
Aymon, 9 Oct. Add.
Azarias, in Babilonia, 16 Dec.

Babylas, Ep. M., Antiochiæ, 24 Jan.
Bacchus, M., Sergiopoli, 7 Oct.
Bacchus ('Bache'), 14 Mai. Add.
Bacchyle, Ep., 14 Apr. Add.
Balbina, filia S. Quirini, V. M., Romæ, 31 Mar.
Baldomerus, vir Dei, Lugduni, 27 Feb.
Balthazar, 6 Jan. Add.
Barala, al. Barula, puerulus M., cum S. Romano, Antiochiæ, 18 Nov.
Barbara, V. M. in Tuscia, Maximiniano Imp., 16 Dec.

Barbara, V. M. in Tuscia, *al.* Nicomediæ, 4 Dec.
Barbarian, C., 2 Jan.
Barbarius, M., 14 Mai. Add.
Barbatianus, Pr. C., 31 Dec. Add.
Barbens, 20 Nov. Add.
Barnabas, Ap., in Cypro, 11 Jun.
Barry, Ep. in Hibernia, 25 Sep. Add.
Bartholomæus, Ap. M., in India, 24 Aug.
Bartholomæus, eius Vigilia, 23 Aug.
Bartholomæus, monachus in Anglia, 24 Jun. Add.
Baruc, propheta, 1 Mai. Add.
Basileus, M., Romæ, 2 Mart.
Basileus, Ep. [M.] Antiochiæ, 22 Dec.
Basilides, M., Romæ, 10 Jun.
Basilides, miles M., Mediolani, 12 Jun.
Basilissa, abbatissa, uxor Juliani [V.] M., Antiochiæ, 9 Jan.
Basilius, eius Depositio, 1 Jan.
Basilius, Ep., Cæsareæ Cappad., eius Ordinatio, 14 Jun.
Basilius, Ep. M., in Hispania, 23 Mai.
Basilla, V. M., Romæ, 20 Mai.
Basilla, Romæ, 11 Jun.
Basolus, C. in territorio Rhemensi, 15 Oct.
Basolus, C., 26 Nov. Add.
Bassa, uxor Claudiani, cum Victore incarcerata, C., Nicomediæ, 6 Mar.
Bassianus, lector. M., Alexandriæ, 14 Feb.
Bassianus, Ep., 19 Jan. Add.
Bassus, M., Alexandriæ, 14 Feb.
Bassus, Ep., M., Nicææ, 5 Dec. Add.
Batyldis, regina, in territ. Parisiensi, 30 Jan.
Baudelius, M., Nemausi in Gallia, 20 Mai.
Bavo, C., Gandavi, 1 Oct.
Beata, V., 29 Jun. Add.
Beatrix, M., soror Faustini, M., Romæ, 29 Jul.
Beda, Pr., Doctor Venerabilis, C. in Brit. 26, *al.* 27 Mai.
Bemonus (*h.e.* Benignus, *ut in.* Add.), eius Translatio, Glastoniæ in Anglia, 27 Jun.
Bene, abbas, 5 Apr. Add.
Benedicta, religiosa femina, M., Romæ, 4 Jan.
Benedicta, V. in territorio Senonensi, 29 Jun.
Benedicta, V. M., Lugduni, 8 Oct.
Benedictus, abbas in Monte Cassino, 21 Mar.
Benedictus, eius Translatio, in monasterio Floriacensi, 14 Jul.
Benedictus, C. in pago Pictaviensi, 23 Oct.
Benedictus, papa, Romæ, 7 Mai.
Benedictus, Ep., 12 Jan. Add.
Benedictus ('Benet'), papa, 21 Mar. Add.
Benedictus, monachus, 21 Mar. Add.
Benedictus, monachus, 20 Jun. Add.
Benjamin, 25 Feb. Add.
Benigne, Pr. M., 17 Jan. Add.
Benignus, M., Tomis in Scythia, 3 Apr.
Benignus, Pr. M., in Divione Castro, 1 Nov.
Benignus, M., 6 Jun. Add.
Benignus, C., 27 Jun. Add.
Bercarus, abbas, 16 Oct. Add.
Berkarus, abbas, M., 1 Sep. Add.
Berenwaldus, Pr. M., in territorio Oxoniensi in Anglia, 21 Dec.
Bernardus, C. abbas Clarevallensis, 20 Aug.
Bernardus, eius Translatio, 17 Mai.
Berno, abbas, 22 Mar. Add.
Bernake, 7 Apr. Add.
Bernardinus, 20 Mai. Add.
Beronicus, M., Antiochiæ in Syria, 19 Oct.
Bertinus, abbas, C., in pago Tarvanensi, 5 Sep.
Bertinus, C., eius depositio, 9 Mai.
Bessia, M., Carthagine, 17 Jul.
Bet[h]urius, M., Carthagine, 17 Jul.
Bibiana ('Vivyane'), M., Romæ, 2 Dec.
Bibianus ('Julian'), Ep. C., apud Santonas, 28 Aug.
Bicor ('Bitro'), Ep. M., in Perside, 22 Apr.
Birgitta, eius Depositio, Romæ, 23 Jul.
Birgitta, eius Translatio in Sueciam, 28 Mai.
Birgitta, eius Canonizatio, 7 Oct.
Birinus, primus Ep. Dorcestriensis, C., Wintoniæ in Anglia, 3 Dec.
Birinus, eius festum aliud, 4 Sep.
Birnstatus ('Brinstane') Ep. Winton. in Anglia, 4 Nov.
Blandina, M., Lugduni, 2 Jun.
Blasius, Ep. M., apud Sebasten in Armenia, 3 Feb.
Boetius, *al.* Severinus, 27 Mai. Add.
Boetius, Ep., C., in Hibernia, 7 Dec. Add.
Bolke, 20 Feb. Add.
Bona ('Boue'), V. Rhemis, 24 Apr. Add.
Bona, *al.* Cordimunda, V., 12 Sep. Add.
Bonifacius, M., apud Tarsum, 5 Jun.; (sepultus Romæ) 14 Mai.
Bonifacius, natione anglus, Ep. M., in Frisia, 5 Jun.
Bonifacius, diac. M., in Africa, 17 Aug.
Bonifacius, C., in Africa, 6 Dec.
Bonifacius, diac., 23 Mar. Add.
Bonifacius, I., papa, 13 Mai. Add.
Bonifacius, IV., papa, 13 Mai. Add.
Bonifacius. Ep., 14 Mai. Add.
Bonifacius, Ep. Carthag., 5 Jun. Add.
Bonitus, Ep. C.,' Avernis in Gallia, 15 Jan.
Bonosa, M., in Portu Romano, 15 Jul.

Bonosus, M., 21 Aug.
Bonus, Pr. M., Romæ, 1 Aug.
Botuphus, abbas, in Britannia, 17 Jun.
Boue, *v.* Bona.
Brandanus, 14 Jun. Add.
Brandanus, abbas in Scotia (*h.e.* 'in Yrelond'), 16 Mai.
Branwallatour, Ep. C., eius translatio, 19 Jan.
Braulius, Ep., Cæsaraugustanus, 12 Nov.
Brictius ('Brythe'), Ep. C., Martulæ, ('marcull'), 9 Jul.
Bri[c]tius, Ep. C., Turonis, 13 Nov.
Brigida ('Bryde'), V., in Scotia, 1 Feb.
Brigwyne, Archiep. Cantuar., in Brit., 26 Aug. Add.
Brinstane *v.* Birnstanus.
Brithyne, abbas Beverlaci, in Brit., 15 Mai. Add.
Brydhestane (h.e. Frithstanus), Ep. C., 10 Sep.
Bythe, *v.* Brictius.
Byryne, *v.* Birinus, Ep. C.

Cæcilia, V. M., Romæ, 22 Nov.
Cæcilianus, M., Cæsaraugustæ in Hisp., 15, *al.* 16 Apr.
Cæcilius, C., in Hispania, 15 Mai.
Cærealis, miles M., Romæ, 14 Sep.
Cæsarius, Ep. C., Arelate in Galliis, 27 Aug.
Cæsarius, diac. M., Tarracinæ in Campania, 1 Nov.
Cæsarius, M. Cæsareæ in Cappad., 3 Nov.
Caius, M. Bononiæ, 4 Jan.
Caius, *al.* Gayus, Romæ, 20 Feb.
Caius, palatinus, M. demersus, 4 Mar.
Caius, M., Apamiæ in Phrygia, 10 Mar.
Caius, M., in Armenia, 19 Apr.
Caius, papa M., Romæ, 22 Apr.
Caius, hospes Pauli, apud Corinthum, 4 Oct.
Caius, miles M., Nicomediæ, 21 Oct.
Caius, Messanæ in Sicilia, 20 Nov.
Caius, Pr. C., Romæ, 22 Apr. Add.
Calapodius, *al.* Calepodius *vel* Calipodius, Pr. M., Alexandriæ, *al.* Romæ, 10 Mai.
Caleb, e xii. a Moyse missis, 1 Sep. Add.
Calixt, *v.* Callistus.
Callinicus, *male* Galericus *vel* Galenicus, M. Apolloniæ, 18, *al.* 28 Jan.
Callistus, *al.* Kalixtus, M., apud Corinthum, 16 Apr.
Callistus, *al.* Calixtus, I. papa, M., Romæ, 14 Oct.
Calocerus, eunuchus, M., Romæ, 19 Mai.
Calocerus, *vel* Calocerius ('Colotery') M., Brixiæ, 19 Mar.
Cælocery, M., Brixiæ, 15 Feb. Add.

Campanus, M., 29 Jul. Add.
Canciane, *v.* Gatianus, 18 Dec.
Candida, uxor S. Artemii, M., Romæ, 6 Jun.
Candida massa ccc Martyrum, 24 Aug.
Candida, V. (? M.), Romæ, 29 Aug.
Candidus, M., Romæ, 2 Feb.
[Candidus], inter xl. milites, Cappadox, M., apud Sebasten in Armenia, 9 Mar.
Candidus, miles, M., Sebastæ in Armenia, 11 Mar.
Candidus, senator militum, ex Thebœorum legione miles, M., Seduni in Gallia, in loco Agauno, 22 Sep.
Candidus, M., Romæ ad Ursum Pileatum, 3 Oct.
Candidus, M., 11 Mar. Add.
Canon, *v.* Conon, M.
Cantianilla, V. M., Cantianus, et Cantius, principes Aniciorum, fratres MM., Aquileiæ, 31 Mai.
Canicus ('Canuke'), abbas in Scotia, 11 Oct.
Capithon, 13 Mar. Add.
Capophorus, *v.* Carpophorus.
Caprasius, abbas in monast. Lirinensi, 1 Jun.
Caprasius, M., Agenni in Galliis, 20 Oct. (vide etiam ad 6 Oct.)
Caradoke, 13 Apr. Add.
Carannus ('Charanny'), M., Carnoti in Gallia, 28 Mai.
Carantoke, *al.* Ceruach, Hibern, 16 Mai. Add.
Caricus, M., 5 Aug. Add.
Carilefus ('Carylef'), Pr. apud Cenoman, 1 Jul.
Carilippus, M., 28 Apr.
Carisius, M., apud Corinthum, 16 Apr.
Carolus Magnus, R., 28 Jan.
Carpoforus, M., 20 Aug. Add.
Carpophorus, e quattuor coronatis, M., Romæ, 8 Nov.
Carpophorus, Pr. M., Spoleti, ('at hyspolitane'), 10 Dec.
Carpus, Ep. Thyatirensis, M., Pergami in Asia, 13 Apr.
Carpus, discip. Pauli, in Troade, 13 Oct.
Cartake, Ep. in Hibernia, 14 Mai. Add.
Carylef, *v.* Carilefus.
Casce, *v.* Castus, M.
Cassia, cum Cassio, M., Damasci, 20 Jul.
Cassiadour, 17 Mar. Add.
Cassianus, Ep. C., Augustoduni, 5 Aug.
Cassianus, M., Romæ, apud forum Syllæ, 13 Aug.
Cassianus, M., Tingitanæ in Mauritania, 3 Dec.
Cassianus, C., in Brit., 21 Jun. Add.
Cassianus (Johannes), eremita, 13 Aug. Add.

Cassius, cum Cassia, M., Damasci, 20 Jul.
Cassius, M., Veronæ, 10 Oct.
Cassius, Ep., 29 Jun. Add.
Castell, uxor Juliani, 27 Jan. Add.
Castor, M., Tarsi, in Cilicia, 28 Mar.
Castor, M., Tarsi, in Cilicia, 27 Apr.
Castor, Nicomediæ, 17 Mar.
Castor, abbas, 13 Feb. Add.
Castorius, M., Romæ, 7 Jul.
Castulus ('Castole'), M. Romæ, 26 Mar.
Castus, M., in Africa, 22 Mai.
Castus, M., Cabilone in Gallia, 4 Sep.
Castus, M., Capuæ, 6 Oct.
Cataldus, Ep., in Hibernia, 8 Mai. Add.
Catharina, V. M., 25 Nov.
Catulinus, diac., M., Carthagine, 15 Jul.
Cathedra S. Petri, Antiochiæ, 22 Feb.
Caynan, 23 Jan. Add.
Ceadda ('Chadde'), Ep. Merciorum, apud Lychefelde in Anglia, 2 Mar.
Cedde, Ep., 2 Mar. Add.
Cedony, 10 Jun. Add.
Celerina, avia Celerini, M., in Africa, 3 Feb.
Celerinus, diac. C., in Africa, 3 Feb.
Celestinus I., papa, 19 Mai. Add.
Celestinus V., papa, 19 Mai. Add.
Celestinus, monachus, 19 Mai.
Celian, Tergeste, 11 Mai. Add.
Celsus, puer, M., Antiochiæ, 9 Jan.
Celsus [puer], M., Mediolani, 12 Jun.
Celsus, puer, M., Mediolani, 28 Jul.
Cena Domini ('the Souper of our Lorde'), 24 Mar.
Censurius, Ep. C., Antisiodori, 10 Jun.
Ceran, Ep., 30 Sep. Add.
Cerealis, M., Romæ, 10 Jun.
Cerberus, M., cum Liberali, 30 Dec. Add.
Cerbonius, Ep., 17 Sep. Add.
Cerbonius, Ep., 10 Oct. Add.
Cercy, v. Tertius.
Chadde, v. Ceadda, Ep. C.
Chæremon ('Chiridon'), Ep. M., Nicopoli in Aegypto, 22 Dec.
Charitas, V. M., Romæ, 1 Aug. ; 17 Jun. Add.
Charannus, v. Carannus.
Charles, 'called Charlemayne,' v. Carolus.
Chaste, v. Castus.
Cheramon, Nicopolitanus, Ep. M., 14 Feb. Add.
Cheramonis uxor, 14 Feb. Add.
Chionia, V. M., Thessalonicæ, 3 Apr.
Chiridon, v. Chæremon.
Christela, al. Christeta ('Aristea'), M. Abulæ in Hispan. 27 Oct
Christina, V. M., Tyri in Ital., 24 Jul.
Christophorus, M., Sami in Lycia, 25 Jul.
Christophorus, monachus M., Cordubæ, 20 Aug.

Chrysanthus, Romæ, 25 Oct. (al. 29 Nov.)
Chrysanthus, M. Romæ, 1 Dec.
Chrysogonus, M. Romæ, 24 Nov.
Chrysotelus, Pr. M., Cordubæ, 22 Apr.
Chutbertus, vide Cuthbertus.
Ciaue, Ep. C., in Hibernia, 5 Mar.
Cilianus, M., 8 Jul. ; 8 Jul. Add.
Ciran, v. Tyrannio.
Circumcisio Domini, 1 Jan.
Cirice, v. Quiriacus.
Ciricus infans cum Julitta, MM., 15 Jul. Add.
Ciricus, Ep. M., ejus Translatio, 8 Aug. Add.
Cirion, et Ciryon, v. Cyrion ; Ciryke, v. Cyrinus ; Ciryne, v. Quirinus.
Cirion, miles M., apud Sebasten in Armenia, 11 Mar.
Cirinus, al. Quirinus, M., Romæ, 25 Mar.
Cirpriane, v. Cyprianus.
Ciryll, 28 Jan. Add.
Clara, V. Assisii, 12 Aug.
Clarus, Pr. M., in pago Vilcassino, 4 Nov.
Clarus, nobilis in Anglia, M. 4 Nov. Add.
Claudianus, M., apud Aegyptum, 25 Feb.
Claudianus, Nicomediæ, 6 Mar.
Claudius, conjux Præpedignæ, M., Ostiæ, 18 Feb.
Claudius, M., Romæ, 26 Apr.
Claudius, commentariensis, M., Romæ, 7 Jul.
Claudius, cum duobus fratribus, MM., Aegæeæ in Cilicia, 23 Aug.
Claudius, marmorum cæsor, M. Romæ, 8 Nov.
Claudius, tribunus, M., Romæ, 3 Dec.
Clemens, papa, M., Romæ, 23 Nov.
Clemens, Pr., Alexandriæ, 4 Dec.
Clemens, Ep. in Gallia, 23 Nov. Add.
Clementinus, M., Heracleæ in Thracia, 14 Nov.
Cleophas, discip. Christi, M., in castello Emmaus, 25 Sep.
Clerici fere cc., MM., in Perside. 22 Apr.
[Clerici] plurimi, MM., Gazæ in Palestina, 4 Mai.
[Clerici] plurimi, MM., in Palestina, 19 Sep.
Clerus, diac., M., Antiochiæ, 7 Jan.
Clerus, diac., 14 Jan.
[Clerus] ecclesiæ Carthag., C., 13 Jul.
Cletus, al. Anacletus, papa, M., Romæ, 26 Apr.
Cletus ('Anaclete') papa, Romæ, 12 Jul. Add.
Clitancus, M. regis filius in Brit. 3 Nov. Add.
Clodoaldus, [Pr.] C., 7 Sep.
Clyse, v. Dius, 12 Jul.
Codoke, 24 Jan.
Cointha, V. M., in Alexandria, 8 Feb.

Cokcydy, *v.* Cottidius.
Colman, Ep. in Hibernia, 7 Jun. Add.
Colmavell [= Colmanel], abbas in Hibernia, 26 Sep. Add.
Colomannus ('Colonare'), Pr. M. Herbipoli in Germania, 8 Jul. ; ('Colonate'), 8 Jul. Add.
Coloterius, M. Brixiæ, 19 Mar.
Columba, V. M., apud Senones, 31 Dec.
Columba ('Columbane'), Pr. C., in Scotia, 9 Jun.
Columbanus, abbas in monast. Bobio in Ital., 21 Nov.
Columbanus alter consanguineus, 21 Nov. Add.
Columbanus, in Italia, 23 Nov.
Columbina, *v.* Columba, V. M.
Columbus, abbas, 13 Dec. Add.
Commemoratio Omnium Fidelium Defunctorum, 2 Nov.
Conace, *v.* Totnanus, M., 8 Jul.
Concordia, nutrix S. Hippolyti, M., Romæ, 13 Aug.
Condedius, C., in monast. Fontanellensi, 21 Oct.
Concordius, Pr. M., Spoleti in Tuscia, 1 Jan.
Confessores (*al.* Martyres), fere 500 cum S. Eugenio in Africa, 10 *al.* 13 Jul.
Confessores (*al.* MM.), 4976, in Africa, 12 Oct.
Confessores alii (tres) cum S. Dionysia, in Africa, 6 Dec.
Congallus, abbas in Hibernia, 10 Mai. Add.
Conon, *al.* Canon, 29 Mai.
Consanguinei duo D.N.J.C., 5 Jan. Add.
Consortia, V., in monast. Cluniacensi, 22 Jun.
Constant, abbas, 14 Nov. Add.
Constantia, M., Nuceriæ, 19 Sep.
Constantinus, Ep. apud Vapingum, 12 Apr.
Constantinus, e septem dormientibus, M., Ephesi, 27 Jul.
Constantinus, Imp., 21 Mai. Add.
Constantius, C., 23 Sep. Add.
Constantius, Ep., 23 Sep. Add.
Corbinianus, Ep. [Frisingensis], 8 Sep. Add.
Cordianus ('Gordiane'), M., Nividuni, 17 Sep.
Corentinus ('Thoremyny'), Ep., 1 Mai.
Coreode, *v.* Curcodomus.
Cornelius centurio, Ep., Cæsareæ, 2 Feb.
Cornelius, papa M., Romæ, 14 Sep.
Corona, V., 24 Apr.
Corona, M., in Syria, 14 Mai.
Corona Domini, 11 Aug. Add.
Coronati Quatuor Fratres, MM. (Severus, Severianus, Carpophorus et Victorianus) Romæ, 8 Nov.

Corporis Christi Festum per Urbanum IV. Papam A.D. 1263, institutum. Quo in anno Feria Quinta post Dominicam Trinitatis occurrit die 25 Mai. Add.
Corsicus, Pr. in Italia, 30 Jun.
Corsy, M., 29 Jul. Add.
Corygenes, M., 29 Jul. Add.
Cosman, C. in deserto, 2 Sep. Add.
Cosmare, *v.* Ursmarus, 19 Apr.
Cosmas, M., frater Damiani. Aegææ, 27 Sep.
Cottidius, diaconus, Reatinæ, in Cappadocia, 6 Sep.
Coynt, V. M., *v.* Cointha, 8 Feb.
Craton, M., Romæ, 15 Feb.
Credane, abbas, 20 Aug. Add.
Crescence, Pr., 23 Mar. Add.
Crescens, discip. S. Pauli, Ep., Galatiæ, 27 Jun. [Viennæ, 29 Dec.]
Crescens, filius Symphorosæ, M., Tibure, 27 Jun.
Crescentia, M. in Lucania, 15 Jun.
Crescentianus, M., Turribus Sardiniæ, 31 Maii.
Crescentianus, C., in Africa, 13 Jun.
Crescentianus, M., in Africa, cum S. Cypriano, 14 Sep.
Crescentianus, M., in Campania, 2 Jul.
Crescentiane, *v.* Crescentio.
Crescentianus, M., Romæ, 24 Nov.
Crescentianus, M., Augustæ, 5 Aug. Add.
Crescentio ('Crescentiane'), M., Romæ, 17 Sep.
Crescentius ('Crescente'), M., Tomis in Ponto, 1 Oct.
Crispina, V.M., Thebeste, in Africa, 5 Dec.
Crispinianus, nobilis, M., Suessione in Gallia, 25 Oct.
Crispinus, nobilis, M., Suessione in Gallia, 25 Oct.
Crispinus, Ep. M., in civitate Astiagensi ('Agens'), 19 Nov.
Crispulus, M., Turribus Sardiniæ, 30 Mai.
Crispus, Pr. [sicut] M., Romæ, 18 Aug.
Crispus, apud Corinthum, 4 Oct.
Cromatius, pater Tiburtii, M., 11 Aug. Add.
Cromatius, Ep., 11 Aug. Add.
Crowne *v.* Corona, M.
Crucifixio Domini nostri Jesu Christi Jerosolymis, 25 Mar.
S. Crucis Inventio, Jerosolymis, 3 Mai.
S. Crucis Exaltatio, Jerosolymis, 14 Sep.
Ctesiphon ('Thesifon'), C. in Hispania, 15 Mai.
Cucufas, M., Barcinone in Hisp., 25 Jul.
Cunibertus ('Cumbert'), Ep. C. (*al.* M.) Coloniæ, 12 Nov.
Cunigunda ('Cungund'), Imperatrix, 14 Jul. Add.

Curcodomus ('Coreode'), diaconus, Antisiodori, 4 Mai.
Cuthbertus, Ep. Lindisfarnensis in Brit., 20 Mar.
Cuthbertus, eius Translatio, 4 Sep.
Cutburga, V., 31 Aug.
Cyprianus ('Cirpriane'). Ep. M., Carthagine, 8 Mar.
Cyprianus, abbas, Petragoricis in Gallia, 9 Dec.
Cyprianus, Ep. M., Carthagine, 14 Sep.
Cyprianus, Ep. M., Romæ, 26 Sep.
Cyprianus, Pr. (al. Ep.) in Africa, 12 Oct.
Cyriacus, v. Quiriacus, Ep. M.
Cyriacus, M., Malacæ in Hispania, 18 Jun.
Cyriacus, M., Tomis in Ponto, 20 Jun.
Cyriacus, al. Quiriacus, M. in Africa, 21 Jun.
Cyriacus, diac., M., Romæ, 16 Mar.
Cyriacus, eius Translatio, Romæ, 8 Aug.
Cyricus, filius Julittæ, M., Antiochiæ, 16 Jun.
Cyrilla, filia Decii imp. V. M., Romæ, 28 Oct.
Cyrillus, M., in Syria, 20 Mar.
Cyrillus, Ep. Alexandriæ, 28 Jan.
Cyrillus, Ep. M., Gortynæ in Creta, 9 Jul.
Cyrillus, M., Philadelphiæ in Arabia, 1 Aug.
Cyrillus, diac, M., 9 Jul. Add.
Cyrinus ('Ciryke'), M. in Hellesponto, 3 Jan.
Cyrinus, miles M., Romæ, al. Mediolani, 12 Jun.
Cyrion, al. Ciryon, Pr. M., 14 Feb.
Cyrion, al. Cirion, inter xl. milites, Cappadox, M., apud Sebasten in Armenia, 9, al. 11 Mar.
Cyrus cum Johanne, M., 31 Jan.
Cythinus ('Stytyny'), Scillitanus M., Karthagine, 17 Jul.

Dacy, v. Dasius.
Dacius, Ep. Mediolan., 19 Jun. Add.
Dafrosa, uxor S. Fabiani, M., Romæ, 4 Jan.
Dalmatius, Ep. M., Papiæ in Italia, 5 Dec.
Dalmatyke, M. in Italia, v. Dalmatius.
Damasus, papa, C., Romæ, 11 Dec.
Damianus, frater S. Cosmæ, M., 27 Sep.
Daniel, propheta, 21 Jul. ; 28 Aug. Add.
Daniel, diac. M., in Padua, 3 Jan. Add.
Daniel, abbas in Egypto, 21 Jul. Add.
Daria, uxor S. Chrysanthi, M., Romæ, 25 Oct.
Daria, Romæ, 29 Nov.
Daria, V. M., Romæ, 1 Dec.
Darius, M., Nicææ, 19 Dec.
Dasius ('Dacy') miles M., Nicomediæ, 21 Oct.
Dativa, C., in Africa, 6 Dec.

Dativus ('Datyve') M., in Africa, 11, al. 12 Feb.
Dativus, M., al. Ep. C., in Africa, 10 Sep.
David, Archiep. C., in Britannia quæ hodie Wallia nuncupatur, 1 Mar.
David, R., 29 Dec. ; propheta, Hierosolymis, 29 Dec. Add.
David, dux xxx latronum, monachus, 29 Dec. Add.
Daygens, C., in Hibernia, 18 Aug. Add.
Debbora, prophetissa, 1 Sep. Add.
Dedicatio Ecclesiæ Sarisburiensis, 30 Sep.
Dedicatio Ecclesiæ S. Pauli Londinensis, 1 Oct.
Demetria, V.M., Romæ, 21 Jun.
Defunctorum Omnium Fidelium Commemoratio, 2 Nov.
Deicolus, abbas, 18 Jan. Add.
Demetrius, M., Thessalonicæ, 8 Oct.
Demetrius cum sociis, Ep. M., Antiochiæ, 10 Nov.
Demetrius, M., apud Ostia Tiberina, 21 Nov.
Demetrius, M., Ostiæ, al. Antiochiæ, 22 Dec.
Demetrius, nobilis, M., 25 Oct. Add.
Demetrius, v. Mitrius.
Denys, v. Dionysius.
Deodatus, abbas, 24 Apr. Add.
Deodorike, Ep., 1 Apr. Add.
Desiderius, Ep. M., apud Lugdunum, 11 Feb.
Desiderius, eius Translatio, Viennæ, 23 Mai.
Desiderius, Ep. M., apud Lingones, 23 Mai.
Desiderius, lector, M., Neapoli in Campania, al. Puteolis, 19 Sep.
Desiderius, Ep. M., Lugduni Gall., 23 Mai. Add.
Desyre, v. Desiderius, Ep. M., 11 Feb., et 23 Mai.
Deusdedit, Archiep. Cantuariensis, in Britannia, 15 Jul.
Dewtrey, v. Demetrius M., 22 Dec.
Didius, v. Dius, M. Alexandriæ, 28 Apr.
Didymus (cum S. Theodora), M., Alexandriæ, 28 Apr.
Digna, discip. S. Afræ, ancilla, M. Augustæ Vindelicorum, 12 Aug.
Diocles ('Dyod'), M., in Istria, 24 Mai.
Diocles, 12 Mar. Add.
Diodole, v. Theodulus, M.
Diodorus, Pr. M., Romæ, 1 Dec.
Diodorus, Ep. C., 1 Dec. Add.
Diogenes, M., in Macedonia, 6 Apr.
Diogenes, 10 Apr. Add.
Diomedes, Nicææ, 9 Jun.
Diomedes, M., Augustæ, 5 Aug. Add.
Dionysia, M., Lampsaci, 15 Mai.
Dionysia, C., in Africa, 6 Dec.

INDEX SANCTORUM. 247

[Dionysia], M. (in Martyrologio Romano nominata, cum Ammonaria) Alexandriæ, 12 Dec.
Dionysius, M., in Armenia minore, 8 Feb.
Dionysius, M., Aquileiæ, 16 Mar.
Dionysius, Ep., Corinthi, 8 Apr.
Dionysius, frater Ammonii, M., Alexandriæ, 14 Feb.
Dionysii et sociorum eius Inventio, 22 Apr.
Dionysius, patruus, *al.* pater, Pancratii, C. *al.* M., Romæ, 12 Mai.
Dionysius, e septem dormientibus, M., Ephesi, 27 Jul.
Dionysius, Ep. C., Mediolani, 25 Mai.
Dionysius, C., 10 Sep.
Dionysius Areopagita, Ep. M., Athenis, *al.* Romæ, 3 Oct.
Dionysius Areopagita, Ep. M., Parisiis, 9 Oct.
Dionysius, Ep. C., Alexandriæ, 17 Nov.
Dionysius, papa, Romæ, 26, *al.* 27 Dec.
Dionysius, M. Romæ, 25 Aug.
Dionysius, M. in Frisia, *al.* Phrygia, 20 Sep.
Dionysius, miles, M., 14 Mai. Add.
Dionysius, M., 29 Jul. Add.
Dionysius, Ep., discipulus S. Thomæ, 21 Dec. Add.
Dioscorus, M., apud Aegyptum, 25 Feb.
Dioscorus, lector, M., in Aegypto, 18 Mai.
Dioscorus, puerulus, M., Alexandriæ, 14 Dec.
Dioscour, abbas, 9 Apr. Add.
Discipuli lxxii, 15 Jul. Add.
Divisio apostolorum xii., 15 Jul. Add.
Dius, *al.* Didius, M., Alexandriæ, 26 Nov.
Dius ('Clyse'), C. Cæsareæ, 12 Jul.
Dode, V., 24 Apr. Add.
Dominicus, C,, eius Depositio, Bononiæ, 4 *al.* 5 Aug.
Dominicus, eius Translatio, Bononiæ, 24 Mai.
Dominicus, M., 21 Jun. Add.
Domitianus, abbas in territ. Lugdun., 1 Jul.
Domitianus, M. Philadelphiæ in Arabia, 1 Aug.
Domitianus, Diaconus, M., Ancyræ in Galatia, 28 Dec.
Domitilla, Flavia, V.M., Tarracinæ in Campania, 7 Mai.
Domitius M., in Syria, 5 Jul.
Domna ('Domnyne'), cum sociis, V.M., Interamnis, 14 Apr.
Domninus, M. Thessalonicæ, 30 Mar.
Domninus, cum Marcellino et Vincentio, Ebreduni in Galliis, 20 Apr.
Domninus, M. apud Juliam in territorio Parmensi, 9 Oct.

Dom[n]ion, Ep. M., Salonæ in Dalmatia, 11 Apr.
Dompne, Ep., 21 Jan. Add.
Donata, M., Carthagine, 17 Jul.
Donatianus, M. Nannete in Galliis, 24 Mai.
Donatianus, Ep. M., *al.* C. in Africa, 6 Sep.
Donatilla, V.M., Tuburbi, in Africa, 30 Jul.
Donate, M. Carthagine, 1 Mar.
Donatus, M., Concordiæ, *al.* Cordubae, 17 Feb.
Donatus, M., Romæ, 4 Feb.
Donatus, M., in Africa, 7 Apr.
Donatus, M., 14 Jul.
Donatus, M., Cæsareæ Cappadociæ, 21 Mai.
Donatus, Ep. M., Aretii in Tuscia, 7 Aug.
Donatus, Pr. C., Sigisterici in Galliis, 19 Aug.
Donatus, M., Antiochiæ, 23 Aug.
Donatus, M., Capuæ, 5 Sep.
Donatus, M., 12 Dec.
Donatus, M. cum Mansueto, Alexandriæ, 30 Dec.
Donatus, Ep. C., 7 Aug. Add.
Donuina ('Dominyne'), M., 23 Aug.
Dormientes Septem, MM., Ephesi, 27 Jun. *al.* Jul.
Dorothe, V., 6 Feb. Add.
Dorothea, V. M., 3 Sep. Add.
Dorothea, V. M., Cæsareæ Cappadoc., 6 Feb.
Dorothene, *v.* Droctoveus, abbas.
Dorotheus, M., Tarsi in Cilicia, 28 Mar.
Dorotheus, præpositus cubiculi regii, M., Nicomediæ, 9 Sep.
Dorythy ('Sythe'), 15 Jan. Add.
Droctoveus ('Dorothene'), abbas Lutetiæ Parisiorum, 10 Mar.
Drusus, M., Antiochiæ, 14 Dec.
Dubritius, Ep. Landavensis, 14 Nov. Add.
Dula, *al.* Theola, ancilla, V. M., Nicomediæ, 25 Mar.
Dunstanus, Archiep. Cantuariensis, 19 Mai; 7 Sept. Add. ; ejus Ordinatio, 21 Oct. Add.
Dydake, Ep., 2 Apr. Add.
Dyod, *v.* Diocles.
Dysmas, C., 25 Mar. Add.

Eanswida, V. in Brit., 31 Aug. Add.
Eadburga. V. in Anglia, 15 Jun.
Eadburga, V., 18 Jul.
Ebba, V. abbatissa, 25 Aug. Add.
Ebba, nobilis, 25 Aug. Add.
Ebrulphus, abbas, C., in pago Oximensi ('Oxforde'), 29 Dec.
Edburt, R., 25 Aug. Add.

Eddune, Pr. M., *al.* Egdunius, 12 Mar.
Edeltrudis ('Audry'), V. in Brit., 23 Jun.
Edilburga, *v.* Ethelburga.
Edisteus, M. Ravennæ, 12 Oct.
Editha, filia Edgari regis, V., Wiltoniæ ('at Wynchester'), 16 Sep.
Edithæ translatio, 3 Nov.
Edmundus, Archiep. Cantuar., eius Translatio in Anglia, 9 Jun.
Edmundus, ejus depositio, Pontiniaci, 16 Nov.
Edmundus, R. M., in Anglia, 29 Apr. ; 20 Nov. Add.
Edwoldus, frater Edmundi R. M., 29 Aug. Add.
Edwardus, R. C., in Anglia, 5 Jan.
Edwardus, ejus translatio, 13 Oct.
Edwardus, R. M., ejus translatio, 13 Feb.
Edwardus, ejus adventus de Perham (Wareham) in Shaftoniam, 18 Feb.
Edwardus, ejus passio, 18 Mar.
Edwardus, ejus translatio, 20 Jun.
Edwoldus, R. M., frater Edmundi, R. M., 29 Aug. Add.
Edwyne, R. M., 12 Oct. Add.
Effam, V. M., 3 Sep. Add.
Effraim, filius Joseph, 5 Feb. Add.
Effrem, *al.* Ephræmus, Edissenæ Eccl. Diaconus, 1 Feb.
Egbertus, 24 Apr. Add.
Egesippus ('Jesyppe'), 7 Apr.
Egwinus ('Ewgyne'), Ep. Wigorn., 30 Dec. Add.
Eiladius, Ep., 31 Aug.
Eiulasius, *v.* Evilasius.
Eldade (*al.* Aldate), Glocestriæ, 4 Feb.
Eleazarus cum filiis, MM., Lugduni Galliæ, 22 *al.* 23 Aug.
Eleazar sacerdos, 1 Jul. Add.
Eleazar, M., tempore Machabæorum, 1 Oct. Add.
Elene (Elgiva?), 18 Mai.
Eleusippus, M., apud Lingonas, 17 Jan.
Eleutherius, *v.* Eutherius, Ep., Tornaci.
Eleutherius, Ep. M., apud Messanam Apuliæ, 18 Apr.
Eleutherius, papa M., Romæ, 25 *al.* 26 Mai.
Eleutherius, abbas, *vel* Ep. C., Romæ, 6 Sep.
Eleutherius, miles M. Nicomediæ. 2 Oct.
Eleutherius, Diac *al.* Pr. M., Parisiis, 9 Oct.
Eleutherius, Ep., 26 Aug. Add.
Elfleda, V. 23 Oct. ; 29 Oct. Add.
Elias, Pr., Cordubæ, 17 Apr.
Eligius, Ep. C., Noviomensis, 1 Dec.
Elisabetha, matrona, 19 Nov.; 19 Nov. Add.
Elizabeth, mater Johannis Præcursoris, 5 Nov. Add.

Elizabeth, Sconaugiæ, V., 17 Jun., Add.
Elizabeth, V., 23 Jun. Add.
Ellad. *v.* Helladius, Ep.
Elisæus, proph. apud Samariam, 14 Jun.
Elphegus ('Alphege'), Ep. Winton. in Anglia, 12 Mar.
Elphegius, Archiep. M., Cantuariæ, in Anglia, 19 Apr. *al.* 28 Dec.
Elpidius ('Helpedy'), Ep. C., Lugduni, 2 Sep.
Emerentiana, V. M., Romæ, 23 Jan.
Emitherius, *vide* Hemitherius.
Emmeramus ('Hamptran'). Ep. M., Ratisponæ, 22 Sep.
Emygdy, Ep. M., 5 Aug. Add.
Enuthere, *vide* Hemitherius.
Enock, 23 Jan. Add.
Enos, 23 Jan. Add.
Eobanus ('Eobanke'), Ep. M., in Frisia, 5 Jun.
Epagathus, M. Lugduni in Gallia, 2 Jun.
Epaphras, Ep. M., Colossis, 19 Jul.
Epaphroditus ('Affrodose'), discipulus S. Pauli, Ep., Tarracinæ, 22 Mar.
Eparchius, abbas C., Engolismæ, 1 Jul.
Ephigena, abbatissa in Egypto, 21 Sep. Add.
Epimachus M., Alexandriæ, 12 Dec. Add.
Ephræm, diac., Edessenus, 1 Feb.
Epictetus ('Epute'), peregrinus M., in Portu Romano, 22 Aug.
Epimachus, M., Romæ, 10 Mai.
Epion, Pr. C., apud Bituricenses, 12 Oct.
Epiphania Domini, 6 Jan.
Epiphaniæ Octava, 13 Jan.
Epiphaniæ Vigilia, 5 Jan.
Epiphanius, Ep. Salaminæ in Cypro, 12 Mai.
Epiphanius, Ep. M., in Africa, 7 Apr.
Epipodius, M., Lugduni in Gallia, 22 Apr.
Epitacius ('Thyke'), Ep. M., in Hispania, 23 Mai.
[Episcopi Septem] cum Nemesiano et Felice, in Africa, 10 Sep.
Epolonius, puer M., cum S. Babila, Antiochiæ, 24 Jan.
Erade, *v.* Heracles.
Eraclius, Ep. C., 14 Nov.
Eracly, *v.* Heraclius, M.
Erasma, V. M., 3 Sep. Add.
Erasmus, Ep. M., in Campania, 3 Jun.
Erasmus, M., Antiochiæ, 25 Nov.
Erastus, Ep. M., Philippis, 26 Jul.
Erblandy, abbas, 18 Oct. Add.
Ercley, *v.* Heraclea, M.
Erculane, *v.* Herculanus.
Erculane, eius Translatio, 14 Nov.
Erhard, Ep., 8 Jan. Add.
Erkengoda, V., filia ('sister') S. Sexburgæ, 7 Jul. Add.

INDEX SANCTORUM. 249

Erkenwaldus, Ep. Londin., 30 Apr. ; 14 Nov.
Ermagory, v. Hermagoras.
Ermenyld, nobilis V., in Britannia, 13 Feb.
Ermete, v. Hermes, M.
Erminygyld, v. Herminigildus, R. M.
Erynbaldus, judex, 10 Dec. Add.
Esaias, propheta, in Judæa, 6 Jul.
Esclepiady, v. Asclepias.
Esdras, propheta, 13 Jul.
Esichy, v. Hesychius, 18 Nov.
Esicy, v. Hesychius, 15 Mai.
Esitius ('Esicy') in Hispania, 15 Mai.
Esterwyne, Abbas, 7 Mar. Add.
Esychius, vide Hesychius.
Ethebyne, in Hibernia, 19 Oct. Add.
Ethelburga ('Alborowe,') V., soror S. Etheldredæ, 7 Jul.
Ethelburga, V., 11 Oct.
Ethelbryght, M., apud Ramsey, 17 Oct. Add.
Etheldreda, Regina V., in Britannia, 23 Jun.
Etheldreda, eius Translatio, 17 Oct.
Ethelred, M., apud Ramsey, 17 Oct. Add.
Ethelwoldus, C., 12 Aug.
Euagrius, Ep. M., Tomis in Scythia, 3 Apr.
Euagrius, M. Tomis in Ponto, 1 Oct.
Euagrye, 3 Apr. Add.
Euanthe, mater Liberalis, M., 30 Dec. Add.
Euaristus, papa, M., Romæ, 27 Oct. ; 26 Oct. Add.
Eubrachius, C., 10 Oct.
Eucherius, Ep. C., Lugdunensis, 16 Nov.
Eudelme, V., 18 Feb. Add.
Eve, 23 Jan. Add.
Eventius, v. Juventius.
Euentius, Pr. M., Romæ, 3 Mai.
Euentius, discip. Hermagoræ, C., Ticini sive Papiæ, 12 Sep.
Euentius, nobilis in Hispania, 12 Sep. Add.
Eufeme, Eufrase, &c. v. Euph—.
Eufrose, v. Aphrodisius, Ep.
Eugendus ('Augend,') abbas, 1 Jan.
Eugence, v. Eugentus, M.
Eugenia, abbatissa, V. M., Romæ, 25 Dec.
Eugenianus, M., Augustoduni, 8 Jan.
Eugenius, Nicomediæ, 17 Mar.
Eugenius, M., in Syria, 20 Mar.
Eugenius, M., Neocæsareæ, 24 Jan.
Eugenius, Ep. C. exulatus (al. M.), Carthagine, 13 Jul.
Eugenius ('Eugyn,') Symphorosæ F., M., Tibure, 27 Jun.
Eugenius, Ep. C. Toleti, 13 Nov.
Eugenius, Ep. Toletan., M. 15 Nov.
Eugenius, barbarus, R. M., 29 Jul. Add.
Eugenius, abbas, Ep., in Hibernia, 23 Aug. Add.
Eugenius, Ep. Cæsariens., discip. Origenis, 15 Nov. Add.
Eugenius, M., 12 Dec. Add.
Eugentus, M., in Africa, 4 Jan.
Eukare, Ep. Aurelianensis. 20 Feb. Add.
Evilasius, al. Ejulasius, judex, M., 20 Sep.
Eulalia, V. M., Barcinonæ, 12 Feb.
Eulalia, V. M., Emeritæ in Hisp., 10 Dec.
Eulether, v. Eleutherius, Ep. M.
Eulogius, diac. M., Tarraconæ in Hisp., 21 Jan.
Eulogius, C., Constantinopoli, 3 Jul.
Eulogius, M., Constantinopoli, 11 Jul. Add.
Eulogius, 11 Jul. Add.
Eulogus, Pr. M., Cordubæ, 20 Sep,
Eumenia, discip. S. Afræ, ancilla, M., Augustæ Vindelicorum, 12 Aug.
Eunomia, v. Eumenia, ancilla M.
Eunus, famulus, M., Alexandriæ, 27 Feb.
Evodius, M., Syracusis, 25 Apr.
Euodius, Ep. M., Antiochiæ, 6 Mai.
Euodius, M., Nicææ in Bithynia, 2 Aug.
Euphronius, C., 3 Aug. Add.
Evortius, al. Evurtius, Ep. C., Aurelianis, 7 Sep.
Euote, al. Eventius, ex xviii. Martt., Cæsaraugustæ, 16 Apr.
Euphemia, ('Eufeme called Effam') V. M., 13 Apr.
Euphemia, V. M., Chalcedone, 16 Sep.
Euphrasia, V., in Thebaide, 13 Mar.
Euphrasia, V., Alexandriæ, 11 Feb.
Euphrasius, Ep. in Africa, 14 Jan.
Euphrasius, Ep. C., in Hispania, 15 Mai.,
Euphrosyna, V., Alexandriæ, 1 Jan.
Euplus, diac. M. Catanæ in Sicilia, 12 Aug.
Euprepia, discip. S. Afræ, ancilla, M., Augustæ Vindelicorum, 12 Aug.
Euprepius, frater SS. Cosmæ et Damiani, M., Aegææ, 27 Sep.
Eusebius, palatinus, M., 5 Mar.
Eusebius, Adrianopoli in Thracia, 22 Oct.
Eusebius, M., 28 Apr.
Eusebius, Ep. Samosatensis, Cæsareæ Cappadociæ, 21 Jun.
Eusebius, Ep. M., Vercellis, 1 Aug.
Eusebius, Pr. C., Romæ, 14 Aug.
Eusebius, M., Romæ, 25 Aug.
Eusebius (papa), Ep. C., Romæ, 26 Sep.
Eusebius, M., Hadrianopoli in Thracia, 22 Oct.
Eusebius, monach., M., Tarracinæ in Campania, 5 Nov.
Eusebius, 31 Mar. Add.
Eusebius, Ep., 15 Aug. Add.
Eusebius, abbas, 15 Aug. Add.
Eusebius, papa, Romæ, 6 Oct. Add.
Eustace, abbas Luxoviensis, 2 Apr.
Eustace, eius Depositio, 29 Mar.
Eustachius, Ep. C., 16 Jul.
Eustachius, Pr. C., in Syria, 12 Oct.
Eustachius M., Romæ, 2 Nov.

Eustachius, abbas, 11 Oct. Add,
Eustachius, Ep. Antiochiæ, 11 Oct. Add.
Eustasius, Luxaviensis abbas, 29 Mar.
Eustochia, V. M., 2 Nov. Add.
Eustochium, abbatissa, 2 Nov. Add.
Eustochius, Ep., Turonis, 19 Sep.
Eustorgius, Pr., Nicomediæ, 11 Apr.
Eustosius, M., Antiochiæ, 10 Nov.
Eustratius, M., 12 Dec. Add.
Eutheme, v. Euthymius.
Euthere, v. Eucherius, Ep. C.
Euthery, Ep. Tornacensis C. in territ. Aspan., 27 Mar.
Euthymius ('Eutheme'), diac. Alexandriæ, 5 Mai.
Eutropes, Ep. M., Santonis in Gallia, 30 Apr.
Eutropia, soror S. Nicasii, M., Rhemis, 14 Dec.
Eutropius, Ep., Arausicæ in Galliis, 27 Mai.
Eutropius, M., in Portu Romano, 15 Jul.
Eutyches ('Euticete'), M., in Italia, 15 Apr.
Eutyches, laicus, M., Puteolis, 19 Sep.
Eutychianus, M., in Campania, 2 Jul.
Eutychianus, M., in Africa, 12 al. 13 Nov.
Eutychianus, papa, M., Romæ, 8 Dec.
Eutychianus, C., 8 Dec. Add.
Eutychius ('Euthyke'), diac. M., Cæsareæ in Mauritania, 21 Mai.
Eutychius, M., in Thracia, 29 Sep.
Eutychius, M., Messanæ in Sicilia, 5 Oct.
Eutychius ('Ewtyke'), nobilis, in Hispania, 11 Dec.
Eutychius, Pr. M., Ancyræ in Galatia, 28 Dec.
Eutychius, M., 4 Jun.
Eutychius ('Ewticy'), abbas, 28 Dec. Add.
Eutymy, 31 Mar. Add.
Ewaldi Duo, Presbyteri MM., in Saxonia, 3 Oct.
Ewlodia, v. Alodia.
Ewyne, Regina, 21 Dec.
Expeditus, M., Militanæ in Armenia, 19 Apr.
Exuperantius, diac. M., Spoleti, 30 Dec.
Exuperia, cum Symphronio, &c., M., Romæ, 26 Jul.
Exuperius, ex legione Thebæorum, M., Seduni in Galliis, 22 Sep.
Exuperius, Ep. C., Tolosæ, 28 Sep.
Exuperius, M. Viennæ, 19 Nov.
Exuper, Ep. C., 1 Aug. Add.
Ezechias, R., Jerosolymis, 24 Jun. Add.
Ezechiel, propheta, in sepulchro Sem et Arphaxat in Babilonia, Apr. 10.

Fabianus, papa M., Romæ, 20 Jan.

Fabian, M., 28 Jan. Add.
Fabius ('Fabiane'), M., Cæsareæ, 31 Jul.
Falek, 28 Jan. Add.
Fandila, Pr. M. Cordubæ, 13 Jun.
Fantinus, C., 31 Jul. Add.
Fare, v. Phara, V.
Faro, al. Pharao, Ep. Ambianensis, C., Meldis, 28 Oct.
Fausta, V. M., Cyzici in Propontide, 20 Sep.
Faust, Abbas, 16 Jan. Add.
Fauster, al. Saturninus, M., ex xviii Martt., Cæsaraugustæ, 16 Apr.
Fawster, Foster ('Sawster'), v. Vedastus.
Faustina, imperatrix, M., Alexandriæ, 23 Nov. Add.
Faustinus, M., Brixiæ, 15 Feb.
Faustinus, M., Romæ, 29 Jul.
Faustinus ('Sawstyne'), M., Romæ, 22 Mai.
Faustinus, C., Alexandriæ, 17 Nov.
Faustinus, alias Faustus, M., Mediolani, 7 Aug.
Faustus, M., Romæ, 24 Jun.
Faustus, M., Romæ, 1 Aug.
Faustus, al. Faustinus, Antiochiæ, 8 Sep.
Faustus, M., Cordubæ in Hisp., 13 Oct.
Faustus, diac. Alexandrinus, M., 19 Nov.
Faustus, Pr. M., Alexandriæ, 26 Nov.
Fayth, v. Fides, V.
Fekyne, 20 Jan. Add.
Felicianus, M., Romæ, 2 Feb.
Felicianus, M., Romæ, 9 Jun.
Felicianus, miles M., Massiliæ in Galliis, 21 Jul.
Felicianus, M., in Lucania, 29 Oct.
Felicianus, M., Viennæ, 19 Nov.
Felicissima, V. M. Falari in Piceno, 12 Aug.
Felicissimus, Tuderti in Tuscia, 26 Mai.
Felicissimus, M. in Campania, 2 Jul.
Felicissimus, diac. M., Romæ, 6 Aug.
Felicissimus, M., in Africa, 26 Oct.
Felicissimus, C. (al. M.) Perusiæ in Tuscia, 24 Nov.
Felicitas, M., Tuburbi in Mauritania, 7 Mar.
Felicitas, cum filiis vii Martt., Romæ, 23 Nov.
Felicula, M., Romæ, 14 Feb.
Felicula, V. M., Romæ, 13 Jun.
Felix, M. in Africa, 11 al. 12 Feb.
Felix, Ep. C. in Anglia Orientali, 8 Mar.
Felix, M., Aquileiæ, 16 Mar.
Felix, M. in civitate Heraclea, 7 Jan.
Felix, Pr. M., Nolæ in Campania, 14 Jan.
Felix, C. (frater Felicis M.), Nolæ in Camp., 14 Jan.
Felix, M., Cæsaraugustæ in Hisp., ex xviii Martt., 15 al. 16 Apr.
Felix, M., Alexandriæ, 21 Apr.
Felix, Pr., Valentiæ in Galliis, 23 Apr.

INDEX SANCTORUM. 251

Felix, Ep. M., Spoleti, 18 Mai.
Felix, papa M., Romæ, 30 Mai.
Felix, M., in Istria, 24 Mai.
Felix, M., in Sardinia, 28 Mai.
Felix, M., Aquileiæ, 11 Jun.
Felix, Pr. M. [S]utrii in Tuscia, 23 Jun.
Felix, M. in Campania, 2 Jul.
Felix, Filius sanctæ Felicitatis, M. Romæ, 10 Jul.
Felix, M., in Africa, 10 Jul.
Felix, M., Carthagine, 17 Jul.
Felix, papa M., Romæ, 29 Jul.
Felix, M., Gerundæ in Hisp., 1 Aug.
Felix, cum sociis, peregrinus, MM. in Portu Romano, 22 Aug.
Felix, Ep., Nolæ, 27 Aug.
Felix, Pr. M., Romæ, 30 Aug.
Felix, M. (al. C.) in Africa, 10 Sep.
Felix, alter, Ep. M. (al. C.), in Africa, 10 Sep.
Felix, M., Nuceriæ, 19 Sep.
Felix, M., Augustoduni, 24 Sep.
Felix, Pr. (al. Ep.) M., in Africa, 12 Oct.
Felix, Ep. M., Venusiæ in Apulia, 24 Oct.
Felix, M., Lutetiæ Parisiorum, 28 Oct.
Felix, Pr. M., Tarracinæ in Campania, 5 Nov.
Felix, M., Tonizæ in Africa, 6 Nov.
Felix, Ep. M., Nolæ, in Campania, 15 Nov.
Felix, Ep. Romæ, 22 al. 30 Dec.
Felix, 14 Jan. Add.
Felix, Ep. M., 16 Jan. Add.
Felix, M., 14 Mai. Add.
Felix, M., 17 Mai. Add.
Felix, M., 12 Jul. Add.
Felix, Pr. C., Nolæ, 31 Aug. Add.
Felix, monachus, 6 Nov. Add.
Felix III, papa, 30 Dec. Add.
Fenan, Ep., 8 Mar. Add.
Ferreolus, Pr. M., Vesontione, 16 Jun.
Ferreolus, tribunus, M., Viennæ, 18 Sep.
Ferreolus, 27 Jan. Add.
Ferrutio, diac. M., Vesontione, 16 Jun.
Festus, diac. M., Neapoli (al. Puteolis) in Campania, 19 Sep.
Festus, in Tuscia, 21 Dec.
Fetyke, Ep. C., 14 Apr. Add.
Fiagry, 11 Apr. Add.
Fiagry, v. Syagrius, Ep. C.
Fidelis, 16 Mai. Add.
Fidentius, Ep. M. 16 Nov. Add.
Fides, filia S. Sapientiæ, V.M., Romæ, 1 Aug.; 17 Jun. Add.
Fides, V. M., Agenni in Galliis, 6 Oct.
Fides, eius Translatio, 14 Jan.
Filiaster, Pr. 18 Jul. Add.
Finanus, abbas in Hibernia, 12 Dec. Add.
Finian, al. Fintanus, Pr. C., in Scotia, 17 Feb.
Firmatus, diac. Antisiodori, 5 Oct.

Firmiliane; Ep., 12 Feb. Add.
Firminus, M., in Africa, 9 Jan.
Firminus, Ep. C., Uzetiæ ('at vrs'), 11 Oct.
Firmus, M., Romæ, 2 Feb.
Firmus, 10 Mar.
Firmus, M., 9 Aug. Add.
Flavia Domitilla, V.M., 7 Mai.
Flaccus, M., 30 Aug. Add.
Flaviana, V., Antisiodori, 5 Oct.
Flavian, M., 30 Jan.
Flavianus, Ep., 24 Nov. Add.
Flavius, M., Nicomediæ, 7 Mai.
Floia, V.M., Cordubæ, 24 Nov.
Flora, V.M., 29 Jul. Add.
Florence, Mar. 19.
Florence, Ep., 3 Apr. Add.
Florentia, M., Cæsarione in territ. Agathensi, 10 Nov.
Florens, Ep., 2 Mai. Add.
Florens, C., 28 Dec. Add.
Florentinus, cum S. Hilario, M., Seduni (' Persewdon ') in Gallia, 27 Sep.
Florentius, M., Carthagine, 15 Jul.
Florentius, Pr. C., in pago Pictaviensi, 22 Sep.
Florentius ('Florentyne'), Ep., Arausicæ in Gallia, 17 Oct.
Florentius. M. apud Tyle castrum, 27 Oct.
Florentius, (' Florens '), C. apud Nursiam, 28 Dec. Add.
Florentius, Ep. C., 26 Oct. Add.
Florentus, M., Karthagine, 15 Jul.
Florianus, M. in Norico Ripensi ('at oricoripens') 4 Mai.
Florianus, M., Gazæ, 17 Dec. Add.
Florus, M., Ostiæ, 22 Dec.
Flosculus (' Frustole') Ep., 2 Feb.
Fors, Ep. in Hibernia, 28 Sep. Add.
Foke, v. Phocas.
Fortunatus, Romæ, 15 Oct.
Fortunatus, M., Romæ, 2 Feb.
Fortunatus, M. Alexandriæ, 21 Apr.
Fortunatus, diac. M., Valentiæ in Galliis, 23 Apr.
Fortunatus, M., Aquileiæ, 11 Jun.
Fortunatus, Ep. C. in territ. Senon., 18 Jun.
Fortunatus, discip. S. Marci, diac. in Aquileia, 12 Jul.
Fortunatus, in Campania, 12 Oct.
Fortunatus, Ep., Tuderti, 14 Oct.
Fortunatus, M., Romæ, 15 Oct.
Fortunatus, Capuæ, 15 Oct.
Fortunatus, lector M., Venusiæ, in Apulia, 24 Oct.
Fortunatus, Alexandriæ, 27 Feb.
Fortunatus, Ep. C., 5 Mai. Add.
Fortunatus, M., 14 Mai. Add.
Fortunatus, M., 17 Mai. Add.
Fortunatus, 14 Oct. Add.

Fotinus, Ep. M., Lugduni, 2 Jun. ; 3 Jun. Add.
Foyllane, 31 Oct. Add.
Franboldus, Ep. C., 16 Aug. Add.
Franciscus, C., fundator Ord. Minorum, Assisii in Umbria, 4 Oct.
Franciscus, eius Translatio, 25 Mai.
Fraternus, Ep., (? M.) Antisiodori, 29 Sep.
Fratres Septem, MM., Romæ, 29 Mai.
Fratres Septem, filii Sanctæ Felicitatis, MM., Romæ, 10 Jul.
Fredeswida, V., Oxonii in Anglia, 19 Oct.
Fremundus, R.M., Britannia. 11 Mai.
Frigidianus ('Frygdiane'), Ep. C. Lucæ. 18 Mar. Add.
Frigidianus, eius Translatio, 18 Nov. Add.
Fronto, abbas, Alexandriæ, 14 Apr.
Fronto, M., ex xviii Martt. Cæsaraugustæ in Hisp., 15 al. 16 Apr.
Fronto, Ep. Petragoricen., in Gallia, 25 Oct.
Fronto, abbas in Thebaide, 19 Apr. Add.
Fructuosa, M., Antiochiæ, 23 Aug.
Fructuosus, Ep. Tarraconæ in Hisp., 21 Jan.
Frumentii Duo, MM. in Africa, 23 Mar.; item 23 Mar. Add.
Frumentius, Ep., 27 Oct. Add.
Frustole, v. Flosculus, Ep. 2 Feb.
Fulgentius, Ep. C., Ruspæ in Africa, 1 Jan.
Fulgence, Ep. Utruculanus, 1 Jan. Add.
Furcey, C., in monast. Perone ('Patron') 16 Jan.
Fusca, V.M., 13 Feb. Add.
Fuscinianus, al. Fustinianus, M., Ambiani in Gallia, 11 Dec.
Fuscolus, Ep. C. in Africa, 6 Sep.
Fyacre, C., 18 Aug. Add.
Fynan, Ep., 16 Mar. Add.
Fynanus (al. Wynyn) in Hibernia, 10 Sep. Add.
Fynchell, 26 March, Add.
Fynian, 6 Feb. Add.
Fyrme, M. 13 Jan. Add.

Gabinius, Pr. M., Romæ, 19 Feb.
Gabinius, M., Turribus Sardiniæ, 30 Mai.
Gabryell, Archang., 25 Mar. Add.
Gadane, 9 Mar. Add.
Gaius, Pr. C. Romæ, 22 Apr. Add.
Galatus, M., Militanæ in Armenia, 19 Apr.
Galenice, v. Callinicus, M., 28 Jan.
Galla, vidua, Romæ. 5 Oct. Add.
Gallicanus, patricius, M., Alexandriæ, 25 Jun.
Gallus ('Gasly') abbas in Alemania, 20 Feb. ; 19 Feb. Add.
Gallus, Pr. C., abbas, in Germania, 16 Oct.
Gamalielis Inventio, Ierosolymis, 3 Aug.
Gasly, v. Gallus.
Gaspar, see Jasper.
Gatianus ('Canciane'), Ep., Turonis, 18 Dec.
Gauberge, v. Walpurgis.
Gaudentia, V. (M.), Romæ, 30 Aug.
Gaudentius, Ep., 3 Feb. Add.
Gaudentius, Ep. M., 14 Oct. Add.
Gaugericus, Ep. C., Cameraci, 11 Aug.
Gawdrysyve, abbatissa, V., 14 Oct. Add.
Gay, v. Caius.
Geate, v. Grata, M.
Gedeon, 1 Sep. ; 1 Sep. Add.
Gelasius, M., Romæ in foro Sempronii, 4 Feb.
Gelasius, I. papa. 18 Nov. Add.
Gelasius, Ep. 20 Dec. Add.
Geminian, Ep. 29 Jan. Add.
Geminianus, M., Romæ, 16 Sep.
Geminus, M. in Africa, 4 Jan.
Geminus, M., Romæ, in foro Sempronii, 4 Feb.
Geminus, Ep. 21 Apr. Add.
Genebadius, Ep. Laudunensis, 7 Dec. Add.
Generalis, femina, M. in Africa, 14 Sep.
Generosa, M. Carthagine, 17 Jul.
Genesius Arelatensis, exceptor, M., Aug.
Gengolfus, C., Lingonis, 11 Mai. Add.
Gengulpus, C., 17 Sep. Add.
Gennand, Ep., 16 Apr. Add.
Genofeva, V., Parisiis, 3 Jan.
Genofeva, eius Translatio, 28 Oct.
Genonius, M., in territ. Lingoniensi, 19 Sep.
Gentianus, hospes SS. Victorici et Fusciani, M., Ambiani, 11 Dec.
Georgius, M. Diospoli in Perside, 23 Apr.
Georgius, diac. monachus, M., Cordubœ, 27 Aug.
Georgii, diac., et Aurelii, MM., reliquiarum receptio, Parisiis, 20 Oct.
Georgius, Pr., cum Frontone, Petragoricis in Gallia, 25 Oct.
Geraldus, C., 10 Oct. Add.
Gerardus, Pannoniæ Ep., 24 Feb. Add.
Gerardus, Lucensis Ep., 24 Feb. Add.
Geremare, abbas, 18 Mar. Add.
Geremarus, abbas, 24 Sep. Add.
Gergenius, Ep. Librensis, 17 Nov. Add.
Gerinus, M., 2 Oct. Add.
Gereon, miles M., Coloniæ Agrippinæ, 10 Oct.
Gergery, v. Gregorius, Ep. Turon.
Gertrudis, V. (? M.), monast. Nivigellæ in Brabantia, 17 Mar.
Gertrude, V.M., eius Translatio, 10 Feb.
Germanicus, M., Smyrnæ, 19 Jan.
Germanus, Ep. C., Parisiis, 28 Mai.

INDEX SANCTORUM. 253

Germanus, eius Translatio, Parisiis, 25 Jul.
Germanus, Ep. C., Antisiodori, 31 Jul.
Germanus, Ep. C., in Africa, 6 Sep.
Germanus, Ep. C., Antisiodori, 1 Oct.
Germanus, M., in Hispania, 23 Oct.
Germanus, Ep. C., Capuæ, 30 Oct.
Germanus, M., Cæsareæ Cappadociæ, 3 Nov.
Gerontius, *al.* Geruntius, Ep. C., Italicæ in Hisp., 25 Aug.
Cervasius, M., Mediolani, 19 Jun.
Getulius, conjux Symphorosæ, M., Romae, 10 Jun.
Gignavus, abbas, in pago Bituricensi, 4 Dec.
Gilbert, *v.* Agilbert, 24 Jun.
Gilbertus, C., 4 Feb.
Gildardus, Ep., Rotomagi, 8 Jun.
Gildardus, C., Nivernis in Hibernia, 24 Aug.
Giles, *v.* Ægidius.
Giraldus, C., 13 Oct.
Gislenus ('Gysleny'), Ep. C., 9 Oct.; Cf., 20 Mar. Add.
Goar, Pr., 6 Jul.
Godricus, C., in Brit., 21 Mai.
Goericus, Ep. (Metensis), 19 Sept. Add.
Golfryde (Ceolfrith), abbas apud Jarrow, 25 Sep. Add.
Gondegrand, M., 5 Sep. Add.
Good Fryday, h.e. Parasceve, 25 Mar.
Goodwale (Gudwal), 6 Jun. Add.
Gordianus, M. Romæ, 10 Mai.
Gordianus, M., Novioduni, 17 Sep.
Gorgonius, M., Sebastæ in Armenia, 10 *al.* 11 Mar.
Gorgonius, M., Nicomediæ, 9 Sep.
Gotardus, Ep. C., 5 Mai. Add.
Gracianus, *vel* Gracilianus, M., Falari in agro Piceno, 12 Aug.
Grata ('Geate'), M., Lugduni, 2 Jun.
Gratianus, M., Ambianensis, 23 Oct. Add.
Gregorii papæ Magni Electio sive Ordinatic, Romæ, 3 Sep.
Gregorius, Ep., Nyssæ, 9 Mar.
Gregorius, Ep. C., Illiberi, 24 Apr.
Gregorius I., papa, Romæ, 12 Mar.
Gregorius, Ep., Nazianzi, 9 Mai.
Gregorius, Ep. M., C., Neocæsareæ in Ponto, 3 Jul.
Gregorius, Ep. M., apud Pontum, 17 Nov.
Gregorius, Ep., Turonis, 17 Nov.
Gregorius, papa, eius Translatio, 9 Dec.
Gregorius, Ep. C., Antisiodori, 19 *al.* 20 Dec.
Gregorius, Pr. M., Spoleti in Tuscia, 24 Dec.
Gregorius, Ep. Lingonensis, 3 Jul. Add.
Gregorius, eques C., in Samo insula, 24 Aug. Add.
Gregorius II, papa, Romæ, 28 Nov. Add.
Gregorius III, papa, Romæ, 28 Nov. Add
Grimbaldus, Pr., apud Wintoniam, 8 Jul.; 7 Jul. Add.
Guddene ('Gundene'), V.M., Carthagine, 18 Jul.
Gulphyle (Ulfilas) Ep. Gothorum, 21 Apr. Add.
Gumpert, Ep., 11 Mar. Add.
Gundleus, R., 29 Mar. Add.
Gungulphus, M., in Burgundia, 6 Oct. Add.
Gundulphus, Ep. C., in pago Bituricensi, 17 Jun.
Gundulphus, *al.* Gundran, Ep. C., Parisiis, 13 Nov.
Guntrannus, R., Cabilione, 28 Mar.
Gurius, M., Edessæ, 20 Nov. Add.
Guthlacus, in Britannia, 11 Apr.
Gwenadius, abbas C., 3 Nov.
Gylbertus (de Sempringham), C., 4 Feb.
Gylbertus, *v.* Agilbertus, M., 24 Jun.
Gyldas, 29 Jan.
Gysleny, *v.* Gislenus.

Habacuc, propheta, in Judæa, 15 Jan.
Habentius ('Avens'), monachus, M., Cordubæ, 7 Jun.
Habetdeum, Ep., 15 Mar. Add.
Habundy, *v.* Abundius.
Habundus, Pr. M., Cordubæ, 8 Jun.
Hadrianus, M., Massiliæ, 1 Mar.
Hadrianus, *al.* Adrianus, M., Nicomediæ, 8 Sep.
Haiot, judex, 1 Sep. Add.
Hailon, judex, 1 Sep. Add.
Hammonius ('Ammon'), M., 14 Feb.
Hamptran, *v.* Emmeranus.
Heber, 28 Jan. Add.
Hedda, Ep. C., 7 Jul.
Hedistius ('Edisty'), M., Ravennæ, 12 Oct.
Hegesippus ('Iesyppe'), historicus, Romæ, 7 Apr.
Helena, R., mater Constantini Imp., Romæ, 18 Aug.
Helena et ejus Translatio, V. Antisiodori, 22 Mai.
Helenus ('Heleny') abbas in Deserto, 17 Apr. Add.
Helewsyppe, *v.* Eleusippus, M.
Helias, miles, Alexandriæ, 22 Jan. Add.
Helimenas, Pr. M., Cordubæ, 22 Apr.
Heliodorus, M., in Africa, 6 Mai.
Helladius ('Ellad'), Ep., Antisiodori, 8 Mai.
Heliodorus, Ep., 3 Jul. Add.
Helpedius, abbas, 2 Sep. Add.
Helpidius, Ep. Lugduni, 2 Sep.

Hely, summus sacerdos, judex Israel, 20 Aug. Add.
Hely, abbas in Deserto, 11 Sep. Add.
Hely, discip. S. Antonii, 11 Sep. Add.
Helyas, propheta, 14 Aug. Add.
Hemitherius, *al.* Emitherius ('Enuthere') miles M., Calagurri, 3 Mar.
Henricus, imperator, 14 Jul. Add.
Henry, 16 Jan. Add.
Hera ('Heroys'), catechumena, M., Alexandriæ, 28 Jun.
Heraclea, M., in Thracia, 29 Sep.
[H]eracles, Ep. Alexandriæ, 14 Jul.
Heraclides, M., Alexandriæ, 28 Jun.
Heraclides, C., in Egypto, 23 Apr. Add.
Heraclius, M., Novioduni, 17 Mai.
Heraclius, M., Tuderti in Tuscia, 26 Mai.
Heraclius, Ep., apud Senones, 8 Jun.
Heraclyte, C., 2 Feb. Add.
Herastus ('Erast'), Ep. M., Philippis, 26 Jul.
Herculanus, M., in Portu Romano, 5 Sep.
Herculanus, miles M., cum S. Alexandro, Romæ, 25 Sep.
Herculanus, Ep. M., Perusii in Italia, 7 Nov.
Herculanus, eius Translatio, Perusii, 1 Mar.
Heren, *al.* Irene, M., Thessalonicæ, 5 Mai.
Hereodarde, *v.* Theodardus.
Herimbertus, Ep. Tolosanus, 14 Mai.
Herina, V., 4 Mai. Add.
Herke, Ep. in Hibernia, 2 Nov. Add.
Hermagoras, Ep. M., discip. S. Marii, Aquileiæ, 12 Jul.
Hermagoras, ejus Translatio, 12 Sep. Add.
Hermas, discip. S. Pauli, Romæ, 9 Mai.
Hermelandus, abbas, 25 Mar.
Hermettus, M., Constantinopoli, 3 Aug.
Hermes, M., Bononiæ, 4 Jan.
Hermes, M., Massiliæ, 1 Mar.
Hermes, præfectus, M., Romæ, 28 Aug.
Hermes, M., Adrianopoli in Thracia, 22 Oct.
Hermes, exorcista, Rhetiariæ, 31 Dec.
Herminigildus, R. M., in Hispania, 13 Apr.
Hermippus ('Hernempy'), 27 Jul.
Hermogenes, Antiochiæ, 17 Apr.
Hermogenes, M., Militanæ in Armenia, 19 Apr.
Hermogenes, M., Syracusis, 25 Apr.
Hermogenes, M., 12 Dec.
Hermocrates ('Hermogiate'), M., 27 Jul.
Hermolaus, Pr. M., Nicomediæ, 27 Jul.
Hero, Ep. M., Antiochiæ, 17 Oct.
Hero, M., Alexandriæ, 14 Dec.

Heros ('Heroys'), M., Alexandriæ, 28 Jun.
Heryne, V., 4 Mai. Add.
Hester, regina, 14 Sep. Add.
Hesychius ('Esicy'), Ep. in Hispania, 15 Mai.
Hesychius, miles M., Dorostori in Mysia, 15 Jun.
Hesychius, *al.* Esychius, M., Antiochiæ, 18 Nov.
Hesychius, Ep. M., 18 Feb. Add.
Hieremias, monachus, Cordubæ, 7 Jun.
Hieremias, M., Cordubæ, 17 Sep.
Hieronymus, Pr. Doctor in Bethleem Juda, 30 Sep.
Hieronymus, ejus Translatio, Romæ, 9 Mai. Add.
Hilaria, mater S. Afræ, M., Augustæ Vindelicorum, 12 Aug.
Hilaria, uxor Claudii, M., Romæ, 3 Dec.
Hilarinus, monachus, M., Aretii in Tuscia, 7 Aug.
Hilarinus, eius Translatio ad Ostia Tiberina, 16 Jul.
Hilarion, eremita, C., 21 Oct.
Hilarius, Ep. C., Gavalis, 25 Oct.
Hilarius, Ep. C., Pictavis, 13 Jan. *et* 1 Nov.
Hilarius, Ep. M., Aquileiæ, 16 Mar.
Hilarius, Ep. C., Arelate in Galliis, 5 Mai.
Hilarius, papa, Romæ, 10 Sep.
Hilarius, abbas, 13 Mai. Add.
Hilda, abbatissa, 18 Nov.; 17 Nov. Add.
Himerius, Ep., 17 Jun. Add.
Hippolytus, Pr. M., Antiochiæ, 30 Jan,
Hippolytus, cum familia sua, M., Romæ, 13 Aug.
Hippolytus, Ep. Africanus, 13 Aug. Add.
Hippolytus, in Portu Romano, 23 Aug.
Hippolytus, Pr. M., Romæ, 20 Nov.
Honesimus, *v.* Onesimus, Ep.
Honestus, M., 16 Feb. Add.
Honoratus, Ep. apud Arelatem, 16 Jan.
Honoratus, Ep., 16 Jan. Add.
Honoratus, abbas, 16 Jan. Add.
Honoratus, Ep. C., Ambiani, 15 Jun. Add.; 1 Sep. Add.
Honoratus, abbas, 16 Jan.
Honoratus, M. Ostiæ ('at antioche'), 22 Dec.
Honorius M. apud Ostia Tiberina, 21 Nov.
Honorius, Archiep. Cantuar., 30 Sep. Add.
Honoryne, V. M., 27 Feb. Add.
Horanus, abbas in deserto Egypti, 12 Nov. Add.
Hormisdas, papa, Romæ, 8 Aug. Add.
Hormisdas, Rex Persarum, M., 8 Aug. Add.
Horres, filius Theusetæ M., Nicææ, 13 Mar.

Hospitius, 21 Mai Add.
Hostianus, Pr. M., in territ. Vivariensi, 30 Jun.
Hukbert, *al* Hubertus, Ep. [Tungrensis], 3 Nov.
Hugo, Ep. Lincoln., 17 Nov.
Hugo, Ep., 31 Mar. Add.
Hugo, abbas, 1 Apr. Add.
Hugo, abbas Cluniacensis, 5 Jul. Add.
Hugo de S. Victore, 5 Jul. Add.
Hugo, puerulus Lincolniæ, 1 Aug. Add, Hundegunda, V., 25 Aug. Add.
Hutbert, Ep. C., 30 Mai.
Hyacinthus ('Iacynct'), M., Romæ, 10 Feb.
Hyacinthus, M., in Portu Romano, 26 Jul.
Hyacinthus, M., Sabinis, 9 Sep.
Hyacinthus, Eunuchus, M., Romæ, 11 Sep.
Hyacinthus, M. in Lucania, 29 Oct.
Hyery, *v*. Pierius, Pr.
Hyginus ('Ygyn'), papa, M., Romæ, 11 Jan. Add.
Hyldebert, Ep., 13 Feb. Add.
Hyldegart, V., 22 Jun. Add.
Hyldelyth, V., 24 Mar. Add.
Hyldentius, Ep., 26 Mai. Add.
Hyrade, M., 11 Mar. Add.
Hyren, *v*. Irenæus, M.
Hyren, *v*. Irene.

Ignatius, avunculus Celerini, M. in Africa, 3 Feb.
Ignatius, Ep. Antioch., M., Romæ, 1 Feb.
Ignatius, eius Translatio, 17 Dec.
Ildefonsus ('Nedolfons'), Ep. Toletanus, 23 Jan. Add. ; ('Hyldefons') 18 Dec. Add.
Iltutus, in Brit., 6 Nov. Add.
Indaletius, [C.] in Hispania, Ep. missus ab apostolis, 15 Mai.
Indrake, R. Hiberniæ, 8 Mai. Add.
Infantes Decem, Martt., Alexandriæ, 15 Jul.
Ingenuinus ('Ingemyne'), Ep. Sabionensis, 5 Feb. Add.
Ingenuus, miles, M., Alexandriæ, 20 Dec.
Ingemyne, *v*. Ingenuinus.
Innocentes, MM., in Bethleem Judæ, 28 Dec.
Innocentes, eorum Octava, 4 Jan.
Innocentius, M. Sirmii, 4 Jul.
Innocentius, papa, C. *al*. M., 28 Jul.
Innocentius, miles M., ex Thebæorum legione, in loco Agauno, Seduni in Galliis, 22 Sep.
Inventio capitis Præcursoris [Jo. Bapt.] Hierosolymis, 24 Feb.
Inventius, *al*. Iuventius ('Vincent'), M., Romæ, 1 Jan.
Irenæus ('Hyerene'), M., Romæ, 10 Feb.
Irenæus, Ep. M., Sirmii, 25 Mar.

Irenæus ('Hyreney'), Diac. apud Pentapolim Libyæ, 26 Mar.
Irenæus, M., Thessalonicæ, 5 Mai.
Irenæus, Ep. M., Lugduni in Galliis, 28 Jun.
Irenæus ('Hyreney'), Diac. M., Clusii in Etruria, 3 Jul.
Irenæus, M., Romæ, 26 Aug.
Irene ('Hyrene'), V. M., Thessalonicæ, 5 Apr.
Isaac, monachus, M., Cordubæ in Hisp., 3 Jun.
Isai, *al*. Jesse, pater David, 29 Dec. Add.
Isay, 26 Feb. Add.
Isidorus, Ep. M., 2 Jan.
Isidorus ('ysydour'), C., 15 Jan.
Isidorus, Ep., Hispali in Hispania, 4 Apr.
Isidorus, monachus, Cordubæ, 17 Apr.
Isidorus, M. (Ep. apud Chium insulam) 15 Mai.
Isidorus, M., Alexandriæ, 14 Dec.
Itamar, Ep. C., 10 Jun.
Ive, *al*. Yve, C. in Britannia, 8 Oct.

Jacob, 5 Feb. Add.
Jacobus, Ap. M. Ierosolymis, 1 Mai.
Jacobus, eius Translatio ab Hierosolymis ad Hispaniam, 25 Jul.
Jacobus, Ep., 15 Mar.
Jacobus, Zebedæi, Ap. M., Ierosolymis, 25 Mar.
Jacobus, Pr. M., in Perside, 22 Apr.
Jacobus, Diac. M., in urbe Lambesitana, 30 Apr.
Jacobus, Ep. C., Nisibi, 15 Jul.
Jacobus, eius Vigilia, 24 Jul.
Jacynct, *v*. Hyacinthus.
Jader, Ep. C., *al*. M., in Africa, 10 Sep.
Jair, judex, 1 Sep. Add.
Januaria, M., Carthagine, 17 Jul.
Januarius, M., in civitate Heraclea, 7 Jan.
Januarius, ex xviii. Martt. Cæsaraugustæ, 16 Apr.
Januarius, M., in Africa, 10 Jul.
Januarius, M., filius S. Felicitatis, Romæ, 10 Jul. ; 23 Nov.
Januarius, M., in Armenia minori, 11 Jul.
Januarius, [Diac. M.] Carthagine, 15 Jul.
Januarius, subdiac. M., Romæ, 6 Aug.
Januarius, Ep. Beneventanæ civitatis, M., Puteolis, *al*. Neapoli in Campania, 19 Sep.
Januarius, M., Cordubæ in Hisp., 13 Oct.
Januarius, Pr. M., Venusiæ in Apulia, 24 Oct.
Jared, 23 Jan. Add.
Jason, filius Claudii, M., Romæ, 3 Dec.
Jason, 11 Mai. Add.
Jasper, e tribus regibus Coloniæ, 6 Jan. Add.
Jephte, judex, 1 Sep. Add.

Jeremias, propheta, 1 Mai.
Jerony, 9 Apr. Add.
Jesus Josedek, 13 Jul. Add.
Jesus Nave, propheta, 1 Sep.
JESU CHRISTI, D. N. Nativitas in Bethleem Juda, 25 Dec. Vigilia, 24 Dec.
JESU Pueri Relatio, 7 Jan.
Jesus, filius Sirach, 1 Aug. Add.
Jesyppe, v. Hegesippus.
Joanna, uxor Chusæ, Antiochiæ, 24 Mai.
Joachim, 26 Jul. Add.
Joannes, abbas, 27 Jan.
Joannes Chrysostomus, Ep., Constantinopoli, 27 Jan.
Joannes, Pr. C., in monast. Reomanensi, 28 Jan.
Joannes, M. cum Cyro, Alexandriæ, 31 Jan.
Joannes, abbas, ex Syria, apud Civit. Penarensem, 19 Mar.
Joannes, eremita in Aegypto, 27 Mar.
Joannes Beverlacensis, Ep. C., Eboraci in Anglia, 7 Mai.; *item* 25 Oct.
Joannes, papa, M., Ravennæ, 27, *al.* 28 Mai.
Joannes, Pr. M., Romæ. 23 Jun.
Joannes Bapt., Nativitas, 24 Jun.; Vigilia, 23 Jun.
Joannes Bapt., ejus Octava, 1 Jul.
Joannes Bapt., ejus Capitis Inventio, 24 Feb.
Joannes Bapt., eius Decollatio, *vel* Inventio Capitis, 29 Aug.
Joannes Bapt., eius Conceptio, 24 Sep.
Joannes, frater Pauli, M., Romæ, 26 Jun.
Joannes, e septem Dormientibus, M., Ephesi, 27 Jul.
Joannes, Pr. sicut M., Romæ, 18 Aug.
Joannes, filius Marcellini, M., Tomis, 27 Aug.
Joannes, nobilis, M., Nicomediæ, 7 Sep.
Joannes, frater Adulphi, M., Cordubæ, 27 Sep.
Joannes, cum Festo, M., in Tuscia, 21 Dec.
Joannes, Ap. & Ev., C., Ephesi, 27 Dec.
Joannes, eius Octava, 3 Jan.
Joannes, ante portam Latinam, Romæ, 6 Mai.
Joannes, Alexandriæ patriarcha, 3 Feb. Add.
Joannes, monachus, 28 Feb. Add.
Joannes, abbas, 28 Feb. Add.
Joannes, abbas in Thebaide, 28 Feb. Add.
Joannes, 28 Feb. Add.
Joannes, de Obedientia vocatus, 28 Mar. Add.
Joannes, Damascenus, 6 Mai. Add.
Joannes, M., Alexandriæ, 19 Mai. Add.
Joannes capistranus, 20 Mai. Add.

Joannes I., papa, 26 Mai. Add.
Joannes II., papa, 26 Mai. Add.
Joannes III., papa, 26 Mai. Add.
Joannes, in deserto Egypti, 11 Jan. Add.
Joannes, monachus cæsus a latronibus, 20 Jun. Add.
Joannes, eremita, 5 Aug. Add.
Joannes, Ep. Augustodunensis, 29 Oct. Add.
Jocundianus, M., in Africa, 4 Jul.
Job, propheta, in terra Ilus, 10 Mai.
Joel, propheta, 13 Jul.
Jomny, abbas, 1 Jun. Add.
Jonas, propheta, 26 Jan. Add.
Jonas, Pr. M., 22 Sep. Add.
Josaphat, filius regis Indiæ, 1 Aug. Add. ; *item* 27 Nov. Add.
Joseph, Diac., Antiochiæ, 15 Feb.
Joseph, sponsus Mariæ, Nutritor Domini, in Judæa, 19 Mar.
Joseph Justus, in Judæa, 20 Jul.
Joseph, 5 Feb. Add.
Joseph ab Arimathia, 27 Mar. Add.
Josias, R. 24 Jun. Add.
Josye, M. scriba apud Judæos, 25 Jul. Add.
Jovilla ('Jonyll '), M. apud Lingones, 17 Jan.
Jovinianus, lector, M., Antisiodori, 5 Mai.
Jovinus, M., Romæ, 2 Mar.
Jovinus, Pr. C., 20 Jun.
Jovitta, Diac. M., Brixiæ, 15 Feb.
Jucundianus, M., in Africa, 4 Jul.
Judalece, v. Indaletius, Ep.
Judith, 14 Sep. Add.
Judocus, eremita, C., 13 Dec. ; *Item*, 25 Jul. Add. ; ejus Translatio (' Nidoke '), 9 Jan. Add.
Judas, Ap. M., 28 Oct.
Julia, V. M., 22 Mai.
Julia, M., Carthagine, 15 Jul.
Julia, V. M., Trecis, 21 Jul.
Julia, soror Verissimi, M., Ulyssipone in Lusitania, 1 Oct.
Julia, V. M., apud Augustam Euphratesiam, 7 Oct.
Julia, socia S. Eulaliæ, V. M., Emeritæ in Hisp., 10 Dec.
Juliana, V. M., Cumis, 16 Feb.
Juliana, M., Romæ, 7 Aug.; 12 Aug.
Julianus, filius Symphorosæ, M., Tibure, 27 Jun.
Julianus, conjux Basilissæ, M. Antiochiæ, 9 Jun.
Julianus, Diac. M., Bellovaci, 8 Jan.
Julianus (*al.* Symon leprosus), Ep. apud Cenommanos, 27 Jan.
Julianus, M., in Aegypto, 16 *al.* 17 Feb.
Julianus, M., in Africa, 19 Feb.
Julianus, M., Alexandriæ, 27 Feb.

Julianus, Ep., Toleti, 6 al. 8 Mar.
Julianus, C., Cæsareæ, 23 Mar.
Julianus, conjux Basilissæ, M., Antiochiæ, 9 Jun.
Julianus, filius Symphorosæ, M., Tibure, 27 Jun.
Julianus, M., Damasci, 20 Jul.
Julianus, Ep., eius Translatio in Cenomanos, 25 Jul.
Julianus, M., Romæ, 7 Aug.
Julianus, C., in Syria, 12 Aug.
Julianus, miles M., 28 Aug.
Julianus, conjux Castell[an]æ, 27 Jan. Add.
Julianus, nobilis M., 27 Jan. Add.
Julianus, M. sub Diocletiano, 27 Jan. Add.
Julianus, eremita, C., 28 Jan. Add.
Julianus, C., 28 Jan. Add.
Julianus, 13 Feb. Add.
Julianus, M., 23 Jun. Add.
Julianus, M. 8 Jul. Add.
Julian (al. Vivianus), Ep. C., apud Santones, 28 Aug.
Julianus, Pr. M., Tarracinæ, 1 Nov.
Julitta, mater Cyrici al. Quiriaci, M., Antiochiæ, 16 Jun. ; item 15 Jul. Add.
Julius, papa C., Romæ, 12 Apr,
Julius, M., Cæsaraugustæ in Hisp., ex xviii Martt., 15 al. 16 Apr.
Julius, miles emeritus, M., Dorostori in Mœsia, 27 Mai.
Julius, senator, M. Romæ. 19 Aug.
Julius, M., Thaguræ in Africa, 5 Dec.
Julius, M., Gedulbæ in Thracia, 20 Dec.
Julius, cognomine Africanus, 10 Apr. Add.
Julius, M. in Brit., 1 Jul. Add.
Ivo, eius Inventio, 24 Apr. Add.
Ivo, 10 Jun. Add.
Justa, M. Carthagine, 15 Jul.
Justa, al. Justina, V. M., Hispali in Hisp., 19 Jul.
Justina, V. M., cum Cypriano, Nicomediæ, 26 Sep.
Justina, V.M., 30 Nov.
Justina, soror S. Aurei, V. M., 16 Jun. Add.
Justina, V. M., 7 Oct. Add.
Justinianus, M. in territ. Belvacensi, 18 Oct.
Justinianus, in Brit. minore, 5 Dec. Add.
Justinus, philosophus, M., apud Pergamum Asiæ, 13 Apr.
Justinus, filius Symphorosæ, M., Tibure, 27 Jun.
Justinus, M., in territ. Parisiensi, 1 Aug.
Justinus, Pr. C. (? M.) Romæ, 17 Sep.
Justinus, Pr., 4 Aug. Add.
Justinus, Pr., 5 Aug.
Justus, M., 12 Feb.
Justus, M., Romæ, 28 Feb.
Justus, M., in Campania, 2 Jul.

Justus, puer M., Compluti in Hisp., 1 Aug.
Justus, Ep. C., Lugduni, 2 Sep.
Justus, eius Depositio, Lugduni, 14 Jul.
Justus, puer M., in territ. Belvacensi, 18 Oct.
Justus, Archiep. [Cantuar.], 10 Nov.
Justus, filius S. Justinæ, M., 1 Aug. Add.
Justus, diaconus, M., 27 Sep. Add.
Justus, Ep. Lugdunensis, 14 Oct. Add.
Justus, M., 2 Nov. Add.
Juthware, V., 13 Jul. Add.
Juvenalis, Ep. C., 3 Mai.
Juvenalis, M., 7 Mai.
Juventius, ('Evence,') Ep., Ticini, 12 Sep.
Juventius ('Vincent'), al. Inventius, M., Romæ, 1 Jun.
Juventius, Pr, in Hispania, 1 Nov. Add.

Kalanyke, M., Gazæ, 17 Dec. Add.
Kalixt, v. Callistus.
Kalixta, V. 27 Feb. Add.
Kalocery, v. Calocerus, M.
Katherina, V. M., Alexandriæ, 25 Nov.
Keby, 8 Nov. Add.
Kenanus, Ep. in Hibernia, 24 Nov. Add.
Keneburga, V. M., Glocestriæ in Britannia, 25 Jun.
Kenede, in Brit., 1 Aug. Add.
Kenelme, 3 Nov. Add.
Kenelmus, R. M., in Britannia, 17 Jul.
Kenfredus, diac. C., 6 Jul. Add.
Kentegerne, Ep., 13 Jan. Add.
Kenyswyde, V., 6 Mar. Add.
Keynyne, abbas in Hibernia, 3 Jun. Add.
Key, v. Caius, Caia.
Keynwyr, V., 8 Oct. Add.
Kilianus, cum sociis, Ep. M., Herbipoli, 8 Jul.
Kunegund, V., 3 Mar. Add.
Kyneburge, abbatissa, 6 Mar. Add.

Laetatius, M., Carthagine, 17 Jul.
Laetus, M., in Africa, 6 Sep.
Laetus, Pr. C., Aurelianis in Gallia, 5 Nov.
Lafreane (= Laisrean), abbas, 18 Apr.
Lambertus, Ep. Tungrensis, M., Leodii, 17 Sep.
Landelme, abbas, 20 Mar. Add.
Lanfrancus, Archiep. Cantuar, 28 Mai. Add.
Lanfrancus, abbas C., 3 Jul. Add.
Lamnomyarus, Pr. in pago Dorcasin. 19 Jan.
Largius, M., Romæ, 12 Aug.
Largius, v. Lorgius.
Largus, M., Aquileiæ, 16 Mar.
Largus, M., Romæ, 16 Mar.
Largus, eius Translatio, 8 Aug.
Largus, M., Augustæ, 5 Aug. Add.

Latro ('Latry') Ep. Laudunensis, 7 Dec. Add.
Latrocinianus, M., Treveris, 28 Apr. Add.
Laudus, Ep. C., Romæ, 21 Sep.
Laurentinus ('Laurence'), patruus Celerini, M., in Africa, 3 Feb.
Laurentinus, M., Aretii in Tuscia, 3 Jun.
Laurentius, Archiep. Doroberniæ in Anglia, 2 Feb.
Laurentius, Archidiac., M., Romæ, 10 Aug.
Laurentius eius Octava, 17 Aug., eius Vigilia, 9 Aug.
Laurentius cum Stephano, 7 Mai. Add.
Laurentius, Ep. 14 Nov. Add.
Laurianus, Ep. Hispalensis, M. in territ. Bituricensi, 4 Jul.
Lazarus, frater Mariæ et Marthæ, in Bethania, 17 Dec.; cf. 10 Jun. Add.
Leander, Ep. C., Hispali in Hisp., 27 Feb.
Leo, M., Romæ, 1 Mar.
Leo I., papa Romæ, 11 Apr.; 22 Apr. Add.
Leo, C., in territorio Tricassino, 25 Mai.
Leo II., papa C. (et Doctor) Romæ, 28 Jun.
Leo, C., in castro Melidunensi, 12 Nov.
Leo X. (al. IX.) papa Romæ, 19 Apr. Add.
Leo, Ep. in Græcia, 29 Apr. Add.
Leo III., papa, 28 Jun. Add.
Leo IV., papa, 16 Jul. Add.
Leo, eques, C., 24 Aug. Add.
Leobinus, al. Leopitus, Ep. Carnutensis, 15 Sep.
Leocadia, V., Toleti, 9 Dec.
Leodegarius, Ep. M., eius Translatio, 15 Mar.
Leodegarius, Ep. Augustodunensis, M., 2 Oct.
Leofridus ('Lewfryde'), C. in pago Ebroicensi, 21 Jun.
Leoncy, C., in Africa, 6 Dec.
Leonardus, eremita, Turonis, 18 Jan.
Leonardus, C., in monast. Wendoper, 26 Nov.
Leonardus, abbas C. 6 Nov.
Leonardus, C., 8 Dec.
Leonardus, 15 Oct. Add.
Leonides, M., 11 Feb. Add.
Leonilla, M. apud Lingones, 17 Jan.
Leonorus, Ep. C., 1 Jul. Add.
Leontia, in Africa, 6 Dec.
Leontius, Ep., Nicomediæ, 19 Mar.
Leontius, M., Aegææ, 27 Sep.
Leontius, M., 20 Aug. Add.
Leontius, C., 30 Oct. Add.
Leorny, Ep., 23 Apr. Add.
Leovigildus, monachus M., Cordubæ, 20 Aug.
Letardus, Ep., 7 Mai. Add.
Lethatius ('Letace') M., Carthagine, 17 Jul.

Leucus ('Lewce') al. Leucius, M., Apolloniæ, 28 Jan.
Lia, uxor Jacob, 5 Feb. Add.
Liberalis, C., Altini, 27 Apr. Add.
Liberalis, Ep. Cannensis, M., 30 Dec. Add.
Liberatus, abbas M., in Africa, 17 Aug.
Liberatus, Amphitr., 20 Dec.
Liberatus, abbas, 23 Mai. Add.
Liberatus, M., 23 Mai. Add.
Liberius, Ep. (papa) Romæ, 23 Sep.
Libertinus, abbas, 31 Mai. Add.
Lidor, al. Littorius, Ep. C., Turonis, 13 Sep.
Ligorius, M., in Græcia, 13 Sep. Add,
Liliosa, M., 27 Aug.
Linus, papa M., Romae, 26 Nov.; item 23 Sep. Add.
Linus, v. Nilus, Ep. M.
Liphardus, Pr. C., in territ. Aurelianensi, 3 Jun.
Litaniæ majores, Romæ, 25 Apr.
Litens, al. Littens ('Luthy'), M. al. Ep. C., in Africa, 10 Sep.
Littorius ('Lidor'), Ep. C., Turonis, 13 Sep.
Liventius, C., in castro Luca, 25 Jan.
Longinus, miles M., Massiliæ in Gallia, 21 Jul.
Longinus, miles M., Cæsareæ Cappad., (1 Sep.) 15 Mar.
Longyse, C., 13 Jan. Add.
Lorgius, M. (al. C.) Cæsareæ in Cappadocia, 2 Mar.
Lot, 5 Feb. Add.
Lotharius, abbas, 14 Dec.
Lucanus, M., 30 Oct. Add.
Lucas, ('Luke') Ep., Mar. 15.
Lucas, diac., M., Cordulæ, 22 Apr.
Lucas, Evang. C., in Bithynia, 18 Oct.
Luceia, V. M., Romæ, 25 Jun.; item 24 Jun. Add.
Lucia, Vidua, M., Romæ, 16 Sep.
Lucia, V.M., Syracusis in Sicilia, 13 Dec.
Lucia, ejus translatio, 18 Jan. Add.
Lucianus, Pr. Antioch., M., Nicomediæ, 7 Jan.
Lucianus, (? Ep. M.) Belvaci, 8 Jan.
Lucianus, M., in Sardinia, 28 Mai.
Lucianus, C., in Africa, 13 Jun.
Lucianus, C. Tripoli, 24 Dec.
Lucianus, Pr., 25 Dec. Add.
Lucifer, Ep., 26 Apr. Add.
Lucilla, V., filia Nemesii, M., Romæ, 31 Oct.
Lucilla, V.M., 29 Jul. Add.
Lucina, discip. Apost., Romæ, 30 Jun.
Lucina, matrona, M., 30 Jun. Add.
Lucinius, ('Lizyne') Ep., Andegavi, 13 Feb.
Lucius, C. Alexandriæ, 11 Jan.

Lucius, M., Romæ, 8 Feb.
Lucius, Ep. M., Cæsareæ in Cappadocia, 2 Mar.
Lucius, papa M., Romæ, 4 Mar.
Lucius, Ep., Cyrenæ, 6 Mai.
Lucius, Ep. M. (al. C.), in Africa, 10 Sep.
Lucius, M., Alexandriæ, 19 Oct,
Lucius, miles M., Romæ, 25 Oct.
Lucius, M., in Lucania, 29 Oct.
Lucius, C., Alexandriæ, 17 Nov.
Lucius, R., in Britannia, 3 Dec. Add.
Ludovicus, Ep., 19 Aug. Add.
Ludovicus, Rex Franciæ, 25 Aug. Add.
Lufyle, Capuæ, 15 Oct.
Lugyde, abbas, 4 Aug. Add.
Luke, v. Lucius, papa.
Luke, Ep. Mar. 15.
Lupercus, M,, Cæsaraugustæ in Hisp., 15 al. 16 Apr.
Lupicinus, abbas in territ. Lugdunensi, 21 Mar.
Lupus, Ep. C., Trecis, 29 Jul.
Lupus, Ep. C., apud Senonas, 1 Sep.
Lupus, Ep. anachorita Lugduni, 25 Sep.
Lupus, C., Cordubæ, 14 Oct.
Lupus, Ep. C., 16 Jun. Add.
Luvianus, C., eius Translatio, 17 Feb.
Lyuence, C., 25 Jan.

Macarius, M. Romæ, 23 Jan.
Macarius, M. Romæ, 28 Feb.
Macarius, Alexandrinus, abbas in Thebaide, 2 Jan.
Macarius, in Aegypto, 15 Jan.
Macarius, M., Alexandriæ (?), 12 Feb.
Macarius, C., in Syria, 12 Aug.
Macarius, M. Alexandriæ, 8 Dec.
Macedonius, Pr. M., Nicomediæ, 13 Mar.
Machabæi, vii fratres, cum matre sua, MM., Antiochiæ, 1 Aug.
Machabæus, Judas, 1 Oct. Add.
Machabæus, Jonathas, 1 Oct. Add.
Machabæus, Simon, 1 Oct. Add.
Machabæus, Johannes, 1 Oct. Add.
Macharius, Pr., 2 Jan. Add.
Machutus, Ep. C., in Britannia minore, 15 Nov.
Mackartyne, 24 Mar. Add.
Macra, V.M., in territ. Rhemensi, 6 Jan.
Macra, al. Martiana, V. M., in Mauritania Cæsariensi, 9 Jan.
Macra, V. M., 18 Jun. Add.
Macrinus, M., Nividuni, 17 Sep.
Macrobius, M., Damasci, 20 Jul.
Macrone, v. Matrona, M.
Maculyne, 6 Sep. Add.
Maeldoke, C., in Hibernia, 13 Mai. Add.
Maglorius, al. Majour, Ep. in Brit. [minori.] 24 Oct. Add.
Magnobonus, Ep., 16 Oct. Add.

Magnus, M. Romæ, 4 Feb.
Magnus, subdiac., M., Romæ, 6 Aug.
Magnus, al. Andreas, M., 19 Aug.
Magnus, M., Cabilone in Gallia, 4 Sep.
Magnus, Rex Norwegiæ, 1 Mai. Add.
Maiolus, abbas Cluniacensis, Silviniaci, 11 Mai.
Majour v. Maglorius.
Malachias, Ep. C., in monast. Clarevall., in territ. Lingonensi, 5 Nov.
Malachias, propheta, 23 Apr. Add.
Malachias, Ep., 2 Nov. Add.
Malchus, M., Cæsareæ Palestinæ, 28 Mar.
Malchus, M., e Septem Dormientibus, Ephesi, 27 Jul.
Malaliel, 23 Jan. Add.
Maldegare, dux, 20 Mar. Add.
Mallosus (Gereon) M., Coloniæ Agrippinæ, Oct.
Mamertus, Ep. C., Viennæ, 11 Mai.
Mamertyne, abbas, 30 Mar. Add.
Mammea, Regina, 11 Feb. Add.
Mammes, M., Cæsareæ Cappadociæ, 17 Aug.
Manahen, Doct. et propheta N. Testamenti, Antiochiæ, 24 Mai.
Manasses, filius Joseph, 5 Feb. Add.
Mandalis, ('Amandale'), M., Romæ, 10 Jan.
Mannea, uxor Marcellini, M., Tomis, 27 Aug.
Mansuetus, Ep. C., Tullensis, 3 Sep.
Mansuetus, Ep. C., in Africa, 6 Sep.
Mansuetus, Ep. M., in Africa, 28 Nov.
Mansuetus, M. Alexandriæ, 30 Dec.
Mansuetus, Ep. C., 2 Sep. Add.
Mappalicus, M., in Africa, 17 Apr.
Marce, v. Martia.
Marcel, v. Mecellus, 24 Jan.
Marcella, M., Alexandrinæ, 28 Jun.
Marcellianus ('Marcell'), M., Romæ, 18 Jun.
Marcellianus, M., Coloniæ in Tuscia, 9 Aug.
Marcellianus, C., 13 Mai. Add.
Marcellinus, puer M., Tomis in Ponto, 2 Jan.
Marcell[inus]. Ep. C., Ebreduni in Gallia, 20 Apr.
Marcellinus, papa M., Romæ, 26 Apr.
Marcellinus, Pr. M., Romæ, 2 Jun.
Marcellinus, tribunus, M., Tomis, 27 Aug.
Marcellinus, Ep., 9 Jan. Add.
Marcell, Ep., 16 Jan. Add.
Marcellus, papa M., Romæ, 16 Jan.
Marcellus, in Africa, 19 Feb.
Marcellus, M. Romæ, 18 Jun.
Marcellus, M., in Castro Argentomacho, 29 Jun.
Marcellus, M., Cabilione, 4 Sep.
Marcellus, M., Capuæ, 6 Oct.

R 2

Marcellus, discip. Petri., M., Romæ, 7 Oct.
Marcellus, C., 13 Oct.
Marcellus, centurio, M., Tingitanæ, in Mauritania, 30 Oct.
Marcellus, Ep., Parisiis, 1 Nov.
Marcellus, diac. M., Spoleti, 30 Dec.
Marcellus, Ep., 16 Jan. Add.
Marcellus, Ep. M., 12 Oct. Add.
Marcesse, v. Narcissus, M.
Marcias, v. Mareas, Ep. M.
Marcilla, famula S. Marthæ, 29 Jul. Add. cf. 10 Jun. Add.
Martia, cum Rufino, M., Syracusis, 21 Jun.
Marcia, M., in Campania, 2 Jul.
Marcus, M. Nicaeæ, 13 Mar,
Marcus ('Marcyll'), cum Quincto, M. Surrenti, 19 Mar.
Marcus, Evang. M., Alexandriæ, 25 Apr.
Marcus, ejus Translatio, 30 Jan. Add.
Marcus, ejus Inventio, 25 Jun. Add.
Marcus, nobilis, M., Romæ, 18 Jun.
Marcus, frater Marciani, M. in Aegypto, 4 Oct.
Marcus, I., papa C., Romæ, 7 Oct.
Marcus, C., 13 Oct.
Marcus, Ep. M., Jerosolymis, 22 Oct.
Marcus, miles M., Romæ, 25 Oct.
Marcus, diac. M., Tergeste, 11 Mai. Add.
Marcus II, papa, 7 Oct. Add.
Marcus, eremita, 7 Oct. Add.
Marcyll, v. Marcus cum Quincto, M.
Mardarius, M., 12 Dec. Add.
Mardonius, M., Neocæsareæ, 24 Jan.
Mareas, Ep. M., in Perside, 22 Apr.
Margareta, V.M., Antiochiæ, 13 al. 20 Jul.
Margareta, regina in Scotia, 10 Jun. Add.
Margareta, V., 8 Oct. Add.
Maria Jacobi, 27 Mar. Add.
Maria Salome, 27 Mar. Add.
Maria a Dioscoro servata, 18 Mai. Add.
Maria de Cegnies, 25 Jun. Add.
Maria soror Moysis, 1 Jul. Add.
Maria consolatrix, V., 1 Aug. Add.
Maria ad Nives, Romæ, 5 Aug. Add.
Maria, eius Purificatio, 2 Feb.
Mariæ, Beatæ V., Annuntiatio in Nazareth Galilaeæ, 25 Mar.
Mariæ Ecclesiæ ad Martyres, Dedicatio Romæ, 13 Mai.
Mariæ (Dormitio), Dei Genitricis, Depositio sive Assumptio, 15 Aug.
Mariæ, Octava Assumptionis B. Mariæ V., 22 Aug.
Mariæ Conceptio, 8 Dec.
Mariæ, Dei Genitricis, Nativituas in Nazareth Galilæeæ, 8 Sep.
Mariæ Nativitatis Octava, 15 Sep.
Mariæ Visitatio ad Elizabetham, 2 Jul.
Mariæ Præsentatio in templo, Hierosolymis, 21 Nov.

Maria Acgyptiaca, peccatrix, in Palæstina, 2 Apr.
Maria Magdalena, eius Translatio, 19 Mar.
Maria Magdalena, 22 Jul. Cf. 10 Jun. Add.
Maria Salome, Hierosolymis, 22 Oct.
Maria ancilla, V.M., 1 Nov.
Maria, V. M., 21 Nov.
Maria, V. M., cum S. Flora, Cordubæ, 24 Nov.
Marianus, lector, M., in urbe Lambesitana, 30 Apr.
Marianus, C., in territ. Bituricensi, 19 Aug.
Marianus, C., 17 Oct.
Marianus, monachus, 29 Apr. Add.
Marina, V. M., Alexandriæ, 18 Jun.
Marinianus, Diac. M., Romæ, 1 Dec.
Marinus, vir Dei, M., Avernis, 25 Jan.
Marinus, miles M., Cæsareæ Palestinæ, 3 Mar.
Marinus, M. in Africa, 10 Jul.
Marinus, patricius, M. Romæ, 26 Dec.
Marinus, C., 4 Sep. Add.
Marius, Persa, nobilis, M., Romæ, 20 Jan.
Marius, al. Maurus, abbas monasterii Bobacensis, 27 Jan.
Maro, M., in Italia, 15 Apr.
Marseus ('Narsey') Alexandriæ, 15 Jul.
Martha, soror Mariæ Magdalenæ, 29 Jul. Cf. June 10. Add.
Martha, eius Translatio, in Bethania, 17 Dec.
Martha, Persis, uxor Marii, M., Romæ, 20 Jan.
Martha, V. M., Coloniæ Agrippinæ, 20 Oct.
Martin ('Marce'), M., Syracusis in Sicilia, 21 Jun.
Martia, M. in Campania, 2 Jul.
Martialis, M., ex xviii Martt., Cæsaraugustæ in Hisp., 15 al. 16 Apr.
Martialis, Ep. C. (al. M.), Lemovicis, 30 Jun.
Martialis, filius S. Felicitatis, M., Romæ, 10 Jul.
Martialis, filius S. Felicitatis, M., Romæ, 23 Nov.
Martialis, peregrinus, M., in Portu Romano, 22 Aug.
Martialis, M., Cordubæ in Hispania, 13 Oct.
Martianus, M. in Africa, 4 Jan.
Martianus, 5 Apr.
Martiana, al. Macra, V. M., in Mauritania Cæsariensi, 9 Jan.
Martiana, V. M., in Mauritania Cæsariensi, 11 Jul.
Martianus, frater Marci, M. in Aegypto, 4 Oct.

INDEX SANCTORUM. 261

Martianus, cum fratribus, M. in Africa, 16 Oct.
Martianus, Ep. M., 6 Mar. Add.
Martianus, M. in Egypto, 5 Jun. Add.
Martina, V. M., Romæ, 1 Jan.
Martina, V., 17 Jul. Add.
Martinian, *v.* Martianus, M., 4 Jan.
Martinianus, M., Romæ, 4 Jul.
Martinianus, e Septem Dormientibus, M., Ephesi, 27 Jul.
Martinus, abbas in monast. Vertano, 24 Oct.
Martinus, papa, exulatus Chersonæ in Lycia, 10 Nov.
Martinus, Ep. C., Turonis in Galliis, 11 Nov.
Martinus, eius Octava, 18 Nov.
Martinus, eius Translatio et Ordinatio, item Dedicatio Basilicæ, Turonis, 4 Jul.
Martinus, abbas, apud Santonas, 7 Dec.
Martinus I. papa, M., Romæ, 12 Nov. Add.
[Martionilla] mater Celsi pueri, M., Antiochiæ, 9 Jan.
Martyres multi, Antiochiæ, 9 Jan.
Martyres tres alii cum Revocato et Firmino, in Africa, 9 Jan.
Martyres lxx. cum Anastas., Romæ, 22 Jan.
Martyres xxxvi., cum Theogene, Hippone in Africa, 26 Jan.
Martyres xii. ex Philadelphia, Smyrnæ. 26 Jan.
Martyres xv., Smyrnæ, 1 Feb.
Martyres (pueri duo, mulieres septem) cum S. Blasio, Sebastæ in Armenia, 3 Feb.
Martyres [innumerabiles] Thmuis in Aegypto, 4 Feb.
Martyres plurimi cum S. Saturnino, in Africa, 11 (*al.* 12) Feb.
Martyres decem milites, Romæ, 10 Feb.
Martyres 5000, in Aegypto, cum S. Juliano, 16 (*al.* 17) Feb.
Martyres 806 (*al.* 86), cum Donato, concordiæ, *al.* Cordubæ, 17 Feb.
Martyres plurimi, apud Tyrum Phœniciæ, Dioclet. Imp., 20 Feb.
Martyres lxxix. in Sicilia, Diocletiano Imp., 21 Feb.
Martyres xx. Adrumeti in Africa, 21 Feb.
Martyres xlii. *al.* lxii. *vel* lxxii. Sirmii, 23 Feb.
Martyres cclx [ii] Romæ, Claudio Imp., 1 Mar.
Martyres plurimi, Alexandro Imp., 2 Mar.
Martyres xxvii. demersi cum S. Caio, 4 Mar.
Martyres Dcccc, Romæ, 4 Mar.
Martyres viii. *alias* ix. *vel* xi. cum Eusebio palatino, 5 Mar.

Martyres tres demersi cum SS. Ariano et Theotico, apud Antinoum in Ægypto, 8 Mar.
Martyres xlii. in Perside, 10 Mar.
Martyres alii (vii.) Nicomediæ, 12 Mar.
Martyres xlvii. *al.* xlix. in carcere Mamertino baptizati, Romæ, Nerone Imp., 14 Mar.
Martyres xx. Romæ, 16 Mar.
Martyres viii. *al.* ix., Surrenti, 19 Mar.
Martyres quatuor cum Paulo et Cyrillo, in Syria, 20 Mar.
Martyres xiii. cum S. Epiphanio in Africa, 7 Apr.
Martyres quinque cum S. Apollonio demersi, Alexandriæ, 10 Apr.
Martyres plurimi, Romæ, Aureliano Imp., 10 Apr.
Martyres multæ mulieres, cum Agathonica, Pergami, 13 Apr.
Martyres vii. demersi Corinthi, 16 Apr.
Martyres multi in Africa, 17 Apr.
Martyres centum, cum S. Symeone, in Perside, 21 Apr.
Martyres plurimi in Perside, Sapore Rege, 22 Apr.
Martyres xxxiv., Lugduni Galliæ, 24 Apr.
Martyres xl., in metallo Phanensi, ('Favence'), 4 Mai.
Martyres lxxv., cum S. Heliodoro, in Africa, 6 Mai.
Martyres cccx., in Perside, 9 Mai.
Martyres xlii., Romæ, Alexandro Imp., 10 Mai.
Martyres alii cum S. Desiderio, apud Lingones, 23 Mai.
Martyres multi, Romæ, 25 Mai.
Martyres duo, Dorostori in Mæsia, 25 Mai.
Martyres xxii. cum Symnitero, Romæ, Antonino Imp., 26 Mai.
Martyres plures cum S. Prisco in territ. Autisiodorensi, 26 Mai.
Martyres vii. Fratres, Romæ, 29 Mai.
Martyres x., Augustoduni, 1 Jun.
Martyres xl. cum Photino, Lugduni in Gallia, 2 Jun.
Martyres xx. apud Tarsum Ciliciæ, 6 Jun.
Martyres iii. cum S. Hieremia, Cordubæ, 7 Jun.
Martyres. xx., cum Basilide, Romæ, Aureliano Imp., 10 Jun.
Martyres x. infantes, 15 Jul.
Martyres cclxii., Romæ, 17 Jun.
Martyres innumerabiles in territorio Parisiensi, 24 Jun.
Martyres xxii. [Virgines cum S. Lucia], Romæ, 25 Jun.
Martyres iii. *vel* viii. cum S. Plutarcho, Alexandriæ, 18 Jun.
Martyres iii., Romæ, Nerone Imp., 2 Jul.

Martyres xii. Christiani cum S. Tryphone, Alexandriæ, 3 Jul.
Martyres xxx., Sirmii, 4 Jul.
Martyres 10203, Romæ, 9 Jul.
Martyres vii. Fratres, filii S. Felicitatis, Romæ, 10 Jul.
Martyres 500 (*al.* Confessores) cum S. Eugenio Ep. in Africa, 13 Jul.
Martyres x. infantes, 15 Jul.
Martyres Scillitani, Carthagine, Saturnino Præfecto, 17 Jul.
Martyres vii. filii S. Symphorosæ, Tibure, 18 Jul.
Martyres x. (*al.* xv.) cum Sabino, apud Damascum, 20 Jul.
Martyres, Philadelphiæ, 1 Aug.
Martyres vii. (*vel.* ix.) cum S. Bono, &c., Romæ, 1 Aug.
Martyres iii., filii S. Theodotæ, in Bithynia, 2 Aug.
Martyres xviii., Romæ, 7 Aug.
Martyres xx. cum S. Cyriaco, &c., 8 Aug.
Martyres, plurimi (*al.* xx. *vel.* xxiv.) cum S. Quirino, &c., 12 Aug.
Martyres xviii. familiares S. Hippolyti, Romæ, 13 Aug.
Martyres multi, in Africa, Hunnerico Rege, 17 Aug.
Martyres 2598. cum Magno et Andrea in Cilicia in Monte Tauro, 19 Aug.
Martyres aliqui, peregrini in Portu Romano, 22 Aug.
Martyres vii., filii Eleazari, Lugduni, 23 Aug.
Martyres xii. (*al.* xv.) Antiochiæ, 23 Aug.
Martyres xxx. (*al.* ccc) sub Valeriano et Gallieno, 23 Aug.
Martyres 300, *v.* 'Massa Candida,' 24 Aug.
Martyres xxiii., Nicomediæ, Maximiano Imp., 8 Sep.
Martyres xxii., 8 Sep.
Martyres xxi. (*al.* xviii.) Romæ, Decio Imp. 14 Sep.
Martyres plurimi in Palestina, 19 Sep.
Martyres 6666 ex Thebæorum legione, Seduni in Gallia, cum S. Cornelio, 22 Sep.
Martyres 504 cum S. Areta, Romæ, 1 Oct.
Martyres innumerabiles, Nicomediæ, Diocletiano Imp., 2 Oct.
Martyres paene innumerabiles in Aegypto, 4 Oct.
Martyres monachi xxx., Messanæ in Sicilia, 5 Oct.
Martyres multi, Viennæ, 9 Oct.
Martyres xviii. cum S. Viatore, Coloniæ Agrippinæ, 10 Oct.
Martyres, vii. *al.* multi, Veronæ, in Gallia, 10 Oct.
Martyres 318, cum S. Gereone, Coloniæ Agrippinæ, 10 Oct.

Martyres et confessores 4,976 in Africa, Hunnerico R., 12 Oct.
Martyres ccc ex legione Thebæorum, Coloniæ Agrippinæ, 15 Oct.
Martyres cclxx., in Africa, Geiserico Rege, 16 Oct.
Martyres 365, *ul.* 375, 16 Oct.
Martyres xlix., Antiochiæ in Syria, 19 Oct.
Martyres multi cum Martha et Saula, Coloniæ Agrippinæ, 20 Oct.
Martyres xlvii.; *Item* cxxi.; Romæ, 25 Oct.
Martyres ccxx., in Africa, 30 Oct.
Martyres xl., *alias* x., Theopoli, 6 Nov.
Martyres tres (ex quibus erant Castorius et Simplicianus) cum S. Claudio, Romæ, 8 Nov.
Martyres xx. cum Demetrio, &c., Antiochiæ, 10 Nov.
Martyres xxx., Nolæ in Campania, Martiano Præside, 15 Nov.
Martyres Dclx., Alexandriæ, Maximino Imp., 25 Nov.
Martyres, omnis familia S. Rufi, Romæ, 28 Nov.
Martyres iii., cum Dionysia, &c., in Africa, *v.* 'Confessores.'
Martyres xxii., 12 Dec.
Martyres duo, femineæ sexus, Alexandriæ, 12 Dec.
Martyres l. Eleutheropoli in Oriente (Gazæ in Palæstina), 17 Dec.
Martyres xxx. (*al.* xx.) Romæ, Diocletiano Imp., 22 Dec.
Martyres xx. (*al.* xxxv.), Nicomediæ, Diocletiano Imp., 23 Dec.
Martyres cc, *al.* Dcc., in insula Palmaria, Diocletiano Imp., 25 Dec.
Martyres feminæ lx, cum S. Anastasia, in insula Palmaria, Diocletiano Imp., 25 Dec.
Martyres x. cum S. Mansueto, Alexandriæ, 30 Dec.
Martyres, uxor Venustiani cum filiis suis, Spoleti, 30 Dec.
Martyres, *vide etiam*, 'Coronati,' 'Milites,' 'Mulieres,' 'Pueri,' 'Virgines.'
Martyres multi cum Tyrso, 17 Jan. Add.
Martyres multi cum Cheramone, 14 Feb. Add.
Martyres multi Alexandriæ, 16 Feb. Add.
Martyres cccc in Italia, 2 Mar. Add.
Martyres multi in Africa, 2 Mar. Add.
Martyres xxiii. cum Adriano, 4 Mar. Add.
Martyres xx., Carthagine, 11 Mar. Add.
Martyres xii. infantes, 23 Mar. Add.
Martyres xl; 4 Mai. Add.
Martyres xl. alii, 4 Mai. Add.
Martyres xliv., 4 Jun. Add.
Martyres Dc. cum Benigno, 6 Jun. Add.

INDEX SANCTORUM. 263

Martyres, 10000 milites, Alexandriæ, 22 Jun. Add.
Martyres M. cum Albano, 25 Jun. Add.
Martyres xvii., Augustæ, 5 Aug. Add.
Martyres mcccc., 11 Aug. Add.
Martyres pene innumerabiles, Cæsaraugustæ, 24 Aug. Add.
Martyres xii. fratres, 1 Sep. Add.
Martyres monachi duo, 15 Sep. Add.
Martyres xlix. cum Euphemia, 24 Sep. Add.
Martyres xxviii. in Perside, 2 Nov. Add.
Martyres cc. cum Porphurio, 24 Nov. Add.
Martyres xl. cum Floriano, 17 Dec. Add.
Martyrius, M., in Anaunia, 29 Mai. Add.
Martyrius, C., 18 Jun. Add.
Massa Candida, Carthagine, 24 Aug.
Materna, ('Mature') M., Lugduni, 2 Jun.
Mathathias, 1 Oct. Add.
Mathusale, 23 Jan. Add.
Matrona, ('Macrone') M., Thessalonicæ, 15 Mar.
Matrona, cum duabus filiabus VV., 15 Feb. Add.
Matthæus. Ap. et Evang. M., in Aethiopia, 21 Sep.
Matthæus, eius Vigilia, 20 Sep.
Matthias, Ep. Ierosolymis, 30 Jan.
Matthias, Ap., in Judæa, 24 Feb.
Maturinus, C. in pago Wastinensi, 1 Nov.
Maturinus, C., 10 Mai. Add.
Maturus, M., Lugduni, 2 Jun.
Matutinus, M., ex xviii. Martt., Cæsaraugustæ, 16 Apr.
Maulean, abbas, 15 Jan.
Maurilio, Ep. C., Andegavi, 13 Sep.
Mauritius, ex Thebæorum legione, M., Seduni in Galliis, 22 Sep.
Maurus, abbas in territ. Andegavensi, 15 Jan.
Maurus, abbas in monast. Bobiacensi, 27 Jan.
Maurus, miles M., Romæ, 29 Jan.
Maurus, M., Romæ, 1 Aug.
Maurus, M., in Istria, 21 Nov.
Maurus, M., Romæ, 22 Nov.
Maurus, Romæ, 29 Nov.
Maurus, M., Narniæ, 1 Dec.
Maurus, filius Claudii, M. Romæ, 3 Dec.
Maxentia, V.M., 20 Nov. Add.
Maxentius, Pr. C., in pago Pictaviensi, 26 Jun.
Maxentius, abbas, 27 Mai. Add.
Maxima ('Maximiane'), M., Sirmii, 26 Mar.
Maxima, V., Calidiani in pago Forojuliensi, 16 Mai.
Maxima, V.M., Tuburbi in Africa, 30 Jul.
Maxima, soror Verissimi, M., Ulyssipone in Lusitania, 1 Oct.

Maxima, V.M., in Africa, 16 Oct.
Maxima, M., 1 Dec. Add.
Maximianus, Pr. M., Bellovaci in Galliis, 8 Jan.
Maximianus, v. Maximus, M., Ostiæ.
Maximianus, M., 21 Aug.
Maximiana, v. Maxima, M., Sirmii.
Maximianus, in Africa, 18 Feb.
Maximianus, e Septem Dormientibus, M., Ephesi, 27 Jul.
Maximianus, Ep., 9 Jun. Add.
Maxim[in]us, Ep., Treveris, 29 Mai.
Maxim[in]us, M., Damasci, 20 Jul.
Maximinus, Pr. C., Aurelianis, 15 Dec.
Maximinus, Aquis in Gallia, 10 Jun. Add.
Maximus, frater Claudii, M., Ostiæ, 18 Feb.
Maximus, M., Romæ, 14 Apr.
Maximus, nobilis, M., Cordulæ, in Perside, 15 Apr.
Maximus, M., Damasci, 20 Jul.
Maximus, Ep. C., Veronæ, 29 Mai.
Maximus, puer M., Karthagine in Africa, 17 Aug.
Maximus, M., Cabilone in Gallia, 4 Sep.
Maximus, levita M., in prov. Ambianensi, 20 Oct.
Maximus, Pr. (al. Ep.) M., Romæ, 19 Nov.
Maximus, pater cœnobii Lerinensis, Ep. C., in civitate Rhegiensi, 27 Nov.
Maximus, 2 Feb. Add.
Maximus, monachus, 23 Mar. Add.
Maximus, Ep. C., 13 Sep. Add.
Maximus, M., 28 Sep. Add.
Maximus, Ep. Taurinensis, 27 Dec. Add.
Maximus, Ep. C., Alexandriæ, 27 Dec.
Mecellus, ('Marcel'), M., Neocæsareæ, 24 Jan.
Medardus, v. Menander.
Medardus, Noviomensis, Ep. C., Suessione in Gallia, 8 al. 9 Jun.
Medericus ('Meryke') Pr. monachus, Parisiis, 29 Aug.
Medericus, abbas, 2 Sep. Add.
Medrisina, V., 22 Nov. Add.
Melan, v. Æmilianus.
Melania, V. sacra, Hierosolymis, 29 Dec.
Melania, 22 Oct. Add.
Melanius, Ep. C., Rhedonis in Gallia, 6 Jan.
Melanius, Ep., Rotomagi, 22 Oct.
Melanius, Ep. C., apud Regidonas, 6 Nov.
Melanius ('Melance'), Ep., 16 Jan. Add.
Melchiades, papa, Romæ, 10 Jan.
Melchiades, papa, Romæ, 10 Dec.
Melchior, 6 Jan. Add.
Melchisedek, 5 Feb. Add.
Mele, Ep., 6 Feb. Add.
Meletius, Ep., C., in Ponto, 4 Dec.

Meletius, Ep., 4 Dec. Add.
Meleusippus, M., apud Lingonas, 17 Jun.
Melisius, Ep. M., in Perside, 22 Apr.
Melke, Ep., 6 Feb. Add.
Mellitus, Ep., Doroberniæ, 24 Apr.
Melour, filius ducis, Cornubiæ, M., 1 Oct.
Memmius ('Neminyne'), Ep. C., Catalannis, 5 Aug.
Menander ('Medard'), M., Philadelphiæ, in Arabia, 1 Aug.
Menelaus, C., 22 Jul. Add.
Mennas, Aegyptius miles, M., 11 Nov.
Mennas, eremita, 11 Nov. Add.
Meny, Ep. C., 5 Aug. Add.
Menye, v. Nimmia, M.
Mercuria, M., Alexandriæ, 12 Dec.
Mercurialis, Ep., 25 Nov. Add.
Mercurius, M., Beneventi, 15 Jun.
Mercurius, M., Cæsaraugustæ, 25 Nov. Add.
Merolus, monachus, 3 Oct. Add.
Merpwyn, V., 10 Feb.
Meryke, v. Medericus, 29 Aug.
Metellus, v. Mecellus.
Methodius, Ep. M., 18 Sep.
Metranus, M., Alexandriæ, 31 Jan.
Metron, C., Veronæ, 9 Mai. Add.
Michael, Archangelus, eius Ecclesiæ Dedicatio, 8 Mai.
Michael, Ecclesiæ eius Dedicatio in Monte Gargano, 29 Sep.
Michael in Monte Tumba, 16 Oct.
Michael, eius Apparitio, 7 Mai. Add.
Michæas, propheta C., 15 Jan.
Micheas, alter, 15 Jan. Add.
Milburga, V., 25 Jun. Add.
Mildreda, V., in Anglia, 13 Jul.
Miles, M., cum S. Albano, in Britannia, 22 Jun.
Milites xxx, al. lx, martyres Romæ, Diocletiano, 1 Jan.
Milites, xl, martyres Romæ, Gallieno Imp., 13 Jan.
Milites, x, martyres Romæ, 10 Feb.
Milites, xl, martyres Cappadoces apud Sebasten Armeniæ, Licinio R., 11 Mar.
Milites viii, martyres cum S. Domnione, Salonæ in Dalmatia, 11 Apr.
Milites iii, martyres cum S. Paulo, Romæ, Nerone Imp., 2 Jul.
Milites 10,203 martyres cum Zenone, Romæ, 9 Jul.
Milites lxxxiii, martyres, Amiterni, 24 Jul.
Milites clxv, martyres Romæ, 10 Aug.
Milites ccc, martyres ex legione Thebæorum, Coloniæ Agrippinæ, 15 Oct.
Milites xii, martyres Nicomediæ, 21 Oct.
Milites xlvii, martyres Romæ, Claudio Imp., 25 Oct.
Milites cxxi, martyres Romæ, 25 Oct.
Milites lxx, martyres Romæ, Numeriano Imp., 3 Dec.

Mimilon, v. Numilo.
Mineatus, M., Florentiæ, 25 Oct.
Minervus, M., Lugduni Galliæ, 23 Aug.
Misael, cum fratribus MM., in Babilonia, 16 Dec.
Mitrius, al. Demetrius M., Aquis in Provincia Narbonensi, 13 Nov.
Modest, C., 24 Jan. Add.
Modesta, filia Macedonii, M., Nicomediæ, 13 Mar.
Modestus, infans, Alexandriæ, 12 Feb.
Modestus, M. in Lucania apud Silarum flumen, 15 Jun.
Modestus, M., Cæsarione in territ. Agathensi, 10 Nov.
Modestus, C., 24 Jan. Add.
Modestus, Ep. Trever., 23 Feb. Add.
Modmund, M., in monast. Glocestriæ, 20 Jul. Add.
Modwenna, V., 5 Jul.
Modwenna, V., 9 Sep.
Moghtewe, abbas in Hibernia, 21 Aug. Add.
Molyng, Ep. in Hibernia, 17 Jun. Add.
Monachi Quinquaginta martyres in Perside, Sapore Rege, 22 Apr.
Monachi duo, 26 Dec. Add.
Monegundes, V. religiosa, Turonis, 2 Jul.
Monica, mater Augustini, 4 Mai.
Monitor, Ep. C., Aurelianis, 10 Nov.
Montanus, Pr. M., apud Sirmium, 26 Mar.
Montanus, 11 Mai.
Moseus, al. Moyses, miles, lector M., in Ponto, 18 Jan.
Moyses, M., Alexandriæ, 14 Feb.
Moyses, propheta, 4 Sep.
Moyses, abbas, 7 Feb. Add.
Moysetes, Ep. in Aegypto, 7 Feb.
Moysetes, M., in Africa, 18 Dec.
Mulier cum Celso puero suo, v. Martionilla, 9 Jan.
Mulier cum suis geminis, MM. in Numidia, Valeriano Imp., 29 Apr.
Mulieres vii, cum duobus pueris, MM. cum S. Blasio, Sebastæ in Armenia, 3 Feb.
Mulieres vii, martyres, Sebastæ, Agricolao Præside, 15 Feb.
Mulieres multæ martyres, cum S. Agathonica, Pergami in Asia, 13 Apr.
Mulieres Sanctæ cum Viduis xl, Eracleæ, 19 Nov.
Mulieres lx, al. dcc., cum S. Anastasia MM. in insula Palmaria, 25 Dec.
Munyse, Ep., 6 Feb. Add.
Murite, M., 24 Mar. Add.
Muritta, C., Carthagine in Africa, 13 Jul.
Musa, V., Romæ, 22 Aug. Add.
Musan, Pr. C., 24 Jan. Add.
Musonius, M., Neocæsareæ, 24 Jan.
Mustiola, matrona nobilis, M., Clusii in Etruria, 3 Jul.

Mutius, diaconus M., Cordulæ, 22 Apr.
Mutius, Pr. M., Constantinopoli, 13 Mai.
Mutius, abbas, 25 Mai. Add.
Mutius, monachus, 25 Mai. Add.
Mycy, v. Mutius, diac.
Myniane, v. Ninianus.

Nabor, miles M., Romæ, al. Mediolani, 12 Jun.
Nabor, M., in Africa, 10 Jul.
Nabor, M., 12 Jul. Add.
Nachor, 28 Jan. Add.
Narcissus ('Marcesse'), puer M., Tomis in Ponto, 2 Jan.
Narcissus, M., Romæ, 17 Sep.
Narcissus, Ep., Jerosolymis, 29 Oct.
Narseus, M., Alexandriæ, 15 Jul.
Narthalus ('Nartaby'), al. Nartalis, Scillitanus, M., Carthagine, 16, al. 17 Jul.
Nason, Discip. Christi, in Cypro, 12 Jul.
Natalia, M., 27 Aug.
Natalia, matrona, 1 Dec.
Natalius, C., Romæ, 31 Oct. Add.
Nathan, propheta, 29 Dec. Add.
Nathanael, e lxii discipulis, 30 Nov. Add.
Nathanael, eremita, 30 Nov. Add.
Nativitas Jesu Christi, 25 Dec.
Nativitas, B.M.V., 8 Sep.
Navalis, cum Valentino, M. Ravennæ, 16 Dec.
Naum, propheta, 24 Dec. Add.
Nazarius, miles M., Romæ, al., Mediolani, 12 Jun.
Nazarius, M., Mediolani, 28 Jul.
Nedolfons, v. Ildefonsus.
Nehemias, propheta, 13 Jul. Add.
Nemelius, v. Nemesius f. Symphorosæ.
Nemesianus, Ep. M., in Africa, 10 Sep.
Nemesius, M., in Cypro, 20 Feb.
Nemesius, filius Symphorosæ, M., Tibure, 27 Jun. (cf. *Mart. Rom.* sub 18 Jul.)
Nemesius, C., in pago Lisuino, 1 Aug.
Nemesius, Diac. M., Romæ, 31 Oct.
Nemesius, M., Alexandriæ in Aegypto, 19 Dec.
Nemesius, nobilis, M., 25 Jul. Add.
Neminyne, v. Memmius.
Neon, M., apud Lingones, 17 Jan.
Neon, M., Aeginæ in Cilicia, 23 Aug.
Neopolis, M., Romæ, 2 Mai.
Neoterius, M., Alexandriæ, 8 Sep.
Neotus, C., 8 Jul.; 31 Jul.
Nereus, eunuchus M., Romæ, 12 Mai.
Nereus, M., 16 Oct.
Nestor, Ep. M., apud Pergen Pamphyliæ, 26 Feb.
Nicæas, Ep. Romatianæ urbis, 22 Jun.
Nicander, M., in Aegypto, 5 Jun.
Nicanor, ex vii Diaconis, M., apud Cyprum, 10 Jan.

Nicanor ('Nichandre'), apud Aegyptum, 5 Apr.
Nicasius, al. Nigasius, Pr. M. in pago Vilcassino, 11 Oct.
Nicasius, Ep. M., Lugduni, al. Rhemis, 14 Dec.
Nice, mater Proculi, M., Puteolis, 19 Oct.
Niceta, V. M., 24 Jul.
Nicetas, M., 25 Mai. Add.
Nicetas, M., Nicomediæ, 12 Sep. Add.
Nicetius ('Nicesy'), Ep., Lugduni, 2 Apr.
Nicetius, Ep. Viennæ, 5 Mai.
Nicetius ('Niceny'), Ep. C., Treviris, 1 Oct.
Nicetius ('Niceny'), Ep. Treviris, 5 Dec.
Nicodemi Inventio, Ierosolymis, 3 Aug.
Nicodemus, 27 Mar. Add.
Nicolas peregrinus, 3 Jun. Add.
Nicolaus, Ep. C., Myri in Lycia, 6 Dec.
Nicolaus, eius Translatio, 9 Mai; *item* 29 Mai. Add.
Nicolaus alter, Ep., 29 Mai. Add.
Nicolaus I., papa, 6 Dec. Add.
Nicomedes, Pr., M., Romæ, 15 Sep.
Nicomedes, eius Dedicatio, 1 Jun.
Nicophorus (al. Nicephorus), in Oriente, M., 17 Apr.
Nicophorus, M., apud Aegyptum, 25 Feb.
Nicostratus, primiscrinius, M., Romæ, 7 Jul.
Nicostratus, M., conjux S. Zoë, 7 Jul. Add.
Nicostratus, marmorum cæsor, M., Romæ, 8 Nov.
Nidoke, v. Judocus.
Nilus ('Line'), Ep. M., apud Tyrum in Phœnicia, 20 Feb.
Nilus, Ep. N., in Palæstina, 19 Sep.
Nimmia ('Menye'), M. Romæ, 12 Aug.
Ninianus ('Mynyane'), Ep. C., 16 Sep. Add.
Nitrand, M. in Egypto, 5 Jun. Add.
Noe, 28 Jan. Add.
Nonos, monachus, 12 Jun. Add.
Norbertus, Ep., 8 Jul. Add.
Novatus, C., Romæ, 20 Jun.
Numilo, V. M., Oscæ in Hispania, 22 Oct.
Nympha, V. M., 10 Nov. Add.
Nymphodora, M., Nicaeæ. 13 Mar.

Octavius, Thebanæ legionis miles, M., Taurini, 20 Nov.
Odalricus, al. Vldaricus, Ep. C., 4 Jul.
Odilion, abbas, 2 Jan.
Odo, abbas Cluniacensis, Turonis, 18 Nov.
Olympias, al. Olympiades, nobilis M., Cordulæ in Perside, 15 Apr.
Odalric, al. Vldaryke, Ep. C., eius Depositio, 4 Jul.
Odilio, abbas Cluniac., 31 Dec. Add.
Odo, Archiep. Cantuar., 2 Jun. Add.

Odulphus ('Adulph'), C. in Frisia, 12 Jun.
Odyle, abbas, 1 Jan. Add.
Olaty (Olavus?), 28 Sep. Add.
Olivierus, eques, Roncevallis, 16 Jun. Add.
Olympius, M. Romæ, 26 Jul.
Omnium Fidelium Defunctorum, 2 Nov.
Omnium Sanctorum Festivitas, 1 Nov.
Omnium Sanctorum Vigilia, 31 Oct.
Ondoce (Oudoceus), Ep., 2 Jul. Add.
Onesimus, Ep. M., Romæ et Ephesi, 16 Feb.
Onesimus, C., 13 Mai. Add.
Onesiphorus, discip. S. Pauli, 6 Sep. Add.
Onias, filius Simonis, 1 Oct. Add.
Oonfrius, eremita, 9 Jun. Add.; *item* 11 Jun. Add.
Opio, *al.* Epion, Pr. C., apud Bituricas, 12 Oct..
Oportuna, V., 22 Apr. Add.
Optatus, M., Cæsaraugustæ in Hisp., 15 Apr., *al.* 16 Apr.
Optatus, Ep. C., Antisiodori, 31 Aug.
Or, eremita, 29 Mar. Add.
Orestius, M., 12 Dec. Add.
Orientius, Ep., Tolosæ, 1 Mai.
Orosiensis, abbas, 14 Mai. Add.
Orontius, M., Ebreduni in Gallia, 22 Jan.
Oseas, propheta, 4 Jul.
Osman, V., in Hibernia, 9 Sep. Add.
Ostianus, *v.* Hostianus, Pr. M. in territorio Vivariensi, 30 Jul.
Oswaldus, Archiep. in Anglia, 28 Feb.
Oswaldus, R. M., in Anglia, 5 Aug.
Oswinus, R. Brit., 20 Aug. Add.
Osythe, V. M., 7 Oct.
Othoniel, judex, 1 Sep. Add.

Pachomius, abbas in Aegypto, 14 Mai.
Pachomius, Ep. M., 18 Feb. Add.
Pachomius, monachus in Scythia, 14 Mai. Add.
Pacianus, Ep., Barcinonæ, 9 Mar.
Pacianus, Ep., 21 Nov. Add.
Pagate, Pr. C., 25 Jan. Add.
Pakamye (Pantamia), 20 Feb.
Pake, M., 29 Jul. Add.
Palatyne, *v.* Caius palatinus, M.
Palatyne, *v.* Eusebius palatinus M.
Palatinus, M., 30 Mai. Add.
Palion, *v.* Pollio.
Palmatius cum familia sua, consul, MM., Romæ, 10 Mai.
Pambo, abbas, 1 Jul. Add.
Pamphilianus, Nicomediæ, 17 Mar.
Pamphilus, Pr. M., Cæsareæ Palestinæ, 1 Jun.
Pamphilus, M., Romæ, 21 Sep.
Panacius, Ep., 24 Jul. Add.

Pancratius, apud Tauromenium Sicil., 3 Apr.
Pancratius, juvenis annorum xiv., M., Romæ, 12 Mai.
Pannucius, 18 Feb. Add.
Pantænus, Alexandriæ, 7 Jul.
Pantaleon, medicus M., Nicomediæ, 28 Jul.
Panutius, abbas, 29 Nov. Add.
Papias, miles M., Romæ, 29 Jan.
Papias, Ep. Hierapoli, 22 Feb.
Papias, M., apud Aegyptum, 25 Feb.
Papinius, Ep. M., in Africa, 28 Nov.
Papyrius, Diac. M., Pergami in Asia, 13 Apr.
Parmenas, ex vii. Diaconis, M., Philippis, 23 Jan.
Parmenius, Pr. M., Cordulæ, 22 Apr.
Parmyn, *v.* Pirminus, Ep.
Parthenus, eunuchus M., Romæ, 19 Mai.
Pascasia, V. M. 9 Jan.
Paschasius, M., in Africa, 12 *al.* 13 Nov.
Passicrates, M., Dorostori in Mæsia ('Mafiaen'), 25 Mai.
Pastor, Nicomediæ, 12 Jan.
Pastor, M., Nicomediæ, 29 Mar.
Pastor, Ep., Aureliæ, 30 Mar.
Pastor, Pr. C., 26 Jul.
Pastor, puer, Compluti in Hisp., 6 Aug.
Paternus, Apr. 15. Add.
Paternianus, Ep. C., 10 Jul. Add.
Paternus, M., in territorio Senonensi 12 Nov.
Patiens, Ep. M. (*al.* C.) Lugduni Galliæ, 11 Sep.
Patricia ('Patryke'), uxor Macedonii, M., Nicomediæ, 13 Mar.
Patriarchæ xii, filii Jacob, 5 Feb. Add.
Patrike, Ep. C., Arvernis, 16 Mar.
Patricius, Ep. C., in Scotia, *h.e.* Hibernia, 17 Mar.
Patricius alter, 24 Aug. Add.
Patricius, abbas in Hibernia, 24 Aug.
Patrinus, Ep. C. Abrincis, 23 Sep.
Patrinus, *v.* Paternus, M.
Patroclus, M. Trecis 21 Jan.
Patryke, *v.* Patricia, Patricius.
Patryke, 4 Jun. *v.* Petrocus.
Paula, V.C., in Bethleem Juda, 27 Jan.
Paula, V.M., Malacæ in Hispania, 18 Jun.
Paula, M., Damasci, 20 Jul.
Paulina, filia Artemii, M., Romæ, 6 Jun.
Paulinus, Ep. C., Nolæ in Campania, 22 Jun.
Paulinus, Ep. M., *al.* C., Treviris, 31 Aug.
Paulinus, Tuderti in Tuscia, 26 Mai.
Paulinus, Ep., Eboraci in Brit., 10 Oct.
Paulus, primus Eremita, in Thebaide, 10 Jan.
Paulus, Ep., Tricassii, 1 Feb.
Paulus, Ep. M., Romæ, 8 Feb.

Paulus, eius Capitis Inventio, Romæ, 25 Feb.
Paulus, M., in Syria, 20 Mar.
Paulus (Sergius), Ep. C., Narbonæ in Gallia, 22 Mar. (al. 22 Jan.).
Paulus, monachus, 17 Apr.
Paulus, M., Lamosaci, 15 Mai.
Paulus, M., Novioduni, 17 Mai.
Paulus, Pr. M., Augustoduni, 1 Jun.
Paulus, Ep. M., Constantinopoli, 7 Jun.
Paulus, M., Tomis in Ponto, 20 Jun.
Paulus, frater Joannis, M., Romæ, 26 Jun.
Paulus, Ap. M., Romæ, 29 Jun.
Paulus, eius Conversio, 25 Jan.
Paulus, eius Celebratio, 29 Jun.
Paulus, eius Commemoratio, 30 Jun.
Paulus, eius primus ingressus in Urbem, Neronis anno ii°., 6 Jul.
Paulus, Ep. C., Narbonæ, 12 Dec.
Paulus ('symple'), 10 Jan. Add.
Paulas, papa, 27 Jan. Add.
Paulus, cum Syro, 26 Feb. Add.
Paulus, Ep. Leonensis, 11 Mar. Add.
Paulus, abbas in Libya, 17 Apr. Add.
Paulus, nobilis, M., 8 Jul. Add.
Paulus, diac. M., Cordubæ, 20 Jul. Add.
Pelagia, M., Nicopoli, Armenia minori, 11 Jul.
Pelagia, poenitens, Hierosolymis, 8 Oct.
Pelagia, M., Antiochiæ in Syria, 19 Oct.
Pelagia, conjux S. Dionysii, M., 21 Dec. Add.
Pelagius, M., 27 Aug. Add.
Pelagius I., papa, 27 Aug. Add.
Pelagius II., papa, 27 Aug. Add.
Peleus, Ep. M., apud Tyrum in Phœnicia, 20 Feb.
Peleus, Ep. M., in Palæstina, 19 Sep.
Peleuse, Pr. M., Alexandriæ, 7 Apr.
Pentecostes festum, 15 Mai. Add.
Peregrinus, M., Thessalonicæ, 5 Mai.
Peregrinus, Ep. Antisiodori, 16 Mai.
Peregrinus, Pr., Lugduni, 28 Jul.
Peregrinus, M., Romæ, 25 Aug.
Perfectus (' Perfyte '), Pr. M., Cordubæ, 18 Apr.
Pergentinus, M., Aretii in Tuscia, 3 Jun.
Permenye, v. Parmenius, Pr. Mr.
Pernell, v. Petronilla, V.
Perpetua, M., Tuburti in Mauritania, 7 Mar.
Perpetuus, Ep. Turonis, 8 Apr.
Perpetuus, Ep. C., Turonis, 30 Dec.
Perseveranda, V., 26 Jun.
Perthemy, v. Parthenus, M.
Petrocus (' Patryke '), C., 4 Jun.
Petronilla (' Pernell '), V. Romæ, 31 Mai.
Petrus, M., crucifixus Aulonæ, 3 Jan.
Petrus, M., Nicomediæ, 12 Mar.
Petrus, M., cum Aphrodisio, in Africa, 14 Mar.
Petrus, diac., Antiochiæ, 17 Apr.

Petrus, ordinis prædicatorum, M., Mediolani, 29 Apr.
Petrus, M., Lamosaci, 15 Mai.
Petrus, exorcista, M., Romæ, 2 Jun.
Petrus, Pr. M., Cordubæ, 7 Jun.
Petrus, Ap. cum Paulo, M., Romæ, 29 Jun.
Petrus cum Paulo, eorum Vigilia, 28 Jun.
Petrus, eius Cathedra Romæ, 18 Jan.
Petrus, eius Cathedra Antiochiæ, 22 Feb.
Petrus, eius Vincula, Romæ, Dedicatio in Esquiliis, 1 Aug.
Petrus, eius Dedicatio in monast. S. Germani, 9 Jun.
Petrus, M. Philadelphiæ in Arabia, 1 Aug.
Petrus, M., Romæ, 7 Aug.
Petrus, filius Marcellini, miles M., Tomis, 27 Aug.
Petrus, Archiep., Tarenti, 11 Sep.
Petrus, miles M., Romæ, 25 Oct.
Petrus, M., Hispali in Hispania, 8 Oct.
Petrus, Ep. M., Alexandriæ, 25 Nov.
Petrus, diac., 12 Mar. Add.
Petrus, Ep., 26 Mar. Add.
Petrus, Ep., Tarentasiensis, 22 Jun. Add.
Petrus, M., 5 Aug. Add.
Petrus, Ep., Tarentasiensis, 18 Oct. Add.
Petrus, Ep., Edessæ, 26 Nov. Add.
Petrus, M. in Persia, 27 Nov. Add.
Petrus, Archiep. Ravennæ, 2 Dec. Add.
Petronius, Ep., Bononiæ, 4 Oct. Add.
Phara, V., in pago Meldensi, 7 Dec.
Pharao, v. Faro, Ep. C.
Philadelphus, M., Augustæ, 5 Aug. Add.
Phileas (' Syle '), Ep. M., 4 Feb.
Philemon, M., apud Antinoum in Aegypto, 8 Mar.
Philibertus, abbas, in Herio (' Nerc ') insula, 20 Aug.
Philippus, Ep., Gortynæ in Creta, 11 Apr.
Philippus, Ap. M., apud Hierapolim 1 Mai.
Philippus, ex vii Diaconis, Cæsareæ, in Palæstina, 6 Jun.
Philippus, filius S. Felicitatis, M., Romæ, 10 Jul.
Philippus, filius S. Felicitatis, M., Romæ, 23 Nov.
Philippus, M., Alexandriæ, 15 Jul.
Philippus, pater S. Eugeniæ, Ep. M. Alexandriæ, 13 Sep.
Philippus, Ep. Adrianopoli in Thracia, 22 Oct.
Philippus, Imp. M., 12 Mai. Add.
Philippus, filius Imp. M. 12 Mai. Add.
Philippus ex deserto Egypti, 11 Jun. Add.
Philomon, v. Philumenus.
Philopolis, Thessalonicæ, 30 Mar.
Philumenus, M., Heracleæ in Thracia, 14 Nov.
Phinees, filius Eleazari, 1 Jul. Add.

Phocas, M., Antiochiæ, 5 Mar.
Phocas, Ep. M., Sinope in Ponto, 14 Jul.
Phocatus, Ep., 14 Jul.
Phoebe (de qua Apostolus ad Rom.), Corinthi, 3 Sep.
Pholcas, Ep., 16 Apr. Add.
Photinus ('Fotyne'), Ep. M., Lugduni, 2 Jun.
Phridiane, v. Frigidianus.
Phyle, Ep. M., 18 Feb. Add.
Phyllorony, M., 4 Feb. Add.
Phyllorrony, Pr., 9 Mar. Add.
Piamon, Pr., 25 Feb. Add.
Piaton ('Plato') Pr. M., Tornaci, 1 Oct.; *item.* 22 Feb. Add.
Piator, Pr. M., 1 Oct. Add.
Pientia, V. M., in pago Vilcassino, 11 Oct.
Pierius ('Hyery') Pr., Alexandriæ, 4 Nov.
Piericus, Pr., 10 Oct. Add.
Pigmenius, Pr. (? Ep.) M., Romæ, 24 Mar.
Pinytus ('Pyncty'), Ep. in Creta, 10 Oct.
Piolius, M., 29 Jul. Add.
Pion, abbas, 23 Feb. Add.
Pionius, P. M., Smyrnæ, 1 Feb.
Piperion, M., 11 Mar. Add.
Pirminus, Ep. Meldensis, 3 Nov.
Pitrion, abbas, 8 Apr. Add.
Pius ('Pituouse'), papa, Romæ, 11 Jul. Add.
Placidia, V., 15 Oct. Add.
Placidus, monachus M., in Sicilia, 5 Oct.
Plato, M., Ancyræ ('Syria') in Galatia, 22 Jul.
Plato, v. Piaton, Pr. M.
Plautus, M., in Thracia, 29 Sep.
Plutarchus, catechumenus M., Alexandriæ, 28 Jun.
Poliact, v. Polyeuctus, M.
Polianus, M., in Africa, 10 Sep.
Polioctus, al. Polyeuctus, Cæsareæ Cappad., 21 al. 22 Mai.
Polius, Diac. M., in Mauritania Cæsariensi, 21 Mai.
Pollio, M., in Pannonia ('at Padway'), 28 Apr.
Polycarpus, Ep., 1 Feb.
Polycarpus, Ep. M., Smyrnæ, 26 Jan.
Polycarpus, eius Reliquiæ, 4 Jul.
Polycarpus, Pr. C., Romæ, 23 Feb.
Polychronius, Ep. M., Babyloniæ in Perside, 17 Feb.
Polycrates, Ep., 31 Jan. Add.
Polyeuctus ('Poliact'), M., Melitenæ in Armenia, 13 Feb.
Polyeuctus, M., Cæsareæ Cappad., 21 Mai.
Polymius, R. Indiæ, 24 Aug. Add.
Pontianus, 14 Jan.
Pontianus, M., Spoleti, 19 Jan.
Pontianus, M. Romæ, 25 Aug.

Pontianus ('Pociane'), Ep. M. in Sardinia, Sepultus Romæ, 19 Nov.
Pontianus, papa M., Romæ, 20 Nov.
Pontianus, M., 11 Dec.
Pontinus, C., 18 Aug.
Pontius ('Ponce') M., 11 Feb.
Pontius, al. Pontianus, diac. Carthagine, 8 Mar.
Pontius, M., in Gallia, 14 Mai.
Porphyrius, magister Agapiti, Romæ, 20 Aug.
Porphyrius, miles, M., Alexandriæ, 24 Nov. Add.
Potamia, M., Thaguræ in Africa, 5 Dec.
Potamiæna ('Potañan'), V. M., Alexandriæ, 28 Jun.
Potamius ('Potamye'), M., in Cypro, 20 Feb.
Potentiana, al. Pudentiana, V., Romæ, 19 Mai.
Potentianus, M., apud Senonas, 19 Oct.
Potentianus, Ep. M., apud Senonas, 31 Dec.
Potitus, M., 22 Jan. Add.
Præjectus, v. Proiectus, Ep., Arvernis, 25 Jan.
Præpedigna, uxor Claudii, M., Ostiæ, 18 Feb.
Præsidius, Ep. C., in Africa, 6 Sep.
Prætextatus, M., 11 Dec.
Pragmatius, ('Pragmas') Ep. C., Augustoduni, 22 Nov.
Praxedes, V., Romæ, 21 Jul.
Priamus, M., in Sardinia, 28 Mai.
Prilidianus, puer cum S. Babylla, M., Antiochiæ, 24 Jan.
Primitivus, ex xviii Martt., M., Cæsaraugustæ in Hisp., 15 al. 16 Apr.
Primitivus, M., Romæ, 10 Jun.
Primitivus, filius Symphorosæ, M., in Tibure, 27 Jun.
Primus, M., in Hellesponto, 3 Jan.
Primus, M., Romæ, 9 Jun.
Primus, Pr. M., 11 Mai. Add.
Prisca, V. M., Romæ, 18 Jan.
Prisca, 4 Sep. Add.
Priscilla, V., Romæ, 16 Jan.
Priscilla, uxor Aquilæ, in Asia minori, 8 Jul.
Priscillianus, clericus M., Romæ, 4 Jan.
Priscillianus, Ep. M., 16 Dec. Add.
Priscus, Pr. M., Romæ, 4 Jan.
Priscus, M., Cæsareæ in Palæstina, 20 Mar.
Priscus, M., in ternt. Antisiodorensi, 26 Mai.
Priscus, discip. Christi, M., Capuæ, 1 Sep.
Priscus, Tomis in Ponto, 1 Oct.
Privatus, Ep. M., in civitate Mimatensi, 21 Aug.

Privatus, M. in Frisia (Phrygia), 2c Sep.
Privatus, miles, Romæ, 14 Oct.
Privatus M., Romæ, 17 Oct. Add.
Probus, M., Tarsi in Cilicia, 11 Oct.
Probus, M., in Africa, 12 al. 13 Nov.
Probus, Ep., Reatinensis, 12 Aug. Add.
Probus, Ep., Ravennæ, 10 Nov. Add.
Processus, M. Romæ, 2 Jul.
Prochorus, ex vii Diaconis, M., Antiochiæ, 9 Apr.
Procopius, M., Cæsareæ in Palæstina, 8 Jul.
Proculus, M., Interamnæ, 14 Apr.
Proculus, Diac. M., Neapoli ('Puteolane') in Campania, 19 Sep.
Proculus, Diac. M., Puteolis, 19 Oct.
Proculus (Ep.) M. Augustoduni, 4 Nov.
Proculus, Pr. (al. Ep. M.) Narniæ, 1 Dec.
Proculus, Ep. C., 9 Dec. Add.
Proiectus (al. Preiectus, Ep.) M., Arvernis, 25 Jan.
Prokor, v. Prochorus.
Prophetæ XII. 4 Jul. Add.
Prosdocimus, Ep. Patav., 7 Nov. Add.
Prosper, Ep., 25 Jun. Add.
Protasius, M., Mediolani, 19 Jun.
Proterus, Pr. M., 21 Aug. Add.
Protolicus, M. Alexandriæ, 14 Feb.
Protus, pædagogus Cantii, M. Aquileæ, 31 Mai.
Protus, eunuchus, M., Romæ, 11 Sept.
Prudens, v. Pudens.
Ptolomæus ('Tholony') M., 19 Oct.
Ptolomæus ('Tholony') miles M., Alexandriæ, 20 Dec.
Publius, in Africa, 19 Feb.
Publius, Ep. M., Athenis, 21 Jan.
Publius, M. ex xviii Martt., Cæsaraugustæ in Hisp., 15 al. 16 Apr.
Publius, M. 20 Apr.
Publy (21 Apr.), v. Pusitius.
Pudens ('Prudent') discip. Pauli, pater S. Pudentianæ, 19 Mai.
Pudentiana, al. Potentiana, V.M., Romæ, 19 Mai.
Pueri duo MM., cum S. Blasio, Sebastæ in Armenia, 3 Feb.
Pueri Tres in Babilonia, 16 Dec.
Pule, lector, 27 Apr. Add.
Punyfyke, abbas, 14 Mar. Add.
Purificatio B. Mariæ V., 2 Feb.
Pusitius ('Publy') artifex regius, M., in Perside, 21 Apr.
Pusitii filia, M., 21 Apr.
Pygasius, M., in Perside, 2 Nov. Add.
Pygmeny, v. Pigmenius (Ep.) M.
Pynitus, al. Pinytus, Ep. in Creta, 10 Oct.
Pyrane (al. Keran), 5 Mar. Add.

Quadratus, M., in Africa, 26 Mai.
Quadratus, Ep. Athenis, 26 Mai.

Quadratus, Ep. C., 21 Aug.
Quartilla, M. apud Surrentum, 19 Mar.
Quartus, M., Romæ, 10 Mai.
Quartus, M. Romæ, 6 Aug.
Quartus, discip. Apostolorum, 3 Nov.
Quatuor Coronati, MM., Romæ, 8 Nov.
Queranus, abbas, in Scotia, 9 Sep.
Quinidius, Ep., 15 Feb.
Quintianus, Pr. M., 14 Jun.
Quintilanus, M., Cæsaraugustæ in Hisp., 15 Apr. al. 16 Apr.
Quintillus, al. Quintilla, M., apud Surrentum, 19 Mar.
Quintinus, M., in Gallia, 31 Oct.
Quint[in]us, M. in Lucania, 29 Oct.
Quintus, M., in Africa, 4 Jan.
Quintus, apud Surrentum, 19 Mar.
Quintus, Romæ, translatus Capuam, 10 Mai.
Quintus, M. Capuæ, 5 Sep.
Quintus, 1 Jun. Add.
Quintyne, v. Quintus, M., 4 Jan.
Quiriacus, al. Cyriacus, Ep. M., Hierosolymis, 4 Mar.
Quiriacus, in Portu Romano, 23 Aug.
Quiriacus, M. Antiochiæ, al. Tarsi in Cilicia, 16 Jun.
Quiriacus, al. Cyriacus, in Africa, 21 Jun.
Quiriacus, M., Romæ, 12 Aug.
Quiriacus, Ep. M., 5 Mar. Add.
Quiriacus, Augustæ, 5 Aug. Add.
Quirinus ('Ciryne'), M., Romæ, 25 Mar.
Quirinus, tribunus, M., Romæ, 30 Mar.
Quirinus, Ep. M., Sciscæ in Illyrico, 4 Jun.
Quirinus, Pr. M., in pago Vilcassino, 11 Oct.
Quirinus, Pr. M., eius Reliquiæ, 4 Jul.
Quirinus, M., Romæ, 26 Mar. Add.

Rachab, 1 Sep. Add.
Rachel, uxor Jacob, 5 Feb. Add.
Radegunda, V. R., Pictavis, 31 Aug.
Ranulphus, M., in pago Atrobatensi, 27 Mai.
Raphael, archangelus, 7 Mar. Add.
Rebecca, 5 Feb. Add.
Rectitius, Ep. Augustodunensis, 21 Oct. Add.
Redemptus, Ep., 28 Jul. Add.
Reges Tres Coloniæ, 6 Jan. Add.
Regina, V. M., Augustoduni, 7 Sep.
Regulus ('Rewle') Arelatensis Ep., in castro Silvanectensi, 30 Mar.; item, ('Rule') 23 Apr.
Relatio Pueri Jesu ex Aegypto, 7 Jan.
Reliquiarum Receptio SS. Polycarpi, Sebastiani, Urbani, et Quirini, MM., 4 Jul.
Remachlewe, 19 Mar. Add.
Remedius, Ep., Vapingi, 3 Feb.

Remigius, Ep. C., Rhemis, 1 Oct.
Remigius, Ep., eius Depositio, Rhemis, 13 Jan.
Reparata, V. M., 8 Oct. Add.
Respicius, M., 10 Nov. Add.
Restitutus ('Rustyke'), M., Romæ, 29 Mai.
Restitutus, Romæ, 11 Jun.
Restitutus, M., Antiochiæ, 23 Aug.
Resurrectio Domini, 27 Mar.
Reverianus, Pr. M., Augustoduni, 1 Jun.
Revocatus, M., Tuburbi in Mauritania, 7 Mar.
Revocatus, M., in Africa, 9 Jan.
Rewe, 28 Jan. Add.
Rewle, *v.* Regulus, Ep.
Richardus, Cicestrensis Ep. C., in Anglia, 3 Apr.
Richardus eius Translatio, Cicestriæ, 16 Jun.
Richardus, R. C., 7 Feb. Add.
Richarius, Pr. C., in monast. Centula, 26 Apr.
Rigobert, 4 Jan. Add.
Robertus, fundator ordinis Cist., 29 Apr. Add.
Robertus, abbas, 7 Jun. Add.
Rogatianus, M., Nannete in Brit. minore, 24 Mai.
Rogatianus, Pr. M., in Africa, 26 Oct.
Rogatus, monachus M., Carthagine in Africa, 17 Aug.
Rogatus, C., 6 Oct.
Rogatus, monachus, 23 Mar. Add.
Rolandus, eques, 16 Jun. Add.
Romanus, abbas in territ. Lugdunensi, 28 Feb.
Romanus, miles M., Romæ, 9 Aug.
Romanus, Archiep. C., Rotomagi in Normannia, 23 Oct.
Romanus, monachus M., Antiochiæ, 18 Nov.
Romanus, Pr. C., in castro Blauio, 24 Nov.
Romanus, abbas, 22 Mai. Add.
Romanus, diac., 8 Jul. Add.
Romanus, Ep. in Hibernia, 18 Nov. Add.
Romericus, abbas, 8 Dec. Add.
Romula, V., Romæ, 12 Aug. Add.
Romulus, M., Concordiæ, 17 Feb.
Romulus, M., in Mauritania, 24 Mar.
Romwaldus, abbas, 19 Jun. Add.
Rophyle, Ep., 18 Jul. Add.
Roseba, V.M., 20 Nov. Add.
Rosula, M., in Africa, 14 Sep.
Rufina, soror Secundæ, V. M., Romæ, 10 Jul.
Rufina, V.M., Hispali in Hispania, 19 Jul.
Rufine, M., 12 Feb.
Rufinus, M., Romæ, 28 Feb.

Rufinus, M., Suessione, 14 Jun.
Rufinus, M., Syracusis in Sicilia, 21 Jun.
Rufinus, puer M., Ancyræ in Galatia, 4 Sep.
Rufinus, filius Wolferi regis, in Britannia, 31 Jul. Add.
Rufus, M., Militanæ in Armenia, 19 Apr.
Rufus, M., Philadelphiæ in Arabia, 1 Aug.
Rufus, patricius, M., Capuæ, 27 Aug.
Rufus, discip. B. Pauli, 21 Nov.
Rufus cum suis, MM., 28 Nov.
Rufus, discip. Christi, M., Philippis in Macedonia, 18 Dec.
Rule, *v.* Regulus.
Rumwoldus, 3 Nov. Add.
Rupertus, Ep., 27 Mar. Add.
Rusticus, subdiac., M., Karthagine in Africa, 17 Aug.
Rusticus, diaconus, *al.* Pr. M., Parisiis, 9 Oct.
Rusticus, subdiaconus, 23 Mar. Add.
Rusticus, M., 9 Aug. Add.
Rusticus, Ep. C., Narbonæ, 26 Oct.
Rustyke, *v.* Restitutus, 29 Mai.
Ruth, vidua sancta, 1 Sep. Add. ; *item* 14 Sep. Add.
Rutulus, M., in Africa, 18 Feb.
Ryoke, abbas, 6 Feb. Add.

Sabas, abbas C., Mutalæ in Cappadocia, 5 Dec.
Sabbatum Sanctum ('Holy Saterdaye'), 26 Mar.
Sabina, uxor Valentini, M., Romæ, 29 Aug.
Sabina, V. in pago Tricassino, 29 Aug.
Sabina, M., Abelæ in Hisp., 27 Oct.
Sabina, V.M., 29 Aug. Add.
Sabinianus ('Saluniane'), M., in Territ. Tricassino, 29 Jan.
Sabi[ni]anus (Ep.) M. apud Senonas, 31 Dec.
Sabinus, in territ. Pictavensi, 11 Jul.
Sabinus, M., Damasci, 20 Jul.
Sabinus, Ep. M., Spoleti, 30 Dec.
Sacerdos, Ep. C., Lugduni, 12 Sep.
Sagar, Ep. M., Laodiceæ, 6 Oct.
Salaberga, abbatissa, 23 Sep. Add.
Sale, 28 Jan. Add.
Saloma, Maria, Ierosolymis, 22 Oct.
Salomon, M., Cordubæ in Lusitania, 8 Feb.
Salomon, filius David, 1 Aug. Add.
Salonius ('Salomon'), Ep. C., Genuæ, 28 Sep.
Saluniane, *v.* Sabinianus, M.
Salustia, uxor Cerealis, Romæ, 14 Sep.
Salustianus, C. in Sardinia, 8 Jun.
Salutaris, archidiac. C. Karthagine exulatus in Africa, 13 Jul.
Salutary, *v.* Solutor, miles, M.

INDEX SANCTORUM. 271

Salvius ('Salver') M., in Africa, 11 Jan.
Salvius, Ep. Engolismensis, apud Valencenas, 26 Jun.
Samdyne, V., 19 Dec. Add.
Samon, M., Edessæ, 20 Nov.
Sampson, Ep. C., Dolæ, in Brit. minore, 28 Jul.
Samson, judex, 1 Sep. Add.
Samuel, propheta, 20 Aug.
Samuel, Pr., 20 Aug. Add.
Sanctinus, Ep. C., 22 Sep. Add.
Sanctorum Omnium Festivitas, 1 Nov.; Vigilia, 31 Oct.
Sanctulus, Pr., 27 Jul. Add.
Sanctus, diaconus M., Lugduni, 2 Jun.
Sapientes Quinquaginta qui cum S. Katerina disputationem inierunt, 13 Nov. Add.
Sapientia, mater S. Fidei &c., M. Romæ, 1 Aug.
Sare, uxor Abraham, 5 Feb. Add.
Sare, abbatissa, 1 Mar. Add.
Sarinus, 4 Dec. Add.
Sarisburiensis (*al.* Sarum) Ecclesiæ Dedicatio, 30 Sep.
Saruke, 28 Jan. Add.
Satary, *v.* Satyrus, M.
Saturianus, M., 16 Oct.
Saturnia, V.M., Coloniæ Agrippinæ, 21 Oct.
Saturninus, Alexandriæ, 31 Jan.
Saturninus, Pr. M., in Africa, 11 *al.*, 12 Feb.
Saturninus, M., Tuburbi in Mauritania, 7 Mar.
Saturnini Quatuor, MM., Cæsaraugustæ in Hisp., 15 *al.* 16 Apr.
Saturninus, M., Alexandriæ, 31 Jan.
Saturninus, M., Romæ, 2 Mai.
Saturninus, peregrinus M., in Portu Romano, 22 Aug.
Saturn[in]us, M., Capuæ, 6 Oct.
Saturninus, C., Cæsareæ in Palæstina, 14 Oct.
Saturninus, M., Romæ. 29 Nov.
Saturninus, M., 16 Oct.
Saturninus, C., Tolosæ, 30 Oct.
Saturninus, Ep. M., Tolosæ, temporibus Decii, 29 Nov.
Saturninus, senex M., Romæ, 29 Nov.
Saturnus, M., 29 Jul. Add.
Satyre, 7 Mar. Add.
Satyrianus, cum fratribus, MM. in Africa, 16 Oct.
Satyrus, M., in Achaia, *alias* Antiochiæ, 12 Jan.
Satyrus, M., *al.* C., in Africa, 29 Mar.
Savina, V., 29 Aug. Add.
Savinianus, Ep. M., apud Senonas, 19 Oct.
Savinianus, M., 29 Aug. Add.

Savinus, Ep. Canosæ ('cawsyne'), 17 Feb. Add.
Savinus, Ep. Placentiæ, 11 Dec. Add.
Saula, V.M., Coloniæ Agrippinæ, 20 *al.* 21 Oct.
Saulus, monachus, Cordubæ, 17 Apr.
Sawster, *v.* Vedastus, Ep., 6 Feb.
Sawstyne, *v.* Faustinus, 22 Mai.
Saynt, *v.* Sanctus, diac.
Scholastica, V., soror S. Benedicti, V., 10 Feb.
Scholastica, eius Translatio, 11 Jul.
Schrysotele, *v.* Chrysotelus.
Schyrion, Ischyrion, *al.* Chiridion, *al.* Chæremon, M. Alexandriæ, 22 Dec.
Scubiculus, diaconus M., in pago Vilcassino, 11 Oct.
Sebastia, *al.* Sabbatia, M., Sirmii, 4 Jul.
Sebastianus, miles M., Romæ, 20 Jan.
Sebastianus, eius reliquiæ, 4 Jul.
Sebastianus, M., in Armenia minore, 8 Feb.
Sebastianus, M., eius Translatio, 9 Dec.
Sebba, R., 24 Mar. Add.
Secunda, soror Rufinæ, V.M., Romæ, 10 Jul.
Secunda, M., Karthagine, 17 Jul.
Secunda, V.M., Tuburbi in Africa, 30 Jul.
Secundianus, M., Concordiæ, 17 Feb.
Secundianus, M., in Tuscia, Coloniæ, 9 Aug.
Secundinus, M., Adrumeti in Africa, 21 Feb.
Secundinus, Ep. M., in Numidia, 29 Apr.
Secundinus, M., Cordubæ, 21 Mai.
Secundole, *v.* Secundus, M.
Secundulus, Tuburbi in Mauritania, 7 Mar.
Secundus ('Secundole'), M., in Mauritania, 24 Mar.
Secundus, Ep. C., in Hispania, 15 Mai.
Secundus, M., Victimilii in Italia, 26 Aug.
Secundus, M., 30 Mar. Add.
Securus, frater Veri, M., in Africa, 2 Dec.
Seledon, *v.* Cheledonius, miles M.
Sem, 28 Jan. Add.
Senator, Albani, 26 Sep.
Seneses, magicus M., 23 Mai. Add.
Sennes, subregulus, M., Romæ, 30 Jul.
Sennes, ('Sisynny'), diaconus, M. Romæ, 29 Nov.
Septem Fratres, MM., Romæ, 29 Mai.
Septem Dormientes, MM., Ephesi, 27 Jul. (*al.* Jun.).
Septem Dormientium resurrectio, 11 Aug. Add.
Septimus, monachus M., Karthagine in Africa, 17 Aug.

Septimus, lector, M., Venusiæ in Apulia, 24 Oct.
Sequanus, *al.* Sygnus, Pr. C., in territ. Lingonensi, 19 Sep.
Seraphia, V. M., Romæ, 29 Jul.
Seraphia, eius Inventio, sive Commemoratio, 3 Sep.
Seraphion, clericus, filius Marcellini, M., Tomis, 27 Aug.
Serapion, M., apud Aegyptum, 25 Feb.
Serapion, anachoreta, Ep. Thmueos, Alexandriæ, 21 Mar.
Serapion, lector apud l'entapolim Libyæ, 26 Mar.
Serapion, ex vii Dormientibus, M., Ephesi, 27 Jul.
Serapion, filius Marcellini, M., Tomis in Ponto, 27 Aug.
Serapion, Ep. C., Antiochiæ, 30 Oct.
Serapion, M. Alexandriæ, 14 Nov.
Serapion, M., 8 Feb. Add.
Serena, uxor Diocletiani, Romæ, 16 Aug.
Serene, Nicomediæ, 17 Mar.
Serenicus, C., 7 Mai. Add.
Serenus, et Serenus alter catechumenus, MM., Alexandriæ, 28 Jun.
Serenus, monachus, M., 24 Feb. Add.
Serenus, abbas, 24 Feb. Add.
Sergius, M., Cæsareæ Cappad., 24 Feb.
Sergius, primicerius, M., Sergiopoli in Augusta Euphratesia, 7 Oct.
Servandus, M., in Hispania, 23 Oct.
Servatius, Ep. Tungrensis, 13 Mai.; ejus Translatio, 7 Jun. Add.
Servilianus ('Servulane'), M., Romæ, 20 Apr.
Servilius, M., in Istria, 24 Mai.
Servus ('Sevy'), subdiac, M., Karthagine in Africa, 17 Aug.
Servulus, M., Adrumeti in Africa, 21 Feb.
Servulus, paralyticus, Romæ, 23 Dec.
Sesary, *v.* Cæsarius, M.
Seth, 23 Jan. Add.
Severianus, conjux Aquilæ, M., Neocæsareæ in Mauritania, 23 Jan.
Severianus, Ep., Gavali, 25 Jan.
Severianus, M., e quatuor coronatis, Romæ, 8 Nov.
Severianus, Ep., Lugduni, 11 Nov.
Severinus, Ep. C., Neapoli in Campania, 8 Jan.
Severinus, abbas monast. Agaunensis in castro Nantoniensi, 11 Feb.
Severinus, C., 2 Oct.
Severinus, Ep., Burdigalæ, 21 Oct.
Severinus, *v.* Severus, Ep., Ravennæ.
Severinus, Ep. C., Coloniæ, 23 Oct.
Severinus, monachus, Tibure, 1 Nov.
Severinus, M., Viennæ, 19 Nov.
Severinus, monachus, Parisiis, 23 Nov.
Severinus, abbas, 8 Jan. Add.

Severinus, Ep., Coloniæ, 5 Jun. Add.
Severinus. *al.* Boëtius, M., 23 Oct. Add.
Severus, C. Alexandriæ, 11 Jan.
Severus ('Severyne'), Ep., Ravennæ, 1 Feb.
Severe, *v.* Sirenus, monachus.
Severus, Pr. C., Viennæ in Gallia, 8 Aug.
Severus, M., e quatuor coronatis, Romæ, 8 Nov.
[Severus], M., cum Mansueto, Alexandriæ, 30 Dec.
Severus, Ep., 1 Feb. Add.
Severus, Pr. M., 1 Feb. Add
Severus, Pr. C., 1 Feb. Add.
Severus, abbas, 25 Aug. Add.
Servanus, Ep., 25 Aug. Add.
Sexburga, V., soror S. Etheldredæ, in Anglia, 6 Jul.
Sewsyppe, *v.* Speusippus, M.
Sextus, C., 10 Feb. Add.
Sicarius ('Sycare'), M., 2 Mai. Add.
Sidonius, Ep., 24 Aug. Add.
Sidronius, M., apud Senones, 11 Jul.
Sigibertus, R., monachus, 16 Jan. Add.
Sigismundus, R. M., Seduni, 1 Mai.
Sigon ('Signy'), Pr., in territ. Lingonicæ civitatis, 19 Sep.
Silas, Ap., in Macedonia, 13 Jul.
Silvanus, Ep. M., apud Tyrum in Phœnicia, 2 *al.* 20 Feb.
Silvanus, M., in Africa, 18 Feb.
Silvanus, Ep. M., Gazæ in Palæstina, 4 Mai.
Silvanus, M., in Istria, 24 Mai.
Silvanus, filius S. Felicitatis, M., Romæ, 10 Jul.
Silvanus, puer M., Ancyræ in Galatia, 4 Sep.
Silvanus, Ep. C., in territorio Bituricensi, 22 Sep.
Silvanus, abbas, 22 Sep. Add.
Silverius ('Syvere'), papa, C. *al.* M., Romæ, 20 Jun.
Silvester ('Sylvere'), Ep. C., Cabilone, 20 Nov.
Silvester, papa, C., Romæ, 31 Dec.
Silvinus, Ep. Tolosanus, 17 Feb.
Silvius, M., Alexandriæ, 21 Apr.
Simeon, monachus, Antiochiæ, 5 Jan.
Simeon, filius Cleophæ, Ep. M., Ierosolymis, 18 Feb.
Simeon, Ep. M., in Perside, 21 Apr.
Simeon, monachus, Treviris, 1 Jun.
Simeon, monachus in Sicilia, 27 Jul.
Simeon Justus, 8 Oct.
Similianus, Ep. C., Nannete in Britannia minori, 16 Jun.
Simitrius ('Symniter'), Pr., cum sociis xxii, M., Romæ, 26 Mai.
Simon Chananæus, cum S. Juda, Ap. M., in Perside, 28 Oct.; eorum Vigilia, 27 Oct.

Simon, filius Oniæ, 1 Oct. Add.
Simplicius, senator, M., Romæ, 10 Mai.
Simplicius, Ep. C., Augustoduni, 24 Jun.
Simplicius, M., Romæ, 29 Jul.
Simplicius, Ep. C., Augustoduni, 19 Nov.
Simplicius, papa, 7 Jan. Add. ; 2 Mar. Add.
Sirenus, *al.* Sinerius, *vel* Syrenus ('Severe'), monachus, M., Sirmii, 23 Feb.
Siricius, papa, 7 Jan. Add.
Siridion, Ep., 2 Jan.
Sisinnius, Cappadox M., in Anaunia, 29 Mai.
Sisinnius, Diaconus [Ep. C.], M., Romæ, 29 Nov.
Sixtus I. (*al.* Xystus), papa, M., Romæ, 6 *al.* 16 Apr.
Sixtus II. (*al.* Xystus), papa, M., Romæ, 6 Aug.
Sixtus (*al.* Xystus), discip. B. Petri, Ep. C., Rhedon. *al.* Rhemis in Gallia, 1 Sep.
Sixtus (' Syxt '), papa, Romæ, 7 Jan. Add.
Sixtus, papa, 28 Mar. Add.
Sixtus III., papa, 6 Aug. Add.
Skumculy, *v.* Scubiculus, Diac.
Smaragdus, M., Romæ, 16 Mar.
Smaragdus, eius Translatio, 8 Aug.
Socrates, in Britanniis, 17 Sep.
Solemnius, Ep. Carnotensis, Blesis, 25 Sep., *item* 24 Sep. Add.
Solutor, M., Ravennæ, 13 Nov.
Solutor (' Solutary'), miles Thebanæ legionis M., Taurini, 20 Nov.
Sophia, matrona, 17 Jun. Add.
Sophonias, propheta, 18 Mai. Add.
Sophronius, C., 3 Mai. Add.
Sophy, 15 Mai. Add.
Sosipater, discip. Pauli, Pyrrhiberoeæ (' at l'uricorea ') 25 Jun.
Sosius, Diac. Misenas, M., in Campania, 23 Sep.
Sosthenes, M., Chalcedone, 10 Sep.
Sosthenes, discip. Fauli, Corinthi, 18 *al.* 28 Nov.
Soter, papa, Romæ, 22 Apr.
Soteris, V., 6 Feb.
Soteris, V. M., in Oriente (? Romæ, via Appia), 10 Feb.
Speciosus, nobilis, monachus, 30 Jul. Add.
Speciosus, monachus in Monte Cassino, 20 Sep. Add.
Speratus, M., Karthagine, 16 *al.* 17 Jul.
Spes, V. M., Romæ, 1 Aug.; *item* 17 Jun. Add.
Spes, abbas, 10 Aug. Add.
Speusippus (' Sewsyppe '), M. apud Lingonas, 17 Jan.
Spiridion, propheta, Ep. C., in Cypro, 14 Dec.
Stactæus, filius Symphorosæ, M., Tibure, 27 Jun.

MARTILO.

Stactæus, M., Romæ, 28 Sep.
Stephana, M., 18 Sep. Add.
Stephanus, M. in Ægypto, 1 Apr.
Stephanus, cum Castore, M., Tarsi in Cilicia, 27 Apr.
Stephanus, in Ægypto, 8 Mai.
Stephanus, papa, M., Romæ, 2 Aug.
Stephanus, subdiac. M., Romæ, 6 Aug.
Stephanus, M., in Britanniis, 17 Sep.
Stephanus, protomartyr, 26 Dec.
Stephanus, eius Octava, 2 Jan.
Stephanus, eius Inventio, Ierosolymis, 3 Aug.
Stephanus, abbas, 13 Feb. Add.
Stephanus, alter abbas, 13 Feb. Add.
Stephanus cum Laurentio, 7 Mai. Add.
Stephanus II., papa C., Romæ, 2 Aug. Add.
Stephanus III., papa, Romæ, 2 Aug. Add.
Stephanus, eremita, 3 Aug. Add.
Stephanus, Pr., 20 Nov. Add.
Stercatius, frater Victoris, M., Emeritæ in Hisp., 24 Jul.
Stratoclianus, *v.* Austriclinianus.
Stytyny, *v.* Cythinus, M.
Successus, M., Cæsaraugustæ in Hisp., 15 *al.* 16 Apr.
Sulpitius Pius, Ep. M., apud Bituricas, 17 Jan.
Sulpitius, M., Romæ, 20 Apr.
Suranus, abbas, M., 27 Sep. Add.
Susanna, V. M., Romæ, 11 Aug.
Susanna, per Danielem liberata, 28 Aug. Add.
Swythunus, Ep., Wintoniæ in Anglia, 2 Jul.
Swythunus, eius Translatio, 15 Jul.
Swythunus, eius Ordinatio, 30 Oct.
Syagrius, (' Fiagry ') Ep. C., Augustoduni, 27 Aug.
Sycare, M., 2 Mai. Add.
Sycus (' Ysyce '), Antiochiæ, 30 Mai. Add.
Sydron, M., in territ. Senonum, 11 Jul.
Sygny, *v.* Sequanus, *vel* Sigon.
Syle, discip. Apostolorum, in Macedonia, 13 Dec.
Syle, Ep. M., *v.* Philæas, 4 Feb.
Sylvanus, &c., *v.* Silvanus, &c.
Sylvia, V., 10 Mar. Add.
Symeon, 4 Feb. Add.
Symmachus (' Symake '), papa, 21 Feb. Add.
Symmachus, M., 27 Mai. Add.
Symmetrius (' Symniter '), Pr. M., Romæ, 26 Mai. ; *item*, 27 Mai. Add.
Symphorianus, M., Augustoduni, 22 Aug.
Symphorianus, Romæ, 9 Nov.
Symphorosa, uxor Getulii cum vii filiis, M., Tibure, 27 Jun. *al.* 18 Jul.
Symphorosa. M., in Campania, 2 Jul.
Symphronianus, M., Romæ, 7 Jul.

S

Symphronius, M., Romæ, 26 Jul.
Symplicius, papa, 2 Mar. Add.
Symylyane, v. Similianus, Ep. C.
Syncletyke, abbatissa, 1 Mar. Add.
Syntyche, V., Philippis, 22 Jul.
Syrenus, alias Sinerius, ('Seuere') monachus M., Sirmii, 23 Feb.
Syuere, v. Silverius.
Syrus, discip. Hermagoræ, C., Ticinii, sive Papiæ, 12 Sep.
Syrus, Ep., 7 Feb. Add.
Syrus, M., 14 Feb. Add. ; 26 Feb. Add.
Syrus, Ep. Papiæ, eius Transla'io, 17 Mai. Add.
Syrus, Ep. C., 9 Dec. Add.
Sysinnius ('Sysyn'), 12 Mar. Add.
Sythe, v. Dorothy, 15 Jan. Add.
Syxt, v. Sixtus, papa.

Tabita, 4 Mar. Add.
Tabra, diac. M., 22 Nov. Add.
Tabrata, diac. M., 22 Nov. Add.
Tarbua, al. Tarbula, 22 Apr.
Tarrasius, C., 17 Sep. Add.
Tatianus, diac. M., Aquileiæ, 16 Mar.
Tatwinus ('Tadwyne') Ep. C., Cantuariæ, 30 Jul. Add.
Taurinus, Ep. C., apud Ebroicenses in Gallia, 11 Aug.
Tecla, v. Thecla, V.
Telesphorus, papa M., Romæ, 5 Jan.
Terentianus, M., 30 Aug. Add.
Tertius ('Cercy'), monachus C., in Africa, 6 Dec.
Tertulla, Virgo sacra, M., in Numidia, 29 Apr.
Tertullianus, M., 4 Aug. Add.
Tertullinus, Pr. M., Romæ, 4 Aug.
Thaddæus, qui et Judas, cum Simone, Ap. M., 28 Oct.
Thaddæus, in deserto Egypti, 11 Jun. Add.
Thais, 8 Oct. Add.
Tharacus, al. Tharacius, M., Tarsi in Cilicia, 11 Oct.
Tharcilla, 17 Aug. Add.
Thare, 28 Jan. Add.
Tharsitius, acolytus, M., Romæ, 15 Aug.
Thebæi, MM., Seduni in Gallia, 22 Sep.
Thecla, al. Tecla, V., 22 Feb.
Thecla, V. M., Iconii, sepulta Seleuciæ, 23 Sep.
Thecla, V., 3 Sep. Add.
Thelesfory, v. Telesphorus, papa M.
Theliaus, v. Eliud, Ep., 9 Feb. Add.
Theobaldus, C., 1 Jul. Add.
Theodoce, v. Theodotus, M.
Theodardus ('Hereodarde'), Ep. Tungrensis, 10 Sep. Add.
Theodora ('Theodour'), M., Nicææ, 13 Mar.
Theodora ('Theodour'), soror Hermetis, M., Romæ, 1 Apr.

Theodora, V. M., Alexandriæ, 28 Apr.
Theodora, al. Theodota, 2 Aug.
Theodora, 17 Jul. Add.
Theodoretus ('Theodour'), Pr. M., Antiochiæ in Syria, 23 Oct.
Theodoricus, Pr. C., in territ. Remensi, 1 Jul.
Theodour, v. Theodotus, M.
Theodorus, Ep., 19 Mar.
Theodorus, Pr. M., Antiochiæ, 23 Mar.
Theodorus, Ep. M., apud Pentapolim Libyæ, 26 Mar.
Theodorus, miles M., Euchaitæ al. Amaseæ in Ponto, 9 Nov.
Theodorus, Ep. Lugduni, 9 Nov.
Theodorus, M., Antiochiæ, 14 Dec.
Theodorus, 12 Feb. Add.
Theodorus, Ep. M., 18 Feb. Add.
Theodorus, Ep., 6 Apr. Add.
Theodorus, 6 Apr. Add.
Theodorus, abbas, 14 Mai. Add.
Theodorus, Consul, M., 26 Mai. Add.
Theodorus, Ep. M., eius Translatio, 29 Mai. Add.
Theodorus, M., 29 Jul. Add.
Theodorus, eques, 24 Aug. Add.
Theodorus, Archiep. Cantuar. 19 Sep. Add.
Theodorus, eques, M., 9 Nov. Add.
Theodorus, Ep. C., 10 Nov. Add.
Theodorus, Ep. Tarsensis, 15 Dec. Add.
Theodoryke, C., Rhemis, 1 Jul.
Theodosia, V. M., Cæsareæ Cappadociæ, 2 Apr.
Theodosia, V. M., 22 Dec.
Theodosius, miles M., Romæ, 25 Oct.
Theodosius, Imp. C., 31 Mai. Add.
Theodota, al. Theodora, matrona, M., in Bithynia, 2 Aug.
Theodotus ('Theodour'), M., in Africa, 4 Jan.
Theodotus ('Theodour'), Ep., Laodiceæ, 2 Nov.
Theodotus ('Théodoce'), M., Heracleæ in Thracia, 14 Nov.
Theodour, v. Theodoretus, Pr. M.
Theodour, v. Theodotus, Ep.
Theodulius ('Theodour'), Pr., Antiochiæ, 23 Mar.
Theodulus ('Diodole'), M., 31 Mar.
Theodulus, Pr. M., Romæ, 3 Mai.
Theodulus, M., Romæ, 26 Jul.
Theogenes, M., in Hellesponto, 3 Jan.
Theogenes, M., 26 Jan.
Theogenes, M., 4 Jan. Add.
Theole, v. Dula, V. M.
Theon, M., apud Lingones, 17 Jan.
Theon, abbas, 23 Aug. Add
Theonas, Ep. C., Alexandriæ, 23 Aug.
Theonilla, M., Aegæe in Cilicia, 23 Aug.
Theonistus, Ep. M., 22 Nov. Add.
Theophanes, C., 29 Sep. Add.

Theophilus, scholasticus, cum S. Dorothea, M., Cæsareæ Cappad., 6 Feb.
Theophilus, M., Alexandriæ, 8 Sep.
Theophilus, Ep., Antiochiæ, 13 Oct.
Theophilus ('Theopholy'), M., Cæsareæ Cappadociæ, 3 Nov.
Theophilus, miles M., Alexandriæ, 20 Dec.
Theophilus, M., Romæ, 28 Feb.
Theophilus, Ep., 5 Mar. Add.
Theophilus, penitens, C., 13 Oct. Add.
Theopista ('Theospita'), filia S. Eustachii, Romæ, 2 Nov.
Theopistes ('Theospis'), uxor S. Eustachii, M., Romæ, 2 Nov. ; *item* ('Theophist'), 20 Mai. Add.
Theopistus ('Theophist'), filius S. Eustachii, M., Romæ, 20 Mai. Add.
Theopompus, Ep. M., 23 Mai. Add.
Theosie, *v.* Theodosia, V. M.
Theoticus, M., apud Antinoum in Ægypto, 8 Mar.
Theotignus, Ep., 21 Jan. Add.
Theotimus, Ep., 22 Dec. Add.
Theremon, abbas, 15 Mar. Add.
Thesifon, *v.* Ctesiphon.
Theuseta, M., Nicææ, 13 Mar.
Thola, judex, 1 Sep. Add.
Tholonius, M., Alexandriæ, 19 Oct.
Thomas, Ap. M., Calaminæ in India, 21 Dec.
Thomas, eius Vigilia, 20 Dec.
Thomas, eius Translatio, Edessæ in Mesopotamia, 3 Jul.
Thomas, Cantuariensis Archiep. M., 29 Dec. Add. ; eius Octava, 5 Jan.
Thomas, Herfordensis Ep., 2 Oct.
Thomas de Aquino, 7 Mar. Add.
Thomas, monachus, M., Dubri ('douer'), 5 Aug. Add.
Thoremyny, *v.* Corentinus, 1 Mai.
Thotist, Ep., 21 Jan. Add.
Thraseas ('Tharsy'), Ep. M., 5 Oct.
Thraso, ('Traso'), M., Romæ, 11 Dec.
Thuran, *v.* Turianus.
Thyke, *v.* Epitacius, Ep. M.
Thyrsus ('Trice') M., Apolloniæ, 28 *al.* 18 Jan.
Thyrsus ('Tyrce'), Alexandriæ, 31 Jan.
Thyrsus, diaconus, M., Augustoduni, 24 Sep.
Tiberius, M., Cæsarione in territ. Agathensi, 10 Nov.
Tiburtius, M., Romæ, 14 Apr.
Tiburtius, filius Chromatii, M., Romæ, 11 Aug.
Tiburtius, M. in Sabinis, 9 Sep.
Tiernake, 4 Apr. Add.
Tigris ('Tygryde'), Ep., in oppido Vapingo, 3 Feb.
Timon, ex vii. diac. M., Corinthi, 19 Apr.

Timon, Ep. M., 19 Apr. Add.
Timotheus, M. in Graecia, 8 Jan.
Timotheus, discip. B. Pauli, Ep. M., Ephesi, 22 *al.* 24 Jan.
Timotheus, M., in Macedonia, 6 Apr.
Timotheus, Constantinopoli, 9 Mai.
Timotheus, diac., M., in Mauritania Cæsariensi, 21 Mai.
Timotheus, M., Romæ, 22 Mai.
Timotheus, M., Romæ, 22 Aug.
Timotheus, M., Rhemis, 23 Aug.
Timotheus, Antiochiæ, 8 Sep.
Timotheus, Ep., 14 Jan. Add.
Timotheus, eremita in Egypto, 11 Jun. Add.
Timotheus, Ep. Alexandriæ, M., 21 Aug. Add.
Titianus, Ep. C., Opitergii ('Odoberg'), 16 Jan.
Titus ('Tyte'), Ep. in Creta, 4 Jan. ; *item*, 25 Aug. Add.
Titus, *v.* Tychicus, 29 Apr.
Titus, Ep., 25 Aug. Add.
Tobias, 14 Sep. Add.
Torpes, M., Pisis in Tuscia, 17 Mai. ; *item* 29 Apr. Add.
Torquatus, Ep. C., in Hispania, 15 Mai.
Totnanus, *al.* Conacus, Diac. M., Herbipoli, 8 Jul.
Trajanus, Imperator, 23 Nov. Add.
Tranquillinus, M., Romæ, 6 Jul.
Transfiguratio Domini N. Jesu Christi, 6 Aug.
Trice, *v.* Thrysus.
Trinitatis SS. festum, secundum quosdam, 15 Mai. Add.
Triphon, *v.* Tryphon.
Tripus ('Tripode'), M., Romæ, 10 Jun.
Trist, V., 27 Feb. Add.
Trojanus ('Trophiane'), Ep., apud Santones, 30 Nov.
Trophimus, Ep. C., Arelate, 29 Dec.
Trudo, Pr. C., 23 Nov. ; *item* 20 Mar. Add.
Trybune, *v.* Quirinus, tribunus, M.
Triphon, M. in Africa, 4 Jan.
Tryphon ('Triphon'), M., Nicææ, 3 Feb.
Tryphon, M., Alexandriæ, 3 Jul.
Tryphon, puerulus, M., 5 Mai. Add.
Tryphon, M., 10 Nov. Add.
Tryphonia, uxor Decii, Romæ, 18 Oct.
Turianus ('Thuran'), Ep. C. in Brit. minore, 13 Jul.
Tybba, V., 6 Mar. Add.
Tychicus, ('Tite') discip. Apostol., apud Paphum, 29 Apr.
Tygryde, *v.* Tigris, Ep.
Tyrannio ('Ciran'), Ep. M., apud Tyrum in Phœnicia, 20 Feb.
Tyrce, *v.* Thyrsus.
Tyrsus ('Tyrs'), M., 17 Jan. Add.

S 2

Ulpius, M., Lugduni, 2 Jun.
Ulmarus, C. in territ. Bononiæ, 20 Jul.
Uran (? Urbanus), M., 2 Jul.
Urbanus, M., ex xviii Martt. Cæsaraugustæ in Hisp., 15, *al.* 16 Apr.
Urbanus, papa M., Romæ, 25 Mai.
Urbanus, eius Reliquiæ, 4 Jul.
Urbanus, M., in Campania, 2 Jul.
Urbanus, puer, 24 Jan. Add.
Urbanus, M., in Campania, 2 Jul. Add.
Ursatius, solitarius C., Nicææ in Bithynia, 16 Aug.
Ursicinus ('Vrcissyne'), M., Ravennæ, 19 Jun.
Ursicinus ('Vrsycyne'), Ep., apud Bituricas, 9 Nov.
Ursinus, Ep., 29 Dec. Add.
Ursmarus, Ep. C. ('Cosmar'), 18 Apr.
Ursulinus, Ep., 24 Jul. Add.
Ursus, miles M., Solodori in Gallia, 30 Sep.
Ursus, M., 21 Jun. Add.
Ursus, C., 28 Jul. Add.
Ursus, Ep. C. (*al.* M.), Antisiodori, 30 Jul. Add.
Ustazedes, *al.* Uskazandus, *s.* Usthazanes, eunuchus M., in Perside, 21 Apr.

Valdetrudis, 20 Mar. Add.
Valentinus, Pr. M., Romæ, 14 Feb.
Valentinus, Ep. M., Interamnæ, 14 Feb.
Valentinus, M., Ravennæ, 13 Nov.
Valentinus, magister militum, M., Ravennæ, 16 Dec.
Valention, M., Dorostori in Moesia, 25 Mai.
Valentius, Pr., 6 Jul. Add.
Valeriana, uxor S. Vitalis, M., 28 Apr. Add.
Valerianus, M., Romæ, 14 Apr.
Valerianus, M., Antiochiæ, 23 Aug.
Valerianus, M., Trenortii in territ. Cabilonensi, 15 Sep.
Valerianus, M., Nividuni, 17 Sep.
Valerianus, Ep. C., in Africa, 15 Dec.
Valerius, ('Valery'), Ep. C., Treviris, 29 Jan.
Valerius. M., Suessione, 14 Jun.
Valery, *v.* Walericus, abbas.
Vanalis, *v.* Navalis.
Vbaldus, Ep., 16 Mai. Add.
Vdalricus, ('Odalryke'), Ep. C., Augustæ, 4 Jul.
Vectius ('Vect'), C., 25 Jan. Add.
Vedastus, Atrebatensium Ep. C., 6 Feb.
Vedastus, Atrebatensis Ep., C., Cameraci, 1 Oct.
Venantius, Ep. M., 1 Apr.
Venantius ('Wynance'), abbas, Turonis, 11, *al.* 13 Oct.
Venantius, M., Camerini, 18 Mai. Add.
Veneranda, V. M., 14 Nov. Add.

Venerandus, M., 14 Nov. Add.
Venerius, abbas, 11 Sep. Add.
Venerius, monachus, 11 Sep. Add.
Venustianus cum uxore et filiis, MM., Spoleti, 30 Dec.
Venustus, M., in Africa, 6 Mai.
Veranus, Ep., 11 Nov. Add.
Verianus, M., Coloniæ in Tuscia, 9 Aug.
Verissimus, M., Ulyssipone in Lusitania, 1 Oct.
Verulio ('Verole'), Adrumeti in Africa, 21 Feb.
Verus, frater Securi, M., in Africa, 2 Dec.
Viator, minister S. Justi, Lugduni, 2 Sep. *item* 21 Oct.
Viconius, C., Verduni, 9 Nov.
Victor, Nicomediæ, 12 Jan.
Victor, M., Ebreduni in Galliis, 22 Jan.
Victor, socius S. Thyrsi, Alexandriæ, 31 Jan.
Victor, Romæ, 20 Feb.
Victor, M., apud Ægyptum, 25 Feb.
Victor, M., Nicomediæ, 6 Mar.
Victor, M., in Ægypto, 1 Apr.
Victor, Ep. M., xv. papa, Romæ, 20 Apr.
Victor, miles M., Mediolani, 8 Mai.
Victor, in Ægypto, 8 Mai.
Victor, M., in Syria, 14 Mai.
Victor, M., Cæsareæ in Cappadocia, 21 Mai.
Victor, miles M., Massiliæ in Gallia, 21 Jul.
Victor, miles M., Emeritæ in Hispania, 24 Jul.
Victor, papa M., 28 Jul.
Victor, M., *al.* Ep. C., in Africa, 10 Sep.
Victor, M., Chalcedone, 10 Sep.
Victor, M., cum Cypriano in Africa, 14 Sep.
Victor, Thebanæ legionis M., Seduni in Gall., 22 Sep.
Victor, miles ex legione Thebanorum M., Solodori in Gall., 30 Sep.
Victor, M., Agrippinæ, 10 Oct.
Victor, C., 17 Oct.
Victor, C., in territ. Belvacensi, 18 Oct.
Victor, M., Ravennæ, 13 Nov.
Victor, *v.* Victoria, M., 23 Dec.
Victor, Ep., Carthagine, 20 Apr. Add.
Victor, M., 29 Jul. Add.
Victor, M., 18 Sep. Add.
Victoria, M., Cordubæ in Hisp., 17 Nov.
Victoria ('Victor'), V. M., Romæ, 23 Dec.
Victorianus, proconsul, M., in Africa, 23 Mar.
Victorianus, in Isauria, 15, *al.* 16 Mai.
Victorianus, 6 Mai. Add.
Victoricus, M., Ambiani in Gall., 11 Dec.
Victorinus, M., apud Ægyptum, 25 Feb.
Victorinus, in carcere M., Nicomediæ, 6 Mar.
Victorinus, M., Nicomediæ, 29 Mar.
Victorinus, M., in Italia, 15 Apr.

Victorinus, M., Romæ, 7 Jul.
Victorinus, Amiterninus Ep. M., Romæ, 5 Sep.
Victorinus, Pictaviensis *seu* Pitabionensis, Ep. M., 2 Nov.
Victorinus, e quatuor coronatis M., Romæ, 8 Nov.
Victorinus, magister S. Hieronymi, 5 Sep. Add.
Victorius ('Victor'), Cæsareæ Cappad., 21 Mai.
Victorius, Ep. C., apud Cenomanos, 1 Sep.
Vigilia Assumptionis, 13 Aug.
Vigilius, Ep. M., apud Tridentum, 26 Jun.
Vigilius, Ep. M., 26 Jun. Add.
Vigilius, papa M., 26 Jun. Add.
Vigilius, diac. monachus, 26 Jun. Add.
Vigor, Ep., apud Baiocas, 1 Nov.
Vincent, *v.* Viventius, 13 Jan. Add.
Vincentius, diac. M., Valentiæ in Hispania, 22 Jan.
Vincentius, M., Ebreduni in Gall., 22 Jan.
Vincentius, M., Caucoliberi in Hisp. Tarraconesi, 19 Apr.
Vincentius, cum Marcello C., Ebreduni in Gallia, 20 Apr.
Vincentius (? Inventius), M., Romæ, 1 Jun.
Vincentius, Levita M., Agenni in Gall., 9 Jun.
Vincentius, M., Romæ, 24 Jul.
Vincentius, subdiaconus M., Romæ, 6 Aug.
Vincentius, M., Romæ, 25 Aug.
Vincentius, C., in Territ. Nivernensi, 17 Oct.
Vincentius, M., Abelæ in Hispania, 27 Oct.
Vincentius, M., 6 Jun. Add.
Vincentius, C., 24 Jul. Add.
Vindemialis, 2 Mai. Add.
Virgilius, Ep., 27 Mar. Add.
Virgines, Septem., MM. apud Sirmium, 9 Apr.
Virgines plurimæ, cum S. Domnina, MM., Interamnæ, 14 Apr.
Virgines Sacræ plurimæ, MM., in Perside, Sapore Rege, 22 Apr.
Virgines, xxii, MM. cum S. Lucia, Romæ, 25 Jun.
Virgines undecim milia, MM., Coloniæ Agrippinæ, 21 Oct.
Virgines Quadraginta, MM., Antiochiæ in Syria, 24 Dec.
Vitalica, puellula M., Ancyræ, 4 Sep.
Vitalis, M., Romæ, 14 Feb.
Vitalis, M., Alexandriæ, 21 Apr.
Vitalis, M., Ravennæ, 28 Apr.
Vitalis, M., in Campania, 2 Jul.
Vitalis, filius S. Felicitatis, M., Romæ, 10 Jul.
Vitalis, C., 24 Oct.

Vitalis, M., Cæsareæ Cappadociæ, 3 Nov.
Vitalis, servus, M., Bononiæ in Italia, 27 Nov.
Vitalis, M., 4 Nov. Add.
Vitus, M., in Sicilia, 15 Jun.
Vivardus, Ep., 1 Sep. Add.
Viventius ('Vincent'), C., 13 Jan. Add.
Viviana, *al.* Bibiana, M., Romæ, 2 Dec.
Vivianus, *al.* Bibianus (? Julianus), Ep. C., apud Santonas, 28 Aug.
Vldaricus, *al.* Odaldricus, Ep. C., Augustæ in Rhætia, 4 Jul.
Vlfrannus, Ep. Senonensis, in monast. Fontanellæ in pago Rotomagensi, 20 Mar.

Walaricus, Pr. C., in pago Niviacensi, 12 Dec.
Walburga, V., 4 Feb., *item*, 1 Feb. Add., 1 Mai. Add.
Walericus ('Valery'), C., Ambiani, 1 Apr.
Wallenus, *al.* Waltheof, Eboraci, 3 Aug. Add.
Walpurge, V., 25 Feb. Add.
Walpurgis, *v.* Walburga.
Wandregesilus, C., eius Translatio, 31 Mar.; *item*, 22 Jul. Add.
Warburga, V., 3 Feb.
Warburga, eius Translatio, 21 Jun.
Wenceslaus ('Wyncesse'), 28 Sep. Add.
Wenefrida, V. M., in Anglia, 3 Nov.; *item*, 22 Jun. Add.
Wilfridus, Archiep. Ebor., 12 Oct.
Wilfridus, eius Translatio, 24 Apr. Add.
Wilfridus junior, Archiep. Ebor. 29 Apr. Add.
Wilibaldus ('Wyllybald'), 7 Feb. Add.
Willibrordus, Trajectensis Ep. C., 7 Nov.
Willielmus, Ep. Bituricensis, 10 Jan. Add.
Willielmus ('Wyllyam'), Pr. 2 Mar. Add.
Willielmus, a Judæis cæsus, Norwici, 15 Apr. Add.
Willielmus, in Brit. natus, 10 Mai. Add.
Willielmus, Dux Aquitaniæ, C., 28 Mai. Add.
Willielmus, Archiep. Ebor., 8 Jun. Add.
Winibaldus ('wenebald'), 7 Feb. Add.
Witburga, V., 17 Mar.
Witburga, eius translatio, 8 Jul.
Wolfadus, filius Wolferi regis, in Brit., 31 Jul. Add.
Wolmare, *v.* Wulmarus.
Wolryke (Wulfrick), Pr. 20 Feb., Add.
Wolsinus, Ep. C., 8 Jan. Add.
Wolstan, *v.* Wulstanus.
Wolsyld (Wulthild), V., 9 Sep. Add.
Wulfrannus, Ep. [Senonensis], in Fontanella monast., 20 Mar.; *item*, 15 Oct.
Wulmarus, C., 17 Jun.
Wulmarus ('Vlmare'), abbas, 20 Jul.

Wulstanus, Ep. C., 'at Wyllenchester,' 18 Jan.
Wulstanus, Ep. Wigorn. in Anglia, 19 Jan.
Wulstanus, Ep. Wigorn., eius Translatio, 7 Jun.
Wydburga, *v.* Witburga, V.
Wynance, *v.* Venantius, abbas C.
Wyncesse, *v.* Wenceslaus.
Wynewale, abbas, Ep., 3 Mar.
Wynyn, *v.* Fynanus.
Wystanus, R. M., apud Evesham, 1 Jun. Add.
Xystus ('Syxt'), papa M., Romæ, 6 Apr.
Xystus, *v.* Sixtus II. papa, M.
Ygyn, *v.* Hyginus.
Yon, M., 5 Aug. Add.
Ypolite, *v.* Hippolytus, M.
Ysidore, Ysydour *v.* Isidorus.
Ysaac, Pr. Antiochiæ, 3 Jun. Add.
Ysaac, 5 Feb. Add.
Ysyce (Sycus) M. in Antiochia, 30 Mai. Add.
Ytamar, Ep. C. 10 Jun.
Yve, Pr. C. in Brit. minori, 19 Mai. Add.
Yve, *v.* Ivo, 24 Apr.; 10 Jun. Add.
Yve, C., 8 Oct.
Zacchœus, Ep. Ierosolymitanus IV.[tus] 23 Aug.
Zacchœus, Ep. Antiochiæ, 23 Aug. Add.
Zacharias, pontifex, Romæ, 14 Mar.
Zacharias, Pr. M., Lugduni, 2 Jun.
Zacharias, M., Nicomediæ, 10 Jun.

Zacharias, propheta, 6 Sep.
Zacharias, pater B. Jo. Baptistæ, 5 Nov.
Zacharias, Pr., 6 Sep. Add.
Zacharias, papa, 5 Nov. Add.
Zeno, M., Romæ, 14 Feb.
Zeno, Ep. M., Veronæ, 12 Apr.
Zeno, Romæ, M., 9 Jul.
Zeno, M., Alexandriæ, 15 Jul.
Zeno, miles M., Alexandriæ, 20 Dec.
Zeno, abbas in Thebaide, 9 Jul. Add.
Zeno, Ep., 8 Dec. Add.
Zenobius, Pr. M., apud Tyrum in Phœnicia, 20 Feb.
Zenobius, Pr. M., Sidone in Phœnicia, 29 Feb.
Zenobius, Ep. Florentinus, 25 Mai. Add.
Zephyrinus, papa [M.] Romæ, 26 Aug.
Zoë, vxor Nicostrati, M., Romæ, 5 Jul.
Zoëllus, *al.* Zoilus, in Istria, 24 Mai.
Zoilus et alii xix., Cordubæ in Hisp. 27 Jun.
Zoilus, Pr. 27 Jun. Add.
Zorobabel, 13 Jul. Add.
Zosima, soror Bonosæ M., 15 Jul.
Zozimas, abbas, 30 Apr. Add.
Zozimus, M., Antiochiæ, 14 Dec.
Zosimus, cum Rufo, ex discipp. Christi, M., 18 Dec.
Zosimus, papa, 7 Jan. Add.
Zosimus, M., 11 Mar. Add.
Zoticus, M., Romæ, 10 Feb.
Zoticus, M. Lugduni, 2 Jun.
Zoticus, miles M., Nicomediæ, 21 Oct.

GLOSSARIAL INDEX

OF

NAMES OF PLACES.

₊ The object of this index being to explain the names, it has not been thought necessary to record every mention of each place. The references are to the pages of the reprint. The words followed by a colon (:) are the adjectives from which many of Whytford's names have been derived.

Abbiens, 174, for Albigens, Albigensis: Albia, Albi.
Abrince, 150, Abrincæ, Avranches.
Aconitane, 7, for Anconitane, Anconitanus: Ancona.
Adartens, 83, Adartensis or Atrebacensis: Atrebati, Arras.
Adrumete, 30, Adrumetum in Africa.
Aganens, 25, for Agaunens, Monasterium Agaunense: Agaunum, now St. Maurice (Valais).
Agathen, 176, Agathensis: Agatha, Agde.
Agen, 157, 165, Ageño, 91, Agens, 181; Agennum, Agen.
Agryppe, 177, Agryppyny, 160: Colonia Agrippina, Cöln (Cologne).
Agunens, 172, see Aganens.
Albane, 152, Albanum, Albano, see Notes, Sept. 26.
Aıbigens, 52, Albigensis: Albia, Alby.
Alexander, passim, Alexandria.
Altyne, 64, 179, Altinum, Altino distrutto, near Venice.
Altynens, 182, Altinensis: see Altyne.
Almayne, 30, Alemannia.
Amase, 175, Amasea in Cappadocia.
Ambian, 94, Ambianum, Amiens.
Ambianens, 11, 138, 151, Ambianensis: Ambianum, Amiens.
Ambience, 137, Amiens.
Amphitre, 196, Amphitrea.
Amphyble, 74, Amphipolis.
Amyterne, 140, Amiternum, S. Vittorino, three miles from Aquila.
Ananyue, 84, Anaunia, Val d'Anagna.
Ancyran, 53, Ancyranus: Ancyra.
Andegaue, 26, 164, Andegavum, Angers.

Andogavence, 10, Andegavensis: Andegavum, Angers.
Andro, yle of, 47, Andros.
Anticyrane, 11, Anticyra.
Antinoum, 15, Antion, 38; Antinous in Egypt.
Antysiodour, 67, Antisiodorum, Auxerre.
Anyse, water of, 68, Anisus, the River Enns, a tributary of the Danube.
Apamya, 139, Apamea.
Apollonia, 17.
Aquens, 92, Aquensis: Aquæ, Aix in Provence.
Aquiley, 41, 85, Aquileia.
Aquis, 177, Aquæ, Aix in Provence.
Aquyne, 20, Aquitania.
Arawsyke, 83, Arausica, Orange.
Arecy, 88, Aretium, Arezzo.
Arelatens, 69, 134, Arelatensis: Arelatum, Arles.
Argentomate, castell of, 102, Castrum Argentomacum, Argenton.
Argentyne, 52, Argentina, Strassburg.
Aspane, 48, Pagus Hasbanius.
Assyse, 127, Assisium, Assisi.
Atens, 82, Athens.
Atrebacens, 154, Atrebatensis: Atrebatum, Arras.
Auare, 192, Auraris (*Cat. Sanct.* i. 61).
Auerne, 10, 16, Averni or Arverni, Clermont (Puy de Dome).
August, 23 (Feb. 5), Augusta, London.
Augustane, 123, Augusta, in Rhœtia, Augsburg.
Augustudune, 6, Augustodunum, Autun.
Auiens, 165, Auiensis: Avia, near Aquila.
Aulane, 3, Aulanus: Aulona in Macedonia.

GLOSSARIAL INDEX OF NAMES OF PLACES.

Aurasyke, 164, Arausica, Orange.
Aurelatens, 11, for Arelatens, *q.v.*
Austrace, 66, for Auch, see Notes, May 1.
Austudune, 99, for Augustodune, Autun.

Baiocas, 171, Baiocæ, Bayeux.
Bapyll, 194, Bapilla (*Cat. Sanct.* xi, 125).
Barcinon, 25, Barcinona, Barcelona.
Bartimon, 116, for Barcinon, *q.v.*
Barum, 72, Bari.
Beame, 153, Bohemia.
Beame, 191, Ambianum, Amiens.
Beluacens, 164, Beluacensis: Beluacum, Beauvais.
Beluake, 6, Beluacum, or Bellovacum, Beauvais.
Beneuent, 94, Beneventum.
Beneuentane, 148, Beneuentana ciuitas: Benevento.
Betony, 196, Bampton, Oxon. See Notes, Dec. 21.
Biryne, 121, for Bithynia.
Biturica, 12, Biturike, 79, Bitury, 95, Byture, 105: Bituricæ, Bourges.
Bituricens, 8, Biturience, 65, Bituriens, 130, Bituricensis: Bituricæ, Bourges.
Blaue, castell of, 183, Castrum Blavium, Blayne near Bordeaux.
Blese, 63, 151, Blesæ, Blois.
Bobacens, 17, Monasterium Bobacense: in Val de Bannez.
Boneuale, 51, Bona Vallis.
Bonony, 4, 156, Bononye, 114; Bononia, Bologna.
Breknoke, 159, Brecknock.
Bredunens, 60, for Ebredunensis: Ebredunum, Embrun.
Bristowe, 30, Bristol.
Brixinens, 22, Brixen. Prussia.
Bruce, 62, Prussia.
Bryxe, 27, Brixia, Brescia.
Buckingham, 173.
Burdegale, 166, Burdigala, Bordeaux.
Burgoyn, 65, Burgundy.
Byterne, 45, Biterræ, Beziers.
Byture, 104, Bituricæ, Bourges.

Cabilon, 140, 181, Cabilony, 65; Cabilo, Châlons-sur-Saone.
Cabilonens, 49, 146, Cabilonensis: Cabilo, Châlons-sur-Saone.
Calagurryn, 35, Calagurris, Calahorra.
Calaritane, 64.
Calcidony, 143, Chalcedon.
Calcydy, 147, Chalcis.
Camber, 193, Camberake, 126; Cameracum, Cambria.
Cameracens, 44, 154, Cameracensis: Camercum, Cambrai.
Cameryn, 77, Camerinum, Camerino.
Campeyn, 10, Campania.
Cañens 201, see Notes, Dec. 30.

Cantiliber, 60, Caucoliberis in Hispania.
Carboyle, 172, Castrum Carboilum.
Carneto, 146, Carnot, 84; Carnotum, Chartres.
Carnotens, 17, Carnotensis: Carnotum, Chartres.
Casary, 8, for Cesary, Cæsarea.
Cassyn, 25, Monte Cassino.
Castelnount, 25, Nantonense Castrum, Chateau Landon.
Cathalamnis, 123, for Cathalauni, Châlons-sur-Marne.
Cathenens, 22, Catania.
Cathyne, 126, Catania.
Cawsyne, 28, Canusium, Canosa.
Cecile, 89, for Cilicia.
Cenoman, 17, 116, 138; Cenomani, Le Mans.
Cenomānyke, 103, Cenomanicus: Cenomani, Le Mans.
Centuncellēs, 153, Centum Cellæ.
Cesaraugust, 133, Caesaraugusta, Saragossa.
Cesare palestyne, 14, Cæsarea Palestinæ.
Cesariens, 7, Mauritania Cæsariensis.
Chechester, 52, Chichester.
Chire, yle of, 76, Chios.
Cicilye, 160, for Cilicia.
Cicyle, 22, Cicyll, 181; Sicilia, Sicily.
Cipres, 30, 74, Cipris, 8; Cyprus.
Circen, 65, Cirta in Numidia.
Cireney, 197, Cyrene.
Cisceter, 95, Chichester.
Ciuilitane, 64.
Clareuale, 131, 174, Claravallis, Clairvaux.
Cluniacens, 45, 106, Cluniacensis: Clugny.
Clusyne, 104, Clusium, Chiusi.
Coket, yle of, 11, Coquet Island on the coast of Northumberland.
Colen, 125, Colonia Tusciæ.
Colen Agryppyne, 160, Colonia Agrippina, Cöln (Cologne).
Colen thebestyne, 188, Colonia Thebestina.
Coleyn, 5, Colonia Agrippina, Cöln (Cologne).
Colose, 113, Colossæ.
Complute, 124, Complutum, Alcalá de Henares.
Corduba, 24, Cordova in Spain.
Corduba, 57, in Persia.
Corsite, 80, for Corsice, Corsica.
Cretens, 4, Cretensis: Crete.
Crispinens, 44.
Cucusse, 90, Cucussum in Cappadocia.
Cume, 28, Cumæ.
Cymele, 75, Cimella.
Cyrenen, 70, Cyrene.
Cyzyke, 4, Cyzicus.

Diuyon, castell of, 171, Diuio Castrum, Dijon.

GLOSSARIAL INDEX OF NAMES OF PLACES. 281

Dole, 118, Dolum, Dol in Brittany.
Dorkasyn, the fraunchest of, 13. Pagus dorcassinus, or durpcassinus, a district north of Chartres.
Doroberne, 20, Dorobernia, Canterbury.
Doroscorens, 83, for Dorostorensis : Dorostorum in Mysia.
Dorostre, 81, Dorostorum in Mysia, now Dora in Bulgaria.
Douer, 123, Dover.
Dymens, 190, "Territorium dunense" A., perhaps for Divionense, Dijon.
Dyospole, 62, Diospolis, Lydda in Palestine.

Ebredune, 14, Ebreduna, Embrun.
Ebroas, castell of, 126.
Edissen, 19, Edessæ.
Ege, 152, Ægæa.
Emerite, 115, Emeryte, 191 ; Emerita, Merida.
Engolisme, 103, Engolisma, Angoulême.
Ephesios, 28, Ephesum, 19, 117, Ephesy, 14 ; Ephesus.
Eracle, 178, Heraclea.
Eufratesi, 158, see Notes, Oct. 7.
Ewgolysme, 101 for Engolisme, *q.v.*
Ewmeny, 157, Eumenia in Phrygia.
Ewsam, 86, Evesham.

Fauence, 68, see Notes, May 4.
Florence, 81.
Fomanel, 75, Fontanell, 166 ; Fontanella.
Fontanellence, 50, Fontanellensis : Fontanella, in diocese of Rouen.
Forcill, 127, Forum Syllæ, Imola.
Fryselond, 93, Frisia ; and elsewhere for Phrygia.
Fynthall, 79, for Fynchall, Finchale, near Durham.

Galace, 35, Galicia.
Galas, 199, Galatia.
Gauale, 16, 168, Gavalis, Mende.
Gaualitan, 131, Gavalitanus : Gavalis, Mende.
Gelduba, 196, see Notes, Dec. 20.
Genecesary, 15, Neo-Cæsarea.
Geneo, 15, see Notes, Jan. 24.
Geneocesarcpont, 104. Neo-Cæsarea Ponti.
Gerūd, 120, Gerunda, Gerona.
Glassenbury, 101, Glastonbury.
Glastingens, 137, Glastonbury.
Glocester, 21, 114, Gloucester.
Golden Mount, 71, Mons Aureus.
Gortyn, 55, Gortyna in Crete.
Granopole, 50, Gratianopolis, Grenoble.
Graundmount, 26, Grandis Mons, Grand-Mont (Haute Vienne).
Grauion, castell of, 9, see Notes, Jan. 13.

Habull, 168, Abula, Avila.
Hamonens, 60, Hannonia, Hainault.
Helionople, 6, for Helenopole, Helenopolis in Bithynia.
Herbipole, 39, Herbipolis, Wurzburg.
Herford, 79, 155, Hereford.
Hermepole, 59, Hermopolis in Egypt.
Horton, 143, in Dorset, 6 m. N. of Wimborne.
Hoste, 29, 165, Ostia.
Hylpane, 25, for Hyspane ; Hispania.
Hylyber, 63, Illiberis, Elvira.
Hypponens, 34, Hipponensis : Hippo.
Hyspale, 33, Hispalis, Seville.
Hyspolitane, 191, see Notes, Dec. 10.
Hystre, 81, Istria.

Iane, 152, Janua, Genoa.
Iarewe, 151, Jarrow.
Interam, 27, Interamnis, 57, Interampnis, 27 ; Interamna, Terni.
Iule, 159, Julia in territorio Parmensi.
Iuliens, 76, for Forojuliensis : Forum Julii, Fréjus or Friuli.

Katacumbe, 13, Catacumbæ, the Catacombs of Rome.
Kayrmyrthyn, 24, Caermarthen.

Lambesitane, 66, Lambesitana urbs, Lambesa, Lambesca in Tunis.
Lamosate, 76, for Lampsacus.
Landens, 13, for Laudens, Laudensis : Lodi.
Laodice, 171, Laudice, 172 ; Laodicea.
Laudui ens, 190, Laudunensis : Laudunum, Laon.
Lauriake, 69, Lauriacum, Enns (in Austria).
Lausemy, 164.
Legionens, 35, Legionensis ; Legio, Leon in Galizia.
Lemonicens, 134, for Lemouicens, Lemovicæ, Limoges.
Lemoniga, 103, Lemouices, Limoges.
Leodicens, 99, Leodiensis : Leodium, Liége.
Leodike, 147, Leodicum, Liége.
Leonens, 39, Saint-Pol-de-Léon.
Librens, 180, Liberiensis (*Cat. Sanct.*, x. 173).
Lice, 132, Lycia.
Lingon, 174, Linguon, 12 ; Lingones, Langres.
Lingoniens, 105, Lingonyke, 148 ; Lingoniensis : Lingones, Langres.
Lirinens, monastery of, 86. Monasterium Lirinense, les Iles de Lérins, near Cannes.
Liuience, 184, Liviensis (*Cat. Sanct.* x. 107).

GLOSSARIAL INDEX OF NAMES OF PLACES.

Lornon, 123, for Bonon, Bononia, Bologna.
Lucas castell, 16.
Lucane, 43, 157, 169, Lucanus ; Lucca.
Lucernary, 119, Lucernaria, in Africa.
Luke, 23, Lucca.
Lunens, 41, Luni.
Luxaniens, 49, Luxoniens, 51 ; for Luxouiensis ; Luxovium, Luxeuil in the diocese of Besançon.
Lychefelde, 35, Lichfield.
Lyndisfarnens, 44, Lindisfarne.
Lyngon, 73, 80, Lingones, Langres.
Lyons, *passim*, Lugdunum.
Lyppary, yle of, 133, Lipara Insula.
Lysyn, 120, pagus Lisuinus, the district round Lisieux.

Machiens, 106.
Madriacens, 97, Madriacense Monasterium: La Croix saint Leufroy in Normandy.
Mafiaen, 81, see Notes, May 25.
Magonce, 186, Magontia, Mainz.
Malact, 96, Malaca, Malaga.
Malbody, 19, 174, Malbodium, Maubeuge in Hainault.
Mamuete, 95, for Nannetes, Nantes.
Marcull, 108, for Martula in Umbria.
Maritymy, 15, Mauritania.
Marsia, 83, for Mesia, see Notes, May 27.
Massely, 92, Massyle, 114, Massylye, 34 ; Massilia, Marseilles.
Maturitane, 8, for Mauritania.
Mauritane, 37, Mauritania.
Melde, 169, Meldæ, Meaux.
Meldence, 137, Meldinens, 189 ; Meldensis : Meldæ, Meaux.
Melidune, castell of, 177, Melodunum, Melun.
Mesennate, 150, Mesenata civitas.
Messany, 59, Messana, Messina ?
Messy, 94, Mysia.
Metens, 129, Metensis : Metæ, Metz.
Mildunens, 81, for Maldunensis : Malmesbury.
Myldynens, 26.
Mirrea, 85.
Misybbe, 111, for Nisibis in Mesopotamia.
Molysme, 65, Monasterium Molesmense, Molesme.
Morast, 11, see Notes, Jan. 15, Add.
Muthon, 75.
Mutyne, 18, Mutina, Modena.
Mylen, 26, Mylytane in armeny, 59 ; Militana in Armenia.
Myllen, 6, 65, Mediolanum, Milan.

Nāmete, 81, Nannetes, Nantes.
Narbon, 192, Narbone, 168 ; Narbona, Narbonne.

Narbonens, 45, Narbonensis : Narbona, Narbonne.
Naryne, 187, for Narnia, Narni.
Nazant, 72, Nazianzus.
Nemause, 79, Nemausus, Nîmes.
Neoconens, 182.
Nere, 130, for Here. Insula Herio, at the mouth of the Loire, now Noirmoutier.
Nice, 21, Nicæa.
Nice, 38, Nyssa.
Nicodeme, 6, 49, for Nicomede, Nicomedia.
Nicopole, 27, Nicopolis.
Nisebene, 61, Nysibena urbs (*Cat. Sanct.* xi, 86). Nisibis.
Niuedune, 77, Noviodunum in Mysia.
Niuedune, 88, 89, Nivedunum or Noviodunum, Noyon, Nyon, or Nivedunum in Mysia.
Niuedune, 147, Noviodunum, Nyon.
Niuiacens, 192, for Pagus Vimacensis.
Nouariens, 21, Novariensis : Novara.
Nouiome, 187 (Dec. 1), Noviomum, Noyon.
Nouiomens, 90, Noviomensis : Noviomum, Noyon.
Nuceria, 148, Nocera de' Pagani.
Numgell, 42, for Nivigella, Nivelle.
Nyenna, 125, for Vienna in Gaul.
Nyuerne, "in yrelond," 133, Nivernum, Nevers.
Nyuernens, 164, Nivernum, Nevers.

Odoberg, 11, Opitergium, Oderzo.
Olisepon, 154, Olisepona or Ulissipona, Lisbon.
Olympyle, 147, for Olympus Lyciæ.
Orchester, 173.
Oricoripens, 68, a corruption of *in N.rico Ripensi*.
Orliaunce, 20, Aurelianum, Orleans.
Oska, 166, Osca, Huesca.
Oste, 111, Ostia.
Oxford, 196.
Oxforde, 52, Oxomensis : Oxoma, Burgo de Osma in Spain.
Oxforde, 200, Oximensis : Oximæ, Exmes in Normandy.

Pade, river of, 192, Padus, the Po.
Padue, 93, Padua.
Padway, 65, for Pannonia.
Padwey, 4, Patavium, Padua.
Palmary, yle of, 144, 198, see Notes.
Pamon, 48, for Pannonia.
Papie, 77, Papye, 34 ; Papia, Pavia.
Paryhenople, 63.
Parys, 39, Paryse, 3, 18 ; Paris.
Patauie, 175 (Nov. 7), Patavium, Padua.
Patras, 186, Patræ in Achaia.
Patron, 11, Perrona.

Penarens, 43.
Perham, 28, Wareham.
Persewdon, castell of, 152, see Notes, Sept. 27.
Peruse, 34, Perusia, Perugia.
Perusyne, 174, Perusinus: Perusia, Perugia.
Petragoryke, 190, Petragorica, Perigueux.
Philadolph, 16, for Philadelphia.
Pictauens, 100, Pictavensis: Pictavi, Poitiers.
Pictauis, 9, Pictauy, 127, 171; Pictavi, Poitiers.
Pitabion, 171, see Notes, Nov. 2.
Placence, 154, Placentyne, 192: Placencia Piacenza.
Pluteolane, 148, for Puteolane, Puteoli, Puzzuoli.
Ponce, yle of, 70, Ponciane, yle of, 57.
Pontia Insula, Isola di Ponza.
Pontiniake, 179, Pontiniacum, Pontigny.
Pontyne, 64, Le Ponthieu.
Portese, 17.
Prenestyne, 113, Præneste, Palestrina.
Preuestyn, 129, for Prenestyn.
Puricoroea, 100, see Notes, June 25.
Puteole, 165, Puteoli, Puzzuoli.

Ramesey, 92, Ramsey, 164; Ramsey in Hunts.
Ratisponens, 7, Ratisponensis: Ratispona, Regensburg.
Rauen, 13, 96, Ravenna.
Reame, 194; Reme, 9, 63; Remys, 138; Remi, Rheims.
Reatyne, 127, Rieti in Umbria.
Rece, 123, Rhætia.
Reciar, 201, Retiaria, Nicopoli on the Danube.
Redon, 161, 174: Redomis, 5; Redones, Rennes.
Regens, 184, Regensis: Regium, Riez in S. France.
Remens, 4, Remensis: Remi, Rheims.
Reomens, 17, Monasterium Reomense, Moutier St. Jean, in the diocese of Langres.
Romaryke, 145, Monasterium Romaricum, Remiremont (Vosges).
Rome, *passim*, Roma.
Rone, 24, 44, Rothomagus, Rouen.
Rouncyuale, 95, Roncevaux.
Rumsey, 170, Romsey in Hants.
Ruspence, 2, Ruspensis: Ruspæ, near Carthage.

Sabionens, 22, Sabiona, Seben.
Sabyn, 143.
Salary, 127, for Faleria in Tuscia.
Salodour, 153, for Solodour, Solodurum, Soleure.
Saloma, 55, Salon, 131, Salona in Dalmatia.

Saltzpurge, 48, Salzburg.
Samon, 116, Samos in Lycia.
Sanctipole, 107, for Scythopolis.
Sanctonas, 66, 135, Santones, Saintes.
Sardyn, 84, Sardinia.
Satale, 192.
Sconange, 95, for Sconaugia, Schönau.
Sebasten, 21, Sebaste.
Sedune, 149, Sedunum, Sion.
Sedunens, 66, Sedunensis: Sedunum, Sion.
Sely, mount of, 91, Mons Celius.
Senon, 91, 109, 138, Senony, 102, Senonyke, 177, Zenon, 96; Senones, Sens.
Sephton, 28, Shaftonia, Shaftesbury.
Septimane, 45, Septimania.
Serentyne, 118.
Shyrborne, 7, Sherborne.
Sigesteryke, 130, Pagus Sigestericus, the district round Sisteron.
Siluiake, 3, for Silviniacum, Souvigny.
Siryne, 31, see Notes, Feb. 23.
Siryne, 46, for Sirmium in Pannonia.
Slepe, 92, St. Ives, Hunts.
Spolete, 2, Spoletum, Spoleto.
Suppentone, 15, Suppentonia near Mount Soracte.
Suretyke, 43, for Surrentum, Sorrento.
Suenuy, 163, see Notes, Oct. 16.
Swesion, 90, Swessy, 94; Swesyon, 168; Suessiones, Soissons.
Syluanect, 62, Silvanectum, Senlis.
Syluanectence, 50, Silvanectensis: Silvanectum, Senlis.
Syluinyake, 73, Silviniacum, Souvigny.
Synade, 119.
Synopole, 110, Synope.
Syryne, 55, for Sirmium.
Sythe, 88, for Siscia.

Tagora, 188, Thagura in Africa.
Tampnis, 58, in Egypt.
Taraston, 118, for Tarascon.
Tarcens, 194, Tarsensis: Tarsus.
Tarentase, 98, Tarentasiens, 164, Tarentaise.
Tarente, 144, Tarentum, Taranto.
Taruernens, 143, Teruens, 28, Teruernens, 141; Pagus Tarvanensis, Therouane.
Taurin, 181, Taurinum, Turin.
Tauromeny, 52, Tauromenium, Taormina in Sicily.
Teracyne, 70, 174, Terracyne, 171, Tarracina, Terracina.
Terascone, 14, Terascona, Tarascon.
Terdon, 37, Terdona, Tortona.
Tergest, 73, Tergeste, Trieste.
Terraconens, 177, Tarraconensis: Tarraco, Tarragona.
Tharsum, 89, 160, Tarsus.
Thebaida, 3, Thebaide, 54, Thebaides, 34; Thebais.

Theopole, 174, Theopolis.
Tholete, 178, Toletum. Toledo.
Thomis, 97, Tomis in Pontus.
Thymus, 21, Thmuis in Egypt.
Ticyne, 135, 144, Ticinum, Pavia.
Tolete, 15, 190, Toletum, Toledo.
Toletane, 195, Toletanus : Toleto, Toledo
Tolane, 28, Tolosane, 75, Tolosanus : Tolosa, Toulouse.
Tolose, 152, Tolosa, Toulouse.
Tornate, 30, for Tornacum, Tournay.
Tonyse, 174, Thinissa in Africa, Tunis.
Toures of sardyne, 85, Turres Sardiniæ, Porto Torre.
Tourney, 154, Tornacum, Tournai.
Traiectens, 23, Trajectensis : Traiectum, Utrecht.
Trecas, 14, 18, 114, Tricas, 19 ; Trecæ, Troyes.
Trecacyne, 18, Trecassyn, 81 ; Trecassyne, 136, Trecassinum territorium, the district round Troyes.
Treuer, 18, 84, Treveri, Trier (Trèves).
Trientyne, 100, Tridentinus : Tridentum, Trent.
Tripole, 198, Tripolis.
Tubabocens, 11.
Tubertyn, 162, for Tudertinus : Tudertum, Todi.
Tudertusce, 82, see Notes, May 26.
Tull, 139, Tullum, Toul.
Tumbe, mount of, 163, Mons Tumba, Mont St. Michel.
Tungrens, 74, 144, Tungrensis : Tungri, Tongres in the diocese of Liège.
Turon, 12, 104, Turyne, 54 : Turones, Tours.
Tyburtyne, 101, 171, Tibur, Tivoli.
Tylecastell, 169, Castrum Tyle, in the diocese of Langres.
Tynge, 187, Tingis, Tangier.
Tyngentyne, 170, Tingis, Tangier.
Tyrason, 177, Turiaso, Tarazona.

Valence, 62, 157, Valencia, Valence.
Valenciane, 101, Valentiana, Valenciennes.
Valentyne, 14, Valentinus : Valentia, Valencia in Spain.
Vasion, 27, Vasio, Vaison.
Venys, 85, Venyse, 78 ; Venice.

Venyse, 167 (Oct. 24), for Venusia, Venosa.
Vercell, 120, Vercelli.
Verdune, 175, Virodunum, Verdun.
Veridiane, 7, for Niridane : Nirida near Naples, see Notes, Jan. 9.
Vermendens, 170, Augusta Veromanduorum, St. Quentin.
Verolane, 97, for Verolame, Verolamium, St. Albans.
Veron, 72, Verona.
Veronens, 56, Veronensis : Verona.
Vertane, 167, Vertanum, Vertou near Nantes.
Vesegoryne, 60, 'in araby.'
Vesuce, 95, for Vesunce, Vesuntio, Besançon.
Victymyle, 134, Victimilium, Ventimiglia.
Vien, 147, 181, Vieñ, 22, 73 ; Vienna, Vienne in Gaul.
Vilcasyne, 173, Vilcassinus, Le Vexin.
Villaren, 105.
Viterbe, 82, Viterbium, Viterbo.
Viuariens, 103, Vivariense territorium, Le Vivarais.
Vrs, 161, for Uzetia, Uzez.
Vtruculane, 3.
Vtryne, 98, for Sutrium, Sutri.
Vulcasyne, fraunchest of, 160, Pagus Vilcassinus, Le Vexin (in diocese of Rouen).

Wapyng, 21, Vapingum, Gap.
Warmaciens, 48, for Wormaciensis: Wormatia, Worms.
Wastinens, 171, Pagus Wastinensis, Le Gâtinois.
Wendoper, 184, Vendopera, Vendœuvre.
Wentane, 7, 40, 107, Wentana civitas or Wintonia, Winchester.
Were, 9, the River Wear.
Wyllenchester, 12, see Notes, Jan. 18.
Wyteby, 90, Whitby.

Ybery, 29, Iberia.
Yconium, 84, Iconium.
Ynde, 5, 133, India.
Ysawre, 84, Ysawry, 76, Isauria.
Ytalyke, 134, Italica, near Seville.

Zenon, 96, see Senon.

GLOSSARY

OF

OBSOLETE OR UNUSUAL WORDS.

The numbers refer to the pages of this reprint.
Italics denote the corresponding words in the Latin Martyrology.

p. = perf. tense of a verb.
p.p. = past participle.

Almeser, 21, a giver of alms.
Almesman, 124, Almes woman, 78 ; a giver of alms.
Amite, 157, friendship.
Ancre, 12, 30, an anker or anchorite.
Anenst, 195, near, *e vicino*.
Apocriphase, 62, Apocrypha.
Auoutry, 112, Aduoutry, 111 ; adultery.
Avoyd, 96, avoid ! get away.
Axe, 104, 186, to ask.

Baptym, 13, 36, 50, baptism.
Battes, 130, *fustes*.
Beneficyall, 6, beneficent.
Bette, 121, p., beat.
Breder, 3, 22, 31, brothers.
Bren, 44, to burn.
Brennynge, 69, burning.
Brent, 28, 40, burnt.

Carayne, 140, carrion.
Chase, 145, p., chose.
Childer, 22, 26, 65, children.
Clausures, 48, enclosures.
Colet, 128, acolyte.
Cressettes, 92, lamps.

Dekey, 41, decay.
Despoused, 79, espoused.
Drabbe of kechyn, 36, kitchen servant.

Eched, 137, p.p., joined.
Edifycatyne, 199, edifying.
Elsyns, 96, shoemakers' awls.
Enflambed, 166, burnt.
Ete, 108, p., ate.

Expowne, 1, to expose ; 58, 174, to expound.
Everyche, 33, every one.
Eysell, 119, vinegar.

Fatigate, 4, weary.
Faute, 103, v., to commit a fault.
Feastfull day, 30, festival day. " Festeful " is used by Caxton in contrast to " feryal," *Golden Legend*, ed. Morris, 1892, p. 1133, l. 12.
Fende, 28, fiend.
Festyuate, 139, kept as a festival.
Flambyng, 149, 150, flaming.
Flaync, 148, flayed.
Frater, 17, refectory.
Fraunchest, territory, *pagus, territorium*, Cf. " Fraunchyse, Libertas, territorium," *Prompt. Parvulorum*, s. v.
Fyrehote, 111, hot from the fyre.

Gentilite, 5, paganism.
Gossyppes, 174, god-parents.
Grette, 46, p., greeted.

Henge, 140, p., hung.
Herborowe, 17, lodging.
Hertned, 182, encouraged.
Hoste, 40, 82, *hostia*.

Improve, 56, reprove.
Insunder, 122, asunder.
Iury, 130, Judæa.

Kepynge, 40, prison.
Kytte, 5, p.p., cut.

GLOSSARY OF OBSOLETE OR UNUSUAL WORDS.

Lap, 35, to wrap.
Laureres, 196, laurels.

Mammelles, 22, breasts, *mamillæ*.
Mo, 79, Moo, 65; more.
Monycyon, 99, advice.
More, 162, greater, "in the more brytayne."

Ne, 31, nor.
Nedely, 158, of necessity.
Nerehande, 5, 102, nearly.
Neuewe, 23, 164, nephew.
Nosethrylles, 192, nostrils.
Nourysshe, 26, bringer up, nurse.
Nouryssher, 43, bringer up, (male).
Noyaunce, 36, 108, injury.
Noyed, 94, injured.
Noyous, 93, 104, injurious.

Obediyenser, 45, one owing obedience.
Ordre, 64, holy orders.
Over teeth, 161, *dentes superiores*.
Overthwarte, 66, across.
Oynted, 121, anointed.

Pace, 48, Pascha.
Palseys, 14, palsied persons.
Papalite, 78, papacy.
Peter pens, 112, Peter's pence.
Pistle, 143, epistle.
Podell, 21, pool.
Promyssyon, 138, promise.
Prycksonge, 9, pricksong.

Quycke, 47, living.

Religyon, 7, 45, 70, 80, a monastic order.
Religyous, 1, belonging to a monastic order.
Reny, 46, deny.
Repaused, 47, rested.
Rote, 62, a wheel.

Sanctiloge, 1. Sanctilogium.
Seacynge, 73, ceasing.
Sell, 201, cell.
Sene, 33, 55, 79, a synod or council. Cf. *Catholicon Anglicum* (E.E.T.S.), p. 330. "A Sene; Sinodus."
Senous, 122, sinews.
Sense, 5, insense.
Sextry, 145, *sacrarium*.
Sherthursday, 52, *Dies Cænæ Domini*.
Shyppe of Noe, 18.
Shryne, 70, v., to place in a shrine.
Soudyour, 3, 97, soldier.
Souerayne, 132, 158, see Notes, Aug. 23.
Sprad, 142, pp., spread.
Stale, 57, 112, p., stole.
Stallacyon, 30, installacion.
Stepdame, 43, stepmother.
Stert, 108, p., started.
Stryplynges, 194, *pueri*.
Stythes, 84, anvils.
Sudary, 113, *sudarium*.

Thrall, 29, slave.
Thrast, 197, p., thrust.
Traitory, 74, treason.
Tronizacyon, 30, enthronement.
Twindles, 65, twins.

Wanne, 17, 152, p., won.
Wawes, 4, waves.
Wemme, 174, damage.
Wilfully, 131, 135, 190, of his own free will, willingly, 96, intentionally.
Wode, 19, mad.
Wombe, 142, belly.
Worship, 74, honour.
Wretche, 1, 150, 158, a sinner.
Wynke, 158, to close the eyes for some time.

Ympne, 162, 180, a hymn.
Yse, 9, ice.

APPENDIX.

EXTRACTS RELATING TO ENGLISH SAINTS IN THE CANTERBURY MARTYROLOGY.

THE following extracts are from the Martyrologium of Christ Church, Canterbury (Brit. Mus. Arundel MS., 68). This MS. which appears to be of the end of the thirteenth century, contains also an Obituarium, an abstract of the Rule of St. Benedict, and other memoranda. About the beginning of the sixteenth century the book was apparently laid aside, and superseded by a beautiful copy made at that time, which is preserved in Lambeth Library (MS. No. 20). In the Arundel book the names of the pope and of St. Thomas of Canterbury have not been erased; but in the Lambeth copy, which was probably in daily use in the time of Henry VIII., the word *papa* has generally been erased and altered to *episcopus* and the name of St. Thomas has been erased, together with the notices of him in 7 July, 2 Dec., and 29 Dec.

The Lambeth copy follows the original so closely even in the punctuation that it is not considered necessary to give a collation, which would only show slight variations in spelling.

With the exception of the few entries relating to English Saints, the Canterbury Martyrology is that of Usuard, and varies from it far less than does the Syon Martyrology.

The additions later than the thirteenth century are printed in italics.

The letter ·U. has been placed after the entries relating to British saints which are found in Usuard.

Non. Jan. [5 Jan.] Ipso die apud westmonasterium depositio sancti ædwardi regis anglorum qui dedit Cherteham et Waleworthe ecclesie christi.

v Id. Jan. [9 Jan.] Cantuarie sancti adriani abbatis.

xvii Kal. Feb. [16 Jan.] Parona monasterio sancti fursei confessoris cuius capud in dorobernia habetur.

xiv Kal. Feb. [19 Jan.] Eodem die sancti wlstani wigorniensis episcopi et confessoris.

iii Kal. Feb. [30 Jan.] In territorio parisiacensi sancte baltildis regine.

Kal. Feb. [1 Feb.] In hibernia sancte brigide uirginis cuius uita miraculis claruit. U.

vii Id. Feb. [7 Feb.]. In britanniis ciuitate augusta natale beati auguli episcopi qui temporis cursum per martyrium explens eterna meruit suscipere premia. U.

vi Kal. Mar. [24 Feb.] *Item in monasterio sancti Augustini Cantuarie deposicio sancti Ethelberti Regis et confessoris ac primi fundatoris huius sancte Cantuariensis ecclesie.*

Kal. Mar. [1 Mar.] *Eodem die meneuie. sancti Dauid eiusdem ciuitatis episcopi et confessoris.*

vi Non Mar. [2 Mar.] In britannia deposicio sancti ceadde episcopi et confessoris.

xvi Kal. Apr. [17 Mar.] In scocia natale sancti patricii episcopi et confessoris qui primus ibidem christum euuangelizauit. U.

xv Kal. Apr. [18 Mar.] Ipso die passio sancti edwardi regis *anglie et martiris.*

[There is a long note here recording the donation of two corrodies by Richard II. to the church of Canterbury, and stating that it was granted to the King that each of the two feasts of St. Edward, K.M., viz., his Passion on this day and his Translation on 20 June, should be observed as *festum principale*. In Arundel 68, this record is in the lower margin, in Lambeth 20 it is placed in the text.]

iii Id. Apr. [11 Apr.] In britannia depositio sancti Guthlaci confessoris christi et anachorite.

xiii Kal. Mai. [19 Apr.] Eodem die sancti Ælphegi cantuariensis archiepiscopi qui ab exercitu paganorum post dirutam illius urbem. post cruentam innocentis populi cedem. post templi expoliationem uinctus abductus est: et per septem menses uariis tormentorum suppliciis cruciatus tandem furencium manibus paganorum lapidatus martyrii coronam suscepit.

xi Kal. Mai. [21 Apr.] Cantuarie depositio anselmi eius ciuitatis archiepiscopi.

viii Kal. Mai. [24 Apr.] Eodem die depositio sancti melliti episcopi in britannia. U.

v. Kal. Mai. [27 Apr.] *Eodem die sancte Sythe uirginis.*

xiiii Kal. Jun. [19 Mai.] In ciuitate dorobernia natale sancti patris nostri Dunstani archiepiscopi. qui ab ipso matris utero sanctificatus. omne tempus uite sue magnifice duxit unde et glorioso fine quieuit.

vii Kal. Jun. [26 Mai.] In anglia ciuitate cantuarie sancti Augustini archiepiscopi et confessoris. qui missus a beato papa gregorio primus genti anglorum christi euuangelium predicauit. crebrisque adhuc refulget miraculis. U. [The last four words are a Canterbury addition.]

iii Kal. Jun. [30 Mai.] Ipso die sancti cuthberti episcopi et confessoris.

iiii Non. Jun. [2 Jun.] In cancia sancti odonis archiepiscopi et confessoris.

vi Id. Jun. [8 Jun.] Eodem die translatio sancti Ælphegi archiepiscopi et martyris de lundonia in canciam ad ecclesiam christi.

v Id. Jun. [9 Jun.] Apud monasterium sancti germani. dedicatio oratorii in honore beati petri apostoli. *Eodem die translacio sancti Eadmundi cantuariensis archiepiscopi et confessoris.*

xvi Kal. Jul. [16 Jun.] *Eodem die translacio sancti Ricardi cicestrensis episcopi et confessoris.*

xv Kal. Jul. [17 Jun.] Ipso die sancti botulfi abbatis.

xii Kal. Jul. [20 Jun.] *Eodem die translacio sancti Edwardi. Regis et martiris.*

x Kal. Jul. [22 Jun.] In britannia sancti Albani martyris qui tempore diocliciani in uerolamio ciuitate post uerbera et tormenta acerba capite plexus est   Passus est cum illo eciam unus de militibus eo quod eum ferire iussus noluerit. U.

ix Kal. Jul. [23 Jun.] In britannia natale sancte etheldrithe uirginis et regine cuius corpus cum undecim annis esset sepultum: incorruptum inuentum est. U.

vi Non. Jul. [2 Jul.] In anglia ciuitate wentonie. sancti swithuni episcopi et confessoris.

iii Non. Jul. [5 Jul.] In scocia sancte moduenne uirginis.

ii Non. Jul. [6 Jul.] Eodem die sancte sexburge sororis sancte etheldride uirginis.

Non. Jul. [7 Jul.] Eodem die translacio. sancti thome archiepiscopi et martyris. Anno gracie. m°. cc°. xx°. passionis autem eiusdem martiris quinquagesimo. feria tercia. Ut eadem die et nasceretur ad penam. et pateretur ad gloriam. et transferetur ad honorem. In cuius translacione passionis ipsius dominus miracula suscitauit ut dum nouis superuenientibus uetera fuissent renouata : ex signis choruscantibus et ipse martyr gloriosior appareret.

viii Id. Jul. [8 Jul.] Wentonie sancti Grimbaldi confessoris.

iii Id. Jul. [13 Jul.] Cantuarie sancte mildrithe uirginis.

xvii Kal. Aug. [16 Jul.] *Eodem die Translacio sancti Osmundi Episcopi Sarum et confessoris.*

iiii Non. Aug. [2 Aug.] Cantuarie deposicio sancti plegemundi archiepiscopi.

Non. Aug. [5 Aug.] Eodem die sancti oswaldi regis anglorum. cuius actus commemorat uenerabilis beda presbiter in gestis eiusdem gentis. U.

xvi Kal. Sept. [16 Aug.] Item dedicatio cripte ecclesie christi cantuarie.

MARTILO.   T ix Kal. Sept. [24 Aug.] In ybernia sancti patricii abbatis. et gildardi confessoris. qui patricius primus ybernensium fertur fuisse magister. sed quia nec eos corexisse potuit in peregrinationem perrexit. ad monasterium glestingense peruenit ibique uitam uirtutibus clarescens finiuit. quod et usque hodie mortua ossa ipsius contestari uidentur.

vii Kal. Sept. [26 Aug.] Cantuarie depositio beate memorie breguini eiusdem ciuitatis archiepiscopi et confessoris.

ii Kal. Sept. [31 Aug.] Eodem die sancti aidani episcopi. cuius animam sanctus cuthbertus in celum ab angelis ferri uidit.

ii Non. Sept. [4 Sept.] Translatio reliquiarum sancti cuthberti episcopi.

v Id. Sept. [9 Sept.] In scocia querani abbatis. U.

Id. Sept. [13 Sept.] Ipso die translatio sancti augustini archiepiscopi et confessoris.

xiii Kal. Oct. [19 Sept.] Cantuarie deposicio beati theodori eiusdem ciuitatis archiepiscopi et confessoris.

vi Non. Oct. [2 Oct.] *Eodem die sancti Thome confessoris herfordensis episcopi.*

ii Non. Oct. [6 Oct.] *Eodem die translacio sancti hugonis lincolniensis episcopi.*

Non. Oct. [7 Oct.] In britannia. natale sancte osythe uirginis et martyris.

vi Id. Oct. [10 Oct.] In britannia sancti paulini archiepiscopi et confessoris. U.

v Id. Oct. [11 Oct.] In scocia sancti camichi abbatis. U.

iv Id. Oct. [12 Oct.] Ipso die deposicio sancti Wilfridi episcopi et confessoris. qui inter ceteras uirtutes mortuo quoque uitam legitur reddidisse.

iii Id. Oct. [13 Oct.] *Apud westmonasterium translacio sancti eadwardi regis et confessoris.*

xiiii Kal. Nou. [19 Oct.] *Item eodem die Oxoniis sancte frideswyde uirginis.*

iii Non. Nou. [3 Nov.] Eodem die sancti wlganii confessoris.

xvi Kal. Dec. [16 Nov.] Ipso die ordinatio sancti Aelphegi cantuariensis archiepiscopi et martyris. quam deus per apostolum suum reuelare dignatus est. Cantuarie. deposicio beate memorie aelfrici eiusdem ciuitatis archiepiscopi et confessoris. *Eodem die sancti Eadmundi cantuariensis archiepiscopi et confessoris.*

xiii Kal. Dec. [19 Nov] In hybernia deposicio sancti ronani episcopi et confessoris. Huius sinistrum brachium ab anigo filio regis auertach a corpore sublatum. cantuariam delatum est. et in ecclesia saluatoris domini christi reconditum. ubi usque hodie in integra carne decenti honore seruatur.

xii Kal. Dec. [20 Nov.] Eodem die sancti edmundi regis et martiris. qui pro confessione christi ab iniquo rege inguuare interfectus est.

iiii Non. Dec. [2 Dec.] Eodem die regressio sancti thome martyris ab exilio. Quem post diuturna supplicia quibus cotidie nouus martyr effulserat. uelut aurum in fornace multipharie probatum in thesauros regis assumptum. septimo anno dominus ad palmam sub gladii cautione reuocauit. ac si ostensis ei gladiis. uoce dominica diceretur. Amice. ecce ad quod uenisti.

Id. Dec. [13 Dec.] Cantuarie depositio sancte ædburgis uirginis.

iv Kal. Jan. [29 Dec.] Eodem die cantuarie passio uenerandi patris thome eiusdem ciuitatis archiepiscopi et martyris gloriosi. Hic post longos exilii labores quos pro iusticia pacienter pertulit: tandem deo miserante reuersus. et in ecclesia sua cum honore susceptus: in eadem pro defensione libertatis ipsius gladiis impiorum percussus occubuit. Tali modo fortis athleta agone suo constanter expleto. proprio sanguine laureatus ac triumphali morte insignis: ad christum pro quo fideliter decertauit. feliciter peruenit. cuius glorie miraculorum frequencia testimonium perhibet. que post passionem ipsius euestigio tanta secuta sunt: et adhuc fere cotidie multiplicantur: quanta retro actis temporibus pro aliquo sanctorum uix uspiam facta leguntur.

www.ingramcontent.com/pod-product-compliance
Lightning Source LLC
Chambersburg PA
CBHW021159230426
43667CB00006B/469